ACTS OF RELIGION

ACTS OF RELIGION

JACQUES DERRIDA

Edited and with an Introduction by
GIL ANIDJAR

ROUTLEDGE
New York and London

Published in 2002 by
Routledge
29 West 35th Street
New York, NY 10001

Published in Great Britain by
Routledge
11 New Fetter Lane
London EC4P 4EE

Routledge is an imprint of the Taylor & Francis Group.

Printed in the United States of America on acid-free paper.

10 9 8 7 6 5 4 3 2 1

Library of Congress Cataloging-in-Publication Data

Derrida, Jacques.
    Acts of religion / Jacques Derrida ; edited by Gil Anidjar.
      p. cm.
    Includes bibliographical references and index.
    ISBN 0-415-92400-6 — ISBN 0-415-92401-4 (pbk.)
    1. Religion—Philosophy.   I. Anidjar, Gil.   II. Title.

B2430.D484 D46 2001
210—dc21   20010119944

CONTENTS

Introduction:
"Once More, Once More": Derrida, the Arab, the Jew
Gil Anidjar

1

(Dates of first publication appear below each selection. "The Eyes of Language: The Abyss and the Volcano" and "Hostipitality" are published here for the first time in any language.)

1
Faith and Knowledge:
The Two Sources of "Religion" at the Limits of Reason Alone
(In French, 1996; in English, 1998)

40

2
Des Tours de Babel
(In French, 1980; in English, 1985)

102

3
Interpretations at War: Kant, the Jew, the German
(In French, 1989; in English, 1991)

135

4

The Eyes of Language: The Abyss and the Volcano

189

5

Force of Law:
The "Mystical Foundation of Authority"
*(Simultaneously in French and English, 1990; complete French version, 1994;
complete English version, 2001)*

228

6

Taking a Stand for Algeria
(In French, 1995; in English, 1998)

299

7

A Silkworm of One's Own
(Points of View Stitched on the Other Veil)
(In English, 1996; in French, 1997)

309

8

Hostipitality

356

Bibliography

421

Permissions

427

Index

429

Introduction
"Once More, Once More": Derrida, the Arab, the Jew

Gil Anidjar

If . . . religion is etymologically that which binds, that which holds together, then what of the non-bond which disjoins beyond unity—which escapes the synchrony of "holding together," yet does so without breaking all relations or without ceasing, in this break or in this absence of relation, to open yet another relation? Must one be nonreligious for that?

—Maurice Blanchot, *The Writing of the Disaster*

But take another Abraham, *aber ein anderer Abraham.*

—Franz Kafka, "Abraham"[1]

It has become a commonplace to assert that religion in Jacques Derrida's works depends upon the range of meanings promoted by terms such as *God, theology,* and even *Judaism.* Under the guise of these terms, we may no longer be hearing simply about the demise of religion, most famously proclaimed by Nietzsche, but we keep hearing a great deal about what has been called its "return." According

I would like to thank Avital Ronell without whom none of this would have been possible; Judith Butler, for having thought of me and for the continued support; Bill Germano, for having thought of *Acts of Religion,* and for going through with it; Ulrich Baer, Peter Connor, Bill Darrow, Brent Edwards, Jill Robbins, Lecia Rosenthal, Gayatri Chakravorty Spivak, and my colleagues in the Department of Middle East and Asian Languages and Cultures at Columbia University, for seeing me through it.

For his immense generosity and kindness, and for more, I thank Jacques Derrida.

1. In her reading of Kafka's parable "Abraham," Avital Ronell shows the importance of attending to "several Abrahams." The task of reading the "deconstitution of the primal patriarch" left unread by the Bible and its commentators engages the possible and impossible openings of a name that cannot be reduced to the same or difference" (Avital Ronell, *Stupidity* [Champaign: University of Illinois Press, 2001]). Derrida recently drew on Ronell's reading in a lecture he gave in Paris entitled "Abraham, l'autre."

1

to this view religion acts, exercising its pressure by reflecting a dominantly theo-logical lexicon that communicates values of spirituality, community, and faith. And since religion inevitably brings up figures of aberrant returns and archaic remnants, figures of familial or ethnic traditions preserved and fossilized, Derrida has been seen as well as performing *acts of religion*, as enacting a return to his own "religious" origins, though within the constraints of a necessarily complicated reappropriation.

Among the developments enabled by these considerations, there is moreover the undeniable fact that the study of religion has already benefited greatly from Derrida's extensive contributions and the growing recognition that, clearly, Derrida has spoken and written on religion, on the following terms of "religion": God, for example, but also theology, negative theology, "a new atheistic discourse," and the touch of Jesus and of Jean-Luc Nancy (in "The Theater of Cruelty," "Violence and Metaphysics," *Of Grammatology*, "On a Newly Arisen Apocalyptic Tone in Philos-ophy," "How to Avoid Speaking: Denials," *On the Name, Aporias, Le toucher, Jean-Luc Nancy*); Islamic alms, circumcision (Arab, Jewish, and other), angels and archangels, Christianity, Judaism, and Islam and other religions (in "Edmond Jabès and the Question of the Book," "Ellipses," *Glas, Post Card*, "Schibboleth: For Paul Celan," "In this Very Work, At this Very Moment," *Ulysse Gramophone, Given Time*, "Circumfession," *Archive Fever, On The Name, Politics of Friendship, Donner la mort*, "Typewriter Ribbon: Limited Ink [2]"); the Kabbalah, the Hebrew Bible and the New Testament, Paul, Augustine, the Talmud, messianism and messianicity, forgiveness, hospitality, prayer, and his prayer shawl (in *Dissemination*, "Des Tours de Babel," *Force de loi, Donner la mort, Memoirs of the Blind, Specters of Marx, Adieu, Of Hospitality*, "A Silkworm of One's Own"); the spirit and the letter, and German Jews and Arab Jews (in *Writing and Difference*, "Interpretations at War," *Of Spirit, Aporias, Monolingualism of the Other*); and more. Derrida, the argument continues, has amply and sufficiently testified to his growing up in an Algerian Jewish, French-speaking family, to the complex impact of a certain Christianity on his surroundings and on himself, and to his being deeply affected by religious per-secution. With various degrees of seriousness, Derrida has also referred to himself as "the last and the least of the Jews" and as "Marrano," and he has said that he watches, on television, "very regularly, on Sunday mornings, from 8:45am to 9:30am, ... the religious, Jewish and Muslim, programs that interest me greatly—and if we had time I would tell you why."[2]

---

2. Jacques Derrida (Avec Bernard Stiegler), *Échographies de la television*, (Paris: Galilée-INA, 1996) 155.

Acts of Religion, then, in which what are put on stage, what are in fact restaged and replayed, are a number of acts, a number of books and plays, deeds and performances, pretenses and obligations. Jacques Derrida's writing on religion has indeed consisted of a manifold and powerful effort to situate and raise again questions of tradition, faith, and sacredness and their relation to the premises of philosophy and political culture.[3] These writings, therefore, do not merely consti-tute an exploration of familiar theologemes, a bringing to light of hidden religious dimensions of language and sociality, the producing and revisiting of exegetical elaborations—be they "traditional" or "heretical"—and ritual body markings; nor do they simply announce, indeed, prophesy, the renewal of faith. Rather, when Derrida writes on religion, it is always on the Abrahamic.

The notion of the Abrahamic, like the notion of "The People of the Book," is of Islamic origin.[4] It is an ancient notion which, as Derrida notes, was on occasion revived in Europe (Kierkegaard, of course), perhaps most recently by the impor-tant Islamicist Louis Massignon.[5] As this ancient notion, the Abrahamic has been considered either the original and gathering root of the three major monotheistic faiths or, more pervasively, as the (three) branches of one single faith. It suggests the reclaiming of territorialized roots, the reoccupation and gathering of a site of welcoming togetherness, where old fallen branches can come back to life: as Paul writes, "God is perfectly able to graft them back again" (*Romans* 11:23). This return may promise, minimally, the resurrected togetherness and enabling of "religion," but it also institutes the possibility of comparison under the allegedly unified figure of Abraham, whose name appears in the three scriptural traditions. The modern discourse of comparative religion, which rendered the incommensurable compara-ble, could hardly have emerged independently of Jewish, Christian, and Muslim

---

3. The most wide-reaching and rigorously compelling discussion of these issues can be found in Hent de Vries, *Philosophy and the Turn to Religion* (Baltimore: Johns Hopkins University Press, 1999); and see, in a different perspective, John D. Caputo, *The Prayers and Tears of Jacques Derrida: Religion without Religion* (Bloomington: Indiana University Press, 1997); but the debate was on from the beginning (since Dufrenne and Taylor, and earlier still), and earlier still, surrounding the way in which "metaphysics, the-ology, and deconstruction have always existed in a covert economy" (K. Hart, *The Trespass of the Sign: Deconstruction, Theology and Philosophy* [New York: Fordham University Press, 2000 [1989] xxxiii).

4. To speak of "Abrahamic religions" is to adopt, as Jonathan Z. Smith explains, "a term from Muslim discourse" ("Religion, Religions, Religious," in Mark C. Taylor, Ed., *Critical Terms for Religious Studies* [Chicago and London: University of Chicago Press, 1998] 276). Consider, however, Gershom Scholem's punctuation when he asserts that the phrase "people of the book" had "originated among none others than the Arabs! It was Mohammed, the founder of Islam, who used this term in many passages in the Koran specifically in reference to the Jews" (Gershom Scholem, "The People of the Book," trans. Jonathan Chipman, in Gershom Scholem, *On the Possibility of Jewish Mysticism in Our Time & Other Essays* [Philadelphia and Jerusalem: Jewish Publication Society, 1997], 167). One should note however that in the Qur'anic text it is not Mohammed but God who uses the term.

5. On Massignon, see Derrida's "Hostipitality," in this volume.

medieval disputations that stage the one/three faith(s) in different and complex ways.[6] However, the Abrahamic is not simply a figure that can be subsumed as one theme among many. The Abrahamic is the very condition of "religion."[7]

Derrida unquestionably pursues this "ancient" notion of the Abrahamic, which is why it is important to underscore (as well as to interrogate and problematize) the Abrahamic's welcoming gathering and its hospitable dimension. Hence also the necessity of exploring the highly articulated images of the Abrahamic that have thus suggested themselves in and to Europe along with the views that conceive of the Abrahamic's relatedness to religion as essential or as resting on matters of essence. Yet if there is a particular urgency and timeliness to an anthology of Derrida's writings on religion, it is because to engage Derrida on religion is to follow "the religious beyond of the concept, in the direction of a certain Abraham;"[8] it is to witness and experience—to read—the irreconcilable and, if not quite the explosion of the Abrahamic, then undoubtedly, and more precisely, the Abrahamic as explosive. And it is "an experience that leaves nothing intact."[9]

At a relative distance from that to which it is inevitably connected, namely the threat of so-called Islamic fundamentalism and the strange promise of messianic-

---

6. On the "confrontational cultures" of medieval polemics, see Amos Funkenstein, *Perceptions of Jewish History* (Berkeley and Los Angeles: University of California Press, 1993), esp. chapter 6. For a compellingly close study of the complexity of relations "between" religions in the exemplary case of Moses Naḥmanides, see Nina Caputo, "'And God Rested on the Seventh Day': Creation, Time, and History in Medieval Jewish Culture" (Ph.D. diss., University of California-Berkeley, 1999). On the great interreligious controversies among Muslim, Jew, Christian, and Manichean, see Steven M. Wasserstrom, *Between Muslim and Jew: The Problem of Symbiosis under Early Islam* (Princeton: Princeton University Press, 1995) 136–64. From Ibn Ḥazm to Peter the Venerable, Petrus Alfonsi, Naḥmanides, Ramon Llull, Ibn al-ʿArabī and Thomas Aquinas, key figures of medieval culture have shaped the issue of "comparative religion" as a series of "Abrahamic" elaborations.

7. On "condition," see Jacques Derrida, *Given Time*, 17–18; Marian Hobson, *Jacques Derrida: Opening Lines* (London: Routledge, 1998) esp. chap. 1; see also Hent de Vries's discussion of "condition and uncondition" where "the conditioned conditions the condition" or where what is made possible in turn makes possible what made it possible as well as, de Vries makes clear, impossible. (*Philosophy*, 141ff.).

8. Jacques Derrida, *Writing and Difference*, trans. Alan Bass (Chicago: University of Chicago Press, 1978) 111.

9. On "irreconcilable monotheisms (whatever people say)" see Jacques Derrida, *Points*, ed. Elizabeth Weber, Trans. Peggy Kamuf et al. (Stanford: Stanford University Press, 1995) 356/F367; trans. modified); on the experience that leaves nothing intact see again *Points*, 120 and *Monolingualism of the Other*, trans. Patrick Mensah (Stanford: Stanford University Press, 1998).

10. "For, furthermore, who has ever been sure that the expectation of the Messiah is not, from the start, by destination and invincibly, a fear, an unbearable terror—hence the hatred of what is thus awaited? And whose coming one would wish both to quicken and infinitely to retard, as the end of the future? And if the thinkers of the 'dangerous perhaps' can be nothing other than dangerous, if they can signify or bring nothing but threat and chance at one and the same time, how could I desire their coming without simultaneously fearing it, without going to all ends to prevent it from ever taking place? Without going to all ends to skip such a meeting? Like telepoiesis, the messianic sentence carries within it an irresistible disavowal. In the sentence, a structural contradiction converts a priori the called into the repressed, the desired into the undesired, the friend into the enemy, *car, de surcroît, qui a jamais été assuré que l'attente du Messie n'était pas, dès l'origine, par destination et invinciblement, une peur, la ter-*

ity,[10] the Abrahamic oscillates between the haunting threat of a volcanic explosion, the no less spectral "seismic turbulence" of aftershocks ("countless tremors, *secousses*"),[11] and the promise of peaceful reconciliation, all of which may yet have to be distinguished. Figuring an unwritten history that is neither that of "Europe and the Jews" nor that of "Islam and the West" (at least not simply), the Abrahamic inscribes the other hyphen, one that mourns and affirms, and uncertainly founds on shaky grounds and abysses the distinction of theological from political, the divisions of the theologico-political: Judaism—always already non-political—would have been the theological other, Islam the political other. From the earliest so-called "encounters" of the three "religions" via the discussions of Thomas

---

reur insoutenable, donc la haine de ce qu'on attend ainsi ? Et dont on voudrait à la fois accélérer et retarder infiniment la venue, comme la fin de l'avenir ? Et si les penseurs du « dangereux peut-être » ne peuvent qu'être dangereux, s'ils ne peuvent signifier ou apporter que la menace en même temps que la chance, comment pourrais-je souhaiter leur venue sans du même coup la redouter et tout faire pour qu'elle n'ait pas lieu, jamais ? Tout pour que le rendez-vous soit à jamais manqué dans le faux bond? Comme la télépoièse, la phrase messianique porte en elle une irrésistible dénégation. Une contradiction structurelle y convertit a priori l'appelé en refoulé, le désirable en indésirable, l'ami en ennemi." (Jacques Derrida, *Politics of Friendship*, trans. George Collins [London: Verso, 1997] 174/F198).

11. Jacques Derrida, *Politics of Friendship*, 263/F294; on the explosive and seismic dimension of "deconstruction" Derrida elsewhere writes, "Here is the entire question of what some people call deconstruction: a seism which *happens* to this truth" ("Interpretations," this volume; see also "Signature, Event, Context," trans. Alan Bass in *Margins of Philosophy* (Chicago: University of Chicago Press, 1982), 309; *The Other Heading*, Trans. Pascale-Anne Brault and Michael B. Naas (Bloomington: Indiana University Press, 1992), 19; *Archive Fever*, 16/F34, "Faith and Knowledge," in this volume, sec. 23.

12. While using similar rhetorical strategies about—or, rather, against—both Jews and Muslims, medieval writers were careful to maintain a strict separation between them, either by thematizing such separation or by treating the two in different treatises. Thomas Aquinas is, here too, exemplary insofar as he separates the Jew from the Muslim in two distinct ways. He first asserts that there is a shared religious discourse between Christians and Jews, lamenting that this is not the case with Muslims and establishing in the process the lack of a "common" *polemical* ground: "Thus, against the Jews we are able to argue by means of the Old Testament, *sicut contra Iudaeos disputare possumus per Vetus Testamentum*, while against heretics we are able to argue by means of the New Testament. But the Mohammedans . . . accept neither the one nor the other, *hi vero neutrum recipiunt*" (Thomas Aquinas, *Summa Contra Gentiles*, book 1, ch. 2, trans. Anton C. Pegis [Notre Dame, Ind.: University of Notre Dame Press, 1975] 62). Aquinas then goes on to assert the lack of any theological or religious basis for Islam's power, thus already construing it as a political and military enemy ("Mohammed said that he was sent by the power of his arms, *sed dixit se in armorum potentia missum*. . . . [He] forced others to become his followers by the violence of his arms, *per quorum multitudinem alios armorum violentia in suam legem coegit*," ibid., ch. 6, 73). Steven Kruger addressed the issue of the dividing line between Muslim and Jew and described how Guibert of Nogent also separates the "private" and "theological" Jew, on the one hand, and the "public" and "political" Muslim, on the other. Thus Guibert writes about the former in his *Memoirs* and theological works and about the later in his history of the First Crusade (Steven F. Kruger, "Medieval Christian (Dis)identifications: Muslims and Jews in Guibert of Nogent," *New Literary History* 28, no. 2 [1997]: 185–203).

13. The explicit comparisons between the three monotheistic religions in Hegel are, of course, numerous and complex. (Moreover, they obviously do not exhaust what Hegel has to say on religion and on other religions.) To the extent that he opposes Islam and Judaism, Hegel does so around the question of universality that Judaism would entirely lack. It is on the question of "world dominion" that Islam is distinguished from Judaism and thus closer to Christianity. Christianity's purpose is "a universal condition of the world, world dominion, universal monarchy"; so too in Islam—"world dominion is the purpose"—even if this dominion is of an "abstract," "spiritual nature." Hegel does note that this abstraction,

Aquinas,[12] G. W. F. Hegel's lectures on the philosophy of religion,[13] and Carl Schmitt's postulation of enemy lines dividing the "political" and "psychological" (and until today), the Abrahamic—split, doubled and divided along the lines of the theologico-political—disrupt the temporality of the Judeo-Christian.[14] The Abrahamic, as it occurs, if it occurs, in Derrida's writings in its quasi-formulaic dimension—"Judaism, Christianity, Islam"—and otherwise, precedes and follows the

the ground of Islam's "fanaticism," is "at the present stage" not so abstract, and that "the purpose is still an external, empirical purpose, an all-encompassing purpose but on the plane of empirical reality—i.e., the purpose is a *world dominion*" (Hegel, *Lectures on the Philosophy of Religion*, Peter C. Hodgson [Berkeley and Los Angeles: University of California Press, 1987] vol. 2, 500). Having been shown to be too universal in its world dominion politics, Islam can then be faulted for lacking particularity, for having "no defining characteristic like the Jewish sense of national value," no "concrete historical content" (vol. 3, 242–43; see also how Islam is described as "being cleansed of nationalism," vol. 2, 158).

14. As already pointed out, the scholarly tradition has not been entirely consistent in addressing the links and ruptures that operate between Islam and Judaism. Moreover, this tradition has virtually ignored—has been unable to read—these links and ruptures as constitutive of what is still called "Christian Europe" (the lines and protocols for such a reading are laid out by Derrida in *The Other Heading* and in *Politics of Friendship* [esp. chaps. 4 and 9], and they clearly bear upon his reflections on the Abrahamic). In a recent work of historiography that may begin to broach the subject, David Nirenberg writes in a footnote that "Muslims and Jews living in Christian lands are rarely treated in comparative perspective" (*Communities of Violence: Persecution of Minorities in the Middle Ages* [Princeton: Princeton University Press, 1996], 10, n. 23). Whereas there are a (limited) number of studies of Western attitudes toward Islam (Norman Daniel, Richard Southern, Edward Said, Alain Grosrichard, Hichem Djaït, Albert Hourani, John Tolan, Benjamin Kedar, and others), and an enormous amount of work has been done on "Europe and the Jews," there is in fact no book-length study that would address, let alone compare, *both* Jew and Muslim in the history of Europe. The explanation for this uncanny silence becomes clearer when considering that it buttresses the dividing lines of the theologico-political. Summarizing this tradition, Dwayne Carpenter reinscribes the Christian distinction and hermetic separation between Jew and Muslim precisely along those lines: "In essence, Jewish-Christian relations were defined and oftimes determined by historico-theological considerations, while Muslim-Christians contacts in the Iberian peninsula were governed by pragmatic concerns resulting from religio-bellicose confrontations" (D. E. Carpenter, "Minorities in Medieval Spain: The Legal Status of Jews and Muslims in the *Siete Partidas*," *Romance Quarterly* 33 [1986]: 276); see also the few pages dedicated to this subject by Jeremy Cohen, who writes of the conception that "Muslims and Jews shared ethnic, linguistic, and, presumably, religious characteristics" yet insists that Muslims were seen as operating "from without" and Jews "from within"—the alleged geographical distance thus remaining constant. More than a religious, theologically defined minority, "the devotees of Islam endangered the Christian world above all *militarily*" (Jeremy Cohen, *Living Letters of the Law: Ideas of the Jew in Medieval Christianity* [Berkeley and Los Angeles: University of California Press, 1999], 158–60). Still, this is not to efface the way in which associations (phantasmatic or not) did at times produce a rapprochement between Muslim (Arab, Moor, Turk) and Jew (most notably, perhaps, in eschatological, polemical and legal writings) only to alter the cathected charges that associate *and* dissociate Islam and Judaism. The threat of such rapprochement thus alternated with apotropaic pronouncements and the promise that the two would remain distant. Hence, the distance never closes but the threat does increase—during the Crusades, for example: "At Rouen one day, some men who had taken the cross with the intention of leaving for the crusade began complaining among themselves. 'Here we are,' they said, 'going off to attack God's enemies in the East . . . when there are Jews right here before our very eyes'" (*A Monk's Confession: The Memoirs of Guibert of Nogent*, trans. Paul J. Archambault [University Park: Pennsylvania State University Press, 1996], 111); see also how some representations had Christ "struck by Mahomet, the prophet of the Muslims, who has wounded and killed him" (Michael Camille, *The Gothic Idol: Ideology and Image-making in Medieval Art* [Cambridge: Cambridge University Press, 1989], 138). Later, Jews were figured as a "fifth column" of the Turkish empire. (Historians like Joshua Trachtenberg and Carlo Ginzburg have explored, if briefly, this

Judeo-Christian and questions the pertinence of hyphenated gatherings and their repetitive doublings, hierarchizations of and within alterity. The Abrahamic confronts us as a divisive and repetitive machine, and an explosive ghost that interrogates hermetic histories and their dividing modes of operation. The Abrahamic—that is to say, Derrida on religion—also articulates a multiplicity of names (Abraham, Maimonides,[15] Marx "the Moor,"[16] Algeria, Levinas, Massignon, Genet, Sultana Esther Georgette,[17] Jerusalem, Shatila, etc.) that silence and voice, erase and memorize, expose and explode religion—the encounter, if it is one, of Judaism, Christianity, Islam. The Abrahamic will also have been Derrida's name.

The Abrahamic ("la coupure abrahamique" as *Glas* has it) dissociates and breaks the dividing movement around which "Europe"—and religion—constitutes itself. The Abrahamic may very well be as unreadable as an explosion, yet the unreadable, as Derrida has shown, is often the trace that summons us time and again to the scene of something significant. In addition to its geotextual implications, the Abrahamic provokes us to reconsider the inscription of the "autobiographical" in

---

association of Jew and Muslim. See Trachtenberg's *The Devil and the Jews* (Philadelphia: Jewish Publication Society of America, 1943) and Ginzburg's *Ecstasies: Deciphering the Witches' Sabbath* (New York: Pantheon, 1991). More recently, consider that Carl Schmitt's distinction between *hostis* and *inimicus*, which clearly and explicitly locates the Muslim as *the* political enemy of "Christian Europe," also begs the question as to where to locate the Jew or the "theological" enemy. (According to Schmitt, "Never in the thousand year struggle between Christians and Moslems did it occur to a Christian to surrender rather than defend Europe out of love toward the Saracens or Turks. The enemy in the political sense need not be hated personally, and in the private sphere only does it make sense to love one's enemy, i.e., one's adversary" (Carl Schmitt, *The Concept of the Political*, trans. George Schwab [Chicago: University of Chicago Press, 1996] 29; and see Derrida, *The Gift of Death*, trans. David Wills (Chicago: University of Chicago Press, 1945) 103–5, and *Politics of Friendship*). Regardless of where Schmitt would locate the Jew along those theologico-political lines (perhaps as a "weak people, *ein schwaches Volk*," which no longer "maintains itself in the sphere of politics" [53]), there is no doubt that the status of the Jew as nonpolitical remains a well-entrenched topos, one that was productively and famously recast in Franz Rosenzweig's *Star of Redemption*. Consider, finally, that the becoming-political (in the narrow sense) of the Jew in the State of Israel has reversed the equation and 'forced' the Muslim out of the political sphere and into the theological and religious ("Islamic fundamentalism"), thus maintaining the split in and of the Abrahamic, its "logic of opposition."

15. "On this subject, have I ever talked to you of *Le guide des égarés—the Perplexed*—that I opened and touched as an eight year old in the glass library of my grandfather?" (Jacques Derrida and Catherine Malabou, *La contre-allée* [Paris: La Quinzaine Litteraire/Louis Vuitton, 1999] 263).

16. Franz Mehring documents the well-known association of Karl Marx with Moors and Turks. Marx, writes Mehring, was treated by his children as a "playmate." The children "called him 'The Moor,' a nickname given to him on account of his jet-black hair and dark complexion" (Franz Mehring, *Karl Marx: The Story of His Life*, trans. Edward Fitzgerald [Ann Arbor: The University of Michigan Press, 1962] 246–47). But this was not the only time Marx was considered as fitting the "ethnic" bill. Mehring reports that Marx met the English diplomat David Urquhart who, upon having read an article by Marx in the *New York Tribune*, "received Marx with the compliment that a Turk might have written the article" (244).

17. "Did I tell you that the maiden name of my mother, *Safar*, accented in a particular way, means in Arabic 'travel' or 'departure'? Otherwise accented, as a friend poetess herself named Safaa (Fathy) teaches me, the word designates the second month of the Muslim and 'lunar' year of the Hegira (*hejireth*, 'flight' [*fuite*] from Mecca by Muhammad): exile, emigration, exodus" (Derrida and Malabou, *La contre-allée*, 42).

Derrida's texts. The question of the "I" in those texts, the question of autobiography insofar as it has been reduced to the inscription of "life only" (the biographical as philosophically irrelevant *fait divers*), this "I" in Derrida's texts, has yet to be fully comprehended. It is indeed surprising to consider how what is commonly referred to as "life" in Derrida (Derrida's so-called life) in spite of its being repeatedly inscribed in his texts, is rarely more than a curiosity that appears to demand only a cursory gloss at best.[18] Derrida's "autobiography" is more often viewed as an unin-terrogated—and undivided—point of departure for identification purposes (e.g., "Derrida the Jew"), or as the occasion for a theory or theorization of the autobio-graphical. Following the dissociative logic of the Abrahamic then, the "autobiograph-ical" in Derrida seems to remain at a distance—to escape, and even to resist, reading.

With the Abrahamic, Derrida continues to interrogate the primacy of essence, but he singularly does so by exhorting us to expose ourselves to a reading field that is also mined. As the unacknowledged nonsite that breaks "Europe" and "religion" at their heart, at their center, and at their headings, the Abrahamic ("two mono-theisms still alien enough, *encore assez étrangers*, at the heart, *au coeur*, of Graeco-Christian, Pagano-Christian Europe")[19] has therefore little—almost nothing—to do with a mere latency, or with any kind of empiricity. The event of its explosive-ness, if it is one, rather maintains its unreadability. It is an event that, in troubling simultaneity, exposes and explodes—as in laughter, a matter of *éclat*—"religion," the Abrahamic, and Derrida, while at the same time constituting each.[20]

But why again, "religion"? And why, "once more, once more,"[21] a bomb, and a specter?

The specter, the bomb to which the Abrahamic exposes "like a disarming explo-sion, *comme une explosion désarmante*,"[22] may have already disabled a reading—any reading—of religion. But the Abrahamic, "older than Abraham,"[23] does more. It does more than conjure a distant Biblical past to which "Judaism" can be and has

---

18. For a notable exception to this general cursoriness and for an important corrective to persistent readings of Derrida's "Jewishness," see Jill Robbins's compelling review of "Circumfession": "Circum-cising Confession: Derrida, Autobiography, Judaism," *Diacritics* 25, no. 4 (winter 1995): 20–38; see also Hent de Vries's important comments on Derrida's "quasi-autobiography" in *Philosophy*, esp. 344–48.

19. Jacques Derrida, "Faith and Knowledge," section 15.

20. On the explosiveness, the "éclats," "ça saute," and other conflagrations found throughout Derrida's text, see David Farell Krell, *The Purest of Bastards: Works of Mourning, Art, and Affirmation in the Thought of Jacques Derrida* (University Park: Pennsylvania State University Press, 2000).

21. William Shakespeare, *Othello*, ed. E. A. J. Honigman, (Walton-on-Thames: The Arden Shakespeare, 1997), 5.2.17.

22. Jacques Derrida, *Post Card*, trans. Alan Bass (Chicago and London: University of Chicago Press, 1987) 188/F203.

23. Jacques Derrida, "Circonfession," trans. G. Bennington, in Jacques Derrida and Geoffrey Bennington, *Jacques Derrida* (Chicago: University of Chicago Press, 1993) 309.

often been referred (this is the anti- and philo-Semitic *topos* of the Jew as Biblical or prophetic, prefigurative, and ante-Christian). The Abrahamic does more than harangue us toward a prophetic and messianic future that, more often than not, comforts because it presents, destroys, or steals no more than the images of the other. The Abrahamic breaks and tears as it utters words that break from their context, finding again a speech that cuts and unbinds. The Abrahamic also affirms a certain silence. It surrounds and articulates an insufficient hyphen that does not bridge anything, the silence of which, moreover, "does not pacify or appease anything, not a single torment, not a single torture. It will never silence their memory. It could even worsen the terror, the lesions, and the wounds. A hyphen is never enough to conceal protests, cries of anger or suffering, the noise of weapons, airplanes and bombs."[24]

The names of the Abrahamic are numerous—perhaps as numerous as legion (French, foreign, or other). The explosiveness to which they expose us in Derrida's writings is compounded in the oscillation whose momentum may have started over with the two sons of Abraham, the two Biblical brothers, Ishmael and Isaac ("Hear, O Ishmael!" as Derrida often quotes Joyce). The figurations of Biblical fraternity open the distance within and between the "Christian roots of the motif of fraternity,"[25] within and between any notion of "fraternity." Commenting on Derrida's work, Fethi Benslama writes that the "being-together" of these brothers, of Ishmael and Isaac, may in fact constitute the unbearable itself.[26] The two brothers, each prefiguring one of two nations that the Bible promises, thus provide the poles of an oscillation that never quite gathers as the Arab Jew.[27] The reading field to which we are transported is therefore that of an impossibility, a non-figure that, in its invisibility and unreadability, reproduces and exceeds the so-called "Jewish-Muslim sym-

---

24. Jacques Derrida, *Monolingualism of the Other*, 11

25. Jacques Derrida, *Politics of Friendship*, 268n10.

26. "C'est donc l'être ensemble de ces deux frères, de ces deux modalités de l'origine qui est intenable, comme si leur réunion menaçait la raison monothéiste dans ces concepts fondamentaux" (Fethi Benslama, "La répudiation originaire," *Idiomes, Nationalités, Déconstructions: Rencontre de Rabat avec Jacques Derrida, Cahiers Intersignes* 13 [Paris & Casablanca: l'Aube-Toubkal, 1998] 134).

27. "What could be more important," Mark Taylor asks, commenting on Derrida, "than speaking of the Jew and the Arab today, here and now?" (Mark C. Taylor, *Nots* [Chicago: University of Chicago Press, 1993] 54). Taylor thus significantly raises the question and acknowledges its importance while suggesting that Derrida responds to it.

28. For a recent and extensive discussion of Judeo-Arabic culture and some of the scholarly and political problems associated with its history, see Ammiel Alcalay, *After Jews and Arabs: Remaking Levantine Culture* (Minneapolis: University of Minnesota Press, 1993). A more circumscribed reading of the issue in the Israeli and Palestinian context appears in Ella Shohat, "Zionism From the Standpoint of its Jewish Victims," *Social Text* 19–20 (1988): 1–35 and more recently in Shohat's "The Invention of the Mizrahim," *Journal of Palestine Studies* 29, no. 1 (autumn 1999). For a discussion of the so-called Jewish-Muslim symbiosis within the specialized scholarly discourse, and for an extensive bibliography, see Wasserstrom, *Between Muslim and Jew*, esp. chapter 1; see also Mark R. Cohen, *Under Crescent and Cross: The Jews in the Middle Ages* (Princeton: Princeton University Press, 1994).

biosis,"[28] at once ancient and new—more ancient and newer than could, strictly speaking, ever appear or become manifest. The Abrahamic exposes us to the nonfigure that was long ago inscribed and erased in "the fold of this Abrahamic or Ibrahimic moment, folded over and again by the Gospels between the two other 'religions of the Book,' *le pli de ce mouvement abrahamique ou ibrahimique replié par l'Évangile entre les deux autres « religions du Livre »*."[29] It was inscribed and erased by "Christian typologists [who] also used Esau, Pharaoh, and Herod to couple the Jew and the Muslim as carnal children of Abraham facing each other across the world-historic break effected by the Incarnation."[30] Figured and failing to figure as the promise and the threat of an alliance—the cut of circumcision—of the Arab and the Jew, the Arab Jew (Muslim and Jew, Moor and Jew, Arab and Jew), the Abrahamic articulates the non-figure of the first as already the last, of the last and of the end, an explosive specter of uncertain and troubling existence ("Judaism and Islam would thus be perhaps, *seraient peut-être alors*, the last two monotheisms to revolt against everything . . .").[31] The Arab Jew, whose silent hyphen will prove both more and less than that of "Judeo-Christianity," fails to fuse and violently opens the field of the Abrahamic that Derrida gives us to read.[32] This, then, is Derrida "on religion."

Unsurprisingly, to read (for) the Abrahamic, as this anthology proposes, will

---

29. Jacques Derrida, *Donner la mort* (Paris: Galilée, 1999) 149. This passage, as well as other sections of *Donner la mort*, were published in the final French version after David Wills's translation (*The Gift of Death*). One significant difference between the English and the French versions has to do with the quite consistent addition of the name of Ishmael, as well as, occasionally, that of the Arabic name of Abraham, Ibrahim (cf., for example, page 100 of the French text, where Ishmael is now mentioned; he was not in *The Gift of Death*, 70).

30. Julia Reinhard Lupton, "*Othello* Circumcised: Shakespeare and the Pauline Discourse of Nations," *Representations* 57 (winter 1997): 78–79.

31. Jacques Derrida, *Religion,* 12/F20.

32. As far as I am aware, Fethi Benslama is the only one to have identified the importance of the Arab Jew in relation to Derrida's work. Benslama writes, "We will be unable to leave in the unthought the collective play of multiple distancings and couplings of these edges, *ces bords à bords*: Greek-Jew, Greek-Arab, Jew-Arab, or Jew-Greek, Arab-Jew, and most particularly this last among them: Jew-Arab, Arab-Jew, from which the Abrahamic origin would become accessible to Deconstruction, *à partir duquel l'origine abrahamique deviendrait accessible à la déconstruction*" (Fethi Benslama, "Editorial," *Idiomes*, 9). In contrast, Jean-François Lyotard considered the specific unbinding of the hyphen to be at work solely in the term *Judeo-Christian*. Here only, Lyotard suggests, is *religion* (or *religions*, as opposed to *nations*) at work: "The hyphen traced by Paul is the one that can be read in the expression 'Judeo-Christian.' It is distinct from all the other hyphens that associate or dissociate the name of the Jew from those of the nations where Jews are dispersed or exiled: Judeo-Arab, Judeo-Spanish, Judeo-Roman" (Jean-François Lyotard and Eberhard Gruber, *The Hyphen: Between Judaism and Christianity*, trans. Pascale-Anne Brault and Michael Naas [Amherst, NY: Humanity Books, 1999] 15). Lyotard seems not to consider how the term *Arab Jew* could singularly disrupt the hyphen of *Judeo-Christian*—not, at least, until Lyotard himself writes how Paul says that "the Israel of the flesh . . . was born in the Sinai (in Arabia, he specifies). . . . Are we to conclude that Jews, like Arabs, are slaves of the flesh, and so are disinherited?" (21). It is precisely the status of this "like" ("*like* Arabs") that reflections on the Abrahamic engage and that will have to be read in—and as a result of—Derrida's work, as I am trying to show.

mean to listen to the recurrence of sounds and lexemes that have escaped attention, have otherwise failed to gather or to coagulate—into words.[33] They have therefore retained the spectrality and explosiveness of a non-history, the spectrality and explosiveness of the Abrahamic. "Recite," then, as the Qur'ān exhorts; "recite," this anthology would say, re-cite and read, read Derrida on "religion," read "once more, once more," along and around the *bord, corps, dors, fors, fort,* fort, *hors, maure, mord,* mord, *mores, mors, mort, sort,* and more. Read Derrida, in other words, still and once more, read Freud on "religion," and read also Shakespeare. Read the incomparable, Shylock and Othello. This will take time, and yes, yes, the clock (or is it a bomb?) is ticking.

MOORINGS

Freud had his ghosts, he confesses it on occasion.

—Jacques Derrida[34]

I was eight or nine, [at] a fair in El-Biar. I could no longer find my parents and blinded by tears I had been guided toward my father's car, up behind the church, by the creatures of the night, guardian spirits, *des fantômes bienveillants.* Spirits, why are spirits always called upon in letter writing? . . . something like speculating with spirits, denuding oneself before them; he wrote only (on) letters that one, one of the last along with Freud finally. This is Europe, *centrale,* the center of Europe . . . .

—Jacques Derrida[35]

At the center of Europe, Central Europe, Freud searches out Europe's other, fixing an alterity defined by a range of sightings and repressive forgettings—what we might call "oversights." At this time, Freud, concerned in his work with the effect of the phantom, oversights, and mental deliberations, is on the verge of an exposure to the Abrahamic, whose ghostly aura he marks out. "Driving away the phantoms that were at that time supposedly haunting [Wilhelm] Fliess," Avital Ronell writes, Freud "was 'seriously' working on specters."[36] By way of a double gesture that conjures and excludes, and from the very opening of *The Psychopathology of Everyday*

---

33. Hobson writes, "something akin to points of accumulation of an argument, places where it was possible to bring complexity together into a word and hence raise as a theme" (Marian Hobson, *Jacques Derrida,* 3).

34. Derrida, *Archive Fever,* 89.

35. Derrida, *Post Card,* 34–35/F40.

36. Avital Ronell, *Dictations: On Haunted Writing* (Lincoln: University of Nebraska Press, 1993) 4.

37. Sigmund Freud, *The Psychopathology of Everyday Life,* trans. James Strachey, in *The Standard Edition of the Complete Psychological Works of Sigmund Freud* (London: Hogarth Press and the Institute of Psychoanalysis, 1960 [1901]), vol. 6.

Life,[37] a peculiar shape "is made to remind the reader of something that cannot be altogether forgotten, something that spooks or haunts (*"Nun ist die Luft von solchem Spuk so voll"*) the text about to be broached. Freud is here calling upon Goethe's text, which names the ghostly stakeout. But, literary as this *West-östliche* gesture may be, it hardly amounts, as Ronell has shown, to a matter of figuration. The haunting shape is not a figure; nor, in the not-quite-logic of spectrality, does it ever achieve ontological stability. The shape is a thing, a "something," that can hardly be identified—and if at all, it could only be ascertained by way of its effects. The stock of Freud's ghostly conjuring engenders a whole field of geopolitical speculation whose borders he probes in the *Psychopathology*.

What takes shape under this heading and, subsequently, under the name "Signorelli," has been altogether overlooked to the extent that it articulates, in Freud's text, an early instance of a haunting of and by religion. By bringing together—suspending for now the status of such "togetherness"—uncertain shapes of Judaism, Christianity, and Islam, Freud's example does not break down but it breaks *out* by unexpectedly providing protocols of reading "religion" and its attendant hyphens. Overlooked, and thus reproducing the (failed) forgetting that constitutes it in Freud's account in the "first" place, the no less spectral and unreadable shape of the *Psychopathology* pivots on the Abrahamic.

Although it appears as a shape, then, the articulated "something" fails to gather into a secured or unified figure. The story of its vanishing appearances—the inscription of a no less failing forgetting—could be said to begin, after the Goethe citation in Freud's text, in the opening pages of his *Psychopathology*. Freud takes us on a car trip in which talking ensues, but he does not describe this occurrence as a "talking-cure." He becomes involved in the story, rather, of a "conversation with a stranger, *ein Gespräch mit einem Fremden*" and a "melancholy event, *traurige Ereignis*" (3). It is a sad occasion, in part no doubt because here even Freud's own "talking out" failed to happen. Freud remains mostly silent, but this is a silence that provides the occasion for a greater clarity in the order of figuration—the revelatory occasion, at any rate, of a famous event, which came to be known as the "Signorelli example."

Freud had notoriously forgotten the artist's name "who painted the magnificent frescoes of the 'Four Last Things, *letzten Dingen* [Death, Judgement, Hell, and Heaven] in the Orvieto cathedral" (2). This serves as more than an "example." Freud calls it an event or *Ereignis*. In connection to this event, Freud tells his readers that he has a lot on his mind about which he cannot talk—Freud says this much: he must remain silent. He was constrained to be silent, he says ("what is there to be said?" [5]), at least on the topic ("I did not want to allude to the topic" [3]) and therefore had to interrupt himself: "It was a motive which caused me to interrupt myself while recounting what was in my mind" (4). Freud had names on his mind. In the Signorelli example, a number of names testify to the strange shape, and to what Freud understands as "a sort of compromise." By way of this compromise, the names, remembered and forgotten, remind Freud "just as much of what I wanted to forget as of what I wanted to remember." The names, he continues, also "show me that my intention to forget something was neither a complete success nor a complete failure, *und zeigen mir, daß meine Absicht, etwas zu vergessen, weder ganz gelungen, noch ganz mißglückt ist*" (4).

Freud furtively begins to assemble a Shakespearean cartography. In the twin spaces of "not complete success" and "not complete failure," what inscribes itself are the impossibly shared destinies of the Arab and the Jew that have been etched by Shakespeare. Freud's unforgettably forgotten moment is occupied by Othello's near success and by Shylock's incomplete failure. Enter the stranger(s). Freud tells us that he was "driving in the company of a stranger, a foreigner, *mit einem Fremden*, from Ragusa in Dalmatia to a place in Herzegovina." Driving East, Freud continues to map Europe's violent "ethnic" conflicts, yet he also turns and veers back, closing in on Italy. His mind is approaching Venice, which is why the "conversation had turned to the subject of travel in Italy" (2). At some point, Freud had turned to his "traveling companion, *Reisegefährte*" and asked him about Orvieto, inquiring about the magnificent frescoes of the cathedral on the "Four Last Things." Freud was changing the subject. He and this by no means extravagant and wheeling "stranger" "had been talking about the customs of the Turks living in *Bosnia* and *Herzegovina*" (3; emphasis in the original). "Those people, *diese Leute*" Freud had reported, "are accustomed to show great confidence in their doctor and great resignation to fate" (3). Freud had neglected, he realized, to pursue the lines of thought that brought him to the Turks and their resignation toward death, and he had therefore refrained from telling—though he wanted to do so—"a second anecdote which lay close to the first in my memory."

Although Freud had suppressed the anecdote when conversing with the stranger, he proceeds to divulge it to his readers. In this anecdote the main characters are not "turning Turk," so much as they could be said to be "turning ghost." "These Turks place a higher value on sexual enjoyment than on anything else, and in the event of sexual disorders they are plunged in a despair which contrasts strangely with their resignation towards the threat of death, *welche seltsam gegen ihre Resignation bein Todesgefahr absticht*. (3)"[38] Thus the "topic" to which Freud did and did not allude, when he interrupted his conversation about the cathedral at

---

38. Although there are clear differences in his account (most notably in the pathological historicization), Freud is already quoting a well-known stereotype. Recall, for example, Hegel's description of Islam's "tendency to let everything take its own course, indifference with respect to every purpose, absolute fatalism, indifference to life; no practical purpose has any essential value" (Hegel, *Lectures*, vol. 3, 243).

Orvieto—a strange contrast that he did and did not relate in his conversation with a stranger. Freud did say that he was talking about the Turks, about their sexuality and their "resignation towards the threat of death." Yet, it is not entirely clear— certainly not to Freud, not for another twenty years—whether, or how, the topic of this anecdote is in fact distinct from "the topic of 'death and sexuality,'" which Freud tells his readers in the next sentence he wishes to leave unspoken. The confusion here may derive from the fact that the later "topic" is figured as an addition, a supplement: "I did *more, ich tat aber* noch mehr, [than suppress the account of the Turks]: I also diverted my attention from pursuing thoughts which might have arisen in my mind from the topic of 'death and sexuality'" (3; emphasis added). Freud allows that his views "have from the very first been *dualistic*," and insists on a certain unbridgeable doubling (of death and sexuality, of Italy and Bosnia, of forgetting and remembering, of success and failure, of Christian and Muslim, etc.).[39] He also begins to alert us to the phantomatic shape of a *trait d'union*, a shape wherein the difference between terms is not simply one of either unity or opposition but of dualistic disjunction.

In Freud's telling, the rumored phantomatic shape of "those people" ("I had told him what I had heard from a colleague practicing among those people") occurs as the partial veiling of the (author of the) Christian figuration of "Death, Judgement, Hell and Heaven." This phantomatic shape, in turn, comes to constitute a larger shape that may hardly be said to gather anything (note, again, that Freud writes about a "strange contrast," not about a gathering. Freud does so, even if being plunged into despair over sexual enjoyment does not necessarily appear—later will perhaps no longer appear—as particularly contrasting with a "resignation toward death"). If this shape indeed gathers in the mode of contrast, it is therefore only covertly, perhaps forgetfully, as "a sort of compromise" that never loses its strangeness. Moreover, what may have become noticeable is the way in which, in Freud's telling, this shape is further haunted by another strange contrast. I have said earlier that the "Signorelli example" constitutes a haunting by religion—indeed, a religion and shape in which the forgetting of unforgettable terms is as necessary as it is succeeding and failing: the spectral shape of the Abrahamic. The Jew (Freud interrupting his telling, [n]either telling [n]or forgetting) the Christian (Signorelli) (about) the Muslim. "Signior," Freud would have said, prayed, or conjured—had he remembered the unpronounceable name of Il Signior—"it is the Moor."

In this shape, the haunting of forgetting (with and by remembering) affects yet

---

39. Sigmund Freud, *Beyond the Pleasure Principle*, in *The Standard Edition*, trans. James Strachey, vol. 18, 53.

another strange contrast that Freud would revisit when, displacing Abraham and the Abrahamic onto another "figure," he associated "in one figure, the father, the founding father and the stranger,"[40] the Jew and the Egyptian, Moses, and inevitably—following insistent fantasmatic projections and complex modes of denegations that were not lost on Freud and on the basis of which Egypt is to this day associated with and dissociated from the "East" and from the "Arab world"—the Jew and the Arab.[41] What associations, what semantic and emotional investments could there be between and within these terms, between what links and dissociates them? Freud, the Arab, the Christian, the Jew. What "mental geography" brings and fails to bring these together in the mode of contrast?

> Two of these scoundrels were Croats who called themselves Jews or Moors, *Juifs et* [*sic*] *Maures*, and who spent their life, as they confessed to me, roaming Spain and Italy, embracing Christianity and having themselves baptized. . . .
> —Jean-Jacques Rousseau[42]

> Why on the sudden is your colour changed?
> —Christopher Marlowe, *The Jew of Malta*, 2.3.323

Freud's mind follows turns and conversions that, at the center of Europe, also remain fixed in an Italian vicinity, never too far from Venice. He brings together, under the heading of a strange contrast, shapes of the Abrahamic. Discreetly sig-

---

40. Fethi Benslama, "La répudiation," in *Idiomes*, 139.

41. Freud reinscribes, in *Moses and Monotheism*, the Abrahamic configuration, which, he says, "tormented me like an unlaid ghost" (Freud, *Moses and Monotheism*, in *The Standard Edition*, vol. 23, 103) and with which he opened his *Psychopathology*. Implying a complex process of memory and forgetting concerning the church (*Moses*, 55–56), Freud also rewrites the Abrahamic, the Turk, and the Jew, by exploring what Moses shared with the Turks. On the basis of Moses' Egyptian identity, Freud compares the Turks' attitude toward circumcision, or rather noncircumcision, with that of Moses and other Egyptians: "Even to this day a Turk will abuse a Christian as an 'uncircumcised dog.' It may be supposed that Moses, who, being an Egyptian, was himself circumcised, shared this attitude" (30, and see also the reference to borrowings from "Arabian tribes," 34). Jan Assmann underscores the momentous division Freud is struggling to undo here, arguing against "the map of memory," on which "Israel and Egypt appear as antagonistic worlds" (Assmann, *Moses the Egyptian: The Memory of Egypt in Western Monotheism* [Cambridge, Mass.: Harvard University Press, 1997] 6).

42. Jean-Jacques Rousseau, *Confessions*, book 2, trans. J. M. Cohen (London: Penguin, 1953) 65. The translation of *et* as *or* instead of *and* is not found in other translations and, although not strictly speaking incorrect (it is not necessarily an exclusive *or*), has no philological basis, or at least none that I could find. That Rousseau is using an inclusive *and* ("Juif *et* Maure") is confirmed when he later writes that he was not given the "white robe" at the conversion ceremony: "Unlike the Moor, I was not given one since I had not the honour to be a Jew" (72). Marian Hobson's comments in another context bear relevance here to a reading of the Arab Jew, the Arab and/or the Jew: "In its passing from *et* to *ou* and back, the phrase exhibits the very kind of instability in discrimination being presently analyzed, for the copula passes over into a disjunction as the strands separate, and back as the focus has stabilized" (Hobson, *Jacques Derrida*, 65).

naling toward both Othello and Shylock, Freud does *more*. He does more than merely confirm that a Turk could turn ghost, that a "blessed Jew" could turn Moor, and that such "Blackmoor" could, in turn, turn "white." The turns of Samuel Marochitanus, the "blessed Jew of Morocco," already tell the story of "a blackamoor turned white," of a Jew turned Muslim but also turned Christian.[43] In this story, the Jew turned Muslim translates into the Jew turned Christian so that the violent substitutions of the Abrahamic (the ram for Isaac) are maintained in their inequalities. This story articulates the indispensable if ungathered premise upon which the comparison, the nonbridging of a strange contrast, could be made ("Fair Jessica" is the story of such turn—"I say my daughter is my flesh and blood" says her father Shylock, to which Salarino replies, "There is more difference between thy flesh and hers than between jet and ivory.")[44] Freud's story of a turn does more than merely add to the comparison Shakespeare's Lorenzo had already made,[45] namely, the comparison between—that is, the impossible figure of another hyphen—Jew and Moor.[46] Minimally, however, Freud *entame*, he broaches and breaches, as Derrida says, he provides an introductory reading of the phantomatic, if unreadable and not entirely forgettable, shape of the Abrahamic at the center of Europe.

---

43. What Norman Daniel refers to as the " 'Rabbi Samuel' literature" seems to have originated in an anti-Jewish polemical treatise called, in the original Arabic, *Ifḥam al-Yahūd* and written by Rabbi Samuel the Moroccan (Samaw'al al-Maghribī), who had converted to Islam (Norman Daniel, *Islam and the West: The Making of an Image* [Edinburgh: Edinburgh University Press, 1960] 189). In the Latin translation of his treatise (and, subsequently, in the numerous translations into Western European languages), Samuel turns, however, Christian. There is, as of yet, no study of "his" book, a heavily edited translation of which appeared in English in the seventeenth century under the title *The Blessed Jew of Marocco: Or, A Blackmoor made White. Being a Demonstration of the true Messias out of the law and prophets, by Rabbi Samuel, a Jew Turned Christian* (York: T. Broad, 1648).

44. William Shakespeare, *The Merchant of Venice*, ed. Jay L. Halio (Oxford: Oxford University Press, 1993) 3.1.35–37.

45. At this point in *The Merchant of Venice*, Lorenzo is answering Lancelot's criticisms regarding his engagement to Jessica. Noting that there are two distinct moments to Lancelot's diatribe, "Fair Jessica" reports to Lorenzo what Lancelot told her first: "He tells me flatly there's no mercy for me in heaven because I am a Jew's daughter, and he says you are no good member of the commonwealth, for in converting Jews to Christians, you raise the prize of pork" (Shakespeare, *The Merchant of Venice*, 3.5.29–33). This second argumentative moment ("you raise the prize of pork"), more directly addressed to Lorenzo, chastizes him for converting Jews. To this accusation, Lorenzo responds by telling Lancelot that he, Lancelot, does, in fact, the "same." Doing so, Lorenzo illustrates ever so fleetingly the comparability of Jew with Moor, of Shylock with Othello: "I shall answer that better to the commonwealth than you can the getting up of the Negro's belly. The Moor is with child by you, Lancelot!" (3.5.34–36).

46. Lorenzo's linking of Jew and Moor appears to maintain the unreadability of the Abrahamic: it remains largely unattended by most readers of Shakespeare, but it is "much that the Moor should be more than reason." Yet there are a few exceptions that broach, but can only begin to elaborate on the link between and the comparison of the two plays. Most notably, Leslie A. Fiedler, *The Stranger in Shakespeare* (New York: Stein and Day, 1972) and Julia Reinhard Lupton, "*Othello* Circumcised." As to the difficulties associated with the term *Moor* in a different but relevant context, see Jack D. Forbes, *Black Africans and Native Americans: Color, Race and Caste in the Evolution of Red-Black Peoples* (Oxford: Basil Blackwell, 1988) and Gayatri Chakravorty Spivak, "Race before Racism: The Disappearance of the American," *Boundary 2* 25, no. 2 (summer 1998): 35–53.

~

An explicit political meaning has also been attributed to the extreme threshold between life and death, the human and the inhuman, that the *Muselmann* inhabits ... At times a medical figure or an ethical category, at times a political limit or an anthropological concept, the *Muselmann* is an indefinite being in whom not only humanity and non-humanity, but also vegetative existence and relation, physiology and ethics, medicine and politics, and life and death continuously pass through each other.

—Giorgio Agamben[47]

Freud directs our reading of the Abrahamic toward a shape of forgetting occurring, a movement of vanishing where that which "turns Turk" also continues to "turn ghost." When it appears or reappears—though the term "appearance" has already proven inadequate—in the texts of survivors of Nazi extermination camps, it remains as unreadable as Kafka's Abrahams,[48] open only to the repeated and uninterpreted inscription of its being-forgotten, the movement of its disappearance. Doing so, the spectral shape of the Abrahamic maintains the complex movement of memory's successes and failures described by Freud. And it does so, as Primo Levi remembers the forgotten and unforgotten forgettable, "without leaving a trace in anyone's memory."[49]

"Those people" are vanishing ghosts and, much further from Venice, they still bring together—but this togetherness is more than ever suspended—disparate theatrical genres (comedy and tragedy, Shylock and Othello, the *Merchant* and the *Moor of Venice*). They are named, as Hélène Cixous recently recalled, "Muslims." They are "the deported, for example, as what were called 'Muslims.'" They are named, then, even if they do not quite figure, although Cixous subtly remarks that

---

47. Giorgio Agamben, *Remnants of Auschwitz: The Witness and the Archive*, trans. Daniel Heller-Roazen (New York: Zone Books, 1999) 47–48.

48. To Kafka's Abrahams one should perhaps add Kafka's "Savages" who actualize in more than one way the promise made to Abraham that his descendants will be "as numerous as the stars of heaven and the sands on the seashore" (*Genesis* 22:17). Kafka's prophetic parable indeed gives pause as it reproduces the rhythmic repetition carrying yet "another Abraham," which punctuates the repetition, this time, with the words "or rather, *oder vielmehr.*" Kafka describes the ghostly and disappearing figure of those "of whom it is recounted that they have no other longing than to die, or rather, they no longer have even that longing, but death has a longing for them, and they abandon themselves to it, or rather, they do not even abandon themselves, but fall into the sand of the shore and never get up again.... Anyone who might collapse without cause and remain lying on the ground is dreaded as though he were the Devil, it is because of the example, it is because of the stench of truth that would emanate from him. Granted nothing would happen; one, ten, a whole nation might very well remain lying on the ground and nothing would happen.... (Franz Kafka, "The Savages," trans. Ernst Kaiser and Eithng Wilkins, in *Parables and Paradoxes* [New York: Schocken, 1961] 121).

49. Primo Levi, *Survival in Auschwitz [If This Is a Man]*, trans. Stuart Woolf (New York: Collier Books, 1961) 81.

50. Hélène Cixous, "We Who Are Free, Are We Free?" *Critical Inquiry* 19, no. 2 (winter 1993): 208.

they did play a "sort of role." "Everyone there has a sort of role, everyone is dressed up, travestied."[50]

In the context of recalling those "Muslims"—Jews "turning Moors" who, though well known, have attracted little critical attention—Cixous reminds us that we are also reading (and not reading) Shakespeare. Cixous thus reiterates and gives to read the *trait d'union* whose haunting shape provides the "strange contrast" of a non-gathering in Freud, reminding us that "one never dares think of Hell as a comedy." "After" the theological and the political, hell and comedy take the haunting shape of a strange contrast, that of "Jews" and "Muslims," Jews and Muslims, Arabs and Jews. The Abrahamic, if that is what this is, remains. It remains a haunting shape that is "made to remind the reader of something that cannot be altogether forgotten, something that spooks or haunts the text about to be opened, and in ways from which no one knows how best he may escape."[51]

"One knows that they are only here on a visit, that in a few weeks nothing will remain of them but a handful of ashes in some near-by field and a crossed-out number on a register."[52] In another description, they are the prisoners "who had been destroyed physically and spiritually, and who had neither the strength nor the will to go on living."[53] Lacking in that they provide no reason to invest in them, those whom Levi described as having turned Muslims provide little hope of "later . . . perhaps" deriving "some benefit."[54] Insistently marked for their failure to submit to a logic of value and capital, the Muslims are "the men in decay [with whom] it is not even worth speaking." They are the "weak, the inept, those doomed to selection," those who stopped fighting, living dead or walking corpses, and were no longer able to fold their legs. Unlike Freud's "Turks" who are "plunged in a despair that contrasts strangely with their resignation towards the threat of death," Levi's "Muslims" (*Muselmann,* or "Mussulmans" in some English translations) are also mostly Jews, but not only (perhaps no longer) Jews, and they are turning ghosts.

---

51. Avital Ronell, *Dictations*, 3.

52. Primo Levi, *Survival in Auschwitz*, 80–81.

53. Tadeusz Borowski, quoted in Cixous, "We Who Are Free," 208, n. 6. Borowski is among the few writers who make explicit the instability of the "Muslim" as more than a terminal stage. Indeed, the "Muslim" can still and always turn or "convert." The "Muslim" can turn ghost, Jew, but most importantly, the "Muslim" can turn back: "In Auschwitz one man knows all there is to know about another: when he *was* a Muslim, how much he stole. . . . " (Borowski, "Auschwitz, Our Home (A Letter)" in *This Way for the Gas, Ladies and Gentlemen*, trans. Barbara Vedder [New York: Penguin, 1967] 102; emphasis added). *Muslim*, the noun, can also turn verb, or at least participle: "The following day, when we were again driven out to work, a 'Muslimized' Jew from Estonia who was helping me haul steel bars tried to convince me all day that human brains are, in fact, so tender you can eat them absolutely raw" ("The Supper," in *This Way*, 156). Finally, "Muslim" (already an analogy?) is carried further by the force of analogy and simile: "What a goddam nuisance for a healthy man to be rotting in bed like a 'Muslim'" ("A True Story," in *This Way*, 158).

54. Levi, *Survival in Auschwitz*, 81.

Various testimonies about the "Muslims" were compellingly reproduced and discussed in Giorgio Agamben's *Remnants of Auschwitz*. These testimonies appear to inscribe no more than the "Muslims'" disappearance. Yet, though forgotten and forgettable (leaving no trace in anyone's memory, as Levi puts it), on the thither side of the human, they remain sites of memory. As problematic as their existence as memory traces seems to have been, they were already memory effects, referential extrapolations that recalled (and still recall) the look of "Arabs praying."[55] Having lost all will to live, "they do not even abandon themselves," and they hardly constitute anything; but out of the issues of naming are multiplied: "one hesitates to call them living: one hesitates to call death a death they do not fear."[56] Their name, though it is only one in a long, often forgotten and disseminated chain, is somehow spared the uncertainty of naming even if it produces added layers of forgotten perplexities. They are "Muslims, that is to say people of absolute fatalism. Their submission was not an act of will, but to the contrary, evidence that their will was broken."[57] Among the many unbearable difficulties that emerge here, one has to do with the impossibility of following the absent web of memory-traces that would philologically and otherwise link "Europe and the Jews," "Islam and the West," and Freud's Turks to the camps' *Muselmänner*.[58] What is indisputable, however, is that memory and its failure constitutes and unravels, exposes and explodes, such links.

This unbearable link can, even if with great difficulties, be named and recalled as the Arab Jew. It is the unreadable link, between life and death, of life and death, that has failed—that cannot but fail—to present itself to this day as the elusive shapes of the Abrahamic. In the following pages, I will pursue this unreadability of the Abrahamic, of "religion" in Derrida as the interplay of an autobiographeme (the utterance of the impossible: no longer, not only "I am dead" but "I am a Muselman," "I am an Arab Jew") and an impossible theological and political entity. The Abrahamic, in Derrida, is a silent, forgotten hyphen that constitutes the secret holding of links between the personal and the political, between the political and

---

55. Agamben, *Remnants*, 51.

56. Levi, quoted in Agamben, *Remnants*, 52.

57. Eugen Kogan, quoted in Agamben, *Remnants*, 53.

58. The philological problem raised by language, and more specifically by the idiom of the concentration camps (drawn primarily from Yiddish and Polish, with some German, Russian, and other Slavic languages), provide some of the context for Levi's discussion of the term *Muslim*, which stands therefore in ever complex relation to its more obvious semantic range. The term *Muselmann* has been erratically transliterated, but only rarely translated. It appears in numerous survivors' accounts, thoroughly cleansed of its "other" semantic value. As such, it offers a complex example of a rhetorical mechanism which, in a proximate context, Giorgio Agamben describes as follows: "Insofar as it implies the substitution of a literal expression with an attenuated or altered expression for something that one does not actually want to hear mentioned, the formation of a euphemism always involves ambiguities. In this case, however, the ambiguity is intolerable" (*Remnants*, 31).

the theological, whose porous boundaries are constantly violated. It inserts itself enigmatically and persistently in an unwritten and unreadable history. This trait of the primal father (Abraham) that splits his offsprings, disseminates his sperm, into already politicized entities, factionalized ethnicities, and "religions" grafted and cut off from one another, testifies to the consistently split origin that in Derrida's text fails to gather while inscribing itself in world historical, political explosions. "Religion," as the Abrahamic, while we claim it as "our own," can only disown us. Following the narrative(s) of Abraham, it is the story of a dissemination that exposes and explodes "religion" as it occurs in Derrida's texts, under yet more— once more, once more—names and shapes of the Abrahamic.

TICKINGS

It is much that the Moor should be more than reason. . . .

—William Shakespeare, *Othello*

This is what I want to show by deporting you as swiftly as possible to the limits of a basin, a sea, where there arrive for an interminable war the Greek, the Jew, the Arab, the Hispano-Moor. Which I am also (following), by the trace, *c'est ce que je veux montrer en vous déportant le plus vite possible aux limites d'un bassin, d'une mer, où s'arrivent pour une guerre interminable, le Grec, le Juif, l'Arabe, l'Hispano-Mauresque. Que je suis aussi, à la trace.*

—Jacques Derrida[59]

"There was, perhaps, what I would have wanted to say . . . by going to Capri. . . ." So begins the concluding paragraph of "Faith and Knowledge: The Two Sources of 'Religion' at the Limits of Reason Alone," a text published in French and English and presented by Jacques Derrida at a 1994 seminar that took place on the Italian island of Capri. As the title of the book that gathered the essays presented there indicates, this seminar was devoted to, at Derrida's initiative, the topic of "religion." This concluding paragraph ("There was, perhaps, what I would have wanted to say") also introduces the possibility that Derrida did not say what he would have wanted to say; that it is therefore not at all certain that Derrida has spoken or not on "religion"; and that what he said, if he did, he may have said on, or to, religion and, differently and more precisely, on, or to, the Abrahamic. The difficulty and uncertainty of the Abrahamic as religion could be alleviated by the argument with which I began this introduction regarding Derrida's contribution to the study of

---

59. Jacques Derrida, *Glas*, trans. John P. Leavey, Jr., and Richard Rand (Lincoln: University of Nebraska Press, 1986) 37/F51.

religion in the current understanding of the term. There is indeed neither reason nor justification to disagree with this line of argumentation. The readings that have sustained it have moreover begun and flourished in compelling scholarly works of varied persuasions.[60] All this may be granted and the slightly contrary claim could even be made that not only has there been no "return" of the religious—not in Derrida—but also that a collection of the central texts among those just mentioned would advance the debates that have already been generated by the individual works.[61] Such a collection would strengthen the merits of considering these works under the heading of "religion." Still, because of what Derrida said when he went to speak "on religion" in, for example, *Religion*, it remains possible that Derrida did not say what he would have wanted to say ("I am saying nothing, then, that can be said or sayable"),[62] on religion among other things. If there are conclusions to be drawn from this possibility, they are anything but certain. They implicate and engage any thinking of religion "in" and even "after" Derrida. It is from this uncertainty that the present anthology takes its point of departure in order to turn toward Derrida's own conclusion—if it is one—the conclusion for what is, in context, his most explicit statement (perhaps) on religion, in *Religion*, in "Faith and Knowledge": "There was, perhaps, what I would have wanted to say. . . ."

TICKINGS (II)

Ḥafiẓa 'an ẓahri qalb.

—Arabic expression

The event cannot be as noisy as a bomb, as garish or blazing as some metal held in the fire. Even were it still an event, here it would be—strict-ure against strict-ure—inapparent and marginal.

—Jacques Derrida[63]

" . . . *et grenades*" (" . . . and pomegranates," but also—"Each time what is involved is a machine, *il s'agit chaque fois de machine*"—[64] " . . . and grenades") is the title of

---

60. Without doing justice to the specificity and diversity of directions pursued in each of them, I am here referring to the works of such scholars and thinkers as Mohammed Arkoun, Christopher Bracken, Pascale-Anne Brault, John Caputo, Thomas Carlson, Harold Coward, Jean-Jacques Forté, Toby Foshay, Rodolphe Gasché, Susan Handelman, Kevin Hart, Abdelkebir Khatibi, Michael Naas, Elisa New, Jill Robbins, Gayatri Spivak, Mark Taylor, Hent de Vries, Elisabeth Weber, Shira Wolosky, and others (see bibliography).

61. Derrida's own reflections on the theological were hard to miss (although, it appears, not hard to misread) from the earliest publications, and could be witnessed as well in a certain reception of his work such as Mikel Dufrenne and Henri Meschonnic.

62. Derrida, *Politics of Friendship*, 70.

63. Derrida, *Glas*, 107.

64. Derrida, "Faith and Knowledge," in this volume, section 37.

the concluding section of Derrida's "Foi et savoir" ("Faith and Knowledge") his contribution to the publication of the seminar's proceedings in *La religion* (*Religion*).

Like the rest of "Faith and Knowledge," " . . . *et grenades*" is fragmented, divided into numbered subsections; but unlike the other subsections, it ends with a short paragraph that was not included in the first published English translation of " . . . *et grenades*." This missing paragraph (but its "being-missing" has now vanished) must be read in order to address the question of religion, which Derrida may have spoken about, or not, and most urgently the question of the Abrahamic and "the Abrahamic religions" in his writings. What this introduction traces is a way of marking a path of entry into the question of the Abrahamic, focusing on moments where the three so-called Abrahamic religions or markers thereof are cross-implicated (by now, it should be clear that they hardly cohabit peacefully) in and around Derrida's texts. Most important to consider in this context is that Derrida's name is also implicated, perhaps no less violently, in these moments—and how it is so (this will turn out to be the case not only here but also, and perhaps most prominently, in *Glas*, "Circumfession," *Monolingualism*, and "A Silkworm of One's Own"). Second, but more importantly, by writing, if not binding, the Abrahamic, Derrida engages in a radical re-thinking and re-reading of what could be called "religious difference," something which exceeds any recognizable religion, and unrecognizable as such, exceeds and haunts even a recognizable *via negativa*, while "locating" the Abrahamic. The Abrahamic, Derrida tells us, exposes and explodes (as) "religion."

> (*Here perhaps is what I would have wanted to say*, ce que j'aurais voulu dire, *of a certain Mount Moriah—by going to Capri, last year, so close to Vesuvius and to Gradiva. Today I recall (to) myself*, je me rappelle, *what I had read long ago in* Genet à Chatila, *of which one would have to recall*, dont il faudrait rappeler, *so many premises in so many languages, agents and victims, and the wakes and consequences, all landscapes and all specters:* "One of the questions I will not avoid, que je n'éviterai pas, *is that of religion*," Laguna, April 26 1995.)[65]

This final and concluding paragraph of " . . . *et grenades*" situates in place and time the writing of the entire essay on religion (Derrida writes early on that the printed text of "Foi et savoir" is "d'un caractère différent" from the one given at the seminar). Unlike the other subsections, this paragraph is unnumbered, italicized, and in parentheses (There are fifty-two numbered subsections in "Faith and Knowledge"—"52 very unequal sequences, as many crypts dispersed in a non-identified field . . . like a desert about which one isn't sure if it is sterile or not, or like a field of ruins and of mines and of wells and of caves and of cenotaphs and of scattered

---

65. Ibid., section 52, translation altered.

seedings"[66]—the first section of which is entitled "Italiques" and written, all sub-sections numbered, in Italic characters). The paragraph begins with the word "Voilà" and, appearing to refer to what precedes, it concludes "Faith and Knowledge": "There was perhaps what I would have wanted to say, *voilà peut-être ce que j'aurais voulu dire. . . .*" The uncertain status of this "missing" paragraph becomes clearer here, for if he spoke this by going to Capri, Derrida did not do so in a simple present tense or past present tense. Hence, the text says neither "what I wanted to say, *ce que j'ai voulu dire*," nor "what I had wanted to say, *ce que j'avais voulu dire.*" Along with the "perhaps," "what I would have wanted to say" not only suspends the ever having been present of the paragraph and of Derrida's words on religion. It also introduces uncertainty regarding whether, and what, Derrida spoke or did not—on what and to (*à*) whom. The phrase and its uncertainty further suggest that the word *voilà* is not simply a conclusion to "Faith and Knowledge"—it does not simply refer to what has, perhaps, been said in Capri. Rather, the suggestion would be that *voilà* refers to what follows, namely the italicized and parenthetical paragraph itself. *Voilà*, therefore, could equally be read as an introduction to a no less non-present time, the time of a conditional: *Voilà*, "There is," perhaps even "Here is," "Here perhaps is . . . ": "Here perhaps is what I would have wanted to say, *voilà peut-être ce que j'aurais voulu dire. . . .* " Derrida may have said or spoken, then, what he wanted to say, and he may also not have or he may have done so only in those concluding lines. In any case, this last paragraph could perhaps give the readers some (other) sense of what Derrida perhaps said, would have said, or would have wanted to say "by going to Capri."

> you'll have nephews neigh to you, you'll have coursers for cousins, and gennets for germans.
>
> —William Shakespeare[67]

With that possibility, the words that precede and follow this "introduction" would thus be placed under the insistent mark of the conditional. Before and after *voilà*, everything would be distinctly inflected, differently punctuated, and, as it were, in quotation marks. "Here is what I would have wanted to say: 'Today, I recall. . . . '" Read this way, these words suggest that part of what Derrida would have wanted to say (*dire*) was not to be spoken (*parler*), may have been not to be spoken, not to be spoken in his name. Rather, what Derrida would have wanted would have been to recall, to cite and to recite, "following a colon,"[68] a quotation from

---

66. Ibid., section 35.
67. Shakespeare, *Othello*, 1.1.112–13.

himself or another, and, in this case, from Jean Genet. It is with such a quotation (within invisible quotations marks as well, then) that Derrida ends this final paragraph of "Faith and Knowledge." Derrida quotes Genet: "'One of the questions that I will not avoid, *une des questions que je n'éviterai pas*, is the question of religion.'"

> Of course, in some respects Abraham does speak. He says a lot. But even if he says everything, he need only keep silent on a single thing for one to conclude that he hasn't spoken.
>
> —Jacques Derrida[69]

Part of what Derrida would have wanted to say, then, was perhaps not to speak but to quote, to recall and quote an assertion of non-avoidance. This assertion, which Derrida himself did not speak but did write and quote, recalls and implicates not only Derrida's own discussions of avoidance, but also the distinct and related issues of his re-deployment of the languages of other religious traditions, of the questions of negative theology/ies, issues to which Derrida himself has often returned, and upon which discussions of his work have tended to focus. Here also, interpretations at war, Derrida re-cites Genet ("For the first time I am afraid, while writing, as they say, 'on' someone, of being read by him. Not to arrest him, not to draw him back, not to bridle him. Yesterday he let me know that he was in Beirut, among the Palestinians at war, encircled outcasts. I know that what interests me always takes (its/his) place over there, but how to show that?").[70] Derrida introduces again his text on religion, and does so in a text that he had previously introduced by citing Hegel, with whom "Faith and Knowledge" began. Had he said what he would have wanted to say, Derrida would have thus also recalled and recited—as he did in the preceding sections—*Glas, Glauben und Wissen*, as well as, "Interpretations at War," Immanuel Kant, Henri Bergson, and Hermann Cohen, "the Jew, the German," and Jean Genet. Still, by going to Capri, Derrida certainly may have wanted to say, to recite and repeat that he, or another, will have been bound by a promise, an affir-

---

68 "But what is literally retained, in a declaration which means to bear witness to a work rather than to a person. . . . But a time of remembrance which recalls, *temps de remémoration qui se remémore*, less the friend than the saying. . . . The incredible audacity . . . , following a colon, opens a solitary subordinate clause; it suspends the entire declaration in an *epokhē* of this intemporal time which is suited to mourning but also annuls in advance everything that could indeed be said in this saying, *tout ce qui pourrait bien être dit en ce dire et déclaré en cette déclaration*. A colon. . . ." (Derrida, *Politics of Friendship*, 301/F334).

69. Jacques Derrida, *The Gift of Death*, 59.

70. Jacques Derrida, *Glas*, 36/F50. On Derrida and Genet, see Abdelkebir Khatibi, "Ultime dissidence de Genet," *Figures de l'étranger dans la littérature française* (Paris: Denoël, 1987) 129–200; Ian H. Magedera, "*Seing* Genet, Citation and Mourning; à propos *Glas* by Jacques Derrida," *Paragraph* 21 (March 1998) 28–44; and Jane Marie Todd, "Autobiography and the Case of the Signature: Reading Derrida's *Glas*," *Comparative Literature* 38:1 (winter 1986) 1–19.

mation to the future, that one will not avoid the question of religion. Doing so, Derrida would have spoken the future or perhaps the promise ("I will not") of a nonavoidance, therefore, that may or may not be his. In addition, had he said what he would have wanted to say by going to Capri, Derrida would also have said, "Today I recall to myself what I had once read in *Genet à Chatila.* . . . " Had he said that, and perhaps he did, Derrida would have spoken, he would not have avoided speaking—he would not have avoided speaking of religion. Here, Derrida would have recalled that day ("today") as a day that, in the manner of Nietzsche's "On this perfect day" in *Ecce Homo*, he may have wanted to mark "otobiographically." Yet, for Derrida speaking here, "this day"—"today"—is one that is not recalled as a perfect day.[71] Unlike Nietzsche, then, had he said what he would have wanted to say on that day, Derrida would not have told his life to himself ("On this perfect day," Nietzsche wrote, "I tell my life to myself"). Rather, Derrida would have called himself, brought close and closer, "so close to Vesuvius and to Gradiva," so close to Europe and to Latin, Christian Rome—he would have recalled to himself (*je me rappelle*), he would have recalled himself and again called himself (*je m'appelle, je me rappelle*), by citing that which an other said and spoke, and that he had read long ago.[72] Had he said what he would have wanted to say, Derrida would also have been put under the obligation to recall (*il faudrait rappeler*) that which was implied and implicated by *Genet à Chatila*, by Genet *at*, but also *to*, Shatila (Genet *à* Chatila): languages, agents, and victims, at Shatila and elsewhere, all of whom and all of which would have had to be recalled.[73] Had he said what he wanted to say, and perhaps he did (recall that the paragraph may be read as a conclusion for " . . . *et grenades*" and of what has been said in it), Derrida would have recalled (to, *à*) himself, he would have named himself and Shatila, and named himself *as* Shatila ("«A I, bien sûr», . . . les voyelles").[74] He would have remembered himself and Shatila, him/itself as a distant *lieu*, as a place in the distance which, like Mount

---

71. Robert Smith, *Derrida and Autobiography* (Cambridge: Cambridge University Press, 1995), esp. 63 & 75–96.

72. "How does one utter a worthwhile 'I recall' when it is necessary to invent both one's language and one's 'I,' to invent them *at the same time*, beyond this surging wave of amnesia, *comment dire un «je me rappelle» qui vaille quand il faut inventer et sa langue et son je, les inventer* en même temps, *par-delà ce déferlement d'amnésie* . . . ?" (*Monolingualism of the Other*, 31/F57; translation altered).

73. "On 14 September 1982, at about eleven o'clock in the morning, French, American and Italian ships started to leave Beirut. . . . The ships were taking the deterrent force away from Lebanon, and the very same day, 14 September 1982, at half-past four, their departure was eclipsed by Bechir Gemayel's assassination. . . . The next morning, Wednesday, and for the next three nights, the Palestinian camps of Sabra, Chatila and Bourj Barajneh were bombed, and the civilian population tortured and massacred. . . . They must have been between two and three thousand, the Palestinian and Lebanese dead, together with a few Syrians and some Jewish women married to Lebanese, all killed in the camps at Sabra, Chatila and Bourj Barajneh" (Jean Genet, *Prisoner of Love*, trans. Barbara Bray [Hanover, N.H.: Wesleyan University Press, 1992] 328).

74. Derrida, "Circonfession," 42.

Moriah—then and *today*[75]—brutally implicates the already bound "Abrahamic religions," their agents and victims, all of whom and to (*à*) all of whom Derrida perhaps spoke, or would have wanted to speak. "At the undiscoverable moment when the proper name breaks into language, destroys itself in language with an explosion—dynamite—and leaves it as a hole,"[76] it is, once again, once more, to a brutal "place" of explosions (" . . . and grenades"), of memory and forgetting ("very quickly recovered: a parasitic vegetation without, *sans,* memory"),[77] to this unreadable non-site of implication (and of dislocation) of the Abrahamic as it emerges from Derrida's writings that we are brought and recalled.

Derrida did not avoid the question of religion. He did not avoid recalling (to) himself, and (to) Shatila, addressing and recalling, therefore, also Islam as well as the other Abrahamic religions. But if recalling is not yet speaking ("what I would have wanted to say"), neither is (not) speaking, avoiding. It is important to note this distinction: Derrida, who may only have wanted to speak of Shatila and thus perhaps did (not) speak of it or to it, nonetheless may not have *avoided* speaking (which is why it is pertinent that the citation speaks in the future tense: "I will not avoid"). It is important to note this because the word *avoiding* evokes Derrida's own reading of it, his reading of Martin—("la tête d'un vieux Juif d'Alger," says *Post Card*)—Heidegger's *vermeiden* (translated as: *éviter,* avoiding) in *Of Spirit,* and may thus suggest a proximity, if not an identity, between (not) avoiding speaking and (not) speaking. In this 1987 book on Heidegger's avoidance, Derrida himself suggests that, here, another chapter of another book could be written, a chapter that, Derrida imagines, would be entitled *Comment ne pas parler.* "Here one could get into writing a chapter destined for a different book. I imagine its title: 'How to Avoid Speaking', *On pourrait s'engager ici dans l'écriture d'un chapitre destiné à un autre livre. J'en imagine le titre:* Comment ne pas parler."[78] At this point, in a footnote, Derrida mentions that in this same year (1987) he is publishing another text entitled "Comment ne pas parler," suggesting that though it bears the same imagined title ("Subtitle: To be or not to be Christian or, more savagely, *The Importance of (not) Being Christian,* as if it were possible"),[79] it may be that this other text is not the said chapter destined for a different book in which the question of avoiding and of Heidegger will have been addressed. Did Derrida then speak of it, did he write it, or did he avoid it? Did he speak "how not to speak" on this day?

---

75. See Derrida, *The Gift of Death,* 69–70.

76. Derrida, *Glas,* 236/F330.

77. Ibid.

78. Jacques Derrida, *Of Spirit,* trans. Geoffrey Bennington and Rachel Bowley (Chicago: University of Chicago Press, 1989) 2/F12.

79. "Sous-titre: Être ou ne pas être chrétien ou, plus sauvagement, *The Importance of (not) Being Christian,* comme si c'était possible" (Jacques Derrida, *Le toucher, Jean-Luc Nancy,* 274, n. 3).

Had he done so, were it what he would have wanted to say, would it have translated as "How to Avoid Speaking"? Would avoidance here recall or not the *via negativa*? Which? Clearly, the answer is neither a simple yes, nor, perhaps, a simple no(t).

Derrida's interrogation of Heidegger's avoidance in *Of Spirit* should not be read as accusation, nor is it one that could be launched as it is at Derrida. Derrida perhaps quoted the word "avoiding" but, as far as I could find, he neither affirmed avoidance nor asserted that he avoided, that he or anyone else should have avoided speaking, nor did he avoid speaking—on the question of religion among others. On the other hand, this does not necessarily mean that Derrida spoke, and it is possible, indeed, that Derrida did (not) speak—of Islam or of the other Abrahamic religions.

Earlier, in "Faith and Knowledge," one of the ways Derrida will have, perhaps, spoken of that which should not be avoided, or should at least be recalled were it spoken about—that which was named by his naming and recalling himself and Shatila (that is, Judaism, Christianity, Islam)—is by asserting another obligation toward Islam (recall that Derrida said: "il *faudrait* rappeler"). To be precise, Derrida writes that, at this moment, it is perhaps toward Islam that one *should,* that one would have to turn first: "at the moment when it is towards Islam, perhaps, that we ought to begin by turning our attention, *au moment où c'est vers l'islam que nous devrions peut-être commencer par tourner notre regard.*"[80] Derrida regrets the absence of Muslims at the meeting at Capri, and asserts that, along with the absence of women, this is something that should be taken into account. Here too it is a matter of obligation, a matter of duty: "We ought to take this into account, *nous devrons en tenir compte.*"[81]

The question of Islam—Islam *as* a question—is brought up again in the very next paragraph of "Faith and Knowledge." This is a matter of memory, of recalling again, or at least of not forgetting which, as in Freud, implicates the name: "Islam is

---

80. Derrida, "Faith and Knowledge," sec. 5; and compare how one would also have to begin again with Islam, how Islam would have to come again, first, to be named and recalled again—in order to be not looked at but, this time, heard—again, first, *d'abord*: "It will one day be necessary, first of all so as to recall and understand Islam, *Il faudra bien un jour, d'abord pour y rappeler et entendre l'Islam . . . ," Adieu,* 145, n. 71/F128, n. 1.

81. Derrida, "Faith and Knowledge," sec. 5; but the question of counting and of taking account, the question of the first and "the question of numbers," and the futural possibility of new and other manners of counting for the future, which is "perhaps the most grave and most urgent for the state and the nations of Israel" is a question that "also concerns all the Jews" and "all the Christians in the world." It is however, also a question that marks "a fundamental difference," a religious difference, between the three Abrahamic religions, since it does not concern the Muslims of the world, not *today,* "not at all Muslims today" (section 44). Today, Islam would have to be taken into an account—would have to be counted—even though counting is not the question of Islam. What counts as an account when counting and accounting are out of the question? Can such an account be settled? Settling accounts, *giving* accounts of that which cannot be counted would then become the question of Islam, the question from and to Islam, what is called Islam *today.* Needless to say, the question of number, *la question du nombre,* is "at the center" of a thinking of politics and of the theologico-political in *Politics of Friendship* (x/F14).

not Islamism, never forget this, but the latter operates in the name of the former, and this is the grave question of the name" (14). What is said and done "in the name of religion, here in the name of Islam" (sec. 6) is said and done, and there is no other remnant, no recalling or remembrance of avoidance, no question of avoiding speaking the name of Islam, which may then also be the Christian name of "religion."[82] Inscribing onto a future memory ("Never") that the force of a call and of a recall, the force of a name, is not to be considered an accident, Derrida writes, "Never to consider as an accident the force of the name in what happens, what is said and done *in the name of* religion, here in the name of Islam, *ne jamais traiter comme un accident la force du nom dans ce qui arrive, se fait ou se dit au nom de la religion, ici au nom de l'islam*" (7). Derrida, who does not recall (his) names by accident, recalls the name of Islam, recalls what is said and done, in the name of Islam—one of the names the recalling of which, the force of which, is no accident. Once again, it becomes difficult to determine whether what is spoken here, on or to religion, is or would have been spoken, here, in and under the Latin, Christian name of religion—that is to say also in and under the name of Islam. Is Derrida speaking here? And, whether or not he does, is it in the name of Islam? Is what Derrida says and does ("here") done in the name of religion ("*ce qui se fait ou se dit ... ici au nom de l'islam*"), in or under the name of Islam as another name for religion? Elsewhere Derrida will name the Muslim as the heir of a divine contradiction, as "the hyperbolic heir of this endless contradiction [of Judaism and Christianity]: contradiction of the Infinite itself. God, as usual, contradicts *himself, Dieu, comme d'habitude, se contredit.*"[83] But by naming Islam here does Derrida speak in the name of Islam? "What of Islam?" This is the (other) question of Islam, and of religion ("one of the questions I will not avoid") that Derrida asked just earlier: what of Islam and of its name? What of its name and of Derrida's name? What of it if, in the name of Islam, there is at work a "hypercritical rationality," one that does not "turn away from what may at least resemble a deconstructive radicalisation of the critical gesture," one that does not avoid the development of "a radical critique of what binds the *contemporary* democracy, *in its limits, in its operative concept and power,* to the market and to the tele-techno-scientific reason that dominates in it" (sec. 37)? What of it if its name is also "Islamism"? And what of it if this

---

82. Derrida explains, "The history of the word 'religion' should in principle forbid every non-Christian from using the name 'religion,' in order to recognize in it what 'we' would designate, identify and isolate there, *L'histoire du mot <<religion>> devrait en principe interdire à tout non-chrétien de nommer <<religion>>, pour s'y reconnaître, ce que <<nous>> désignerions, identifierions et isolerions ainsi*" ("Faith and Knowledge," section 34), and: "globalatinization, religion that does not speak its name, *mondialatinisation, religion qui ne dit pas son nom*" (section 42).

83. Jacques Derrida, *Le toucher*, 302, n. 1, re-citing "Edmond Jabès and the Question of the Book" where Derrida had famously written "*Dieu déjà se contredit*, God already contradicts himself."

is also Derrida's name, the name Shatila, the name of a place that like Moriah, then and today, is a brutal and explosive encounter between the three Abrahamic religions? What if this is indeed the name of the Abrahamic?

"Comment ne pas parler"—a text that is at once "terribly autobiographical" and concerned with exploring and deploying language (at) the sources and resources of negative theology, and with reading its languages—raises the question of "how not to speak." In it, Derrida speaks also of avoidance (évitement). The two questions raised in this title, and rendered more acute in the English translations ("how not to speak" and "how to avoid speaking") are distinct questions, and perhaps they are not questions at all, but there is a difference—one that is perhaps hardly tenable, but a difference nonetheless—between them. Recalling some of J. L. Austin's most difficult but also richest titles, "how not to speak" speaks of something other than avoidance, otherwise than avoidance. If it is the case that there is avoidance in "how not to speak," there is also, as Derrida explains, a speaking, an affirmation of the impossibility not to speak, indeed, an obligation to speak ("Comment ne pas parler, how could one not speak?"). How not to speak would then be neither a question nor an order, or both at the same time, as well as a prayer, a plea and a response to an obligation, an obligation to speak—which may be impossible to fulfill—but without avoidance, perhaps beyond or otherwise than avoidance.

In "How to Avoid Speaking," Derrida takes great care to distinguish between avoidance, specifically Heidegger's avoidance, and his own (not) speaking. Derrida translates his French title with the English "how to avoid speaking" but takes their difference one step further when he asks about Heidegger's relation to avoidance: "with regard to the traditions and texts [of apophatic theologies] that I have just evoked . . . does Heidegger stand in a relation of avoidance? What abyss would this simple word, avoidance, then designate?"[84] Thus showing the difficulty of reading the word or the notion of "avoidance," in Heidegger as well as in the Greek and Christian traditions of negative theology, Derrida proceeds to open parentheses again: "(To say nothing, once again, of the mysticisms or theologies in the Jewish, Islamic, or other traditions)" (55). Can this italicized and parenthetical saying nothing, this—perhaps—nonspeaking (which was not spoken when asking the question of Heidegger's avoidance), this naming of Islam and of an other Abrahamic religion in the language of a third ("chrétien latin français" says "Circonfession"), be equated with the "abyss" designated by the word "avoidance"? Can it be said to

---

84. Jacques Derrida, "How to Avoid Speaking: Denials," trans. Ken Frieden in Derrida and Negative Theology, ed. Harold Coward and Toby Foshay (Albany: SUNY Press, 1992); hereafter page numbers will be cited parenthetically in the text.

have been spoken, not spoken, or avoided, in any of the manners or senses pursued by the texts Derrida reads? Could this saying nothing, once again, this calling again, be equated with (not) speaking?

Earlier in "Comment ne pas parler" Derrida elaborates on his decision not to speak: "*I thus decided* not to speak *of negativity or of apophatic movements in, for example, the Jewish or Islamic traditions. To leave this immense place empty, and above all that which can connect such a name of God with the name of the Place,* ce qui peut y lier tel nom de Dieu au nom du Lieu, *to remain thus on the threshold—was this not the most consistent possible apophasis? Concerning that about which one cannot speak, isn't it best to remain silent? I let you answer this question. It is always entrusted to the other*" (53). The answer to the question, the decision, is the other's. The threshold, where Derrida may remain by speaking and not speaking, names a place, but it does not have one proper name (least of all "Arab Jew"). This nameless threshold would be where Derrida stays, where he would have wanted to remain, when he stood and delivered the lecture entitled "Comment ne pas parler" in Jerusalem (where Derrida however also asks: "Am I in Jerusalem or elsewhere, very far from the Holy City?"—the question is entrusted to the other) at the place where the connections and coimplications—if there are any, and they may be brutal, and brutally or harmlessly explosive—between the Abrahamic religions are yet to be unraveled. The place, which we have seen may be Moriah or Shatila, so close to the volcano Vesuvius, and to Gradiva, where connections are made between the name of God and the name of that place—there would be perhaps the "truth" that Derrida, like Augustine, "makes" by calling himself again (*je me rappelle*) a place and a name he says one should recall, to which one should recall oneself. Of that space, of that "resonant space," Derrida here says that "nothing, almost nothing will be said, *un espace de résonance dont il ne sera jamais rien dit, presque rien*" (31/F563). This is not, or at least not simply, almost not, an avoidance, nor is it simply (not) saying, (not) speaking, and only with great difficulties a speaking of nothing (*Nichts*). Indeed, this recalls Islam and the other Abrahamic religions, which are not necessarily something, but a place, which must be recalled and cannot be spoken of. But is to recall (not) to speak (of, to, at)? To whom and where? More precisely, one could ask, How is to recall (oneself) (not) to speak to and of? And is it possible? Will it always be impossible? Here, *là, voilà,* where he cites the speech of another, Derrida also calls himself again, he names himself and his discourse as "autobiographical," perhaps as the site of his *confession sans vérité,* writing, "*But if one day I had to tell my story, nothing in this narrative would start to speak of the thing itself if I did not come up against this fact,* si je ne butais sur ce fait: *for lack of capacity, competence, or self-authorization, I have never yet been able to speak of what*

my birth, as one says, should have made closest to me: the Jew, the Arab" (66, n.13).
Here, then, if he could, Derrida would tell his story—something he may have done,
or not, later on, on that day in which he remembered the name of Il Signior
("Monsignior Mourning" as David Farell Krell recasts *Cinders*'s "His Highness
Mourning"),[85] the day he recalled God and what he had read long ago in "mon com-
patriote" Augustine's *Confessions* ("Tiens, je me rappelle Dieu ce matin, le nom, une
citation . . ."). Derrida would tell his story, then, if not his life, to himself perhaps. On
this day, which has not yet, or perhaps already, come, Derrida would perhaps speak,
and speak his non-avoidance, of the question (but what does it mean, not to avoid a
question?). Derrida would say something, and yet, this does not mean that his story
would speak—nor of what—for by the same token, "nothing in this narrative would
start to speak of the thing itself." This story, Derrida's story, would not speak, not at
least for as long as Derrida did not—not address, but, rather, fall, stop, or rest upon,
as if by chance ("Mes chances") stumble upon and knock, *"si je ne butais sur"* (not
contre, not simply "come up against") the fact that he cannot, that he has not been
able to speak.[86] And speak of what? Of that which should have been given to him. By
what or whom? By what is called his birth. If Derrida was able to tell his story, then,
and in order for that story to be able to speak, at least to start speaking of the thing
itself (and it may never), it would have been necessary for "his birth"—what is said to
be his birth—to give him something. What is called, *was heißt,* "his birth"? And what
gives birth? What does birth give? What is called his birth would have had to, it would
have been obligated to give him something, to give him that which should have been
the closest. What one calls, speaks of or names "my birth" ("my birth, as one says")
would have been under the obligation of giving Derrida the ability to write, perhaps
in "chrétien latin français," his *Confessions,* and that which was, or rather should have
been, and therefore is (not) the closest to him, of giving him therefore what it/he does
not have but comes or remains in the proximity, that also goes by the name of "religion," the Abrahamic, the Christian, Derrida, the Jew, the Arab.[87] And, "I am not even
speaking of a Jewish-Arab psyche."[88]

---

85. David Farell Krell, *The Purest of Bastards,* 142.

86. On the word *buter* see Derrida's extended comments in "Lettres sur un aveugle: *Punctum caecum*"
in Jacques Derrida and Safaa Fathy, *Tourner les mots: Au bord d'un film* 91, n. 1.

87. The Arabic expression, quoted earlier in the epigraph, also means "to learn (or, to remember) by
heart." It is quoted in Jacques Derrida's "Che cos'è la poesia?" (Reprinted in *Points,* 290/F304). It can also
be found in handwriting on a loose napkin in Box C.66 of the Derrida archive at the Critical Theory
Library, University of California-Irvine. I cannot tell whether the Arabic handwriting is Derrida's. About
Arabic, which is not quite reducible to—not entirely identical with—the language of Islam but is also
that language, Derrida once spoke of how he came not to speak, not to speak it while remaining, one
could say, *proche,* not too far: "Thus I was raised in a monolingual milieu—absolutely monolingual.

MOORINGS (II): POURSUITES DE DERRIDA

Did Derrida's story begin to speak, and did it say, could it say what it—what *he*—would have wanted to say? In "Encre blanche et Afrique originelle: Derrida et la postcolonialité," Chantal Zabus takes on and passes over the question of autobiography. Zabus quotes a sentence by Jacques Derrida in which the figure of an "Africain deraciné" seems to allow for straightforward biographical identification. Commenting upon this sentence, Zabus asserts that "l'identité première" for Derrida, namely, the "Judeo-Algerian," would have been delivered over to us by Derrida himself. Derrida, then, did tell. He would not only have inscribed his "I" in identity, but he would have done so in postcoloniality and a reconciled Arab Jewishness as well. Derrida, then, would have "described himself as an uprooted African ... born in Algiers, *se décrit comme 'Africain deraciné ... né à Algers.'*"[89]

Is such an "identity," however, so available to determination?[90] Can one henceforth simply consider that Derrida has finally spoken, said what he would have wanted to say, finally told the story and given the last word, regarding his "identity"? Alternatively, should we reinscribe Freud's *Moses* and the place of Egypt and affirm, with Geoffrey Bennington, that "Derrida is neither Jew nor Greek, but 'Egyptian,'"—i.e., "North-African, analogically 'Egyptian'" as Bennington writes

---

Around me, although not in my family, I naturally heard Arabic *spoken, j'entendais* parler *l'arabe,* but except for a few words, *I do not speak* Arabic, *mais* je ne parle pas, I do not speak—*à part quelques mots*—je ne parle pas *l'arabe.* I tried to learn it later but I didn't get very far. Moreover, one could say, *on peut dire,* in a general way, without exaggerating, that learning Arabic was something that was virtually forbidden at school. Not prohibited by law, but practically *impossible.*" ("'There is No *One* Narcissism' [Autobiophotographies]" [1986], in *Points,* 204/F217; emphases added).

The expression *ḥafiẓa 'an ẓahri qalb,* which Derrida leaves untranslated in "Che cos'è la poesia," is a complex one and could be translated "literally" in a variety of ways. I will only suggest some of them by noting that the word *ẓahr* means "back" (French, *dos:* "il n'y a que les *dos* qui comptent," as *Post Card* has it). In the phrase *ẓahru l-qur'ā n,* it refers to "the letter of the Qur'ān" in distinction from *batnu l-qur'ān,* "the inner meaning or interpretation [also: *ta'wīl*] of the Qur'ān." The expression quoted by Derrida could therefore mean "to keep the heart to the letter" or "defending the letter of the heart." When one says "she reads *min ẓahri l-qalbi*" it can mean "she reads without a book" or "from memory." or, alternatively, "she knows this so well that she knows it *'ala ẓahri lisāniha,* like the back of her tongue," which is not quite the same as, though not far from, the French: "je l'ai au bout de la langue," or the English "it's on the tip of my tongue". Whether and how the phrase relates to what Derrida can or cannot say, what he has or has not spoken, or would have wanted to say or read from, on, or to Islam among other things, is what I am trying to explore, by also recalling the (same?) question of (not) speaking (or is it [not] hearing?) raised by Abdelkebir Khatibi in "Le point de non-retour": "La question est la suivante: le silence de la pensée sur la colonisation européenne ... serait-il de l'ordre d'une aphasie et d'une surdité, elles aussi miraculeuses?" (Khatibi, "Le point de non-retour," in *Le passage des frontières: Autour du travail de Jacques Derrida,* ed. Marie-Louise Mallet [Paris: Galilée, 1994], 448, n. 4).

88. Jacques Derrida, "Interpretations at War," in this volume p. 135.

89. Chantal Zabus, "Encre blanche et Afrique originelle: Derrida et la postcolonialité," in *Passions de la littérature: Avec Jacques Derrida* (Paris: Galilée, 1996) 262.

90. The suspension of the word "identity" in quotation marks is, as we will see, Derrida's; see his *Monolingualism of the Other,* 13.

earlier—"in a non-biographical sense to be explored"?[91] It was to Bennington, among others, that Derrida had addressed a description of himself as "a little black and very Arab Jew, *un petit Juif noir et très arabe*," having, in the same text, asserted his readiness to think like certain Muslims ("I am ready even to think like certain Muslims, *je suis prêt même à penser comme certains musulmans*").[92] To the extent that the biographical sets as its goal—but also fails—to situate the subject *chez lui*, "at home," what of biography, what of life, what one calls "life" *chez* Derrida?

These are the questions that are raised once again, once more, by the Abrahamic, and though they do not, could not, substitute for a reading of the unreadable, they may attend to the reading field to which Derrida exposes (and explodes) us "with," one could say, the Abrahamic. Following these questions "*chez* Derrida" implies however that we note that "*chez*" here means the impossibity of inhabiting and remaining at home, the impossibility of *demeure*, and therefore the impossibility of an appropriate use of the word *chez*.[93] Like a secret that "doesn't belong, [that] can never be said to be at home or in its place [*chez soi*]," the question of "life" here extends "beyond an axiomatic of the self or the *chez soi* as *ego cogito*. . . . the question of the self: 'who am I?' not in the sense of 'who am I' but 'who is this "I" that can say "who"? What is the "I," and what becomes of responsibility once the identity of the "I" trembles *in secret*?'"[94] Here, as in many North African homes, the *chez* in the expression "Viens mon petit, viens chez ta mère" will mean "near" (*près de*) and not "at" (*dans la demeure de*).[95]

Let us continue by considering the passage of *Du droit à la philosophie* quoted by Zabus, one that could be thought of as a rare explicit autobiographical moment, prior at least to "Circumfession." What Derrida writes is that he speaks, this time, that he says what he says and writes ("and I say it in a word, *et je le dis d'un mot*") "*comme* une *sorte* d'Africain, *like* a *kind* of African."[96] Yet, the double precaution ("comme" and "une sorte") is important. When Derrida invokes a phrase such as "in a word, *d'un mot*" it hides metonymically an elaborate web of meanings. The irony of Derrida saying anything "in a word" requires therefore no further comment. Derrida's word, if it is one, will therefore be complicated, as it is here,

---

91. Geoffrey Bennington, "Mosaic Fragment: If Derrida were an Egyptian . . . " in *Legislations: The Politics of Deconstruction* (London: Verso, 1994), 209.

92. Jacques Derrida, "Circumfession," 58/F57 and 142/F135.

93. See the discussion of *chez* in, for example, *The Other Heading* and *Politics of Friendship*, and see also Samuel Weber, "Reading and Writing *chez* Derrida," in *Institution and Interpretation* (Minneapolis: University of Minnesota Press, 1987).

94. Jacques Derrida, *The Gift of Death*, 92.

95. This is Samuel Weber's example drawing from Belgian usage ("Reading and Writing," 88). The North African version, of course, would more likely be "*Va chez ta mère.*"

96. Jacques Derrida, "La crise de l'enseignement philosophique," in *Du droit à la philosophie* (Paris: Galilée, 1990) 160.

complicated by figuration (*comme*) and lacking, precisely, a precise identity (*une sorte*). Derrida will not assert, he will not assert (himself), nor identify (himself), not simply, (as) "I" nor (as) "African." Derrida—if the "I" in these texts can simply or ever be read as "Derrida"—and the "I" in the text will perhaps speak *comme* (like, as) an "African," but because of the undecidability of the word *comme*, we will be unable to say of which kind, by way of which figuration, this "African" will be, of what kind and what uprooting will he be (*sera*), or what he will follow (*suivra*).[97]

It should therefore be concluded that when Derrida says "*comme* un Africain," the operative gesture is one that speaks the African as other rather than as a measure of identity. One ought not to lose sight of the rhetoricity of the *comme*, which also separates at the moment it appears to join.

But why "will be, *sera*" or "follow, *suivra*"? Because when Derrida says that he writes "like an African" he writes "comme cette sorte d'Africain déraciné que je suis." This is an almost untranslatable phrase written in a language, French, that one could call "suspended" regarding its meaning. Since "je suis" can be translated as both "I am" and "I follow," the phrase complicates the possibility of deciding conclusively whether or not Derrida *is* (*je suis*) this "African" or whether he follows him (*je suis*) and yet others, following (by) the trace of a number of so-called identities (African, Algerian, Arab Jew, Hispano-Moor, and more recently, Franco-maghrebian, and later "animal" in "l'animal que je suis"). In the final analysis, Derrida's "je suis" is more destabilizing than his use of the word *like—comme*. In other words, to say "I am African" or "l'Africain que je suis," for Derrida, is ever more distant from the assertion of identity that would appear to take place in "like an African."[98]

During a discussion that circled around the question of the "so-called life of the author, *la soi-disant vie de l'auteur*," that is to say, around the tendency to confuse this life with "the corpus of empirical accidents making up the life of an empirically real person,"[99] Derrida said, "If one pursues carefully the questions that have been opened up here, then the very value of empiricalness, the very contours

---

97. Derrida has invoked this duality often, of course, and it has been noted by critics as well; see for example, Krell, *The Purest of Bastards*, 193.

98. Another way of pursuing what Derrida wants to say in what could be called his autobiographical thought has been suggested by Robert Smith, who leaves aside what Zabus considers "autobiographical" and produces instead an elaborate and impressive Derridean "contribution" to a *theory* of autobiography. Smith does so while spending surprisingly little time reading the manner in which Derrida inserts the "I" in his texts, the manner in which the appearance of empiricity takes place in the texts (Smith, *Derrida and Autobiography* [Cambridge: Cambridge University Press, 1995]). But to express wariness over the forgetting of the "I" in the reading of the Derridean text by Smith and others is not to criticize them as if from the opposed vantage point. It does not warrant the restitution of a naively empirical "I" in the so-called autobiographical text; in Smith's wording, "appeals to biological knowledge" should indeed not be "reduced immediately to empirical data concerning the biological" (91); not "immediately," but then what is still required is to address what could be called, after Derrida, "empirical effects."

99. Rodolphe Gasché, in Jacques Derrida, *The Ear of the Other*, trans. Peggy Kamuf (Lincoln: University of Nebraska Press, 1985), 41.

of an empirical text or any empirical entity, can perhaps no longer be determined. I can no longer say what an empirical text is, or the empirical given of a text, *je ne sais plus ce que c'est qu'un texte empirique ou que la donnée empirique d'un texte*" (ibid., 44/62–63). The "I" here can no longer say, the "I" no longer knows, it knows itself no longer as an empirical moment. It is not that the "I" abandons speech or knowledge; it does not even abandon itself. Rather, the "I" fails and falls to empiricity itself, to "accidents" that are said to be empirical and that abandon the "I," abandon it outside of all determinations and all foundations, determinations and foundations that can no longer be maintained. In this abandonment, the auto-biographical genre—if such exists—is unsettled and revealed as a problem. More-over, if the "I" no longer knows what this empiricity might be, what remains of the so-called life is precisely that which, no longer determinable, cannot be read.

It is therefore by way of a different step, an other "step not beyond," non-mimetic or other than mimetic, that Derrida has been following and pursuing paths, roads, and sites that cannot be arrested or frozen into any kind of essence, any simple, recognizable, resemblance or "identity." It is therefore permissible to doubt the possibility of localizing him, of claiming or reclaiming him for a post-coloniality, be it Arab, Jewish, African, or other. Thus, to speak of "Derrida the Jew, *Derrida ha-yehudi*" as Gideon Ofrat has, for example, while following an already well established tradition, or of "Derrida the Algerian," "the French philosopher," or even "the Arab Jew" would perhaps not be wrong. It would, however, indicate, an all too hasty reading, the persistence of a referential moment—the "autobiograph-ical"—that as such testifies to its unreadability.

Derrida closely follows the ends (and perhaps there is only one), the end of the book, of man, and of the Jew. If I am (*je suis*) a Jew, Derrida seems to be saying, it cannot be other than the last, to the extent that I, a Jew, come always too late. But if I follow (*je suis*) him, the Jew is perhaps not only the last, or another last. Let us practice our declensions, then: *je suis, nous suivons*, I am, we follow—together?—a thin line that binds and separates, the end of which is to follow, *à suivre*, to be con-tinued. This end *is* not, therefore, and the last (and least) of the Jews, and with him the "I" if it is the only one, cannot be confused with a figure nor with a figure of apocalypse. Like the Abrahamic, I remain, if anything remains at all, to follow, to be followed and (to be) read—there where it is unreadable, impossible.

Derrida clearly insists on the rhetoricity of the word ("ce je dont je parle en un mot") and on the rhetoricity of the "I," the rhetoricity of the word "I." "What I am saying, the one I am speaking, in a word, this *I* of whom I speak is someone, as I more or less recall.... *Ce que je dis, celui que je dis, ce je dont je parle en un mot, c'est quelqu'un, je m'en souviens à peu près....*"[100] One needs therefore to consider

---

100. Derrida, *Monolingualism of the Other*, 30/F56.

how, in *Monolingualism* for example, the one who speaks—but is this, in fact, someone?—remains singularly distant from, a vague memory of, the "I" who is said (I do not say "that says itself"). We are invited, received, and hosted, into a mise-en-scène and a figuration of memory and forgetting ("je m'en souviens à peu près"), which take the form, familiar to readers of Derrida, of a dialogue, but moreover, that makes a particular use of citation. It is not that Derrida does not say "I" but rather that any identificatory affirmation of this "I" is only offered as a citation, suspended within quotation marks. This citational dimension already appears in "Circumfession" where the sayings of the "I" are, for the most part, citations of *carnets* contemporary with the years of *Post Card*. One encounters a similar dimension in the opening lines of *Monolingualism*:

> —Picture this, imagine someone who would cultivate the French language, *Imagine*
> *le, figure toi quelqu'un qui cultiverait le français . . .*
> [and who] were to tell you, for example, in good French:
> "I only have one language; it is not mine."
> Or rather, and better still: I am monolingual,
> *[et qui] viendrait te dire, par exemple, en bon français,*
> *«Je n'ai qu'une langue, ce n'est pas la mienne».*
> *Et encore, ou encore:*
> *«Je suis monolingue.*
> (*Monolingualism*, 1/F13)

At the risk of confusion, I am here reproducing the punctuation exactly as it appears in both the English and the French texts. The reader will immediately note that the quotation marks, the *guillemets*, are not inscribed in the same way in the two versions. In French, the last quotation marks, opened just before "I am monolingual" are in fact never closed. The English version, on the other hand, has resolved the difficulty thus produced by the open-ended citation by not opening the quotation marks at all. Still, because of the colon introducing it, the sentence thus begun ostensibly functions as a citation. We are only at the beginning of the book and this particular citation will not end, and although quotation marks will be multiplied, strictly speaking, they will never close. This is all the more striking since, as pointed out earlier, this suspension of citation proved unbearable to the English translation, which opted instead for a suspension of the quotation marks. However, what is important to consider here is the very fact of the quoted "I." At the moment he makes the "I," one could say, recognizable, Derrida is already quoting. Such can always be the case, as Derrida demonstrated long ago. What is added here, however, is this: That which (indeed, he who) is "recognized" in these affirmations of an "I" cannot simply be read as "Derrida," cannot simply be read as the

truth of Derrida's place. It is therefore not simply—not *only*—Derrida who speaks
and says that he is "the only Franco-Maghrebian" but also the language who speaks
and declares, the language of an "I" who says, under cover of a hypothesis, "So let us
form a hypothesis.... Let us suppose that without wishing to hurt Abdelkebir
Khatibi's feelings ... I make him a declaration.... What would this public declaration declare to him? *Que lui déclarerait cette déclaration publique?* Approximately
the following: 'You see, dear Abdelkebir, between the two of us, I consider myself to
be the *most* Franco-Maghrebian, and perhaps even the *only* Franco-Maghrebian
here,' «*Cher Abdelkebir, vois-tu, je me considère ici comme le* plus *franco-maghrébin
de nous deux, et peut-être le* seul *franco-maghrébin*»" (12/F29).

It would require much more space and time to read here this citation, thrown
like an enigmatic challenge, that enacts the movement of the Abrahamic as it
addresses itself to the author of *Love in Two Languages* (*Amour bilingue*) and organizes itself around the rhetoric of the *comme* (*je me considère comme*, I consider
myself as). What is of interest here, is the status of the *déclaration* itself, a declaration that, strictly speaking, speaks—and it is indeed the sole speaker—that speaks
the "I" who is spoken here.

Nonetheless, is it truly impossible to identify the "I" spoken here, the "I" that
speaks and asserts that it is as, *comme*, the "most" or the "only" (among a group of
two)? Isn't Derrida after all inscribing a new identity, and, with the Abrahamic, a
new hyphen, to be added to the already long list of hyphenated identities? Derrida
seems to insist and lean in this direction: as we have seen earlier, he speaks, and says
that he speaks of a hyphen, the silence of which "does not pacify or appease anything, not a single torment, not a single torture, *ne pacifie ou n'apaise rien, aucun
tourment, aucune torture.* ... A hyphen is never enough to conceal protests, cries of
anger or suffering, the noise of weapons, airplanes, and bombs, *un trait d'union ne
suffit jamais à couvrir les protestations, les cris de colère ou de souffrance, le bruit des
armes, des avions et des bombes*" (11/F27). But why then, why again, bombs?

This question brings us toward a conclusion, but prior to it, it seems necessary to
return to the issue of following and pursuing (*je suis/je suis*) as an alternative, as an
otherwise than identity. Indeed, the "I" which I am trying to follow is, I have said, not
méconnaissable—it is never a matter of saying that "I" is not—but remains rather difficult to arrest and contain to the extent that "I" follows and pursues an identity and
prior to it an ipseity: "What is identity" asks Derrida, "this concept of which the
transparent identity to itself is always dogmatically presupposed by so many debates,
*qu'est-ce que l'identité, ce concept dont la transparente identité à elle-même est toujours
dogmatiquement présupposée par tant de débats* ... and before the identity of the subject, what is ipseity? The latter is not reducible to an abstract capacity to say 'I,' which
it will always have preceded, *et avant l'identité du sujet, qu'est-ce que l'ipséité? Celle-ci*

ne se réduit pas à une capacité abstraite de dire 'je' qu'elle aura toujours précédée" (14/F31–32). Identity is therefore not denied but indeed affirmed insofar as it remains a question ("Our question is still identity"), and to the extent that it is secondary, because preceded by—that it follows, therefore—an ability to say "I" to which it is not reducible. Derrida will therefore speak of the manner in which "it is always *imagined* that the one who writes should know how to say *I, on se* figure *toujours que celui ou celle qui écrit doit savoir déjà dire* je" (28/F53). This ability and this knowledge follow in their turn a power, the *–pse* of *ipse*, and it is a power, Derrida continues, that "troubles identity, *trouble l'identité*": "To be a Franco-Maghrebian, one "like myself" *l'être 'comme moi'*, is not, not particularly, and particularly not, a surfeit of richness of identity . . . in the first place, it would rather betray a *disorder of identity, cela trahirait plutôt, d'abord, un trouble de l'identité"* (14/F32). It is this "trouble" that I follow and that the "je suis" of Derrida operates.

With this trouble, or rather with these *troubles* (in French, one will often hear of *troubles* rather than of *révoltes*), the question of the Abrahamic returns. For why again, surrounding the hyphen, bombs?

I hesitate to answer and to conclude—if there is here a conclusion—with a text, with the effects, of what can only with great difficulty be called "autobiographical." With the Abrahamic, we are confronted, on the one hand, with a Derrida preoccupied with ethical concerns and with what one could call an 'ethics of memory.' On the other hand, there is here a Derrida who has painfully inscribed incineration, suffering, and who exhorts us to an exp(l)osure, to a reading field that is also a minefield. In this field, around the Abrahamic, the outline of an answer can be found, following (*suivant*) a logic that does not appear, but that nonetheless constitutes an apparition, a shadow or a specter, which Derrida "on religion" conjures and invokes when inscribing an "I" that one could still call, though differently, "autobiographical." This phantomization stages the Abrahamic, a certain *outre-tombe*, even an *outre-bombe* that Derrida calls and recalls, calls himself again, and indicates something that Derrida is not, not simply, even if he follows it, even if the "I" of his text follows. The apparition therefore does not as such appear, but intervenes in "Circumfession" and elsewhere, at the moment where there emerges "a little black and very Arab Jew, *un petit Juif noir et très arabe*," enigmatic site of his "life," of "religion," and of the Abrahamic.[101] It concerns what Derrida calls the closest, the "chez," the most proximate that also remains infinitely distant, separated by no more but also no less than punctuation, there a hyphen, here a comma: "what my birth, as one says, should have made closest to me: the Jew, the Arab, *ce que ma naissance, comme on dit, aurait dû me donner de plus proche: le Juif, l'Arabe."*

---

101. Derrida, "Circumfession," 58/F57.

~

If the Abrahamic is the condition of religion, the texts included in this anthology can be said to dwell within and read the self-divided and dividing limits of this condition in its differential dimensions. In these texts religion—the Abrahamic—carries Derrida's reflections from negative theology to the theologico-political (and here one cannot reduce the "theology" of either term to one signifier of the "same" religion or religiosity) and to a hospitality in which "each concept opens itself to its opposite, reproducing or producing in advance, in the rapport of one concept to the other, the contradictory and deconstructive law of hospitality. Each concept becomes hospitable to its other, to an other than itself that is no longer *its* other" (see "Hostipitality," in this volume). The course of this complex development from a more recognizable concept and configuration of "religion" to the unsettling problematic of the theologico-political also follows the course of seminars that have been partly elaborated upon in publications or alluded to in the form of articles ("Interpretation at War"), interviews ("Eating Well"), and books (*Politics of Friendship*). These texts and seminars not only show some of the underlying rhythm of a teaching career that marks Derrida's writing in general, but also provide a distinct perspective on his writings on religion in particular. In this development, religion—the Abrahamic—will carry the call for an "effective dissociation of the political and the theological" ("Taking a Stand for Algeria"), a dissociation that remains wanting in Algeria and elsewhere. It is at this site of association and dissociation that the Abrahamic appeals to the proximity—and thus to the distance—of Abraham and Abrahamic hospitality in Levinas and Massignon ("Hostipitality"), and to the explosive and welcoming features of an encounter—if there is one—between Jews and their others. Thus, the famous "dialogue" between Jews and Germans signals, in a way that is distinct from what historical studies have unearthed so far, toward the troubled encounter ("Oh, if Maimonides had only known . . .") between "the Jew, the Arab" *and* "the German, the Jew" ("Interpretation at War"). Pursuing the reflections on war that he elaborates in *Politics of Friendship*, Derrida on religion pursues other dissociations such as the set of complex relations between the Jew and the Greek ("Force of Law"), the human and the divine ("Des tours de Babel"), the living and the dead, destruction and preservation ("The Eyes of Language"), and more. As condition, the Abrahamic cannot quite be said to structure, certainly not in any exclusive way, the distinct operations that are at work between all of these terms, and yet, "could I explain anything without it, ever?"[102]

---

102. Derrida, *Monolingualism of the Other*, 71.

1

A Note on "Faith and Knowledge"

"Faith and Knowledge," Derrida's most explicit treatment of "religion," addresses the sites of religion—that most Latin and Christian of names—as it circulates in the world. Religion, in its "globalatinization," associates and dissociates itself from salvation, the social, sacrifice, radical evil, translation, the West, spectrality, so-called fundamentalisms, messianicity, sexual difference, the living and the surviving, and the machine. None of these terms, Derrida shows, can be thought of without the other, or without the "Other." Such impossibility—the impossibility of the unaccountable and of the incalculable—is the testimony of religion, the testimonial space that exceeds religion and within which it inscribes itself, and to which it responds.

As Derrida shows, religion counts. Religion (Is there one? Is it one and of the one? Perhaps *religions*, but then, still, religion) counts. Religion is a matter of number, of calculability and incalculability. One (and already, one has begun the count) can only count—that is to say also count on, trust, have faith and confidence in— where there is the incalculable, where one can no longer count *on* one's own, where one is no longer alone, nor all one. *Plus d'un* (more than one, no more than one, no longer one), the one that counts makes itself. And in making itself, it makes violence of itself: the one (religion) "makes violence of itself, does violence to itself and keeps itself from the other, *se fait violence et se garde de l'autre*" (section 52). Religion and counting. Counting on and counting the incalculable and the unaccountable, "Faith and Knowledge" attends in its fifty-two (weekly?) sections, to the name and the number, the names and numbers of religion counting the "Two Sources of 'Religion' at the Limits of Reason Alone." Religion counts, again; it accumulates returns and thus returns. Religion and its others, religion as its others (itself and that from which it could not be dissociated: "the concepts of ethics, of the juridical, of the political or of the economic" [section 28]), indemnifies and immunizes itself from its others, gathers itself in its dissociations from itself, making itself in a process where "the same unique source divides itself mechanically, automatically, and sets itself reactively in opposition to itself: whence the two sources in one" (section 29). This process, which begins with a response ("Religion, in the singular? Response: 'Religion is the response,'" [section 29]), in which religion begins by counting and counting on itself, by trusting and distrusting itself and giving itself indemnity, immunity and immunization, is what Derrida calls here a "general logic of auto-immunization" (section 37, n. 27). "But the auto-immunitary haunts the community and its system of immunitary survival like the hyperbole of its own possibility. Nothing in *common,* nothing immune, safe and sound, *heilig* and holy, nothing unscathed in the most autonomous living present without a risk of auto-immunity. As always, the risk charges itself twice, the same finite risk. Two times rather than one: with a menace and with a chance. In two words, it must take charge of—one could also say: take in trust—the *possibility* of that radical evil without which good would be for nothing" (section 37).

"Faith and Knowledge" can be read as Derrida's own introduction to the question of religion in his work. His footnotes alone can guide the reader through Derrida's major texts on issues such as negative theology, the holy and the sacred, spirit, messianicity, and other major themes of religion that Derrida has addressed since the earliest of his writings. But "Faith and Knowledge," in which Derrida draws on Immanuel Kant, G. W. F. Hegel, Henri Bergson, and Martin Heidegger while dissociating himself from these sources, is hardly a simple continuation of Derrida's previous arguments. Rather, it recasts Derrida's earlier texts, refiguring the politics of religion, technology (the text is also one of Derrida's most extensive discussions of technology in its contemporaneity), and our understanding of "life."

G. A.

FAITH AND KNOWLEDGE

The Two Sources of "Religion"
at the Limits of Reason Alone

ITALICS

(1) *How 'to talk religion'? Of religion? Singularly of religion, today? How dare we speak of it in the singular without fear and trembling, this very day? And so briefly and so quickly? Who would be so imprudent as to claim that the issue here is both identifiable and new? Who would be so presumptuous as to rely on a few aphorisms? To give oneself the necessary courage, arrogance or serenity, therefore, perhaps one must pretend for an instant to abstract, to abstract from everything or almost everything, in a certain way. Perhaps one must take one's chance in resorting to the most concrete and most accessible, but also the most barren and desert-like, of all abstractions.*

Should one save oneself by abstraction or save oneself from abstraction? Where is salvation, safety? (In 1807, Hegel writes: "Who thinks abstractly?": "Thinking? Abstract?—Sauve qui peut!" he begins by saying, and precisely in French, in order to translate the cry—'Rette sich, wer kann!'—of that traitor who would flee, in a single movement, thought and abstraction and metaphysics: like the "plague.")

(2) Save, be saved, save oneself. *Pretext for a first question: can a discourse on religion be dissociated from a discourse on salvation: which is to say, on the holy, the sacred, the safe and sound, the unscathed <indemne>,[1] the immune (sacer, sanctus, heilig, holy, and their alleged equivalents in so many languages)? And salvation, is it necessarily*

---

1. *Translator's note*: the use of angle brackets < > indicates interpolations of the translator. Such brackets contain either a few words from the original or short emendations. Parentheses and square brackets reproduce those in the French text. All footnotes stem from the author except where otherwise indicated (as here).

redemption, before or after evil, fault or sin? Now, where is evil <le mal>? Where is evil today, at present? Suppose that there was an exemplary and unprecedented figure of evil, even of that radical evil which seems to mark our time as no other. Is it by identifying this evil that one will accede to what might be the figure or promise of salvation for our time, and thus the singularity of the religious whose return is proclaimed in every newspaper?

Eventually, we would therefore like to link the question of religion to that of the evil of abstraction. To radical abstraction. Not to the abstract figure of death, of evil or of the sickness of death, but to the forms of evil that are traditionally tied to radical extirpation and therefore to the deracination of abstraction, passing by way—but only much later—of those sites of abstraction that are the machine, technics, technoscience and above all the transcendence of tele-technology. "Religion and mechane," "religion and cyberspace," "religion and the numeric," "religion and digitality," "religion and virtual space-time": in order to take the measure of these themes in a short treatise, within the limits assigned us, to conceive a small discursive machine which, however finite and perfectible, would not be too powerless.

In order to think religion today abstractly, we will take these powers of abstraction as our point of departure, in order to risk, eventually, the following hypothesis: with respect to all these forces of abstraction and of dissociation (deracination, delocalization, disincarnation, formalization, universalizing schematization, objectification, telecommunication etc.), "religion" is at the same time involved in reacting antagonistically and reaffirmatively outbidding itself. In this very place, knowledge and faith, technoscience ("capitalist" and fiduciary) and belief, credit, trustworthiness, the act of faith will always have made common cause, bound to one another by the band of their opposition. Whence the aporia—a certain absence of way, path, issue, salvation—and the two sources.

(3) To play the card of abstraction, and the aporia of the no-way-out, perhaps one must first withdraw to a desert, or even isolate oneself on an island. And tell a short story that would not be a myth. Genre: "Once upon a time," just once, one day, on an island or in the desert, imagine, in order to "talk religion," several men, philosophers, professors, hermeneuticians, hermits or anchorites, took the time to mimic a small, esoteric and egalitarian, friendly and fraternal community. Perhaps it would be necessary in addition to situate such arguments, limit them in time and space, speak of the place and the setting, the moment past, one day, date the fugitive and the ephemeral, singularize, act as though one were keeping a diary out of which one were going to tear a few pages. Law of the genre: the ephemeris (and already you are speaking inexhaustibly of the day). Date: 28 February 1994. Place: an island, the isle of Capri. A hotel, a table around which we speak among friends, almost without any order,

without agenda, *without order of the day, no watchword* <mot d'ordre> *save for a single word, the clearest and most obscure: religion. We believe we can pretend to believe—fiduciary act—that we share in some pre-understanding. We act as though we had some common sense of what "religion" means through the languages that we believe (how much belief already, to this moment, to this very day!) we know how to speak. We believe in the minimal trustworthiness of this word. Like Heidegger, concerning what he calls the* Faktum *of the vocabulary of being (at the beginning of* Sein und Zeit*), we believe (or believe it is obligatory that) we pre-understand the meaning of this word, if only to be able to question and in order to interrogate ourselves on this subject. Well—we will have to return to this much later—nothing is less pre-assured than such a* Faktum *(in both of these cases, precisely) and the entire question of religion comes down,* perhaps, *to this lack of assurance.*

(4) *At the beginning of a preliminary exchange, around the table, Gianni Vattimo proposes that I improvise a few suggestions. If I may be permitted, I would like to recall them here, in italics, in a sort of schematic and telegraphic preface. Other propositions, doubtless, emerged in a text of different character that I wrote afterwards, cramped by the merciless limits of time and space. An utterly different story, perhaps, but, from near or afar, the memory of words risked in the beginning, that day, will continue to dictate what I write.*

I had at first proposed to bring to the light of day of reflection, misconstruing or denying it as little as possible, an effective and unique situation—that in which we then found ourselves: facts, a common commitment, a date, a place. We had in truth agreed to respond to a double proposition, *at once philosophical and editorial, which in turn immediately raised a* double question*: of language and of nation. Now if, today, the "question of religion" actually appears in a new and different light, if there is an unprecedented resurgence, both global and planetary, of this ageless thing, then what is at stake is language, certainly—and more precisely the idiom, literality, writing, that forms the element of all revelation and of all* belief, *an element that ultimately is irreducible and untranslatable—but an idiom that above all is inseparable from the social nexus, from the political, familial, ethnic, communitarian nexus, from the nation and from the people: from autochthony, blood and soil, and from the ever more problematic relation to citizenship and to the state. In these times, language and nation form the historical body of all religious passion. Like this meeting of philosophers, the international publication that was proposed to us turns out to be first of all "Western," and then confided, which is also to say confined, to several European languages, those that "we" speak here in Capri, on this Italian island: German, Spanish, French, Italian.*

(5) *We are not far from Rome, but are no longer in Rome. Here we are literally isolated for two days, insulated on the heights of Capri, in the difference between the Roman*

and the Italic, the latter potentially symbolizing everything that can incline—*to a cer*-
tain remove from the Roman in general. To think "religion" is to think the "R*oman*."
This can be done neither in Rome nor too far from Rome. A chance or necessity for
recalling the history of something like "religion": everything done or said in its name
ought to keep the critical memory of this appellation. European, it was first of all Latin.
Here, then, is a given whose figure at least, as limit, remains contingent and significant
at the same time. It demands to be taken into account, reflected, thematized, dated.
Difficult to say "Europe" without connoting: Athens—Jerusalem—Rome—Byzantium,
wars of Religion, open war over the appropriation of Jerusalem and of Mount Moriah,
over the "here I am" of Abraham or of Ibrahim before the extreme "sacrifice" demanded
of him, the absolute offering of the beloved son, the demanded putting-to-death or
death given to the unique descendant, repetition suspended on the eve of all Passion.
Yesterday (yes, yesterday, truly, just a few days ago), there was the massacre of Hebron
at the Tomb of the Patriarchs, a place held in common and symbolic trench of the religions called "Abrahamic." We represent and speak four different languages, but our
common "culture," let's be frank, is more manifestly Christian, barely even Judaeo-
Christian. No Muslim is among us, alas, even for this preliminary discussion, just at the
moment when it is towards Islam, perhaps, that we ought to begin by turning our attention. No representative of other cults either. Not a single woman! We ought to take this
into account: speaking on behalf of these mute witnesses without speaking for them, in
place of them, and drawing from this all sorts of consequences.

(6) Why is this phenomenon, so hastily called the "return of religions," so difficult to
think? Why is it so surprising? Why does it particularly astonish those who believed
naïvely that an alternative opposed Religion, on the one side, and on the other, Reason,
Enlightenment, Science, Criticism (Marxist Criticism, Nietzschean Genealogy, Freudian
Psychoanalysis and their heritage), as though the one could not but put an end to the
other? On the contrary, it is an entirely different schema that would have to be taken as
one's point of departure in order to try to think the "return of the religious." Can the
latter be reduced to what the doxa confusedly calls "fundamentalism," "fanaticism" or,
in French, "integrism"? Here perhaps we have one of our preliminary questions, able to
measure up to the historical urgency. And among the Abrahamic religions, among the
"fundamentalisms" or the "integrisms" that are developing universally, for they are at
work today in all religions, what, precisely, of Islam? But let us not make use of this
name too quickly. Everything that is hastily grouped under the reference to "Islam"
seems today to retain some sort of geopolitical or global prerogative, as a result of the
nature of its physical violences, of certain of its declared violations of the democratic
model and of international law (the "Rushdie case" and many others—and the "right
to literature"), as a result of both the archaic and modern form of its crimes "in the

name of religion," as a result of its demographic dimensions, of its phallocentric and theologico-political figures. Why? Discernment is required: Islam is not Islamism and we should never forget it, but the latter operates in the name of *the former, and thus emerges the grave question of the name.*

(7) *Never treat as an accident the force of the name in what happens, occurs or is said in the name of religion, here in the name of Islam. For, directly or not, the theologico-political, like all the concepts plastered over these questions, beginning with that of democracy or of secularization, even of the right to literature, is not merely European, but Graeco-Christian, Graeco-Roman. Here we are confronted by the overwhelming questions of the name and of everything "done in the name of": questions of the name or noun "religion," of the names of God, of whether the proper name belongs to the system of language or not, hence, of its untranslatability but also of its iterability (which is to say, of that which makes it a site of repeatability, of idealization and therefore, already, of* techné, *of technoscience, of tele-technoscience in calling at a distance), of its link to the performativity of calling in prayer (which, as Aristotle says, is neither true nor false), of its bond to that which, in all performativity, as in all address and attestation, appeals to the faith of the other and deploys itself therefore in a pledge of faith.*

(8) Light takes place. *And the day. The coincidence of the rays of the sun and topographical inscription will never be separated: phenomenology of religion, religion as phenomenology, enigma of the Orient, of the Levant and of the Mediterranean in the geography of appearing* <paraître>. *Light (*phos*), wherever this* arché *commands or begins discourse and takes the initiative in general (phos, phainesthai, phantasma, hence spectre, etc.), as much in the discourse of philosophy as in the discourses of a revelation (*Offenbarung*) or of a revealability (*Offenbarkeit*), of a possibility more originary than manifestation. More originary, which is to say, closer to the source, to the sole and same source. Everywhere light dictates that which even yesterday was naïvely construed to be pure of all religion or even opposed to it and whose future must today be rethought (*Aufklärung, Lumières, Enlightenment, Illuminismo*). Let us not forget: even when it did not dispose of any common term to "designate," as Benveniste notes, "religion itself, the cult, or the priest, or even any of the personal gods," the Indo-European language already concurred in "the very notion of 'god' (deiwos), of which the 'proper meaning' is 'luminous' and 'celestial.'*[2]

---

2. Emile Benveniste, *Indo-European Language and Society*, trans. Elizabeth Palmer Faber and Faber, (London, Faber and Faber, 1973), pp. 445–46. We shall often cite Benveniste in order to leave him a responsibility—that of speaking for example with assurance of "proper meaning," precisely in the case of the sun or of light, but also with regard to everything else. This assurance seems greatly exaggerated and more than problematic. *Translator's note*: the published English translation has been modified throughout in the interest of greater literalness.

(9) *In this same light, and under the same sky, let us this day name three places: the island, the Promised Land, the desert. Three aporetical places: with no way out or any assured path, without itinerary or point of arrival, without an exterior with a predictable map and a calculable programme. These three places shape our horizon, here and now. (But since thinking and speaking are called for here, they will be difficult within the assigned limits, and a certain absence of horizon. Paradoxically, the absence of horizon conditions the future itself. The emergence of the event ought to puncture every horizon of expectation. Whence the apprehension of an abyss in these places, for example a desert in the desert, there where one neither can nor should see coming what ought or could—perhaps—be yet to come. What is still left to come.)*

(10) *Is it a coincidence if we—almost all of us* Mediterranean *by origin and each of us* Mediterranean *by a sort of magnetism—have, despite many differences, all been oriented by a certain phenomenology (again light)? We who today have come together to meet on this island, and who ourselves must have made or accepted this choice, more or less secretly, is it a coincidence if all of us, one day, have been tempted both by a certain dissidence with respect to Husserlian phenomenology and by a hermeneutics whose discipline owes so much to the exegesis of religious texts? Hence the even more pressing obligation: not to forget those <of either gender> whom this implicit contract or this "being-together" is obliged to exclude. We should have, we ought to have, begun by allowing them to speak.*

(11) *Let us also remember what, rightly or wrongly, I hold provisionally to be evident: that, whatever our relation to religion may be, and to this or that religion, we are not priests bound by a ministry, nor theologians, nor qualified, competent representatives of religion, nor enemies of religion as such, in the sense that certain so-called Enlightenment philosophers are thought to have been. But we also share, it seems to me, something else—let us designate it cautiously—an unreserved taste, if not an unconditional preference, for what, in politics, is called republican democracy as a universalizable model, binding philosophy to the public "cause," to the* res publica, *to "public-ness," once again to the light of day, once again to the "lights" of the Enlightenment <aux Lumières>, once again to the enlightened virtue of public space, emancipating it from all external power (non-lay, non-secular), for example from religious dogmatism, orthodoxy or authority (that is, from a certain rule of the* doxa *or of belief, which, however, does not mean from all faith). In a less analogical manner (but I shall return to this later) and at least as long and in so far as we continue speaking here together, we shall doubtless attempt to transpose, here and now, the circumspect and suspensive attitude, a certain* épochè *that consists—rightly or wrongly, for the issue is serious—in thinking religion or making it appear "within the limits of reason alone."*

(12) *Related question: what of this 'Kantian' gesture today? What would a book be like today which, like Kant's, is entitled,* Religion within the Limits of Reason Alone? *This* epoché *also gives its chance to a political event, as I have tried to suggest elsewhere.*[3] *It even belongs to the history of democracy, notably when theological discourse was obliged to assume the forms of the* via negativa *and even there, where it seems to have prescribed reclusive communities, initiatic teachings, hierarchy, esoteric insularity or the desert.*[4]

(13) *Before the island—and Capri will never be Patmos—there will have been the Promised Land. How to improvise and allow oneself to be surprised in speaking of it? How not to fear and how not to tremble before the unfathomable immensity of this theme? The figure of the Promised Land—is it not also the essential bond between the promise of place and historicity? By historicity, we could understand today more than one thing. First of all, a sharpened specificity of the concept of religion, the history of its history, and of the genealogies intermingled in its languages and in its name. Distinctions are required: faith has not always been and will not always be identifiable with religion, nor, another point, with theology. All sacredness and all holiness are not necessarily, in the strict sense of the term, if there is one, religious. We will have to return to the emergence and the semantics of this noun 'religion', passing by way both of its Roman Occidentality and of the bond it has contracted with the Abrahamic revelations. The latter are not solely events. Such events only happen by taking on the meaning of engaging the historicity of history—and the eventfulness <événementialité > of the event as such. As distinct from other experiences of "faith," of the "holy," of the "unscathed" and of the "safe and sound," of the "sacred," of the "divine"; as distinct from other structures that one would be tempted to call by a dubious analogy "religions," the Testamentary and Koranic revelations are inseparable from a historicity of revelation itself. The messianic or eschatological horizon delimits this historicity, to be sure, but only by virtue of having previously inaugurated it.*

(14) *With this emerges another historical dimension, a historicity different from what we evoked a moment ago, unless the two overlap in an infinite mirroring <en abyme>. How can this history of historicity be taken into account so as to permit the treatment today of* religion within the limits of reason alone? *How can a history of political and technoscientific reason be inscribed there and thus* brought up to date, *but also a history of radical evil, of its figures that are never simply figures and that—*

---

3. Cf. "Sauf le nom," in Jacques Derrida, *On the Name,* ed. Tom Dutoit, trans. David Wood, John P. Leavey Jr., and Ian McLeod (Stanford: Stanford University Press, 1995), notably p. 80 ff.

4. In "How to avoid speaking: denials," in *Languages of the Unsayable: the Play of Negativity in Literature and Literary Theory,* ed. by Sanford Budick and Wolfgang Iser (New York: Columbia University Press, 1989), pp. 3–70, I treat in a more precise manner, in an analogous context, the themes of hierarchy and of "topolitology."

this is the whole evil—are always inventing a new evil? The radical "perversion of the human heart" of which Kant speaks,[5] *we now know is not one, nor given once and for all, as though it were capable only of inaugurating figures or tropes of itself. Perhaps we could ask ourselves whether this agrees or not with Kant's intention when he recalls that Scripture does indeed "represent" the historical and temporal character of radical evil even if it is only a "mode of representation"* (Vorstellungsart) *used by Scripture in function of human "frailty";*[6] *and this, notwithstanding that Kant struggles to account for the rational origin of an evil that remains inconceivable to reason, by affirming simultaneously that the interpretation of Scripture exceeds the competence of reason and that of all the "public religions" that ever were, only the Christian religion will have been a "moral" religion (end of the first* General Remark). *Strange proposition, but which must be taken as seriously as possible in each of its premises.*

(15) *There are in effect for Kant, and he says so explicitly, only* two *families of religion, and in all* two *sources or two* strata *of religion—and hence two genealogies of which it still must be asked why they share the same name whether proper or common* <noun>: *the* religion of cult alone (des blossen Cultus) *seeks "favours of God," but at bottom, and in essence, it does not act, teaching only prayer and desire. Man is not obliged to become better, be it through the remission of sins.* Moral (moralische) *religion, by contrast, is interested in the good conduct of life* (die Religion des guten Lebenswandels); *it enjoins him to* action, *it* subordinates *knowledge* to it and *dissociates it from itself, prescribing that man become better by* acting *to this end, in accordance with the following principle: "'It is not essential and hence* not *necessary for everyone to know what God does or has done for his salvation,' but it is essential to know* what man himself must do *in order to become worthy of this assistance." Kant thus defines a "reflecting* (reflektierende) *faith," which is to say, a concept whose possibility might well open the space of our discussion. Because it does not depend essentially upon any historical revelation and thus agrees with the rationality of purely practical reason,* reflecting faith *favours* good will *beyond all knowledge. It is thus opposed to "dogmatic* (dogmatische) *faith." If it breaks with this "dogmatic faith," it is insofar as the latter claims to know and thereby ignores the difference between faith and knowledge.*

Now the principle of such an opposition—and this is why I emphasize it—could not be simply definitional, taxonomic or theoretical; it serves not simply to classify heterogeneous religions under the same name; it could also define, even for us today, a place of conflict, if not of war, in the Kantian sense. Even today, albeit provisionally, it could help us structure a problematic.

---

5. I. Kant, *Religion Within the Limits of Reason Alone*, Book I, section 3.
6. Ibid., Book I, section 4.

Are we ready to measure without flinching the implications and consequences of the Kantian thesis? The latter seems strong, simple and dizzying: the Christian religion would be the only truly "moral" religion; a mission would thus be reserved exclusively for it and for it alone: that of liberating a "reflecting faith." It necessarily follows therefore that pure morality and Christianity are indissociable in their essence and in their concept. If there is no Christianity without pure morality, it is because Christian revelation teaches us something essential about the very idea of morality. From this it follows that the idea of a morality that is pure but non-Christian would be absurd; it would exceed both understanding and reason, it would be a contradiction in terms. The unconditional universality of the categorical imperative is evangelical. The moral law inscribes itself at the bottom of our hearts like a memory of the Passion. When it addresses us, it either speaks the idiom of the Christian—or is silent.

This thesis of Kant (which we would like later to relate to what we will call "globalatinization" <mondialatinisation>)[7]—is it not also, at the core of its content, Nietzsche's thesis at the same time that he is conducting an inexpiable war against Kant? Perhaps Nietzsche would have said "Judaeo-Christian," but the place occupied by Saint Paul among his privileged targets clearly demonstrates that it was Christianity, a certain internalizing movement within Christianity, that was his primary enemy and that bore for him the gravest responsibility. The Jews and European Judaism even constituted in his eyes a desperate attempt to resist, in so far as there was any resistance, a last-ditch protest from within, directed against a certain Christianity.

This thesis doubtless tells us something about the history of the world—nothing less. Let us indicate, rather schematically, at least two of its possible consequences, and two paradoxes among many others:

1. *In the definition of "reflecting faith" and of what binds the idea of pure morality indissolubly to Christian revelation, Kant recurs to the logic of a simple principle, that which we cited a moment ago verbatim: in order to conduct oneself in a moral manner, one must act as though God did not exist or no longer concerned himself with our salvation. This shows who is moral and who is therefore Christian, assuming that a Christian owes it to himself to be moral: no longer turn towards God at*

---

7. *Translator's note:* It should be noted that the French neologism created by Derrida—*"mondialatin-isation"*—emphasizes the notion of "world," whereas the English word used in this translation: "global-atinization"—stresses that of "globality." Since "globe" suggests "earth" rather than "world," the use of "globalatinization" here tends to efface an important distinction made throughout this chapter. This interest of this problem, however, is that it may not "simply" be one of translation. For if, as Derrida argues in this chapter, the major idiom and vehicle of the process of *mondialatinisation* today is precisely Anglo-American, then the very fact that the notion of "globality" comes to supplant that of "world" in the most common usage of this language must itself be highly significant. This difficulty of translation, in short, adds a new question to those raised in this chapter: what happens to the notion of "world," and to its distinction from "earth" and "globe," if the predominant language of "mondialatinization" tends to speak not of "world" but of "globality"?

the moment of acting in good faith; act as though God had abandoned us. In enabling us to think (but also to suspend in theory) the existence of God, the freedom or the immortality of the soul, the union of virtue and of happiness, the concept of "postulate" of practical reason guarantees this radical dissociation and assumes ultimately rational and philosophical responsibility, the consequence here in this world, in experience, *of this abandonment. Is this not another way of saying that Christianity can only answer to its moral calling and morality, to its Christian calling if it endures in this world, in phenomenal history, the death of God, well beyond the figures of the Passion? That Christianity is the death of God thus announced and recalled by Kant to the modernity of the Enlightenment? Judaism and Islam would thus be perhaps the last two monotheisms to revolt against everything that, in the Christianizing of our world, signifies the death of God, death in God, two non-pagan monotheisms that do not accept death any more than multiplicity in God (the Passion, the Trinity etc.), two monotheisms still alien enough at the heart of Graeco-Christian, Pagano-Christian Europe, alienating themselves from a Europe that signifies the death of God, by recalling at all costs that "monotheism" signifies no less faith in the One, and in the living One, than belief in a single God.*

2. *With regard to this logic, to its formal rigour and to its possibilities, does not Heidegger move in a different direction? He insists, indeed, in* Sein und Zeit *upon the character of originary conscience* (Gewissen), *being-responsible-guilty-indebted* (Schuldigsein) *or attestation* (Bezeugung) *as both* pre-moral *(or pre-ethical, if "ethical" still refers to that meaning of* ethos *considered by Heidegger to be derivative, inadequate and of recent origin) and* pre-religious. *He would thus appear to go back before and beyond that which joins morality to religion, meaning here, to Christianity. This would in principle allow for the repetition of the Nietzschean genealogy of morals, but dechristianizing it where necessary and extirpating whatever Christian vestiges it still might contain. A strategy all the more involuted and necessary for a Heidegger who seems unable to stop either settling accounts with Christianity or distancing himself from it—with all the more violence in so far as it is already too late, perhaps, for him to deny certain proto-Christian motifs in the ontological repetition and existential analytics.*

What are we calling here a "logic," its "formal rigour" and its "possibilities"? The law itself, a necessity that, it is clear, undoubtedly programmes an infinite spiral of outbidding, a maddening instability among these "positions." The latter can be occupied successively or simultaneously by the same "subjects." From one religion to the other, the "fundamentalisms" and the "integrisms" hyperbolize today this outbidding. They exacerbate it at a moment when—we shall return to this later— globalatinization (this strange alliance of Christianity, as the experience of the death of God, and tele-technoscientific capitalism) is at the same time hegemonic and finite, ultra-powerful and in the process of exhausting itself. Simply, those who are involved in this outbidding can pursue it from all angles, adopting all "positions," either simultaneously or successively, to the uttermost limit.

Is this not the madness, the absolute anachrony of our time, the disjunction of all self-contemporaneity, the veiled and cloudy day of every today?

(16) *This definition of reflecting* faith *appears in the first of the four* Parerga *added at the end of each section of* Religion within the Limits of Reason Alone. *These* Parerga *are not integral parts of the book; they "do not belong within" "religion in the limits of pure reason," they "border upon" it. I stress this for reasons that are in part theo-topological, even theo-architectonic: these* Parerga *situate perhaps the fringe where we might be able, today, to inscribe our reflections. All the more since the first* Parergon, *added in the second edition, thereby defines the secondary task* (parergon) *which, concerning what is morally indisputable, would consist in surmounting all the difficulties connected to transcendent questions. When translated into the element of religion, moral ideas pervert the purity of their transcendence. They can do this in two times two ways, and the resulting square could today frame, providing that the appropriate transpositions are respected, a programme of analysis of the forms of evil perpetrated at the four corners of the world "in the name of religion." We will have to limit ourselves to an indication of the titles of this programme and, first, of the criteria* (nature/supernatural, internal/external, theoretical elucidation/practical action, constative/performative): (a) the allegedly internal *experience (of the effects of grace): the* fanaticism *or* enthusiasm *of the illuminated* (Schwärmerei); *(b) the allegedly* external *experience (of the miraculous):* superstition (Aberglaube); *(c) the alleged elucidations of the* understanding *in the consideration of the supernatural (secrets,* Geheimnisse): illuminatism, *the frenzy of the initiates; (d) the risky attempt of acting upon the supernatural (means of obtaining grace): thaumaturgy.*

When Marx holds the critique of religion to be the premise of all ideology-critique, when he holds religion to be the ideology par excellence, even for the matrix of all ideology and of the very movement of fetishization, does his position not fall, whether he would have wanted it or not, within the parergonal framework of this kind of rational criticism? Or rather, more plausible but also more difficult to demonstrate, does he not already deconstruct the fundamentally Christian axiomatics of Kant? This could be one of our questions, the most obscure one no doubt, because it is not at all certain that the very principles of the Marxist critique do not still appeal to a heterogeneity between faith and knowledge, between practical justice and cognition. This heterogeneity, by the way, may ultimately not be irreducible to the inspiration or to the spirit of Religion within the Limits of Reason Alone. *All the more since these figures of evil discredit, as much as they accredit, the "credit" which is the act of faith. They exclude as much as they explain, they demand perhaps more than ever this recourse to religion, to the principle of faith, even if it is only that of a radically fiduciary form of the "reflecting faith" already mentioned. And it is this mechanics, this machine-like return of religion, that I would here like to question.*

(17) *How then to think—within the limits of reason alone—a religion which, without again becoming "natural religion," would today be effectively universal? And which, for that matter, would no longer be restricted to a paradigm that was Christian or even Abrahamic? What would be the project of such a 'book'? For with* Religion within the Limits of Reason Alone, *there is a World involved that is also an Old–New Book or Testament. Does this project retain a meaning or a chance? A geopolitical chance or meaning? Or does the idea itself remain, in its origin and in its end, Christian? And would this necessarily be a limit, a limit like any other? A Christian—but also a Jew or a Muslim—would be someone who would harbour doubts about this limit, about the existence of this limit or about its* reducibility *to any other limit, to the current figure of limitation.*

(18) *Keeping these questions in mind, we might be able to gauge two temptations. In their schematic principle, one would be "Hegelian": ontotheology which determines absolute knowledge as the truth of religion, in the course of the final movement described in the conclusions of* The Phenomenology of Spirit *or of* Faith and Knowledge, *which announces in effect a "religion of modern times"* (Religion der neuen Zeit) *founded on the sentiment that "God himself is dead." "Infinite pain" is still only a "moment"* (rein als Moment), *and the moral sacrifice of empirical existence only dates the absolute Passion or the speculative Good Friday* (spekulativer Karfreitag). *Dogmatic philosophies and natural religions should disappear and, out of the greatest "asperity," the harshest impiety, out of kenosis and the void of the most serious privation of God* (Gottlosigkeit), *ought to resuscitate the most serene liberty in its highest totality. Distinct from faith, from prayer or from sacrifice, ontotheology destroys religion, but, yet another paradox, it is also perhaps what informs, on the contrary, the theological and ecclesiastical, even religious, development of faith. The other temptation (perhaps there are still good reasons for keeping this word) would be "Heideggerian": beyond such ontotheology, where the latter ignores both prayer and sacrifice. It would accordingly be necessary that a "revealability"* (Offenbarkeit) *be allowed to reveal itself, with a light that would manifest (itself) more originarily than all revelation* (Offenbarung). *Moreover, the distinction would have to be made between theo-logy (the discourse on God, faith or revelation) and theio-logy (discourse on being-divine, on the essence and the divinity of the divine). The experience of the*

sacred, the holy or the saved (heilig) would have to be reawakened unscathed. We would have to devote all our attention to this chain, taking as our point of departure this last word (heilig), this German word whose semantic history seems to resist the rigorous dissociation that Levinas wishes to maintain between a natural sacredness that would be "pagan," even Graeco-Christian, and the holiness <sainteté>[8] of (Jewish) law, before or under the Roman religion. As for the "Roman,"[9] does not Heidegger proceed, from Sein und Zeit on, with an ontologico-existential repetition and rehearsal of Christian motifs that at the same time are hollowed out and reduced to their originary possibility? A pre-Roman possibility, precisely? Did he not confide to Löwith, several years earlier, in 1921, that in order to assume the spiritual heritage that constitutes the facticity of his "I am," he ought to have said: "I am a 'Christian theologian'"? Which does not mean "Roman." To this we shall return.

(19) In its most abstract form, then, the aporia within which we are struggling would perhaps be the following: is revealability (Offenbarkeit) more originary than revelation (Offenbarung), and hence independent of all religion? Independent in the struc-

---

8. The Latin (even Roman) word used by Levinas, for example in Du sacré au saint [From the Sacred to the Holy] (Paris: Editions de Minuit, 1977) is, to be sure, only the translation of a Hebrew word (kidouch).

9. Cf., for example, M. Heidegger, Andenken (1943): "Poets, when they are in their being, are prophetic. But they are not 'prophets' in the Judaeo-Christian sense of the word. The 'prophets' of these religions do not restrict themselves to the anticipatory-founding word of the Sacred (das voraufgründende Wort des Heiligen). They immediately announce the god upon whom one can subsequently count as upon the certain guarantee of salvation in superterrestrial beatitude. The poetry of Hölderlin should not be disfigured with the 'religious' element of 'religion,' which remains the business of the Roman way of interpreting (eine Sache der römischen Deutung) the relations between humans and gods." The poet is not a "Seer" (Seher) nor a Diviner (Wahrsager). "The Sacred (das Heilige) that is uttered in poetic prediction only opens the time of an apparition of the gods and indicates the region where it resides (die Ortschaft des Wohnens) on this earth of man required by the destiny of history .... His dream [the poet's] is divine, but it does not dream a god." (Gesamtausgabe, vol. IV, p. 114.)

More than twenty years later, in 1962, this protest is renewed against Rome, against the essentially Roman figure of religion. It brings together into a single configuration modern humanism, technics, politics and law. In the course of his trip to Greece, after visiting the orthodox monastery of Kaisariani, above Athens, Heidegger notes: "What the little church possesses that is Christian remains in harmony with ancient Greece, a pervasive spirit that does not bow before the theocratic thought seeped in canon law (dem kirchenstaatlich-juristischen Denken) of the Roman Church and its theology. On the site where today there is the convent, there was formerly a 'pagan' sanctuary (ein "heidnisches" Heiligtum) dedicated to Artemis" (Aufenthalte, Séjours, [Paris, Éditions du Rocher, 1989], French translation by F. Vezin slightly modified, p. 71).

Prior to this, when his journey brings him close to the island of Corfu—yet another island— Heidegger recalls that another island, Sicily, appeared to Goethe to be closer to Greece; and the same recollection associates in two phrases the "traits of a romanized, Italian (römisch-italienischen) Greece," seen in the "light of modern humanism," and the coming of the "machine age" (ibid., p. 19). And since the island also figures our gathering-place <lieu d'insistance>, let us not forget that for Heidegger, this Greek voyage remains above all a "sojourn" (Aufenthalt), a modest (Scheu) stopover <halte> in the vicinity of Delos, the visible or manifest, a meditation of unveiling via its name. Delos is also the "saintly" or "sacred" island (die heilige Insel); ibid., p. 50).

tures of its experience and in the analytics relating to them? Is this not the place in which "reflecting faith" at least originates, if not this faith itself? Or rather, inversely, would the event of revelation have consisted in revealing revealability itself, and the origin of light, the originary light, the very invisibility of visibility? This is perhaps what the believer or the theologian might say here, in particular the Christian of originary Christendom, of that Urchristentum *in the Lutheran tradition to which Heidegger acknowledges owing so much.*

(20) *Nocturnal light, therefore, more and more obscure. Let us step up the pace in order to finish: in view of a* third *place that could well have been more than archi-originary, the most anarchic and anarchivable place possible, not the island nor the Promised Land, but a certain desert, that which makes possible, opens, hollows or infinitizes the other. Ecstasy or existence of the most extreme abstraction. That which would orient here "in" this desert, without pathway and without interior, would still be the possibility of a* religio *and of a* relegere, *to be sure, but before the "link" of* religare, *problematic etymology and doubtless reconstructed, before the link between men as such or between man and the divinity of the god it would also be like the condition of the "link" reduced to its minimal semantic determination: the holding-back <halte> of scruple* (religio), *the restraint of shame, a certain* Verhaltenheit *as well, of which Heidegger speaks in the* Beiträge zur Philosophie, *the respect, the responsibility of repetition in the wager <gage> of decision or of affirmation (re-legere) which links up with itself in order to link up with the other. Even if it is called the social nexus, link to the other in general, this fiduciary "link" would precede all determinate community, all positive religion, every onto-anthropo-theological horizon. It would link pure singularities prior to any social or political determination, prior to all intersubjectivity, prior even to the opposition between the sacred (or the holy) and the profane. This can therefore resemble a desertification, the risk of which remains undeniable, but it can—on the contrary—also* render possible *precisely what it appears to threaten. The abstraction of the desert can thereby open the way to everything from which it withdraws. Whence the ambiguity or the duplicity of the religious trait or retreat, of its abstraction or of its subtraction. This deserted re-treat thus makes way for the repetition of that which will have given way precisely for that in whose name one would protest against it, against that which only resembles the void and the indeterminacy of mere abstraction.*

Since everything has to be said in two words, let us give two names to the duplicity of these origins. For here origin is duplicity itself, the one and the other. Let us name these two sources, these two fountains or these two tracks that are still invisible in the desert. Let us lend them two names that are still "historical," there where a certain concept of history itself becomes inappropriate. To do this, let us refer—provisionally, I emphasize this, and for pedagogical or rhetorical reasons—first to the "messianic," and second to the chora, *as I have tried to do more minutely, more patiently and, I hope, more rigorously elsewhere.*[10]

(21) First name: *the* messianic, *or* messianicity without messianism. *This would be the opening to the future or to the coming of the other as the advent of justice, but without horizon of expectation and without prophetic prefiguration. The coming of the other can only emerge as a singular event when no anticipation sees it coming, when the other and death—and radical evil—can come as a surprise at any moment. Possibilities that both open and can always interrupt history, or at least the* ordinary course *of history. But this ordinary course is that of which philosophers, historians and often also the classical theoreticians of the revolution speak. Interrupting or tearing history itself apart, doing it by deciding, in a decision that can consist in letting the other come and that can take the apparently passive form of the* other's *decision: even there where it appears in itself, in me, the decision is moreover always that of the other, which does not exonerate me of responsibility. The messianic exposes itself to absolute surprise and, even if it always takes the phenomenal form of peace or of justice, it ought, exposing itself so abstractly, be prepared* (waiting without awaiting itself) *for the best as for the worst, the one never coming without opening the possibility of the other. At issue there is a "general structure of experience." This messianic dimension does not depend upon any messianism, it follows no determinate revelation, it belongs properly to no Abrahamic religion (even if I am obliged here, "among ourselves," for essential reasons of language and of place, of culture, of a provisional rhetoric and a historical strategy of which I will speak later, to continue giving it names marked by the Abrahamic religions).*

(22) *An invincible desire for justice is linked to this expectation. By definition, the latter is not and ought not to be certain of anything, either through knowledge, consciousness, conscience, foreseeability or any kind of programme as such. This abstract messianicity belongs from the very beginning to the experience of faith, of believing, of a credit that is irreducible to knowledge and of a trust that "founds" all relation to the other in testimony. This justice, which I distinguish from right, alone allows the hope, beyond all "messianisms," of a universalizable culture of singularities, a culture in which the abstract possibility of the impossible translation could nevertheless be announced. This justice inscribes itself in advance in the promise, in the act of faith or in the appeal to faith that inhabits every act of language and every address to the other. The universalizable culture of this faith, and not of another or before all others, alone permits a "rational" and universal discourse on the subject of "religion." This messianicity,*

---

10. See "Khora," in Derrida, *On the Name,* and *Specters of Marx,* trans. Peggy Kamuf (New York and London: Routledge, 1994) and "Force of law," in this volume.

stripped of everything, as it should, this faith without dogma which makes its way through the risks of absolute night, cannot be contained in any traditional opposition, for example that between reason and mysticism. It is announced wherever, reflecting without flinching, a purely rational analysis brings the following paradox to light: that the foundation of law—law of the law, institution of the institution, origin of the constitution—is a "performative" event that cannot belong to the set that it founds, inaugurates or justifies. Such an event is unjustifiable within the logic of what it will have opened. It is the decision of the other in the undecidable. Henceforth reason ought to recognize there what Montaigne and Pascal call an undeniable "mystical foundation of authority." The mystical *thus understood allies belief or credit, the fiduciary or the trustworthy, the secret (which here signifies "mystical") to foundation, to knowledge, we will later say also, to science as "doing," as theory, practice and theoretical practice—which is to say, to a faith, to performativity and to technoscientific or tele-technological performance. Wherever this foundation founds in foundering, wherever it steals away under the ground of what it founds, at the very instant when, losing itself thus in the desert, it loses the very trace of itself and the memory of a secret, "religion" can only begin and begin again: quasi-automatically, mechanically, machine-like, spontaneously. Spontaneously, which is to say, as the word indicates, both as the origin of what flows from the source,* sponte sua, *and with the automaticity of the machine. For the best and for the worst, without the slightest assurance or anthropo-theological horizon. Without this desert in the desert, there would be neither act of faith, nor promise, nor future, nor expectancy without expectation of death and of the other, nor relation to the singularity of the other. The chance of this desert in the desert (as of that which* resembles to a fault, *but without reducing itself to, that* via negativa *which makes its way from a Graeco-Judaeo-Christian tradition) is that in uprooting the tradition that bears it, in atheologizing it, this abstraction, without denying faith, liberates a universal rationality and the political democracy that cannot be dissociated from it.*

(23) *The* second name *(or first name prior to all naming), would be* chora, *such as Plato designates it in the* Timaeus,[11] *without being able to reappropriate it in a consistent self-interpretation. From the open interior of a corpus, of a system, of a language or a culture,* chora *would situate the abstract spacing,* place *itself,* the place of absolute exteriority, *but also the place of a bifurcation between two approaches to the desert. Bifurcation between a tradition of the "via negativa" which, in spite of or within its Christian act of birth, accords its possibility to a Greek—Platonic or Plotinian—tradition that persists until Heidegger and beyond: the thought of that which is beyond being* (epekeina tes ousias). *This Graeco-Abrahamic hybridization*

---

11. I must refer here to the reading of this text, in particular to the 'political' reading of it, that I propose in "How to avoid speaking: denials," "Khora," and "Sauf le nom."

remains anthropo-theological. In the figures of it known to us, in its culture and in its history, its "idiom" is not universalizable. It speaks solely at the borders or in view of the Middle-Eastern desert, at the source of monotheistic revelations and of Greece. It is there that we can try to determine the place where, on this island today, "we" persist and insist. If we insist, and we must for some time still, upon the names that are given us as our heritage, it is because, in respect of this borderline place, a new war of religions is redeploying as never before to this day, in an event that is at the same time both interior and exterior. *It inscribes its seismic turbulence directly upon the fiduciary globality of the technoscientific, of the economic, of the political and of the juridical. It brings into play the latter's concepts of the political and of international right, of nationality, of the subjectivity of citizenry, of the sovereignty of states. These hegemonical concepts tend to reign over a world, but only from their finitude: the growing tension of their power is not incompatible, far from it, with their precariousness any more than with their perfectibility. The one can never do anything without recalling itself to the other.*

(24) *The surge <déferlement> of "Islam" will be neither understood nor answered as long as the exterior and interior of this borderline place have not been called into question; as long as one settles for an internal explanation (interior to the history of faith, of religion, of languages or cultures as such), as long as one does not define the passageway between this interior and all the apparently exterior dimensions (technoscientific, tele-biotechnological, which is to say also political and socioeconomic, etc.).*

 For, in addition to investigating the ontotheologico-political tradition that links Greek philosophy to the Abrahamic revelations, perhaps we must also submit to the ordeal of that which resists such interrogation, which will have always resisted, from within or as though from an exteriority that works and resists inside. Chora, the "ordeal of chora"[12] *would be, at least according to the interpretation I believed justified in attempting, the name for place, a place name, and a rather singular one at that, for that spacing which, not allowing itself to be dominated by any theological, ontological or anthropological instance, without age, without history and more "ancient" than all oppositions (for example, that of sensible/intelligible), does not even announce itself as "beyond being" in accordance with a path of negation, a* via negativa. *As a result,* chora *remains absolutely impassible and heterogeneous to all the processes of historical revelation or of anthropo-theological experience, which at the very least suppose its abstraction. It will never have entered religion and will never permit itself to be sacralized, sanctified, humanized, theologized, cultivated, historicized. Radically heterogeneous to the safe and sound, to the holy and the sacred, it never admits of any* indemnification. *This cannot even be formulated in the present, for* chora *never presents itself as such. It*

---

12. See "Sauf le nom," p. 76. *Translator's note:* In the published English version, "*l'épreuve de Khôra*" is translated more idiomatically as "the test of Chora."

is neither *Being, nor the Good, nor God, nor Man, nor History. It will always resist them, will have always been (and no future anterior, even, will have been able to reappropriate, inflect or reflect a* chora *without faith or law) the very place of an infinite resistance, of an infinitely impassible persistence* <restance>: *an utterly faceless other.*

(25) Chora *is nothing (no being, nothing present), but not the Nothing which in the anxiety of* Dasein *would still open the question of being. This Greek noun says in our memory that which is not reappropriable, even by our memory, even by our "Greek" memory; it says the immemoriality of a desert in the desert of which it is neither a threshold nor a mourning. The question remains open, and with it that of knowing whether this desert can be thought and left to announce itself "before" the desert that we know (that of the revelations and the retreats, of the lives and deaths of God, of all the figures of kenosis or of transcendence, of* religio *or of historical "religions"); or whether, "on the contrary," it is "from" this last desert that we can glimpse that which precedes the first* <l'avant-premier>, *what I call the desert in the desert. The indecisive oscillation, that reticence (*epoché *or* Verhaltenheit*) already alluded to above (between revelation and revealability,* Offenbarung *and* Offenbarkeit, *between event and possibility or virtuality of the event), must it not be respected for itself? Respect for this singular indecision or for this hyperbolic outbidding between two originarities, the order of the "revealed" and the order of the "revealable," is this not at once the chance of every responsible decision and of another "reflecting faith," of a new "tolerance"?*

(26) *Let us suppose it agreed upon, among ourselves, that all of us here are for "tolerance," even if we have not been assigned the mission of promoting it, practising it or founding it. We would be here to try to think what "tolerance" could henceforth be. I immediately place quotation marks around this word in order to abstract and extract it from its origins. And thereby to announce, through it, through the density of its history, a possibility that would not be solely Christian. For the concept of tolerance, stricto sensu, belongs first of all to a sort of Christian domesticity. It is literally, I mean behind this name, a secret of the Christian community. It was printed, emitted, transmitted and circulated in the name of the Christian faith and would hardly be without relation to the rise, it too Christian, of what Kant calls "reflecting faith"—and of pure morality as that which is distinctively Christian. The lesson of tolerance was first of all an exemplary lesson that the Christian deemed himself alone capable of giving to the world, even if he often had to learn it himself. In this respect, the French Enlightenment, les Lumières, was no less essentially Christian than the Aufklärung. When it treats of tolerance, Voltaire's* Philosophical Dictionary *reserves a dual privilege for the Christian religion. On the one hand it is exemplarily tolerant; to be sure, it teaches tolerance better than any other religion, before every other religion. In short, a little in the manner of Kant, believe it or not, Voltaire seems to think that Christianity is the*

sole "moral" religion, since it is the first to feel itself obliged and capable of setting an example. Whence the ingenuity, and at times the inanity of those who sloganize Voltaire and rally behind his flag in the combat for critical modernity—and, far more seriously, for its future. For, on the other hand, the Voltairian lesson was addressed above all to Christians, "the most intolerant of all men."[13] *When Voltaire accuses the Christian religion and the Church, he invokes the lesson of originary Christianity, "the times of the first Christians," Jesus and the Apostles, betrayed by "the Catholic, Apostolic and Roman religion." The latter is "in all its ceremonies and in all its dogmas, the opposite of the religion of Jesus."*[14]

Another "tolerance" would be in accord with the experience of the "desert in the desert"; it would respect the distance of infinite alterity as singularity. And this respect would still be religio, religio *as scruple or reticence, distance, dissociation, disjunction, coming from the threshold of all religion in the* link of repetition to itself, *the threshold of every social or communitarian link.*[15]

Before and after the logos *which was in the beginning, before and after the Holy Sacrament, before and after the Holy Scriptures.*

POST-SCRIPTUM

Crypts . . .

(27) [. . .] **Religion?** Here and now, this very day, if one were still supposed to *speak* of it, of religion, perhaps one could attempt to think it in *itself* or to devote oneself to this task. No doubt, but to try above all to *say* it and to *utter a verdict* concerning it, with the necessary rigour, which is to say, with the reticence, modesty, respect or fervour, in a word the scruple *(religio)* demanded at the very least by that which is or claims

---

13. Even if Voltaire responds to the question "What is tolerance?" by stating that "It is the prerogative of humanity," the example of excellence here, the most elevated inspiration of this "humanity" remains Christian: "Of all the religions, Christianity is without doubt that which ought to inspire the greatest tolerance, even if until now Christians have been the most intolerant of men" (*Philosophical Dictionary*, article "Tolerance").

The word "tolerance" thus conceals a story: it tells above all an intra-Christian history and experience. It delivers the message that Christians address to other Christians. Christians ("the most intolerant") are reminded, by a co-religionist and in a mode that is essentially co-religionist, of the word of Jesus and of the authentic Christianity at its origins. If one were not fearful of shocking too many people all at once, one could say that by their vehement anti-Christianity, by their opposition above all to the Roman Church, as much as by their declared preference, sometimes nostalgic, for primitive Christianity, Voltaire and Heidegger belong to the same tradition: proto-Catholic.

14. Voltaire, "Tolerance," *Philosophical Dictionary*.

15. As I have tried to do elsewhere (*Specters of Marx*, p. 23 ff.), I propose to think the condition of justice in relation to a certain sundering <*déliaison*>, in relation to the always-safe, always-to-be-saved possibility of this secret of disassociation, rather than through the bringing-together (*Versammlung*) towards which Heidegger retraces it, in his concern, doubtless legitimate in part, to extract *Dike* from the authority of *Ius*, which is to say, from its more recent ethico-juridical representations.

to be, in its essence, a religion. As its name indicates, it would be necessary, therefore, one would be tempted to conclude, to speak of this essence with a sort of *religio*-sity. In order not to introduce anything alien, leaving it thus intact, safe, *unscathed*. Unscathed in the experience of the unscathed that it will have wanted to be. Is not the unscathed <*l'indemne*>[16] the very matter—the thing itself—of religion?

But no, on the contrary, someone will say. One would not be speaking *of* it if one were to speak *in its name*, if one were to settle for *reflecting* religion as in a mirror specularly, religiously. Moreover, someone else might say, or is it the same one, to break with it, even to suspend for an instant one's religious affiliation, has this not been the very resource, since time immemorial, of the most authentic faith or of the most originary sacredness? One must in any case take into account, if possible in an areligious, or even irreligious manner, what religion at present might *be*, as well as what is *said* and *done*, what *is happening* at this very moment, in the world, in history, *in its name*. Wherever religion can no longer reflect or at times assume or bear its name. And one should not say lightly, as though in passing, 'this very day', "at this very moment" and "in the world," "in history," while forgetting what happens *there*, returning to or surprising *us*, still under the name of religion, even in the name of religion. What *happens to us there* concerns precisely the experience and radical interpretation of everything that these words are felt to mean: the unity of a "world" and of a "being-in-the-world," the concept of world or of history in its Western tradition (Christian or Graeco-Christian, extending to Kant, Hegel, Husserl, Heidegger), and no less that of *day* as well as that of the *present*. (Much later we will have to get around to scrutinizing these two motifs, each as enigmatic as the other: *presence* unscathed by the present, on the one hand, *and believing* unscathed by belief, on the other; or yet again: the sacrosanct, the safe and sound on the one side, *and* faith, trustworthiness or credit on the other.) Like others before, the new "wars of religion" are unleashed over the human earth (which is not the world) and struggle even today to control the sky *with finger and eye*: digital systems and virtually immediate panoptical visualization, "air space," telecommunications

---

16. *Indemnis*: that which has not suffered damage or prejudice, *damnum*; this latter word will have given in French "*dam*" ("*au grand dam*": to the detriment or displeasure of) and comes from *dap-no-m*, tied to *daps, dapis*, that is, to the sacrifice offered the Gods as ritual compensation. In this latter case, one could speak of *indemni-fication* and we will use this word here or there to designate both the process of compensation and the restitution, sometimes sacrificial, that *re*constitutes purity intact, renders integrity safe and sound, restores cleanliness <*propreté*> and property unimpaired. This is indeed what the word "unscathed" <*indemne*> says: the pure, non-contaminated, untouched, the sacred and holy before all profanation, all wound, all offence, all lesion. It has often been chosen to translate *heilig* ("sacred, safe and sound, intact") in Heidegger. Since the word *heilig* will be at the centre of these reflections, we therefore had to elucidate here and now the use that we shall be making of the words "unscathed," "indemnity," "indemnification," In what follows, we shall associate them regularly with the words "immune," "immunity," "immunization," and above all, "auto-immunity."

satellites, information highways, concentration of capitalistic-mediatic-power—in three words <*en trois mots*>, *digital culture, jet* and *TV* without which there could be no religious manifestation today, for example no voyage or discourse of the Pope, no organized emanation <*rayonnement*> of Jewish, Christian or Muslim cults, whether 'fundamentalist'[17] or not. Given this, the cyberspatialized or cyberspaced wars of religion have no stakes other than this determination of the "world," of "history," of the "day" and of the "present." The stakes certainly can remain implicit, insufficiently thematized, poorly articulated. By repressing them, on the other hand, many others can also be dissimulated or displaced. Which is to say, as is always the case with the topics of repression, inscribed in other places or other systems; this never occurs without symptoms and fantasies, without spectres (*phantasmata*) to be investigated. In both cases and according to both logics, we ought to take into account every *declared* stake in its greatest radicality as well as asking ourselves what the depths of such radicality might virtually encrypt, down to its very roots. The *declared* stakes already appear to be without limit: what is the "world," the "day," the "present" (hence, all of history, the earth, the humanity of man, the rights of man, the rights of man and of woman, the political and cultural organization of society, the difference between man, god and animal, the phenomenality of the day, the value or 'indemnity' of life, the right to life, the treatment of death, etc.)? What is the present, which is to say: what is history? time? being? being in its purity <*dans sa*

---

17. There is insufficient space to multiply in this regard the images or the indications, one could say the icons, of our time: the *organization, conception* (generative forces, structures and capital) as well as the *audiovisual representation* of cultic or socio-religious phenomena. In a digitalized 'cyberspace', prosthesis upon prosthesis, a heavenly glance, monstrous, bestial or divine, something like an eye of CNN, watches permanently: over Jerusalem and its three monotheisms, over the multiplicity, the unprecedented speed and scope of the moves of a Pope versed in televisual rhetoric (of which the last encyclical, *Evangelium vitae*, against abortion and euthanasia, for the sacredness or holiness of a life that is safe and sound—unscathed, *heilig*, holy—for its reproduction in conjugal love—sole immunity admitted, with priestly celibacy, against human immuno-deficiency virus (HIV)—is immediately transmitted, massively "marketed" and available on CD-ROM; everything down to the signs of presence in the mystery of the Eucharist is "cederomized"; over airborne pilgrim-ages to Mecca; over so many miracles transmitted live (most frequently, healings, which is to say, returns to the unscathed, *heilig*, holy, indemnifications) followed by commercials, before thousands in an American television studio; over the international and televisual diplomacy of the Dalai Lama, etc.

So remarkably adapted to the scale and the evolutions of global demography, so well adjusted to the technoscientific, economic and mediatic powers of our time, the power of all these phenomena to bear witness finds itself formidably intensified, at the same time as it is collected in a digitalized space by supersonic airplanes or by audiovisual antennae. The ether of religion will always have been hospitable to a certain spectral virtuality. Today, like the sublimity of the starry heavens at the bottom of our hearts, the "cederomized" "cyberspaced" religion also entails the accelerated and hypercapitalized relaunching of founding spectres. On CD-ROM, heavenly trajectories of satellites, jet, TV, e-mail or Internet networks. Actually or virtually universalizable, ultra-internationalizable, incarnated by new 'corporations' that are increasingly independent of the powers of states (democratic or not, it makes little difference at bottom, all of that has to be reconsidered, like the "globalatinity" of international law in its current state, which is to say, on the threshold of a process of accelerated and unpredictable transformation).

propriété> (that is, unscathed, safe, sacred, holy, *heilig*)? What of holiness or of sacredness? Are they the same thing? What of the divinity of God? How many meanings can one give to *theion*? Is this a good way to pose the question?

(28) **Religion?** *In the singular?* Perhaps, *may-be* (this should always remain possible) there is *something else*, of course, and other interests (economic, politico-military, etc.) behind the new "wars of religion," behind what presents itself under the name of religion, beyond what defends or attacks in its name, kills, kills itself or kills one another and for that invokes declared stakes, or in other words, names *indemnity* in the light of day. But inversely, if what is thus *happening to us*, as we said, often (but not always) assumes the figures of evil and of the worst in the unprecedented forms of an *atrocious* "war of religions," the latter in turn does not always speak its name. Because it is not certain that in addition to or in face of the most spectacular and most barbarous crimes of certain "fundamentalisms" (of the present or of the past), *other* over-armed forces are not *also* leading "wars of religion," albeit unavowed. Wars or military "interventions," led by the Judaeo-Christian West in the name of the best causes (of international law, democracy, the sovereignty of peoples, of nations or of states, even of humanitarian imperatives), are they not also, from a certain side, wars of religion? The hypothesis would not necessarily be defamatory, nor even very original, except in the eyes of those who hasten to believe that all these just causes are not only secular but *pure* of all religiosity. To determine a war of religion *as such*, one would have to be certain that one can delimit the religious. One would have to be certain that one can distinguish all the predicates of the religious (and, as we shall see, this is not easy; there are at least *two* families, two strata or sources that overlap, mingle, contaminate each another without ever merging; and just in case things are still too simple, one of the two is precisely the drive to remain unscathed, on the part of that which is allergic to contamination, *save by itself, auto-immunely*). One would have to dissociate the essential traits of the religious as such from those that establish, for example, the concepts of ethics, of the juridical, of the political or of the economic. And yet, nothing is more problematic than such a dissociation. The fundamental concepts that often permit us to isolate or to *pretend* to isolate the *political*—restricting ourselves to this particular circumscription—remain religious or in any case theologico-political. A single example. In one of the most rigorous attempts to isolate in its purity the sphere of the political (notably by separating it from the economic and the religious), in order to identify the political and the political enemy in wars of religion, such as the Crusades, Carl Schmitt was obliged to acknowledge that the ostensibly purely political categories to which he resorted were the product of a secularization or of a theologico-political heritage. And when he denounced the process of "depoliticization" or of

neutralization of the political that was underway, it was explicitly with respect to a European legal tradition that in his eyes doubtless remained indissociable from "our" thought of the political.[18] Even supposing that one accepts such premises, the unprecedented forms of today's wars of religion could also imply radical challenges to our project of delimiting the political. They would then constitute a response to everything that our idea of democracy, for example, with all its associated juridical, ethical and political concepts, including those of the sovereign state, of the citizen-subject, of public and private space, etc., still entails that is religious, inherited in truth from a determinate religious stratum.

Henceforth, despite the ethical and political urgencies that do not permit the response to be put off, reflection upon the Latin noun "religion" will no longer be held for an academic exercise, a philological embellishment or an etymological lux-ury: in short, for an alibi destined to suspend judgement or decision, at best for another *epoché*.

(29) Religion, in the *singular*? Response: 'Religion is **the response.**' Is it not there, perhaps, that we must seek the beginning of a response? Assuming, that is, that one knows what *responding* means, and also *responsibility*. Assuming, that is, that one knows it—and believes in it. No response, indeed, without a principle of responsi-bility: one must respond to the other, before the other and for oneself. And no responsibility without a *given word*, a sworn faith <*foi jurée*>, without a pledge, without an oath, without some *sacrament* or *ius iurandum*. Before even envisaging the semantic history of testimony, of oaths, of the given word (a genealogy and interpretation that are indispensable to whomever hopes to think religion under its proper or secularized forms), before even recalling that some sort of "I promise the truth" is always at work, and some sort of "I make this commitment before the other from the moment that I address him, even and perhaps above all to commit perjury," we must formally take note of the fact that **we are already speaking Latin**. We make a point of this in order to recall that the world today speaks Latin (most often via Anglo-American) when it authorizes itself in the *name* of *religion*. Presupposed at the origin of all address, coming from the other to *whom it is also addressed*, the wager <*gageure*> of a sworn promise, taking immediately God as its witness, cannot not but have already, if one can put it this way, engendered God quasi-mechanically. *A priori* ineluctable, a descent of God *ex machina* would stage a transcendental addressing machine. One would thus have begun by posing, retrospectively, the absolute right of anteriority, the absolute "birthright" <*le droit*

---

18. Without even speaking of other difficulties and of other possible objections to the Schmittian theory of the political, and thus also of the religious. I take the liberty of referring here to *Politiques de l'amitié*, (Paris: Galilée, 1994; English trans. *Politics of Friendship*, London: Verso Books, 1997).

d'aînesse absolu> of a One who is not born. For in taking God as witness, even when he is not named in the most 'secular' *<laïque>* pledge of commitment, the oath cannot *not* produce, invoke or convoke him as already there, and therefore as unengendered and unengenderable, prior to being itself: unproducible. And absent in place. Production and reproduction of the unproducible absent in place. Everything begins with the presence of *that* absence. The "deaths of God," before Christianity, in it and beyond it, are only figures and episodes. The unengenderable thus re-engendered is the empty place. Without God, no absolute witness. No absolute witness to be taken as witness in testifying. But with God, a God that is present, the existence of a third (*terstis, testis*) that is absolute, all attestation becomes superfluous, insignificant or secondary. Testimony, which is to say, testament as well. In the irrepressible invoking of a witness, God would remain then one *name of the witness*, he would be *called* as witness, thus *named*, even if sometimes the named of this name remains unpronounceable, indeterminable, in short: unnameable in his very name; and even if he ought to remain absent, non-existent, and above all, in every sense of the word, unproducible. God: the witness as "nameable-unnameable," present-absent witness of every oath or of every possible pledge. As long as one supposes, *concesso non dato*, that religion has the slightest relation to what we thus call God, it would pertain not only to the general history of nomination, but, more strictly here, under its name of *religio*, to a history of the *sacramentum* and of the *testimonium*. It would *be* this history, it would merge with it. On the boat that brought us from Naples to Capri, I told myself that I would begin by recalling this sort of too luminous evidence, but I did not dare. I also told myself, silently, that one would blind oneself to the phenomenon called "of religion" or of the "return of the religious" *today* if one continued to oppose so naïvely Reason *and* Religion, Critique or Science *and* Religion, technoscientific Modernity *and* Religion. Supposing that what was at stake was to understand, would one understand anything about "what's-going-on-today-in-the-world-with-religion" (and why "in the world"? What is the "world"? What does such a presupposition involve?, etc.) if one continues to believe in this opposition, even in this incompatibility, which is to say, if one remains within a *certain* tradition of the Enlightenment, one of the many Enlightenments of the past three centuries (not of an *Aufklärung*, whose critical force is profoundly rooted in the Reformation), but yes, this light of Lights, of the *Lumières*, which traverses like a single ray a *certain* critical and anti-religious vigilance, anti-Judaeo-Christiano-Islamic, a *certain* filiation "Voltaire–Feuerbach–Marx–Nietzsche–Freud–(and even)–Heidegger"? Beyond this opposition and its determinate heritage (no less represented on the other side, that of religious authority), perhaps we might be able to try to "understand" how the imperturbable and interminable development of critical and technoscientific reason, far from

opposing religion, bears, supports and supposes it. It would be necessary to demonstrate, which would not be simple, that religion and reason have the same source.
(We associate here reason with philosophy and with science as technoscience, as
critical history of the production of knowledge, of knowledge *as* production, know-
how and intervention at a distance, teletechnoscience that is always high-performance and performative by essence, etc.) Religion and reason develop in tandem,
drawing from this common resource: the testimonial pledge of every performative,
committing it to respond as much *before* the other as *for* the high-performance performativity of technoscience. The same unique source divides itself mechanically,
automatically, and sets itself reactively in opposition to itself: whence the two
sources in one. This reactivity is a process of *sacrificial indemnification*, it strives to
restore the unscathed (*heilig*) that it itself threatens. And it is also the possibility of
the two, of *n* + 1, the same possibility as that of the *testimonial deus ex machina*. As
for the *response*, it is *either or*. *Either* it addresses the absolute other as such, with an
address that is understood, heard, respected faithfully and responsibly; *or* it retorts,
retaliates, compensates and *indemnifies itself* in the war of resentment and of reactivity. One of the two responses ought always to be able to contaminate the other. It
will never be proven whether it is the one or the other, never in an act of determining, theoretical or cognitive judgement. This might be the place and the responsibility of what is called belief, trustworthiness or fidelity, the fiduciary, "trust" <*la
"fiance"*> in general, the tribunal <*instance*> of faith.

(30) But **we are already speaking Latin**. For the Capri meeting, the "theme" I
believed myself constrained to propose, religion, was named in Latin, let us never
forget it. Does not "the question of *religio*," however, quite simply merge, one could
say, with the question of Latin? By which should be understood, beyond a "question of language and of culture," the strange phenomenon of Latinity and of its
globalization. We are not speaking here of universality; even of an idea of universality, only of a process of universalization that is finite but enigmatic. It is rarely
investigated in its geopolitical and ethico-juridical scope, precisely where such a
power finds itself overtaken, deployed, its *paradoxical* heritage revived by the global
and still irresistible hegemony of a "language," which is to say, also of a culture that
in part is not Latin but Anglo-American. For everything that touches religion in
particular, for everything that speaks "religion," for whoever speaks religiously or
about religion, Anglo-American remains Latin. *Religion* circulates in the world,
one might say, like an *English word* <*comme un mot anglais*> that has been to Rome
and taken a detour to the United States. Well beyond its strictly capitalist or
politico-military figures, a hyper-imperialist appropriation has been underway
now for centuries. It imposes itself in a particularly palpable manner within the

conceptual apparatus of international law and of global political rhetoric. Wherever this apparatus dominates, it articulates itself through a discourse on religion. From here on, the word "religion" is calmly (and violently) applied to things which have always been and remain foreign to what this word names and arrests in its history. The same remark could apply to many other words, for the entire "religious vocabulary" beginning with "cult," "faith," "belief," "sacred," "holy," "saved," "unscathed" (*heilig*). But by ineluctable contagion, no semantic cell can remain alien, I dare not say "safe and sound," "unscathed," in this apparently borderless process. *Globalatinization* (essentially Christian, to be sure), this word names a unique event to which a meta-language seems incapable of acceding, although such a language remains, all the same, of the greatest necessity here. For at the same time that we no longer perceive its limits, we know that such globalization is finite and only projected. What is involved here is a Latinization and, rather than globality, a globalization that is running out of breath <*essoufflée*>, however irresistible and imperial it still may be. What are we to think of this running out of breath? Whether it holds a future or is held in store for it, we do not know and by definition cannot know. But at the bottom of such non-knowing, this expiring breath is blasting the ether of the world. Some breathe there better than others, some are stifled. The war of religions deploys itself there in its element, but also under a protective stratum that threatens to burst. The co-extensiveness of the two questions (religion and worldwide Latinization) marks the dimensions of what henceforth cannot be reduced to a question of language, culture, semantics, nor even, without doubt, to one of anthropology or of history. **And what if *religio* remained untranslatable?** No *religio* without *sacramentum*, without alliance and promise of testifying truthfully to the truth, which is to say, to speak the truth: that is to say, to begin with, no religion without the promise of keeping one's promise to tell the truth—and to have already told it!—in the very act of promising. To have already told it, *veritas*, in Latin, and thus to consider it told. The event to come has already taken place. The promise promises *itself*, it is *already* promised, that is the sworn faith, the given word, and hence the response. *Religio* would begin there.

(31) **And if *religio* remained untranslatable?** And if this question, and *a fortiori* the response to which it appeals, were to inscribe us already in an idiom whose translation remains problematic? What does it mean to respond? It is to swear—the faith: *respondere, antworten, answer, swear (swaran)*: "to be compared with the got. *swaran* [from which come *schwören, beschwören*, "swear," "conjure," "adjure," etc.], 'to swear, to pronounce solemn formulas': this is almost literally *respondere*."[19]

---

19. Benveniste, *Indo-European Language*, p. 475, article "Libation, 1: sponsio."

"Almost literally . . . " he says. As always, recourse to knowledge is temptation itself. Knowing is *temptation*, albeit in a somewhat more singular sense than believed when referring habitually (habitually, at least) to the Evil Genius or to some original sin. The temptation of knowing, the temptation of knowledge, is to believe not only that one knows what one knows (which wouldn't be too serious), but also that one knows what knowledge is, that is, free, structurally, of belief or of **faith**—of the fiduciary or of trustworthiness. The temptation to believe in knowledge, here for example in the precious authority of Benveniste, can hardly be separated from a certain fear and trembling. Before what? Before a scholarship that is recognized, no doubt, and legitimate and respectable, but also before the confidence with which, authorizing himself without trembling through this authority, Benveniste (for example) proceeds with the cutting edge of assured distinction. For example, between the *proper* meaning and its other, the *literal* sense and its other, as though precisely *that itself* which is here in question (for example the response, responsibility or religion, etc.) did not arise, in a quasi-automatic, machine-like or mechanical manner, out of the hesitation, indecision and margins between the two ostensibly assured terms. *Scruple*, hesitation, indecision, reticence (hence modesty <*pudeur*>, respect, *restraint* before that which should remain sacred, holy or safe: unscathed, immune)—this too is what is meant by *religio*. It is even the meaning that Benveniste believes obliged to retain with reference to the "proper and constant usages" of the word during the classical period.[20] Let us nevertheless cite this page of Benveniste while emphasizing the words "proper," "literally," an "almost literally" that is almost mind-boggling, and finally what is said to have "disappeared" and the "essential" that "remains." The places to which we call attention situate in our eyes chasms over which a great scholar walks with tranquil step, as though he knew what he was talking about, while at the same time acknowledging that at bottom he really doesn't know very much. And all this *goes on*, as we can see, in the enigmatic Latin derivation, in the "prehistory of Greek and Latin." All that *goes on* in what can no longer be isolated as a *religious vocabulary*, which is to say, in a relationship of right to religion, in the experience of the promise or of the indemnificatory offering, of a word committing a future to the present but concerning an event that is past: 'I promise you that it happened.' What happened? Who, to be precise? A son, yours. How beautiful to have an example. Religion, nothing less:

---

20. Ibid., p. 521. For example, "This is where the expression *religio est*, 'to have scruples.' comes from. . . . This usage is constant during the classical period. . . . In sum, *religio* is a hesitation that holds back, a scruple that prevents, and not a sentiment that guides an action or that incites one to practice a cult. It seems to us that this meaning, demonstrated by ancient usage beyond the slightest ambiguity, imposes a single interpretation for *religio*: that which Cicero gives in attaching *religio* to *legere*."

Together with *spondeo*, we must consider *re-spondeo*. The *proper* meaning of *respondeo* and the relation with *spondeo* emerge *literally* from a dialogue of Plautus (*Captiui*, 899). The parasite Ergasilus brings Hegion good news: his son, long disappeared, is about to return. Hegion *promises* Ergasilus to feed him all his days, *if what he says is true*. And the latter *commits himself* in turn:

898 [. . .] sponden tu istud?—Spondeo.
899 At ego tuum tibi aduenisse filium respondeo.

"Is this a *promise?*—It's a *promise.*—And I, for my part, promise you that your son has arrived."

This dialogue is constructed according to a legal formula: a *sponsio* by the one, a *re-sponsio* by the other, forms of a security that are henceforth reciprocal: "I guarantee you, in return, that your son has really arrived."

This exchange of guarantees (cf. our expression *answer for . . .*) gives rise to the meaning, already well established in Latin, "respond." *Respondeo, responsum*, is said of the interpreters of the gods, of priests, notably of the haruspices, *giving a promise in return for the offering*, depositing a security in return for a gift; it is the "response" of an oracle, of a priest. This explains a legal usage of the verb: *respondere de iure*, "to give a legal consultation." The jurist, with his competence, guarantees the value of the opinion he gives.

Let us note a symmetrical Germanic expression: old engl. *and-swaru* 'response' (engl. answer), compared to the got. *swaran* 'to swear, pronounce solemn words': it is *almost literally respondere*.

Thus we can determine precisely, in the prehistory of Greek and of Latin, the meaning of a term that is of the *greatest importance in religious vocabulary*, and the value that is derived from the root **spend* with respect to other verbs that indicate offering in general.

In Latin, *an important part of the initial distinction has disappeared, but the essential remains* and this is what determines the juridical notion of *sponsio* on the one hand, and on the other, the link with the Greek concept of *spondé*.[21]

(32) But religion does not follow the movement of **faith** any more necessarily than the latter rushes towards faith in God. For if the concept of "religion" implies an institution that is separable, identifiable, circumscribable, tied through its letter to the Roman *ius*, its essential relation both to faith and to God is anything but self-evident. When we speak, **we Europeans**, so ordinarily and so confusedly today about a "return of the religious," what do we thereby name? To what do we refer?

---

21. Ibid., pp. 475–76. Only the foreign words and the expression 'answer for' are emphasized by Benveniste.

The "religious," the religiosity that is vaguely associated with the experience of the sacredness of the divine, of the holy, of the saved or of the unscathed (*heilig*)—is it religion? In what and to what extent does a "sworn faith," a belief have to be *committed* or *engaged*? Inversely, not every sworn faith, given word, trustworthiness, trust or confidence in general is necessarily inscribed in a "religion," even if the latter does mark the convergence of two experiences that are generally held to be equally religious:

1. the experience of *belief*, on the one hand (believing or credit, the fiduciary or the trustworthy in the act of faith, fidelity, the appeal to blind confidence, the testimonial that is always beyond proof, demonstrative reason, intuition); and
2. the experience of the unscathed, of *sacredness* or of *holiness*, on the other?

These two veins (or two strata or two sources) of the religious should be distinguished from one another. They can doubtless be associated with each other and certain of their possible co-implications analysed, but they should never be confused or reduced to one another as is almost always done. In principle, it is possible to sanctify, to sacralize the unscathed or to maintain oneself *in the presence* of the sacrosanct in various ways without bringing into play an act of belief, if at least belief, faith or fidelity signifies here acquiescing to the testimony of the other—of the *utterly other* who is inaccessible in its absolute source. And there where every other is utterly other <*où tout autre est tout autre*>. Conversely, if it carries beyond the presence of what would offer itself to be seen, touched, proven, the acquiescence of trust still does not in itself necessarily involve the sacred. (In this context two points deserve consideration: first, the distinction proposed by Levinas between the sacred and the holy; we shall do that elsewhere; secondly, the necessity for these two heterogeneous sources of religion to mingle their waters, if one can put it that way, without ever, it seems to us, amounting simply to the same.)

(33) We met, thus, at Capri, **we Europeans**, assigned to languages (Italian, Spanish, German, French) in which the same word, *religion*, should mean, or so we thought, the same thing. As for the trustworthiness of this word, we shared our presupposition with Benveniste. The latter seems in effect to believe himself capable of recognizing and isolating, in the article on *sponsio* that we evoked a moment ago, what he refers to as "religious vocabulary." But everything remains problematic in this respect. How can discourses, or rather, as was just suggested, "discursive practices," be articulated and made to cooperate in attempting to take the measure of the question, "What is religion?"

"What is . . . ?" which is to say, *on the one hand,* what is it in its *essence?* And *on the other,* what *is* it (present indicative) at present? What is it doing, what is being done with it at present, today, today in the world? So many ways of insinuating, in each of these words—*being, essence, present, world*—a response into the question. So many ways of imposing the answer. Of pre-imposing it or of prescribing it *as* religion. There we might have, perhaps, a pre-definition: however little may be known of religion *in the singular,* we do know that it is always a response and responsibility that it is always a response and responsibility that is prescribed, not chosen freely in an act of pure and abstractly autonomous will. There is no doubt that it implies freedom, will and responsibility, but let us try to think this; will and freedom *without autonomy.* Whether it is a question of sacredness, sacrificiality or of faith, the other makes the law, the law is other: to give ourselves back, and up, to the other. To every other and to the utterly other.

The said "discursive practices" would respond to several types of programme:

1. Assuring oneself of a provenance by **etymologies**. The best illustration would be given by the divergence concerning the *two possible etymological sources* of the word *religio*: (a) *relegere,* from *legere* ("harvest, gather"): Ciceronian tradition continued by W. Otto, J.-B. Hofmann, Benveniste; (b) *religare,* from *ligare* ("to tie, bind"). This tradition would go from Lactantius and Tertullian to Kobbert, Ernout-Meillet, Pauly-Wissowa. In addition to the fact that etymology never provides a law and only provides material for thinking on the condition that it allows itself to be thought as well, we shall attempt later to define the implication or tendency *<charge> common to the two sources* of meaning thus distinguished. Beyond a case of simple synonyms, the two semantic sources perhaps overlap. They would even repeat one another not far from what in truth would be the origin of repetition, which is to say, the division of the same.

2. The search for historico-semantical **filiations** or **genealogies** would determine an immense field, with which the meaning of the word is put to the test of historical transformations and of institutional structures: history and anthropology of religions, in the style of Nietzsche, for example, as well as in that of Benveniste when he holds "Indo-European institutions" as "witnesses" to the history of meaning or of an etymology—which in itself, however, proves nothing about the effective use of a word.

3. An analysis above all concerned with **pragmatic** and functional effects, more structural and also more political, would not hesitate to investigate the usages or applications of the lexical resources, where, in the face of new regularities, of unusual recurrences, of unprecedented contexts, discourse liberates words and meaning from all archaic memory and from all supposed origins.

These three biases seem, from different points of view, legitimate. But even if they respond, as I believe they do, to irrefutable imperatives, my provisional hypothesis (which I advance all the more prudently and timidly for not being able to justify it sufficiently in the limited space and time available) is that here, in Capri, the last type ought to dominate. It should not exclude the others—that would lead to too many absurdities—but it should privilege the signs of what in the world, *today*, singularizes the use of the word "religion" as well as experience of "religion" associated with the word, there where no memory and no history could suffice to announce or gather it, at least not at first sight. I would have had therefore to invent an operation, a discursive machine, if one prefers, whose economy not only does justice, in the space and time available, to these three demands, to each of the imperatives that we feel, at least, to be irrefutable, but which would also organize the hierarchy and the urgencies. At a certain speed, at a rhythm given within the narrow limits <available>.

(34) **Etymologies, filiations, genealogies, pragmatics.** We will not be able to undertake here all the analyses required by distinctions that are indispensable but rarely respected or practised. There are many of them (religion/faith, belief; religion/piety; religion/cult; religion/theology; religion/theiology; religion/ontotheology; or yet again, religious/divine—mortal or immortal; religious/sacred–saved–holy–unscathed–immune—*heilig*). But among them, before or after them, we will put to the test the quasi-transcendental privilege we believe ourselves obliged to grant the distinction between, *on the one hand*, the experience of belief (trust, trustworthiness, confidence, faith, the credit accorded the *good faith of the utterly other* in the experience of witnessing) and, *on the other*, the experience of sacredness, even of holiness, of the unscathed that is safe and sound (*heilig*, holy). These comprise two distinct sources or foci. "Religion" figures their *ellipse* because it both comprehends the two foci but also sometimes shrouds their irreducible duality in silence, in a manner precisely that is secret and *reticent*.

In any case, the history of the word 'religion' should in principle forbid every non-Christian from using the name "religion," in order to recognize in it what "we" would designate, identify and isolate there. Why add here this qualification of "non-Christian"? In other words, why should the concept of religion be solely Christian? Why, in any case, does the question deserve to be posed and the hypothesis taken seriously? Benveniste also recalls that there is no "common" Indo-European term for what we call "religion." The Indo-Europeans did not conceive "as a separate institution" what Benveniste, for his part, calls "the omnipresent reality that is religion." Even today, wherever such a "separate institution" is not recognized, the word "religion" is inadequate. There has not always been, therefore, nor is there always and everywhere, nor will there always and everywhere ("with humans" or elsewhere) be *something*, a thing that is *one and identifiable*, identical with itself, which, whether religious or irreligious, all agree to call "religion." And yet, one tells oneself, **one still must respond**. Within the Latin sphere, the origin of *religio* was the theme of challenges that in truth were interminable. Between two readings or two lessons, therefore, two provenances: on the one hand, supported by texts of Cicero, *relegere*, what would seem to be the avowed formal and semantic filiation: bringing together in order to return and begin again; whence *religio*, scrupulous attention, respect, patience, even modesty, shame or piety—and, on the other hand (Lactantius and Tertullian) *religare*, etymology "invented by Christians," as Benveniste says,[22] and linking religion to the *link*, precisely, to obligation,

---

22. Ibid., p. 516 ff. The Indo-European vocabulary does not dispose of any "common term" for "religion" and it is in "the nature itself of this notion not to lend itself to a single and constant appellation." Correlatively, we would have considerable difficulty in discovering, as such, what one would retrospectively be tempted to identify under this name, which is to say, an institutional reality resembling what we call "religion." We would in any case have difficulty in finding anything of that order in the form of a socially separable entity. Moreover, when Benveniste proposes to study solely *two terms*, Greek and Latin, which, he says, "can pass for *equivalents* of 'religion,'" we ought for our part to underscore two significant traits, two paradoxes as well, even two logical scandals:

1. Benveniste presupposes thus an assured meaning of the word "religion," since he authorizes himself to identify its "equivalents." However, it seems to me that he at no point thematizes or problematizes this pre-comprehension or this presupposition. Nothing permits one to authorize the hypothesis that in his eyes the "Christian" meaning provides here the guiding reference, since, as he himself says, "the interpretation by *religare* ('bond, obligation') . . . invented by Christians [is] historically false."

2. On the other hand, when, after the Greek world *threskeia* ("cult and piety, ritual observance," and much later "religion"), Benveniste retains—and this is the other term of the pair—the word *religio*, it is only as an "equivalent" (which could hardly mean identical) to "religion." We find ourselves confronted by a paradoxical situation that describes very well, at an interval of one page, the double and disconcerting use that Benveniste makes, deliberately or not, of the word "equivalent"—which we emphasize thus:

   (a) "We shall retain solely two terms [*threskeia* and *religio*] which, one in Greek and the other in Latin, can pass for equivalents of 'religion'" (p. 517). Here, then, are two words that can pass, in short, for equivalents of one of them, which itself, on the following page, is said not to have any equivalent in the world, not at least in "Western languages," which would render it "infinitely more important in all respects"!

   (b) "We now come to the second term, infinitely more important in all respects: it is the Latin *religio*, which remains, in all Western languages, the sole and constant word, for which no *equivalent* or substitute has ever been able to impose itself" (p. 518; emphasis added). It is a "proper meaning" (attested to by Cicero), and it is the "proper and constant usages" (pp. 519, 521) that Benveniste intends to identify for this word which is in short an equivalent (among others, but without equivalent!) for that which cannot be designed in short by anything but itself, which is to say, by an equivalent without equivalent.

At bottom, is this not the least deficient definition of religion? In any case, what Benveniste's formal or logical inconsistency designates is perhaps the most faithful reflection, even the most theatrical symptom of what actually occurred in the "history of humanity," and what we here call the "globalatinization" of "religion."

ligament, and hence to obligation, to debt, etc., between men or between man and God. At issue would still be, in an entirely different place, on an entirely different theme, a division of the source and of the meaning (and we are not yet done with this dualization). This debate on the *two sources*, etymological but also "religious," of the word *religio* is without doubt fascinating and passionate (it is related to the Passion itself, in so far as one of the two disputed sources has been claimed to be Christian). But whatever its interest or necessity might be, such a divergence is for us limited in scope. In the first place, because nothing gets decided at the source, as we have just suggested.[23] Secondly, because the two competing etymologies can be retraced to the same, and in a certain manner to the possibility of repetition, which produces the same as much as it confirms it. In both cases (*re-legere* or *re-ligare*), what is at issue is indeed a persistent bond that bonds itself first and foremost to itself. What is at issue is indeed a reunion <*rassemblement*>, a re-assembling, a re-collecting. A resistance or a reaction to dis-junction. To ab-solute alterity. "Recollecting," *recollecter*, is moreover the translation proposed by Benveniste,[24] who glosses it thus: "return for a new choice, return to revise a previous operation," whence the sense of "scruple," but also of choice, of reading and of election, of intelligence, since there can be no selectivity without the bonds of collectivity and recollection. Finally, it is in the bond to the self, marked by the enigmatic "re-," that one should perhaps try to reconstrue the passage between these different meanings (*re-legere, re-ligare, re-spondeo*, in which Benveniste analyses what he also calls, elsewhere, the "relation" to *spondeo*). All the categories of which we could make use to translate the common meaning of the "re-" would be inadequate, and first of all because they can only *re*-introduce into the definition what has to be defined, as though it already had been defined. For example, in pretending to know what is the "proper meaning," as Benveniste says, of words such as repetition, resumption, renewal, reflection, re-election, recollection—in short, religion, "scruple," response and responsibility.

Whatever side one takes in this debate, it is to the ellipse of these double Latin foci that the entire modern (geo-theologico-political) problematic of the "return of the religious" refers. Whoever would not acknowledge either the legitimacy of this double foci or the Christian prevalence that has imposed itself globally within the said Latinity would have to refuse the very premises of such a debate.[25] And with them, any attempt to *think* a situation in which, as in times past, there will perhaps

---

23. See Section 33, points 1 and 2.

24. Benveniste, *Indo-European Language*, p. 521.

25. Something that Heidegger doubtless would have done, given that in his eyes the claimed "return of the religious" would signify nothing but the persistence of a Roman determination of "religion." The latter would go together with a dominant juridical system and concept of the state that themselves would be inseparable from the "machine age" (see Section 18, and note 9).

no longer exist, just as once it did not yet exist, any "common Indo-European term for 'religion.'"[26]

(35) But, **one still must respond**. And without waiting. Without waiting too long. **In the beginning**, Maurizio Ferraris at the Hotel Lutétia. "I need," he tells me, "we need a theme for this meeting in Capri." In a whisper, yet without whispering, almost without hesitating, machine-like, I respond, "Religion." Why? From where did this come to me, and yes, mechanically? Once the theme was agreed upon, discussions were improvised—between two walks at night towards Faraglione, which can be seen in the distance, between Vesuvius and Capri. (Jensen refers to it, Faraglione, and Gradiva returns perhaps, the ghost of light, the shadowless shadow of noon, *das Mittagsgespenst*, more beautiful than all the great ghosts of the island, better "habituated" than they, as she puts it, "to being dead," and for a long time.) I had thus subsequently to justify an answer to the question, why I had named, all of a sudden, machine-like, "religion"? And this justification would have become, today, my response to the question of *religion*. Of religion today. For, of course, it would have been madness itself to have proposed to treat religion *itself*, in general or in its essence; rather the troubled question, the common concern is: "What is going on today with it, with what is designated thus? What is going on there? What is happening and so badly? What is happening under this old name? What in the world is suddenly emerging or re-emerging under this appellation?" Of course, this form of question cannot be separated from the more fundamental one (on the essence, the concept and the history of religion *itself*, and of what is called "religion"). But its approach, first of all, should have been, according to me, more direct, global, massive and immediate, spontaneous, without defence, almost in the style of a philosopher obliged to issue a brief press release. The response that I gave almost without hesitation to Ferraris must have come back to me from afar, resonating from an alchemist's cavern, in whose depths the word was a precipitate. "Religion," a word dictated by who knows what or whom: by everyone perhaps, by the reading of the nightly news televised on an international network, by the everyman we believe we see, by the state of the world, by the whole of what is as it goes (God, its synonym in short, or History as such, and so on). Today once again, today finally, today otherwise, the great question would still be religion and what some hastily call its "return." To say things in this way and to believe that one knows of what one speaks, would be to begin by no longer understanding anything at all: as though religion, the question of religion was *what succeeds in returning*, that which all of a sudden would come as a surprise to what one believes one knows: man, the earth, the world,

---

26. Benveniste, *Indo-European Language*, p. 516.

history falling thus under the rubric of anthropology, of history or of every other form of human science or of philosophy, even of the "philosophy of religion." First error to avoid. It is typical and examples of it could be multiplied. If there is a question of religion, it ought no longer to be a "question-of-religion." Nor simply a response to this question. We shall see why and wherein the question of religion is first of all the question of the question. Of the origins and the borders of the question—as of the response. "The thing" tends thus to drop out of sight as soon as one believes onself able to master it under the title of a discipline, a knowledge or a philosophy. And yet, despite the impossibility of the task, a demand is addressed to us: it should be delivered <*tenir*>, done, or left to "deliver itself" <*se tenir*>—this discourse, in a few traits, in a limited number of words. Economy dictated by publishing exigencies. But why, always the question of number, where there ten commandments, subsequently multiplied by so and so many? Where here would be the just ellipsis we are enjoined to say in keeping it silent. Where the reticence? And what if the ellipsis, the silent figure and the "keeping quiet" of reticence were precisely, we will come to that later, religion? We are asked, in the collective name of several *European* publishers, to state a position in a few pages on religion, and that does not appear monstrous today, when a serious treatise on religion would demand the construction of new Libraries of France and of the universe, even if, not *believing that one is thinking* anything new, one would content oneself with remembering, archiving, classifying, taking note in a memoir, of what one *believes* one already *knows*.

Faith and knowledge: between believing one knows and knowing one believes, the alternative is not a game. Let us choose, then, I told myself, a quasi-aphoristic form as one chooses a machine, the least pernicious machine to treat of *religion* in a certain number of pages: 25 or a few more, we were given; and, let us say, arbitrarily, to de-cipher or anagrammatize the 25, 52 very unequal sequences, as many *crypts* dispersed in a non-identified field, a field that is nonetheless already approaching, like a desert about which one isn't sure if it is sterile or not, or like a field of ruins and of mines and of wells and of caves and of cenotaphs and of scattered seedings; but a non-identified field, not even like a world (the Christian history of this word, "world," already puts us on guard; the world is not the universe, nor the cosmos, nor the earth).

(36) **In the beginning**, the title will have been my first aphorism. It condenses two traditional titles, entering into a contract with them. We are committed to deforming them, dragging them elsewhere while developing if not their negative or their unconscious, at least the logic of what they might have let speak about religion independently of the meanings they wanted to say. In Capri, at the beginning of the session, improvising, I spoke of light and in the name of the island (of the necessity

of dating, that is, of signing a finite meeting in its time and in its space, from the singularity of a place, of a Latin place: Capri, which is not Delos, nor Patmos-nor Athens, nor Jerusalem, nor Rome). I had insisted on the light, the relation of all religion to fire and to light. There is the light of revelation and the light of the Enlightenment. Light, *phos*, revelation, orient and origin of *our* religions, photographic instantaneity. Question, demand: in view of the Enlightenment of today and of tomorrow, in the light of other Enlightenments (*Aufklärung, Lumierès, illuminismo*) how **to think religion** in the daylight of today without breaking with the philosophical tradition? In our "modernity," the said tradition demarcates itself in an exemplary manner—it will have to be shown why—in basically Latin titles that name religion. First of all in a book by Kant, in the epoch and in the spirit of the *Aufklärung,* if not of the *Lumières: Religion within the Limits of Reason Alone* (1793) was also a book on radical evil. (What of reason and of radical evil today? And if the "return of the religious" was not without relation to the return—modern or postmodern, for once—of certain phenomena, at least, of radical evil? Does radical evil destroy or institute the possibility of religion?) Then, the book of Bergson, that great Judaeo-Christian, *The Two Sources of Morality and of Religion* (1932), between the two world wars and on the eve of events of which one knows that one does not yet know how to think them, and to which no religion, no religious institution in the world remained foreign or survived *unscathed, immune, safe and sound.* In both cases, was the issue not, as today, that of thinking religion, the possibility of religion, and hence of its interminable and ineluctable return?

(37) "**To think religion?**" you say. As though such a project would not dissolve the very question in advance. To hold that religion is properly *thinkable,* and even if thinking is neither seeing, nor knowing, nor conceiving, is still to hold it in advance in respect; thus, over short or long, the affair is decided. Already in speaking of these notes as of a machine, I have once again been overcome by a desire for economy, for concision: by the desire to draw, in order to be quick, the famous conclusion of the *Two Sources* ... towards another place, another discourse, other argumentative stakes. The latter could always be—I do not exclude it—a hijacked translation, or a rather free formalization. The book's concluding words are memorable: "**the effort required to accomplish, down to our refractory planet, the essential function of the universe, which is a machine for the making of gods**." What would happen if Bergson were made to say something entirely different from what he believed he wanted to say but what perhaps was surreptitiously dictated to him? What would happen if he had, as though despite himself, left a place or a passage for a sort of symptomatic *retraction,* following the very movement of hesitation, indecision and of scruple, of that turning back (*retractare,* says Cicero to define the *religious* act or

being) in which perhaps the *double source*—the double stratum or the double root—of *religio* consists? Were such the case, then that hypothesis would receive perhaps a doubly *mechanical* form. "Mechanical" would have to be understood here in a meaning that is rather "mystical." Mystical or secret because contradictory and distracting, both inaccessible, disconcerting and familiar, *unheimlich*, uncanny to the very extent that this machinality, this ineluctable automatization produces and re-produces what *at the same time detaches from and reattaches to* the family (*heimisch*, homely), to the familiar, to the domestic, to the proper, to the *oikos* of the ecological and of the economic, to the *ethos*, to the place of dwelling. This quasi-spontaneous automaticity, as irreflective as a reflex, repeats again and again the double movement of abstraction and attraction that *at the same time detaches and reattaches* to the country, the idiom, the literal or to everything confusedly collected today under the terms "identity" or "identitarian"; in two words, that which at the same time ex-propriates and re-appropriates, de-racinates and re-enracinates, *ex-appropriates* according to a logic that we will later have to formalize, that of auto-immune auto-indemnification.

Before speaking so calmly of the "return of the religious" today, two things have to be explained in one. Each time what is involved is a machine, a tele-machine:

1. The said "return of the religious," which is to say the spread of a complex and overdetermined phenomenon, is not a simple *return*, for its globality and its figures (tele-techno-media-scientific, capitalistic and politico-economic) remain original and unprecedented. And it is not a *simple* return *of the religious*, for it comports, as one of its two tendencies, a radical destruction of the religious (*stricto sensu*, the Roman and the statist, like everything that incarnates the European political or juridical order against which all non-Christian "fundamentalisms" or "integrisms" are waging war, to be sure, but also certain forms of Protestant or even Catholic orthodoxy). It must be said as well that in face of them, another self-destructive affirmation of religion, I would dare to call it auto-immune, could well be at work in all the projects known as "pacifist" and economic, "catholic" or not, which appeal to universal fraternization, to the reconciliation of "men, sons of the same God," and above all when these brothers belong to the monotheistic tradition of the Abrahamic religions. It will always be difficult extricating this pacifying movement from a *double horizon* (the one hiding or dividing the other):

   (a) The *kenotic* horizon of the death of God and the anthropological re-immanentization (the rights of man and of *human* life above all obligation towards absolute and transcendent truth of commitment before the divine order: an Abraham who would henceforth refuse to sacrifice his son and would no longer envisage what was always madness). When one hears the official representatives of the religious hierarchy, beginning with the most mediatic and most Latinoglobal and cederomized of all, the Pope, speak of this sort of ecumenical reconciliation, one also hears (not only, to be sure, but also) the announcement or reminder of a certain "death of God." Sometimes one even has the impression that he speaks only of that—which speaks through his mouth. And that another death of God comes to haunt the Passion that animates him. But what's the difference, one will say. Indeed.

(b) This declaration of peace can also, pursuing war by other means, dissimulate a *pacifying* gesture, in the most European-colonial sense possible. Inasmuch as it comes from Rome, as is often the case, it would try first, and first in Europe, upon Europe, to impose surreptitiously a discourse, a culture, a politics and a right, to impose them on all the other monotheist religions, including the non-Catholic Christian religions. Beyond Europe, through the same schemes and the same juridico-theologico-political culture, the aim would be to impose, in the name of peace, a globalatinization. The latter become henceforth European-Anglo-*American* in its idiom, as we said above. The task seems all the more urgent and problematic (incalculable calculation of religion for our times) as the demographic disproportion will not cease henceforth to threaten external hegemony, leaving the latter no strategems other than internalization. The field of this war or of this pacification is henceforth without limit: all the religions, their centres of authority, the religious cultures, states, nations or ethnic groups that they represent have unequal access, to be sure, but often one that is immediate and potentially without limit, to the same world market. They are at the same time producers, actors and sought-after consumers, at times exploiters, at times victims. <At stake in the struggle> is thus the access to world (transnational or trans-state) networks of telecommunication and of tele-technoscience. Henceforth religion "in the singular" accompanies and even precedes the critical and tele-technoscientific reason, it watches over it as its shadow. It is its wake, the shadow of light itself, the pledge of faith, the guarantee of trustworthiness, the fiduciary experience presupposed by all production of shared knowledge, the testimonial performativity engaged in all technoscientific performance as in the entire capitalistic economy indissociable from it.

2. The same movement that renders indissociable religion and tele-technoscientific reason in its most critical aspect reacts inevitably *to itself*. It secretes its own antidote but also its own power of auto-immunity. We are here in a space where all

self-protection of the unscathed, of the safe and sound, of the sacred (*heilig*, holy) must protect itself against its own protection, its own police, its own power of rejection, in short against its own, which is to say, against its own immunity. It is this terrifying but fatal logic of the *auto-immunity of the unscathed* that will always associate Science and Religion.[27]

On the one hand, the 'lights' and Enlightenment of tele-technoscientific critique and reason can only suppose trustworthiness. They are obliged to put into play an irreducible "faith," that of a "social bond" or of a "sworn faith," of a testimony ("I promise to tell you the truth beyond all proof and all theoretical demonstration, believe me, etc."), that is, of a performative of promising at work even in lying or perjury and without which no address to the other would be possible. Without the performative experience of this elementary act of faith, there would neither be 'social bond' nor address of the other, nor any performativity in general: neither convention, nor institution, nor constitution, nor sovereign state, nor law, nor above all, here, that structural performativity of the productive performance that binds from its very inception the knowledge of the scientific community to doing, and science to technics. If we regularly speak here of technoscience, it is not in order to cede to a contemporary stereotype, but in order to recall that, more clearly than ever before, we now know that the scientific act is, through and through, a practical intervention and a technical performativity in the very energy of its essence. And for this very reason it plays with place, putting distances and speeds to work. It delocalizes, removes or brings close, actualizes or virtualizes, accelerates or decelerates. But wherever this tele-technoscientific critique develops, it brings into play and confirms the fiduciary credit of an elementary faith which is, at least in its essence

---

27. The "immune" (*immunis*) is freed or exempted from the charges, the service, the taxes, the obligations (*munus*, root of the common of community). This freedom or this exemption was subsequently transported into the domains of constitutional or international law (parliamentary or diplomatic immunity), but it also belongs to the history of the Christian Church and to canon law; the immunity of temples also involved the inviolability of the asylum that could be found there (Voltaire indignantly attacked this "immunity of temples" as a "revolting example" of "contempt for the laws" and of "ecclesiastical ambition"); Urban VIII created a congregation of ecclesiastical immunity: against taxes and military service, against common justice (privilege designated as that of the *for*) and against police searches, etc. It is especially in the domain of biology that the lexical resources of immunity have developed their authority. The immunitary reaction protects the "indemnity" of the body proper in producing antibodies against foreign antigens. As for the process of auto-immunization, which interests us particularly here, it consists for a living organism, as is well known and in short, of protecting itself against its self-protection by destroying its own immune system. As the phenomenon of these antibodies is extended to a broader zone of pathology and as one resorts increasingly to the positive virtues of immuno-depressants destined to limit the mechanisms of rejection and to facilitate the tolerance of certain organ transplants, we feel ourselves authorized to speak of a sort of general logic of auto-immunization. It seems indispensable to us today for thinking the relations between faith and knowledge, religion and science, as well as the duplicity of sources in general.

or calling, religious (the elementary condition, the milieu of the religious if not religion itself). We speak of trust and of credit or of trustworthiness in order to underscore that this elementary act of faith also underlies the essentially economic and capitalistic rationality of the tele-technoscientific. No calculation, no assurance will ever be able to reduce its ultimate necessity, that of the testimonial signature (whose theory is not necessarily a theory of the subject, of the person or of the ego, conscious or unconscious). To take note of this is to give oneself the means of understanding why, in principle, today, there is no incompatibility, in the said "return of the religious," between the "fundamentalisms," the "integrisms" or their "politics" and, on the other hand, rationality, which is to say, the tele-techno-capitalistico-scientific fiduciary, in all of its mediatic and globalizing dimensions. This rationality of the said "fundamentalisms" can also be hypercritical[28] and not recoil before what can sometimes resemble a deconstructive radicalization of the critical gesture. As for the phenomena of ignorance, of irrationality or of "obscurantism" that are so often emphasized and denounced, so easily and with good reason, they are often residues, surface effects, the reactive slag of immunitary, indemnificatory or auto-immunitary reactivity. They mask a deep structure or rather (but also at the same time) a fear of self, a reaction against that with which it is partially linked: the dislocation, expropriation, delocalization, deracination, disidiomatization and dispossession (in all their dimensions, particularly sexual—*phallic*) that the tele-techno-scientific machine does not fail to produce. The reactivity of resentment opposes this movement to itself by dividing it. It *indemnifies* itself thus in a movement that is at once immunitary and auto-immune. The reaction to the machine is as automatic (and thus machinal) as life itself. Such an internal splitting, which opens distance, is also peculiar or "proper" to religion, appropriating religion for the "proper" (inasmuch as it is also the *unscathed*: heilig, holy, sacred, saved, immune and so on), appropriating religious indemnification to all forms of property, from the linguistic idiom in its "letter," to blood and soil, to the family and to the nation. This internal and immediate reactivity, at once immunitary and auto-immune, can alone account for what will be called the religious resurgence in its double and contradictory phenomenon. The word *resurgence <déferlement>*

---

28. This is testified to by certain phenomena, at least, of "fundamentalism" or of "integrism," in particular in "Islamism," which represents today the most powerful example of such fundamentalisms as measured by the scale of global demography. The most evident characteristics are too well known to dwell on (fanaticism, obscurantism, lethal violence, terrorism, oppression of women, etc.). But it is often forgotten that, notably in its ties to the Arab world, and through all the forms of brutal immunitary and indemnificatory reactivity against a techno-economical modernity to which a long history prevents it from adapting, this "Islamism" also develops a radical critique of what ties democracy *today, in its limits, in its concept and its effective power*, to the market and to the tele-technoscientific reason that dominates it.

imposes itself upon us to suggest the redoubling of a wave that appropriates even that to which, enfolding itself, it seems to be opposed—and simultaneously gets carried away itself, sometimes in terror and terrorism, taking with it precisely that which protects it, its own "antibodies." Allying itself with the enemy, hospitable to the antigens, bearing away the other with itself, this resurgence grows and *swells* with the power of the adversary. From the shores of whatever island, one doesn't know, here is the resurgence we believe we see coming, without doubt, in its spontaneous swelling, irresistibly automatic. But we believe we see it coming without any horizon. We are no longer certain that we see and that there is a future where we see it coming. The future tolerates neither foresight nor providence. It is therefore in it, rather, caught and surprised by this resurgence, that "we" in truth are carried away—and it is this that we would like to *think*, if this word can still be used here.

Religion today allies itself with tele-technoscience, to which it reacts with all its forces. It *is, on the one hand*, globalization; it produces, weds, exploits the capital and knowledge of tele-mediatization; neither the trips and global spectacularizing of the Pope, nor the interstate dimensions of the "Rushdie affair," nor planetary terrorism would otherwise be possible, at this rhythm—and we could multiply such indications *ad infinitum*. But, *on the other hand*, it reacts immediately, *simultaneously*, declaring war against that which gives it this new power only at the cost of dislodging it from all its proper places, *in truth from place itself*, from the *taking-place* of its truth. It conducts a terrible war against that which protects it only by threatening it, according to this double and contradictory structure: immunitary and auto-immunitary. The relation between these two motions or these two sources is ineluctable, and therefore automatic and mechanical, between one which has the form of the machine (mechanization, automatization, machination or *mechane*), and the other, that of living spontaneity, of the *unscathed* property of life, that is to say, of another (claimed) self-determination. But the auto-immunitary haunts the community and its system of immunitary survival like the hyperbole of its own possibility. Nothing in *common*, nothing immune, safe and sound, *heilig* and holy, nothing unscathed in the most autonomous living present without a risk of auto-immunity. As always, the risk charges itself twice, the same finite risk. Two times rather than one: with a menace and with a chance. In two words, it must take charge of—one could also say: take in trust—the *possibility* of that **radical evil** without which good would be for nothing.[29]

---

29. *Translator's note, "sans lequel on ne saurait bien faire"*: in addition to the ambiguity of the more literal meaning of this phrase, (a) "without which nothing good could be done," and (b) "without which nothing could be done well," the French expression here recalls the colloquial idiom "ça commence à bien faire: y en a marre," which adds the ironic connotation of "that's enough!" to the dialectic of good and evil.

... *and pomegranates*

(Having posed these premises or general definitions, and given the diminishing space available, we shall cast the fifteen final propositions in a form that is even more granulated, grainy, disseminated, aphoristic, discontinuous, juxtapositional, dogmatic, indicative or virtual, economic; in a word, more than ever telegraphic.)

(38) Of a discourse to come—on the to-come and repetition. Axiom: no to-come without heritage and the possibility of *repeating*. No to-come without some sort of *iterability*, at least in the form of a covenant with oneself and *confirmation* of the originary *yes*. No to-come without some sort of messianic memory and promise, of a messianicity older than all religion, more originary than all messianism. No discourse or address of the other without the possibility of an elementary promise. Perjury and broken promises require the *same* possibility. No promise, therefore, without the promise of a confirmation of the *yes*. This *yes* will have implied and will always imply the trustworthiness and fidelity of a faith. No faith, therefore, nor future without everything technical, automatic, machine-like supposed by iterability. In this sense, the technical is the possibility of faith, indeed its very chance. A chance that entails the greatest risk, even the menace of **radical evil**. Otherwise, that of which it is the chance would not be faith but rather programme or proof, predictability or providence, pure knowledge and pure know-how, which is to say annulment of the future. Instead of opposing them, as is almost always done, they ought to be thought together, as *one and the same possibility:* the machine-like and faith, and the same holds for the machinal and all the values entailed in the sacrosanct (*heilig*, holy, safe and sound, unscathed, intact, immune, free, vital, fecund, fertile, strong, and above all, as we will soon see, "swollen") —more precisely in the sacrosanctity of the **phallic** effect.

(39) This double value, is it not, for example, that signified by a phallus in its differentiality, or rather by the **phallic**, the effect of the phallus, which is not necessarily the property of man? Is it not the phenomenon, the *phainesthai*, the day of the *phallus?*—but also, by virtue of the law of iterability or of duplication that can *detach* it from its pure and proper presence, it is not also its *phantasma*, in Greek, its ghost, its spectre, its double or its fetish? Is it not the *colossal automaticity* of the erection (the maximum of life to be kept unscathed, indemnified, immune and safe, sacrosanct), but also and precisely by virtue of its reflex character, that which is most mechanical, most separable from the life it represents? The phallic—is it not also, as distinct from the penis and once detached from the body, the marionette that is erected, exhibited, festishized and paraded in processions? Is this not where one grasps, virtuality of virtuality, the power or potency of a logic powerful

enough to account for (*logon didonai*)—counting on and calculating the incalculable—everything that binds the tele-technoscientific machine, this enemy of life in
the service of life, to the very source and resource of the religious: to faith in the
most living as dead and automatically *sur-viving*, resuscitated in its spectral *phantasma*, the holy, safe and sound, unscathed, immune, sacred—in a word, everything
that translates *heilig*? Matrix, once again, of a cult or of a culture of the generalized
fetish, of an unlimited fetishism, of a fetishizing adoration of the Thing itself. One
could, without being arbitrary, read, select, connect everything in the semantic
genealogy of the unscathed—"saintly, sacred, safe and sound, *heilig, holy*"—that
speaks of force, **life**-force, fertility, growth, augmentation, and above all *swelling*, in
the spontaneity of erection or of pregnancy.[30] To be brief, it does not suffice to

---

30. Let us worry <*Egrenons*> the premises here of a work to come. Let them be drawn first, and once
again, from that rich chapter of Benveniste's *Indo-European Language and Society*, addressing the Sacred
and the Holy after having opportunely recalled several "methodological difficulties." It is true that to us
these "difficulties" seem even more serious and more fundamental than to Benveniste—even if he is
willing to acknowledge the risk of "seeing the object of study dissolve bit by bit" (p. 445). Maintaining
the cult of "original meaning" (religion itself, and the "sacred"), Benveniste identifies, through the enor-
mously complex network of idioms, filiations and etymologies studied, the recurrent and insistent
theme of the "fertility" of the "strong," of the "powerful," in particular in the figure or the imaginal
scheme of *swelling*.
   We may be permitted the following long citation, while referring the reader to the article itself for the
rest: "The adjective *sura* does not signify merely 'strong'; it is also a qualification of a number of gods, of
several heroes including Zarathustra, and of certain notions such as 'dawn.' Here, comparison with
related forms of the same root can lead us to the original meaning. The Vedic verb *su-sva* signifies 'to
swell, grow,' implying 'force' and 'prosperity'; whence *sura-*, 'strong, valiant.' The same conceptional relation joins in Greek the present *kueîn*, 'to be pregnant, carry in the womb,' the noun *kûma*, 'swelling (of
waves), flood,' on the one hand, and *kûros*, 'force, sovereignty,' *kúrios*, 'sovereign,' on the other. This juxtaposition brings out the initial identity of the meaning of 'swell' and, in each of the three languages, a specific evolution ... In Indo-Iranian no less than in Greek the meaning evolves from 'swelling' to 'strength'
or 'prosperity' ... Between gr. *kuéo*, 'to be pregnant,' and *kúrios*, 'sovereign,' between Av. *sura*, 'strong,' and
spénta, relations are thus restored which, little by little, make more precise the singular origin of the
notion of 'sacred' ... The holy and sacred character is thus defined through a notion of exuberant and
fecund force, capable of bringing to life, of causing the productions of nature to burst forth" (pp. 448–49).
   One could also inscribe under the title of the "two sources" the remarkable fact, often emphasized by
Benveniste, that "almost every-where" there corresponds to the "notion of the 'sacred' not one but two
distinct terms." Benveniste analyses them, notably in German (the Gothic *weihs*, "consecrated," and the
Runic *hailag*, ger. *heilig*) in Latin *sacer* and *sanctus*, in Greek *hágios* and *hierós*. At the origin of the
German *heilig*, the Gothic adjective *hails* translates the idea of "soundness, health, physical integrity,"
translation of the Greek *hygies, hygiainon*, "in good health." The corresponding verbal forms signify
"render or become healthy, heal." (One might situate here—although Benveniste does not—the necessity for every religion or all sacralization also to involve healing—*heilen*—health, hail or promise of a
cure—*cura, Sorge*—horizon of redemption, of the restoration of the unscathed, of indemnification).
The same for the English, "holy," neighbour of "whole" ("entire, intact," therefore "safe, saved, unscathed
in its integrity, immune"). The Gothic *hails*, "in good health, in possession of physical integrity," carries
with it a wish, as does the Greek *khaîre*, "hail!". Benveniste underscores its "religious value": "Whoever
possesses 'hail' <*le 'salut'*>, that is, whose physical integrity is intact, is also capable of conferring 'hail.'
'To be intact' is the luck that one wishes, predicts or expects. It is natural to have seen in such perfect
'integrity' a divine grace, a sacred meaning. By its very nature, divinity possesses the gift of integrity, of
being hail, of luck, and can impart it to human beings .... In the course of history the primitive Gothic
term *weihs* was replaced by *hails, hailigs*" (pp. 451–52).

recall here all the phallic cults and their well-known phenomena at the core of so many religions. The three "great monotheisms" have inscribed covenants or founding promises in an *ordeal of the unscathed* that is always a circumcision, be it "exterior or interior," literal or, as was said before Saint Paul, in Judaism itself, "circumcision of the heart." And this would perhaps be the place to enquire why, in the most lethal explosions of a violence that is inevitably ethnico-religious —why, on all sides, women in particular are singled out as victims (not "only" of murders, but also of the rapes and mutilations that precede and accompany them).

(40) The religion of the living—is this not a tautology? Absolute imperative, holy law, law of salvation: saving the living intact, the unscathed, the safe and sound (*heilig*) that has the right to absolute respect, restraint, modesty. Whence the necessity of an enormous task: reconstituting the chain of analogous motifs in the sacrosanctifying attitude or intentionality, in relation to that which is, should remain or should be allowed to be what it is (*heilig*, living, strong and fertile, erect and fecund: safe, whole, unscathed, immune, sacred, holy and so on). Salvation and health. Such an intentional attitude bears several names of the same family: respect, modesty, restraint, inhibition, *Achtung* (Kant), *Scheu, Verhaltenheit, Gelassenheit* (Heidegger), restraint or *holding-back* <halte> in general.[31] The poles, themes, causes are not the same (the law, sacredness, holiness, the good to come and so on), but the movements appear quite analogous in the way they relate to them, *suspending* themselves, and *in truth interrrupting themselves*. All of them

---

31. Elsewhere, in a seminar, I attempt to reflect in a more sustained manner on this value of the hold and on its lexical ramifications, in particular surrounding the use of *halten* by Heidegger. In addition to *Aufenthalt* (stopover, ethos, often involving the *heilig*), *Verhaltenheit* (modesty or respect, scruple, reserve or silent discretion that suspends itself in and as reticence) would be only one example, albeit a major one for what concerns us here and taking into account the role played by this concept in the *Beiträge zur Philosophie* with respect to the "last god," or the "other god," the god who comes or the god who passes. I refer here, in particular regarding this last theme, to the recent study by Jean-François Courtine, "Les traces et le passage de Dieu dans les *Beiträge zur Philosophie* de Martin Heidegger" ("The traces and passing of God in Heidegger's *Contributions to Philosophy*"), in *Archivio di filosofia*, 1994, nos. 1–3. When he refers to Heidegger's insistence on modern nihilism as "uprooting" (*Entwürzelung*), Courtine rightly associates it with what is said of—and always implicitly against—the *Gestell* and all "technical-instrumental manipulation of beings" (*Machenschaft*), with which he even associates "a critique of the idea of creation directed primarily against Christianity" (p. 528). This seems to go in the direction of the hypothesis developed above: Heidegger directs suspicion at the same time against "religion" (especially Christian-Roman), against belief, and against that in technics which menaces the safe and sound, the unscathed or the immune, the sacrosanct (*heilig*). The interest of his "position" consists, simplifying considerably, in the way it tends to take its distance <se déprendre> from *both* religion and technics, or rather from what is called *Gestell* and *Machenschaft*, as though they were the same. The *same*, yes, as what we are trying to say here as well, modestly and in our fashion. And the *same* neither excludes not effaces any of the differential folds. But once this *same possibility* is recognized or thought, it is not certain that it calls only for a Heideggerian "response," nor that the latter is alien or exterior to this *same possibility*, be it the logic of the unscathed, or the auto-immune indemnification that we are trying to approach here. We shall return to this later in this text and elsewhere.

involve or mark a restraint <*halte*>. Perhaps they constitute a sort of universal, not "religion" as such, but a universal structure of religiosity. For if they are not in themselves properly religious, they always open the possibility of the religious without ever being able to limit or restrain it. This possibility remains divided. On the one hand, to be sure, it is respectful or inhibited abstention before what remains sacred mystery, and what ought to remain intact or inaccessible, like the mystical immunity of a secret. But in thus holding back, the same halting also opens an access without mediation or representation, hence not without an intuitive violence, to that which remains unscathed. That is another dimension of the mystical. Such a universal allows or promises perhaps the global translation of *religio*, that is: scruple, respect, restraint, *Verhaltenheit*, reserve, *Scheu*, shame, discretion, *Gelassenheit*, etc.—all stop short of that which must or should remain safe and sound, intact, unscathed, before what must be allowed to be what it ought to be, sometimes even at the cost of sacrificing itself and in prayer: the other. Such a universal, such an "existential" universality, could have provided at least the mediation of a *scheme* to the globalatinization of *religio*. Or in any case, to its possibility.

What would then be required is, in the same movement, to account for a double postulation: *on the one hand,* the absolute respect of **life**, the "Thou shalt not kill" (at least thy neighbour, if not the living in general), the "fundamentalist" prohibition of abortion, of artificial insemination, of performative intervention in the genetic potential, even to the ends of gene therapy, etc.; *and on the other* (without even speaking of wars of religion, of their terrorism and their killings) the no less universal sacrificial vocation. It was not so long ago that this still involved, here and there, human **sacrifice**, even in the "great monotheisms." It always involves sacrifice of the living, more than ever in large-scale breeding and slaughtering, in the fishing or hunting industries, in animal experimentation. Be it said in passing that certain ecologists and certain vegetarians—at least to the extent that they believe themselves to have remained pure of (unscathed by) all carnivorousness, even symbolic[32]— would be the only "religious" persons of the time to respect one of these two pure sources of religion and indeed to bear responsibility for what could well be the future of a religion. What are the *mechanics* of this double postulation (respect of life and sacrificiality)? I refer to it as *mechanics* because it reproduces, with the regularity of a technique, the instance of the non-living or, if you prefer, of the dead in the living. It was also the automation according to the phallic effect of which we spoke above. It was the marionette, the dead machine yet more than living, the spec-

---

32. That is, of what in Western cultures remains sacrificial, up to and including its industrial, sacrificial and "carno-phallogo-centric" implementation. On this latter concept, I take the liberty of referring to "'Eating Well,' or the calculation of the subject," in Jacques Derrida, *Points . . . Interviews*, 1974–94, ed. Elisabeth Weber, trans. Peggy Kamuf et al. (Stanford, Stanford University Press, 1995), pp. 255–87.

tral fantasy of the dead as the principle of life and of sur-vival <*sur-vie*>. This mechanical principle is apparently very simple: life has absolute value only if it is worth *more than* life. And hence only in so far as it mourns, becoming itself in the labour of infinite mourning, in the indemnification of a spectrality without limit. It is sacred, holy, infinitely respectable only in the name of what is worth more than it and what is not restricted to the naturalness of the bio-zoological (sacrificeable)— although true sacrifice ought to sacrifice not only "natural" life, called "animal" or "biological," but also that which is worth more than so-called natural life. Thus, respect of life in the discourses of religion as such concerns "human life" only in so far as it bears witness, in some manner, to the infinite transcendence of that which is worth more than it (divinity, the sacrosanctness of the law).[33] The price of human life, which is to say, of anthropo-theological life, the price of what ought to remain safe (*heilig*, sacred, safe and sound, unscathed, immune), as the absolute price, the price of what ought to inspire respect, modesty, reticence, this price is priceless. It corresponds to what Kant calls the dignity (*Würdigkeit*) of the end in itself, of the rational finite being, of absolute value beyond all comparative market price (*Marktpreis*). This dignity of life can only subsist beyond the present living being. Whence, transcendence, fetishism and spectrality; whence, the religiosity of religion. This excess above and beyond the living, whose life only has absolute value by being worth more than life, more than itself–this, in short, is what opens the space of death that is linked to the automaton (exemplarily "phallic"), to technics, the machine, the prosthesis: in a word, to the dimensions of auto-immune and self-sacrificial sup-plementarity, to this death-drive that is silently at work in every community, every *auto-co-immunity*, constituting it as such in its iterability, its heritage, its spectral tra-dition. Community as *com-mon auto-immunity:* no community <is possible> that would not cultivate its own auto-immunity, a principle of sacrificial self-destruction ruining the principle of self-protection (that of maintaining its self-integrity intact), and this in view of some sort of invisible and spectral sur-vival. This self-contesting attestation keeps the auto-immune community alive, which is to say, open to some-thing other and more than itself: the other, the future, death, freedom, the coming or the love of the other, the space and time of a spectralizing messianicity beyond all messianism. It is there that the possibility of religion persists: the *religious* bond (scrupulous, respectful, modest, reticent, inhibited) between the value of life, its absolute "dignity," and the theological machine, the "machine for making gods."[34]

---

33. Concerning the association and disassociation of these two values (*sacer* and *sanctus*), we refer below to Benveniste and to Levinas.

34. *Translator's note*: Henri Bergson, *The Two Sources of Morality and Religion*, trans. R. Ashley Audra and Cloudesley Brereton, with the assistance of W. Horsfall Carter (Notre Dame: University of Notre Dame Press, 1986), p. 317.

(41) Religion, as a response that is both ambiguous and ambi-valent <*à double détente et à double entente*> is thus an ellipsis: the ellipsis of **sacrifice**. Is a religion imaginable without sacrifice and without prayer? The sign through which Heidegger believes ontotheology can be recognized is when the relation to the absolute Being or to the supreme Cause has freed itself of both, thereby losing access to sacrificial offering no less than to prayer. But there as well, two sources: the dividual law, the *double bind*, also the dual foci, the ellipsis or originary duplicity of religion, consists therein, that the law of the unscathed, the salvation of the safe, the humble respect of that which is sacrosanct (*heilig*, holy) *both requires and excludes* sacrifice, which is to say, the indemnification of the unscathed, the price of immunity. Hence: auto-immunization and the sacrifice of sacrifice. The latter always represents the same movement, the price to pay for not injuring or wronging the absolute other. **Violence** of sacrifice in the name of non-violence. Absolute respect enjoins first and foremost sacrifice of self, of one's most precious interest. If Kant speaks of the "holiness" of the moral law, it is while explicitly holding a discourse on "sacrifice," which is to say, on another instantiation of religion "within the limits of reason *alone*": the Christian religion as the only "moral" religion. Self-sacrifice thus sacrifices the most proper in the service of the most proper. As though *pure* reason, in a process of auto-immune indemnification, could only oppose religion as such to a religion or *pure* faith to this or that belief.

(42) In our "wars of religion," **violence** has two ages. The one, already discussed above, appears "contemporary," in sync or in step with the hypersophistication of military tele-technology—of "digital" and cyberspaced culture. The other is a "new archaic violence," if one can put it that way. It counters the first and everything it represents. Revenge. Resorting, in fact, to the same resources of mediatic power, it *reverts* (according to the return, the resource, the repristination and the law of internal and autoimmune reactivity we are trying to formalize here) as closely as possible to the body proper and to the premachinal living being. In any case, to its desire and to its phantasm. Revenge is taken against the decorporalizing and exproriating machine by resorting—reverting—to bare hands, to the sexual organs or to primitive tools, often to weapons other than firearms <*l'arme blanche*>. What is referred to as "killings" and "atrocities"—words never used in "clean" or "proper" wars, where, precisely, the dead are no longer counted (guided or "intelligent" missiles directed at entire cities, for instance)—is here supplanted by tortures, beheadings and mutilations of all sorts. What is involved is always avowed vengeance, often declared as **sexual** revenge: rapes, mutilated genitals or severed hands, corpses exhibited, heads paraded, as not to long ago in France, impaled on the end of stakes (phallic processions of "natural religions"). This is the case, for example,

but it is only an example, in Algeria today, in the name of Islam, invoked by both belligerent parties, each in its own way. These are also symptoms of a reactive and negative recourse, the vengeance of the body proper against an expropriatory and delocalizing tele-technoscience, identified with the globality of the market, with military-capitalistic hegemony, with the globalatinization of the European democractic model, in its double form: secular and religious. Whence—another figure of double origin—the foreseeable alliance of the worst effects of fanaticism, dogmatism or irrationalist obscurantism with hypercritical acumen and incisive analysis of the hegemonies and the models of the adversary (globalatinization, religion that does not speak its name, ethnocentrism putting on, as always, a show of "universalism," market-driven science and technology, democratic rhetoric, "humanitarian" strategy or "keeping the peace" by means of peace-keeping forces, while never counting the dead of Rwanda, for instance, in the same manner as those of the United States of America or of Europe). This archaic and ostensibly more savage radicalization of 'religious' violence claims, in the name of "religion," to allow the living community to rediscover its roots, its place, its body and its idiom intact (unscathed, safe, pure, proper). It spreads death and unleashes self-destruction in a desperate (auto-immune) gesture that attacks the blood of its own body: as though thereby to eradicate uprootedness and reappropriate the sacredness of life safe and sound. Double root, double uprootedness, double eradication.

(43) Double rape. A *new cruelty* would thus ally, in wars that are also wars of religion, the most advanced technoscientific calculability with a reactive savagery that would like to attack the body proper directly, the **sexual** thing that can be raped, mutilated or simply denied, desexualized—yet another form of the same violence. Is it possible to speak today of this double rape, to speak of it in a way that wouldn't be too foolish, uninformed or inane, while "ignoring" "psychoanalysis"? To ignore psychoanalysis can be done in a thousand ways, sometimes through extensive psychoanalytic knowledge that remains culturally disassociated. Psychoanalysis is ignored when it is not integrated into the most powerful discourses today on right, morality, politics, but also on science, philosophy, theology, etc. There are a thousand ways of avoiding such consistent integration, even in the institutional milieu of psychoanalysis. No doubt, "psychoanalysis" (we have to proceed more and more quickly) is receding in the West; it never broke out, never really crossed the borders of a part of "old Europe." This "fact" is a legitimate part of the configuration of phenomena, signs, symptoms that we are questioning here under the title of "religion." How can one invoke a new Enlightenment in order to account for this "return of the religious" without bringing into play at least some sort of logic of the unconscious? Without bringing it to bear on the question of radical evil and working out

the reaction to radical evil that is at the centre of Freudian thought? This question can no longer be separated from many others: the repetition-compulsion, the "death-drive," the difference between "material truth" and "historical truth" that imposes itself upon Freud with respect to "religion," precisely, and that works itself out above all in closet proximity to an interminable **Jewish question**. It is true that psychoanalytic knowledge can in turn uproot and reawaken faith by opening itself to a new space of testimoniality, to a new instance of attestation, to a new experience of the symptom and of truth. This new space would have to be also, although not exclusively, legal and political. We shall have to return to this.

(44) We are constantly trying to think the interconnectedness, albeit otherwise, of knowledge *and* faith, technoscience *and* religous belief, calculation *and* the sacrosanct. In the process we have not ceased to encounter the alliance, holy or not, of the calculable and the incalculable. As well as that of the immunerable and of number, of the binary and of the digital. Demographic calculation, for instance, today concerns *one* of the aspects, as least, of the "religious question" in its geopolitical dimension. As to the future of a religion, the question of number concerns as much the quantity of "populations" as the living indemnity of "peoples." This does not merely signify that the religious factor has to be taken into account, but that the manner in which the faithful are counted must be changed in an age of globalization. Whether it is "exemplary" or not, the **Jewish question** continues to be a rather good example (sample, particular case) for future elaboration of this demographic-religious problematic. In truth, this question of *numbers* obsesses, as is well known, the Holy Scriptures and the monotheisms. When they feel themselves threatened by an **expropriative and delocalizing** tele-technoscience, "peoples" also fear new forms of invasion. They are terrified by alien "populations," whose growth as well as presence, indirect or virtual—but as such, all the more oppressive—becomes incalculable. New ways of counting, therefore. There is more than one way of interpreting the unheard-of survival of the small "Jewish people" and the global extension of its religion, single source of the two monotheisms which share in a certain domination of the world and of which, in dignity at least, it is the equal. There are a thousand ways of interpreting its resistance to attempts at extermination as well as to a demographic disproportion, the like of which is not known. But what will come of this survival the day (already arrived, perhaps) when globalization will be saturated? Then, "globalization," a term so frequently encountered in American discourse,[35] will perhaps no longer allow the surface of the human earth

---

35. *Translator's note*: Although Derrida uses the English word "*globalisation*," here, elsewhere he consistently uses the French term "*mondialisation*" and the neologism "*mondialatinisation*," which have been translated throughout as "globalization" and "globalatinization."

to be segmented into micro-climates, those historical, cultural, political micro-zones, little Europe and the Middle East, in which the Jewish people had such great difficulty surviving and bearing witness to its faith. "I understand Judaism as the possibility of giving the Bible a context, of keeping this book readable," says Levinas. Does not the globalization of demographic reality and calculation render the probability of such a "context" weaker than ever and as threatening for survival as the worst, the radical evil of the "final solution"? "God is the future," says Levinas also—while Heidegger sees the "last god" announcing himself in the every absence of future: "The last god: his occurring (*Wesung*) is found in the hint (*im Wink*), in the onset of an arrival still outstanding (*dem Anfall und Ausbleib der Ankunft*), as well as in the flight of the gods that are past and of their hidden metamorphosis."[36]

This question is perhaps the most grave and most urgent for the state and the nations of Israel, but it concerns also all the Jews, and doubtless also, if less obviously, all the Christians in the world. Not at all Muslims today. And to this day, this is a fundamental difference between the three original "great monotheisms."

(45) Is there not always another *place* of dispersion? Where the source today divides itself again, like *the same* dissociating itself between faith and knowledge? The original reactivity to an **expropriative and delocalizing** tele-technoscience must respond to at least two figures. The latter are superimposed upon one another, they relay or replace each other, producing in truth at the very place of the emplacement nothing but indemnifying and auto-immune supplementarity:

1. Violent sundering <*arrachement*>, to be sure, from the radicality of roots (*Entwürzelung*, Heidegger would say; we cited him above) and from all forms of originary *physis*, from all the supposed resources of a force held to be authentically generative, sacred, unscathed, "safe and sound" (*heilig*): ethnic identity, descent, family, nation, blood and soil, proper name, proper idiom, proper culture and memory.

2. But also, more than ever, the counter-fetishism of the same desire inverted, the animist relation to the tele-technoscientific machine, which then becomes a machine of evil, and of radical evil, but a machine to be manipulated as much as to be exorcised. Because this evil is to be domesticated and because one increasingly *uses* artifacts and prostheses of which one is totally ignorant, in a growing disproportion between knowledge and know-how, the space of such technical experience tends to become more animistic, magical, mystical. The spectral

---

36. *Beiträge zur Philosophie*, p. 256, French translation and cited by J.-F. Courtine, "Les traces et le passage de Dieu," p. 533. On a certain question of the future, Judaism and Jewishness, I permit myself to refer to *Archive Fever: A Freudian Impression*, trans. Eric Prenowitz, (Chicago: University of Chicago Press, 1995), pp. 9–63.

aspect of this experience persists and then tends to become—in proportion to this disproportion, one might say—increasingly **primitive and archaic**. So much so that its rejection, no less than its apparent appropriation, can assume the form of a religiosity that is both structural and invasive. A certain ecologist spirit can participate in this. (But a distinction must be drawn here between a vague ecologist ideology and ecological discourses and politics that are often both competent and rigorous.) Never in the history of humanity, it would seem, has the disproportion between scientific incompetence and manipulatory competence been as serious. It is not even measurable any longer with respect to machines that are used everyday, with a mastery that is taken for granted and whose proximity is ever closer, more interior, more domestic. To be sure, in the recent past every soldier did not *know* how his firearm functioned although he *knew* very well how to use it. Yesterday, all the drivers of automobiles or travellers in a train did not always know very well how "it works." But their relative incompetence stands in no common (quantitative) measure nor in any (qualitative) analogy with that which today characterizes the relationship of the major part of humanity to the machines by which they live or with which they strive to live in daily familiarity. Who is capable of explaining scientifically to children how telephones function today (by undersea cables or by satellite), and the same is true of television, fax, computer, electronic mail, CD-ROMS, magnetic cards, jet planes, the distribution of nuclear energy, scanners, echography, etc.?

(46) The same religiosity is obliged to ally the reactivity of the **primitive and archaic** return, as we have already said, *both* to obscurantist dogmatism *and* to hypercritical vigilance. The machines it combats by striving to appropriate them are also machines for destroying historical tradition. They can displace the traditional structures of national citizenship, they tend to efface both the borders of the state and the distinctive properties of languages. As a result, the religious reaction (rejection and assimilation, introjection and incorporation, impossible indemnification and mourning) normally follows two avenues that compete with each other and are apparently antithetical. Both of them, however, can as easily oppose or support a "democratic" tradition: *either* the fervent return to national citizenship (patriotism of the home in all its forms, affection for the nation-state, awakening of nationalism or of ethnocentrism, most often allied with Churches or religious authorities), *or*, on the contrary, a protest that is universal, cosmopolitan or ecumenical: "Ecologists, humanists, believers of all countries, unite in an International of anti-tele-technologism!" What is involved here, moreover, is an International that—and it is the singularity of our time—can only develop through the networks it combats, using the means of the adversary. At the same speed against an adver-

sary that in truth is the same. The same <but> double, which is to say, what is called the contemporary in the blatant anachrony of its dislocation. Auto-immune indemnification. This is why these "contemporary" movements are obliged to search for their salvation (the safe and sound as the sacrosanct), as well as their health in the paradox of a new alliance between the tele-technoscientific and the **two** sources of religion (the unscathed, *heilig*, *holy*, on the one hand, and faith or belief, the fiduciary on the other). The 'humanitarian' would provide a good example of this. "Peacekeeping forces" as well.

(47) Of what should one take particular note in trying to formalize, in a concise manner, the axiom of the **two** sources around each of the two "logics" if you like, or each of the two distinct "resources" of what in the West goes by the Latinate name, "religion"? Let us remember the hypothesis of these two sources: on the one hand, the fiduciar-*ity* of confidence, trustworthiness <*fiabilité*> or of trust <*fiance*> (belief, faith, credit and so on), and on the other, the unscathed-*ness* of the unscathed (the safe and sound, the immune, the holy, the sacred, *heilig*). Perhaps what in the first place ought be stressed is this: each of these axioms, as such, already reflects and presupposes the other. An *axiom* always affirms, as its name indicates, a value, a price; it confirms or promises an evaluation that should remain intact and entail, like every value, an act of faith. Secondly, both of these two axioms renders possible, but not necessary, something like a religion, which is to say, an instituted apparatus consisting of dogmas or of articles of faith that are both determinate and inseparable from a given historical *socius* (Church, clergy, socially legitimated authority, people, shared idiom, community of the faithful committed to the same faith and sanctioning the same history). But the gap between the opening of this *possibility* (*as a universal structure*) and the *determinate necessity* of this or that religion will always remain irreducible; and sometimes <it operates> within each religion, between on the one hand that which keeps it closest to its "pure" and proper possibility, and on the other, its own historically determined necessities or authorities. Thus, one can always criticize, reject or combat this or that form of sacredness or of belief, even of religious authority, in the name of the most originary possibility. The latter can be *universal* (faith or trustworthiness, "good faith" as the condition of testimony, of the social bond and even of the most radical questioning) or already *particular*, for example belief in a specific originary event of revelation, of promise or of injunction, as in the reference to the Tables of the Law, to early Christianity, to some fundamental word or scripture, more archaic and more pure than all clerical or theological discourse. But it seems impossible to deny the *possibility* in whose name—thanks to which—the derived *necessity* (the authority or determinate belief) would be put in question, suspended, rejected or

criticized, even deconstructed. One can *not* deny it, which means that the most one can do is to deny it. Any discourse that would be opposed to it would, in effect, always succumb to the figure or the logic of denial <*dénégation*>. Such would be the place where, before and after all the Enlightenments in the world, reason, critique, science, tele-technoscience, philosophy, **thought** in general, retain the *same* resource as religion in general.

(48) This last proposition, in particular in so far as it concerns **thought**, calls for several essential qualifications. It is impossible here to devote to it the necessary elaborations or to multiply, which would be easy, references to all those who, before and after all the Enlightenments in the world, believed in the independence of critical reason, of knowledge, technics, philosophy and thought with respect to religion and even to all faith. Why then privilege the example of Heidegger? Because of its extreme character and of what it tells us, in these times, about a certain "extremity." Without doubt, as we recalled it above, Heidegger wrote in a letter to Löwith in 1921: "I am a 'Christian theologian.'"[37] This declaration would merit extended interpretation and certainly does not amount to a simple declaration of faith. But it neither contradicts, annuls nor excludes this other certainty: Heidegger not only declared, very early and on several occasions, that philosophy was in its very principle "atheistic," that the idea of philosophy is "madness" for faith (which at the least supposes the converse), and the idea of a Christian philosophy as absurd as a "squared circle." He not only excluded the very possibility of a philosophy of religion. He not only proposed a radical separation between philosophy and theology, the positive study of faith, if not between thought and theiology,[38] the discourse on the divinity of the divine. He not only attempted a "destruction" of all forms of the ontotheological, etc. He also wrote, in 1953: "Belief [or faith] has no place in thought (*Der Glaube hat im Denken keinen Platz*)."[39] The context of this firm declaration is,

---

37. This letter to Löwith, dated 19 August 1921, was recently cited in French by J. Barash, *Heidegger et son siècle* (Paris: PUF, 1995), p. 80, n. 3, and by Françoise Dastur, in "Heidegger et la théologie," *Revue philosophique de Louvain*, May–August 1994, nos. 2–3, p. 229. Together with that of Jean-François Courtine cited above, the latter study is one of the most illuminating and richest, it seems to me, that have been published on this subject in recent years.

38. I take the liberty, in regard to these questions, of referring once again to "How to avoid speaking." As to the divinity of the divine, the *theion*, which would thus be the theme of a theology, distinct both from theology and from religion, the multiplicity of its meanings should not be overlooked. Already in Plato, and more specifically in the *Timaeus*, where there are no less than four concepts of the divine (see on this point the remarkable work of Serge Margel, *Le Tombeau du dieu artisan*, Paris, Éditions de Minuit, 1995). It is true that this multiplicity does not prevent but on the contrary commands one to return to the unitary pre-comprehension, to the horizon of meaning as it is called, of the same word. Even if, in the final accounting, this horizon itself must be abandoned.

39. "The Anaximander fragment," in Martin Heidegger, *Early Greek Thinking*, trans. David Farrell Krell and Frank A. Capuzzi (San Francisco: Harper, 1984), p. 57; "Der Spruch des Anaximander," *Holzwege*, Klostermann, 1950, p. 343.

to be sure, rather particular. The word *Glaube* seems to concern *first of all* a form of belief: credulity or the blind acceptance of authority. Heidegger was concerned with translating a *Spruch* (a saying, a sentence, decree, decision, poem, in any case a saying that cannot be reduced to its statement, whether theoretical, scientific or even philosophical, and that is tied in a singular and performative way to language). In a passage that concerns presence (*Anwesen, Präsenz*) and presence in the representation of representing (*in der Repräsentation des Vorstellens*), Heidegger writes: "We can not scientifically prove (*beweisen*) the translation nor ought we simply by virtue of any authority put our trust in it [accredit it, believe it] (*glauben*). The reach of proof [inferred as "scientific"] is too short. Belief has no place in thinking (*Der Glaube hat im Denken keinen Platz*)." Heidegger thus dismisses, back to back, scientific proof (which might suggest that to the same extent he accredits non-scientific testimony) and belief, here credulous and orthodox confidence that, closing its eyes, acquiesces and dogmatically sanctions authority (*Autorität*). Certainly, and who would contradict this? But Heidegger still extends with force and radicality the assertion that belief *in general* has no place in the experience or the act of thinking *in general*. And there we would have difficulty following him. First along his own path. Even if one succeeds in averting, in as rigorous a manner as possible, the risk of confusing modalities, levels, contexts, it still seems difficult to dissociate faith in general (*Glaube*) from what Heidegger himself, under the name of *Zusage* ("accord, acquiescing, trust or confidence"), designates as that which is most irreducible, indeed most originary in thought, prior even to that questioning said by him to constitute the piety (*Frömmigkeit*) of thinking. It is well known that without calling this last affirmation into question, he subsequently explained that it is the *Zusage* that constitutes the most proper movement of thinking, and that without it (although Heidegger does not state it in this form) the question itself would not emerge.[40] This recall to a sort of faith, this recall to the trust of the *Zusage*, "before" all questioning, thus "before" all knowledge, all philosophy, etc., finds a particularly striking formulation relatively late (1957). It is formulated in the form—rare for Heidegger, whence the interest often attached to it—not of self-criticism or remorse but of a return to a formulation that demands to be nuanced, refined, let us say, to be reengaged differently. But this gesture is less novel and singular than it might seem. Perhaps we will try to show elsewhere (it would require more time and space) that it accords with everything which, beginning with the existential analytics of the thought of being and of the truth of being, reaffirms continuously what we will call (in Latin, alas, and in a manner too Roman for Heidegger) a certain *testimonial*

40. On these issues—and since I am unable to develop them here—I take the liberty of referring to *Of Spirit: Heidegger and the Question*, trans. Geoffrey Bennington and Rachel Bowlby (Chicago and London: University of Chicago Press, 1989), p. 129 ff. Cf. also Dastur, "Heidegger et la théologie," p. 233, n. 21.

sacredness or, we would even go so far as to say, a sworn word *<foi jurée>*. This reaffirmation continues throughout Heidegger's entire work. It resides in the decisive and largely underestimated motif of attestation (*Bezeugung*) in *Sein und Zeit* as well as in all the other motifs that are inseparable from and dependent upon it, which is to say, *all* the existentials and, specifically, that of conscience (*Gewissen*), originary responsibility or guilt (*Schuldigsein*) and *Entschlossenheit* (resolute determination). We cannot address here the immense question of the ontological repetition, in all these concepts, of a so markedly Christian tradition. Let us therefore limit ourselves to situating a principle of reading. Like the experience of authentic attestation (*Bezeugung*) and like everything that depends upon it, the point of departure of *Sein und Zeit* resides in a situation that cannot be radically alien to what is called *faith*. Not religion, to be sure, nor theology, but that which in faith acquiesces before or beyond all questioning, in the already common experience of a language and of a "we." The reader of *Sein und Zeit* and the signatory who takes him as witness are already situated in this element of faith from the moment that Heidegger says "we" to justify the choice of the "exemplary" being that is *Dasein*, the questioning being that must be interrogated as an exemplary witness. And what renders possible, for this "we," the positing and elaboration of the question of being, the unfolding and determining of its "formal structure" (*das Gefragte, das Erfragte, das Befragte*), *prior to all questioning*—is it not what Heidegger then calls a *Faktum*, that is, the vague and ordinary pre-comprehension of the meaning of being, and first of all of the words "is" or "be" in language or in a language (§ 2)? This *Faktum* is not an empirical fact. Each time Heidegger employs this word, we are necessarily led back to a zone where acquiescence is *de rigueur*. Whether this is formulated or not, it remains a requirement prior to and in view of every possible question, and hence prior to all philosophy, all theology, all science, all critique, all reason, etc. This zone is that of a faith incessantly reaffirmed throughout an open chain of concepts, beginning with those that we have already cited (*Bezeugung, Zusage*, etc.), but it also communicates with everything in Heidegger's way of thinking that marks the reserved holding-back of restraint (*Verhaltenheit*) or the sojourn (*Aufenthalt*) in modesty (*Scheu*) in the vicinity of the unscathed, the sacred, the safe and sound (*das Heilige*), the passage or the coming of the last god that man is doubtless not yet ready to receive.[41] That the movement proper to this faith does not constitute a religion is all too evi-

---

41. On all these themes, the corpus that would have to be invoked is immense and we are incapable of doing justice to it here. It is above all determined by the discourse of a conversation between the Poet (to whom is assigned the task of saying, and hence of saving the unscathed, *das Heilige*) and the Thinker, who searches for the signs of the god. On the *Beiträge*, particularly rich in this respect, I refer once again to the study of Jean-François Courtine and to all the texts that it evokes and interprets.

dent. Is it, however, untouched <*indemne*> by all religiosity? Perhaps. But by all "belief," by that "belief" that would have "no place in thinking"? This seems less certain. Since the major question remains, in our eyes, albeit in a form that is still quite new: "What does it mean to believe?" we will ask (elsewhere) how and why Heidegger can at the same time affirm one of the possibilities of the "religious," of which we have just schematically recalled the signs (*Faktum, Bezeugung, Zusage, Verhaltenheit, Heilige*, etc.) and reject so energetically "belief" or "faith" (*Glaube*).[42] Our hypothesis again refers back to the two sources or two strata of religion which we distinguished above: the experience of sacredness and the experience of belief. More receptive to the first (in its Graeco-Hölderlinian or even archeo-Christian tradition), Heidegger was probably more resistant to the second, which he constantly reduced to figures he never ceased to put into question, not to say "destroy" or denounce: dogmatic or credulous belief in authority, to be sure, but also belief according to the religions of the Book and ontotheology, and above all, that which in the belief in the other could appear to him (wrongly, we would say) to appeal necessarily to the egological subjectivity of an *alter ego*. We are speaking here of the belief that is demanded, required, of the faithful belief in what, having come from the utterly other <*de l'autre tout autre*>, there where its originary presentation in person

---

42. Samuel Weber has reminded me, and I thank him for doing so, of the very dense and difficult pages devoted by Heidegger to "The Thought of the Eternal Return as Belief (*als ein Glaube*)" in his *Nietzsche* (Neske, 1961, vol. I, p. 382; English trans. David Farrell Krell [San Francisco: Harper, 1991], pp. 121–32). In re-reading these passages it strikes me as impossible in a footnote to do justice to their richness, complexity and strategy. I will try to return to this elsewhere. While waiting, however, just these two points: (1) Such a reading would suppose a patient and thoughtful sojourn with the holding (*Halt, Haltung, Sichhalten*) discussed above (n. 31), throughout Heidegger's way of thinking. (2) This "holding" is an essential determination of belief, at least as Heidegger interprets it in his reading of Nietzsche and notably of the question posed in *The Will to Power*: "What is a *belief*? How is it born? All belief is a *holding-for-true* (*Jeder Glaube ist ein* Für-Wahr-halten)." No doubt that Heidegger remains very careful and suspensive in his interpretation of this "concept of belief" (*Glaubensbegriff*) in Nietzsche, which is to say of the latter's "concept of truth and of 'holding-himself (*Sichhalten*) in truth and for truth.'" He even declares that he abandons the task, as well as that of representing the Nietzschean grasp of the difference between religion and philosophy. Nevertheless, he multiplies preliminary indications in referring to sentences dating from the period of *Zarathustra*. These indications reveal that in his eyes, if belief is constituted by "holding-for-true" and by "holding-oneself in truth," and if truth signifies for Nietzsche the "relation to the entity in its totality," then belief, which consists in "taking for true something represented (*ein Vorgestelltes als Wahres nehmen*)," remains therefore metaphysical in some way, and therefore unequal to what in thought should exceed both the order of representation and the totality of the entity. This would be consistent with the affirmation cited above: "*Der Glaube hat im Denken keinen Platz*." Of the Nietzschean definition of belief (*Für-Wahr-halten*), Heidegger declares first that he retains only one thing, but "the most important," which is to say, "holding to what is true and maintaining oneself in it" (*das Sichhalten an das Wahre und im Wahren*). And a little further on he adds: "If maintaining-oneself in the true constitutes a modality of human life, then no decision concerning the essence of belief and Nietzsche's concept of belief in particular can be made before his conception of truth as such and its relation to 'life' has been elucidated, which is to say, for Nietzsche: its relation to the entity in its totality (*zum Seienden im Ganzen*). Without having acquired a sufficient notion of the Nietzschean conception of belief, we would not attempt to say what the word 'religion' signifies for him . . . . " (p. 386; trans. p. 124).

would forever be impossible (**witnessing** or given word in the most elementary and irreducible sense, promise of truth up to and including perjury), would constitute the condition of *Mitsein*, of the relation to or address of the other in general.

(49) Beyond the culture, semantics or history of law—moreover intertwined—which determine this word or this concept, the experience of **witnessing** situates a convergence of *these* two sources: the *unscathed* (the safe, the sacred or the saintly) and the *fiduciary* (trustworthiness, fidelity, credit, belief or faith, "good faith" implied in the worst "bad faith"). We speak of *these* two sources there, in one place of their convergence, for the figure of the two sources, as we have verified, proliferates, can no longer be counted, and therein lies perhaps another reason of our questioning. In testimony, truth is promised beyond all proof, all perception, all intuitive demonstration. Even if I lie or perjure myself (and always and especially when I do), I promise truth and ask the other to believe the other that I am, there where I am the only one able to bear witness and where the order of proof or of intuition will never be reducible to or homogeneous with the elementary trust <*fiduciarité*>, the "good faith" that is promised or demanded. The latter, to be sure, is never pure of all iterability nor of all technics, and hence of all **calculability**. For it also promises its repetition from the very first instant. It is involved <*engagé*> in every address of the other. From the first instant it is co-extensive with this other and thus conditions every "social bond," every questioning, all knowledge, performativity and every tele-technoscientific performance, including those of its forms that are the most synthetic, artificial, prosthetic, calculable. The act of faith demanded in bearing witness exceeds, through its structure, all intuition and all proof, all knowledge ("I swear that I am telling the truth, not necessarily the 'objective truth,' but the truth of what I believe to be the truth, I am telling you this truth, believe me, believe what I believe, there, where you will never be able to see nor know the irreplaceable yet universalizable, exemplary place from which I speak to you; perhaps my testimony is false, but I am sincere and in good faith, it is not false <as> testimony"). What therefore does the promise of this axiomatic (quasi-transcendental) performative do that conditions and foreshadows "sincere" declarations no less than lies and perjuries, and thus all address of the other? It amounts to saying: "Believe what I say as one believes in a miracle." Even the slightest testimony concerning the most plausible, ordinary or everyday thing cannot do otherwise: it must still appeal to faith as would a miracle. It offers itself like the miracle itself in a space that leaves no room for disenchantment. The experience of disenchantment, however indubitable it is, is only one modality of this "miraculous" experience, the reactive and passing effect, in each of its historical determinations, of the testimonially miraculous. That one should be called upon to believe in testi-

mony as in a miracle or an "extraordinary story"—this is what inscribes itself without hesitation in the very concept of bearing witness. And one should not be amazed to see examples of "miracles" invading all the problematics of testimony, whether they are classical or not, critical or not. *Pure* attestation, if there is such a thing, pertains to the experience of faith and of the miracle. Implied in every "social bond," however ordinary, it also renders itself indispensable to Science no less than to Philosophy and to Religion. This source can collect or scatter itself, rejoin or disjoin itself. Either at the same time or successively. It can appear contemporaneous with itself where testimonial trust in the pledge <*gage*> of the other unites belief in the other with the sacralization of a presence-absence or with a sanctification of the law, as law of the other. It can divide itself in various ways. First of all, in the alternative between sacredness without belief (index of this algebra: "Heidegger") and faith in a holiness without sacredness, in a desacralizing truth, even making of a certain disenchantment the condition of authentic holiness (index: "Levinas"— notably the author of *From the Sacred to the Holy*). As a follow-up, it can dissociate itself when what constitutes the said "social bond" in belief is also an interruption. There is no opposition, fundamentally, between "social bond" and "social unraveling." A certain interruptive unraveling is the condition of the "social bond," the very respiration of all "community." This is not even the knot of a reciprocal condition, but rather the possibility that every knot can come undone, be cut or interrupted. This is where the *socius* or the relation to the other would disclose itself to be the secret of testimonial experience—and hence, of a certain faith. If belief is the ether of the address and relation to the utterly other, it is <to be found> in the experience itself of non-relationship or of absolute *interruption* (indices: "Blanchot," "Levinas" . . .). Here as well, the hypersanctification of this non-relation or of this transcendence would come about by way of desacralization rather than through secularization or laicization, concepts that are too Christian; perhaps even by way of a certain "atheism," in any case by way of a radical experience of the resources of "negative theology"—and going beyond even this tradition. Here we would have to separate—thanks to another vocabulary, for example Hebraic (the holiness of *kidouch*)—the sacred and the holy, and no longer settle for the Latinate distinction, recalled by Benveniste, between the natural sacredness in things and the holiness of institutions or of the law.[43] This interruptive dis-junction enjoins a sort of incommensurable equality within absolute dissymmetry. The law of this untimeliness interrupts and makes history, it undoes all contemporaneity and opens the very space of faith. It designates disenchantment as the *very resource of the religious*.

---

43. Benveniste, *Indo-European Language*, particularly pp. 449, 453–56, 468.

The first and the last. Nothing seems therefore more uncertain, more difficult to sustain, nothing seems here or there more imprudent than a self-assured discourse on the age of disenchantment, the era of secularization, the time of laicization, etc.

(50) **Calculability**: question, apparently arithmetic, of two, or rather of n + One, through and beyond the demography of which we spoke above. Why should there always have to be *more than one* source? There would not have to be two sources of religion. There would be faith and religion, faith or religion, because *there are at least two*. Because there are, for the best and for the worst, division and iterability of the source. This supplement introduces the incalculable at the heart of the calculable. (Levinas: "It is this being-two <*être à deux*> that is human, that is spiritual.") But the more than One <*plus d'Un*>[44] is at once more than two. There is no alliance of two, unless it is to signify in effect the pure madness of pure faith. The worst violence. The more than One is this n + One which introduces the order of faith or of trust in the address of the other, but also the mechanical, machine-like division (testimonial affirmation and reactivity, "yes, yes," etc., answering machine and the possibility of **radical evil**: perjury, lies, remote-control murder, ordered at a distance even when it rapes and kills with bare hands).

(51) The possibility of **radical evil** both destroys and institutes the religious. Ontotheology does the same when it suspends sacrifice and prayer, the truth of this prayer that maintains itself, recalling Aristotle one more time, beyond the true and the false, beyond their opposition, in any case, according to a certain concept of truth or of judgement. Like benediction, prayer pertains to the originary regime of testimonial faith or of martyrdom that we are trying to think here in its most "critical" force. Ontotheology en**crypts** faith and destines it to the condition of a sort of Spanish Marrano who would have lost—in truth, dispersed, multiplied—everything up to and including the memory of his unique secret. Emblem of a still life: an opened pomegranate, one Passover evening, on a tray.

(52) At the bottom without bottom of this **crypt**, the One + n incalculably engenders all these supplements. *It makes violence of itself, does violence to itself and keeps itself from the other*. The auto-immunity of religion can only indemnify itself without assignable end. On the bottom without bottom of an always virgin impassibility, *chora* of tomorrow in languages we no longer know or do not yet speak. This place is unique, it is the One without name. It *makes way, perhaps*, but without the slightest generosity, neither divine nor human. The dispersion of ashes is not even promised there, nor death given.

$\sim$

---

44. *Translator's note: 'Plus d'un'* can also mean "one no more." See: *Specters of Marx*, passim.

(This, perhaps, is what I would have liked to say of a certain Mount Moriah—while going to Capri, last year, close by the Vesuvius of Gradiva. Today I remember what I had just finished reading in Genet at Chatila, *of which so many of the premises deserve to be remembered here, in so many languages, the actors and the victims, and the eves and the consequence, all the landscapes and all the spectres: "One of the questions I will not avoid is that of religion."*[45] Laguna, 26 April 1995.)

Translated by Samuel Weber

---

45. J. Genet, *Genet à Chatila* (Paris: Solin, 1992), p. 103.

2

A Note on "Des Tours de Babel"

"Des Tours de Babel" is Derrida's first, and perhaps most explicit, extended discussion of the name of God. Along with "Of an Apocalyptic Tone," *Memoirs of the Blind*, "Circumfession," and *Donner la Mort*, "Des Tours de Babel" is also one of Derrida's most significant contributions to a reading and re-reading of the Bible. Babel—the site, the story, the text, but also "the name of God as name of the father"—is in that regard "exemplary." It is exemplary of religion as law (Heb. *dat*, Ar. *din*), of divine law as it institutes and forbids translation. Carrying religion, with which it bears no necessary relation, translation "as holy growth of languages" (a phrase Derrida borrows from Walter Benjamin) is the law in which a name that remains untranslatable nonetheless circulates across languages and cultures: "At the very moment when pronouncing 'Babel' we sense the impossibility of deciding whether this name belongs, properly and simply, to *one* tongue." This is the predicament of the name and of the name "religion" that Derrida explores in "Faith and Knowledge," for example. Here it is the predicament of translation, as Derrida reads it in Benjamin's "Task of the Translator." (Interestingly, in "Force of Law," Derrida will continue to pursue the name of the Hebrew God while also reading the name of Walter Benjamin, and Benjamin's discussion of divine violence.) "The religious code is essential here." Translation enacts this predicament insofar as it encounters in the sacred text its very limit. An insistent preoccupation with the name, the proper name and, most importantly, the proper name of God, has remained at the center of Derrida's work at least since—"once again, it is not theological"—*différance* put into question "the name of the name," even that of "an ineffable Being which no name could approach: God, for example."

With Babel, with the name of God, the God who "would have marked with his patronym a communal space," translation promises, it "promises a kingdom to the reconciliation of languages." As "holy growth of languages," translation "announces the messianic end." But, like the law that simultaneously grants and forbids, this promise grants and forbids from you ("this gate was made only for you," said the gatekeeper of Kafka's "Before the Law") the shared and the common of community: "'That is what is named from here on Babel: the law imposed by the name of God who in one stroke commands and forbids you to translate by showing *and* hiding from you the limit." This limit is the sacred text "itself," the law of the sacred text in which "the sacred surrenders itself to translation," and translation "devotes itself to the sacred."

G. A.

DES TOURS DE BABEL

"Babel": first a proper name, granted. But when we say "Babel" today, do we know what we are naming? Do we know whom? If we consider the sur-vival of a text that is a legacy, the narrative or the myth of the tower of Babel, it does not constitute just one figure among others. Telling at least of the inadequation of one tongue to another, of one place in the encyclopedia to another, of language to itself and to meaning, and so forth, it also tells of the need for figuration, for myth, for tropes, for twists and turns, for translation inadequate to compensate for that which multiplicity denies us. In this sense it would be the myth of the origin of myth, the metaphor of metaphor, the narrative of narrative, the translation of translation, and so on. It would not be the only structure hollowing itself out like that, but it would do so in its own way (itself *almost* untranslatable, like a proper name), and its idiom would have to be saved.

The "tower of Babel" does not merely figure the irreducible multiplicity of tongues; it exhibits an incompletion, the impossibility of finishing, of totalizing, of saturating, of completing something on the order of edification, architectural construction, system and architectonics. What the multiplicity of idioms actually limits is not only a "true" translation, a transparent and adequate interexpression, it is also a structural order, a coherence of construct. There is then (let us translate) something like an internal limit to formalization, an incompleteness of the constructure. It would be easy and up to a certain point justified to see there the translation of a system in deconstruction.

One should never pass over in silence the question of the tongue in which the question of the tongue is raised and into which a discourse on translation is translated.

First: in what tongue was the tower of Babel constructed and deconstructed? In a tongue within which the proper name of Babel could also, by confusion, be translated by "confusion." The proper name Babel, as a proper name, should remain untranslatable, but, by a kind of associative confusion that a unique tongue rendered possible, one thought it translated in that very tongue, by a common noun signifying what *we* translate as confusion. Voltaire showed his astonishment in his *Dictionnaire philosophique*, at the *Babel* article:

> I do not know why it is said in *Genesis* that Babel signifies confusion, for *Ba* signifies father in the Oriental tongues, and *Bel* signifies God; Babel signifies the city of God, the holy city. The Ancients gave this name to all their capitals. But it is incontestable that Babel means confusion, either because the architects were confounded after having raised their work up to eighty-one thousand Jewish feet, or because the tongues were then confounded; and it is obviously from that time on that the Germans no longer understand the Chinese; for it is clear, according to the scholar Bochart, that Chinese is originally the same tongue as High German.

The calm irony of Voltaire means that Babel means: it is not only a proper name, the reference of a pure signifier to a single being—and for this reason untranslatable—but a common noun related to the generality of a meaning. This common noun means, and means not only confusion, even though "confusion" has at least two meanings, as Voltaire is aware, the confusion of tongues, but also the state of confusion in which the architects find themselves with the structure interrupted, so that a certain confusion has already begun to affect the two meanings of the word "confusion." The signification of "confusion" is confused, at least double. But Voltaire suggests something else again: Babel means not only confusion in the double sense of the word, but also the name of the father, more precisely and more commonly, the name of God as name of father. The city would bear the name of God the father and of the father of the city that is called confusion. God, the God, would have marked with his patronym a communal space, that city where understanding is no longer possible. And understanding is no longer possible when there are only proper names, and understanding is no longer possible when there are no longer proper names. In giving his name, a name of his choice, in giving all names, the father would be at the origin of language, and that power would belong by right to God the father. And the name of God the father would be the name of that origin of tongues. But it is also that God who, in the action of his anger (like the God of Böhme or of Hegel, he who leaves himself, determines himself in his finitude and thus produces history), annuls the gift of tongues, or at least embroils it, sows confusion among his sons, and poisons the present (*Gift*-gift). This is also the origin of tongues, of the multiplicity of idioms, of what in other words are usually called mother tongues. For this entire history deploys filiations, generations and genealogies: all Semitic. Before the deconstruction of Babel, the great Semitic family was establishing its empire, which it wanted universal, and its tongue, which it also attempts to impose on the universe. The moment of this project immediately precedes the deconstruction of the tower. I cite two French translations. The first translator stays away from what one would want to call "literality," in other words, from the Hebrew figure of speech for "tongue," where the second, more concerned about literality (metaphoric, or rather metonymic), says "lip," since in Hebrew "lip" designates what we call, in another metonymy, "tongue." One will have to say multiplicity of lips and not of tongues to name the Babelian confusion. The first translator, then, Louis Segond, author of the Segond Bible, published in 1910, writes this:

> Those are the sons of Sem, according to their families, their tongues, their countries, their nations. Such are the families of the sons of Noah, according to their generations, their nations. And it is from them that emerged the nations which spread over the earth after the flood. All the earth had a single tongue and the same words. As they had left the origin they found a plain in the country of Schinear, and they dwelt there. They said to one another: Come! Let us make bricks, and bake them in the fire. And brick served them as stone, and tar served as cement. Again they said: Come! Let us build ourselves a city and a tower whose summit touches the heavens, and let us make ourselves a name, so that we not be scattered over the face of all the earth.

I do not know just how to interpret this allusion to the substitution or the transmutation of materials, brick becoming stone and tar serving as mortar. That already resembles a translation, a translation of translation. But let us leave it and substitute a second translation for the first. It is that of Chouraqui. It is recent and wants to be more literal, almost *verbum pro verbo*, as Cicero said should not be done in one of those first recommendations to the translator which can be read in his *Libellus de Optimo Genera Oratorum*. Here it is:

> Here are the sons of Shem
> for their clans, for their tongues,
> in their lands, for their peoples.
> Here are the clans of the sons of Noah for their exploits,
> in their peoples:
> from the latter divide the peoples on earth, after the flood.
>
> And it is all the earth: a single lip, one speech.
> And it is at their departure from the Orient: they find a canyon,
> in the land of Shine'ar.
> They settle there.
> They say, each to his like:
> "Come, let us brick some bricks.

Let us fire them in the fire."
The brick becomes for them stone, the tar, mortar.
They say:
"Come, let us build ourselves a city and a tower.
Its head: in the heavens.
Let us make ourselves a name,
that we not be scattered over the face of all the earth."

What happens to them? In other words, for what does God punish them in giving his name, or rather, since he gives it to nothing and to no one, in proclaiming his name, the proper name of "confusion" which will be his mark and his seal? Does he punish them for having wanted to build as high as the heavens? For having wanted to accede to the highest, up to the Most High? Perhaps for that too, no doubt, but incontestably for having wanted thus to make a name for themselves, to give themselves the name, to construct for and by themselves their own name, to gather themselves there ("that we no longer be scattered"), as in the unity of a place which is at once a tongue and a tower, the one as well as the other, the one as the other. He punishes them for having thus wanted to assure themselves, by themselves, a unique and universal genealogy. For the text of Genesis proceeds immediately, as if it were all a matter of the same design: raising a tower, constructing a city, making a name for oneself in a universal tongue which would also be an idiom, and gathering a filiation:

They say:
"Come, let us build ourselves a city and a tower.
Its head: in the heavens.
Let us make ourselves a name,
that we not be scattered over the face of all the earth."
YHWH descends to see the city and the tower
that the sons of man have built.
YHWH says:
"Yes! A single people, a single lip for all:
that is what they begin to do! . . .
Come! Let us descend! Let us confound their lips,
man will no longer understand the lip of his neighbor."

Then he disseminates the Sem, and dissemination is here deconstruction:

YHWH disperses them from here over the face of all the earth.
They cease to build the city.

Over which he proclaims his name: Bavel, Confusion,
for there, YHWH confounds the lip of all the earth,
and from there YHWH disperses them over the face of all the earth.

Can we not, then, speak of God's jealousy? Out of resentment against that
unique name and lip of men, he imposes his name, his name of father; and with this
violent imposition he opens the deconstruction of the tower, as of the universal language; he scatters the genealogical filiation. He breaks the lineage. He *at the same
time* imposes and forbids translation. He imposes it and forbids it, constrains, but
as if to failure, the children who henceforth *will bear* his name, the name that *he*
gives to the city. It is from a proper name of God, come from God, descended from
God or from the father (and it is indeed said that YHWH, an unpronounceable
name, *descends* toward the tower) and by him that tongues are scattered, con-
founded or multiplied, according to a descendance that in its very dispersion
remains sealed by the only name that will have been the strongest, by the only idiom
that will have triumphed. Now, this idiom bears within itself the mark of confusion,
it improperly means the improper, to wit: Bavel, confusion. Translation then becomes necessary and impossible, like the effect of a struggle for the appropriation of
the name, necessary and forbidden in the interval between two absolutely proper
names. And the proper name of God (given by God) is divided enough in the
tongue, already, to signify also, confusedly, "confusion." And the war that he declares
has first raged within his name: divided, bifid, ambivalent, polysemic: God decon-
structing. "And he war," one reads in *Finnegans Wake*, and we could follow this
whole story from the side of Shem and Shaun. The "he war" does not only, in this
place, tie together an incalculable number of phonic and semantic threads, in the
immediate context and throughout this Babelian book; it says the declaration of
war (in English) of the One who says I am the one who am, and who thus was
(*war*); it renders itself untranslatable in its very performance, *at least in the fact* that
it is enunciated in more than one language at a time, at least English and German. If
even an infinite translation exhausted its semantic stock, it would still translate into
one language and would lose the multiplicity of "he war." Let us leave for another
time a less hastily interrupted reading of this "he war," and let us note one of the
limits of theories of translation: all too often they treat the passing from one language to another and do not sufficiently consider the possibility for languages to be
implicated *more than two* in a text. How is a text written in several languages at a
time to be translated? How is the effect of plurality to be "rendered"? And what of
translating with several languages at a time, will that be called translating?

Babel: today we take it as a proper name. Indeed, but the proper name of
what and of whom? At times that of a narrative text recounting a story (mythical,

symbolic, allegorical; it matters little for the moment), a story in which the proper name, which is then no longer the title of the narrative, names a tower or a city but a tower or a city that receives its name from an event during which YHWH "proclaims his name." Now, this proper name, which already names at least three times and three different things, also has, this is the whole point, as proper name the function of a common noun. This story recounts, among other things, the origin of the confusion of tongues, the irreducible multiplicity of idioms, the necessary and impossible task of translation, its necessity *as* impossibility. Now, in general one pays little attention to this fact: it is in translation that we most often read this narrative. And in this translation, the proper name retains a singular destiny, since it is not translated in its appearance as proper name. Now, a proper name as such remains forever untranslatable, a fact that may lead one to conclude that it does not strictly belong, for the same reason as the other words, to the language, to the system of the language, be it translated or translating. And yet "Babel," an event in a single tongue, the one in which it appears so as to form a "text," also has a common meaning, a conceptual generality. That it be by way of a pun or a confused association matters little: "Babel" could be understood in one language as meaning "confusion." And from then on, just as Babel is at once proper name and common noun, confusion also becomes proper name and common noun, the one as the homonym of the other, the synonym as well, but not the equivalent, because there could be no question of confusing them in their value. It has for the translator no satisfactory solution. Recourse to apposition and capitalization ("Over which he proclaims his name: Bavel, Confusion") is not translating from one tongue into another. It comments, explains, paraphrases, but does not translate. At best it reproduces approximately and by dividing the equivocation into two words there where confusion gathered in potential, in all its potential, in the internal translation, if one can say that, which works the word in the so-called original tongue. For in the very tongue of the original narrative there is a translation, a sort of transfer, that gives immediately (by some confusion) the semantic equivalent of the proper name which, by itself, as a pure proper name, it would not have. As a matter of fact, this intralinguistic translation operates immediately; it is not even an operation in the strict sense. Nevertheless, someone who speaks the language of Genesis could be attentive to the effect of the proper name in effacing the conceptual equivalent (like *pierre* [rock] in *Pierre* [Peter], and these are two absolutely heterogeneous values or functions); one would then be tempted to say *first* that a proper name, in the proper sense, does not properly belong to the language; it does not belong there, *although and because* its call makes the language possible (what would a language be without the possibility of calling by a proper name?); consequently it can properly inscribe itself in a language only by allowing itself to be translated therein, in other words, *interpreted* by its semantic equivalent: from this moment it can no longer be taken as proper name. The noun *pierre* belongs to the French language, and its translation into a foreign language should in principle transport its meaning. This is not the case with *Pierre*, whose inclusion in the French language is not assured and is in any case not of the same type. "Peter" in this sense is not a *translation* of *Pierre*, any more than *Londres* is a translation of "London," and so forth. And *second*, anyone whose so-called mother tongue was the tongue of *Genesis* could indeed understand Babel as "confusion"; that person then effects a *confused* translation of the proper name by its common equivalent without having need for another word. It is as if there were two words there, two homonyms, one of which has the value of proper name and the other that of common noun: between the two, a translation which one can evaluate quite diversely. Does it belong to the kind that Jakobson calls intralingual translation or rewording? I do not think so: "rewording" concerns the relations of transformation between common nouns and ordinary phrases. The essay *On Translation* (1959) distinguishes three forms of translation. *Intralingual* translation interprets linguistic signs by means of other signs of the *same* language. This obviously presupposes that one can know in the final analysis how to determine rigorously the unity and identity of a language, the decidable form of its limits. There would then be what Jakobson neatly calls translation "proper," *interlingual* translation, which interprets linguistic signs by means of some other language—this appeals to the same presupposition as intralingual translation. Finally there would be intersemiotic translation or *transmutation*, which interprets linguistic signs by means of systems of nonlinguistic signs. For the two forms of translation which would not be translations "proper," Jakobson proposes a definitional equivalent and another word. The first he translates, so to speak, by another word: intralingual translation or *rewording*. The third likewise: *intersemiotic* translation or *transmutation*. In these two cases, the translation of "translation" is a definitional interpretation. But in the case of translation "proper," translation in the ordinary sense, interlinguistic and post-Babelian, Jakobson does not translate; he repeats the same word: "interlingual translation or translation proper." He supposes that it is not necessary to translate; everyone understands what that means because everyone has experienced it, everyone is expected to know what is a language, the relation of one language to another and especially identity or difference in fact of language. If there is a transparency that Babel would not have impaired, this is surely it, the experience of the multiplicity of tongues and the "proper" sense of the word "translation." In relation to this word, when it is a question of translation "proper," the other uses of the word "translation" would be in a position of intralingual and inadequate translation, like metaphors, in short, like twists or turns of translation in the proper sense. There would thus be a translation in the proper sense and a translation in the figurative sense. And in order to translate the one into the other, within the same tongue or from one tongue to another, in the figurative or in the proper sense, one would engage upon a course that would quickly reveal how this reassuring tripartition can be problematic. Very quickly: at the very moment when pronouncing "Babel" we sense the impossibility of deciding whether this name belongs, properly and simply, to *one* tongue. And it matters that this undecidability is at work in a struggle for the proper name within a scene of genealogical indebtedness. In seeking to "make a name for themselves," to found at the same time a universal tongue and a unique genealogy, the Semites want to bring the world to reason, and this reason can signify simultaneously a colonial violence (since they would thus universalize their idiom) and a peaceful transparency of the human community. Inversely, when God imposes and opposes his name, he ruptures the rational transparency but interrupts also the colonial violence or the linguistic imperalism. He destines them to translation, he subjects them to the law of a translation both necessary and impossible; in a stroke with his translatable-untranslatable name he delivers a universal reason (it will no longer be subject to the rule of a particular nation), but he simultaneously limits its very universality: forbidden transparency, impossible univocity. Translation becomes law, duty and debt, but the debt one can no longer discharge. Such insolvency is found marked in the very name of Babel: which at once translates and does not translate itself, belongs without belonging to a language and indebts itself to itself for an insolvent debt, to itself as if other. Such would be the Babelian performance.

This singular example, at once archetypical and allegorical, could serve as an introduction to all the so-called theoretical problems of translation. But no theorization, inasmuch as it is produced in a language, will be able to dominate the Babelian performance. This is one of the reasons why I prefer here, instead of treating it in the theoretical mode, to attempt to translate in my own way the translation of another text on translation. The preceding ought to have led me instead to an early text by Walter Benjamin, "On Language as Such and on the Language of Man" (1916), translated by Maurice de Gandillac (*Mythe et Violence*, Paris: Denoël, 1971). Reference to Babel is explicit there and is accompanied by a discourse on the proper name and on translation. But given the, in my view, overly enigmatic character of that essay, its wealth and its overdeterminations, I have had to postpone that reading and limit myself to "The Task of the Translator" (also translated by Maurice de Gandillac in the same volume). Its difficulty is no doubt no less, but its unity remains more apparent, better centered around its theme. And this text on translation is also the preface to a translation of the *Tableaux parisiens* by Baudelaire, and I refer first to the French translation that Maurice de Gandillac gives us. And yet, translation—is it only a theme for this text, and especially its primary theme?

The title also says, from its first word, the task (*Aufgabe*), the mission to which one is destined (always by the other), the commitment, the duty, the debt, the responsibility. Already at stake is a law, an injunction for which the translator has to be responsible. He *must* also acquit himself, and of something that implies perhaps a fault, a fall, an error and perhaps a crime. The essay has as horizon, it will be seen, a "reconciliation." And all that in a discourse multiplying genealogical motifs and allusions—more or less than metaphorical—to the transmission of a family seed. The translator is indebted, he appears to himself as translator in a situation of debt; and his task is to *render*, to render that which must have been given. Among the words that correspond to Benjamin's title (*Aufgabe*, duty, mission, task, problem, that which is assigned, given to be done, given to render), there are, from the beginning, *Wiedergabe*, *Sinnwiedergabe*, restitution, restitution of meaning. How is such a restitution, or even such an acquittance, to be understood? Is it only to be restitution of meaning, and what of meaning in this domain?

For the moment let us retain this vocabulary of gift and debt, and a debt which could well declare itself insolvent, whence a sort of "transference," love and hate, on the part of whoever is in a position to translate, is summoned to translate, with regard to the text to be translated (I do not say with regard to the signatory or the author of the original), to the language and the writing, to the bond and the love which seal the marriage between the author of the "original" and his own language. At the center of the essay, Benjamin says of the restitution that it could very well be impossible: insolvent debt within a genealogical scene. One of the essential themes of the text is the "kinship" of languages in a sense that is no longer tributary of nineteenth-century historical linguistics without being totally foreign to it. Perhaps it is here proposed that we think the very possibility of a historical linguistics.

Benjamin has just quoted Mallarmé, he quotes him in French, after having left in his own sentence a Latin word, which Maurice de Gandillac has reproduced at the bottom of the page to indicate that by "genius" he was not translating from German but from the Latin (*ingenium*). But of course he could not do the same with the third language of this essay, the French of Mallarmé, whose untranslatability Benjamin had measured. Once again: how is a text written in several languages at a time to be translated? Here is the passage on the insolvent (I quote as always the French translation, being content to include here or there the German word that supports my point):

> Philosophy and translation are not futile, however, as sentimental artists allege. For there exists a philosophical genius, whose most proper characteristic is the nostalgia for that language which manifests itself in translation.

Les langues imparfaites en cela que plusieurs, manque la suprême: penser étant écrire sans accessoires ni chuchotement, mais tacite encore l'immortelle parole, la diversité, sur terre, des idiomes empêche personne de proférer les mots qui, sinon, se trouveraient, par une frappe unique, elle même matérielle-ment la vérité.

If the reality that these words of Mallarmé evoke is applicable, in full rigor, to the philosopher, translation, with the seeds [*Keimen*] that it carries within itself of such a language, is situated midway between literary creation and theory. Its work has lower relief, but it impresses itself just as profoundly on history. If the task of the translator appears in this light, the paths of its accomplishment risk becomming obscure in an all the more impenetrable way. Let us say more: of this task that consists, in the trans-lation, in ripening the seed of a pure language ["den Samen reiner Sprache zur Reife zu bringen"], it seems impossible ever to acquit onself ["diese Aufgabe ... scheint niemals lösbar"]; it seems that no solution would permit defining it ["in keiner Lösung bestimmbar"]. Does not one deprive it of any basis if rendering meaning ceases to be the standard?

Benjamin has, first of all, forgone translating the Mallarmé; he has left it shining in his text like the medallion of a proper name; but this proper name is not totally insignificant; it is merely welded to that whose meaning does not allow transport without damage into another language or into another tongue (and *Sprache* is not translated without loss by either word). And in the text of Mallarmé, the effect of being proper and thus untranslatable is tied less to any name or to any truth of ade-quation than to the unique occurrence of a performative force. Then the question is posed: does not the ground of translation finally recede as soon as the restitution of meaning ("Wiedergabe des Sinnes") ceases to provide the measure? It is the ordinary concept of translation that becomes problematic: it implied this process of restitution, the task (*Aufgabe*) was finally to render (*wiedergeben*) what was first *given*, and what was given was, one thought, the meaning. Now, things become obscure when one tries to accord this value of restitution with that of maturation. On what ground, in what ground will the maturation take place if the restitution of the meaning given is for it no longer the rule?

The allusion to the maturation of a seed could resemble a vitalist or geneticist metaphor; it would come, then, in support of the genealogical and parental code which seems to dominate this text. In fact it seems necessary here to invert this order and recognize what I have elsewhere proposed to call the "metaphoric catas-trophe": far from knowing first what "life" or "family" mean whenever we use these familiar values to talk about language and translation; it is rather starting from the notion of a language and its "sur-vival" in translation that we could have access to the notion of what life and family mean. This reversal is operated expressly by Benjamin. His preface (for let us not forget: this essay is a preface) circulates without cease among the values of seed, life, and especially "sur-vival." (*Überleben* has an essential relation with *Übersetzen*). Now, very near the beginning, Benjamin seems to propose a simile or a metaphor—it opens with "just as . . . "—and right away everything moves in and about *Übersetzen, Übertragen, Überleben:*

> Just as the manifestations of life are intimately connected with the living, without signifying anything for it, a translation proceeds from the original. Indeed not so much from its life as from its survival [*Überleben*]. For a translation comes after the original and, for the important works that never find their predestined translator at the time of their birth, it characterizes the stage of their survival [*Fortleben*, this time, sur-vival as continuation of life rather than as life *post mortem*]. Now, it is in this simple reality, without any metaphor ["in völlig unmetaphorischer Sachlichkeit"], that it is necessary to conceive the ideas of life and survival [*Fortleben*] for works of art.

And according to a scheme that appears Hegelian, in a very circumscribed passage, Benjamin calls us to think life, starting from spirit or history and not from "organic corporeality" alone. There is life at the moment when "sur-vival" (spirit, history, works) exceeds biological life and death: "It is rather in recognizing for everything of which there is history and which is not merely the setting for history that one does justice to this concept of life. For it is starting from history, not from nature . . . , that the domain of life must finally be circumscribed. So is born for the philosopher the task [*Aufgabe*] of comprehending all natural life starting from this life, of much vaster extension, that is the life of history."

From the very title—and for the moment I stay with it—Benjamin situates the *problem*, in the sense of that which is precisely *before oneself* as a task, as the problem of the translator and not that of translation (nor, be it said in passing, and the question is not negligible, that of the translatoress). Benjamin does not say the task or the problem of translation. He names the subject of translation, as an indebted subject, obligated by a duty, already in the position of heir, entered as survivor in a genealogy, as survivor or agent of sur-vival. The sur-vival of works, not authors. Perhaps the sur-vival of authors' names and of signatures, but not of authors.

Such sur-vival gives more of life, more than a surviving. The work does not simply live longer, it lives more and better, beyond the means of its author. Would the translator then be an indebted receiver, subject to the gift and to the given of an original? By no means. For several reasons, including the following: the bond or obligation of the debt does not pass between a donor and a donee but between two texts (two "productions" or two "creations"). This is understood from the opening of the preface, and if one wanted to isolate theses, here are a few, as brutally as in any sampling:

1. The task of the translator does not announce itself or follow from a *reception*. The theory of translation does not depend for the essential on any theory of reception, even though it can inversely contribute to the elaboration and explanation of such a theory.

2. Translation does not have as essential mission any *communication*. No more than the original, and Benjamin maintains, secure from all danger of dispute, the strict duality between the original and the version, the translated and the translating, even though he shifts their relation. And he is interested in the translation of poetic or sacred texts, which would here yield the essence of translation. The entire essay extends between the poetic and the sacred, returning from the first to the second, the one that indicates the ideal of all translation, the purely transferable: the intralinear version of the sacred text, the model or ideal (*Urbild*) of any translation at all possible. Now, this is the second thesis: for a poetic text or a sacred text, communication is not the essential. This putting into question does not directly concern the communicative structure of language but rather the hypothesis of a communicable content that could be strictly distinguished from the linguistic act of communication. In 1916, the critique of semiotism and of the "bourgeois conception" of language was already directed against that distribution: means, object, addressee. "There is no content of language." What language first communicates is its "communicability" ("On Language as Such," trans. M. de Gandillac, 85). Will it be said that an opening is thus made toward the performative dimension of utterances? In any case this warns us against precipitation: isolating the contents and theses in "The Task of the Translator" and translating it otherwise than as the signature of a kind of proper name destined to ensure its sur-vival as a work.

3. If there is indeed between the translated text and the translating text a relation of "original" to version, it could not be *representative* or *reproductive*. Translation is neither an image nor a copy.

These three precautions now taken (neither reception, nor communication, nor representation), how are constituted the debt and the genealogy of the translator? Or first, how those of that which is *to-be-translated*, of the to-be-translated?

Let us follow the thread of life or sur-vival wherever it communicates with the movement of kinship. When Benjamin challenges the viewpoint of reception, it is not to deny it all pertinence, and he will undoubtedly have done much to prepare for a theory of reception in literature. But he wants first to return to the authority of what he still calls "the original," not insofar as it produces its receiver or its translators, but insofar as it requires, mandates, demands or commands them in establishing the law. And it is the structure of this demand that here appears most unusual. Through what does it pass? In a literary—more strictly speaking in this case, "poetic"—text it does not pass through the said, the uttered, the communicated, the content or the theme. And when, in this context, Benjamin still says "communication" or "enunciation" (*Mitteilung, Aussage*), it is not about the act but about the content that he visibly speaks: "But what does a literary work [*Dichtung*] 'say'? What does it communicate? Very little to those who understand it. What it has that is essential is not communication, not enunciation."

The demand seems thus to pass, indeed to be formulated, through the *form*. "Translation is a form," and the law of this form has its first place in the original. This law first establishes itself, let us repeat, as a demand in the strong sense, a requirement that delegates, mandates, prescribes, assigns. And as for this law as demand, two questions can arise; they are different in essence. First question: in the sum total of its readers, can the work always find the translator who is, as it were, capable? Second question and, says Benjamin, "more properly" (as if this question made the preceding more appropriate, whereas, we shall see, it does something quite different): "by its essence does it [the work] bear translation and if so—in line with the signification of this form—does it require translation?"

The answers to these two questions could not be of the same nature or the same mode. *Problematic* in the first case, not necessary (the translator capable of the work may appear or not appear, but even if he does not appear, that changes nothing in the demand or in the structure of the injunction that comes from the work), the answer is properly *apodictic* in the second case; necessary, a priori, demonstrable, absolute because it comes from the internal law of the original. The original requires translation even if no translator is there, fit to respond to this injunction, which is at the same time demand and desire in the very structure of the original. This structure is the relation of life to sur-vival. This requirement of the other as translator, Benjamin compares it to some unforgettable instant of life: it is lived as unforgettable, it *is* unforgettable even if in fact forgetting finally wins out. It will have been unforgettable—there is its essential significance, its apodictic essence; forgetting happens to this unforgettableness only by accident. The requirement of the unforgettable—which is here constitutive—is not in the least impaired by the finitude of memory. Likewise the requirement of translation in no way suffers from not being satisfied, at least it does not suffer in so far as it is the very structure of the work. In this sense the *surviving* dimension is an *a priori*—and death would not change it at all. No more than it would change the requirement (*Forderung*) that runs through the original work and to which only "a thought of God" can respond or correspond (*entsprechen*). Translation, the desire for translation, is not thinkable without this *correspondence* with a thought of God. In the text of 1916, which already accorded the task of the translator, his Aufgabe, with the response made to the gift of tongues and the gift of names ("Gabe der Sprache," "Gebung des Namens"), Benjamin named God at this point, that of a correspondence authorizing, making possible or guaranteeing the correspondence between the languages engaged in translation. In this narrow context, there was also the matter of the relations between language of things and language of men, between the silent and the speaking, the anonymous and the nameable, but the axiom held, no doubt, for all translation: "the objectivity of this translation is guaranteed in God" (trans. M. de Gandillac, 91). The debt, in the beginning, is fashioned in the hollow of this "thought of God."

Strange debt, which does not bind anyone to anyone. If the structure of the work is "sur-vival," the debt does not engage in relation to a hypothetical subject-author of the original text—dead or mortal, the dead man, or "dummy," of the text—but to something else that represents the formal law in the immanence of the original text. Then the debt does not involve restitution of a copy or a good image, a faithful representation of the original: the latter, the survivor, is itself in the process of transformation. The original gives itself in modifying itself; this gift is not an object given; it lives and lives on in mutation: "For in its survival, which would not merit the name if it were not mutation and renewal of something living, the original is modified. Even for words that are solidified there is still a postmaturation."

Postmaturation (*Nachreife*) of a living organism or a seed: this is not simply a metaphor, either, for the reasons already indicated. In its very essence, the history of this language is determined as "growth," "holy growth of languages."

4. If the debt of the translator commits him neither with regard to the author (dead insofar as his text has a structure of survival even if he is living) nor with regard to a model which must be reproduced or represented, to what or to whom is he committed? How is this to be named, this what or who? What is the proper name if not that of the author finite, dead or mortal of the text? And who is the translator who is thus committed, who perhaps finds himself *committed* by the other before having committed himself? Since the translator finds himself, as to the survival of the text, in the same situation as its finite and mortal producer (its "author"), it is not he, not he himself as a finite and mortal being, who is committed. Then who? It is he, of course, but in the name of whom or what? The question of proper names is essential here. Where the act of the living mortal seems to count less than the sur-vival of the text in the *translation*—translated and translating—it is quite necessary that the signature of the proper noun be distinguished and not be so easily effaced from the contract or from the debt. Let us not forget that Babel names a struggle for the sur-vival of the name, the tongue or the lips.

From its height Babel at every instant supervises and surprises my reading: I translate, I translate the translation by Maurice de Gandillac of a text by Benjamin who, prefacing a translation, takes it as a pretext to say to what and in what way every translator is committed—and notes in passing, an essential part of his demonstration, that there could be no translation of translation. This will have to be remembered.

Recalling this strange situation, I do not wish only or essentially to reduce my role to that of a passer or passerby. Nothing is more serious than a translation. I rather wished to mark the fact that every translator is in a position to speak *about* translation, in a place which is more than any not second or secondary. For if the structure of the original is marked by the requirement to be translated, it is that in laying down the law the original begins by indebting itself *as well* with regard to the translator. The original is the first debtor, the first petitioner; it begins by lacking and by pleading for translation. This demand is not only on the side of the con- structors of the tower who want to make a name for themselves and to found a uni- versal tongue translating itself by itself; it also constrains the deconstructor of the tower: in giving his name, God also appealed to translation, not only between the tongues that had suddenly become multiple and confused, but first *of his name,* of the name he had proclaimed, given, and which should be translated as confusion to be understood, hence to let it be understood that it is difficult to translate and so to understand. At the moment when he imposes and opposes his law to that of the tribe, he is also a petitioner for translation. He is also indebted. He has not finished pleading for the translation of his name even though he forbids it. For Babel is untranslatable. God weeps over his name. His text is the most sacred, the most poetic, the most originary, since he creates a name and gives it to himself, but he is left no less destitute in his force and even in his wealth; he pleads for a translator. As in *La Folie du jour* by Maurice Blanchot, the law does not command without demanding to be read, deciphered, translated. It demands transference (*Übertra- gung* and *Übersetzung* and *Überleben*). The *double bind* is in the law. Even in God, and it is necessary to follow rigorously the consequence: *in his name.*

Insolvent on both sides, the double indebtedness passes between names. It sur- passes a priori the bearers of the name, if by that is understood the mortal bodies which disappear behind the sur-vival of the name. Now, a proper noun does and does not belong, we said, to the language, not even, let us make it precise now, to the corpus of the text to be translated, of the to-be-translated.

The debt does not involve living subjects but names at the edge of the language or, more rigorously, the trait which contracts the relation of the aforementioned living subject to his name, insofar as the latter keeps to the edge of the language. And this trait would be that of the to-be-translated from one language to the other, from this edge to the other of the proper name. This language contract among several languages is absolutely singular. First of all, it is not what is generally called a language contract: that which guarantees the institution of *one* language, the unity of its system, and the social contract which binds a community in this regard. On the other hand, it is generally supposed that in order to be valid or to institute anything at all, a contract must take place in a single language or appeal (for example, in the case of diplomatic or commercial treaties) to a transferability already given and without remainder: there the multiplicity of tongues must be absolutely dominated. Here, on the contrary, a contract between two foreign languages as such engages to render possible a translation which *subsequently* will authorize every sort of contract in the originary sense. The signature of this singular contract needs no written document or record: it nevertheless takes place as trace or as trait, and this place takes place even if its space comes under no empirical or mathematical objectivity.

The topos of this contract is exceptional, unique, and practically impossible to think under the ordinary category of contract: in a classical code it would have been called transcendental, since in truth it renders possible every contract in general, starting with what is called the language contract within the limits of a single idiom. Another name, perhaps, for the origin of tongues. Not the origin of language but of languages—before language, languages.

The translation contract, in this transcendental sense, would be the contract itself, the absolute contract, the contract form of the contract, that which allows a contract to be what it is.

Will one say that the kinship among languages presupposes this contract or that the kinship provides a first occasion for the contract? One recognizes here a classic circle. It has always begun to turn whenever one asks oneself about the origin of languages or society. Benjamin, who often talks about the kinship among languages, never does so as a comparatist or as a historian of languages. He is interested less in families of languages than in a more essential and more enigmatic connection, an affinity which is not sure to precede the trait or the contract of the to-be-translated. Perhaps even this kinship, this affinity (*Verwandschaft*), is like an alliance, by the contract of translation, to the extent that the sur-vivals which it associates are not natural lives, blood ties, or empirical symbioses.

This development, like that of a life original and elevated, is determined by a finality original and elevated. Life and finality—their correlation apparently evident, yet almost beyond the grasp of knowledge, only reveals itself when the goal, in view of which all singular finalities of life act, is not sought in the proper domain of that life but rather at a level more elevated. All finalized vital phenomena, like their very finality, are, after all, finalized not toward life but toward the expression of its essence, toward the representation [*Darstellung*] of its signification. Thus translation has finally as goal to express the most intimate relation among languages.

A translation would not seek to say this or that, to transport this or that content, to communicate such a charge of meaning, but to re-mark the affinity among the languages, to exhibit its own possibility. And that, which holds for the literary text or the sacred text, perhaps defines the very essence of the literary and the sacred, at their common root. I said "re-mark" the affinity among the language to name the strangeness of an "expression" ("to express the most intimate relation among the languages"), which is neither a simple "presentation" nor simply anything else. In a mode that is solely anticipatory, annunciatory, almost prophetic, translation renders *present* an affinity that is never present in this presentation. One thinks of the way in which Kant at times defines the relation to the sublime: a presentation inadequate to that which is nevertheless presented. Here Benjamin's discourse proceeds in twists and turns:

> It is impossible that it [the translation] be able to reveal this hidden relation itself, that it be able to restitute [*herstellen*] it; but translation can represent [*darstellen*] that relation in actualizing it in its seed or in its intensity. And this representation of a signified ["*Darstellung eines Bedeuteten*"] by the endeavor, by the seed of its restitution, is an entirely original mode of representation, which has hardly any equivalent in the domain of nonlinguistic life. For the latter has, in analogies and signs, types of reference [*Hindeutung*] other than the intensive, that is to say anticipatory, annunciatory [*vorgreifende, andeutende*] actualization. But the relation we are thinking of, this very intimate relation among the languages, is that of an original convergence. It consists in this: the languages are not foreign to one another, but, a priori and abstracted from all historical relations, are related to one another in what they mean.

The entire enigma of that kinship is concentrated here. What is meant by "what they mean"? And what about this presentation in which nothing is presented in the ordinary mode of presence?

At stake here are the name, the symbol, the truth, the letter.

One of the basic foundations of the essay, as well as of the 1916 text, is a theory of the name. Language is determined starting from the word and the privilege of naming. This is, in passing, a very strong if not very conclusive assertion: "the originary element of the translator" is the word and not the sentence, the syntactic articulation. As food for thought, Benjamin offers a curious "image": the sentence (*Satz*) would be "the wall in front of the language of the original," whereas the word, the word for word, literality (*Wörtlichkeit*), would be its "arcade." Whereas the wall braces while concealing (it is *in front of* the original), the arcade supports while letting light pass and the original show (we are not far from the Parisian passages). This privilege of the word obviously supports that of the name and with it what is proper to the proper name, the stakes and the very possibility of the translation contract. It opens onto the *economic* problem of translation, whether it be a matter of economy as the law of the proper or of economy as a quantitative relation (is it translating to transpose a proper name into several words, into a phrase or into a description, and so forth?).

There is some to-be-translated. From both sides it assigns and makes contracts. It commits not so much authors as proper names at the edge of the language, it essentially commits neither to communicate nor to represent, nor to keep an already signed commitment, but rather to draw up the contract and to give birth to the pact, in other words to the *symbolon*, in a sense that Benjamin does not designate by this term but suggests, no doubt with the metaphor of the amphora, let us say, since from the start we have suspected the ordinary sense of metaphor with the *ammetaphor.*

If the translator neither restitutes nor copies an original, it is because the original lives on and transforms itself. The translation will truly be a moment in the growth of the original, which will complete itself in enlarging itself. Now, it has indeed to be, and it is in this that the "seminal" logic must have imposed itself on Benjamin, that growth not give rise to just any form in just any direction. Growth must accomplish, fill, complete (*Ergänzung* is here the most frequent term). And if the original calls for a complement, it is because at the origin it was not there without fault, full, complete, total, identical to itself. From the origin of the original to be translated there is fall and exile. The translator must redeem (*erlösen*), absolve, resolve, in trying to absolve himself of his own debt, which is at bottom the same—and bottomless. "To redeem in his own tongue that pure language exiled in the foreign tongue, to liberate by transposing this pure language captive in the work, such is the task of the translator." Translation is a poetic transposition (*Umdichtung*). We will have to examine the essence of the "pure language" that it liberates. But let us note for the moment that this liberation itself presupposes a freedom of the translator, which is itself none other than relation to that "pure language"; and the liberation that it operates, eventually in transgressing the limits of the translating language, in transforming it in turn, must extend, enlarge, and make language grow. As this growth comes also to complete, as it is *symbolon*, it does not reproduce: it adjoins in adding.

Hence this double simile (*Vergleich*), all these turns and metaphoric supplements: (1) "Just as the tangent touches the circle only in a fleeting manner and at a single point, and just as it is this contact, not the point, that assigns to the tangent the law according to which it pursues to infinity its course in a straight line, so the translation touches the original in a fleeting manner and only at an infinitely small point of meaning, to follow henceforth its proper course, according to the law of fidelity in the liberty of language movement." Each time that he talks about the contact (*Berührung*) between the bodies of the two texts in the process of translation, Benjamin calls it "fleeting" (*flüchtig*). On at least three occasions, this "fleeting" character is emphasized, and always in order to situate the contact with meaning, the infinitely small point of meaning which the languages barely brush ("The harmony between the languages is so profound here [in the translations of Sophocles by Hölderlin] that the meaning is only touched by the wind of language in the manner of an Eolian lyre"). What can an infinitely small point of meaning be? What is the measure to evaluate it? The metaphor itself is at once the question and the answer. And here is the other metaphor, the metamphora, which no longer concerns extension in a straight and infinite line but enlargement by adjoining along the broken lines of a fragment. (2) "For, just as the fragments of the amphora, if one is to be able to reconstitute the whole, must be contiguous in the smallest details, but not identical to each other, so instead of rendering itself similar to the meaning of the original, the translation should rather, in a movement of love and in full detail, pass into its own language the mode of intention of the original: thus, just as the debris become recognizable as fragments of the same amphora, original and translations become recognizable as fragments of a larger language."

Let us accompany this movement of love, the gesture of this loving one (*liebend*) that is at work in the translation. It does not reproduce, does not restitute, does not represent; as to the essential, it does not *render* the meaning of the original except at that point of contact or caress, the infinitely small of meaning. It extends the body of languages, it puts languages into symbolic expansion, and symbolic here means that, however little restitution there be to accomplish, the larger, the new vaster aggregate, has still to *reconstitute* something. It is perhaps not a whole, but it is an aggregate in which openness should not contradict unity. Like the urn which lends its poetic topos to so many meditations on word and thing, from Hölderlin to Rilke and Heidegger, the amphora is one with itself though opening itself to the outside—and this openness opens the unity, renders it possible, and forbids it totality. Its openness allows receiving and giving. If the growth of language must also reconstitute without representing, if that is the symbol, can translation lay claim to the truth? Truth—will that still be the name of that which still lays down the law for a translation?

Here we touch—at a point no doubt infinitely small—the limit of translation. The pure untranslatable and the pure transferable here pass one into the other— and it is the truth, "itself materially."

The word "truth" appears more than once in "The Task of the Translator." We must not rush to lay hold of it. It is not a matter of truth for a translation in so far as it might conform or be faithful to its model, the original. Nor any more a matter, either for the original or even for the translation, of some adequation of the language to meaning or to reality, nor indeed of the representation to something. Then what is it that goes under the name of truth? And will it be that new?

Let us start again from the "symbolic." Let us remember the metaphor, or the ammetaphor: a translation espouses the original when the two adjoined fragments, as different as they can be, complete each other so as to form a larger tongue in the course of a sur-vival that changes them both. For the native tongue of the translator, as we have noted, is altered as well. Such at least is my interpretation— my translation, my "task of the translator." It is what I have called the translation contract: hymen or marriage contract with the promise to produce a child whose seed will give rise to history and growth. A marriage contract in the form of a seminar. Benjamin says as much, in the translation the original becomes larger; it grows rather than reproduces itself—and I will add: like a child, its own, no doubt, but with the power to speak on its own which makes of a child something other than a product subjected to the law of reproduction. This promise signals a kingdom which is at once "promised and forbidden where the languages will be reconciled and fulfilled." This is the most Babelian note in an analysis of sacred writing as the model and the limit of all writing, in any case of all Dichtung in its being-to-be-translated. The sacred and the being-to-be-translated do not lend themselves to thought one without the other. They produce each other at the edge of the same limit.

This kingdom is never reached, touched, trodden by translation. There is something untouchable, and in this sense the reconciliation is only promised. But a promise is not nothing, it is not simply marked by what it lacks to be fulfilled. As a promise, translation is already an event, and the decisive signature of a contract. Whether or not it be honored does not prevent the commitment from taking place and from bequeathing its record. A translation that manages, that manages to promise reconciliation, to talk about it, to desire it or make it desirable—such a translation is a rare and notable event.

Here two questions before going closer to the truth. Of what does the untouchable consist, if there is such a thing? And why does such a metaphor or ammetaphor of Benjamin make me think of the hymen, more visibly of the wedding gown?

1. The always intact, the intangible, the untouchable (*unberührbar*) is what fascinates and orients the work of the translator. He wants to touch the untouchable, that which remains of the text when one has extracted from it the communicable meaning (point of contact which is, remember, infinitely small), when one has transmitted that which can be transmitted, indeed taught: what I do here, after and thanks to Maurice de Gandillac, knowing that an untouchable remnant of the Benjaminian text will also remain intact at the end of the operation. Intact and virgin in spite of the labor of translation, however efficient or pertinent that may be. Pertinency has no bearing here. If one can risk a proposition in appearance so absurd, the text will be even more virgin after the passage of the translator, and the hymen, sign of virginity, more jealous of itself after the other hymen, the contract signed and the marriage consummated. Symbolic completeness will not have taken place to its very end and yet the promise of marriage will have come about—and this is the task of the translator, in what makes it very pointed as well as irreplaceable.

But again? Of what does the untouchable consist? Let us study again the metaphors or the ammetaphors, the *Übertragungen* which are translations and metaphors of translation, translations (*Übersetzungen*) of translation or metaphors of metaphor. Let us study all of these Benjaminian passages. The first figure which comes in here is that of the core and the shell, the fruit and the skin (*Kern, Frucht/Schale*). It describes in the final analysis the distinction that Benjamin would never want to renounce or even bother to question. One recognizes a core (the original as such) by the fact that it can bear further translating and restranslating. A translation, *as such*, cannot. Only a core, because it resists the translation it attracts, can offer itself to further translating operations without letting itself be exhausted. For the relation of the content to the language, one would also say of the substance to the form, of the signified to the signifier—it hardly matters here (in this context Benjamin opposes tenor, *Gehalt*, and tongue or language, *Sprache*)— differs from the original text to the translation. In the first, the unity is just as dense, tight, adherent as between the fruit and its skin, its shell or its peel. Not that they are inseparable—one should be able to distinguish them by rights—but they belong to an organic whole, and it is not insignificant that the metaphor here be vegetal and natural, naturalistic:

> This kingdom it [the original in translation] never fully attains, but it is there that is found what makes translating more than communicating. More precisely one can define this essential core as that which, in the translation, is not translatable again.

For, as much as one may extract of the communicable in order to translate it, there always remains this untouchable towards which is oriented the work of the true translator. It is not transmissible, as is the creative word of the original ["übertragbar wie das Dichterwort des Originals"], for the relation of this tenor to the language is entirely different in the original and in the translation. In the original, tenor and language form a determinate unity, like that of the fruit and the skin.

Let us dissect a bit more the rhetoric of this sequence. It is not certain that the essential "core" and the "fruit" designate the same thing. The essential core, that which in the translation is not translatable again, is not the tenor, but this adherence between the tenor and the language, between the fruit and the skin. This may seem strange or incoherent (how can a core be situated between the fruit and the skin?). It is necessary no doubt to think that the core is first the hard and central unity that holds the fruit to the skin, the fruit to itself as well; and above all that, at the heart of the fruit, the core is "untouchable," beyond reach and invisible. The core would be the first metaphor of what makes for the unity of the two terms in the second metaphor. But there is a third, and this time one without a natural provenance. It concerns the relation of the tenor to the language in the translation and no longer in the original. This relation is different, and I do not think I give in to artifice by insisting on this difference in saying that it is precisely that of artifice to nature. What in fact is it that Benjamin notes, as if in passing, for rhetorical or pedagogical convenience? That "the language of the translation envelops its tenor like a royal cape with large folds. For it is the signifier of a language superior to itself and so remains, in relation to its own tenor, inadequate, forced, foreign." That is quite beautiful, a beautiful translation: white ermine, crowning, scepter, and majestic bearing. The king has indeed a body (and it is not here the original text but that which constitutes the tenor of the translated text), but this body is only promised, announced and dissimulated by the translation. The clothes fit but do not cling strictly enough to the royal person. This is not a weakness; the best translation resembles this royal cape. It remains separate from the body to which it is nevertheless conjoined, wedding it, not wedded to it. One can of course embroider on this cape, on the necessity of this *Übertragung*, of this metaphoric translation of translation. For example, one can oppose this metaphor to that of the shell and the core just as one would oppose technology to nature. An article of clothing is not natural; it is a fabric and even—another metaphor of metaphor—a text, and this text of artifice appears precisely on the side of the symbolic contract. Now, if the original text is demand for translation, then the fruit, unless it be the core, insists upon becoming the king or the emperor who will wear new clothes: under its large folds, *in weiten Falten*, one will imagine him naked. No doubt the cape and the folds protect the king against the cold or natural aggressions; but first, above all, it is, like his scepter, the eminent visibility of the law. It is the index of power and of the power to lay down the law. But one infers that what counts is what comes to pass under the cape, to wit, the body of the king, do not immediately say the phallus, around which a translation busies its tongue, makes pleats, molds forms, sews hems, quilts, and embroiders. But always amply floating at some distance from the tenor.

2. More or less strictly, the cape weds the body of the king, but as for what comes to pass under the cape, it is difficult to separate the king from the royal couple. This is the one, this couple of spouses (the body of the king and his gown, the tenor and the tongue, the king and the queen) that lays down the law and guarantees every contract from this first contract. That is why I thought of a wedding gown. Benjamin, we know, does not push matters in the direction that I give to my translation, reading him always already in translation. More or less faithfully I have taken some liberty with the tenor of the original, as much as with its tongue, and again with the original that is also for me, now, the translation by Maurice de Gandillac. I have added another cape, floating even more, but is that not the final destination of all translation? At least if a translation is destined to arrive.

Despite the distinction between the two metaphors, the shell and the cape (the royal cape, for he said "royal" where others could have thought a cape sufficed), despite the opposition of nature and art, there is in both cases a *unity* of tenor and tongue, natural unity in the one case, symbolic unity in the other. Simply in the translation the unity signals a (metaphorically) more "natural" unity; it promises a tongue or language more originary and almost sublime, sublime to the distended extent that the promise itself—to wit, the translation—there remains inadequate (*unangemessen*), violent and forced (*gewaltig*), and foreign (*fremd*). This "fracture" renders useless, even "forbids," every *Übertragung*, every "transmission," exactly as the French translation says: the word also plays, like a transmission, with transferential or metaphorical displacement. And the word *Übertragung* imposes itself again a few lines down: if the translation "transplants" the original onto another terrain of language "ironically" more definitive, it is to the extent that it could no longer be displaced by any other "transfer" (*Übertragung*) but only "raised" (*erheben*) anew on the spot "in other parts." There is no translation of translation; that is the axiom without which there would not be "The Task of the Translator." If one were to violate it, and one must not, one would touch the untouchable of the untouchable, to wit, that which guarantees to the original that it remains indeed the original.

This is not unrelated to truth. Truth is apparently beyond every *Übertragung* and every possible *Übersetzung*. It is not the representational correspondence between the original and the translation, nor even the primary adequation between the original and some object or signification exterior to it. Truth would be rather the *pure language* in which the meaning and the letter no longer dissociate. If such a place, the taking place of such an event, remained undiscoverable, one could no longer, even by right, distinguish between an original and a translation. In maintaining this distinction at all cost, as the original given of every translation contract (in the quasi-transcendental sense we discussed above), Benjamin repeats the foundation of the law. In so doing he exhibits the possibility of copyright for works and author, the very possibility by which actual law claims to be supported. This law collapses at the slightest challenge to a strict boundary between the original and the version, indeed to the identity or to the integrity of the original. What Benjamin says about this relation between original and translation is also found translated in a language rather wooden but faithfully reproduced as to its meaning at the opening of all legal treatises concerning the actual law of translations. And then whether it be a matter of the general principles of the difference original/ translation (the latter being "derived" from the former) or a matter of the translations of translation. The translation of translation is said to be "derived" from the original and not from the first translation. Here are some excerpts from the French law; but there does not seem to be from this point of view any opposition between it and the rest of Western law (nevertheless, a study of comparative law should also concern the translation of legal texts). As we shall see, these propositions appeal to the polarity expression/expressed, signifier/signified, form/substance. Benjamin also began by saying: translation is a form, and the symbolizer/symbolized split organizes his whole essay. Now, in what way is this system of oppositions indispensable to this law? Because only it allows, starting from the distinction between original and translation, acknowledgment of some originality in the translation. This originality is determined, and this is one of the many classic philosophemes at the foundation of this law, as originality of *expression*. Expression is opposed to content, of course, and the translation, which is not supposed to touch the content, must be original only in its language as *expression*; but expression is also opposed to what French jurists call the *composition* of the original. In general one places composition on the side of form, but here the form of expression in which one can acknowledge some originality to the translator, and for this reason the rights of author-translator, is only the form of linguistic expression, the choice of words in the language, and so forth, but nothing else of the form. I quote Claude Colombet, *Propriété littéraire et artistique* (Paris: Dalloz, 1976), from which I excerpt only a few lines, in accordance with the law of March 11, 1957, recalled at the opening of the book and "authorizing . . . only analyses and short quotations for the purpose of example or illustration," because "every representation or reproduction, integral

or partial, made without the consent of the author or of his beneficiaries or execu-
tors, is illegal," constituting "therefore an infraction punishable under articles 425
and following of the Penal Code."

54. —Translations are works which are original only by expression; [very paradoxical
restriction: the cornerstone of copyright, it is indeed that only the form can become
property, and not the ideas, the themes, the contents, which are common and universal property. (Compare all of chapter 1 in this book, *L'absence de protection des idées
par le droit d'auteur.*) If a first consequence is good, since it is this form that defines
the originality of the translation, another consequence could be ruinous, for it would
lead to abandoning that which distinguishes the original from the translation if,
excluding expression, it amounts to a distinction of substance. Unless the value of
composition, however lax it may be, were still to indicate the fact that between the
original and the translation the relation is neither of expression nor of content but of
something else beyond these oppositions. In following the difficulty of the jurists—
sometimes comic in its casuistic subtlety—so as to draw the consequences from
axioms of the type "Copyright does not protect ideas; but these can be, sometimes
indirectly, protected by means other than the law of March 11, 1957" (ibid., 21), one
measures better the historicity and conceptual fragility of this set of axioms] article 4
of the law cites them among the protected works; in fact it has always been admitted
that a translator demonstrates originality in the choice of expressions to render best
in one language the meaning of the text in another language. As M. Savatier says, "The
genius of each language gives the translated work its own physiognomy; and the
translator is not a simple workman. He himself participates in a derived creation for
which he bears his own responsibility"; it is that in fact translation is not the result of
an automatic process; by the choices he makes among several words, several expressions, the translator fashions a work of the mind; but, of course, he could never mod-
ify the composition of the work translated, for he is bound to respect that work.

In his language, Desbois says the same thing, with some additional details:

Derived works which are original in expression. 29. The work under consideration, to
be *relatively original* [emphasized by Desbois], need not bear the imprint of a personality at once in composition and expression, like adaptations. It is enough that the
author, while following step by step the development of a preexistent work, have performed a personal act in the expression: article 4 attests to this, since, in a nonexhaus-
tive enumeration of derived works, it puts *translations* in the place of honor.
"Traduttore, traditore," the Italians are wont to say, in a bit of wit, which, like every
coin, has two sides: if there are bad translators, who multiply misreadings, others are

cited for the perfection of their task. The risk of a mistake or an imperfection has as counterpart the perspective of an authentic version, which implies a perfect knowledge of the two languages, an abundance of judicious choices, and thus a creative effort. Consulting a dictionary suffices only for mediocre candidates to the baccalaureate: the conscientious and competent translator "gives of himself" and *creates* just like the painter who makes a copy of a model. —The verification of this conclusion is furnished by the comparison of several translations of one and the same text: each may differ from the others without any one containing a misreading; the variety in modes of expression for a single thought demonstrates, with the possibility of choice, that the task of the translator gives room for manifestations of personality. [*Le droit d'auteur en France* (Paris: Dalloz, 1978)]

One will note in passing that the *task of the translator*, confined to the duel of languages (never more than two languages), gives rise only to a "creative effort" (effort and tendency rather than achievement, artisan labor rather than artistic performance), and when the translator "creates," it is like a painter who copies his model (a ludicrous comparison for many reasons; is there any use in explaining?). The recurrence of the word "task" is remarkable enough in any case, for all the significations that it weaves into a network, and there is always the same evaluative interpretation: duty, debt, tax, levy, toll, inheritance and estate tax, nobiliary obligation, but labor midway to creation, infinite task, essential incompletion, as if the presumed creator of the original were not—he too—indebted, taxed, obligated by another text, and a priori translating.

Between the transcendental law (as Benjamin repeats it) and the actual law as it is formulated so laboriously and at times so crudely in treatises on copyright for author or for works, the analogy can be followed quite far, for example in that which concerns the notion of derivation and the translations of translations: these are always derived from the original and not from previous translations. Here is a note by Desbois:

The translator will not even cease to fashion personal work when he goes to draw advice and inspiration from a preceding translation. We will not refuse the status of author for a work that is derived, *in relation to anterior translations*, to someone who would have been content to choose, among several versions already published, the one that seemed to him the most adequate to the original: going from one to the other, taking a passage from this one, another from that one, he would create a new work, by the very fact of the combination, which renders his work different from antecedent productions. He has exercised creativity, since his translation reflects a new form and results from comparisons, from choices. The translator would still deserve a hearing in our opinion, even if his reflection had led him to the same result as a predecessor, whose work, by supposition, he would not have known: his unintentional replica, far from amounting to plagiarism, would bear the mark of his personality, would present a "subjective novelty," which would call for protection. The two versions, accomplished separately and each without knowledge of the other, gave rise, separately and individually, to manifestations of personality. *The second will be a work derived vis-à-vis the work that has been translated, not vis-à-vis the first.* [ibid., 41; my emphasis in the last sentence]

Of this right to the truth, what is the relation?

Translation promises a kingdom to the reconciliation of languages. This promise, a properly symbolic event adjoining, coupling, marrying two languages like two parts of a greater whole, appeals to a language of the truth ("Sprache der Wahrheit"). Not to a language that is true, adequate to some exterior content, but to a true tongue, to a language whose truth would be referred only to itself. It would be a matter of truth as authenticity, truth of act or event which would belong to the original rather than to the translation, even if the original is already in a position of demand or debt. And if there were such authenticity and such force of event in what is ordinarily called a translation, it is that it would produce itself in some fashion like an original work. There would thus be an original and inaugural way of indebting oneself; that would be the place and date of what is called an original, a work.

To translate well the intentional meaning of what Benjamin means to say when he speaks of the "language of the truth," perhaps it is necessary to understand what he regularly says about the "intentional meaning" or the "intentional aim" ("Intention der Meinung," "Art des Meinens"). As Maurice de Gandillac reminds us, these are categories borrowed from the scholastics by Brentano and Husserl. They play a role that is important if not always very clear in "The Task of the Translator."

What is it that seems intended by the concept of intention (*Meinen*)? Let us return to the point where in the translation there seems to be announced a kinship among languages, beyond all resemblence between an original and its reproduction and independently of any historical filiation. Moreover, kinship does not necessarily imply resemblence. With that said, in dismissing the historical or natural origin, Benjamin does not exclude, in a wholly different sense, consideration of the origin in general, any more than a Rousseau or a Husserl did in analogous contexts and with analogous movements. Benjamin specifies quite literally: for the most rigorous access to this kinship or to this affinity of languages, "the concept of origin [*Abstammungsbegriff*] remains indispensable." Where, then, is this original affinity to be sought? We see it announced in the plying, replying, co-deploying of intentions. Through each language something is intended which is the same and yet which none of the languages can attain separately. They can claim, and promise themselves to attain it, only by coemploying or codeploying their intentional modes, "the whole of their complementary intentional modes." This codeployment toward the whole is a replying because what it intends to attain is "the pure language" ("die reine Sprache"), or the pure tongue. What is intended, then, by this cooperation of languages and intentional *modes* is not transcendent to the language; it is not a reality which they would besiege from all sides, like a tower that they would try to surround. No, what they are aiming at intentionally, individually and jointly, in translation is the language itself as a Babelian event, a language that is not the universal language in the Leibnizian sense, a language which is not the natural language that each remains on its own either; it is the being-language of the language, tongue or language *as such*, that unity without any self-identity, which makes for the fact that there are languages and that they are languages.

These languages relate to one another in translation according to an unheard-of mode. They complete each other, says Benjamin; but no other completeness in the world can represent this one, or that symbolic complementarity. This singularity (not representably by anything in the world) comes no doubt from the intentional mode or from what Benjamin tries to translate in a scholastico-phenomenological language. Within the same intentional aim it is necessary to distinguish rigorously between the thing intended, the intended (*Gemeinten*), and the mode of intention ("die Art des Meinens"). As soon as he sights the original contract of languages and the hope for the "pure tongue," the task of the translator excludes the intended or leaves it between brackets.

The mode of intention alone assigns the task of translation. Every "thing," in its presumed self-identity (for example, bread *itself*) is intended by way of different modes in each language and in each text of each language. It is among these modes that the translation should seek, produce or reproduce, a complementarity or a "harmony." And since to complete or complement does not amount to the summation of any worldly totality, the value of harmony suits this adjustment, and what can here be called the accord of tongues. This accord lets the pure language, and the being-language of the language, resonate, announcing it rather than presenting it. As long as this accord does not take place, the pure language remains hidden, concealed (*verborgen*), immured in the nocturnal intimacy of the "core." Only a translation can make it emerge.

Emerge, and above all develop, make grow. Always according to the same motif (in appearance organicist or vitalist), one could then say that each language is as if atrophied in its isolation, meager, arrested in its growth, sickly. Owing to translation, in other words to this linguistic supplementarity by which one language gives to another what it lacks, and gives it harmoniously, this crossing of languages assures the growth of languages, even that "holy growth of language" "unto the messianic end of history." All of that is announced in the translation process, through "the eternal sur-vival of languages" ("am ewigen Fortleben der Sprachen") or "the infinite rebirth [*Aufleben*] of languages." This perpetual reviviscence, this constant regeneration (*Fort-* and *Auf-leben*) by translation is less a revelation, revelation itself, than an annunciation, an alliance and a promise.

This religious code is essential here. The sacred text marks the limit, the pure even if inaccessible model, of pure transferability, the ideal starting from which one could think, evaluate, measure the essential, that is to say poetic, translation. Translation, as holy growth of languages, announces the messianic end, surely, but the sign of that end and of that growth is "present" (*gegenwärtig*) only in the "knowledge of that distance," in the *Entfernung, the remoteness* that relates us to it. One can know this remoteness, have knowledge or a presentiment of it, but we cannot overcome it. Yet it puts us in contact with that "language of the truth" which is the "true language" ("so ist diese Sprache der Wahrheit—die wahre Sprache"). This contact takes place in the mode of "presentiment," in the "intensive" mode that renders present what is absent, that allows remoteness to approach as remoteness, *fort:da*. Let us say that the translation is the experience, that which is translated or experienced as well: experience is translation.

The to-be-translated of the sacred text, its pure transferability, that is what would give *at the limit* the ideal measure for all translation. The sacred text assigns the task to the translator, and it is sacred *inasmuch as* it announces itself as transferable, simply transferable, to-be-translated, which does not always mean immediately translatable, in the common sense that was dismissed from the start. Perhaps it is necessary to distinguish here between the transferable and the translatable. Transferability pure and simple is that of the sacred text in which meaning and literality are no longer discernible as they form the body of a unique, irreplaceable, and untransferable event, "materially the truth." Never are the call for translation, the debt, the task, the assignation, more imperious. Never is there anything more transferable, yet by reason of this indistinction of meaning and literality (*Wört-lichkeit*), the pure transferable can announce itself, give itself, present itself, let itself be translated as untranslatable. From this limit, at once interior and exterior, the translator comes to receive all the signs of remoteness (*Entfernung*) which guide him on his infinite course, at the edge of the abyss, of madness and of silence: the last works of Hölderlin as translations of Sophocles, the collapse of meaning "from abyss to abyss," and this danger is not that of accident, it is transferability, it is the law of translation, the to-be-translated as law, the order given, the order received— and madness waits on both sides. And as the task is impossible at the approaches to the sacred text which assigns it to you, the infinite guilt absolves you immediately.

That is what is named from here on Babel: the law imposed by the name of God who in one stroke commands and forbids you to translate by showing *and* hiding from you the limit. But it is not only the Babelien situation, not only a scene or a structure. It is also the status and the event of the Babelian text, of the text of *Genesis* (a unique text in this regard) as sacred text. It comes under the law that it recounts and translates in an exemplary way. It lays down the law it speaks about, and from abyss to abyss it deconstructs the tower, and every turn, twists and turns of every sort, in a rhythm.

What comes to pass in a sacred text is the occurrence of a *pas de sens*. And this event is also the one starting from which it is possible to think the poetic or literary text which tries to redeem the lost sacred and there translates itself as in its model. *Pas de sens*—that does not signify poverty of meaning but no meaning that would be itself, meaning, beyond any "literality." And right there is the sacred. The sacred surrenders itself to translation, which devotes itself to the sacred. The sacred would be nothing without translation, and translation would not take place without the sacred; the one and the other are inseparable. In the sacred text "the meaning has ceased to be the divide for the flow of language and for the flow of revelation." It is the absolute text because in its event it communicates nothing, it says nothing that would make sense beyond the event itself. That event melds completely with the act of language, for example with prophecy. It is literally the literality of its tongue, "pure language." And since no meaning bears detaching, transferring, transporting, or translating into another tongue as such (as meaning), it commands right away the translation that it seems to refuse. It is transferable and untranslatable. There is only letter, and it is the truth of pure language, the truth as pure language.

This law would not be an exterior constraint; it grants a liberty to literality. In the same event, the letter ceases to oppress insofar as it is no longer the exterior body or the corset of meaning. The letter also translates itself of itself, and it is in this self-relation of the sacred body that the task of the translator finds itself engaged. This situation, though being one of pure limit, does not exclude—quite the contrary—gradations, virtuality, interval and in-between, the infinite labor to rejoin that which is nevertheless past, already given, even here, between the lines, already signed.

How would you translate a signature? And how would you refrain, whether it be Yahweh, Babel, Benjamin when he signs right next to his last word? But literally, and between the lines, it is also the signature of Maurice de Gandillac that to end I quote in posing my question: can one quote a signature? "For, to some degree, all the great writings, but to the highest point sacred Scripture, contain between the lines their virtual translation. The interlinear version of the sacred text is the model or ideal of all translation."

Translated by Joseph F. Graham

Translator's Note

Translation is an art of compromise, if only because the problems of translation have no one solution and none that is fully satisfactory. The best translation is merely better than the worst to some extent, more or less. Compromise also precludes consistency. It would have been possible, and it once seemed plausible, to maintain regular equivalents at least for those terms that figure prominently in the argument. But the result was not worth the sacrifice. There was consolation for so much effort to so little effect in that whatever we did, we were bound to exhibit the true principles of translation announced in our text. And so this translation is exemplary to that extent. To the extent that we were guided in translation, the principles were also those found in the text. Accordingly, a silhouette of the original appears for effect in many words and phrases of the translation.

Publication of the French text is also significant in telling of our situation. Among the many differences in this translation, a few appear already in the original.

The quotations from Walter Benjamin are translated from the French, not the German. The biblical passages are also translated from their French versions, since Derrida works from translations in both cases.

Here are some of the problems for which I found solutions least satisfactory:

"Des Tours de Babel." The title can be read in various ways. *Des* means "some"; but it also means "of the," "from the," or "about the." *Tours* could be towers, twists, tricks, turns, or tropes, as in a "turn" of phrase. Taken together, *des* and *tours* have the same sound as *détour*, the word for detour. To mark that economy in language the title has not been changed.

langue/langage. It is difficult to mark this difference in English where "language" covers both. Whenever possible, "tongue" has been used for *langue*, and "language" only in those cases that are clearly specific rather than generic. *Langage* is then translated as "language" in the singular and without modifier, though not always. The German *Sprache* introduces further complications.

survie. The word means "survival" as well as "afterlife"; its use in the text also brings out the subliminal sense of more life and more than life. The hyphenation of "sur-vival" is an admitted cheat.

performance. The French has not the primarily dramatic connotation of the English but rather the sense of prowess and success; its use here also relates to the "performative" of speech acts.

pas-de-sens. With this expression Derrida combines the *pas* of negation with the *pas* of step in a most curious figure. My English suggested a skip.

De ce droit à la vérité quel est le rapport? This sentence could be translated by any and all of the following: What is the relation between this law and the truth? What is the gain from this law to the truth? What is the relation between this right to the truth and all the rest?

3

A Note on "Interpretations at War"

"Interpretations at War" was given as a lecture in Jerusalem in 1988, during the Palestinian uprising that began in 1987. From the outset, Derrida insists on the importance of the "institutional context" in which he speaks and of which he will speak, a context determined "by a university, a State, an army, a police force, religious authorities, languages, peoples, and nations." These institutions are at the center of his lecture; they constitute, he says, the very subject of "Interpretations at War." Derrida chose this subject because it would allow him to ask "some questions about what is going on here and now."

The summary of "Interpretations at War," distributed in advance, bore the title "The Jewish-German Psyche: The Examples of Hermann Cohen and Franz Rosenzweig." The institutional war of interpretations is thus located not only between two entities—one religious, one national—but also within one entity, national and religious, here a psyche. Common to Jews and Germans, this psyche may be the result of what has been called the Jewish-German symbiosis, or it may be the self-reflection (as Derrida here reminds his readers, a *psyché* is, in French, "a great pivoting mirror") of German-Jews who, according to some (Gershom Scholem prominent among them), were involved in a deluded self-reflection they called "dialogue." (Aside from the Israelo-Palestinian conflict, the seminar on the theologico-political provides a significant background to "Interpretations" and announces much that is to come in *Politics of Friendship*.) Between religion and nation, but also "within" the religious (Jewish, Catholic, or Protestant, and the difference may be difficult to circumscribe: "and the Catholics are already Protestant . . . just like the Jews: they are all Neoplatonic Kantians"), and within Kant ("Kant against Kant, or Kant without Kant") a war is on—a "war within the spirit," a "fratricidal war" that Cohen's *Deutschtum und Judentum* sought to avert. Is the locus of this war "Jewish" or "German," and, if the difference holds, where is it to be located? In religion? In politics? In order to answer these questions "one would have to be certain that one can delimit the religious. One would have to be certain that one can distinguish all the predicates of the religious" ("Faith and Knowledge," section

28). The abyss that opens the space of questioning is here as explosive as a volcano, and as vertiginously "delirious": "the Germans are Jews," Cohen's discourse maintains, "the Jew himself being, as we shall verify, a Protestant and the Protestant a Platonic Jew." What remains of the notion of a religious nation, or of a national religion? And who is its subject? Cohen maintained that the exemplary subject is "the Jew and the German": "Their *socius* (alliance, spiritual symbiosis, psyche, and so on) is that very *socius* which makes of the *subjectum* a moral being and a legal being, a freedom, a person." And this subject implicates all Jews who therefore already have a state, and a homeland: "This homeland, however, is not Israel but Germany." Germany, in Cohen's words, "is the motherland of their [the Jews'] soul, if however religion is their soul." The discourse of "religion" is also the discourse of nationalism and of the state. And although religion and politics are undoubtedly "interpretations at war," their strict distinction is anything but certain.

G. A.

INTERPRETATIONS AT WAR
Kant, the Jew, the German

As will soon become easily apparent, the choices I have made for this paper bear *a necessary* relation to *this very place*: the university, an Israeli institution of Jerusalem. They bear a necessary relation to *this very moment*: the terrible violence marking once again the history of this land and pitting against each other all those who believe they have the right to inhabit it.

Why is this relation a *necessary* one?

Like other papers, mine will consist of a set of interpretive hypotheses on the subject, precisely, of the institutions of interpretation. Consequently it will stand, certainly and *de facto*, in a relation with an *institutional context*, the one which is determined today, here, now, by a university, a State, an army, a police force, religious authorities, languages, peoples, and nations. But this *de facto* also calls for interpretation and responsibility. I therefore did not think I should accept the fact of this situation passively. I have chosen to treat a subject which would allow me, while touching directly on the themes stated in the agenda of this conference (The Institutions of Interpretation), to ask at least indirectly, and as carefully as possible, some questions about what is going on here now. But although between the discourse I am about to hold forth and the current violence, here and now, the mediations required are numerous, complicated, and difficult to interpret, although these mediations call for as much patience as caution on our part, I shall not use them as a pretext to wait and remain silent before that which demands *immediate* response and responsibility.

I had already communicated my anxiety to the organizers of this meeting. I had expressed to them my wish to participate in a conference where Arab and Palestinian colleagues would be officially invited and effectively involved. The organizers of this meeting, Professors Sanford Budick and Wolfgang Iser, shared my concern. I thank them for the understanding they have shown in this regard. With all the gravity this requires, I wish to state right now my solidarity with all those, in this land, who advocate an end to violence, condemn the crimes of terrorism and of military and police repression, and advocate the withdrawal of Israeli troops from the occupied territories as well as the recognition of the Palestinians' right to choose their own representatives to negotiations now more indispensable than ever. This cannot be accomplished without unceasing, well-informed, courageous reflection. This reflection should lead to new or not-necessarily-new interpretations of what—three years ago, while this conference was being planned here—I had proposed to call the "institutions of interpretation." But that same reflection should also lead us to interpret that dominant institution which is the State, here the Israeli State (whose existence, it goes without saying, must henceforth be recognized by all and definitively guaranteed), along with its prehistory, the conditions of its recent founding, and the constitutional, legal, political foundations of its present functioning, the forms and limits of its *self-interpretation*, and so forth.

As is evident by my presence right here, this declaration is inspired not only by my concern for justice and by my friendship toward both the Palestinians and the Israelis. It is meant also as an expression of respect for a certain image of Israel and as an expression of hope for its future.

I am not saying this, of course, in order to tailor my purpose artificially to some external circumstance. The call for such a historical reflection, anxiety-laden as it might appear, courageous as it must be, seems to me to be inscribed in the most strictly determining context of our meeting. It constitutes in my view its very sense—and its urgency.

I

Taking for granted familiarity with the advance text which defined the most general horizon of this paper,[1] let me state without further introduction the reasons which

1. The following summary was distributed, by prior arrangement, during the weeks preceding the conference:

The Jewish-German Psyche:
The Examples of Hermann Cohen and Franz Rosenzweig

Jacques Derrida

Insisting on the word *example*, we open onto several questions. (1) What is exemplarity (rather than paradigm) in the history of national self-affirmation? What happens when a "people" presents itself as exemplary? Or when a "nation" declares itself endowed with a mission by virtue of its very uniqueness; as of

induce me to compare and contrast, in a manner still partial and preliminary, two German Jewish thinkers, in a highly determined politico-institutional context.

(1) Hermann Cohen and Franz Rosenzweig both assumed their Jewishness radically, although in opposite ways.

(2) Neither one of them was a Zionist, and Rosenzweig was even frankly hostile, so it seems, to the project of an Israeli state.

(3) Both having privileged the reference to Kant, both took a certain distance from Kant—a different sort of distance in each case.

(4) Although they belonged to different generations, they did share something of their time. Rosenzweig followed Cohen's teaching. He declared his admiration for the grand master of neo-Kantianism in a text that I shall quote shortly. He then moved away from Cohen, even turned against him, at least as far as his thinking about and relation to Judaism were concerned. He produced a critical reading of Deutschtum and Judentum, that text by Cohen that we shall begin to analyze in a moment.

---

bearing testimony, and of having a responsibility, all of which are exemplary; in other words, of bringing a universal message? (2) In what sense and how have the Jewish and German people been able to declare themselves as exemplary in terms of this "exemplarity"? In what sense and how, since the *Aufklärung* (Mendelssohn, Kant, etc.) has a certain modern pair, both singular and impossible (which was judged "mythic" and "legendary" by Scholem, the Jewish-German pair, been doubly exemplary in terms of this exemplarity? What happened in regard to this in the politico-institutional context of the Emancipation, of the two world wars, of Zionism and of Nazism, etc.? What we call the "psyche" is both a psychic locus of the fantasies that drive us [*fantasmatique pulsionnelle*] (love, hate, madness, projection, rejection, etc.), which has constituted the strange pair of these two cultures, of these two "histories," of these two "peoples," and what is called in French a "psyche," i.e., a great pivoting mirror, a device of specular reflection. (3) In what way are these examples, and particularly the example of the corpus that we shall be treating (one certain corpus signed by Cohen and by Rosenzweig), exemplary as to the general questions which will be on the horizon of this presentation? What is a context? How can we determine its openness and its closedness? How can we delimit the institutionality of a context? What does it mean to render an account of an institutional context in an interpretation, when a context remains always "open" and inexhaustible, stabilizable but only because of its being essentially unstable and mutable?

In the case of the texts we shall analyze (*Deutschtum und Judentum* by Cohen 1915, certain pages from *Der Stern der Erlösung* by Rosenzweig), and the contextual dimensions abysmally enveloped are at least (1) the "whole" of the two traditions (Jewish and German); (2) the history of the Emancipation of the German Jews; (3) the history of Western philosophy, with Kant being privileged in an exemplary way by Cohen, Rosenzweig, and other German Jews (Benjamin and Adorno) (we'll speak of "Kant, the Jew, the German"); (4) the respective situation of the two thinkers (in their relationship to each other, in their relationship to Judaism, to Zionism, to German culture, and—it has to be emphasized—to the discourse or the institution of the university, to academic philosophy in general); (5) finally and most importantly the war of 1914–18: the nationalistic German text (Jewish-German) of Cohen is in fact a very special text, in other words, a powerful, violent, and troubling interpretation of the whole history of philosophy and of Western religions, and above all of the Jewish-German pair. This interpretation was primarily addressed [*destinée*] to the American Jews to ask them to prevent the United States from entering the war against Germany. But what does "primarily concerning a destination" mean here for the question of a text and a context?

This text was said to be "cursed." It is certainly not so simple. Is there an "actual" "context"—and which one—to reread this text today? Instead of answers to these numerous questions precipitously raised we shall rather multiply preliminary warnings as to the very positioning of these questions.

(5) Two different generations, two different situations, indeed; and yet the two texts that will serve us as a guideline are more or less contemporaneous. Both date, as to the publication of the one and the preparation and "composition" of the other, from the war of 1914. Both are caught up and rooted in that war: in a war, one might say, which neither of the two thinkers has survived—not, in any case, to the extent of reaching the next stage alive, the next stage being the moment when Nazism casts over that whole adventure, over what I would call the Jewish-German psyche of the war of 1914, a revealing and at the same time a deforming light. The future-in-the-past may lead to retrospective distortions, and it may also tear down veils. Cohen died at the end of the war, in 1918, three years after the publication of *Deutschtum und Judentum*. Rosenzweig was struck with aphasia, then total paralysis from 1922 on, by a disease which was to cause his death seven years later in December 1929.

By way of introduction to this context, let us first read a tribute rendered by Rosenzweig to Cohen upon the latter's death in 1918. Noticeable at once is a certain mistrust towards this highly respected, great academic, this master of neo-Kantianism who had already left such a deep mark on German philosophy during the half-century separating two Franco-German wars (1870–1920). It is too often forgotten, when one is interested in Husserl and Heidegger, that this neo-Kantian sequence has largely determined the context *in* which, that is to say also *against* which, Husserl's phenomenology, later the phenomenological ontology of the early Heidegger (who, besides, succeeded Cohen in his Marburg chair—and this also marks an institutional context in the strictest sense), in a way arose: against neo-Kantianism and in another relation to Kant.

Rosenzweig recalls his initial distrust towards this great academic philosopher whose authority, in Jewish and non-Jewish circles, stemmed from a respectable professorial image which, having radiated its light from the University of Marburg, continued to do so from Berlin, where Cohen taught, in 1913, at another institution, the Institute of Judaism. The work published by Cohen during those years bears an extremely Kantian title (in fact it is like the book of a Jewish Kant on religion within the limits of simple reason: *Religion der Vernunft aus den Quellen des Judentums*) and was to have a certain influence on Rosenzweig. Rosenzweig had begun attending Cohen's lectures in 1913 with a limited, or rather a distrustful, interest. This distrust is directed first at a sort of institutional entity, "the marketplace of German academic philosophy":

> I have attended Hermann Cohen's lectures only during the years when he was in Berlin. Apart from some occasional works on Jewish theology, I had read practically nothing by him. These few readings, which have left me with a dull impression without

moving me and mostly with a growing distrust, gradually becoming systematic, towards everything on the marketplace of German academic philosophy that succeeded in mustering a handful of admirers, had dissuaded me from seeking better acquaintance with him. So I had no special expectations when in November 1913 I went to attend his course, driven not by keen interest but by mere curiosity.[2]

Distrust gave way to delighted astonishment. Certain points of the encomium recall or anticipate the experience that some have described of the encounter with Heidegger's teaching during the years immediately following the war. All of this tells something of his cultural context and his relation to academic philosophy. It is, then, a typical reaction, one whose typicality appears interesting here, for it amounts to saying, At last, here is a philosopher who is no longer a professional from academia: he thinks in front of us, he speaks to us of what is at stake in existence, he reminds us of the abysmal risk of thought or existence. Rosenzweig speaks of the sense of the abyss (*Abgrund*) in order to describe this experience. One expected a professor, and here is a man walking the edge of a precipice, a flesh-and-blood man, a man who does not forget his body. This *aura* surrounds the teaching of his successor, Heidegger, too, from its beginnings in the lectures of his early years. In those lectures he speaks of the university, he calls for a thought that, within the university, would be a thought of existence and not an abstract and comfortable, ultimately irresponsible exercise. And this is just Rosenzweig's language: where he expected to see a professor *in cathedra*, he discovers a man, a unique man sensitive to the uniqueness of each existence, a man and a body over the abyss:

I then had an uncommon surprise. Being used to encounter in chairs of philosophy intelligent people of fine, sharp, elevated, profound mind ... I then met a philosopher. Instead of tightrope-walkers, showing off their more or less audacious, clever or graceful tricks on the high wire of thought, I saw a man. There was nothing there of that disconcerting vacuity or of that useless character which seemed to me to encumber nearly all the academic philosophical proceedings of the period, and which forced everyone to keep wondering why such and such an individual among all others, why just this one went in for philosophy rather than something else. With Cohen, the question no longer arose, and there was an unfailing sense that he, for one, could do nothing but philosophy, that he was inhabited by that precious force which the powerful word compels to manifest itself. That which, led astray by what the present had

2. Franz Rosenzweig, "Un hommage," in *Franz Rosenzweig, Les cahiers de la nuit surveillée*, no. 1 (1982); subsequent references to this work will be identified parenthetically in the text without pagination. (Here and elsewhere, unless otherwise noted, the English version of quoted material is my translation of Derrida's French—Tr.)

to offer, I gave up looking for long since except in the Great Dead, that learned and rigorous mind that knows how to meditate over the abyss, of a world still plunged in the confusion of a reality threatened by chaos, that is what I all of a sudden met in Cohen, face to face, incarnated in a living speech ("Un hommage").[3]

What is thus being revealed to Rosenzweig? A Jew, nothing less than the essence of the Jew, but also of the German Jew. And one cannot very well tell whether he is more purely Jewish because he is a German Jew or essentially Jewish and on top of that, by some accident or otherwise, also a German Jew. The ambiguity is remarkable; for it is with this German Jew, with a particular way of being a German Jew, Jewish *and* German (I shall return to one of Rosenzweig's letters which says, "Let us then be Germans and Jews. Both at the same time, without worrying about the *and*, without talking about it a great deal, but really both"), that Rosenzweig, like Scholem and Buber in a different way, will eventually break, despite the respect that Cohen still inspired, this great figure of rationalist German Judaism, liberal and non-Zionist if not assimilationist, this Jewish *and* German thinker.

For the moment, we can pay attention to the most salient features of this encomium of a German Jew by Rosenzweig. In the following paragraph we distinguish at least three.

A. As Scholem was to do later in a now famous letter addressed to him,[4] Rosenzweig associates rather strangely and in just such a biblical manner the figure of the abyss with that of volcanic fire. Boiling over, eruption, gushing forth out of untold depths, mixture of water and fire, but especially the convulsive rhythm of the flow of lava—such is Cohen's speech.

B. Convulsion, the convulsive tremor which marks the rhythm of volcanic production and scans the jet or projection of lava, the ejaculation of liquid fire, is also the tempo of discontinuous rhetoric, and that too is Cohen's speech. In it Rosenzweig recognizes that caesura in rhetorical composition, the aphoristic quality of a speech that cares nothing for composition or is composed of an irregular series of aphoristic interruptions. But he recognizes it primarily as a property of *Jewish* speech—an interpretation for which, as I do throughout, I leave him the responsibility.

This interruption, this interruptive quality in which Rosenzweig sees something essentially Jewish, calls for at least two comments.

---

3. A somewhat different English version of this passage is to be found in Franz Rosenzweig, *Franz Rosenzweig: His Life and Thought,* ed. Nahum Glatzer (New York: Schocken, 1961) p. 29–Tr.

4. "An Unpublished Letter from Gershom Scholem to Franz Rosenzweig. Concerning Our Language. A Confession," 26 Dec. 1926; French translation by Stéphane Mosès, in *Archives des sciences sociales et des religions,* 60, no. 1 (July–September 1985). I shall propose elsewhere a reading of this letter. [See "The Eyes of Language," in this volume.]

(1) It ought to mark, as a circuit breaker might, the essence of the conjunction "and," which not only defines the relation of the Jew to the German ("Let us be Jewish *and* German") but also determines the Jewish in the German: ruptivity, a dissociative and irruptive power. The volcano is irruption, but irruption is that which the coming of an event initiates, rupture and hence interruption in the totalizing synthesis. We know that Rosenzweig's thought is characterized first and foremost both by this thought of the "and" *and* by that within it which dislocates any totalizing synthesis. It does not forbid any in-gathering [*rassemblement*] but interrupts in-gathering by the *syn* of the synthesis or of the system, notably in the form of the State. The "and" of "Jewish and German" is perhaps a "*syn*" or a "*with*" but without an identifying or a totalizing synthesis. It carries disjunction as much as it does conjunction. It is this "lack of transition" which Rosenzweig believes to have noticed in Cohen and of which he will say that "nothing is more Jewish." This has to do primarily with Cohen's manner of speaking and teaching: lack of transition also, he notes, hence of mediation between thought and feeling, the coldest thought and the most passionate feeling. This "logic" is as paradoxical as that of the "and." The lack of transition signifies omission of the middle term and everything that plays the role of mediation in a dialectic, whether by this word one means the process of being and absolute knowledge or of the art of language. But his nonmediation may translate itself into two apparently contradictory effects: on the one hand, discontinuity—the abrupt juxtaposition of two heterogenous elements, the relationless relation between two terms with no continuity, no analogy, no resemblance, not susceptible to any genealogical or deductive derivation; but on the other hand and for the very same reason, the lack of transition produces a sort of immediate continuity which joins one to the other, the same to the same and to the nonsame, the other to the other.

(2) This disjunctive conjunction, this "lack of transition," is a way of connecting without connection in rhetoric and in argumentation, for instance philosophical argumentation: "a single word or a very short sentence of five or six words," he says. An aphoristic seriality, in short. Now is it not nearly at the same time as he writes this about Cohen in 1918 that Rosenzweig himself, in an eruptive manner, like a series of brief volcanic tremors, writes *The Star of Redemption* on postcards, so it is said, while serving at the front? In any case, the conjunctive-disjunctive texture of this book clearly exhibits this rhythm: lack of transition, continuity and discontinuity, a style which is rather alien to that of the classic presentation of the philosophical system or treatise, an argumentation, a rhetoric and connecting devices unlike those which dominate the history of Western philosophy. This history, this philosophy, these canons, are quite familiar to Rosenzweig. He must have reasoned with them, then broken with them somehow, and not only to the extent of not becoming an academic.

(3) The tribute is not rendered to the writing but to the speech; it is addressed not to an author of books but to a man, a particular existence in which thought and feeling are one. The author left Rosenzweig cold and distrustful, the living speech surprises and excites him. This speech is enchanted as well as enchanting, and the rhythm-inflected motion of the body involves the hands as much as the voice. We know what attention Rosenzweig paid to phonic rhythm, especially Rosenzweig the translator, and not only in translating the Bible.

> By what enchantment was this man's speech inhabited? His speech rather than his writings, which a certain distance tarnished somewhat. His speech gave the impression of a volcano smouldering under a smooth surface; as it would sometimes be weaving its web, placing itself squarely in the rigorous treatment of some problem, while the audience saw the flow of thoughts stream under the powerful brow, Cohen's personality would at a certain moment erupt like lightning, suddenly and without transition, unexpectedly and unpredictably. An attitude struck infrequently, a gesture of the hand—although he spoke with hardly a gesture, in fact it was necessary not to take one's eyes off him—a single word or a very brief sentence of five or six words and the sluggish flow would expand to the dimensions of an overflowing sea, the light of a world brought back to life from the bottom of the human heart would gush out of the web of thought. It is precisely the total immediacy of these eruptions which endowed them with a decisive power. This perfectly spontaneous boiling over of a pathos emerging out of underground sources, the close coexistence of the coldest thought and the most passionate feeling—*surely there is nothing more Jewish than this lack of transition.* In fact this German, this German Jew of such a straight, such a free, such an elevated conscience [or consciousness—tr.], was undoubtedly, in the deepest attachments of his soul, much more Jewish and purely so than all those who today claim with evident nostalgia that they are purely Jewish ("Un hommage"; my italics).

The last paragraph seems rather odd. I would underline its allusion to the system. The encomium emphasizes primarily Cohen's *uniqueness* and *solitariness*: he is *the only one* today, *the only one* of his generation to do this or that, he stands apart from the "crowd" and from "the crowd of his contemporaries."

What is he the only one to do? First, not to dissociate feeling and intellect. Thus he confronts the great problems of concrete humanity, of life and death. But since he never dissociates—*that* is his greatness and his uniqueness—he is the only one to propose a system. What does this mean? To propose a system is not merely to promise one, as has so often been done in the history of philosophy, it is to provide it. Cohen has a system, Rosenzweig seems to say. Not only does he have it, he provides it, he delivers what he promised, what others have promised without keeping their promise, or what others have provided without ever having had it. Cohen provides what he has, he has what he provides, and what he has and provides is the system. The system is his generosity, the sign of an overabundance which did not content itself with promising or having but was able to produce, to provide, in this case to teach.

Now, let us not forget, the author of *The Star of Redemption* directed his entire thought against or rather beyond the system—in any case, against or beyond systemic totality, especially in its Hegelian form. He cannot, therefore, simply praise a thinker for having promised, produced, or provided a system. The system may even well be that which cannot be provided, that which forbids the possibility of a gift, reappropriating it in advance and in a circular manner. The highest praise that he himself can confer, the most generous gift, is to have thought, to have allowed thinking *beyond* the system. Whether it is true or false, this at any rate is what he dedicates to Cohen's memory. But also to the Jew. For in this move beyond the system Rosenzweig believes he can recognize the Jew, someone who is not just the rationalist philosopher, the neo-Kantian of the Jewish religion of the Enlightenment, of the (Jewish) religion within the limits of simple reason, but the man of piety.

> It is precisely there that his scientific personality is rooted and this is what distinguishes him from the crowd of his contemporaries. He was undoubtedly the only one of his generation, and even of the following one, not to have pushed aside with a falsely knowledgeable air the basic questions which humanity has always asked itself and which turn around the problems of life and death, the only one to have not given in to the weakness of wrapping them up in a tangled skein of feelings and intellectualism; on the contrary, he has met them in their fullest extent and true sense. It is therefore impossible that there should have been mere chance in the fact that there too he was *the only one*, among those who during the past few decades continued to accord philosophy a scientific autonomy, *not only to promise a system but really to provide one*. It is precisely the fact that he did not avoid the essential thing which allowed him not to shirk the age-old obligation of the question of totality. He was able from the start, without having learnt it at all, to approach ultimate problems, that which, *beyond the system* led him, finally, during his last theological period, to an immediate confrontation with such questions. It is only then, in this septuagenarian, that the most profoundly child-like characteristic of this great soul made its appearance, "child-like" in the sense of the Marienbad Elegy: "therefore you are all, you are unsurpassable." And in fact, he was basically altogether simple. He was a pious man ("Un hommage", my italics).

This posthumous homage allowed us to glimpse the relation without relation (but in many respects exemplary for what interests us here) that existed between these two German Jews, neither of whom knew Nazism, neither of whom was a

Zionist, but both of whom had undoubtedly so much to tell us, whether they knew it or not, about what was to follow after their death.

II

A few years before his death, in the middle of the war, the man whom Rosenzweig describes as a "child-like septuagenarian" writes a text entitled *Deutschtum und Judentum.*[5] Following its publication in 1915, this essay was reprinted three times within a year. It became a sort of best seller in its class (ten thousand copies) and in 1924, in Berlin, was taken up again, with a preface by Rosenzweig, in volume 2 of the *Jüdische Schriften.* Another text by Cohen bears the same title and takes up the same arguments in a less polemical and a less political manner in 1916. As has often been pointed out, and the fact is well known, the concern with defining the relation between Germanity and Judaism did not originate in this period. An enormous literature, which dealt also with the problems of emancipation, assimilation, conversion, and Zionism, had been devoted to it.

This text has been described as "*maudit*" (this is the word that the French translator, Marc B. de Launay, risks within quotation marks at the outset of his presentation in *Pardes* 5/1987). Professing a sort of German hypernationalism, alleging a Jewish-German symbiosis occasionally defined in terms which collide with common sense, it is addressed primarily to American Jews. Once convinced, American Jews ought to exercise the strongest pressure in order to prevent the United States from entering the war in support of England and especially of France, which, by forming an alliance with tzarist barbarianism, betrayed the ideals of the French Revolution. These ideals would be better represented by Kantianism and by German socialism (and let us not forget that Cohen is socialist). This text may well be "*maudit*"; condemned by Rosenzweig, Scholem, Buber, and many Zionists, it nevertheless does represent, in a form both learned and at times extravagant, well-worked-out, and excessive, something then typical of a certain Jewish-German intelligentsia, that very same class that would end up either in exile (often precisely in America) or in the camps some twenty-five years later (like Hermann's wife, for example, Martha Cohen, who died in Theresienstadt at the age of eighty-two). It is because he represents, in a manner so remarkably worked out, a certain type of militant patriotism in the Jewish-German community, it is also because to this end he mobilizes the Kantian reference, indeed the socialist, national, and neo-Kantian reference, that he seemed to me to deserve a special attention, a strategically moti-

---

5. See Hermann Cohen, *Deutschtum und Judentum* (Giessen, 1915); hereafter cited in text by section number.

vated attention, in our context. At that period, during the First World War and probably the years immediately following it, the militant patriotism of Scheler or Husserl, for instance, belongs, all differences considered, to the same configuration. Such at least is the hypothesis.

This strategy also dictates to us a principle of selective reading in a text which deals with the whole history of the Greek, Jewish, and Christian West, the whole history of philosophy, literature, and the arts, all of Jewish and German culture, politics, law, morality, religion, the categorical imperative and messianism, the State and the nation, the army or school, and university education. By granting a privilege to the Kantian core of this text, we shall radiate around several Kantian or neo-Kantian cells. Neo-Kantianism in this case may mean two things: sometimes Kantianism as adopted and adapted, tailored or appropriated, sometimes a critique of the Kantian critique in Kant's name, Kantianism as a matter of right and inspiration which claims to be opposed to Kantianism of fact or to go beyond it. Kant against Kant, or Kant without Kant.

Let us go directly, by way of a beginning, to the clearest proposition, the firmest and, for us, the most interesting one: the close, deep internal kinship (*die innerste Verwandschaft*) between Judaism and Kantianism. That is to say also between Judaism and the historical culmination (*geschichtliche Höhepunkt*) of idealism as the essence of German philosophy, namely the Kantian moment, the *inner sanctum* (*innerste Heiligtum*) which Kantianism is, with its fundamental concepts (the autonomy of universal law, liberty, and duty). It is that same Kant of whom Adorno will say, in "Replying to the Question: Who is German?" that he is the best "witness" of the German tradition or the German mind.[6] How then is this proposition maintained (especially §§ 6 to 12)? What placing-in-perspective, in other words, what historical contextualization is it which claims to justify such an interpretation?

It is first of all, within a comparative logic which has its own history and its own institutions, the argument of the *tertium comparationis*. In hazarding a comparison (*Vergleichung*) between different peoples or the spirit of different peoples (*Volkgeister*), one must avoid error and provide a legitimation for such a science of the spirit (*Geisteswissenschaft*). To this end one must make sure that the two terms had entertained an intimate relation, an intrinsic alliance (*innerliche Verbindung*) with a third term (*tertium comparationis*). The third term, in this case, is nothing other than Hellenism most particularly Greek philosophy. Both Jewish and German idiosyncrasies have had fruitful, internal relations with Greek philosophy. Far from

---

6. Theodor W. Adorno, "Réponse à la question: qu'est-ce qui est allemand?" (Replying to the Question: Who Is German?), in his *Modèles critiques*, French translation by Marc Jimenez and Elaine Kaufholz (Paris: Payot, 1984), p. 221; *Modèles critiques* is a translation of *Eingriffe: neun Kritische Modelle* (Frankfurt am Main: Suhrkamp, 1963) and *Stichworte: Kritische Modelle 2* (Frankfurt am Main, 1969).

being placed in opposition to the Jewish, according to an old habit, the Greek is interpreted rather as consubstantial with the Jewish idiom, which presumably received from the Greek a new force and a new imprint (*Aufprägung*). This is not merely a relation of mixture, identity, or reciprocity (the "Jewgreek is Greekjew" in *Ulysses*). Cohen invokes here the great figure of Philo Judaeus. The exile of Judaism to Alexandria brought the destiny of Israel up to a worldwide level. It universalized it, cosmopolitanized it somehow in its world mission (*Weltmission*) without putting its foundations in question. This cosmopolitical moment has become essential to Judaism. Philo is supposed to have been Plato's Jewish heir who, through the logos, the new "holy spirit" (*heilige Geist*), paved the way for Christianity. The logos, which in effect acts as a mediator in Philo's philosophy, becomes the mediator (*Mittler*) between God and man, between God and the world. Undoubtedly Philo is not Jewish insofar as he is a Platonist. But this disciple of Plato's (and discipline here has an institutional character) dominates a Judeo-Alexandrian current which reconciles Hellenism and Judaism through the mediation of the logos and the holy spirit. This influence was not only speculative but also institutional. It marked the entire social life of the Jews. With respect to Alexandrian Judaism, Philo is supposed to have been not just a member, much less a "mentor" (as de Launay, reluctant to overburden the text, translates it with discretion), but a *"Mitglieder"*—a member in effect, and espe-cially a *Führer*—a guide and a leader. To translate *Führer* as "mentor" is to wish to spare this German hypernationalist text a disturbing connotation (might the Jews, too, have a *Führer*?), but it is also to neglect that which can be so current in the use of the word *Führer* in the German language.

The Neoplatonic logos then puts the seal on the Judeo-Hellenic alliance. It is also that without which the Church, the institution of Christianity, if not Christi-anity itself, is unthinkable. Now, by the same stroke, within the element of the logos and of Christianity, Greece becomes the fundamental source (*Grundquelle*) of Germanity. Whether they know it or not, willy-nilly, the Germans are Jews. At any rate it would be impossible to uproot Judaism from their genealogy. Whatever the violence or the artificiality of the syllogism, it would tend to whisper the following, which Cohen evidently does not say, at least not in these terms: there is in the German unconscious, that is to say deep inside the German spirit, a proposition which cannot be uprooted, destroyed, or denied, a German *cogito*—"ergo sumus all German Jews." Cohen, for his part, assumes quite literally the middle term of the syllogism, the Christian logos which will serve as mediator between Judaism and Germanity, between the Jewish spirit and the German spirit.

This, once again, may be conscious or unconscious. This hypothesis of uncon-sciousness—which we would need in order to evoke a psyche that surely must have worked, to the point of genocide, as an ultimate murderous denial of origin, of resemblance and of a dark history of a crucified father or mediator—one cannot say that it is excluded by Cohen, even though he does not use the word "unconscious." This word matters little here, since Cohen refers to a fundamental historical force (*Grundkraft*) which can never "run out or dry up" and to something which "never ceases to keep alive the original force by which it is imbued throughout the history of a nation." It is, says Cohen in fact, "what must have repeatedly occurred (*ereignen*) within the relation between Germanity and Judaism, even if this relation was mediated by Christianity *at the turning points which profoundly marked the history of the German spirit.*" Cohen underlines this last part of the sentence: "*an inneren Wendepunkten in der Geschichte des deutschen Geistes ereignen*" (§2). A strong sentence and an odd one: it says that there is a German spirit, that this spirit has or is a history marked by events, decisive events, which constitute turns or turning points. At each turning point, each curve, each turn or bent of the German mind, an originary "force," namely the Jewish genealogy or lineage, must have played a marking role. The German comes to terms (*auseinandersetzt*) with the Jew at each decisive turn of his history, in history as history of the spirit, and, in an exemplary manner, as history of the German spirit. In coming to terms with the Jew, the German comes to terms with himself since he carries and reflects Judaism within himself: not in his blood but in his soul. Or in his spirit. Not in his blood, for this genealogy is not a natural but an institutional, cultural, spiritual, and psychic one. Assuming that in this argumentation race may be reduced to biologico-naturalist schemas (let us keep in mind Rosenzweig's enigmatic thought of the blood), the question of racism is neither raised nor undoubtedly necessary. On the other hand, at least in this moment of the syllogism, Cohen seems already to appeal to a theory of the Jewish-German psyche: psyche, because the genealogy which somehow twins the Jew and the German, culminating in Kant, is not at all a natural, physical, genetic genealogy. Rather it comes down by way of the association of the religious and the philosophical, by way of that interlingual contract which consigns the Judeo-Hellenic heritage in line with the essential mediation of the logos to the form of an absolute logocentrism. What is in question is indeed a psyche, since that association is not natural but rather sealed within the whole semantic family of the logos: reason, discourse or speech, gathering, and so forth. Furthermore, it is indeed a psyche which is in question, not only a mirror, but a soul which holds the spirit, the holy spirit, without necessarily implying consciousness or representative knowledge. Cohen speaks of a force which acts at the great turning points of the history of the German spirit, but a force of which the Jewish or German "subjects" need not be conscious. Hence the need for a pedagogy, for a didactic analysis concerning that which alternates between sleeping and walking in that logocentered psyche.

We have barely begun our reading of this strange text. We have at least the sense of a text worked through by intuitions or by symptoms, by sensitivity to decisive symptoms later rationalized, interpreted often forcibly, artificially, in a naively ingenious manner, but then still according to schemas or gestures whose extravagance, indeed delirium, may well be saying something quite essential. One question might then be the following: in order to render an account (*logon didonai*, a Greek and Platonic formula invoked by Cohen on the next page) of the Jewish-German phenomenon (and who will deny the existence of such a "phenomenon?") in its often delirious forms, is it possible not to involve logic, the logos, in this delirium? Can one dispense with entering into it in order to give an account of it? How to avoid sliding into this psyche and its phantasy life in trying to explain, describe and speak of it? Is not *everything* artificial or in any case non-natural in what we are here calling psyche?

Let us try to make this series of questions more accessible by way of two distinct propositions pertaining to two different levels.

First Proposition

Perhaps it is unimportant to decide whether Cohen takes his story seriously or not, whether he believes in it or not. Undoubtedly he did seriously believe in it, but the question, precisely, is perhaps not there, as long as it remains concerned with the trivial determination of what such belief of such seriousness can be. If one were to prove to Cohen that all this is delirious, he might always say: but, after all, who told you that this was the "objective" truth and that I believe in it as in something objectifiable? I explain the German spirit, within the Jewish-German psyche which constitutes it. If, with the entire Judeo-Graeco-Christian underpinning which structures it, this psyche looks delirious to you, if it gives rise to some delirium, to all types of violence, to the highs (*Höhepunkten*) and the lows, the depressions, the crises, the historical turning points, the expulsions, the murders or the suicides, the reappropriations by emancipation or by genocide, well then, I am just telling you what this thing you call delirium is made of. And my discourse must appear delirious because it reflects a psyche which is itself a reflexive delirium. Whether I, a German Jew, believe in it or not, is an uninteresting or an irrelevant question. Whether or not my discourse is implicated in its object, that is a (positive or negative) sign which makes no difference for the interest of its content. Since we are dealing with something like the German spirit or the Judeo-Graeco-Christian psyche, we are not here involved in a plain instance of the scientific "subject-object" relation, as if my own discourse (which is also a discourse on the origin of the value of objectivity and a history of reason) ought to submit to the requirements of objectivity. You have the right to consider my discourse as a symptom of the madness it describes—this makes no difference for its value, its relevance as a *true symp-*

tom in some sense. If it is a symptom of what it describes, it is perhaps all the more revealing of the unconscious truth of which it speaks or—and this amounts to the same thing—which speaks through it. In this region, the symptom is knowledge, knowledge is a symptom. Between the two there would no longer be a borderline such as a particular rationalism—objectivistic, positivistic, or scientific—would like to impose, with as much artificiality as violence. And the artificiality of this violence cannot come about except through institutions. There is nothing natural in it, by definition. This kind of rationalism has no understanding of the spirit or the psyche; it does not see that they cannot be made into an object. The object itself is caught in a structure of interpretation and institution, of "artificial" reflection, what we also call a psyche. Most notably, this form of rationalism (which we shall not confuse with reason itself or reason in general and will nonetheless interpret in the name of a certain reason, by no means in favor of some irrationalism) is amnesia itself, with regard to its own genealogy, that very same genealogy, Cohen might say, that we are describing here: all of philosophy, reason or the logos in its demand for rendering an account (*logon didonai*), indeed the principle of reason itself. Far from possibly becoming, Cohen might say further, the object of rational knowledge as a symptom of an alleged delirium, it is my discourse that renders an account of so-called objective knowledge. That is why a symptom may be true, true of a truth which it says and which is no longer of the order of positive objectivity. A little further on, in an even more hallucinated or hallucinating moment of his interpretation, Cohen writes: "Maimonides is, within Medieval Judaism, the symptom of Protestantism (§9). The word translated as "symptom" is precisely *Wahrzeichen.*

Second Proposition

This region, in which the symptom has a chance of being truth, of speaking as the truth, is not one we can consider as merely a region among others. It is the one I am talking about, Cohen might say, and properly speaking, both for me and for those to whom I address myself, it is not a region. It is nothing less than the logos, that which is in the beginning and which holds together speech and reason. The logos speaks *of and by itself* [*de lui-même*]. *By itself,* that is to say spontaneously, on its own account, as a principle, for one need not render an account of that which is a principle and answers for itself. Of itself, for through my mouth, the logos truly speaks of the logos, of itself. Any claim to objective knowledge that one might wish to place in opposition to it is still nothing but a "logical" manifestation of it.

This "logic," then, remains rather strong. For it is less a "logic" than the ambition to talk about logic, to say the truth about the origin of logic, namely the logos. There is perhaps a "meta-logic," there is no meta-logos.

III

We have deliberately stuck to the initial *syllogism* of this discourse. It is indeed a sort of syllogism: being by [*auprès de*] itself, the being with (*syn*) itself of the logos which gathers and gathers itself [*rassemble et se rassemble*] in order to speak of itself. The originary syllogism of the logos itself when it produces its own logic. How and through what mediations can this originary syllogism lead one to conclude of the greatness of the German army, the necessity of mandatory military service, the duty of the Jews throughout the world to recognize Germany as their real homeland [*patrie*] and to prevent America from allying itself with England, with Russia, and with France, which betrayed its own revolution? We are only at the beginning and we begin, as is befitting, by the logos. But before going any further, and in order to understand the necessity of going further, we must perhaps worry ourselves with what, at first glance, looks like a sort of flaw in this deduction of the Judeo-German psyche. If the starting point for its constitution is the Greek logos, if the logos is its principal mediator allied with both Alexandrian Judaism and Christianity, a Christianity that has as much need of the Greek as of the Jew, then where has the German gone in all this story? How goes it with the German? Does he add anything essential to this plot? With this kind of logic, why not talk of the *same* psyche wherever Hellenism, Judaism, and Christianity existed? Given the wealth of that culture, but also the instances of historical violence to which it gave rise, why not be interested in a Judeo-Spanish psyche? Why not accord it a decisive role in the history of the West? I am not even speaking of a Jewish-Arab psyche, which seems to be excluded from the very principle of this powerful fable.

Although Cohen does not ask this essential question as such and in these terms, one can say that his argumentation does implicitly take it on. The point is to prove that not only is the German moment of this syllogism essential and necessary, but that there is no other Judeo-X psyche (Spanish, Italian, French—still less Arab, that is, non-Christian) which measures up to this syllogism. Briefly, there can be no Judeo-Moslem or Judeo-Catholic (Spanish, French, or Italian) psyche. The psyche we are talking about is not even Judeo-Christian in general; it is strictly Judeo-Protestant—that is to say, thanks to Luther, Judeo-German.

This, for at least two reasons.

The first is easy to formulate; it concerns a German tradition which survives as far as Heidegger: the German holds an absolutely privileged relation to the Greek—descent, *mimesis*, and rivalry with all the consequent paradoxes. I have tried to approach one of these paradoxes in my reading of Heidegger.[7] No other

---

7. See Jacques Derrida, *De l'esprit. Heidegger et la question* (Paris: Galilée, 1987).

European people is supposed to share this competitive affinity with Greece. If the Greek tradition is safeguarded in a privileged manner within German culture and more specifically within German philosophy, then the syllogism implies the German spirit. Cohen emphasizes this already at the end of the first paragraph: "Now, as Christianity is unthinkable without the logos, Hellenism is one of its sources. *But thus, and with equal impact, Hellenism appears as one of the fundamental sources* (Grundquelle*) of Germanity.*"

The second reason concerns the deep and specific mainspring of this text, its rhetoric, the mechanics of proof and persuasion that happens to be at work in it, the one we are analyzing here while emphasizing the privileged reference to Kant. What happens to be at stake is nothing less than an interpretation of the sense of being. At a level and in a style that are not Heidegger's—far from it—but that could call for some cautious analogies, Cohen intends an answer to the question of being. He, too (for the same may be said of Heidegger), does so through an interpretation of Platonism, an interpretation of the instituted interpretations of Platonism, of the Platonic logos, *eidos*, and especially the *hypotheton*. This history of the interpretations gives a double privilege to the German spirit in its process of becoming, in the concatenation of its spiritual events, both philosophical and religious. It is on the one hand the privilege of German idealism, as a philosophy or, rather, as a moral consciousness of philosophy and science. It constitutes the ideal interpretation of Platonic idealism. It is on the other hand, and primarily, the Lutheran Reformation. The latter must be recognized as the religious form of the rationality that opposes the logos, the *eidos* and especially the hypothesis to the dogma of ecclesiastical institution. One could consider the Reformation from this point of view as a critique of instituted truth, of the institutional dogmatism which freezes the interpretation of Scripture. This critique, in turn, can only, inevitably, give rise to institutions, and we could follow the progress of the Protestant motif in several modern hermeneutics. But this German Reformation would then be side by side with, on the side of, the *Aufklärung*—not opposite it. The French Lumières, which ought to be distinguished from the *Aufklärung* in this respect, were not able to oppose the Catholic Church. In allying itself with critical science, with the hypothesis, with doubt, with the history of knowledge, with the putting-in-question of institutional authorities, and so on. "The Reformation placed the German spirit at the center of world history" (*Mit der Reformation tritt der deutsche Geist in den Mittelpunkt der Weltgeschichte*) (§7).

How does Cohen intend to prove this? The comparative method, when it comes to determining national spirits, appeals not only to the *tertium comparationis*. It is necessary for it to be interested also in the essential depth of each national spirit (*Nationalgeist*), beyond extrinsic properties such as its political, social, moral determinations (in the sense of "mores": *sittliche Eigenschaften*), which are extrinsic properties. This depth manifests itself in spiritual culture: religion, art, philosophy. Pure science—for example, mathematics—is excluded from it since it is universal by essence. The reciprocal "influence" (*Einwirkung*) and "interaction" (*Wechselwirkung*) between Judaism and Germanity will be analyzed in the element of this spiritual culture. Cohen begins neither by religion nor by art but by philosophy, which is "scientifically the most graspable" (*wissenschaftlich fassbarsten*). The question "Was ist deutsch?" which runs from Wagner to Nietszche, Adorno, and so on, amounts here essentially to the question "What is German philosophy?" The simple, straightforward, unequivocal answer: the essence of German philosophy is idealism. "Was bedeutet aber Idealismus?" (But what does idealism mean?) The answer, as one may suspect, is more complicated than the question. It is this answer which assumes a historical displacement within what can safely be called an institution of interpretation, namely the dominant interpretation of Platonism. Idealism is no mere theory of ideas in contrast with the sensible or with matter, it is not an antisensualism or antimaterialism. Despite his maturity and his didactic precision, Plato did not determine the idea (*eidos*) with complete clarity. If he asked the question of Being, of substance, of the eternal being [*l'étant éternel*], he used terms among which privilege was mistakenly given to those that referred to vision (*Schauen*) or to intuition (*Anschauung*) in accordance with the etymology of the word *eidos*. The most fundamental determination, however, one which is to be found in Plato but has nevertheless been covered up and neglected throughout the renewals of Neoplatonism and the Renaissance, the one which founded idealism as a scientific project and a method, is the *hypothesis*, the concept of hypothesis. Without expanding on Plato's complicated discourse on the subject of the hypothesis and the anhypothetic, Cohen assumes rather bluntly the hypothesis, precisely, of an affiliation between the Platonic concept of the hypothesis and Kepler's astronomy or physics. Through Kepler, after him, German thought is supposed to have given the authentically scientific idealism (which Platonism had not yet been) its full effectiveness.

The property of the German spirit plays itself in the interpretation of the sense of Being *or* the sense of the Idea. Heidegger linked (for example in his *Nietzsche*) the destiny of the German people also to the answerability [*responsabilité*] of this type of question. But one of the many radical differences between Cohen and Heidegger (his successor, let us not forget, in that institution, the University of Marburg), is that in the eyes of the former, *the interpretation of the Idea as Being is not German*, it is less German in any case than the interpretation of the Idea as hypothesis. This latter interpretation would be more "critical," it would suspend the naive ontology of the Idea in favor of its methodologico-scientific interpretation. For philosophical (that is, German) idealism must be a project of scientific philosophy: not science itself but philosophy as scientific (*wissenschaftlich*). Such is the answer to the question: "What meaning (*welche Bedeutung*) does it have for the characterization of the German spirit that the Idea should be known only as Being or as hypothesis?"

It is a subtle wrinkle. What is German is not science or the hypothesis. These, as we have seen, are universal. But the inaugural philosophical interpretation, the determination of the Idea as hypothesis, opening the problematic of scientific knowledge, *that* is supposed to be Platonico-German; *that* is the historical event which properly institutes and constitutes the German spirit in its exemplary mission, hence in its responsibility. If, as Cohen recognizes, science in its methodic hypothetic procedures is universal, if it is the "condition of all natural thought in human life, as in the historical conduct of peoples" (§5), the property of the German spirit and of philosophical idealism, which it has somehow marked, is to have *borne within itself* this universal possibility, to have made it come about by testifying for it. Here again lies its exemplarity.

> It is thanks to this concept [the Platonic concept of the hypothesis] that Kepler developed his astronomy and his mechanics . . . it is through Kepler that German thought was able to make out of the authentically scientific *idealism*, founded upon the Idea as hypothesis, the moving force of science. . . . The sense of this introduction, which sets off from the hypothesis, will become clear later. Being is not grasped as an immediate datum—a prejudice on which sensualism is founded—but it is thought as a universal project, as a problem that scientific research must solve and whose reality it must prove. As a hypothesis, the idea is then by no means the solution of the problem, but only the exact definition of the problem itself. (§4)

What we have here, then, under the name of hypothesis, is indeed a determination of the idea as an opening to the infinite, an infinite task for "philosophy as a rigorous science" (this had already been for years the title of a famous text by Husserl) or else, Idea in the Kantian sense, an expression which was to guide Husserl too in diagnosing the crisis of European sciences and in defining the infinite task, but also in several other contexts, the most "teleologist" of his discourses.

> Consequently, nor is it true *a priori* and in itself, still less is it the final truth; on the contrary, it must undergo the test of its own truth to be decided by this test alone.
>
> That is why, in order to designate this method of the idea, Plato used another expression: that of rendering account (*Rechenschaftsablegung*) (*logon didonai*).

The idea (*idea*) is so far from being synonymous with the concept (*eidos* = *logos*) that it is only thanks to it and to the account it renders that the concept (*logos*) itself may be verified.

One understands now what depth this truly authentic interpretation of idealism reveals and guarantees to the deontological consciousness of scientific thought.... This procedure is the prejudicial condition of any authentic science and, therefore, of any philosophy, any scientific fecundity; but for all that, it is no less the condition of any natural thought in life in general, as in the historical conduct of peoples.

§6. This sober lucidity is the deep, true meaning of German idealism, which has always been the mark both of its science and its philosophy in their classic productions. From this fundamental feature of the scientific spirit we must now draw conclusions—by showing the validity of such a generalization—for the historical conduct as a whole and, more particularly, for the political conduct of the German people.

This movement leads, then, to Kant. Who is Kant? He is the holiest saint of the German spirit, the deepest, innermost inner sanctum of the German spirit (*in diesem innersten Heiligtum des deutsches Geistes*), but he is also the one who represents the innermost affinity (*die innerste Verwandschaft*) with Judaism. This kinship is sealed in the most intimate depth and the most essential interiority. This seal is sacred, sacredness itself, the historical sacredness of the spirit. But if it is necessary here to insist on "*die innerste*," the innermost and most intimate, it is precisely because underlying this sacred alliance is interiority itself. This alliance is not simply internal like the spirit, it is concluded in the name of moral consciousness (*Gewissen*) as absolute interiority. It was surely made possible by the Greek third term or by the logocentered triangle of Graeco-Judeo-Christianity; but it is at the moment of the Reformation that this Judeo-German kinship is born in being reborn [*en renaissant*]. It then experiences one of its many births, which, like German idealism, scan this teleological process, from Kepler to Nicholas of Cusa to Leibniz and finally to Kant. The Reformation, something irreducibly German in Cohen's eyes, places the German spirit "at the center of world history" (*in den Mittelpunkt der Weltgeschichte*). A rather indisputable proposition, if we accept a certain number of protocols, but one I shall not analyze here. In its spirit, this Reformation is presumably at bottom the faithful heiress of Platonic hypotheticism: respect for the hypothesis, cult of the doubt, suspicion towards dogma (and if you prefer also towards *doxa*) and towards institutions based on dogma, a culture of interpretation but of a *free* interpretation, one which, in its spirit, at least, tends to liberate itself from any institutional authority. The Reformation wants to render an account and justify (*logon didonai*). It holds nothing as established, it submits everything to an examination. To render an account of and to justify, the rendering of reason (*Rechenschaft*) and justification, this is the slogan (*Schlagwort*) of the Reformation. It is the exercise of the logos, of the *logon didonai*, or, in Latin, of the *ratio*, the *rationem reddere*. We might confront this schema with Heidegger's schema concerning a Principle of Reason which, after a period of incubation, finds the event of its formulation with Leibniz in order to dominate later on all of modernity. It so happens that Heidegger's text (*Der Satz vom Grund*) is also, among other things, a meditation on the institution of the modern university within the tenure [*mouvance*] of the Principle of Reason.

What does Cohen say when he names the event of Protestantism? He speaks cautiously of the "historical spirit of Protestantism" (*der geschichtliche Geist des Protestantismus*). This spirit is not to be confused with the empirical history of factual events; it is a current, a force, a telos. It is so strong, internal, and undeniable that even the non-Protestants, the Catholics and the Jews, must recognize it. It is as if Cohen were saying to the latter: become Protestant enough to recognize, beyond the institutional dogma, scientifically, rationally, philosophically, by consulting nothing but your conscience, the very essence of Protestantism, of this Protestant spirit that you have already become. The hidden axiom of this provocation is not only the paradox of some logico-speculative perversity. It is also like a grand maneuver: that of philosophy, of the conversion to Protestantism, of conversion in general. If you recognize that Protestantism is basically the truth, the very demand for truth beyond instituted dogma, the demand for knowledge and freedom of interpretation without institution, then you are already Protestant in submitting to this demand for truth; you are such whatever the religious and dogmatic institution to which you think you otherwise belong. It is because you were *already* Protestant (and this temporal modality is the entire question of truth) that you converted. And you converted secretly, even if ostensibly, dogmatically, institutionally, you are Catholic, Jewish, Moslem, Buddhist, or even atheist. Likewise, you are Kantian but also Jewish, Jewish and German, the Jew himself being, as we shall verify, a Protestant and the Protestant a Platonic Jew, if only you are a philosopher and have within you, conscientiously [*en conscience*], the demand for hypothesis for truth, for science.

Before proceeding further, let us try to formalize one of the laws of this "logic," such logic as is at work in Cohen's interpretation. Cohen analyzes not only alliances, genealogies, marriages, spiritual minglings of blood, graftings, cuttings, derivations. He does not analyze some chemico-spiritual composition of the German, the Jew, or the Christian. No, he has a thesis, which is also a hypothesis, an underlying and a substantial thesis, the hypothesis of any possible thesis on the subject of any spiritual genealogy of peoples, of any possible alliance among the spirits of peoples. What is this absolute hypothesis, which may ultimately resemble Cohen's anhypothetic, all the more so as it involves morality and the Good, that is to say the *agathon* where Plato located the anhypothetic? It is that the general possibility of spiritual kinships, of this general *economy* of the spirit, hence of spiritual families (*oikonomia* here names the law, the law of the family *oikos* as the *law*, period), the possibility of this genealogy *without limit* does not merely find an example or an application in the Judeo-German or rather in the Judeo-Protestant case. Judeo-Protestant Platonism or logocentrism is the very event which makes possible this general economy, this spiritual hybridization as world genealogy. I say, indeed, world *logocentrism*. "Logocentrism" is not Cohen's word, but I believe I have justified its use. "World" because spiritual worldwideness [*mondialisation*] is supposed to have its origin in this Judeo-Protestant psyche which, in the name of the logos, of the spirit, of philosophy as idealism, hence of knowledge and scientificity, as moral "consciousness of philosophy and science" (*Gewissen der Philosophie und der Wissenschaft*), would have become the "center of the world."

The abstract form of these propositions should not mislead us. This is an economic formalization, of course, and Cohen's language, too, is a composite one: extremely concrete notations together with the boldest metaphysical shortcuts. But some may be tempted, like myself, to translate or theatricalize these theorems.

This might perhaps produce the following scenario, and some would say: "Indeed yes, this is what is going on: if . . . the process of things becoming worldwide [*mondialisation*], if . . . the homogenization of planetary culture involves techno-science, rationality, the principle of reason (and who can seriously deny this?), if the great family of anthropos is being gathered together thanks to this general hybridization—through the greatest instances of violence, no doubt, but irresistibly—and if it becomes unified and begins to gather itself and gather not as a genetic family but as a 'spiritual' family, trusting in this set called science and the discourse of human rights, in the unity of techno-science and the ethico-juridico-political discourse of human rights, namely in its common, official, and dominant axiomatic, . . . then humanity does indeed unify itself around a Platonico-Judeo-Protestant axis (and the Catholics are already Protestant, as we have seen, just like the Jews: they are all Neoplatonic Kantians). The Platonico-Judeo-Protestant axis is also the one around which revolves the Jewish-German psyche, heir, guardian, and responsible for the Platonic hypothesis, itself relayed by the principle of reason. This unification of *anthropos* in fact involves what is called European culture—now represented, in its indivisible unity, by the economic-technical-scientific-military power of the United States. Now if one considers the United States to be a society essentially dominated, in its spirit, by Judeo-Protestantism, not to mention even an American-Israeli axis, then—one might go on within the same hypothesis— Cohen's hypothesis concerning the Platonic hypothesis and its lineage would not seem quite so mad. If it is mad, this is because it translates the 'real' madness, the truth of real madness, this logocentric psychosis which presumably got hold of humanity over twenty-five centuries ago, confusing or articulating science, technique, philosophy, religion, art, and politics all together within the same set [*ensemble*]." End of fable—or truth of the truth.

But from what external location can one claim to pronounce upon this truth of the truth? This logocentrico-Judeo-Protestant truth? Here is the entire question of what some people call deconstruction: a seism which *happens* to this truth, without one being able truly to decide if it comes from inside or from outside, if it is happening now or has always been happening, or in what sense and to what extent the label "deconstruction in America," currently so widespread, is a fable, a rhetorical convenience, a metonymy, or an allegory. Is not history, in its hardest reality, its most murderous aspect, also made of these displacements of figures?

It is clear what additional [*supplémentaire*] reason I had for putting an allusion to the United States of America into the mouth of my imaginary interlocutor, this man both so sensible and so mad, this man without place who still inhabits, and already does so no longer, neither the old world nor the new world. This is because the hypothesis about hypothesis, Cohen's anhypothetical hypothesis, is surely addressed, as an open letter, to all of mankind—and it is as such that it reaches us now, right here (and what is our here-and-now made of? How could we keep it in parentheses?). But the anhypothetical hypothesis was first meant for America, for the American Jews at a certain precise moment, during a real war inside Europe, but only a possible one between Germany and the United States. Cohen wants to prevent this war. He wants to intervene in order to avert the confrontation between two brothers, in any case two members of the great Judeo-Protestant family. He has even two other hypotheses on this subject, perhaps a hypothesis and a certainty, perhaps even two certainties: (1) If the United States enters the war, Germany will lose (and indeed this is what has happened twice). (2) Pressure exercised by the American Jews can determine the American decision: they are powerful in the United States and their link to Judaism is still very strong. It all seems as though the First so-called World War up until 1917, then the Second so-called World War up until 1941, so long as the United States did not take part in them, remained secondary, local wars. Why is that? Not for quantitative or geographical reasons, but because they had not yet split up the spiritual world; they had not yet pitted one against the other the two great sons or brothers of the family, the two major members of the great Judeo-Protestant body in the world, the two lobes of the Jewish-German psyche or of its powerful Judeo-Americano-German prosthesis. This psyche, as psyche has always done, guards the spirit. When it breaks between the United States and Germany, this war will be an enormous family feud, a dissension, a war of secession: not between *two* opposite blocks, X versus X, nor between Jews and Protestants, but between Judeo-Protestants and Judeo-Protestants. Cohen's rhetoric is being raised like a white flag: stop this fratricidal war. Would this Jewish, socialist, German, pacifist, nationalist, internationalist, and neo-Kantian philosopher have said that the Second World War brought about what he had feared, what already happened just before his death in 1917, namely *a war within the spirit*? Within the spirit as the spirit of philosophy, consciousness and conscience of science, the Judeo-Protestant logos under the charge of the Jewish-German psyche?

We have spoken of the soul or psyche. We have spoken of the spirit—the German spirit, the holy spirit, the spirit of Judaism. But we have only alluded to consciousness, precisely to *Gewissen*, that conscience which is supposed to situate, in history, the becoming-German of philosophy. As the authentic, full-fledged form of Platonic idealism, German idealism arises, in sum, with Protestantism, namely in the tendency to recognize no authority other than the authority of *Gewissen*.

On the one hand, idealism is the conscience, the *Gewissen* of philosophy and science. On the other hand, Protestantism commands us to put no trust either in the Church itself and its works, that is, in the institution, or in its priests, but "only in conscience's own labor" (*allein die eigene Arbeit des Gewissens*).

But to put one's trust in the incessant "labor" of conscience only is in the view of "religious thought" (*das religiose Denken*) a double, equivocal gesture. And this partly explains how the German Reformation could have been at the source of an *Aufklärung* which, in contrast to the French *Lumières* and *Encyclopaedia*, does not go against faith. This is because the labor of conscience at one and the same time frees and encumbers religious thought. Liberation and overburdening at one and the same time. *Befreien* and *Belasten*, because in delivering it from dogmatico-ecclesiastical authority and the external weight of the institution, it charges conscience with taking upon its own self, all alone, a purely internal responsibility. It must *institute* itself, stand up and hold itself up all by itself, assume a faith offered to the blows and objections of knowledge [*la connaissance*]. Faith is like an auto-instituting decision whose authenticity seeks no external guarantee, at least not in institutions of this world. Whence the double sense (*Doppelsinn*) of this faith (*Glaube*) to which Luther appeals against the Church: an anti-institutional and an archi-institutional faith. Let us not forget, by the way, the enormous respect Luther has always inspired among the Jewish German intelligentsia. Rosenzweig and Buber, for example, when it comes to translating the Bible from Hebrew into German, consider Luther as the great ancestor, the formidable rival, the unequaled master. Rosenzweig speaks of him at times in a tone of crushed fervor.

In its double sense, such a faith constitutes idealism precisely insofar as it is opposed to the instituted data of the Church. But the Church will be reluctant to part with the force of idealism. Thus, at least as a polemical pretext, it too internalizes that which contests it, both from without and from within, from an outside which precisely claims the authority of the inside, of the most intimate *Gewissen*. After having up to a certain point consecrated the Reformation, the Church assigns itself a duty (*Pflicht*) of justification (*Rechtfertigung*, which refers back to *logon didonai*). This duty of justification is the only source of bliss, of salvation (*Seligkeit*). It confers on religion a new authenticity, a new truth, a new truthful truth, a truthfulness (*Wahrhaftigkeit*). This is a historical event, since this truthfulness or this authenticity is new. Such an event institutes a new relation of religion to truth as truthfulness, as authenticity rather than as truth of correspondence in the sense of science or of objective knowledge. This instituting event, whose reach cannot be overestimated, makes faith (*Glauben*) come alive to its authenticity. By the same token, it assigns a "new destination" (*eine neue Bestimmung*) to the German spirit.

The concept of *Wahrhaftigkeit* is clearly an ambiguous one. It signals simultaneously both towards the true and towards the truthful, both towards the truth of knowledge [*connaissance*] and towards the authenticity of a certain existence, here existence in a state of faith. The Reformation exposes the quick, it vivifies in modern man (and in sum Cohen raises the question of modernity, it may even be said that he claims to define the advent of Modern Times [*Temps Modernes*]) two types of certainty (*Gewissheit*). (Let us not forget that for Heidegger, who would rather tend to suspect it, the value of certainty, which he associates rather with the idealism of the Cartesian *cogito*, also marks the advent of a certain modernity.) It is better to retain here the German word *Gewissheit*. Unlike "certainty" [*certitude*], it maintains a certain communication between knowledge (*Wissen*), science (*Wissenschaft*), conscience (*Gewissen*), self-consciousness (*Selbst-bewusstsein*) and certainty (*Gewissheit*). There is the *Gewissheit*, the certainty of scientific knowledge, and there is the *Gewissheit* in the realm of faith. As soon as the questions of faith are no longer exposed to skepticism, as they might have been when only the dogmatism of the ecclesiastical institution guaranteed them, they are gathered together and held fast (*zusammengefasst und festgehalten*) within a doctrine of morality, as that very doctrine (*als Lehre der Sittlichkeit*). Henceforth morality stands on the side of religion, side by side with it, flush with religion, inseparable from a sort of "religion within the limits of simple reason," as Kant the *Aufklärer* might say. Morality is no longer the rival but the ally of religion. Religion is no longer the "wretch" that the French *Lumières* (still too Catholic because anti-Catholic, and I can add: too French in 1915!), with Voltaire, wished to get rid of. The ideal of Protestantism structures and founds the cultural and scientific consciousness of the modern nations on these two types of *Gewissheit*. Consequently, the development of ethics, like that of religion, becomes conditioned by this idealism of modern culture. Without it there is no rectitude or justice (*Aufrichtigkeit*), no honesty, no personal conscience for the man of modernity.

What becomes of Judaism in all this?

If it is not prepared in a scientific manner, if it does not stem from positive science itself, idealism tends naturally toward philosophical speculation. That is to say also toward ontology and the thought of being itself. Now Judaism begins by the self-presentation of God in the burning bush. God said: "*Ich bin der Ich bin.*" In translating the Hebrew formula into German, Cohen notes that the tense of the original version is marked by the future. God names him*self*, he calls himself *being*. But he calls himself (into) being in the future, a future which is not simply the modification of a present, just another present yet to come. And this being yet to come is unique. Cohen goes on to translate the "*Ich bin der Ich bin*" without any further precaution, into the Platonic idiom: God is being, he alone; there is no being beside him; any other being, "as Plato would say (*wie Platon sagen würde*) is but pure appearance; a mere phenomenon (*Erscheinung*)." God is being; it is in him that the world and humanity have their foundation, that which guards and maintains them. Judaism would thus merge with Platonism, Yahweh with the *agathon* or the *anhypotheton*. Like the Good, God escapes any image, any comparison, any perception. He remains unrepresentable. The purely intuitive thought relating to him is not a thought of knowledge (*Denken der Wissenschaft*), but a thought of love (*Denken der Liebe*): "The knowledge of God is love," says Cohen. Love is presumably the authentic word for faith in reformed biblical language. This is the Greco-Platonic Eros, at the source of knowledge and of the aesthetic sense. This is also the vocabulary of so many Christian texts, primarily evangelical ones.

Hence the initial kinship of Judaism with Idealism. This kinship is explored and developed, from Philo to the twelfth century with Maimonides, the source of the great scholastics, of Nicholas of Cusa in his doctrine of divine attributes and of Leibniz, who also quotes him when he speaks of the divine being. Hence this odd formula: Maimonides is the "symptom" (the revealing sign, the mark, *Wahrzeichen*) of a Medieval Jewish Protestantism. There was presumably a Jewish Reformation before the letter of the Christian Reformation. Maimonides is its proper name; he is the emblem and the seal of the alliance between these two Reformations. Between them, he signs for the first time the alliance or the contract. It is the figure of the first signatory or the first delegate to the signing of this alliance, an alliance which forms the Jewish-German psyche, the mirror or the reflexive consciousness of modernity. All of this goes with the grain of an "authentic" (*echten*) Platonic idealism.

Oh, if Maimonides had only known, if he had only seen himself in advance carried away along the course of this fantastic cavalcade, this galloping of a Jewish-German historian of philosophy, running through all of Western history in one breath without stopping for a single moment, all in front of an American public! If he had only known, he who considered himself rather Judeo-Maghrebian, Judeo-Arab, or Judeo-Spanish, that one day he would see himself recruited for this strange struggle, having unwittingly signed an alliance with post-Lutheran Germany, having consigned the great Jewish alliance to that alliance between the two alleged Reformations, would his soul rest in peace? I mean, would his psyche? And if only Plato had known? If all of them had?

Their protesting against Cohen, that is to say against Protestantism, would not perhaps have been quite unjust. But who can say that it would have been quite right [*dans le vrai*] for all that? For ultimately what is the truth in this case? Is it not precisely a matter of interpreting the truth of truth itself in the origin of its institution?

How does Cohen rationalize this recruitment of Maimonides for the Jewish-German cause? He does not rationalize; he thinks he does not have to. He speaks of reason itself—and of the historical institution of rationalism. Although he does not challenge the religious institutions, as Luther might do, Maimonides still seeks the foundations of religion. He founds religion upon a grand, rigorous rationalism. It is in the name of reason that he founds the Jewish Reformation.

When it comes to Maimonides, an abstention by Cohen may seem astonishing. In this text, which overflows with learning and cites just about every canonized philosopher (provided he is not French, with the exception of Rousseau, of whom we shall speak later), one philosopher is never named. No significant place is recognized for him. He is, however, a great rationalist philosopher, Jewish in his own way, and precisely a critic of Maimonides: Spinoza. Cohen knows him well, he has written about him a great deal. Why doesn't he grant him any place? Here is a feature that he will have in common with Heidegger in what is for both a meditation on the *logon didonai* and on the Principle of Reason. There would be a great deal to say about this common silence. All the more so since Cohen talks abundantly about Mendelssohn. This is particularly difficult to do without mentioning the man who for Mendelssohn was a master, a disputed one, no doubt, but still a master. The last lines of the article seem to take aim at a certain Spinozism, without naming Spinoza, as if to excommunicate it from the Jewish-German psyche, along with mysticism and pantheism. At the moment of celebrating the unity of the unique God, Cohen writes: "The future of German culture (*Gesittung*) rests on the force that the national spirit can muster to resist all the charms of mysticism, but also the pantheistic illusions of monism: our future depends on the ability to comprehend in their pure rational difference both nature and morality, 'the starry sky above me and the moral law within me,' and not to seek their unity (unification, *Vereinigung*) except in the idea of the one God."

The absence of Spinoza seems all the more blatant since Cohen speaks of a religion and a morality founded upon the love of God and on Pauline law: these are also the essential motifs of the *Theologico-Political Treatise.*

Cohen will have often named the *spirit*: the German spirit and the Holy Spirit. I, for my part, have often spoken of a Jewish-German psyche, of symbiosis or spiritual alliance. But has Cohen said nothing of the soul, of the Jewish or the German soul, of the Jewish psyche or the German psyche? We are coming to it.

There are presumably two principles of Judaism. One is God's oneness, the other that of the "purity of the soul" (*Reinheit der Seele*). The Jewish morning prayer says: "My Lord, the soul you gave me is pure. You created it, you formed it inside me, you breathed it into me [and the psyche is breath], you preserve it inside of me and it is you who will take it back again some day in order to return it to me in the life to come." The purity of the soul, says Cohen, is the "foundation pillar" (*Grundpfeiler*) of Jewish piety. Hence the immediacy of the relation to God, without intercessor, without mediator. After Maimonides, Cohen cites another Jew, Ibn Ezra, the earliest and the most important among the critics of the Bible. The authority of this Ibn Ezra, let me note in passing in order to recall Spinoza once more, is invoked at some length in the *Theologico-Political Treatise*, particularly in Chapter 8, when the issue is the authorship of the Holy Scripture, especially of the Pentateuch. Everybody used to believe it was Moses, notably the Pharisees, who resorted to an accusation of heresy against anyone who doubted this. Ibn Ezra, however, "a man of a rather free spirit and of immense erudition," says Spinoza, "was the first who, to my knowledge, has noticed this prejudice." But he dared not say so openly, and in order to dodge what was also the authority of an institution, he said it cryptically. Spinoza meant to lift this self-censorship and disclose his true intentions.

What, however, does Ibn Ezra say, the one whom Cohen now cites? One of his maxims states that there is no mediator between God and man other than human reason. The Holy spirit is equally man's spirit as it is God's. Man's spirit is holy because the holy God deposited it in him. Involved in the spirit are both the reconciliation (*Versöhnung*) between God and man and the redemption of sins: purity of soul and holiness of spirit. Quoting one of David's psalms, Cohen means to show (§11) that, in Judaism, redemption assumes a concept of human psyche.

This Jewish concept of the soul implies an immediate relation to a unique God. No mediator is necessary. But if it permits an understanding of freedom and of what morality assumes of freedom, how can this philosophy of immediacy account for duty, obligation, commandment? What is to be made of the law, so essential to Judaism after all? Cohen's way of posing and resolving the problem in three sentences (a war is on) is marvelous. A marvel of elliptical simplification, not to say distressing simple-mindedness, the more so when one knows that this economy conceals enormous exegetic problems, hermeneutic debates still open despite the libraries and the institutions growing rich by them by the day. Cohen knows them well, he inhabits them, teaches in them, and occasionally writes about them.

What does he say? The following: I have just shown a "point of support" (*Stutzpunkt*) of Idealism, but there is another fundamental conception (*Grundgedanke*) of Judaism. Since Paul, it has been opposed to the former through the concept of the law. This is a single sentence, in the beginning of §12. It is true that in very well-known and extremely complex texts (which, moreover, Spinoza interprets in his way around the problem of circumcision in Chapter 3 of the *Treatise*), Paul says some rather negative things about obedience to the law in Judaism, at least to the external and transcendent law which is supposed to be at the origin of sin and to which Paul opposes love and internal law.

The fundamental thought of Judaism, if there is one and if one interprets along with Cohen, would thus be stretched between two poles: freedom of the soul in the immediate relation to God, respect for transcendent law, duty, and commandment. Now, who has done this? Who has thought, *en bloc*, like a single revolution, that which revolves about these two poles, both freedom and duty, autonomy and universal law? Kant, and this thinker presumably delved deep into Judaism, into its spirit or its soul. Since he is the holiest saint of the German spirit, it is in "this innermost sanctum of the German spirit" (*in diesem innersten Heiligtum des deutschen Geistes*) that we find "the innermost kinship" (*die innerste Verwandschaft*) or affinity of the German spirit with Judaism. "Duty is God's commandment, and in Jewish piety, it must be on an equal footing, for the free service of love, with respect [here not *Achtung*, Kant's word, but *Ehrfurcht*]: for the love of God in the love of men." The spiritual consanguinity, the psycho-spiritual symbiosis is sealed in the *Critique of Practical Reason* and in everything which accords with it in Kant's work and elsewhere.

The gesture is not new. Kant's thought, whose Protestant descendance is so evident, has very rapidly been interpreted as a profound Judaism. It may be recalled both that he was saluted as a sort of Moses and that Hegel saw in him a shameful Jew.[8] This philosophical anti-Semitism or rather this anti-Judaism will reappear, with scarcely different motivations, in Nietzsche's *contra* Kant. On the other hand, *Religion within the Limits of Pure Reason* does resemble that Judeo-Reformationist *Aufklärung* of which Cohen speaks. *The Critique of the Faculty of Judgment* describes

---

8. I permit myself to refer the reader to long developments devoted to this scene in my *Glas* (Paris: Galilée, 1974).

the exemplarity of the Jewish experience in its relation to the sublimity of moral law. The fact that the *Anthropology from a Pragmatic Point of View* includes at least one properly anti-Semitic note (literally anti-Palestinian) is not incompatible with Kant's quasi-Judaism. Besides, what is anti-Semitism not compatible with? This is a terrible question, for it is directed at Jews, at those who call themselves such, as well as at non-Jews, at the anti-Semites and at those who are not such, still more perhaps at the philo-Semites. Without being able to formalize here the strange logic of this question, or prove that one is not to expect any positive and determinate answer, I would say only that the essential excess [*démesure*] of this thing called anti-Semitism makes itself known in it. It has a form and it does not have one. Its form consists in deforming and de-limiting itself ceaselessly in order to make contracts with everything that is opposed to it. Instead of deploying this logic, which we cannot do here, let us make do with an image and a fact: the tribute of a bouquet of flowers which, during a public demonstration in Nice, the Jewish militants of the Front Populaire thought fit to present to Mr. Le Pen (the man who dared speak of a "detail" in relation to the Shoah and captured 14 percent of the vote in the first round of the latest presidential election in France). One can explore all the possible combinations implicit in the positions thus taken, and the matrix of strategies gathered together in this bouquet.

Cohen, whether he wants to or not, presents at each moment a bouquet to all the dormant—or rather ever-wakeful—Le Pens, who do not concern themselves overmuch with detail. Concerning details and anti-Semitism in its most visible empirico-political manifestation, Cohen is well aware that at the very moment he is writing to celebrate his sense of sublime sacredness and of moral law, this German culture or society practices, officially and institutionally, legal anti-Semitism. This anti-Semitism touches Cohen quite closely in his own institution: it takes the form of excluding Jewish students from corporate student associations. Cohen devotes to it no more than a brief allusion, and this in no way disorganizes his discourse, which would like to remain "spiritual," not factual. He claims not to be able to embark on this question "in detail" (*wir hier keine Einzelförderungen aufstellen*) (§42). There is a war on, this is not the time to open fronts at home, national and Jewish-German solidarity must come first, we shall see later, there is still progress to be made, our Jewish American coreligionists are well aware of this (and it is true that a certain *numerus clausus* was for a long time applied to Jews in a practically official manner in the United States, and in fact still after the Second World War with regard to full professors in Ivy League universities). Cohen is aware then, as a university professor (and, to recall once more, he was the first Jewish professor of that rank in Germany), of the existence of this embarrassing detail, the exclusion of Jewish students from the corporate community. He puts the analysis off: "We are living in the great German patriotic hope that the unity between Judaism and Germanity, to which all the past history of German Jewry committed itself, should finally be brought to full light and radiate, like a *truth of cultural history* [my italics] in German politics and in life but also in the feeling of the German people [*im deutschen Volkgefühl*: we shall return to *Gefühl* shortly]" (§41).

This already amounts to recognizing that the psycho-spiritual truth, like the truth of cultural history, is not yet incarnated in historical effectivity: the truth has not yet been recognized. Cohen goes on:

§12. We have no intention of examining here in detail that complex question (*diese komplizierte Frage*) of determining in what way the conditions of national cohesion [rather than consensus, as one might say: *nationale Einmütigkeit*] must be rooted in social life. However this may be, the great educational establishments which are the universities ought to make it their imperative duty [unconditional: *unbedingte Verpflichtung*], in view of the dignity and the preservation of the sense of national honor, to eliminate, without any further formality, because it goes "against good manners" (*gegen die guten Sitten*), the exclusion of Jewish students from student associations and corporations. This exclusion damages in the first place the respect [*Achtung* this time] due to the Jewish teachers. He who does not hold me worthy of his socio-academic community [and here, in an exemplary manner, the professor uses the first person], should also not follow my lectures and disdain my teaching. This demand is then pressingly directed at the academic authorities as well as at the students having the benefit of their academic freedom.

In all logic, Cohen couldn't but appeal to academic freedom. In a manner equally formal and perverse, it was in the name of this freedom that the exclusion was practiced: one has the right to set freely the conditions of association. Cohen's appeal is at the same time both very dignified and somewhat humiliating: first for himself, but also for the Jewish students, whose rights would have to be protected and guaranteed by the prestige or the authority of the great Jewish professors.

But this, for him, is only a contextual and an institutional question. It remains a relatively minor question; dealing with it "in detail" may be put off until later. What counts, in the order of urgencies of a time of war, is the most fundamental thing, namely Judeo-Kantian law and its correlation to the freedom, the autonomy of the subject as spirit, soul, and conscience [or consciousness, *conscience*]. The choice here is not between two realms [*ordres*] of interpretation and institutionality, since what I call the Judeo-Kantian also belongs to the realm of historical events. These do not go without instituting moments and are always incarnated, if we can follow Cohen, in peoples, nations, languages, and even in juridico-political structures. We shall come to this. As the deepest foundation of all morality, God's law is also the foundation of legal justice [*droit*] and the State. The Mosaic code [*le droit mosaïque*] has always been recognized, even if, when Grotius's jurisnaturalism first arose, it was rejected on account of its formal justifications. In fact, this divine law and this Mosaic code were, according to Cohen, at the origin of legal justice. They have made possible the correct [*juste*] establishment, the institution of legal justice, and first of all the juridical sense. The latter exhibits some analogy, at a level other than that of the moral law, with the sense of respect defined by Kant. It commands the universal consciousness of rightness [*conscience universelle du juste*], even beyond the Judeo-Christian cultures, for instance in Islam (here Cohen cites Trendelenburg, author of a *Naturrecht* [1860]). By uniting freedom and duty in "personality," Kant states simultaneously both the difference and the intimate link, a new "*Verbindungslinie*" between ethics and religion. In religion, this new "line of alliance" gathers together "the soul and the spirit" (*die Seele und der Geist*).

IV

Kant, the Jew, the German. In this title, then, none of the attributes can be made minor, none is more essential. This is a cosubstantial reciprocity rather than a coattribution. This fundamental identification or this substantial alliance may rather be said to be *subjectal*. It is in the very subjectivity of the Kantian subject, of man as a subject of morality and justice [*droit*], free and autonomous, that the Jew and the German are associated. Their *socius* (alliance, spiritual symbiosis, psyche, and so on) is that very *socius* which makes of the *subjectum* a moral being and a legal being [*un être de droit*], a freedom, a person.

At this point, a leap seems to me to be required in this reading. It is necessary to bring out the strategy and the pragmatics of this text, the contextual and institutional aim of its rhetoric, at the moment when a new line of alliance between the soul and the spirit has just been named. This will permit us also to recall that German, if not Jew, is also German as a language, German as it is spoken.

Cohen's strategy aims at demonstrating to all the Jews of the world, primarily but not only to American Jews, that the universality of the moral subject came to be rooted in an event: the history of the German spirit and the German soul. So that Germany is the true homeland of every Jew in the world, "the motherland of their soul (*das Mutterland seiner Seele*)." If religion is their soul, the homeland of their soul is Germany. The old accusation against Jewish internationalism or cosmopolitanism rests upon an obscure prejudice. We ought not to take it into account when we wish to elucidate questions of principle. If there is a Jewish internationalism, this is insofar as all the Jews of the world have a common homeland for their psyche (*Seele*). This homeland, however, is not Israel but Germany: "I believe that, if we abstract the problem of naturalization (*Naturalisierung*), the Jews of France, England, and Russia are bound by obligations of piety (*Pflichten der Pietät*) toward Germany; for it is the motherland of their soul, if however religion is their soul."

Cohen does not wish to avoid the contradiction into which he locks these poor non-German Jews in a time of war, for similar discourses might be held at the same time, for example in France or in America. He goes on to develop an argument which I give up paraphrasing—it remains so inimitable. Before quoting a paragraph, let me briefly note that, in the name of what is advertised as "the finest political tact" (*Freilich bedurf es des feinsten politischen Taktes*), it comes down to demanding of all the Jews of the world to recognize Germany as the motherland of their soul, without betraying the other one, but while still working toward universal peace, that is, the end of a war to be won by Germany, and of a war in which the sacred obligation to love one's neighbor, be he even one's enemy, would be maintained.

> To say the truth, it takes the finest political tact in order for this piety not to hurt or give umbrage to the higher duty of love for one's country. Nevertheless, this difficulty, which is proper to the war situation, is not fundamentally of a different nature: everyone conducts a war *without losing sight of the peace latent in deep humanity*. Wars of extermination are humanity's shame. Is the duty of piety felt toward his original homeland by whoever has been naturalized, if only in part, perhaps so different from this international and universal duty of humanity?
>
> Surely it is the most concrete meaning of the obligation to *love one's enemies*, that there should be preserved, in the enemy people, its participation not only in humanity in general, but also in the most complex ramifications of this idea. And there is no discontinuity, a *fortiori* no gap, between this general duty of humanity and the piety owed to his real cultural and spiritual, even physical motherland by anyone whom destiny led to a foreign State or caused to be born there.
>
> It is from such a principle that the peace efforts undertaken at the international level must draw the only essential and indisputable foundation which would confer upon them an efficacity that none of the parties involved would contest. The humanity proper to one's birthplace can become the mother tongue of a true internationalism so as to establish firmly a spirit of peace. (§40)

The last sentence says that "humanity [*Humanität*: and Fichte recalled that, in its abstraction, this Latin word was not equivalent to *Menschheit*, an immediately sensible and intelligible essence to a German] can become the maternal ground (*Mutterboden*) of a true internationality in view of founding, establishing, or justifying, of firmly instituting by right [*en droit*] (*Begrundung*) a spirit of peace, a sense of peace (*Friedesgesinnung*)."

Precisely as to language, however, the statement is rather odd. Why should the American Jews, who are Cohen's primary addressees and who came by the thousands from Germany or Russia, still have a pious duty towards Germany, even though they are American citizens? Why should they piously (*pietätsvol*) respect (*achten* this time) their psycho-spiritual motherland (*als ihr seelisch-geistiges Mutterland*)? Because of language; more precisely and even more significantly, because of the so-called "Jargon," the Yiddish language. Even though it maims, mutilates, truncates (*verstummelt*) the mother tongue, it still signals back to the language to which it owes the originary force of reason (*Urkraft der Vernunft*) as originary force of the spirit (*Urkraft der Geistes*). It is through the mediation of this language, German, that man (and here, in an exemplary manner, the German Jew) has been able to spiritualize his thoughts and ennoble his religious habits. He must not deny the people that gave him such a rebirth [*renaissance*] (*Wiedergeburt*) his inner loyalty.

Addressing himself thus to the American Jews, Cohen indicts the attitude of certain French or English Jews (those, by the way, who, for their part, indulged in analogous—and for essential reasons, only analogous—rhetoric). These Jews have presumably shown themselves to be weak with regard to Russia, which annexes their brethren, and ungrateful with regard to Germany. Such is for example the case of "Mister Bergson," who puts his talent and his credit into the service to France. This renegade loses his soul in forgetting that he is the son of a Polish Jew (not even a German!) and especially that his parents spoke Yiddish (not even pure German, which Cohen, like every self-respecting member of a certain Jewish-German intelligentsia, puts way above that degraded [*verstummelt*] form of the noble German idiom):

> Outstanding in this context are the invectives of a French philosopher who, using all the devices of virtuosity and of advertising (*der Virtuosität und der Reklame*), which unfortunately work only too well for him in Germany [one hears analogous things today from certain German philosophers], puts up the act of an original philosopher: he is the son of a Polish Jew who spoke Yiddish. What may be happening in the soul of this Mister Bergson when he remembers his father and denies Germany its "ideals!" (*Er ist der Sohn eines polnisches Juden, der den Jargon sprach. Was mag in der Seele dieses Herrn Bergson vorgehen, wenn er seines Vaters gedenkt und Deutschland die "Ideen" abspricht!*)

Our analysis must become more refined in order to come still nearer to the sharpest specificity of *this* interpretation, in *this typical* contextual and institutional situation (*this* war, *this* Jewish-German Professor, *this* neo-Kantian philosopher, and so on), and in order to better determine the articulation between the "external" and the "internal" institution of *these* interpretations. There are several ways to do this. Having chosen to privilege the reference *to Kant, the Jew, the German,* we shall underline first the ambivalence which, despite the hyperbolic tribute, continues to mark this reference. This ambivalence corresponds also to a general type. It is not the property of neo-Kantianism, of Cohen, or of Jewish-German thinkers of the period. We do not have enough time and space to better situate Rosenzweig's thought in this respect, in its double relation to Kant and to Cohen. In the course of a brief detour, we shall then be content to invoke not only Rosenzweig's ambivalence toward Kant, but also—what is more interesting at this point—his awareness of it and the interpretation, diagnosis even, he proposed for it.

In 1923 Buber had just published his lectures on Judaism.[9] Rosenzweig wrote to thank him for the book. Of this long letter, dealing mainly with Jewish law, I shall quote first a tribute to Buber. It announces a sort of double bind in filiation or rather in *discipline.* Just as, for "our spiritual Judaism," it is both possible and impossible to inherit Kant, both possible and impossible to be Kant's *disciple,* so it will be both possible and impossible to follow Buber (and *a fortiori* Cohen): "The preceding centuries had already reduced Study to genteel poverty, to a handful of fundamental concepts; it was left to the 19th century to complete this development methodically and with the highest seriousness. You have liberated Study from this limited sphere, and in doing that, protected us from the imminent danger of making our spiritual Judaism depend on the possibility and impossibility for us to be Kant's pupils."[10]

Possibility and impossibility: we could and could not be Kant's heirs. This translates perhaps into "we could but we shouldn't," or "shouldn't have." Or else: "toward Kant, the man who gave its categorical formulation to the law and to the imperative of that name, we have contradictory attitudes, perhaps contradictory duties. Kant was and should not have been the institutor and the law of our relation to the law. And from this Moses to whom Kant had so often been compared, from this idol or effigy of Moses and from the necessarily troubled and ambiguous link we had to him, you, Buber, have emancipated us."

In truth, you have emancipated us and you have not. For in turn the same ambivalence is declared with regard to Buber's teaching. Buber would have shut the relation to the law in a space of teaching, that is to say ultimately in a theoretical or an epistemological space. The law, however, is no mere object of knowledge, any more than a text one should be content to read or study:

This is why, it is all the more curious, that after you have liberated us and shown us the way toward a new kind of Study, your answer to the other side of the question

---

9. See Martin Buber, *Reder über das Judentum* (Frankfurt am Main, 1923).
10. Franz Rosenzweig, *Kleinere Schriften* (Berlin, 1937), pp. 106–21; subsequent references to this work will be identified parenthetically in the text, without pagination, as *KS.*

concerning the Law—"What should we do?"—that your question had to leave this Law still locked in shackles, the same ones as those the 19th century imposed on Study as well [having no access, at the moment, to the original, I am quoting a French translation which seems strange and may be inadequate]. For is it really with the Jewish Law that you are trying to reach an accord, and are unable to do so? Is it really upon this law that you turn your back simply in order to tell yourself and to tell us, who had expected the answer from you, that our only task must be to take cognizance of this Law, reverentially, with a reverence that in no way affects our selves or our way of living? Is it really the Jewish Law, that age-old Law, studied and experienced, searched and celebrated, the Law of everyday and of the Last Day, meticulous and yet sublime, sober and yet woven with legends; a Law that knows both the flame of the Sabbath candles and that of the martyrs' stake? (*KS*)

What is the place, in this letter, where the double bind ties up with the question of nation? The "unheard of" uniqueness of the Jewish nation in its relation to the law is that its birth pertains not to nature but precisely to the Law. Rosenzweig dissociates nature and nation, birth by nature and birth by law. This distinction actually is still a Kantian one. All nations, he says, are born in the bosom of nature, in the bowels of Mother Nature. This is why they are in need of historical development. At the moment of their birth, of course, they do not yet have a history, they do not even have a face. The Jewish nation does have a history, so to speak, *before* being born. It does not come to be born naturally but by being taken out from another nation, having been known, having been called by God's Law even before its birth. It comes to be born out of this calling in a non-natural way. Its face had already been shaped, its birth already inscribed in a history that had begun before it even though it was already its own. That is why the history of this nation is somehow supernatural or, if one prefers, transhistorical. Its path remains unique. Like Heidegger, Rosenzweig thinks all this in the form of the *path* [*chemin*] and as a new thought of the path, thought as path. He links the path to the Law. This passage of the letter is a passage on the path where we are, the path that we are. It is a passage on the path and on the leap: "We can attain both Study and the Law only by becoming aware that we are still in the first part of the path and that it is up to *us* to choose to go ahead. But what then is the path leading up to the Law?" (*KS*)

This is Kafka's question in *Vor dem Gesetz* [Before the Law] (written a few years earlier): How to gain access to the Law? How can one touch it? What is progress toward the Law? Rosenzweig questions this path toward the Law as a path toward the unreachable. He does so using words and a tone that are very close to Kafka's. The "track" is "open" to someone who, having traveled "the entire length" of the path, would not even have "the right to claim that he thereby attains his goal."

"Such a man would have to be content with saying that he travelled the entire path, but that even for him the goal is one step beyond—in the unreachable. So why call it a path? Can a path lead to the unreachable?" Does it still deserve the name "path"? A "tiresome, goalless detour through knowable Judaism gives us the certainty that the ultimate leap from what we know already to what we need to know at any price, the leap into Study, has led us to *Jewish* Study." What is the need for this ultimate leap? The answers tell of the "unheard of" uniqueness of the Jewish nation. Its relation to the Law is, but is not, the relation determined by Kant:

Other nations do not feel this kind of need. When a member of one of the nations teaches, he is teaching out from amongst his people and toward his people, even if he has learned nothing. All he teaches becomes the possession of his people. For the nations have a face still in the making—each its own. None of them knows at birth just what it is to be; their faces are not molded while they are still in nature's lap.

But our people, the only one that did not originate from the womb of nature that bears nations, but—and this is unheard of!—was led forth "a nation from the midst of another nation" (*Deuteronomy* 4:34)—our people was decreed a different fate. Its very birth became the great moment of its life, its mere being already harbored its destiny. Even "before it was formed," it was "known," like Jeremiah its prophet. And so only he who remembers this determining origin can belong to it; while he who no longer can or will utter the new word he has to say "in the name of the original speaker," he who refuses to be a link in the golden chain, no longer belongs to his people. And that is why this people must learn what is knowable as a condition for learning what is unknown, for making it his own.

All this holds also for the Law, for doing.[11]

After this detour, let us come back to Cohen to stake out some points of reference within this relation to Kant. As we have seen, Cohen, in his way of telling the story [*raconter l'histoire*], regularly assigned a variety of origins to what he calls the German spirit or German idealism: the Platonic hypothesis, its adoption or anticipation by Judaism, notably by Philo, the Christian logos, the Reformation, Kepler, Nicholas of Cusa, Leibniz, Kant. Each time its birth did but announce another birth. At one particular moment, the peak, the high point (*Höhepunkt*) of this chain of births or mountains, was Kant ("until it [German idealism] reaches with Kant its historical high point" [*seinen geschichtlischen Höhepunkt*]) (§6). Now here is the ambiguity: it appears now (§44) that the real high point is not Kant. It is

---

11. Franz Rosenzweig, "The Builders: Concerning the Law," in his *On Jewish Learning*, ed. Nahum Glatzer (New York: Schocken, 1965), p. 81.

Fichte: he discovered that the social Self is a national Self (*"Das soziale Ich hat er als das nationale Ich entdeckt"*; Cohen's italics). In seeking and finding in the "national Self" the "supra-empirical foundation of the Self," he thus constituted "in fact" (*in der Tat*) the peak of German philosophy (*So budet Fichte in der Tat einen Höhepunkt der deutschen Philosophie*).

How is this possible? What does it mean? Let us first note that, as for Rosenzweig, it is the thought of the national [*la pensée du national*] which makes it possible here to go beyond the Kantian peak. But this time it is in view of a summit which identifies the national with the essence of the German or of the Jewish-German couple. Its representative figure is a thinker of the German nation, the very man who considered the German nation a chosen nation and who used occasionally the reference to Jewish prophecy in order to intimate what he wished to intimate of the German nation to the German nation. In his *Address to the German Nation* he also speaks of a path of human history. He even specifies that "midway point" where the second half of human history must begin:

> The real destiny of the human race on earth . . . is in freedom to make itself what it really is originally. Now this making of itself deliberately, and according to rule, must have a beginning somewhere and at some moment in space and time. Thereby a second great period, one of free and deliberate development of the human race, would appear in place of the first period, one of development that is not free. We are of opinion that, in regard to time, this is the very time, and that now the race is exactly midway between the two great epochs of its life on earth. But in regard to space, we believe that it is first of all the Germans who are called upon to begin the new era as pioneers and models for the rest of mankind.[12]

It is not insignificant that this *Address* (the third) ends with "the vision of an ancient prophet":

> Thus says the prophet by the river of Chebar, the comforter of those in captivity, not in their own, but in a foreign land. "The hand of the Lord was upon me, and carried me out in the spirit of the Lord, and set me down in the midst of the valley which was full of bones, and caused me to pass by them round about: and, behold, there were very many in the open valley; and, lo, they were very dry. And He said unto me, Son of man, can these bones live? And I answered, O Lord God, thou knowest. Again He said unto me, Prophesy upon these bones, and say unto them O ye dry bones, hear the

---

12. Johan Gottlob Fichte, *Addresses to the German Nation*, ed. George Armstrong, tr. R. F. Jones and G. H. Turnbull (New York, 1968), p. 40; hereafter cited in text.

word of the Lord. Thus saith the Lord God unto these bones, Behold, I will cause breath to enter into you, and ye shall live: and I will lay sinews upon you, and will bring up the flesh upon you, and cover you with skin, and put breath in you, and ye shall live; and ye shall know that I am the Lord ... "

Though the elements of our higher spiritual life may be just as dried up, and though the bonds of our national unity may lie just as torn asunder and as scattered in wild disorder as the bones of the slain in the prophecy, though they may have whitened and dried for centuries in tempests, rainstorms, and burning sunshine, the quickening breath of the spiritual world has not yet ceased to blow. It will take hold, too, of the dead bones of our national body, and join them together, that they may stand glorious in new and radiant life. (43–44)

How does Cohen analyze Fichte's relation to Kant? And how does he account for this duality of peaks? (1) By the dissociation of the theoretical from the practical; (2) by recalling the social point of view presumably latent in Kantian ethics; (3) by showing that the manifestation of the latent unites the national with the social, nationalism with socialism (§44).

Cohen recognizes that, theoretically speaking, no one has gone beyond Kant. Fichte's philosophy of the Self (*Die Ich-Philosophie Fichtes*) is a theoretical regression in relation to Kant. It would be superficial or inconsistent to fail to recognize this. He puts himself in opposition to those academics who, in the name of purely patriotic considerations, out of concern for "patriotic merit," would then be prepared, in this context, to prefer the nationalist Fichte at any price. Cohen's complex gesture consists of recognizing the national question as an essential and an essentially philosophical question, but at the same time also emphasizing that, theoretically speaking, Fichte's philosophy of the Self is regressive. Cohen also admits that philosophy is a "national matter" (*eine nationale Sache*) and one must be grateful to Fichte, his "theoretical regression" notwithstanding, for having made some progress (*Fortschritt*): he brought out the latent socialism of Kantian ethics into "explicit display." Let us not forget that this 1915 nationalist discourse is also a socialist discourse. Fichte's great "discovery" is that the Self is social, but also that the social Self is in its origin and essence a national Self.

In other words, the "I" in "I think," in the *cogito*, is not a formal one, as Kant presumably had believed. It appears to itself in its relation to the other, and this *socius*, far from being abstract, manifests itself to itself originally in its national determination, as belonging to a spirit, a history, a language. I—the Self—sign first in its spiritual language. The nationality of the *ego* is not a characteristic or an attribute that happens to a subject who was not national-social to begin with. The subject is in its origin and through and through, substantially, subjectally national. The ego cogito discovered by Fichte is a national one. It has a universal form, but this universality does not occur to its truth except as nationality. This "new truth (*neue Warheit*) completes" in fact (*in der Tat*) what was latent in the *Ich* of the Kantian *Ich denke*, because it is a "new realization (*Verwirklichung*) of the I." It goes beyond the ethical abstraction of humanity and provides the "*Lebensgrund*" of Fichte's Idealism.

These statements pivot around themselves—like a psyche. If the essence of egological effectivity is nationality, if there lies the truth of idealism, namely of philosophy itself of which German idealism is also the realization, then one must say, conversely, that the nation is an ego. It relates to itself in the form of egological subjectivity. The truth of nationality asserts itself as idealism. And since the truth of philosophical idealism, that is, of philosophy in general, is German idealism, the truth of nationality *in general* is German idealism. When one says "in general" one must think that the realization (*Verwirklichung*) of this generality is nationality— German nationality. The truth of the *I* inasmuch as it *posits itself* is German. If in the act of positing itself by itself as nationality one finds something of *reflection* and therefore of the narcissistic structure where a "new truth" "discovers" (*entdeckt*) itself, if that structure posits itself in unveiling itself, then the mirror of a certain psyche is thus to be found in the pivoting center of the relation to itself of the *ego* as national ego. Hence the literally cosmopolitan proposition which happens to be [*se trouve*] deduced, in accordance with Fichte's best logic, from this national-socialist German idealism. This is the exemplary superiority of German idealism as of German nationalism. The German spirit is the spirit of humanity: "The spirit of humanity is the originary spirit of our ethic. In this ethical determinacy, the German spirit is the spirit of the cosmopolitanism and of the humanity (*der Geist der Weltburgertums und der Humanität*) of our classical period" (§45), that is to say, of the eighteenth century.

At the peak of the Fichtean peak, Cohen dreads, certainly, the narcissistic effects of this exaltation of the German spirit and of the national *ego*. This fear and its formulation pertain moreover to the program or the typology of all nationalisms. There is always a moment when one must issue a warning, as does Cohen, against a national enthusiasm or excitation (*nationale Begeisterung*) which shows every appearance of narcissistic infatuation (*Eigendunkel*) and sentimental complacency for one's property. Cohen remains Kantian enough to suspect this *Begeisterung*. He is for balancing enthusiasm by the consciousness of the law, the harshness of obligation, the sense of responsibility. Privilege also assigns a mission, it even consists of this mission. The national Self is, of course, also a "We" and first of all the subject of rights, especially of duties. With no other transition, Cohen moves on to a list of consequences that seem to follow [*se déduire*], in a quasi-analytical way, from this German idealism: mandatory military service, the right to vote, compulsory education.

While taking care not to give way to misleading analogies, one might be tempted to recall here the three "services" deduced by Heidegger, in his *Rectorate Speech* (1933)—another war discourse in sum, postwar and prewar—from the self-affirmation, not to say self-positing of the German university. The content of these two times three duties is undoubtedly not exactly the same, although both knowledge and the army are there. Heidegger does not mention the right to vote, which is moreover not a duty, but in both cases all of these obligations or services (*Aufgabe, Dienste*) are deduced from national self-affirmation. And although the democratic theme is absent from Heidegger's text, the socialist, even populist theme spans both texts.

Let us not imprudently bring these two gestures together. The differences between them are considerable. But they are re-marked [*elles se remarquent*] within the common web of a tradition that should never be forgotten. All the more since Cohen's text is also, in many respects, a text about the academic institution. This can be recognized by the crucial role that the German university plays in the argument. First, because German idealism has no sense, no *effectivity*, precisely, outside the effectivity of the German university and its history during the nineteenth century (which is also the century of the emancipation of the Jews, let us never forget, and Cohen is still a nineteenth-century man). Then, because, as Cohen literally says, the university must become the people's thing, a truly popular school: "*Die Universität muss die wahrhafte Volksschule werden*" (§44; Cohen's italics). The self-positing of the German spirit, the reflexive psyche that ensures its keeping and tradition, finds its effective truth nowhere else than in the people's university. Let us try yet another cautious and limited analogy. Just as for the 1933 Heidegger, among the three obligations (*Bindungen*) or services (*Arbeits-, Wehr-, Wissens-dienste*)—all as originary as any of the others and of equal dignity—the service of knowledge maintains [*garde*] a privilege inasmuch as it molds the guardians and the guides of the German people in its university, so it is to the "higher institutions of education" (*höheren Bildungsstätten*) that Cohen wants to entrust this pedagogical function. It must be accessible to the popular classes, ensure social justice and national unity.

These three duties link together the consciousness of the national subject. They limit the risks of the exaltation into which one might be pushed by a dangerous interpretation of Fichte's thought. From one peak to another. One before the other, and Cohen returns regularly from one to the other. In defining the three duties and this cohesion of the national consciousness (*Einheitlichkeit des Nationalbewusst-seins*) which constitutes the living core of the "national sentiment" he emphasizes the word "sentiment" (*Gefühl*) but insists on the necessity of understanding Kant's thought, which is not merely a sentimental thought about duty and responsibility.

(It is, however, also that: respect for the law must remain a sentiment.) "Every German must know, with an intimacy such as love offers, his Schiller and his Goethe, must always keep them in his mind as well as in his heart. But this intimacy presupposes his having also acquired a familiarity and a basic understanding of his Kant" (§44).

Here the question of military service, that is, the first of the three obligations mentioned earlier, deserves special attention. This for three reasons. First, of course, because this text is being written and published during wartime by a socialist who wishes despite everything to remain pacifist and cosmopolitan. Then, because Cohen links this question specifically to Kant. Finally, because his link to the Jewish question is at that time rather peculiar in Germany. Let us follow these three threads.

There is no exaggerating the importance of music in this problematic of the German nation—of any nation, for that matter. Now, we note the appearance of the military thematics at the very heart of what we are being told about the soul, about the national psyche, and about music. The latter is in the first place the law of the breath and of pneumatic structures (*Lufthauch, Luftgebilde*), that is to say, psychic as well. Music is the locus of the "spiritual sublime" (*geistige Erhabenheit*). Now the fusion of spirit and soul (*Verschmelzung von Geist und Seele*) does not achieve its ultimate fulfillment (*Vollendung*) except in German music (*einzig in der deutschen Musik*). This must be demonstrated in order to reply to the question of the unique property of German music and to the question of knowing why it should have such an impact on the unique property (*die Eigenart*) of the German spirit. Music is the most ideal of the arts (*die idealste der Künste*). This hierarchy of the arts, according to their degrees of ideality, is assumed by this entire discourse. It should call for a comparative analysis of classifications of the arts, from Hegel to Heidegger at least. Here this higher ideality of music puts it in tune with the whole idealistic purpose of this discourse on German idealism. If music is the most ideal art, this is precisely because of its psychic character. The structure, the architecture or the edification (*Gebäude*) of music is pure breath (*reiner Hauch*), respiration, *spiritus* and psyche. Mindful as he is of rhythm, Cohen is equally so of the vast empire of mathematical forms which organize music. Rosenzweig pays Cohen the tribute of having been, perhaps unwittingly, a great mathematical thinker: "Hermann Cohen, contrary to his own conception of himself and contrary to the impression his works make, was something quite different from a mere epigone to this movement [begun with Plato], which had truly run its course. And it remained for him to discover in mathematics an organum of reasoning, just because it creates its elements out of the definite Nought of the differential, each time assigned to that required Element, not out of the empty Nought of the one and universal Zero. The differential combines in itself the characteristics of the Nought and the Aught."[13]

In the same development Rosenzweig speaks of Cohen as a "master." A master because he is supposed to have truly broken with that idealism to which he nevertheless laid claim, to have broken with Hegel, precisely, by his return to Kant. Rosenzweig then means to introduce into the heart of the idealist tradition rifts to which Cohen is supposed not to have given enough consideration. That same development concerns no less than a thought to nothingness which would also call for a debate with Heidegger:

> Mathematics is the guide for the sake of these two paths. It teaches us to recognize the origin of the Aught in the Nought. Thus even if Cohen, the master, would be far from admitting it, we are continuing to build on the great scientific achievement of his logic of origins, the new concept of the Nought. For the rest he may have been, in the execution of his ideas, more of a Hegelian than he admitted—and thereby as much of an "Idealist" as he claimed to be. Here, however, in this basic idea, he broke decisively with the idealistic tradition. He replaced the one and universal Nought, that veritable "no-thing" (*Unding*) which, like a zero, really can be nothing more than "nothing," with the particular Nought which burst fruitfully onto reality. There he took his stand in most decided opposition precisely to Hegel's founding of logic on the concept of Being [I will say, Heidegger did so too in his own way in *Was ist Metaphysik?*], and thereby in turn to the whole philosophy into whose inheritance Hegel had come. For here for the first time a philosopher who himself still considered himself an "Idealist" (one more indication of the force of what happened to him) recognized and acknowledged that what confronted reasoning when it set out in order "purely to create" was not Being but—Nought.
>
> For the first time—even if it remains true that here too, as everywhere, Kant, alone among all the thinkers of the past, showed the way which we are now to follow, and showed it, as always, in those comments to which he gave utterance without drawing their systematic consequences. (21)

Need we point out again the institutional dimension of these so-overdetermined interpretations? They concern the system, the unity of the corpus, the way in which interpretive, auto- or hereto-interpretive traditions, hence academic institutions, evaluate, manage, conceal, rank, canonize—founding themselves by these operations. And, let us not forget, what we have here, in appearance, is a

---

13. Franz Rosenzweig, "Origins," in his *The Star of Redemption*, tr. from 2nd ed. by William W. Hallo (Notre Dame: University of Notre Dame Press, 1971), p. 20; hereafter cited in the text.

nonacademic speaking of the academy. But it is not sufficient to be by profession foreign to the university in order to be simply outside of it. Neither as a civilian nor as a military man, still to use convenient yet problematic distinctions, especially during wartime. But what is wartime? Nothing that is military is foreign to knowledge, to the matheme and to mathematics. Especially not military music. The greatness of German music appeals to the sublimity of spiritual forms (*Erhabenheit der geistigen Forme*). This whole discourse about nationalism is also a discourse about the sublime. This sublime edifice (*dieser erhabene Formenbau*) plunges its beams into the deepest sources of originary feeling [*sentiment*]. This sublimity of spiritual forms goes hand in hand with the mathematization of rhythms. It links up with the sources of feeling and thus makes for the originality of German music. Now, to what must this structuring of feeling be compared? Cohen's answer: to that of a *Heerzug*, a military array, a military train, procession, or parade (§15).

Here we must recall the history that Cohen places in perspective: not only that of the emancipation of the German Jews, but also that of a world Jewry interpreted according to German Jewry in its link to the *Aufklärung* and to Kant. Cohen has no doubt about this, so he says: Mendelssohn's influence and Kant's were simultaneous and of the same nature. This influence reaches beyond Germany, to Judaism in all its depth "as well as to the cultural life of the Jews, at least of those who were living in the modern Western countries" (§33). (This final restriction appears to be very significant, especially if one considers the essentially European character of early Zionism.) Having noted this influence, Cohen emphasizes once more the "very internal or very profound moral affinity" between Germanity and Judaism. It concerns political socialism. It corresponds both to the generalization of priesthood, both a Lutheran and a Jewish motif, and to messianism. The German State is supposed to be in its modernity both priestly and messianic. This is recognizable in its social policy, more precisely by the fact that social policy is recognized by it as a duty: an ethical duty prior to being a political one, a duty already prescribed by natural law. Socialism is not a policy among others, and it is the German policy *par excellence*, by essence [*par essence*]. Socialism is national and it is German. There may be different modes of policy or politics, different strategies in the implementation of such and such a socialism, but as to its end there is no doubt whatever. This socialist policy, this morality inspired by universal priesthood, serves a fundamental messianism: Jewish-German messianism.

To illustrate this truth (some indices of which are undeniable anyhow), Cohen gives some examples. First of all, Bismarck made universal suffrage a right written into the constitution. (Let me recall here a remark by Blanchot, who wonders, in connection with the alliance between nationalism and socialism, in connection with national socialism, whether Heidegger in 1933 did not mistake Hitler for

Bismarck.[14]) Bismarck, according to Cohen, draws a logical conclusion written into the very idea of a German *Reich*. The other example is that toward which we have been heading for a while. The same logic has led disciples of Kant to make obligatory military service a major institution deserving to be written into the German constitution. And if Cohen emphasizes that these were disciples of Kant's, it is in order to recall their being in principle pacifists. Because of the war for Schleswig-Holstein and the war against Napoleon, they have had to surrender themselves to this necessity. This necessity is still marked by democracy, by social democracy rather than by militarism. The obligatory character of military service corresponds to a democratization of the military institution. The founding of social democracy is besides an essential property (*Eigenart*) of the German spirit in Cohen's eyes; he recalls furthermore that the Jews proved their military patriotism in the wars of liberation, whereas at the time of Frederick II they had been barred from military service. This patriotic zeal is supposed then to have lucidly anticipated and prepared, in spirit, the letter of the legal apparatus. As to social democracy, as an ethical phenomenon (once purged of its "material cinders"), being the essence of the German spirit in its alliance with Judaism, Cohen sees many signs for this fact, such as for example Marx's Jewish origin or the religious orientation of Ferdinand Lassalle in his youth.

V

Interpretations at war, we were saying. The status, the date, and the purpose [*finalité*] of this text justify the attention we pay to that in it which concerns the philosophy of the army as well as the philosophy of war. Cohen wants to reconcile at least three apparently incompatible things: (1) He wishes, quite openly, for Germany's victory. (2) He wishes for it also as a German Jew and so must interpret such a victory as a victory for Judaism, knowing full well that the majority of world Jews are not German. (3) As a good Kantian, he is committed not only to cosmopolitanism but also to pacifism. How does he go about it?

(1) He wishes clearly for victory by force of arms, "the heroic victory of our fatherland" (*den Heldensig unseres Vaterlandes*). When he says "our," he is addressing himself to the Germans, to the German Jews, but also to the Jews of the world, who should recognize, we remember, their being or their having to be German. This "we" bears within it, in this usage—its pragmatics, its rhetoric—the teleological force of the "we" in the *Discourse to the German Nation*. This "we" is at the same time invoked as that which is yet to be constituted—and presupposed as the most originary instance. The hope for victory definitely concerns an actual military

---

14. See Maurice Blanchot, "Les intellectuels en question," *Le Débat*, no. 29 (March 1984).

triumph by German arms ("*Wir hoffen auch den Triumph der deutschen Waffen*")
(§41). But Cohen's discourse is more embarrassed when it has to deal with justifying this war. Is it a "just" one? As a socialist pacifist Cohen begins by asking himself:
Was it necessary? Is war in general necessary? His apparently calm reply: we shall
not discuss these questions here. They pertain to historical judgment and to the
philosophy of history. As to the causes of the war, the question is left to the historians and to the disciplines that deal simultaneously with history, economics, and the
State. A strange move, but one based, in any case, on the division of labor as a division of problematic regions, of disciplines of knowledge, and of academic departments. All of which are presuppositions and, furthermore, institutional ones.

How can someone whose major point is the justification of the victory of one
side, and who also calls himself a pacifist, leave these questions to others or postpone [*différer*] them till later? How can he reserve them to constituted disciplines,
thus to institutions that are external to the one that underwrites his own discourse?
May we talk here of evasion or denial? For this question is both posed and evaded
by Cohen in a gesture that, while perhaps not rigorously Kantian, still maintains a
Kantian style. Cohen is saying, in short, I am here renouncing the philosophy of
history, the theodicy of universal history, as well as the regional sciences (economics, political science, and so on). But I may still, having thus turned back by a neo-
criticist gesture, maintain a reflecting and a teleological attitude by asking myself:
the event of the war *having occurred*, whatever its causes (for this see the work of
historians, economists, political scientists) or final aims (for this see philosophers
of history or theologians), "what lesson can one draw from the event of the war
(*aus der Tatsache der Kriege*) and the events of the present conflict that would lead
to a better understanding of the destiny of mankind (*Bestimmung des Menschen-
geschlechts*), and of the destiny of Germanity (*Bestimmung der Deutschtum*) within
it, in order to illuminate and accomplish the moral purpose of Germanity (*um dem
sittlichen Zweck der Deutschtums zu erhellen und zu erfüllen*)?" (§43).

Cohen calls this a "teleological" method (§43). A method, merely, since by
renouncing knowledge of ultimate ends, human or divine, one recoils towards this
question: What is the purpose of this war with regard to our national *Dasein*
(*suchen wir den Zweck dieses Krieges für unser nationales Dasein zu erforschen*)?
Immediate reply: from this war we expect a national rebirth (*nationale Wiedergeburt*) and the social rejuvenation of our entire people (*die soziale Verjungung
unseres gesamten Volkes* [Cohen's italics]. This is why, in the view of a German, a triumph of arms is to be wished for.

(2) But this German teleology is also a Jewish teleology. Since this war is occurring, the same question arises: Why must a Jew wish for the triumph of German
arms? And what can this mean for the destiny of Judaism? In reply, this war is not

far from being presented as a war of liberation. Such, at least, is one's hope—or trust. By the "heroic victory of our fatherland," the "God of justice and love will put an end to the barbarous servitude" that the tzarist empire imposes upon our brethren (§41). The political existence of those poor Russian Jews is a shameful challenge to human right, dignity, and respect. But if he seems to place German Jewry higher than others, higher than downtrodden Russian Jewry for example, Cohen hopes precisely that the German victory will also advance the emancipation of the German Jews. He is well aware that progress remains to be made on the German side, for example, concerning the unreserved recognition of the Jewish religion, which cannot stop at mere legal equality. A German victory, thinks Cohen, should even enhance the life and the truth of the Jewish-German psyche. One knows why he was unable to submit his hypothesis to the test of experience.

(3) Finally, how can this approval of a just war, this hope for a German—one should say Jewish-German—victory, be reconciled with a fundamental pacifism, a pacifism associated besides with an originally Kantian cosmopolitanism? Thanks to the following major idea, which resembles, at least, an Idea in the Kantian sense: this war must be inscribed within the perspective of a messianic idea and bring about an international understanding, peace among nations. What should be the foundation of this peace? Let us pay close attention to the letter of these propositions. It provides exemplarism—which constitutes the very center of our reflection on nationality—with one of its most economical formulations. Our example (*unser Beispiel*), says Cohen (§41), must be capable of serving as a model (*als Vorbild dienen dürfen*). Our example must serve as an example—in other words, as a model, an exemplary example, a paradigm, or an ideal: *the Beispiel, as a Vorbild*. It must serve as an example for the acknowledgement (*Anerkennung*) of German hegemony, predominance, preponderance (*der deutschen Vormacht*: this last word italicized by Cohen) in all fundamentals or foundations of spiritual and psychic life (*in allen Grundlagen des Geistes- und des Seelenslebens*). The logic here is more extraordinary than ever: there will be no understanding and no peace among nations unless our example is followed. But let us follow the progression, which is also a redundant tautology, between the a priori synthesis and the analytic explicitation: our example (*Beispiel*) must be followed as an example (*Vorbild*) in order to acknowledge our *Vormacht*, German hegemony or preeminence. The progression from *Beispiel* to *Vorbild* to *Vormacht* is tautologous, since an example is not an indifferent case in a series. It is exemplary, a premodel, a preformatory model. To acknowledge it as such is to acknowledge German hegemony (*Vormacht*). Acknowledgement cannot remain merely theoretical. It doesn't go without political subjection—in the spiritual and psychic domain, of course, where all this teleological discourse belongs, while nevertheless proliferating purifying remarks vis-à-vis

foreigners and the alien, vis-à-vis "false allogenous glories," and so on, that is to say, remarks rarely pure of all xenophobia (see, notably, §45).

This spiritualist determination of national exemplarity does not belong to the German nation only. What would one say were it to be stated that it does not belong to it except in an exemplary manner? In *What Is a Nation?* (*Qu'est-ce qu'une nation?*), Renan too emphasizes this spiritual characteristic. "Nothing material" is sufficient for defining a nation. "A nation is a spiritual principle": neither race, nor even language, nor interests, nor religious affinity, nor geography, nor military necessities are sufficient to exhaust its definition. This spiritual principle is also called by Renan "soul": "A nation is a soul, a spiritual principle."

For reasons that are not only of time and space we shall point out only two of the motives which make us quote Renan here. Both lead us back to Cohen.

A. The first concerns memory and forgetting. For Cohen, to become aware of a sort of spiritual Jewish-German nation is to practice anamnesis of a rather peculiar kind. This anamnesis goes back to Plato, to Philo, to the Christian logos, to Maimonides, to Luther, to Kant, and Fichte, and so forth. Memory is possible. But it is also necessary and obligatory, which means that it is not taken for granted: forgetting is therefore equally constitutive of the history that will have formed a nation. Now, Renan's thesis, simultaneously paradoxical and sensible, is that forgetting makes the unity of a nation, not memory. More interestingly, Renan analyzes this forgetting as a sort of repression: it is active, selective, meaningful, in one word interpretive. Forgetting is not, in the case of a nation, a simple psychological effacement, a wearing out or a meaningless obstacle making access to the past more difficult, as when an archive has been accidentally destroyed. No, if there is a forgetting, this is because there is no bearing something which was at the origin of the nation, surely an act of violence, a traumatic event, some sort of a curse one does not admit. In the midst of historical narratives, that we should all find interest in rereading, whatever our nationality (I can count at least four here), Renan writes, for example:

> Forgetting, and I would say even historical error, are an essential factor in the formation of a nation, and thus the progress of historical study is often a danger for nationality. Historical investigation, in effect, brings back to light the violent deeds which took place at the origin of all political formations, even those whose consequences have been beneficial. Unity is always achieved brutally: the union of Northern and Southern France was the result of extermination and of terror continued for nearly a century. The King of France, who is, I dare say, the ideal type of a crystallizer, the King of France who has achieved the most perfect national unity ever achieved; the King of France, too closely seen, has lost his prestige; the nation he had formed has cursed him, and today none but the cultivated minds know what he was worth and what he has done.

A series of examples (French, Slavic, Czech, and German) allows Renan to conclude: "Now, the essence of a nation is that all individuals should have many things
in common and that all should have forgotten quite a few things. No French citizen
knows whether he is a Burgundian, an Alainian, a Tifalian, a Visigoth; every French
citizen must have forgotten Saint Bartholomew, the 13th century massacres in the
South. There are not ten families in France that can furnish evidence of a Frankish
origin, and any such evidence would still be totally defective, as a result of a thousand unknown interbreedings capable of undoing all our genealogical systems."

These truths, always worth saying, remind us of at least two things. On the one
hand, a nation does not exist as long as there is no certainty that "all should have
forgotten quite a few things"; as long as some remember originary deeds of violence, a nation remains unassured of its essence and of its existence. On the other
hand, as long as some remember and recall the purity of their origin (Burgundian,
Alainian, Visigothic, for example), the nation remains unassured of its essence or of
its existence.

These truths, however, we should not forget. They did not prevent the French
historian Renan from forgetting in his turn (QED), and from being rather violent,
when he dares to state the following blatant untruth: "An honorable fact for France
is that it has never sought to obtain unity of language by coercive measures." We
know that this is not so (QED). The objectivity of historical science, an interpretive
discipline through and through, is here affected at a given moment in one of its
representatives by its [or his] belonging to a national institution, the French language, to begin with. Limits of self interpretation.

This discourse about forgetting is interesting not only for what it says of an originary violence, constitutive and still vaguely active. Even though Renan does not do
so, one may even put it in communication with a comment located elsewhere in the
same text. If a nation has a soul or a spiritual principle, this is not only, says Renan,
because it is not founded upon anything of what is called race, language, religion,
place, army, interest, and so on. It is because a nation is at the same time both memory (and forgetting pertains to the very deployment of this memory) and, in the
present, promise, project, a "desire to live together." Isn't this promise in itself, by
structure, a relation to the future which involves forgetting, indeed, a sort of essential indifference to the past, to that in the present which is not present, but also an
ingathering, that is, a memory of the future? "A remembered future," one might say,
twisting perhaps the title of a book you are well familiar with.[15] This is not Renan's
language. I propose it nevertheless in order to interpret this statement of his:

---

15. The reference is to a book by Harold Fish, a professor from Bar-Ilan University in Israel, who participated in the conference.

186 ACTS OF RELIGION

> A nation is a soul, a spiritual principle. Two things which, truly speaking, are one constitute this soul, this spiritual principle. [Thus we have the spirit and the psyche, the latter being divided in two, we shall soon see, thus being reflected in time: the past and the future turn around a present pivot.] One is in the past, the other in the present. One is the possession in common of a rich legacy of memories; the other is the present assent, the desire to live together, the wish to continue to make the most out of the heritage one has received undivided. Man, gentlemen, does not improvise.

The "present assent," the "desire to live together" are performative commitments, promises which must be renewed daily, inscribing the necessity of forgetting in memory itself, one within the other inseparably. And further on: "The existence of a nation is (forgive me this metaphor) a daily plebiscite, just as the existence of the individual is a perpetual affirmation of life. Oh, I know, this is less metaphysical than divine right, less brutal than supposedly historical right."

Is this quite so certain? Here I leave this question suspended.

B. Another theme recalls Cohen's discourse: that of the European confederation. Appearing after the 1870 war, referring to it (something it has in common with Cohen's later discourse, with which it is from this viewpoint contemporaneous), Renan's text takes stock, in 1882, of what he calls the secession, the crumbling of nations:

> We have driven out of politics the metaphysical and theological abstractions. What remains after that? Man remains, his desires, his needs. The secession, you will tell me, and in the long run the crumbling of nations, are the consequences of a system which puts these old organisms at the mercy of wills that are often hardly enlightened.... Nations are not something eternal. They began and they shall end. The European confederation will probably replace them. But such is not the law of the century we live in. At the present time, the existence of nations is good, even necessary. Their existence guarantees liberty, which would be lost were the world to have but one master.

～

This leads us back to our third question: How can Cohen reconcile his hope for a Jewish-German victory with his cosmopolitan pacifism inspired by Kant? How can the German spirit become the center of a confederation that would guarantee world peace? How to legitimize a war by claiming that it is just (*gerechte*) because it is also the preparation (*Vorbereitung*) for perpetual peace?

If the spirit of universal humanity is, *in an exemplary manner*, the origin of *our* Jewish-German ethic, the German spirit is surely, from a moral viewpoint, the spirit of cosmopolitanism as it was formed in the eighteenth century. If a national development serves universal justice, the use of force is legitimate if it in turn serves this national development in its exemplary singularity. In this war, says Cohen, every German is conscious of both national right and universal justice. From this consciousness he draws a "sublime energy" (*mit erhabener Energie*) (§46), and in this too this letter to the American Jews definitely resembles a treatise on the sublime. (Let it be said in passing, this description of the soldier's "consciousness" is undoubtedly sufficiently correct to have been also that in which the French soldier had been educated at the same moment—like every nonmercenary soldier in every war in the world.) In this consciousness [*conscience*, also "conscience"], force is not opposed to right. Here enters an analogy between the individual and the State. "What the organism is for the spirit of the individual, force is for the State, that spirit of peoples" (§46). Just as the individual should not thwart humanity, the individual power of each State should not thwart the universal State, that is, the confederation of States which ought to be the ideal of every State. According to natural right or according to positive and historical right, the concept of State requires federation. This requirement is written into it and must lead to its maturity. The project of an international socialism must not remain a utopia. And war is there in order to make it finally emerge out of utopia! The power of the State is necessary in order to make socialism effective, to make it into something other than a "blunt weapon and a half-truth." One sees the working of the same logic, less and less a Kantian one, Hegelian rather, or quasi-Hegelian: the logic of effectivity or of effecting of the State, just that logic that Rosenzweig will have broken with. The force of the State is here supposed to render effective a socialist and internationalist ideal, which otherwise would remain abstract, in a state of pure subjective representation.

Whereas he had bracketed off the philosophy of history, Cohen now declares, so it seems, just the opposite: the concept of "confederation," or of "the achievement of the ideal of the state" must be erected into the "*principle of the philosophy of History*" (§47).

Let us provisionally conclude our discussion of this point. Like all the others, the problem of confederation is everywhere a pressing matter of the moment.

Why does Cohen cease taking his cue from Kant when he goes into the problem of confederation and perpetual peace? Because he believes, unlike Kant, in the necessity of permanent armies. Kant, for his own part, put it in principle that the constitution of permanent armies (*miles perpetuus*) must "disappear in time": "No peace treaty may be considered such, if one secretly reserves in it some subject for resuming war." Condemning any "*reservatio mentalis*" in peace treaties, he speaks of a sparrow, and this surely addresses itself to hawks and doves of all nations:

"Expecting a universal lasting peace from what is called the balance of European powers is purely a chimera, similar to that house in Swift, built by an architect in a manner so conforming to the rules of equilibrium, that a sparrow having alighted upon it, it crumbled instantly."[16]

Cohen thinks, unlike Kant, that the existence of permanent armies is not in itself the cause for wars. He incriminates militarism rather, and condemns those who see militarism wherever there is anything military. Militarism is a depravation of the military. It arises when people exalt an army that, rather than serve a State worthy of this name, serves economic powers and the interests of capitalist expansionism. An antinomy may exist between the State and the military when the army puts itself in the service of private economic forces or a fraction of civilian society. But once it has become effective, the ideal State—that is, ethical and confederative in its orientation, hence German in spirit—has no reason to give up its permanent army. Cohen thus opposes "our conception of military service" to that of the English enemy, whose social policy gave an impetus to the war. It is true that in passing, and this will forbid us once more to simplify our reading, he calls upon a Kantian proposition in the domain of right, if not morality: the exercise of right implies a capacity for constraint.

> If each State is therefore founded so that it cannot renounce its army, this is not only because it means to protect itself, but also because it wants to reserve the ideal of confederation, since the latter, like every constitution founded on right, implies that force should be put to the service of its protection. Consequently the State, a separate entity endowed with an army, remains, from the legitimate viewpoint that takes into account the history of nations both in a genealogical and a teleological perspective, the original force (*ursprungliche Kraft*) that must give the initial impetus to the achievement of the moral task incumbent upon humanity. It is all too certain that confederation is the end that the State must pursue so that the ideal of the State can be achieved elsewhere than in itself (§48).

Earlier on (§46), the State had been described as the summit (*Gipfel*), the summit of the nation as well as the summit of humanity. "The ideal of the State culminates in the confederation of States."

Translated by Moshe Ron

---

16. Immanuel Kant, *Théorie et pratique* (*Critique of Practical Reason*), French translation by Jean-Michel Muglioni (Paris: Vrin, 1990).

4

A Note on "The Eyes of Language"

In this previously unpublished text, Derrida delivers a reading he announced in "Interpretations at War" and in *Monolingualism of the Other*, a reading of a letter written by Gershom Scholem to Franz Rosenzweig in 1926. At that time, Scholem had already been awarded the chair for the study of Jewish mysticism at Hebrew University, and Rosenzweig's fortieth birthday was celebrated with a series of texts, among which was this letter. Written in German on the subject of Hebrew as the "sacred language," on Hebrew as it is thought to be "revived" and even "resuscitated" in Palestine, the letter is a confession as to the possibility and impossibility of this revival, the possibility and impossibility of secularizing the sacred language. Derrida here continues to explore the "name of God," as well as the struggle, the interpretations at war within the "Jewish-German psyche," between Scholem and Rosenzweig, and the "uprising" of and within the sacred language "itself" as it figures in Scholem's text. At stake are interpretations of Judaism, Zionism, spectrality, apocalypse and messianism, technology, sacrifice and generations, vengeance, and the theologico-political. More importantly, perhaps, the letter, as Derrida reads it, is about a "catastrophe of language" that, far from being contained in the linguistic

---

Translator's note: In its present form, the text is an extensive revision of an unpublished translation prepared by Joseph Adamson and Jean Wilson for Derrida in the 1980s. I gratefully acknowledge their work.

As a matter of rule, by providing the French in brackets, I have sought less to "ground" the translation than to signal a difficulty that is already there in the French, a situation of originary, and impossible, translation. Throughout the text I translate the French *langue* to the English *language*. This is, in part, because Derrida shows the oscillation in Scholem's own text between a general language and a specific tongue, speech (*langue*) or language (namely Hebrew). This oscillation is both based on and troubled by the distinction between "sacred" and "secular" languages, as well as the distinction between a language spoken or written, a language spoken or written about, and moreover, spoken or written about in yet another language such as is repeatedly the case here. With these qualifications in mind, one could nonetheless take note of Scholem's writing between German and a Hebrew that is and is not spoken, that is and is not Hebrew, while in turn being read and written between German, Hebrew, and French by Derrida here translated into an English which also falls (and fails as) in between. The abyssal condition of translation therefore leaves little room for certainty, and resembles nothing less than a "gathering of languages."

sphere, threatens to explode, threatens to contaminate at once sacred and secular language(s). Yet the question that Derrida raises by commenting on Scholem is whether there could be such a thing as a "secular" language. Could there be a language in which one could speak of language, and of sacred language in particular? "Secular language as meta-language," Derrida writes, "does not exist in itself; it has neither presence nor consistency of its own. Its title is that of a 'façon de parler,' thus of comporting itself toward the only language that is or that matters—the sacred language." Yet, sacred language cannot be faced, for one is either blind to its power and violence or one falls into its threatening abysses.

G. A.

p. 200 no Archimedean point - true → o

the sacralization of secular
languag - what Derrida does

comment
on appdix

Mpltfying
power relations
where is Arabic?

the true landscape

PP.
210-211

Is what
our usual
language
on
time
dependence

START c p. 209

THE EYES OF LANGUAGE
The Abyss and the Volcano

Language
Time →
dormancy

Arabic)
Latin)

sacred
secular

language
time
dependence
place
dependence

This letter has no testamentary character, though it was found after Scholem's death, in his papers, in 1985. Here it is, nonetheless, arriving and returning to us, speaking to us *after* the death of its signatory, and something in it henceforth resonates like the voice of a ghost [*fantôme*].

Benveniste

What gives this resonance a kind of depth is yet something else: Here is this ghostly voice that cautions, warns, predicts the worst, announces the return or the reversal, the revenge and the catastrophe, the resentment, the retaliation, the punishment—and it resurges at a moment in the history of Israel that makes one sensitive more than ever to this imminence of the apocalypse. The letter was written in December 1926, long before the birth of the State of Israel, but what constitutes its theme, namely, the secularization of the language, had already been systematically undertaken in Palestine from the beginning of the century.

One has at times the impression that a *revenant* proclaims to us the terrifying return of a ghost.

P. 227 → # biblical
place names

P. 213
214

This "Confession on the Subject of Our Language (*Bekenntnis über unsere Sprache*)" has thus been translated and published by Stéphane Mosès (who, since then, had the kindness to send me the original) in 1985 in the *Archives des sciences sociales et religieuses* under the title "An Unpublished Letter from Gershom Scholem to Franz Rosenzweig, on the Subject of Our Language, a Confession [*Une lettre inédite de Gershom Scholem à Franz Rosenzweig, à propos de notre langue, une confession*]." The letter is followed by an invaluable article by Stéphane Mosès, "Language and Secularization in Gershom Scholem [*Langage et sécularisation chez Gershom Scholem*]" to which I am, of course, greatly indebted.

the problem of modern Israel →
secular rests on sacred
settler movement

191

In order to broach a presentation of the signatory and of the addressee of this letter, in order to announce it while renouncing it, I begin by reading a page from Scholem's book of memoirs, *From Berlin to Jerusalem,* that traces precisely the territory and one of the geographical, political, historical and cultural trajectories I am attempting to follow in this seminar:

I had been in Frankfurt for three days the previous year and had seen Franz Rosenzweig there several times. Rudolf Hallo, a young man who, like Rosenzweig, was from Kassel and had for some time been deeply influenced by him, had been my fellow student in Munich. From Hallo I learned much about Rosenzweig, his development and turning to Judaism, and early in 1920 Hallo brought me a copy of Rosenzweig's recently published main work *Der Stern der Erlösung* [The Star of Redemption],[1] undoubtedly one of the central creations of Jewish religious thought in this century. Thus I started corresponding with Rosenzweig, who had in the meantime heard about me from various sources. At that time Rosenzweig still had his health and had started to study the Talmud with the famous rabbi Dr. Nobel in Frankfurt.[2] Every encounter with him furnished evidence that he was a man of genius (I regard the abolition of this category, which is popular today, as altogether foolish and the "reasons" adduced for it as valueless) [There would be much to say about this remark made in passing. It is not without relation to the content of our letter and the critique of a kind of secularizing rationalization that flattens, levels, evens out, with the language, the resistance of any singularity or any exception, a certain geniality which could be shown to be not unrelated to sacredness, but also a certain originarity and a certain original engendering —J. D.] and also that he had equally marked dictatorial inclinations [I would add: as obviously marked as those of Scholem himself — J. D.]. Our decisions took us in entirely different directions. He sought to reform (or perhaps I should say revolutionize) German Jewry from within. I, on the other hand, no longer had any hopes for the amalgam known as *"Deutschjudentum,"* i.e., a Jewish community that considered itself German, and expected a renewal of Jewry only from its rebirth in Eretz Yisrael. Certainly we found each other of interest. Never before or since have I seen such an intense Jewish orientation as that displayed by this man, who was midway in age between Martin Buber and me. What I did not know was that he regarded me as a nihilist [I do not know what Rosenzweig may have thought of the 1926 letter addressed to him by Scholem. But, as paradoxical as this may seem, it could have confirmed this diagnosis: nihilism. It is true that the very "logic," the "pro-

---

1. Franz Rosenzweig, *The Star of Redemption,* trans. William W. Hallo (New York: Rinehart & Winston, 1971).
2. Nehemiah Anton Nobel (1871–1922), German rabbi who served in Cologne from 1896 to 1899 and in Frankfurt from 1910.

gram" of "nihilism"—and these words must be put within quotation marks—always give it the most gripping resemblances with its opposite —J. D.]. My second visit, which involved a long conversation one night about the very German Jewishness that I rejected, was the occasion for a complete break between us. I would never have broached this delicate topic, which stirred such emotions in us both, if I had known that Rosenzweig was then already in the first stages of his fatal disease, a lateral sclerosis. He had had an attack which had not yet been definitely diagnosed, but I was told that he was on the mend, and the only thing left was a certain difficulty in speaking [This remark, yet again, over-imprints [*surimprime*] an "unheimlich," "uncanny" note to this account of a stormy and crepuscular debate on a certain historical experience of which one might say, without exaggeration, that it touches on *Unheimlichkeit* in general and on the "manner of speaking [*façon de parler*]," even on a diagnosis of aphasia —J. D.[3]]. Thus I had one of the stormiest and most irreparable arguments of my youth. Three years later, however, Buber and Ernst Simon asked me to contribute to a portfolio of very short essays which was to be presented to Rosenzweig,[4] who was then already paralyzed and unable to speak, on his fortieth birthday, and I did so. When I was in Frankfurt in August of 1927, Ernst Simon said to me: "Rosenzweig would be very pleased if you visited him." I went and told the terminally ill man about my work. He could move only one finger and with it directed a specially constructed needle over an alphabet board, while his wife translated his motions into sentences. It was a heartrending visit. Yet Rosenzweig produced very impressive work even in those years, participated in the Bible translation project inaugurated by Buber, and corresponded copiously with many.[5]

Rosenzweig is ill, therefore, partially paralyzed, and aphasic when, in 1926, Scholem sends him this "confession" for his fortieth birthday, from Jerusalem, where he has settled for the past three years. As Mosès reminds us, "Rosenzweig reproached Scholem for thinking that 'the Judaism of the Diaspora is in a state of clinical death and that it is only "over there" that it will return to life'" (in a letter from Rosenzweig to Scholem, dated January 6, 1922).[6] According to Rosenzweig, Zionism is a "secular form of Messianism," which itself attempts to "normalize," and thus also to secularize, Judaism—whence the strange chiasmus and the double unilaterality of a

3. *Translator's note:* the word "uncanny" is in English in the text.

4. Ernst Akiba Simon (1899–1988), born in Berlin, was coeditor of the newspaper *Der Jude* in 1918. He emigrated to Palestine in 1928 but responded to the appeal launched by Martin Buber in 1934 to take charge of the education of Jews excluded from public institutions by Adolf Hitler.

5. Gershom Scholem, *From Berlin to Jerusalem: Memories of My Youth*, trans. Harry Zohn (New York: Schocken Books, 1980), 139–41.

6. Quoted in Stéphane Mosès, "Langage et sécularisation chez Gershom Scholem," in *Archives de Science Sociales des Religions* 60: 1 (July–September 1985), 87.

correspondence without correspondence: accused of being on the side of secularization, Scholem writes a "confession" addressed to Rosenzweig in order to confide in
him his concerns about that very secularization. On the one hand, Rosenzweig re-
proaches Zionism—and consequently Scholem at the moment when the latter is
preparing to emigrate to Palestine—as a secularization of Jewish Messianism, a
secularization and a historical, if not a historicist integration, not to say a profanation, of messianic sacredness. But, a few years later, after three years in Palestine,
Scholem's "confession" seems to avow that secularization is indeed a certain risk run
by Zionism, and it is one that passes first through language. Naturally, this movement in the form of an avowal is no doubt marked [*accentué*] to some extent: it is
destined to erase some of the violence of the discussion with Rosenzweig that leaves
Scholem with a guilty conscience. Before receiving this letter, in 1926, Rosenzweig
wrote, "Scholem projects onto me the guilty conscience he has on my account and
imagines that I hold a grudge against him."[7] Here again, these movements, these
folds of remorse, this affect of guilt between these two German Jews who stand on
opposite sides of history, of eschatology, of the State of Israel, and so forth do not, it
seems to me, form only the *exterior* decor of the drama that is being played out and
over which they struggle: the revenge or the return of the sacred, the reproach of the
sacred in the face of a "politicolinguistic" profanation.

What does Scholem confess? What does he avow and in what sense is this an
avowal or a confession—that is to say, at the same time, a recognition in the sense
of an avowal and an avowal in the sense of a profession of faith? It is a confession
before Rosenzweig the anti-Zionist, because Scholem is a Zionist—that is what he
wants to be, that is what he remains and confirms being. Yet, he cannot but recognize in Zionism an *evil*, an inner evil, an evil that is anything but accidental [*un mal
qui n'a rien d'accidentel*]. More precisely, one cannot but recognize that the accident that befalls Zionism or that lies in wait for it threatens it essentially, in its closest proximity: *in its language* [*au plus proche de lui-même*: dans sa langue], and as
soon as a Zionist opens his mouth. This evil has the triple form of threat or danger,
first, then of failure, and finally, at the root of the danger and the failure, the form
of profanation, of corruption and sin. It is a matter of what used to be called then,
in Palestine, the "actualization (*Aktualisierung*)" of the Hebrew language, its modernization, the transformation undertaken since the beginning of the century (Ben
Yehuda) and pursued systematically toward adapting biblical Hebrew to the needs
of everyday communication, be it technical and national, but also, for a modern
nation, international and interstate communication. This linguistic evil does not

---

7. Quoted in Mosès, "Langage et sécularisation," 88.

let itself be localized or circumscribed. It does not only affect one means of communication precisely because it degrades into a means of communication a language originarily or essentially destined for something entirely distinct from information. One transforms a language and, first of all, names, into an informative medium (as we will see, all this is supported by a very Benjaminian interpretation of the essence of language as nomination). The linguistic evil is total; it has no limit, first of all because it is entirely political. The evil stems from the fact that Zionists—those who believe themselves Zionists and who are, in fact, no more than holding this power, nothing other than falsifiers of Zionism—do not understand the essence of language. They treat this abyssal mystery as a problem—worse, as a local, specific, circumscribed, technolinguistic or technopolitical problem. This is why they are asleep and why one day they will wake up on the verge, even in the midst, of the catastrophe, at the moment when the sacred language will return, as punishment and return/ghostliness [*revenance*].

It is indeed a matter of "catastrophe"—the word is Scholem's—a turn and a return, a reversal: the evil will not only consist in the loss of the sacred language, thus of Hebrew, and thus of what is essential to Zionism, but in an avenging return of the sacred language that will violently turn against those who speak it (*gegen ihre Sprecher ausbrechen*), against those who have desecrated it. Then, terrible things will not fail to happen. Events will be produced by this linguistic sin. The catastrophe will depend on this added turn, this return of the sacred, an unavoidable return whose shape [*forme*] will be revenge and the spectral *revenant*. This catastrophe of language will not only be linguistic. From the beginning of the letter, the political and national dimension is staged.

"This country is like a volcano in which language boils (*Dies Land ist ein Vulkan. Es beherbergt die Sprache*)."[8] In Palestine, one speaks much about language; one is very occupied and preoccupied with languages. Everything that concerns the linguistic is boiling. Language is overheated, words burn, one can hardly touch them and yet one does nothing but that. The allusion to the figure of the volcano, in the very first words, signifies both this boiling and the imminence of an eruption that will swallow the whole country. Imminence of the reversal, imminence of the catastrophe, and the value [*valeur*] of imminence is here very striking [*marquante*], which connotes all the Messianic, apocalyptic or eschatological discourses. The confession announces, warns, and cautions against what will not fail to happen tomorrow. Imminence, therefore, of an outpouring that risks releasing a lava that

---

8. *Translator's note:* Derrida here follows Mosès's translation which has, "Ce pays est pareil à un volcan où bouillonnerait le language."

boils still in the crater where are gathered the energies of this little country. This volcano is language, that which labors, happens, and suffers within language, the passion of a language, what a sacred language *suffers* [*souffre*].

The staging that blends the passion of language with the elements (earth, boiling water, air and water afire) nevertheless privileges fire. In this respect, it is already a very biblical figuration. "It speaks [*ça parle*]" through the volcano, language will speak through fire, it will come out of itself and return through this fire hole: mouthpiece, trumpet, and mouth of fire, a jealous and revengeful God who is a God of fire (one recalls here Spinoza's fright before the jealousy of this God of fire). Not to mention a burning bush. Can one not say, consequently, that Scholem speaks, in a certain manner ("a manner of speaking [*une façon de parler*]"), a sacred language? Yet that he does so in German (Hebrew figures in the German language) and in order to speak the evil that has happened, that will happen [*pour dire le mal qui vient d'arriver, qui va arriver*] to the sacred language, but will happen [*advenir*] to it as much through a certain return of the sacred language that will *come back* as through its departure, through the experience in which we separate ourselves from this language or depart from it? This country is a volcano, then, and language inhabits it. Language dwells, as one says, *on top of* a volcano. And Scholem continues, "One speaks more than ever today about the Arabs. But more uncanny than the Arab people (*unheimlicher als das arabisches Volk*) another threat confronts us that is a *necessary* consequence [I emphasize and insist: *mit notwendigkeit* —J. D.] of the Zionist undertaking: What about the "actualization (*Aktualisierung*)" of Hebrew? Must not this abyss (*Abgrund*) of a sacred language handed down to our children break out again [*wieder aufbrechen*, the phrase will often recur —J. D.]?

After the volcano, the "abyss." The volcano is only named once. It is the first word after *Land*. But the abyss, if I have counted well, reappears five times in the letter. Scholem does not collapse the figure of the volcano with that of the abyss, though I would be tempted to do so. In both cases it is a matter of an invisible chasm [*gouffre*], a resounding hollow at the bottom of which a catastrophe is literally stirred up [*fomentée*] (*fovimentum; foment*, this is a certain work of fire), either that fire comes out of it or that one falls into it. In any case, one does not see what occurs there. One is blind at the bottom of the abyss and at the bottom of the volcano. One can only interpret, indirectly, the signs that one hears coming from the bottom of the chasm, the fumes that escape and announce that which is coming and which, precisely, one does not see coming.

One must speak, therefore, to the blind. That is the act of this confession. But in a confession, the one who announces, cautions, warns, and even accuses does not exclude himself from the whole [*ensemble*] of his addressees. He accuses himself as well, and he avows his having been blind to the Zionist blindness that he does not, however, renounce. He only opposes an essential Zionism or a Zionism to come to actual Zionism [*un sionisme de fait*], to the Zionism that blindly practices an "actualization" of the sacred language without seeing the abyss. Scholem figures as a kind of singular, solitary Zionist: not only alone but the only Zionist; one could almost say that he is preaching in the desert. Or, rather: he insists simply on the verge of the abyss—this is his desert, his place without place [*son lieu sans lieu*]— he insists and sojourns at this improbable border. And one shall never know—this at least will be the question guiding my reading but, for essential reasons, it will also remain unanswered—whether at this limit where no settlement is possible Scholem asks for a *shibboleth* in order to get out of the abyss or, finally, in order to rush into it and be engulfed by it [*pour s'y engouffrer*]. There will be some difficulty in identifying his desire here. And the desire of this "we," the site of this "we" in the name of which he speaks when he specifies, for instance: "And on the day this eruption occurs, which generation will suffer its effects (*Und welches Geschlecht wird dieser Ausbruch finden*)? We do live inside this language ["this language" is Hebrew—and he says this in German to another German Jew? It is true that the original does not say here "our language, *unsere Sprache*" as does—and this amounts to the same thing—the title (*Bekenntnis über unsere Sprache*). Here it is "*Wir leben ja in dieser Sprache*, we live inside this language"; there is no possible equivocation —J. D.], most of us as blind men [*pareils, pour la plupart d'entre nous, à des* aveugles] walking confidently above an abyss.[9] But when our sight is restored, we or those who come after us, must we not fall to the bottom of this abyss? And no one knows whether the sacrifice (*das Opfer*) of individuals who will be annihilated in this abyss will suffice to close it."

I will come back later to these last words, the sacrifice and the fall (*hineinstürtzen*), and to the strange logic of such a sacrifice. The overstatement, the *mise-en-abyme* of the abyss, the supplement of catastrophe relates to this abyss of language—that will soon take the name of *name*—into which one falls at the moment of seeing, at the moment when one has just seen, at the moment of lucidity, when one becomes aware of the essence of language, to wit, that it is either sacred or it is not [*à savoir de ce qu'elle est sacrée ou elle n'est pas*], which for Scholem means: It consists of names, it returns/amounts to naming [*elle revient à nommer*], without which it *does not* consist at all and it *never* returns, it returns/amounts to nothing [*ne revient à rien*], returns to no one, and no longer returns/amounts to itself [*ne revient plus à elle*].

It is thus lucidity that threatens to engulf us, not blindness. The blind men that we are, *almost all of us*, live in this language, above an abyss. (*Wir leben ja in dieser*

---

9. *Translator's note:* Here again, Derrida follows the French translation.

Sprache über einem Abgrund, fast alle mit der Sicherheit des Blinden). But the seers, the lucid ones, fall into it—this is what we must understand.

What should language be, then, and first of all the sacred language (but we will see that, according to Scholem, there is no other)? What should the language be such that *seeing it and falling into it* would be the *same* event? What is the relation between light and lucidity, between the essence of language and the fall to the bottom of the abyss? How shall we hear this name of abyss about which we will see that it opens up on the name itself, the name of *name*, and the name of which returns so often in the letter? We have just encountered it for the first time. A few lines later, Scholem denounces those who have had the demonic and blind courage to restore life to the sacred names, to resuscitate a language destined to become an Esperanto, there where only an Esperanto was possible. Scholem describes them as "spellbound" (but they are also sorcerers, sorcerers' apprentices) who walk "above the abyss," above the silent abyss, at the moment when they transmit to our youth the ancient names and seals. But these sacred names, precisely those that the blind men bequeath to our youth without seeing and without knowing [*sans voir et sans savoir*], they *are* the abyss. They conceal the abyss—in them the abyss is sealed. And it is the abyss that they bequeath thus to our children without seeing and without knowing. The abyss is in the name, one could say, if such a topology were representable, if the bottomlessness [*sans-fond*] of the *Abgrund* could still let itself be included, inscribed, comprehended. At bottom, at the bottom of this bottomlessness [*au fond de ce sans-fond*], what the blind sorcerers of secularization do not see, is not so much the abyss itself, over which they walk like madmen, but rather that the abyss does not, any more than language, let itself be dominated, tamed, instrumentalized, secularized. The abyss no more than language, for both take place, *their* place, without objectifiable topology, in the name: "*Sprache ist Namen*, language is Name." *Sprache* is at the same time language and speech [*la langue et le langage*]. It is not enough to say that language [*la langue*] is or consists of the names. Speaking is naming; it is calling [*parler, c'est nommer, c'est appeler*]. What does this mean? What does Scholem himself want to name in this letter? And in the face of the abyssal character of this question, how to read this letter [*comment lire cette lettre*]?

I am here attempting a reading that is as internal as possible. I do not believe in purely internal readings, nor do I believe that they are rigorously possible. Without recourse to the many other arguments proper to demonstrate this, and in order to stay as close as possible to this letter, the simple event of the name would suffice to produce a breach in this supposed interiority of the text. And yet, the document constituted by this letter is sufficiently rich and visibly abyssal, as it were, for us first of all to make the effort of reading it as closely to its letter as possible, and to do so in order to lose from it as little as possible. We have begun to do this, first, by making ourselves attentive to the fact that this is a letter and that this fact is marked in the letter of this letter; second, by taking into account its apparently principal destination, its addressee, and the relationship between Scholem and Rosenzweig, which turns this gesture into a confession; and third, by underlining the unusual nature of this writing, which recalls through certain of its traits the language, the figures and the pathos of the sacred text of which it speaks, it names, but through a foreign language—German—that, as a nonsacred language, as a vehicular language, happens to be the nonetheless maternal tongue [*la langue néanmoins maternelle*] of the two correspondents, Scholem and Rosenzweig.

Whence the general form of the question that confronts us on the—internal and external—edge [*bord*] of this reading, as on the edge of those abysses of abysses: In what language *can* or *must* the appeal be launched, this appeal that is also a warning, in the face of the threat of a secularization of the sacred language? This appeal to guard oneself (from secularization) in order to safeguard the sacred language figures an event about which one must ask where it takes place [*où il a lieu*]: is it in the sacred language or outside it? And what is the nature of the limit between the two sites [*les deux lieux*]? This question complicates or augments itself by way of the following: Can one speak a sacred language as a foreign language? This question in turn perverts or deepens itself thus: Is a sacred language more proper or more foreign [*plus propre ou plus étrangère*] in general? And are we dealing in this case with an alternative, with an oppositional logic?

For example, can Scholem claim to speak "*out of* [*depuis*]" the experience of the sacred language, of the sacred names, while putting forward what he says about it, while putting himself forward "*out of* [*depuis*]" the enigmatic fact that he is speaking through German [*qu'il parle à travers l'allemand*]? I now leave to these "out of's [*depuis*]" in quotation marks all their volcanic potential. It is another dimension of the question that we had formulated in the course of our reading of Spinoza: where to locate the sacred? If one speaks—incorrectly, according to Spinoza—of a sacred language, must one consider that the words or the names of the language are themselves sacred? Or only the signifieds? Or only the things named, aimed at [*visées*] through these names? Spinoza rejects all these hypotheses: the sacred is neither in the words nor in the things—only, one could say, in the intentional sense, in the attitude or the usage that brings us toward the ones and the others, toward the ones through the others [*qui nous rapporte aux uns et aux autres, aux uns à travers les autres*].

In what language, then, does this letter write itself? One cannot be content with the *phenomenon*: it is written in German. But neither can one reduce this phenomenon to some inconsistent or secondary appearance. The letter *presents itself* in

German but this self-presentation is also the confession of someone for someone who partakes with him of a rapport to Hebrew that is intense, cultivated, refined and *engagé*. Hebrew is not, for either of them, a mother tongue, but they live it as an archimaternal or patriarchal language. It is a language in the name of which, in view of which, out of which [*depuis laquelle*] they speak together, they have been corresponding for a long time. And this language, then, is, in several senses of the word, the *subject of the letter*.

One might let oneself be tempted here by what I take the risk of calling the hypothesis of the third language [*l'hypothèse de la troisième langue*]. By these words I do not mean a foreign language, German, in which would be formulated a *warning* that would concern two practices of Hebrew, the sacred and the secular. The expression *third language* would rather name a differentiated and differentiating element, a *medium* that would not be *stricto sensu* linguistic but the middle/milieu of an experience of language that, being neither sacred nor profane, permits the passage from one to the other—and to tell one and the other [*et de dire l'un et l'autre*], translating one into the other, appealing from one to the other. In other words, according to the logic of this hypothesis (which Scholem would no doubt judge unacceptable and badly formed; we shall see why in a moment), one would really have *to suppose*, precisely, that signatory and addressee locate themselves between the two languages, and that the former, the one who warns, presents himself as ferryman [*passeur*], as translator, as mediator. Partaking of the two languages, the intercessor only speaks them out of the experience of a third, or, at any rate, out of something in language that, not yet or already no longer sacred *or* secular, or *already still* both at once, permits one to take this step [*ce pas*] on the edge of the abyss.

What, then, would this language be in general, this third language that lets surge within itself the adversity—sacred/nonsacred? holy/not-holy? (Levinas).

But immediately, a question about this question, about the form and the logic—at once transcendental and dialectical—of this question: What if, in fact, *there were no* third language, no language in general, no neutral language within which were possible, in order to take place within it [*dans laquelle serait possible, pour y avoir lieu*], the contamination of the sacred by the profane, the corruption of names (Spinoza), the opposition of the holy and the secular? And what if the dialectico-transcendental hypothesis were already to carry, in its very neutrality, an effect of desacralization, the very thing that the letter incriminates? What if this neutralization by recourse to the third, already to a kind of metalinguistic referee, were also a positivist naturalization of the supernatural?

The axiomatics governing Scholem's letter is wholly other [*tout autre*], and wholly other is its rhetoric as well.

And the wholly other of the letter's rhetoric relates, in a paradoxical and fascinating way, to its treatment of the opposition between sacred language and secular
language as a *rhetorical effect*. At bottom, Scholem seems to say—but this is the bottom of the abyss—there is only sacred language [*il n'y a jamais que de la langue
sacrée*]. Language is one, it suffered no opposition and, at least in the case of
Hebrew (which is not one case in a series), there is only sacred language. It was
born sacred and does not let itself be desacralized without ceasing to be what it is.
This secularization one is talking about, that I am talking about, Scholem seems to
say, that I accuse and of which I complain, that I warn against, this secularization
does not exist; it is but a "*façon de parler*, a manner of speaking." This expression,
façon de parler is also a manner of speaking. It is used by Scholem in French in the
German text. We will return to this rhetorical manner of saying rhetoric [*cette
manière rhétorique de dire la rhétorique*]. That the secularization one talks about
would be only a "manner of speaking" does not render the phenomenon—or the
symptom—less grave or more inconsistent, on the contrary.

This is played out from the very first lines of the letter, after the figure of the volcano and the allusion to the danger more uncanny (*unheimlicher* [*inquiétant*])
than the Arab people, to the "necessary consequence" of the Zionist undertaking
Scholem has therefore just recognized—and recognition is the gravity of his confession [*et de reconnaître c'est toute la gravité de sa confession*]—in front of the noto-
rious anti-Zionism of his addressee, that the evil is worse and more uncanny than
any other properly political danger [*tout autre danger proprement politique*]. This
evil of language is also a political evil but it is not an infantile illness of Zionism.
This "necessary consequence" is congenital to every Zionist project for a nation-
state. Scholem continues, "[W]hat about the 'actualization' of Hebrew? Must not
this abyss of a sacred language handed down to our children break out again?
Surely, no one knows what is being done here. One believes that language has been
secularized, that its apocalyptic thorn has been pulled out. But this is surely not
true; this secularization of language is only a *façon de parler*, a ready-made phrase."

Between the metaphor or the rhetoric of the abyss and the affirmation according to which secularization is, in sum, nothing but a turn of rhetoric, the link is
perhaps necessary. There is no real secularization [*il n'y a pas de sécularisation effective*], is what this strange confession suggests, in sum. What one lightly calls "secularization" does not take place [*n'a pas lieu*]. This surface effect does not affect
language itself, which remains sacred in its abyssal interior. Epiphenomenality is
characteristic of this manner of moving along the surface. Such is also the epiphenomenality of a *manner of speaking of language* [*une manière de parler du langage*],
our metalanguage, our manner of speaking of language. The secularized language

would thus only be a metalinguistic epiphenomenon, a rhetoric, a façon de parler, a rhetorical effect of metalanguage. We must not try to hide this from ourselves; this effect is massive enough to concern, in principle, the totality of the language called technical, objective, scientific, and even philosophical.

But in his own manner Scholem maintains that there is no metalanguage. Secular language as metalanguage, therefore, does not exist in itself; it has neither presence nor consistency of its own. Its title is that of a façon de parler, thus of comporting itself toward the only language that is or that matters [*donc de se comporter à l'égard de la seule langue qui soit ou qui tienne*]—the sacred language. To comport oneself, to bring oneself to it, to carry oneself toward it [*se comporter, se rapporter à elle, se porter vers elle*]—this is still to comport oneself *in* it, still to speak it, even if to deny it. One cannot avoid speaking the sacred language, one can at most *avoid* speaking it, which is to say still speak it in denial, avoidance, distraction, like sleepwalkers above the abyss.

We must presuppose, therefore, in this unique dimension that is the sacredness of language, the power to produce, to engender, to carry these surface effects, this apparent secularization, this belief [*croyance*] in secularizing neutralization, this forgetting of the sacred and this linguistic sleepwalking. It must be [*il faut bien*] that language lends itself to this surface effect, which is not a surface effect, an effect *on the surface*, but an effect that consists in producing surface, this banal flatness (*platitude*), on the surface of which the sleepwalker walks. But we walk on the surface, we sleepwalk, only because we *believe* we are walking on the surface: we believe in the surface. In truth—and this truth no longer belongs to the order of objectivity or of knowledge that is conveyed by the secular language of the surface—there is no surface. There is only the abyss. Sacred language is an abyss. We walk as blind men [*en aveugles*] on its surface when we speak about it [*quand nous parlons à son sujet*]. In this, we are blind to the abyssal essence of the sacred language. I read again a passage that we have already touched on: "We do live inside this language above an abyss, almost all of us with the certainty of the blind"; [the "we" situates itself out of [*depuis*] this interiority of the "*in dieser Sprache*" that does not suffer any exit, any extra- or metalanguage. But when our sight is restored, we or those who come after us, must we not fall to the bottom of this abyss? And no one knows whether the sacrifice of individuals who will be annihilated in this abyss will suffice to close it."

What is it that grants its essential *Unheimlichkeit* to this situation, to this experience of the site [*cette expérience du site*]? Beyond this motif of the fall that awaits us, it is difficult to know whether what is more terrible is to walk on the surface as a blind man or to fall into the abyss as a man of lucid speech, awake, vigilant, awakened to the abyssal essence of language. It is difficult to know whether evil, the fall itself, consists in falling or in staying on the surface. What is it that anguishes Scholem and gives his letter its properly apocalyptic tone? Is it the fact that we, the majority of us, almost all of us, are walking as blind men on the surface of the sacred language? Or is it the fact that this language will fatally come back, or rather that it will open itself upon its own abyss, upon itself, upon its essence, inasmuch as this essence remains abyssal? Does Scholem wish that the abyss remain open, or does he hope that it will close one day since the vigilant and immediate experience of an abyssal language risks becoming properly unlivable? (One thinks here of Spinoza's fright before the hypothesis of a jealous God, a God of fire, and of the fact that this fright, as I have suggested, repeats in a strange way the one that Spinoza attributes to the Hebrews who flee the direct experience of being devoured by the divine word [fire, gulf, mouth] and who delegate it by thus constructing the political plan of action that the *Theological-Political Treatise* describes.)

This equivocation cannot, I believe, be resolved in this letter. It is the letter's entire power of fascination—and the fascination always relates to Scholem's indecision, one that he neither can nor wants to master. This is what gives this *envoi* its apocalyptic tone.

Scholem himself uses the word *apocalyptic* in a manner that is indeed equivocal, as if the apocalyptic should be saved, guarded in the language but as the very thing from which one must save and guard oneself. He uses it twice, and in an enigmatic manner [*façon*].

The first time, we have already heard, is just before the remark on the secularization of Hebrew as only a façon de parler, an equivocal expression in itself. One can hear it in its most probable sense (there is no secularization, properly speaking, whether possible or real; one speaks of it but there isn't any [*il n'y en a pas*]) or in a more artificial and twisted sense (the secularization of the language, as one could have suspected, consists of a rhetorization and a manner of speaking); in one case, *façon de parler* names the name of secularization; in the other case it designates the secularization of language itself. Just before noting this, Scholem was saying, "Indeed, people here don't know what they are doing. They believe they have secularized (*verweltlicht*) the language, pulled out its apocalyptic thorn (*ihr den apokalyptischen Stache ausgezogen zu haben*). But this is surely not true; this secularization (*Verweltlichung*) of the language is only a *façon de parler*, a ready-made phrase."

This leads one to think first [*cela donne d'abord à penser*] that to secularize or desacralize is to decapitate the language by removing its point, its sting (*Stachel*), its apocalyptic thorn. This apocalyptic sting, this point or this teleological aim [*visée*] would institute the sacredness of the language. A sacred language, *this* sacred language (for Scholem does not talk about sacredness in general but of *this* sacredness or this holiness undissociable from the semantic content of Hebrew, from the names, from the covenant) would be nothing without this magnetized pointer of apocalypse [*cette pointe aimantée d'apocalypse*].

All the semantic components of apocalypse must cross each other here and not let themselves be dissociated in this letter: First, the value of revelation or unveiling, the decrypting of what is hidden (*apocalyptô*); second, the current meaning of the end of time and the last judgment; third, catastrophe and cataclysm.

If, for the moment, we did not hold ourselves to a reading as internal as possible, we would have to invoke here a great number of studies by Scholem himself on Jewish apocalypticism. The first essay in the collection entitled *The Messianic Idea in Judaism* ("Toward an Understanding of the Messianic Idea in Judaism") tends to protest against, while correcting, a Christianizing interpretation of Jewish Messianism and prophetism: Christianizing, that is, interiorizing and spiritualizing, an interpretation that "appeared to the Jew ... as a flight which sought to escape verification of the Messianic claim within its most empirical categories by means of a non-existent pure inwardness."[10] Jewish Messianism would have been divided between or pulled by several tendencies that Scholem distinguishes and opposes as conservative, restorative and utopian Messianisms, even if these are sometimes intermingled. Messianism allies faith to an awaiting that is both living and acute; the apocalypse "appears as the form necessarily created by acute Messianism" (4). The writers of apocalypse are distinct from the prophets in that the seer receives a divine revelation that does not concern specific events of the end of history. The apocalypses speak of the whole of history, from the origin to the end, and in particular of the coming of a new aeon (Greek *aiôn*, Hebrew *'olam*) that must reign in Messianic time. "The Greek word *aiôn* translates in the Greek Bible the Hebrew term *'olam* whose value is mainly temporal."[11] The prophets distinguish between the "present aeon (*'olam hazeh*)" and the "aeon to come (*'olam habah*)," between a first and a last time. But the latter, a new age that recalls the time of paradise (Hosea, Isaiah) is not beyond time for the prophets, whereas after the exile, the distinction will be clearer, says Scholem, between the present time and the time to come. The apocalypses are above all turned toward the time of the end of which Daniel speaks (*'eth qetz*, Daniel 11:40).[12] The eschatology of these apoca-

---

10. Gershom Scholem, "Toward an Understanding of the Messianic Idea," trans. Michael A. Meyer, *The Messianic Idea in Judaism And Other Essays on Jewish Spirituality* (New York: Schocken, 1971), 2.

11. *Translator's note:* Derrida is quoting here from a note by the French translator of Scholem's text (see G. Scholem, *Le messianisme juif: Essais sur la spiritualité du judaïsme*, trans. Bernard Dupuy (Paris: Calmann-Lévy, 1974), 28–29. Further quotations are from the English translation, to which the page numbers in the text refer.

12. *Translator's note:* The text of *Daniel* (11:40) reads as follows: "When the time comes for the end [*ube'eth qetz*], the king of the South will try conclusions with him; but the king of the North will come storming down on him with chariots, cavalry, and a large fleet."

lypses, the content of which exceeds that of the ancient prophecies (Hosea, Amos, Isaiah), is no longer of a national character. If the prophets announce the reestablishment of the House of David, then in ruins, and of the "future glory of an Israel returned to God," of an "everlasting peace," of the "turning of all nations toward the one God of Israel" (6), the end of paganism and of idolatry, the aeons of the apocalypses follow each other while opposing each other: present/future [*avenir*], darkness/light, Israel/nations, holiness/sin, pure/impure, life/death. It is against the cosmic and cosmopolitan background of the apocalypses that the ideas of the resurrection of the dead, of the last judgment, of paradise and hell, have appeared. Yet the organizing theme of Scholem's letter, the return of the sacred language and the kind of ultimate punishment that would ensue, seems to have this apocalyptic eschatology as its horizon. No doubt this preserves its root in the ancient prophecies, but these were—at least if one is willing to believe Scholem—clear and distinct in their original context. They now become enigmas, allegories, mysteries, and they ask to be deciphered. The apocalyptic discourse has become esoteric. The authors conceal, they cipher their visions instead of throwing them "into the face of the enemy" as the prophets did: esotericism, elitism, therefore, initiation, a whole politics and a whole hierarchy (7). A role appropriate to apocalyptic knowledge has always been maintained in rabbinic Judaism. It held a place to the side of the gnostic knowledge of the *Merkabah,* the throne-word of God and its mysteries: a knowledge so "explosive"—this is Scholem's word—that it could only be transmitted by word of mouth without passing through writing (7). Writing is here not only profanation but the betrayal of a secret (in an analogous manner, Scholem's positive or scientific work on the Kabbalah has often been felt as such by living cabbalists).

I will only underscore this: the cryptic or esoteric character of the Messianic message, its elitist and initiatory politics, was accentuated when the Jews had to renounce their national existence after the destruction of the second temple. This duplicity in Messianism carries all the problems raised for us by the reading of this letter. Scholem acknowledges that Messianism aims at the "re-establishment of a lost [historical] reality," even though "it also went beyond that" (7). Scholem denounces all those scholars, Christian or Jewish, who deny the permanence of the apocalyptic tradition in rabbinic Judaism. When, in his letter, he takes on those who believe they have secularized the Hebrew language and removed its apocalyptic thorn, he is not far from reducing them to those, Jews or Christians, who have wanted to erase Jewish apocalypticism from the bosom of the rabbinic tradition since the Middle Ages. They have not achieved this, they have only occulted or denied. But by doing so, they have confirmed that the apocalyptic persisted, at once cryptic and occulted, ready to reappear, to return. It is no longer perceptible to the present, by definition, and the occultation, the cryptic veil is its very phenomenality, its state and its efficacy.

Scholem therefore appeals, apparently, to the apocalypse. He calls it and calls upon it as the sharpened point of the sacred language. This lends an accent, one of the accents of the apocalyptic tone of his letter. But there is another accent. For, inversely, Scholem seems to fear this apocalyptic return as a terrifying test and ordeal.

This is the second occurrence of the word *apocalyptic*. The last words of the text are in the form of a prayer: "May the carelessness, which has led us to this apocalyptic path, not bring about our ruin (*Möge uns denn nicht der Leichtsinn, der uns auf diesem apokalyptischen Weg geleitet, zum Verderb werden*)." And the letter is signed, and dated the 7 Teveth 5687.

One does not know, therefore—and this indeterminacy will never be removed—whether the apocalyptic path upon which we are, in any case [*de toutes les façons*], engaged, will save us or lose us. This indeterminacy remains what is proper to the apocalyptic experience. For those who believed that they secularized the sacred language did not do so in order to desacralize. They believed, thoughtlessly, that they were going to "resuscitate," to reanimate the language of origin in a modern world and in a modern state. But the sorcerers' apprentices of this renaissance of the sacred Hebrew did not believe in the reality of the judgment, and thus of the apocalypse to which they are subjecting us all. In the conclusion of the letter, in the future [*futur*] of its grammar, one cannot decide whether, at bottom, Scholem fears or calls the "inescapable," what he calls the inescapable, the fatality of this revolution of the language (*Diese unausbleibliche Revolution der Sprache*): may the voice of God let itself be heard anew through this awakened language (cf. Spinoza, again, and the fright of the Jews before the devouring voice of God):

Each word which is not newly created (*neu geschaffen*) but taken from the "good old" treasure is full to bursting. A generation (*Geschlecht*) that takes upon itself the most fruitful in our sacred tradition—our language—cannot live, were it to wish it a thousandfold, without tradition. The moment the power stored at the bottom of the language deploys itself (*entfalten wird*), the moment the "said" (*das "Gesprochene"*), the content of the language, assumes its form anew, then the sacred tradition will again confront our people as a decisive sign (*als entscheidendes Zeichen*) of the only available choice: to submit or to go under. In a language where he is invoked a thousandfold back (*zurückbeschworen wird*) into our life, God will not stay silent (*wird . . . nicht stumm bleiben*). But this inescapable revolution of the language, in which the voice will be heard again, is the sole object of which nothing is said in this country. Those who called the Hebrew language back to life did not believe in the judgment (*an das Gericht*) that was thus conjured upon us. May the carelessness, which has led us to this apocalyptic path, not bring about our ruin.

SECULARIZING LANGUAGE:
THE VOLCANO, THE FIRE, THE ENLIGHTENMENT

Who speaks here? And how does this confession *present itself*? How does the identification of the "we" in this letter operate? Otherwise put, and at least according to
convention, how does identification operate for the subject of this letter and its signatory, for he who pledges his responsibility, in his own name or rather in his name
and in the name of a "we" who says frequently "we," "all of us or almost," "our children," "our generation," and so on? By provisionally suspending the instance of the
addressee—which has something to do with this identification—I retreat here
toward the side of the apparent signatory and I link my question, on the one hand,
to the question of sacrifice (the word, or the concept, "sacrifice" appears in the confession, once in the original, twice in [Stéphane Mosès' French] translation), and,
on the other hand, to the question of generation given that the logic of vengeance
necessarily plays with generations. How are these two questions tied together?

This letter speaks of the *avenir*. The temporality of *imminence* gives it its apocalyptic tone. The *avenir* has the face of "our children (*unsere Kinder*)." If vengeance
takes place, if the evil done to the holy tongue must one day be avenged by the
properly revolutionary return of language, it is "our children" who will have to
pay. They *will have to* [*ils devront*]: necessity, fatality, and debt—they will have to
acquit a debt that *we* have contracted, by our fault or our crime, in their place. The
illogical logic of vengeance, as soon as it goes through language [*dès lors qu'elle
passe par la langue*], cannot let itself be contained, and therefore comprehended,
within the limits of individual responsibility. The debt, here the guilt, is inscribed
in the language where it leaves its signature. If one generation has to pay for
another, thus disturbing the entire metaphysics of the *cogito*, of the Cartesian
subject, of the practico-transcendental egology that is incapable, in sum, of
understanding something like language, it doesn't only have to do with a logic
proper to vengeance, with the unboundedness in the dynamic of vengeance of
which Hegel speaks. This unboundedness itself, beyond what Hegel says about
it, has to do perhaps with the fact that vengeance goes through language. Language
prescribes, *assigns* but in the same stroke [*du même coup*] *exceeds* individual
responsibility. Before the vengeance of language, one could say, there is a language
of vengeance that traverses generations and speaks beyond them. In the present
case, this apocalyptic confession describes a language of vengeance that avenges
an evil done to language. There is always a language of vengeance; vengeance
always implicates language. Yet in this case the offense, the dispute, the crime
concern language itself. If one asks "who" is language here, what is its name, the
answer leaves no doubt: it is the name of God naming itself through the voice of

God. The crime takes place against God; vengeance is the vengeance or the punishment of God. This is the only subject of punishment, the "only subject" (as the [French] translation says) that is not spoken about in this country—the sole object (*Gegenstand*); the letter literally says, "God will not stay silent. But this inescapable revolution of the language, in which the voice will be heard again, is the sole object (*der einzige Gegenstand*) of which nothing is said in this country." Here is the only object, one can even say the unique subject, of this confession. And perhaps its ultimate addressee.

Our children will have to, they will have to pay. "Children"—this means "*avenir*" [*cela veut dire "avenir"*], the generation to come, but also—in the logic of individual responsibility with which Scholem must always negotiate—innocence. In the *avenir* (and here is, in sum, the essence of the *avenir*), innocent ones will pay and children are innocent because they have not yet spoken (*infants*) at the moment when language has already contracted the debt for them. They do not choose their language and afterward become subjects of language, out of this debt [*depuis cette dette*], as guilty "before the letter," archiguilty.

There are two main occurrences of the expression "our children," sometimes relayed by the expression "our youth," or "youth (*Jugend*)." The two occurrences are located in the two middle paragraphs, while those of the word *generation* are found in the first and last paragraphs, as if the unpredictable turn or the para-Kabbalistic artifice of this composition inscribed—framed—the children between the generations.

Here is the first evocation of "children" who risk being properly sacrificed by our fault, literally by their fathers, if God wills it, that is to say, *in saying*—but it is undecidable in this case, and in this "fear and trembling" of Scholem, one doesn't know whether God will let the child be sacrificed by saying or not saying, by keeping quiet or making his voice be heard.

"The creators of this new linguistic movement (*die Schöpfer der neuen Sprachbewegung*) believed blindly, and stubbornly, in the miraculous power of the language (*an die Wunderkraft der Sprache*)." The "neue Sprachbewegung"—which Stéphane Mosès was right to translate "mouvement de renaissance de l'hébreu"[13]— is indeed a movement for the re-turn, the re-birth, the resurrection even, the *re-* of repetition implying reawakening as much as revolt (thus the *re*-turn, one more time, one more turn [*volte*]), revolution, not to mention the *revenant* whose sign is marked by the return of the word *gespenstisch* (spectral, ghostly) on two occasions in the confession. This semantic chain of *re-* (return, repetition, reawakening, res-

---

13. *Translator's note:* "Hebrew renaissance movement."

urrection, revolt, revolution, *revenance*) crosses the essential question of *re*
language, *as* language insofar as it inaugurates the possibility of vengea....
revenge, punishment, or retaliation.

The originators of this reawakening believed blindly (*glaubten blind*) in the
miraculous power (*Wunderkraft*) of language. This letter is a letter on the *power* and
the *violence* of language, with all the trials of strength [*épreuves de force*] engaged in
it; and this is marked by the return of the words *Kraft, Macht, Gewalt*. And if belief
in this force is blind, one must recognize that blindness is another major motif. This
catastrophic blindness absolves no one; one does not know whether it is better to
keep to it or to escape from it, whether it is better to be lucid or nonseeing, and
whether seeing [*voyance*] has an ordinary meaning or the sense of the seer [*voyant*]
in apocalypse. If you now conjugate this theme of guilty blindness with that of generation, you have the premises of an anti-oedipal scenario (Oedipus being here on
the father's side, if one can still decide) that I will not abuse here.

One should not throw oneself too quickly into sophisticated interpretations of
this letter, not, in any case, before having reconstructed the daily, concrete, pathetic
landscape, but also the paradigmatic scene of this Berliner intellectual from the
diaspora, living two cultures, familiar, as are so many others, with sacred nonspo-
ken texts reserved for study and liturgy, and who all at once hears, in the Palestine
of the 1920s, these sacred names in the street, on the bus, at the corner store, in the
newspapers that every day publish lists of new words to be inscribed in the code of
secular Hebrew. One must imagine the desire and the terror in the face of this outpouring, this prodigious, unbridled prodigality that flooded everyday life with
sacred names, language giving itself out [*la langue se donnant elle-même*], like a
miraculous manna but also like the profanatory *jouissance*, in the face of which a
sort of religious concupiscence recoils in fright.

The blindness of the creators was their "good fortune (*Glück*)," adds Scholem.
"For no one clear-sighted would have mustered the demonic courage (*den dämon-
ischen Mut*) to revive a language, there where only an *Esperanto* could emerge." The
demonic horror of these sorcerers' apprentices gifted with an unconscious courage
that pushes them to manipulate forces which surpass them—here is this horror
commensurate with a kind of death [*à la mesure d'une certaine mort*], the death of
the living dead. As sacred, Hebrew was both a dead language—as a language one
didn't or shouldn't speak in daily life—and a language more living than what is generally called a living language. The new *Sprachbewegung* resuscitates this living dead
reserved for study and prayer and only brings it out of the temple or funerary vault
[*caveau*] for a sinister masquerade, this quasi Esperanto or Volapük, as if the return
to life were only a simulacrum for which one was going to disguise the dead as a

caricature of itself for the *funeral home*,[14] a nonlanguage, the frozen grin of a semiotics, a disincarnated, fleshless [*décharnée*], and formally universal exchange value, an instrument in the commerce of signs,[15] without a proper place, without a proper name, a false return to life, a shoddy resurrection.

And Scholem continues, "[These demonic sorcerers' apprentices] walk, and walk still today, spellbound (*gebannt*) above the abyss. The abyss was silent and they have delivered the ancient names and seals over to the youth. We [we who are neither these bewitched sorcerers' apprentices nor "our youth" —J. D.] sometimes shudder when, out of thoughtless conversation, a word from the religious sphere terrifies us, just there where it was perhaps intended to comfort [Scholem denounces both the evacuation and the perversion of meaning —J. D.]. Hebrew is pregnant with catastrophes (*unheilschwer*). It cannot and will not remain in its current state [it is therefore not a matter of a poor state of things, but rather of a fatal process, of a dynamic that nothing can stop —J. D.]. Our children no longer have another language [we germanophones who know not only a second language but a third, in addition to the two Hebrews, are still able to defend ourselves —J. D.], and it is only too true that they, and they alone, will pay for the encounters which we have initiated without asking, without even asking ourselves [a general irresponsibility, innocent on the side of our children, guilty on ours —J. D.]. If and when the language turns against its speakers (*gegen ihre Sprecher wenden wird*). . . ."

This turning, this *Wendung* of language against those who speak it, presupposes some initiative. Whence would come this initiative of a language that does not return to its subjects? Here is a dead language, which in truth was not dead but *surviving*, living over and above what one calls a living language, a language that one pretends to resuscitate by giving it this masked body, this gesticulation of an Esperantist masquerade, this puppet of a technological and cadaveric instrumentality; here is a language that turns against those who speak it but who, in truth, only believe that they are speaking it and are doubly irresponsible: irresponsible because they are dominated by language, as one always is; but also because they are not aware of their responsibility toward the legacy of a language [*le legs d'une langue*] and have not asked themselves any questions about it [*à son sujet*]. Here, then, is a language that takes the initiative of turning against those who mistreat or ignore it; here is a false cadaver that will animate itself, that will rid itself of its carnival disguises and will in its turn unleash itself upon [*se déchaîner contre*] the demonic sorcerers, who are themselves spellbound. How is this possible?

---

14. *Translator's note:* "funeral home" is in English in the text.

15. Cf. Walter Benjamin, "On Language as Such and on the Language of Man," trans. E. Jephcott, in *Reflections: Essays, Aphorisms, Autobiographical Writings*, ed. Peter Demetz (New York: Schocken, 1986), 314–32.

[handwritten marginalia: "the problem may be linguistic, but arts ... itself"]

To attempt to answer this question, one must begin by drawing out two axioms or two presuppositions in this interpretation of language.

1. In order for it to take the initiative of thus avenging itself, language has to be someone; I am not saying a subject, but it must be speech [*la parole*] speaking in the name of someone, bearing the name of someone: obviously the speech and the name of God. Something of this language must therefore remain attached, in an indissoluble manner [*façon*], to its creator and first signatory, to the name of God, on the one hand, to the things and to the meaning that the names of this language—*singularly*—designate. This opens onto the interpretation of the name by Scholem and by Walter Benjamin.

2. Second presupposition. As sacred, such a language would have to be radically, essentially non-conceptual, at least if by concept one understands a generality of meaning that is dissociable from proper names and transmittable in a universal semiotics, a formalizable language, a characteristic one or an Esperanto. From this point of view at least, the sacred language would have to be nonconceptual, noninstrumentalizable, noninformational, noncommunicational, and nontechnological. Technological contamination, equivalent here to secularizing actualization, can only happen [*advenir*] to it after the fact [*après coup*], and can only befall [*survenir*] it secondarily as an evil, as this accidental death that occurs [*arrive*] here to a dead-living language, in truth more living than the masquerading ghost in whose guise one claims to resuscitate it. In this way, Scholem excludes the possibility of contamination from the origin. Instrumentalizing technicalization (iterability) or desacralization has not always already befallen language. Scholem excludes that language be precisely this possibility of iteration, this iterability.

This interpretation of language and of technology obviously should be, in my view, problematized—at least.

To this second presupposition concerning the nontechnological and nonconceptual essence of language that renders impossible the distinction between body and meaning (since meaning is the concept, the generality that ensures instrumentalization), one would have to add the following consequence: the dissociation between originary and technological language—and therefore the implicit devalorization of technology as profanatory, secularizing, contaminating exteriority—also aims at a Christian idealism, an interiorization of spiritual meaning separated from the body in general, from time, from the letter or the carnal signifier. According to a law that can be regularly verified, technicism would be on the same side as idealism—in its entire tradition, up to Hegel and beyond—and as Christian interiority.

Thus, "if and when the language turns against its speakers—it already does so for certain minutes in our lifetime, and these are difficult to forget, stigmatizing moments [*stigmatisierende Minuten*: wounds of the instant—*stigmè* that recall the apocalyptic thorn <*point*> —J. D.] in which the daring lack of measure of our undertaking reveals itself to us (*in denen sich die ganze Vermessenheit unseres Unterfangens uns offenbart*)—will we then have a youth capable of withstanding the revolt of a sacred language [*Aufstand einer heiligen Sprache*, the uprising, the insurrection of a sacred language —J. D.]?"

The presumption, the lack of measure, the hubris, the madness have to do with what we have dared to desacralize. We have committed a profanation by extracting the sacred language from the sacred text. We have let it out into the street and into everyday life. We have made it serve [*servir*], we have enslaved it [*asservir*], a little as if we had transformed the infinite value attached to a sacred thing into a commercial value or into a value *tout court*, both use and exchange value. Iconoclasm and idolatry at the same time, if that is possible. Those who uphold actualization claim to adore the sacred language, since they want to reactualize it, resuscitate it, but they turn it into a current exchange value and transform it into a monetary sign. The enormous problematic of the analogy between linguistic sign and monetary sign would here graft itself legitimately. There is also the problematic of fetishism. Unfortunately, the "logic" of fetishism being what it is, one no longer knows who is fetishizing the sacred language, whether it is those whom Scholem implicitly accuses of idolatry or the accuser who wants the sacred signifiers to remain out of commerce, dedicating a cult to them that keeps them safe from all current trade, even from all exchange. In the Enlightenment tradition here prepared by Spinoza, there can be no doubt that the main accused would be Scholem.

As for "the daring lack of measure of our undertaking," it is only measured, precisely, like all excessiveness [*démesure*], against the abyssal sublime of language. Since one risks going over the abyss, the bottomlessness [*sans-fond*], and the infinity of names opened onto the bottomlessness, one either walks blindly above the abyss, or is swallowed up by it, and the undertaking is without measure. And when Scholem asks, "Will we then have a youth capable of withstanding the uprising of a sacred language?" one does not know, in 1926, what responsibility "our youth" will be able to assume in the face of this violent insurrection, this irrepressible return of the sacred. Will "our youth" let itself be crushed or will it show itself worthy of the heritage? One can gloss at leisure and speculate upon the concrete figure that, in his innermost heart, Scholem gave to these possibilities, upon the resemblances of this figure with what actually became of, what the youth of that time became, the Israeli people today, for example. Among all the catastrophes that Scholem is predicting— one could say prophesying—what can be neither denied nor affirmed is that there was, with the Nazi genocide, this indirect consequence that was also perhaps the founding and becoming of the State of Israel. The hypothesis of Stéphane Mosès is that "the danger is great, according to Scholem, of seeing their return [that of the "ancient names and seals" —J. D.], after a long period of collective repression, take the form of an anarchic explosion of uncontrolled religious forces."[16] I will return to this.

The second occurrence of the expression "our children"—"woe to our children (*wehe unseren Kindern*)" appears in the following paragraph. It tells us much more about the interpretation of the language that sustains this entire letter, and also about the thinking of Scholem, at this moment and in the *avenir*. It is about a thinking of the name. In a definitional, sententious mode, which contrasts sharply with the remainder of the letter, a theoretical or philosophical utterance speaks the essence of speech [*langage*] and of language [*langue*]. It consist in one word, one name, the name of name: *Sprache ist Namen*. The being of language resides neither in the verb (in the grammatical sense), in the attributes, in the syncategoremes, nor in the phrase [*proposition*]. What does not have the grammatical form of the name (in this case not the substantive but the nominal reference) belongs to language only to the extent that the verb, adjective, preposition, and adverb can let themselves be nominalized. The name does not have the grammatical value of the substantive; it signifies the power of naming, of calling in general. I cannot pursue this direction here. On the ground of the internal reading to which I am here trying to keep, this thinking of the name has to be linked, it seems to me, to this thought of the spectral and of haunting which obsesses this confession. There is a specter because there is language, a language which names, calls, summons [*convoque*], invokes. Language can haunt because names, first of all, haunt our sentences. Names are neither present nor absent in these sentences, neither perceptible nor imperceptible, nor hallucinated either. The category of the spectral *revenant* is not a flower of rhetoric; it *figures*, more or less discreetly, thematically—and the word "ghostly (*gespenstisch*)," we have said, recurs twice—that which extracts the entire logic of this confession from oppositional onto-logic or from the dialectic of presence and absence.

"Speech [or *language* —J. D.] is name [*Sprache ist Namen*. It is, it consists of names, in the names —J. D.].[17] In the names, the power of language is enclosed; in them, its abyss is sealed (*versiegelt*)." There is a power of language, therefore, at once a *dynamis*, an enveloped virtuality, a potentiality that can be brought or not to

---

16. Mosès, "Langage et sécularisation," 93.
17. *Translator's note:* The French text reads as follows, brackets included: "Le langage [ou la langue] est nom [Sprache ist Namen]. [Elle est, elle consiste en noms, dans les noms]."

actuality; it is hidden, buried, dormant. This potentiality is also a power (*Macht*), a particular efficacy that acts on its own, in a quasi- autonomous manner [*façon*], without the initiative and beyond the control of speaking subjects. Scholem will not cease to develop this theme in his works on the name of God, Jewish mysticism, and above all on the Kabbalah. This is indeed an explicit motif in certain trends of the Kabbalah. The magical power of the name produces effects said to be real and over which we are not in command. The name hidden in its potency possesses a power of manifestation and of occultation, of revelation and encrypting [*crypte*]. What does it hide? Precisely the abyss that is enclosed within it. To open a name is to find in it not something but rather something like an abyss, the abyss as the thing itself. Faced with this power, once we have awakened it, we must recognize our impotence. The name is transcendent and more powerful than we are: "After invoking the ancient names daily, we can no longer hold off their power." This last sentence speaks of the ancient names as spirits that one invokes (*nachdem die alten Namen täglich beschworen haben*) for instance in daily prayer. *Beschwörung* sometimes designates the invocation of spirits (*Geistern*). Once it is called, the power of these spirits can no longer be kept at a distance; that possibility is no longer in our power, in our hands: *Es steht nicht mehr in unserer Hand . . . ihre Potenzen zu halten.* The word *power* will be relayed in the same paragraph by those of violence (it is a matter this time of violence, *Gewalt*, with which we have invoked, *beschworen*, once again, the names, a violence against which the power of names will retaliate), and of force, strength (*Kraft*): "and often, out of the ghostly (*gespenstisch*) shame of our language, the power of the sacred speaks out."

By secularizing the sacred language, we are thus playing with ghosts, denying that at stakes are very grave matters. By writing—and whether we are writers or journalists matters little here—we believe that it doesn't matter [*que ce n'est pas grave*]. Writing dissimulates the gravity of the matter; it neutralizes a fatality, the proper place [*le lieu propre*] of which is the name in speech [*la parole*]. The gravest thing, Scholem then says in a very unusual sentence, is that the one who writes thus, playing with the names of this spectral language in writings and newspapers, is not only lying to himself, pretending to believe (*lügt sich*), but is also lying before God, feigning, the [French] translation says, to make God believe (*lügt sich oder Gott vor . . .*) that this is of no importance, that it means nothing (*es habe nichts zu bedeuten*). This remark well stages a language that, in a certain manner, always addresses itself to God, speaks to God, and must let God speak, corresponding with him whether one knows it or not, whether one wants it or not. There is no language, there is no speech outside of these names thus addressed, by themselves: "Truly, we speak in rudiments; truly we speak a ghostly language (*eine Gespenstische Sprache*). The names haunt our sentences. One or another plays with them in writings and newspapers, lying to themselves or to God that this means nothing, and often, out of the ghostly shame of our language (*aus der gespenstischen Schande unserer Sprache*), the power of the sacred speaks out. For the names have their own life. Had they not, woe to our children, who would be hopelessly abandoned to the void."

Two possible and indefinitely competing interpretations: the "void (*Leere*)" to which our children would be hopelessly (*hoffnungslos*) abandoned, sacrificed (*preisgegeben*), is both the loss of signification, the loss of language and of names on the one hand, and, on the other, the abyss into which one falls precisely for not having understood that language and the names are abyssal. There would be two abysses, each one in abyss [*en abîme*] in the other, two abysses of language—the abyss of life and the abyss of death.

I provisionally abandon this question of haunting and of the name that would have to be reconstructed on the basis of other texts by Scholem. For today, in this quasi-internal reading of the letter, I will draw out a last thread, the one which paradoxically ties the value of sacredness [*sacralité*] to that of sacrifice on the one hand, and to the mission or the responsibility of a generation on the other.

The allusion to sacrifice makes itself heard twice as well, in the first paragraph of the letter. What of sacrifice, then, as to sacred language? In German the two words (for example *Opfer* and *heilig*) do not share the same kinship that do "*sacré*" and "*sacrifice*" in French. To kill, to put to death the sacred language—a living dead language but sur-viving, "hyperliving," let us not forget this—this would be to sacrifice it; and doing so, to sacrifice not only something sacred, but that by which and in which the sacred can be called sacred and emerge as such.

I would first say that this sacrifice—as a putting to death—appears quite simply impossible to Scholem. But he evokes the eventuality of what would be impossible, the possibility of the impossible. This confession is, moreover, entirely governed by the haunting of the possibility of the impossible. It constantly posits that the impossible is possible, that the possible is impossible—as such. Whence what I will call the sacred madness [*la folie sacrée*], the damned madness [*la sacrée folie*] of this letter, a letter compulsively animated by the fatal desire that the catastrophe occur [*arrive*] and that apocalypse take place [*ait lieu*] and that, however, they never take place: a frightened awaiting, desire and fright before the possibility of the impossible: that is to say of the *saying* [*dire*], nothing less than the response of God deciding to emerge from his silence. Such is what one hears at the end of the confession: "God will not stay silent . . . the voice will be heard again." It will be the apocalypse, then, unleashed by these other madmen, the spellbound sorcerers [*les sorciers ensorcelés*] of secularization. In the face of this apocalypse, the voice of God speaking to us directly in the fire, Scholem all of a sudden resembles both the Hebrews of whom Spinoza speaks, and Spinoza himself. One would have to analyze here the competition between these two discourses and between these two postures in Scholem. He trembles and says so, as if he felt what Spinoza—whom he opposed, however, radically—feels before this God of fire who would set out to speak immediately to his people, in the very fire of his vindictive jealousy.

If the possible sacrifice remains impossible, it is because secularization, in which the sacrifice should consist, never actually takes place. Secularization "is only a *façon de parler*," Scholem has just said, "a ready-made phrase (*eine Phrase*). It is absolutely impossible to empty out the words filled to bursting, unless one does so at the sacrifice of the language itself (*es sei denn um den Preis der Sprache selbst*). The ghostly Volapük [*das gespenstische Volapük*—I would say spectral, ghostly; further on it will be Esperanto, another mark of contempt for these national nonlanguages, these nonidioms, artificial universal languages scorned by Charles De Gaulle with the same tone when he too spoke of the Volapük of the United Nations —J. D.] spoken here in the streets points precisely to the expressionless linguistic world in which the 'secularization' of language could alone be possible (*möglich*)."

According to the logic of this argumentation, a mad logic in terms of any philosophy, Scholem seems to be saying the most incompatible, "incom-possible" [*incompossibles*] things:

1. Secularization is only a "façon de parler, *eine Phrase*," phraseology. It does not take place [*elle n'a pas lieu*]; to speak of it is to say nothing, to think nothing, to make use of ready-made expressions, of fancy words [*faire des phrases*]. And Scholem adds: this secularization is "impossible," absolutely, simply impossible (*schlechthin unmöglich*), as it is impossible to empty out the content of overloaded words, unless one sacrifices the language itself.

2. Yet, what appears to be impossible does take place. This ghostly Volapük—this phraseology that permits speaking of a nevertheless impossible secularization— is possible, and that is what secularization is.

Thus, from one sentence to the next, Scholem affirms these two contraries: the secularization of language is impossible but it is possible to speak of it only because it takes place, because language has become so inexpressive, vacant, degraded, and corrupted. In sum, it is secularization that allows us to speak of a secularization that does not take place. Secularization leads to mistake for actual secularization what is only a "*façon de parler*," a rumor, mere words on the subject of secularization. Secularization speaks of itself [*parle d'elle-même*], but there is nothing else.

This bizarre logic, at once contradictory and tautological, makes of the impossible the condition of possibility and of existence of the impossible; it speaks of the event of an impossible that consists in a "manner of speaking." What is it that occurs [*advient*] in this way? Not quite a bad [*mauvaise*] language that would come to corrupt the sacred language, but rather a nonlanguage in which or *to* which the sacred language—the only language that speaks—is sacrificed.

Now this sacrifice, which Scholem has just said is impossible unless we renounce the language, does take place, even if it gives place to nothing, to this nonspeech that speaks of secularization, that is to say of nothing [*c'est-à-dire du rien*], of this inexpressive language that produces talk [*qui fait parler*] of secularization. Such will have been the sacrifice: it engulfs and damages [*il abîme*], it makes a sacred language perish in the void by letting it speak in the void of ready-made expressions, phrases as empty, names as mute as "secularization." The empty expression "secularization" brings about the emptying out of meaning of which the would-be, the so-called, the inconsistent secularization consists. It is as if the *nothing* [*le rien*] said *I am nothing* and one were to ask then whether anything had come to pass. What comes to pass is then at least this astonishment and this question. What has come to pass is a sacrifice of language, the destruction of the sacred language as an experience of the sacred language, perhaps the only and the most *unheimlich*, but also the sacrifice of sacrifice, the self-destruction of the sacrificial function, of the sacredness still presupposed, manifested, or sought by every sacrificial operation.

The pre-logical logic, or archi-logic, of this argumentation consists in saying: nothing occurs, *therefore* the nothing occurs, or, *but* the nothing occurs, and what is grave and bears a *Bedeutung*, what is *significant* is that one talks of nothing. The nonlanguage, the simulacrum of the name occurs. Does the madness or the *Unheimlichkeit* consist only in this logical contradiction? Perhaps, but also, and before that, in something else. Sacrifice does not destroy the sacred language itself. By threatening it, on the edge [*bord*] of what Scholem speaks about in sum, and which occurs without occurring, while occurring [*et qui arrive sans arriver, tout en arrivant*] enough for one to be able to speak of it in referring both to the sacred and the nonsacred, it produces an experience of the edge, the edge of the abyss, between two places [*entre deux lieux*]. The imminent sacrifice, at once past and impossible, makes appear, or rather announces, the sacred language as such, the very sacredness that is *of language* [*qui est de la langue*]. According to a logic that is not fortuitously analogous to that of Heidegger's *Was ist Metaphysik* and that concerns the whole of Being in its rapport to speech, nothingness, here the nothingness of the language, the nonlanguage, announces the essence of what it threatens and causes to recoil in totality.

Sacrifice, therefore, has two significations or two virtues. It can destroy the sacred but, in so doing, it can—in what by definition is actualized only as threat, imminence, nonpresence—make the sacred as such manifest, save it thus in the sacrifice, pay homage with, or give the gift of, a destruction [*faire hommage ou don d'une destruction*], indeed of a murder or of a death, to the sacred.

Henceforth, the madness of which we speak no longer has the meaning of a disorder of reason, of an illness or an extravagance. Beyond all the psychopolitical oppositions of a psychiatric or psychoanalytic rationalism, at issue is the experience of the sacred, the approach or the announcement of the sacred. All logical discourses claiming the Enlightenment—the so-called rationalist, even socio-psychophilosophical discourses destined to denounce or to circumscribe this madness[18]—would only translate fear and denegation before the irruption or the promise of the sacred. These rationalities would have the consistency and the inconsistency of secularization: the forgetting, quite simply, of the language and the name.

This "madness" thus moves forward in the still undecidable place where, as always, responsibility must be taken. Responsibility is always taken in a place of absolute undecidability, on the edge [bord] of this double possibility—where it is not a responsibility, but only a calculation, and therefore on the program of secularization. It is a matter here of responding to the call of a sacred language, a call which, according to Scholem, has in any case [de toute façon] taken place. It has already resonated, or we would not even be speaking, and above all not of secularization. By responding in a responsible way to this language, to the call of the name, by guarding this language against the nonlanguage that threatens it, we will decide and assume the historical singularity which is that of our generation.

One must therefore tie what we have just said of sacrifice to the responsibility proper to our generation, the one undergoing the trial of this nonlanguage that secular Hebrew is—a generation of transition (das Geschlecht des Übergangs), a generation of passage and of access. The transition is not interpreted solely according to the current sense of the biological or natural chain of generations. It situates the place of the intermediate space [entre-deux], the "mi-lieu," midway between place and nonplace, the undecidable edge where the greatest risk is taken. The gravest responsibility must be exercised at the moment of the greatest danger: without rule and without guarantee on the edge of the abyss, above the abyss. On the edge of the abyss or above the abyss—it comes down to the same thing [cela revient au même]. There again, we should follow the thread of an analogy—only an analogy, of course, between a certain movement of this Scholem of 1926 and that of a certain Heidegger in the years that are going to follow: the Heidegger of Was ist Metaphysik and Sein und Zeit who relates anxiety and the abyss to responsibility and to Entschlossenheit (resoluteness, the "resolute-decision" determination), but also the more "political" Heidegger, in particular the one who, you remember, signs the text on Nietzsche and the "sign" that our people must understand, failing which history would take revenge.

---

18. Translator's note: The French text has "circonscire," perhaps a neologism, midway between "circoncire (to circumcise)" and "circonscrire (to circumscribe)," or perhaps a typo.

The "we" who signs this confession belongs, then, to this *Geschlecht des Über-gangs*. He engages himself both in this passage and in this responsibility. More precisely: it is because he has engaged himself, even before deciding about it, in this passage, that he must take this responsibility. The responsibility is ineluctable, and as paradoxical as this may appear, it finds the sign of its freedom in this fatality, in the bond of this obligation, which is not the formal or formalizable obligation of a practical universality in the Kantian sense. This is the responsibility of a generation. It does not replace itself, does not delegate itself. It is unique: in a place, at a moment of history, in a language, before [*devant*] a language; but also and of course first of all, and by way of all this, before God, the voice of whom will have marked the covenant in the experience of *this* language. The signature of this "we" countersigns the covenant; it says "our generation" by so countersigning, by so responding to a commitment already taken, to a promise, and it sees its autobiography assigned, the autobiographicity [*l'autobiographicité*] of the "we," out of the call that resonates in this sacred language, out of what has already consecrated this language and allowed one to hear in it the imminence of the voice's return, in its sacrificial instance. One cannot hear or situate this "we," its relation to itself in the confession, without setting out from this experience of sacrificial responsibility. One cannot translate this "we" with, for example, the expression "subject," "communal subject [*sujet commu-nautaire*]." All the philosophemes constructing these two expressions of subject and of community, of the sign as well, belong to the secularizing axiomatic here denounced and displaced, carried into the paradoxes that we are analyzing. The "who" of this "we"—who is neither a subject nor a community—announces itself to itself; it only institutes or undergoes a relation to self out of [*depuis*] the menacing interpellation of a *Geschlecht* by apocalyptic speech [*parole*].

Let us approach once more two passages that I propose to bring together around the word *Geschlecht*. This word is visibly governed in this context by its obvious meaning of "generation." But whatever the authority, the force and the prescription of said context, how to avoid hearing in the language (German) of this word, the resonance, at least virtual, of other associated significations (those that haunt, like this word, and have done so for a long time, in this seminar: family, group, stock, line, sex, race, species, with all the meanings [*valeurs*] that Heidegger tracks down—following Georg Trakl—in this word around *Schlag, verschlagen, zer-schlagen*, etc.: stroke [*coup*], stamp [*frappe*], imprint, impression, *typos*, and so on)?

" . . . this secularization of the language is only a façon de parler, a ready-made phrase (*die Verweltlichung der Sprache ist ja nur eine* façon de parler, *eine Phrase*)." The word *Verweltlichung*, sometimes substituted for "*Säkularisierung*," as a German word for a word of Latin origin—and moreover placed in quotation marks—raises grave problems. First of all, problems point toward these platonic and Christian values that interpret the world according to the opposition of the here below and the beyond, of the sensible or temporal world and the spiritual world, the *Verweltlichung* or secularization deriving all its meaning from this interpretation of transcendence. One knows that Heidegger tried to think a "worldhood" of the world that would not be dependent on the platonic or Christian interpretation that dominates our culture. But must not this platonic-Christian interpretation be still more or otherwise problematic, and even more so for a Jewish thinker? Yet here Scholem speaks in the German language, and like Heidegger also recognizes the necessity of this; he has to maneuver, compromise, negotiate with the significations, the concepts and the words themselves that he must still use at the very moment he radically contests them. The principle of the question that I would like to pose here, in my very incompetence, would be the following: how can one translate, in the sacred Hebrew or in the semantics enjoined by it, the word *Verweltlichung*? What is the Jewish equivalent for the spiritual/worldly, sacred/secular opposition, etc.? Is there such an equivalent, and what is at stake in it for this "confession on the subject of our language (*Bekenntnis über unsere Sprache*)"?

Further down, instead of *Verweltlichung*, the usual word for "laicization," "secularization," Scholem uses, in quotation marks, the word "Säkularisierung," as if there were a German or Latin play on words around the sacred Hebrew, the untouchable language, a language of study or a liturgical language.

"[S]ecularization is only a *façon de parler* [in French, therefore, in the text —J. D.]." A curious shift into French in order to express a sort of rhetorical perversion, as if only the French language could name in proper, idiomatic manner [*façon*], a production of the French spirit, to the extent that it is tied to the practice of the French language. I intentionally say "French spirit" in order to recall that Kant—at the moment he is dealing with invention, which he distinguishes from discovery and from genius, in his *Anthropology from a Pragmatic Point of View*— makes the remark that "in the French language, spirit (*Geist*) and wit (*Witz*) have the same name, *Esprit*. It is different in the German language."[19] *Esprit* is, in fact, in French in the text. Viewed from Germany, and from the viewpoint of German, there is of course an essential link between the French spirit and the *façon de parler*, between the word *esprit* and the expression *façon de parler*. While putting it aside, I submit this remark to the case of national character and the problems it poses. But also to the case of *Deutschjudentum*. It turns out that in parts of the *Anthropology* from which I have just quoted, a very long note (doubtlessly the longest in the book) lets itself be entirely inspired by the most calmly characteristic anti-Semitism. This is section 46, "On Mental Deficiencies in the Cognitive Power."

---

19. Immanuel Kant, *Anthropology from a Pragmatic Point of View*, trans. Mary J. Gregor (The Hague: Martinus Nijhoff, 1974), 13.

I will quote the first and last words of it. Here is what the friend and admirer of Mendelssohn writes:

> The Palestinians living among us have, for the most part, earned a not unfounded reputation for being cheaters, because of their spirit of usury since their exile. Certainly, it seems strange to conceive of a *nation* [Kant's emphasis —J. D.] of cheaters; but it is just as odd to think of a nation of merchants, the great majority of whom, bound by an ancient superstition that is recognized by the State they live in, seek no civil dignity and try to make up for this loss by the advantage of duping the people among whom they find refuge, and even one another. The situation could not be otherwise, given a whole nation of merchants, as non-productive members of society (for example, the Jews in Poland). So their constitution, which is sanctioned by ancient precepts and even by the people among whom they live (since we have certain sacred writings in common with them), cannot consistently be abolished—even though the supreme principle of their morality in trading with us is "Let the buyer beware." (77)

Following this Kant undertakes to explain—without moralizing—the origin of this inclination to commerce, and he concludes, "So their dispersal throughout the world, with their union in religion and language, cannot be attributed to a curse that befell this people. It must rather be considered a blessing, especially since their per capita wealth is probably greater than that of any other people of the same number" (77). In apposition to *façon de parler*, we read *eine Phrase*, again another non-Germanic language, in order to designate an effect of discourse, a purely verbal turn of phrase, an empty expression [*une phrase*] or hollow phraseology, an affectation or aberration of language. It is "impossible," Scholem continues, absolutely impossible, simply impossible (*schlechthin unmöglich*) to "empty out words filled to bursting, unless it be at the sacrifice of the language itself." It is impossible to empty out words filled to bursting (*die zum Bersten erfüllten Worte zu entleeren*)—Scholem does not say filled "with meaning" (and here we come across once again the question of meaning and of the name)—for that would be, that could only be done, at the price of the language itself, in losing or sacrificing thereby the language itself (*es sei denn um den Preis der Sprache selbst*), a language that does not separate itself from words that themselves do not part from that which fills them to bursting. This sacrifice of the language degrades it to a "Volapük." The Volapük thus defines a language emptied of its fullness, a language that has henceforth become a nonlanguage, but this negativity remains haunted, is not an absolutely negative negativity. The "ghostly Volapük" remains inhabited by the *revenant*, wrought by the haunting that permeates [*qui traverse*], as we have seen, the entire text. Here is one of the two occurrences of the word *gespenstisch* (*das gespenstische Volapük*). This phantom of a language, this phantom language spoken here in the streets points precisely to the expressionless linguistic world (*jene ausdruckslose Sprachwelt*) in which the 'secularization' ('*Säkularisierung*') of the language could alone be possible. Were we to transmit to our children the language that has been transmitted to us, were we—the generation of transition (*das Geschlecht des Übergangs*)—to resuscitate the language of the ancient books so that it can reveal itself anew to them [*so daß sie sich an ihnen neu offenbaren kann*; here again, I do not know how far we should take into account the fact that Scholem does not literally say "meaning,"[20] but the question remains of knowing whether one should or should not bring about the manifestation, revelation, and resuscitation of language —J. D.)— must then not the religious violence of this language (*die religiöse Gewalt dieser Sprache*) one day break out against those who speak it [*gegen ihre Sprecher, ausbrechen*: explode, burst forth like lava —J. D.]? And on the day this eruption occurs, which generation (*welches Geschlecht*) will suffer its effects? We do live inside this language (*in dieser Sprache*) on top of an abyss, almost all of us with the certainty of the blind (*über einem Abgrund fast alle mit der Sicherheit des Blinden*). But when our sight is restored, we or those who come after us, must we not fall to the bottom of this abyss? And no one knows whether the sacrifice (*das Opfer*) of individuals who will be annihilated in this abyss (*in diesem Abgrund vernichtet werden*) will suffice to close it (*genügen wird, um ihn zu schliessen*).

With the last paragraph, the question from and of the *revenant* returns [*la question revient du revenant*] and that of revolution as a question of force and meaning, of form and meaning, of force and form. This question of the decision and the responsibility is also that of our generation, and it returns to us out of the undecidable bottom [*nous revient depuis le fond indécidable*]. At bottom [*au fond*], undecidable.

Each word which is not newly created [*Jedes Wort, das nicht eben neu geschaffen wird*— and Scholem does not concern himself here with these new words, nor with the question of knowing to what language they belong; everything occurs as if these were either non-words or absolutely foreign words —J. D.) but taken from the "good old" treasure (*aus dem "guten alten" Schatz*) is full to bursting (*ist zum Bersten voll*). A generation that takes upon itself the most fruitful in our sacred tradition (*unserer heiligen Tradition*)—our language—cannot live, were it to wish it a thousandfold, without tradition. The moment the *power* [*Macht*; emphasis in the original —J. D.] stored at the bottom of the language *deploys itself* [*entfalten wird*, emphasis original—J.D.],

---

20. *Translator's note:* Derrida is referring to the French translation, which includes here, on a few occurrences, the word *sens*, meaning.

the moment the "said" (das "Gesprochene"), the content (*Inhalt*) of the language, assumes its form (*Gestalt*) anew, then the sacred tradition will again confront our people as a decisive sign [*wird jene heilige Tradition wieder als entscheidendes Zeichen vor unser Volk stellen:* this must be compared to Heidegger's text mentioned earlier: the people, the sign to be interpreted, the decision and the vengeance of history —J. D.] of the only available choice: to submit or to go under [*sich zu beugen oder unterzugehen:* to sink into the abyss —J. D.]. In a language where he is invoked back a thousandfold into our life [*in der er tausendfach in unser Leben zurückbeschworen wird:* God is thus begged, sworn, invoked when we call him again to himself while making him return, God *revenant* —J. D.)—God will not stay silent (*wird ... nicht stumm bleiben*).

God speaks in the language, his voice sealed, deposited, on reserve in the sacred language that contains, like a signature, the oath of the covenant or of the faith which ties us to God. The "said" (*das "Gesprochene"*) is locked in the treasure of the sacred language. It is the said of God or the said of the phrases by which we have spoken [*nous avons dit*] our faith, by which we have sworn and taken an oath before God. The content of this hidden speech will take form again, this speech will awaken and God will speak anew, we will answer him by the same words. To hear and to say the words, to listen to them, all of this constitutes one and the same experience, one that renews the covenant. Then one will have to submit to the law of the language in which the form of the word will no longer be, will in truth never have been separated from its meaning. Meaning will again take on form in manifestation; it will awaken and reveal itself.

But the interpretation of language here implies that the separation of content and form (*Inhalt/Gestalt*) does not take place in language. More precisely, it only takes place in the degradation that contaminates language with [*par*] nonlanguage, Volapük or Esperanto. One finds here again the Benjaminian critique of semiotics or of the semiotism that he also calls "bourgeois," with its traditional oppositions: sensible/intelligible, form/meaning, content/form, signified/signifier, whether understood in their platonic tradition or in their modernization, that of the Aufklärung, to say it very quickly. All these dissociations mediatize, they provide means, they instrumentalize language. They are themselves also means, essentially means destined to reduce to silence the speech of God, and our speech toward God. They deafen, they make us deaf to the sacred word or, what comes down to the same thing, they reduce God to muteness. They suppress or, if you will, repress (but repression is still a psychoscientific, positivist category, and therefore borrowed from a secular and fundamentally semiotist realm) something like a conjuration between God and us. This sacred language is "con-juration" itself.

The language of which philosophy speaks, to the extent that the latter lives off the oppositions that we have just evoked, is a language for deaf-mutes. To return, beyond [par-delà] philosophy, to the speaking essence of the sacred language, is to go through [passer par] sacred writing which keeps the speech of God, the voice of God, in trust. And this return is nothing less than a revolution, revolution itself—and we have to hear this word of Scholem's, in the last lines of his confession, as the word of return and as the name of this political movement, more political, as a revolution of language, than the political topoi that, like the Arab problem, for example, occupy the so-called political discourses of the period in Palestine. Like every political revolution, this return marks the moment of judgment, the instance of a court (Gericht, the last judgment [Das jüngste Gericht]) with apocalyptic value. This apocalypse is named in the last lines that take the form of a prayer, of a non-theoretical, nonconstative utterance, which does not judge at the moment it announces judgment. "But this inescapable revolution of the language (diese unausbleibliche Revolution der Sprache), in which the voice will be heard again, is the sole object of which nothing is said in this country. Those who called the Hebrew language back to life did not believe in the judgment that was thus conjured upon us [uns beschworen: convoking us, calling us, assigning us —J. D.]. May the carelessness (Leichtsinn) which has led us to this apocalyptic path not bring about our ruin (Verderb: to the corruption that engulfs and damages [qui abîme])."

I will not, in concluding, insist on the equivocality of this conclusion. We have already analyzed it: ruin [la perte]—is this the punishment deserved for having secularized, profaned, ruined, for having done, in sum, the impossible itself? Or indeed the contrary, the terrifying return of the sacred? And of what, finally, would the punishment consist?

I will mention here Stéphane Mosès's hypothesis, which seems to me to be interesting and illuminating for several reasons. First of all, this hypothesis crosses an internal reading of Scholem with Benjaminian motifs (the protest against the instrumentalization of the language) and psychoanalytic motifs (repression and return of the repressed). Second, it may enable us to formalize the givens of a general problem that I will leave open in concluding, How would a kind of explanation that, to be quick, we would describe as psychoanalytic, psychoanalyticohistorical, a scientific explanation, therefore, depending on a [relevant d'un] modern rationalism, on a new determination of historical subjectivity articulated around a theory of the sign—how would such an explanation, precisely because it is in principle inadmissible by the axiomatic of this confession, enable a sharpening of the paradox that, I would be tempted to say, too quickly, we inhabit today? And what would this paradox be? A thinking of language, an experience of language that enables a deconstruction of the philosophical oppositions that govern a semiotism inherited from both Platonism and the Enlightenment can, while furthering a critique of critique and enabling progress beyond the given limits of a certain scientificity, run the risk—a scientific, philosophical, and political risk—of a rejection of science, of philosophy, to say nothing of the nationalist risk.

Here, then, is this passage from Mosès, from which a new light may be shed on these problems:

good phrase

It seems that in his text of 1926 Scholem wants to say that the unchecked use [*l'usage incontrôlé*] of the Hebrew language implies, in a way, the danger of an involuntary "practical magic" [Mosès just presented Scholem's exposition of the theory of language of Spanish Kabbalist Abraham Abulafia—J. D.]. Indeed, the symbolic dimension of Hebrew, as it appears in the sacred texts, disappears for the benefit of a purely utilitarian use of language. To be sure, in our desacralized world it is no longer a matter of consciously manipulating the magical virtualities of language in order to derive from it some personal gain. But when an entire society hijacks [*détourne*] the language of its religious tradition to purely material ends, when it makes it into a mere instrument in the service of its immediate interests, it returns [*elle retrouve*], without knowing it, to the attitude of the sorcerers of old. A "crude imitation" of the sacred texts' language, modern Hebrew has emptied out the ancient words of their symbolic and religious signification in order to reduce them to mere indices of material reality. For Scholem, however, these symbolic significations continue to live at the bottom of language or, if one will, in the unconscious of the culture that claims to deny them. The question, then, is to know whether there will not be one day a "return of the repressed," in which the religious contents will return under a form that is today unpredictable, but which threatens to be—to use a term which Scholem himself would not have used but which translates his thought—that of a collective neurosis.

"If and when the language turns against its speakers": in this formula, one in which the mystical theory of language is fulfilled as eschatology, the intention of Scholem's text dedicated to Franz Rosenzweig is summed up. For if the symbolic significations sheltered by the sacred language threaten, if they reappear in the full light of day, to reveal themselves as fatal and destructive, it is paradoxically because they are, in themselves, devoid of an identifiable content. According to Jewish mysticism, the semantic dimension of language appears only with the exercise of discourse by man; the specificity of the significations is linked to the multiplicity that characterizes the material world in which man, a finite creature, is immersed. Divine speech, on the contrary, as it reveals itself in the text of the Torah, above all in its secret linguistic texture, is of such a generality that it presents itself in the form of abstract structures (which correspond to the divine names and their diverse combinations). These structures do not transmit a determinate, and consequently limited, meaning, but carry rather an infinity of virtual significations that correspond to the infinity of possible interpretations. To say that the Torah is a divine text signifies that it is infinitely open to interpretation. The day when "the ancient names and seals"—today buried away in the unconscious of secular culture—will emerge anew into the light of day, no one can say how they will be re-interpreted. But the risk is great, according to Scholem, of seeing their return, after a long period of collective repression, take the form of an anarchic explosion of uncontrolled religious forces.[21]

APPENDIX

Gershom Scholem

"Confession on the Subject of Our Language [*Bekenntnis über unsere Sprache*]"

A Letter to Franz Rosenzweig, December 26, 1926.

This country is a volcano. It houses language. One speaks here of many things that could make us fail. One speaks more than ever today about the Arabs. But more uncanny than the Arab people [*unheimlicher als das arabische Volk*] another threat confronts us that is a *necessary* consequence [*mit Notwendigkeit*] of the Zionist undertaking: What about the "actualization [*Aktualisierung*]" of Hebrew? Must not this abyss of a sacred language handed down to our children break out again [*wieder aufbrechen*]? Truly, no one knows what is being done here. One believes that language has been secularized, that its apocalyptic thorn has been pulled out [*ihr den apokalyptischen Stache ausgezogen zu haben*]. But this is surely not true. The secularization of language is only a *façon de parler*, a ready-made phrase. It is absolutely impossible to empty out words filled to bursting, unless one does so at the expense of language itself. The ghostly Volapük spoken here in the streets points precisely to the expressionless linguistic world in which the "secularization" of language could alone be possible. If we transmit to our children the language that has been transmitted to us, if we—the generation of transition [*das Geschlecht des Übergangs*]— resuscitate the language of the ancient books so that it can reveal itself anew to them, must then not the religious violence of this language one day break out against those who speak it [*gegen ihre Sprecher ausbrechen*]? And on the day this eruption occurs, which generation will suffer its effects [*und welches Geschlecht wird dieser Ausbruch finden*]? We do live inside this language, above an abyss, almost all of us with the certainty of the blind. But when our sight is restored, we or those who come after us, must we not fall to the bottom of this abyss? And no one knows whether the sacrifice of individuals who will be annihilated in this abyss will suffice to close it.

---

21. Mosès, "Langage et sécularisation," 92–93.

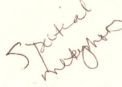

The creators of this new linguistic movement believed blindly, and stubbornly, in the miraculous power of the language, and this was their good fortune. For no one clear-sighted would have mustered the demonic courage to revive a language there where only an Esperanto could emerge. They walk, and walk still today, spellbound [*gebannt*] above the abyss. The abyss was silent and they have delivered the ancient names and seals over to the youth. We sometimes shudder when, out of the thoughtless conversation, a word from the religious sphere terrifies us, just there where it was perhaps intended to comfort. Hebrew is pregnant with catastrophes. It cannot and will not remain in its current state. Our children no longer have another language, and it is only too true to say that they, and they alone, will pay for the encounter which we have initiated without asking, without even asking ourselves. If and when the language turns against its speakers—it already does so for certain moments in our lifetime, and these are difficult to forget, stigmatizing moments in which the daring lack of measure of our undertaking reveals itself to us—will we then have a youth capable of withstanding the uprising of a sacred language?

Language is Name [*Sprache ist Namen*]. In the names, the power of language is enclosed; in them, its abyss is sealed. After invoking the ancient names daily, we can no longer hold off their power. Called awake, they will appear since we have invoked them with great violence. Truly, we speak in rudiments; we truly speak a ghostly language [*wir freilich sprechen eine gespenstische Sprache*]: the names haunt our sentences. One or another plays with them in writings and newspapers, lying to themselves or to God that this means nothing, and often, out of the ghostly shame of our language, the power of the sacred speaks out. For the names have their own life—had they not, woe to our children, who would be hopelessly abandoned to the void.

Each word which is not newly created but taken from of the "good old" treasure is full to bursting. A generation that takes upon itself the most fruitful in our sacred traditions—our language—cannot live, were it to wish it a thousandfold, without tradition. The moment the *power* stored at the bottom of the language *deploys itself*, the moment the "said [*das Gesprochene*]," the content of language, assumes its form anew, then the sacred tradition will again confront our people as a decisive sign of the only available choice: to submit or to go under. In a language where he is invoked back a thousandfold into our life, God will not stay silent. But this inescapable revolution of the language [*diese unausbleibliche Revolution der Sprache*], in which the voice will be heard again, is the sole object of which nothing is said in this country. Those who called the Hebrew language back to life did not believe in the judgment that was thus conjured upon us. May the carelessness, which has led us to this apocalyptic path, not bring about our ruin [*Möge uns dann nicht der Leichtsinn, der uns auf diesem apokalyptischen Weg geleitet, zum Verderb werden*].

Jerusalem, 7 Teveth 5687
Gerhard Scholem

Translated by Gil Anidjar

5

A Note on "Force of Law"

Since at least "Force and Signification" ("the creativity of the classical God appears all too poor") and "Violence and Metaphysics" ("God, therefore, is implicated in war"), and by way of "Signature, Event, Context," *Of Spirit*, and "Ce qui reste à force de musique" (in *Psyché*) and still other texts, Derrida has read the theological threads that are woven by and around force and violence, violence and authority, force and law. "Force of Law" renews these considerations with a scrupulous reading of Walter Benjamin's "Critique of Violence." Published in its final form in the same year as *Politics of Friendship*, "Force of Law" is an explicit rethinking of the notion of force, a rethinking that radically reconfigures the threads that link force and violence to language, law, and the theologico-political. As in *Politics*, Carl Schmitt's argument is furthered that law (*loi* and *droit*, *Gesetz* and *Recht*)—the juridical—constitutes the site where the complex history of the theologico-political comes to the fore. Derrida alters this history, however, by reading "into it" the impossible "force of weakness," the "experience of the impossible" that is justice.

Justice, however, is not "in" the course of history: "Its very moment of foundation or institution, besides, is never a moment inscribed in the homogeneous fabric [*tissu*] of a story or history, since it rips it apart with one decision. Yet, the operation that amounts to founding, inaugurating, justifying law, to *making law*, would consist of a *coup de force*, of a performative and therefore interpretative violence that in itself is neither just nor unjust and that no justice and no earlier and previously founding law, no preexisting foundation, could, by definition, guarantee or contradict or invalidate." This lack of foundation is the "mystical foundation of authority," and it directs us further toward Derrida's notion of the "mystical," toward "a silence walled up in the violent structure of the founding act. Walled up, walled in because this silence is not exterior to language."

But "Force of Law" is, perhaps, first of all, a reading—a reading of Walter Benjamin. It is a reading that extends Derrida's thinking of the name (God, violence [Germ. *Gewalt*], and Walter) as well as Derrida's insistent preoccupation with the Holocaust and with the "final solution." In his conclusion, Derrida may be said to add another aporia to those he explores throughout "Force of Law," a pedagogical aporia: "I do not know whether from this nameless thing that one calls the 'final solution' one can draw something that still deserves the name of a lesson. But if there were a lesson to be drawn, a unique lesson among the always singular lessons of murder, from even a single murder, from all the collective exterminations of history (because each individual murder and each collective murder is singular, thus infinite and incommensurable), the lesson that we could draw today—and if we can do so then we *must*—is that we must think, know, represent for ourselves, formalize, judge the possible complicity among all these discourses and the worst (here the 'final solution')."

The 1989 translation by Mary Quaintance has been revised here mostly in order to include the changes made in the latest French edition of the text, published in 1994 (revisions include translator's notes).

G. A.

FORCE OF LAW

The "Mystical Foundation of Authority"

Note: The first part of this text, "Of the Right to Justice/From Law to Justice [*Du droit à la justice*],"[1] was read at the opening of a colloquium organized by Drucilla Cornell at the Cardozo Law School in October 1989 under the title "Deconstruction and the Possibility of Justice," which gathered philosophers, literary theorists and legal scholars (notably representatives of the movement called, in the U.S., "Critical Legal Studies"). The second part of the text, "First Name of Benjamin [*Prénom de Benjamin*]," was not read aloud, but the text itself was distributed among the participants.

On April 26, 1990, the second part of the same lecture was read at the opening of another colloquium organized at the University of California-Los Angeles by Saul Friedlander under the title "Nazism and the 'Final Solution': Probing the Limits of Representation."[2] To this second part were added a foreword and a postscript that are here reproduced. This version adds a few developments and some notes to the prior versions published in prior editions and foreign languages in the form of article or book.

---

1. *Translator's note:* The translation of the word *droit* into English is notoriously difficult, as this subtitle makes clear. The word carries the sense of "law" and "code of law," and the sense of "right" (as in "the philosophy of right" but also of course as in the "right to strike" or "human rights"). The word *law* has seemed here the most economical translation, even if not entirely appropriate in all instances. One should also keep in mind that this choice for translation does raise the problem of differentiating between law (*droit*) and law (*loi*). To indicate this difference, and since the word *droit* is used with much greater frequency in Derrida's text, I have included the French *loi* in brackets only when relevant. In all other cases, when the words "law" (in the singular) or "right" appear in the present translation, it is consistently as a translation of *droit*.

2. *Translator's note:* Cf. *Probing the Limits of Representation: Nazism and the "Final Solution,"* ed. Saul Friedlander (Cambridge, Mass.: Harvard University Press, 1992).

I: OF THE RIGHT TO JUSTICE/FROM LAW TO JUSTICE

C'est pour moi un devoir, je dois *m'adresser* à vous en anglais. This is for me a duty, I must *address* myself to you in English.

The title of this colloquium and the problem that I must—as you transitively say in your language—address, have had me dreaming for months. Although I have been entrusted with the formidable honor of the "keynote address," I had nothing to do with the invention of this title, nor with the implicit formulation of the problem. "Deconstruction and the Possibility of Justice": The conjunction "and" brings together words, concepts, perhaps things that do not belong to the same category. A conjunction such as *and* dares to defy order, taxonomy, and classificatory logic, no matter how it operates—by analogy, distinction or opposition. An ill-tempered speaker might say, "I do not see the connection; no rhetoric could bend itself to such an exercise. I am quite willing to try to speak of each of these things or these categories ('deconstruction,' 'possibility,' 'justice') and even of these syncategoremes ('and,' 'the,' 'of'), but not at all in this order, this taxonomy or this syntagm."

Such a speaker would not merely be in a bad temper, he would be in bad faith. And even unjust. For one could easily propose a just interpretation, that is to say in this case an adequate and lucid—and so rather suspicious—interpretation, of the title's intentions or of its *vouloir-dire*. This title suggests a question that itself takes the form of a suspicion: Does deconstruction ensure, permit, authorize the possibility of justice? Does it make justice possible, or a discourse of consequence on justice and on the conditions of its possibility? Yes, some would reply; no, would the other party. Do the "deconstructionists" have anything to say about justice, anything to do with it? Why, basically, do they speak of it so little? Does it interest them, finally? Is it not, as some suspect, because deconstruction does not in itself permit any just action, any valid discourse on justice but rather constitutes a threat to law, and ruins the condition of possibility of justice? Yes, some would reply; no, replies the adversary.

With this first fictive exchange one can already find equivocal slippages between law and justice. The suffering of deconstruction, what makes it suffer and what makes suffer those who suffer from it, is perhaps the absence of rules, of norms, and definitive criteria to distinguish in an unequivocal manner between law and justice. It is therefore a matter of these concepts (normative or not) of norm, of rule or criteria. It is a matter of judging what permits judgment, of what judgment itself authorizes.

Such would be the choice, the "either/or," "yes or no" that one can suspect in this title. To this extent, the title would be virtually violent, polemical, inquisitorial. One can fear that it contains some instrument of torture, a manner of interrogation that would not be the most just. Needless to say already, I will not be able to offer any response, at least no reassuring response, to any questions put in this way ("either/or," "yes or no"), to either of the two expectations formulated or formalized in this way.

Je dois, donc, c'est ici un devoir, m'adresser à vous en anglais. So I must, it is here a duty, address myself to you in English. *Je le dois*—this means several things at once:

1. *Je dois parler anglais* (how does one translate this "*dois,*" this duty? I must? I should, I ought to, I have to?) because one has made this for me a sort of obligation or condition by a sort of symbolic force or law [*loi*] in a situation I do not control. A sort of *pólemos* already concerns the appropriation of language: if, at least, I want to make myself heard and understood, it is necessary [*il faut*] that I speak your language; *je le dois,* I have to do it.

2. I must speak your language because what I shall say will thus be more *juste,* or will be judged more *juste,* and be more justly appreciated, that is to say, this time, *juste* in the sense of *justesse,* in the sense of an adequation between what is and what is said or thought, between what is said and what is understood, indeed between what is thought and said or heard and understood by the majority of those who are here and who manifestly make the law [*loi*]. "Faire la loi" ("making the law") is an interesting expression about which we shall have to speak again.

3. I must speak in a language that is not my own because it will be more just, in another sense of the word *juste,* in the sense of justice, a sense which, without thinking about it too much for now, one could call *juridico-ethico-political:* it is more just to speak the language of the majority, especially when, through hospitality, it grants speech to the stranger or foreigner. We are referring here to a law [*loi*] of which it is hard to say whether it is a rule of decorum, politeness, the law of the strongest [*la loi du plus fort*], or the equitable law [*loi*] of democracy. And whether it depends on justice or on law. Still, in order for me to bend to this law [*loi*] and accept it, a certain number of conditions are necessary: for example, I must respond to an invitation and manifest my desire to speak here, something that no one apparently has constrained me to do; then, I must be capable, up to a certain point, of understanding the contract and the conditions of the law [*loi*]—that is to say, of at least minimally appropriating to myself your language, which then ceases, at least to this extent, to be foreign to me. It must be the case [*il faut*] that you and I understand, in more or less the same fashion, the translation of my text, initially written in French; this translation, however excellent it may be,[3] necessarily remains a translation—that is to say an always possible but always imperfect compromise between two idioms.

---

3. *Translator's note:* In the previous English version, Derrida here thanks the translator, Mary Quaintance.

This question of language and idiom will doubtless be at the heart of what I propose for discussion tonight.

There are a certain number of idiomatic expressions in your language that have always appeared precious to me as they have no strict equivalent in French. I will cite at least *two* of them, even before I begin. They are not unrelated to what I would like to try to say tonight.

A. The first is "to enforce the law," or "the enforceability of the law or contract." When one translates "to enforce the law" into French,—as by *appliquer la loi*, for example—one loses this direct or literal allusion to the force that comes from within to remind us that law is always an authorized force, a force that justifies itself or is justified in applying itself, even if this justification may be judged from elsewhere to be unjust or unjustifiable. No law without force, as Immanuel Kant recalled with the greatest rigor. Applicability, "enforceability," is not an exterior or secondary possibility that may or may not be added as a supplement to law. It is the force essentially implied in the very concept of *justice as law*, of justice as it becomes law, of the law as law [*de la loi en tant que droit*].

I want to insist at once to reserve the possibility of a justice, indeed of a law [*loi*] that not only exceeds or contradicts law but also, perhaps, has no relation to law, or maintains such a strange relation to it that it may just as well demand law as exclude it.

The word "enforceability" recalls us therefore to the letter. It literally reminds us that there is no law that does not imply *in itself, a priori, in the analytic structure of its concept*, the possibility of being "enforced," applied by force. Kant recalls this as early as the *Introduction to the Theory of Right* (paragraph E, which concerns law "in its strict sense, *das stricte Recht*").[4] There are, to be sure, laws [*lois*] that are not enforced, but there is no law [*loi*] without enforceability and no applicability or enforceability of the law [*loi*] without force, whether this force be direct or indirect, physical or symbolic, exterior or interior, brutal or subtly discursive—even hermeneutic—coercive or regulative, and so forth.

How to distinguish between this force of the law [*loi*], this "force of law [*force de loi*]" as one says in English as well as in French, I believe, and the violence that one always judges unjust? What difference is there between, *on the one hand*, the force

---

4. This exteriority distinguishes right from morality but it is insufficient to found or justify it. "This right is certainly based on each individual's awareness of his obligations within the law; but if it is to remain pure, it may not and cannot appeal to this awareness as a motive which might determine the will to act in accordance with it, and it therefore depends rather on the principle of the possibility of an external coercion which can coexist with the freedom of everyone in accordance with universal laws" (Immanuel Kant, "Introduction to the Theory of Right," trans. H. B. Nisbet, in *Political Writings* [Cambridge: Cambridge University Press, 1991], 134). On this point, I allow myself to refer the reader to *Du droit à la philosophie* (Paris: Galilée, 1990), 77ff.

that can be just, or in any case judged legitimate (not only an instrument in the service of law but the practice and even the fulfillment, the essence of law), and, *on the other hand*, the violence that one always judges unjust? What is a just force or a nonviolent force?

In order not to leave the question of idiom, I will refer here to a German word that will soon be occupying much of our attention: *Gewalt*. In English, as in French, it is often translated as "violence." The text by Walter Benjamin that I will be speaking about soon is entitled "Zur Kritik der Gewalt," translated in French as "Pour une critique de la violence" and in English as "Critique of Violence." But these two translations, while not altogether unjust, and so not entirely violent, are very active interpretations that do not do justice to the fact that *Gewalt* also signifies, for Germans, legitimate power, authority, public force. *Gesetzgebende Gewalt* is legislative power, *geistliche Gewalt* the spiritual power of the church, *Staatsgewalt* the authority or power of the state. *Gewalt*, then, is both violence and legitimate power, justified authority. How to distinguish between the force of law [*loi*] of a legitimate power and the allegedly originary violence that must have established this authority and that could not itself have authorized itself by any anterior legitimacy, so that, in this initial moment, it is neither legal nor illegal—as others would quickly say, neither just nor unjust? The words *Walten* and *Gewalt* play a decisive role in a few texts by Martin Heidegger—where one cannot simply translate them as either *force* or *violence*—and in a context, where Heidegger will try to show that, for Heraclitus, for example, *Dikē*, (justice, right, trial, penalty or punishment, vengeance, and so forth)—is *eris* (conflict, *Streit*, discord, *pólemos* or *Kampf*); that is, it is *adikia*, injustice, as well.[5]

Since this colloquium is devoted to deconstruction and the possibility of justice, I recall first that in the many texts said to be "deconstructive," and particularly in some of those that I have published myself, recourse to the word "force" is both very frequent and, in strategic places, I would even say decisive, but at the same time always or almost always accompanied by an explicit reserve, a warning [*mise en garde*]. I have often called for vigilance, I have recalled myself to it, to the risks spread by this word, whether it be the risk of an obscure, substantialist, occulto-mystic concept or the risk of giving authorization to violent, unjust, arbitrary force. (I will not cite these texts—it would be self-indulgent and it would waste time—but I ask you to trust me.) A first precaution against the risks of substantialism or irrationalism is to recall the differential character of force. In the texts I just evoked, it is always a matter of differential force, of difference as difference of force, of force

---

5. Cf. "Heidegger's Ear: Philopolemology (*Geschlecht IV*) in *Reading Heidegger*, ed. John Sallis (Bloomington: Indiana University Press, 1993).

as *différance* or force of *différance* (*différance* is a force *différée-différante*); it is always a matter of the relation between force and form, between force and signification, of "performative" force, illocutionary or perlocutionary force, of persuasive force and of rhetoric, of affirmation of signature, but also and above all, of all the paradoxical situations in which the greatest force and the greatest weakness strangely exchange places [*s'échangent étrangement*]. And that is the whole story, the whole of history. What remains is that I have always been uncomfortable with the word *force* even if I have often judged it indispensable—and so I thank you for thus pressing me to try and say a little more about it today. Indeed, the same thing goes for justice. There are no doubt many reasons why the majority of texts hastily identified as "deconstructionist" seem—I do say *seem*—not to foreground the theme of justice (as theme, precisely), nor even the theme of ethics or politics. Naturally this is only *apparently* so, if one considers, *for example*, (I will only mention these) the many texts devoted to Levinas and to the relations between "violence and metaphysics," or to the philosophy of right, that of Hegel's, with all its posterity in *Glas*, of which it is the principal motif, or the texts devoted to the drive for power and to the paradoxes of power in "To Speculate—on Freud," to the law [*loi*], in "Before the Law" (on Kafka's *Vor dem Gesetz*) or in "Declarations of Independence," in "The Laws of Reflection: Nelson Mandela, In Admiration," and in many other texts. It goes without saying that discourses on double affirmation, the gift beyond exchange and distribution, the undecidable, the incommensurable or the incalculable, on singularity, difference and heterogeneity are also, through and through, at least oblique discourses on justice.

Besides, it was normal, foreseeable, and desirable that studies of deconstructive style should culminate in the problematic of right, of law [*loi*] and justice. Such would even be the most proper place for them, if such a thing existed: a deconstructive questioning that starts, as has been the case, by destabilizing or complicating the opposition between *nomos* and *physis*, between *thesis* and *physis*—that is to say, the opposition between law [*loi*], convention, the institution on the one hand, and nature on the other, with all the oppositions that they condition. An example—and this is only an example—is that between positive law and natural law (*différance* is the displacement of this oppositional logic). It is a deconstructive questioning that starts—as has been the case—by destabilizing, complicating, or recalling the paradoxes of values like those of the proper and of property in all their registers, of the subject, and thus of the responsible subject, of the subject of right, the subject of law, and the subject of morality, of the juridical or moral person, of intentionality, and so forth, and of all that follows from these; Such a deconstructive questioning is through and through a questioning of law and justice, a questioning of the foundations of law, morality, and politics.

This questioning of foundations is neither foundationalist nor antifoundation-alist. Sometimes it even questions, or exceeds the very possibility, the ultimate necessity, of questioning itself, of the questioning form of thought, interrogating without confidence or prejudice the very history of the question and of its philo-sophical authority. For there is an authority—and so, a legitimate force of the ques-tioning form of which one might ask oneself whence it derives such great force in our tradition.

If, hypothetically, it had a proper place, which precisely cannot be the case, such a deconstructive questioning or metaquestioning would be more "at home" ["*chez lui*"] in law schools, perhaps also, as it does happen, in theology or architecture departments, than in philosophy and literature departments. That is why, without knowing them well from the inside, for which I feel guilty, without pretending to any familiarity with them, I judge that developments in "critical legal studies" or in such works as those of Stanley Fish, Barbara Herrstein-Smith, Drucilla Cornell, Sam Weber, and others, located at the articulation between literature, philosophy, law and politico-institutional problems, are, today, from the point of view of a certain deconstruction, among the most fertile and the most necessary. They respond, it seems to me, to the most radical programs of a deconstruction that would like, in order to be consistent with itself, not to remain enclosed in purely speculative, theo-retical, academic discourses but rather—contrary to what Stanley Fish suggests—to aspire to something more consequential, to *change* things and to intervene in an efficient and responsible (though always, of course, in a mediated way), not only in the profession but in what one calls the city, the *pólis*, and more generally the world. Not to change things in the no doubt rather naive sense of calculated, deliberate and strategically controlled intervention, but in the sense of maximum intensification of a transformation in progress, in the name of neither a simple symptom nor a simple cause; other categories are required here. In an industrial and hypertechnologized society, academic space, is less than ever the monadic or monastic ivory tower that in any case it never was. And this is particularly true of law schools.

I hasten to add here *three* very brief *points*:

1. This conjunction or conjuncture is no doubt inevitable between, on the one hand, a deconstruction of a style more directly philosophical or motivated by literary theory and, on the other hand, juridicoliterary reflection and critical legal studies.
2. It is certainly not by chance that this conjunction has developed in such an interesting way in this country. This is another problem—urgent and com-pelling—that I must leave aside for lack of time. There are no doubt profound and complicated reasons of global dimensions—I mean geopolitical and not

merely domestic—for the fact that this development should be first and fore-most North American.

3. Above all, if it seems urgent to pay attention to this joint or concurrent develop-ment and to participate in it, it is just as vital that we do not confound largely het-erogeneous and unequal discourses, styles, and discursive contexts. The word *deconstruction* could in certain cases induce or encourage such confusion. The word itself gives rise to enough misunderstandings that one would not want to add to them by reducing—between themselves, first of all—the styles of critical legal studies, or by making them examples or extensions of *Deconstruction* with a capital *D*. However unfamiliar they may be to me, I know that these works in Critical Legal Studies have their own history, context, and idiom; that in relation to such a philosophico-deconstructive questioning they are often (we shall say for the sake of brevity) uneven, timid, approximating or schematic, not to mention belated, whereas their specialization and the acuity of their technical competence puts them, on the other hand, very much in advance of whatever state decon-struction finds itself in a more literary or philosophical field. Respect for contex-tual, academico-institutional, discursive specificities, and mistrust for analogies and hasty transpositions, for confused homogenizations, seem to me to be the first imperative in the current state of things. I am convinced, I hope in any case, that this encounter will leave us with the memory of differences and *différends* at least as much it leaves us with encounters, with coincidences or consensus.

Thus, it only appears that *deconstruction*, in its best-known manifestations under that name, has not "addressed," as one says in English, the problem of justice. It only appears that way, but one must account for appearances, "keep up appear-ances" in the sense Aristotle gave to this necessity. That is how I would like to employ myself here: to show why and how what one currently calls deconstruction, while seeming not to "address" the problem of justice, has done nothing else while unable to do so directly but only in an oblique fashion. I say *oblique*, since at this very moment I am preparing to demonstrate that one cannot speak *directly* about justice, thematize or objectivize justice, say "this is just," and even less "I am just," without immediately betraying justice, if not law.[6]

B. I have not yet begun. I believed that I ought [*j'avais cru devoir*] to start by say-ing that I must [*il me faut bien*] address myself to you in your language; and I announced at once that I have always judged very precious, even irreplaceable, at least two of your idiomatic expressions. One was "to enforce the law," which always

6. On the *oblique*, see my *Du droit à la philosophie*, esp. 71ff, and "Passions: An Oblique Offering" in *On the Name*, trans. David Wood (Stanford: Stanford University Press, 1995).

reminds us that if justice is not necessarily law or the law [*le droit ou la loi*], it cannot become justice legitimately or *de jure* [*de droit ou en droit*] except by holding [*détenir*] force or rather by appealing to force from its first moment, from its first word. At the beginning of justice there will have been *logos*, speech or language, but this is not necessarily in contradiction with another *incipit*, which would say, "In the beginning there will have been force." What must be thought, therefore, is this exercise of force in language itself, in the most intimate of its essence, as in the movement by which it would absolutely disarm itself from itself.

Blaise Pascal says so in a fragment I may return to later, one of his famous "*pensées*," which is always more difficult than it seems. "Justice, force—Il est juste que ce qui est juste soit suivi, il est nécessaire que ce qui est le plus fort soit suivi. [*Justice, Force—It is right that what is just should be followed; it is necessary that what is strongest should be followed*]."[7]

The beginning of this fragment is already extraordinary, at least in the rigor of its rhetoric. It says that what is just *must* [*doit*]—and it is just—be followed: followed by consequence, followed by effect, applied, *enforced*;[8] and then that what is "strongest" *must* also be followed: by consequence, effect, and so on. In other words, the common axiom is that the just and the strongest, the most just as or as well as the strongest, *must* be followed. But this "must be followed," common to the just and the strongest, is "just" in one case, "necessary" in the other: "It is just that what is just be followed [in other words, the concept or idea of the just, in the sense of justice, implies analytically and *a priori* that the just be "followed," enforced,[9] and it is just—also in the sense of *justesse*—to think this way —J. D.], it is *necessary* that what is strongest be followed (enforced)."

Pascal continues, "*La justice sans la force est impuissante* [Justice without force is powerless—in other words, justice is not justice, it is not achieved if it does not have the force to be "enforced"; a powerless justice is not justice, in the sense of law —J. D.]; la force sans la justice est tyrannique. La justice sans force est contredite, parce qu'il y a toujours des méchants; la force sans la justice est accusée. Il faut donc mettre ensemble la justice et la force; et pour cela faire que ce qui est juste soit fort, ou que ce qui est fort soit juste [force without justice is tyrannical. Justice without force is gainsaid, because there are always offenders; force without justice is condemned. It is necessary then to combine justice and force; and for this end make what is just strong, or what is strong just]."

---

7. Blaise Pascal, *Pensées et opuscules*, ed. Léon Brunschvicg (Paris: Hachette, 1961), frag. 298, 470. Blaise Pascal, *Thoughts*, trans. W. F. Trotter (New York: Collier, 1910), 107. *Translator's note:* I have altered the English translation to remain closer to Derrida's phrasing.

8. *Translator's note:* The word *enforced* is in English in the text.

9. *Translator's note:* The word *enforced* is in English in the text.

It is difficult to decide or conclude whether the "it is necessary [*il faut*]" in this conclusion ("And so it is necessary to put justice and force together") is an "it is necessary" prescribed by what is just in justice or by what is necessary in force. One could also consider this hesitation secondary. It hovers above the surface of an "it is necessary" that is deeper, if one could say so, since justice demands, as justice, recourse to force. The necessity of force is implied, then, in the *juste* of justice.

What follows and concludes this pensée is known: "Et ainsi ne pouvant faire que ce qui est juste fût fort, on a fait que ce qui est fort fût juste [And thus being unable to make what is just strong, we have made what is strong just]." The principle of the analysis or rather of the (active and anything but nonviolent) interpretation that I will *indirectly* propose in the course of this lecture, would run, I am convinced, counter to tradition and to its most obvious context. This dominant context and the conventional interpretation that it seems to govern goes, precisely, in a conventionalist direction, toward the sort of pessimistic, relativistic and empiricist skepticism that drove Arnaud to suppress these pensées in the Port Royal edition, alleging that Pascal wrote them under the impression of a reading of Montaigne, according to whom laws [*lois*] are not in themselves just but are rather just only because they are laws. It is true that Montaigne used an interesting expression, which Pascal takes up for his own purposes and which I would also like to reinterpret and retrieve from its most conventional and most conventionalist reading. The expression is "mystical foundation of authority [*fondement mystique de l'autorité*]." Pascal cites Montaigne without naming him when he writes, in *pensée* 293, "l'un dit que l'essence de la justice est l'autorité du législateur, l'autre la commodité du souverain, l'autre la coutume présente; et c'est le plus sûr: rien, suivant la seule raison, n'est juste de soi; tout branle avec le temps. La coutume fait toute l'équité, par cette seule raison qu'elle est reçue; c'est le fondement mystique de son autorité. Qui la ramène à son principe, l'anéantit [one affirms the essence of justice to be the authority of the legislator; another the interest of the sovereign; another, present custom, and this is the most sure. Nothing according to reason alone, is just in itself; all changes with time. Custom creates the whole of equity, for the simple reason that it is accepted. It is the *mystical foundation* of its *authority*. Whoever carries it back to first principles destroys it]."[10]

Montaigne was in fact speaking, these are his words, of a "mystical foundation" of the authority of laws, "Or les loix se maintiennent en credit, non parce qu'elles sont justes, mais parce qu'elles sont loix: c'est le fondement mystique de leur authorité, elles n'en ont poinct d'autre.... Quiconque leur obeyt parce qu'elles sont justes, ne leur obeyt pas justement par où il doibt [Lawes are now maintained

10. Pascal, *Pensées*, no. 294, 467/*Thoughts*, 104; emphasis added.

in credit, not because they are just, but because they are lawes. It is the mystical foundation of their authority; they have none other ... Whosoever obeyeth them because they are just, obeyes them not justly the way as he ought]."[11]

Clearly Montaigne is here distinguishing laws [lois], that is to say law [droit], from justice. The justice of law, justice as law is not justice. Laws are not just in as much as they are laws. One does not obey them because they are just but because they have authority. The word *credit* carries all the weight of the proposition and justifies the allusion to the mystical character of authority. The authority of laws rests only on the credit that is granted them. One believes in it; that is their only foundation. This act of faith is not an ontological or rational foundation. Still one has yet to think what *believing* means [encore faut-il penser ce que croire veut dire].

Little by little what will be clarified—if it is possible and if it is a matter here of a value of clarity—is what one can understand by this expression "mystical foundation of authority." It is true that Montaigne also wrote the following, which must, again, be interpreted by going beyond its simply conventional and conventionalist surface: "nostre droict mesme a, dict-on, des fictions legitimes sur lesquelles il fonde la vérité de sa justice [and our law hath, as some say, certaine lawfull fictions, on which it groundeth the truth of justice]." What is a legitimate fiction? What does it mean to found the truth of justice? These are among the questions that await us. Montaigne proposed an analogy between this supplement of a legitimate fiction, that is, the fiction necessary to found the truth of justice, and the supplement of artifice called for by a deficiency in nature, as if the absence of natural law called for the supplement of historical or positive (that is to say, an addition of fictional) law just as—and that is the proximity [rapprochement] proposed by Montaigne—"les femmes employent des dents d'yvoire où les leurs naturelles leur manquent, et, au lieu de leur vray teint, en forgent un de quelque matiere estrangere ... s'embellissent d'une beauté fauce et empruntée: ainsi faict la science (et nostre droict mesme, a dict-on, des fictions legitimes sur lesquelles il fonde la verité de sa justice) [Even as women, when their naturall teeth faile them, use some of yvorie, and in stead of a true beautie, or lively colour, lay-on artificiall hew ... embellish themselves with counterfeit and borrowed beauties; so doth learning (and our law hath, as some say, certaine lawfull fictions, on which it groundeth the truth of justice)]."[12]

The Pascal pensée that "puts together" justice and force and makes force an essential predicate of justice—by which he means *droit* more than justice—perhaps goes beyond a conventionalist or utilitarian relativism, beyond a nihilism, ancient

---

11. Montaigne, *Essais* 3, ch. 13, "De l'expérience" (Paris: Bibliothèque de la Pléiade, 1962), 1203/*The Essayes of Montaigne*, trans. John Florio (New York: Modern Library, 1933), 970.

12. *Essais* 2, ch. 12, p. 601/*Essayes*, 482.

or modern, that would make the law [*loi*] what one sometimes calls a "masked power," beyond the cynical moral of La Fontaine's "The Wolf and the Sheep," according to which "La raison du plus fort est toujours la meilleure [The reason of the strongest is always the best—i.e., might makes right]."

In its principle, the Pascalian critique refers back to original sin and to the corruption of natural *laws* [*lois*] by a reason that is itself corrupt: "Il y a sans doute des lois naturelles; mais cette belle raison a tout corrompu [Doubtless there are natural laws; but good reason has corrupted all]."[13] And elsewhere, "notre justice [s'anéantit] devant la justice divine [our justice (is annihilated) before divine justice]."[14] These pensées prepare us for the reading of Benjamin.

But if one sets aside the functional mechanism of the Pascalian critique, if one dissociates this simple analysis from the presupposition of its Christian pessimism (something that is not impossible to do), then one can find in it, as in Montaigne, the premises of a *modern* critical philosophy, even a critique of juridical ideology, a desedimentation of the superstructures of law that both hide and reflect the economic and political interests of the dominant forces of society. This would always be possible and sometimes useful.

But beyond its principle and its mechanism, this Pascalian pensée concerns perhaps a more intrinsic structure. A critique of juridical ideology should never neglect this structure. The very emergence of justice and law, the instituting, founding, and justifying moment of law implies a performative force, that is to say always an interpretative force and a call to faith [*un appel à la croyance*]: not in the sense, this time, that law would be *in the service* of force, its docile instrument, servile and thus exterior to the dominant power, but rather in the sense of law that would maintain a more internal, more complex relation to what one calls force, power or violence. Justice—in the sense of *droit* (right or law)[15]—would not simply be put in the service of a social force or power, for example an economic, political, ideological power that would exist outside or before it and that it would have to accommodate or bend to when useful. Its very moment of foundation or institution, besides, is never a moment inscribed in the homogeneous fabric [*tissu*] of a story or history, since it rips it apart with one decision. Yet, the operation that amounts to founding, inaugurating, justifying law, to *making law*, would consist of a *coup de force*, of a performative and therefore interpretative violence that in itself is neither just nor unjust and that no justice and no earlier and previously founding law, no preexisting foundation, could, by definition, guarantee or contradict or invalidate. No

---

13. *Pensées*, no. 294, 466/*Essayes*, 101.
14. *Pensées*, no. 233, 435/*Thoughts*, 80.
15. *Translator's note:* "right or law" is in English in the text.

justificatory discourse could or should ensure the role of metalanguage in relation to the performativity of institutive language or to its dominant interpretation.

Discourse here meets its limit—in itself, in its very performative power. It is what I propose to call here the *mystical*. There is here a silence walled up in the violent structure of the founding act; walled up, walled in because this silence is not exterior to language. Here is the sense in which I would be tempted to interpret, beyond simple commentary, what Montaigne and Pascal call the *mystical foundation of authority*. One will always be able to return upon—or turn against—what I am doing or saying here, the very thing that I am saying is done or occurs [*cela même que je dis qui se fait*] at the origin of every institution. I would therefore take the use of the word *mystical* in a sense that I would venture to call rather Wittgensteinian. These texts by Montaigne and Pascal, along with the tradition to which they belong, like the rather active interpretation of them that I propose, could be invited to a discussion with Stanley Fish in "Force" about H. L. A. Hart's *Concept of Law*, and several others, implicitly including John Rawls, himself criticized by Hart, as well as to many debates illuminated by some texts of Sam Weber on the agnostic and not simply intra-institutional or mono-institutional character of certain conflicts in *Institution and Interpretation*.[16]

Since the origin of authority, the founding or grounding [*la fondation ou le fondement*], the positing of the law [*loi*] cannot by definition rest on anything but themselves, they are themselves a violence without ground [*sans fondement*]. This is not to say that they are in themselves unjust, in the sense of "illegal" or "illegitimate." They are neither legal nor illegal in their founding moment. They exceed the opposition between founded and unfounded, or between any foundationalism or antifoundationalism. Even if the success of performatives that found a law (for example, and this is more than an example, of a state as guarantor of a law) presupposes earlier conditions and conventions (for example, in the national and international arena), the same "mystical" limit will reemerge at the supposed origin of said conditions, rules or conventions, and at the origin of their dominant interpretation.

In the structure I am here describing here, law is essentially *deconstructible*, whether because it is founded, that is to say constructed, upon interpretable and transformable textual strata (and that is the history of law, its possible and necessary transformation, sometimes its amelioration), or because its ultimate foundation is by definition unfounded. The fact that law is deconstructible is not bad news. One may even find in this the political chance of all historical progress. But

---

16. Samuel Weber, *Institution and Interpretation* (Minneapolis: University of Minnesota Press, 1987).
    Translator's note: The references are to Stanley Fish, *Doing What Comes Naturally: Change, Rhetoric, and the Practice of Theory in Literary and Legal Studies* (Durham, N.C.: Duke University Press, 1989), in which Fish engages H. L. A. Hart, *The Concept of Law* (Oxford: Clarendon, 1961).

the paradox that I would like to submit for discussion is the following: it is this deconstructible structure of law or, if you prefer, of justice as law, that also ensures the possibility of deconstruction. Justice in itself, if such a thing exist, outside or beyond law, is not deconstructible. No more than deconstruction itself, if such a thing exist. *Deconstruction is justice.* It is perhaps because law (which I will therefore consistently try to distinguish from justice) is constructible, in a sense that goes beyond the opposition between convention and nature, it is perhaps insofar as it goes beyond this opposition that it is constructible—and so deconstructible and, better yet, that it makes deconstruction possible, or at least the exercise of a deconstruction that, fundamentally, always proceeds to questions of law and to the subject of law. Whence these three propositions:

1. The deconstructibility of law (for example) makes deconstruction possible.
2. The undeconstructibility of justice also makes deconstruction possible, indeed is inseparable from [*se confond avec*] it.
3. *Consequence*: Deconstruction takes place in the interval that separates the undeconstructibility of justice from the deconstructibility of law. Deconstruction is possible as an experience of the impossible, there where, even if it does not exist, if it is not *present*, not yet or never, *there is* justice [il y a *la justice*]. Wherever one can replace, translate, determine the *X* of justice, one would have to say: deconstruction is possible, as impossible, to the extent (there) where *there is X* (undeconstructible), thus to the extent (there) where *there is* (the undeconstructible).

In other words, the hypothesis and propositions toward which I am tentatively moving here would rather call for the subtitle: justice as the possibility of deconstruction, the structure of right or of the law [*la structure du droit ou de la loi*], the founding or the self-authorizing of law as the possibility of the exercise of deconstruction. I am sure this is not altogether clear. I hope, without being sure of it, that it will become a little clearer in a moment.

I have said, then, that I have not yet begun. Perhaps I will never begin and perhaps this colloquium will have to do without a "keynote." Yet I have already begun. I authorize myself—but by what right?—to multiply protocols and detours. I began by saying that I was in love with at least two of your idioms. One was the word *enforceability*, the other was the transitive use of the verb *to address*. In French, one addresses oneself to someone, one addresses a letter or a word, also a transitive use, without being sure that they will arrive at their destination; but one does not address a problem. Even less does one address someone. Tonight, I have agreed by contract to "address," in English, a problem, that is to say, to go straight toward it and straight toward you, thematically and without detour, in addressing myself to you in your language. In between the law or right [*droit*], the rectitude of address, direction and straightforwardness [*droiture*], one should find a direct line of communication and find oneself on the right track. Why does deconstruction have the reputation, justified or not, of treating things *obliquely*, indirectly, in indirect style, with so many "quotation marks," and while always asking whether things arrive at the indicated address? Is this reputation deserved? And, deserved or not, how does one explain it?

And so we have already, in the fact that I speak the language of the other and break with mine, in the fact that I give myself up to the other, a singular mixture of force, *justesse* and justice. And I must, it is a duty, "address" in English, as you say in your language, infinite problems, infinite in their number, infinite in their history, infinite in their structure, covered by the title *Deconstruction and the Possibility of Justice*. But we already know that these problems are not infinite simply became they are infinitely numerous, nor because they are rooted in the infinity of memories and cultures (religious, philosophical, juridical, and so forth) that we shall never master. They are infinite, if one may say so, *in themselves*, because they require the very experience of the aporia that is not unrelated to what we just called the *mystical*.

By saying that they even require the *experience of aporia*, one can understand two things that are already quite complicated:

1. As its name indicates, an *experience* is a traversal, something that traverses and travels toward a destination for which it finds a passage. The experience finds its way, its passage, it is possible. Yet, in this sense there cannot be a full experience of aporia, that is, of something that does not allow passage. *Aporia* is a nonpath. From this point of view, justice would be the experience of what we are unable to experience. We shall soon encounter more than one aporia that we shall not be able to pass.

2. But I believe that there is no justice without this experience, however impossible it may be, of aporia. Justice is an experience of the impossible: a will, a desire, a demand for justice the structure of which would not be an experience of aporia, would have no chance to be what it is—namely, a just *call* for justice. Every time that something comes to pass or turns out well, every time that we placidly apply a good rule to a particular case, to a correctly subsumed example, according to a determinant judgment, law perhaps and sometimes finds itself accounted for, but one can be sure that justice does not.

Law is not justice. Law is the element of calculation, and it is just that there be law, but justice is incalculable, it demands that one calculate with the incalculable; and aporetic experiences are the experiences, as improbable as they are necessary, of justice, that is to say of moments in which the *decision* between just and unjust is never insured by a rule.

And so I must *address* myself to you and "address" problems; I must do it briefly and in a foreign language. To do it briefly, I ought to do it as directly as possible, going straight ahead, without detour, without historical alibi, without oblique proceeding [*démarche oblique*], on the one hand toward you, supposedly the primary addressees of this discourse, but at the same time and on the other hand toward the essential place of decision for said problems. Address, like direction, like *rectitude*, says something about law [*droit*] and about what one must not miss when one wants justice, when one wants to be just—it is the *rectitude* of address. *Il ne faut pas manquer d'adresse*, one must not lack address or skill, one might say in French, but, above all, *il ne faut pas manquer l'adresse*, one must not miss the address, one must not mistake the address. But the address always turns out to be singular. An address is always singular, idiomatic, and justice, as law, seems always to suppose the generality of a rule, a norm or a universal imperative. How to reconcile the act of justice that must always concern singularity, individuals, groups, irreplaceable existences, the other or myself *as* other, in a unique situation, with rule, norm, value, or the imperative of justice that necessarily have a general form, even if this generality prescribes a singular application in each case? If I were content to apply a just rule, without a spirit of justice and without in some way and each time inventing the rule and the example, I might be sheltered from criticism, under the protection of law, my action conforming to objective law, but I would not be just. I would act, Kant would say, *in conformity* with duty but not *through* duty or *out of respect* for the law [*loi*]. Is it ever possible to say that an action is not only legal, but just? A person is not only within his rights [*dans son droit*] but within justice? That such a person is just, a decision is just? Is it ever possible to say, "I know that I am just"? I would want to show that such confidence is essentially impossible, other than in the figure of good conscience and mystification. But allow me yet another detour.

To address oneself to the other in the language of the other is both the condition of all possible justice, it seems, but, in all rigor, it appears not only impossible (since I cannot speak the language of the other except to the extent that I appropriate it and assimilate it according to the law [*loi*] of an implicit third) but even excluded by justice as law, inasmuch as justice as law seems to imply an element of universality, the appeal to a third party who suspends the unilaterality or singularity of the idioms.

When I address myself to someone in English, it is always a test and an ordeal for me and for my addressee, for you as well, I imagine. Rather than explain to you why and lose time in doing so, I begin in medias res, with several remarks that for me tie the anguishing gravity of this problem of language to the question of justice, of the possibility of justice.

On the one hand, for fundamental reasons, it seems to us just to *rendre la justice*, as one says in French, in a given idiom, in a language in which all the "subjects" concerned are supposed competent, that is to say, capable of understanding and interpreting; all the "subjects," so to say, are those who establish the laws [*lois*], those who judge and those who are judged, witnesses in both the broad and narrow sense—all those who are guarantors of the exercise of justice, or rather of law. It is unjust to judge someone who does not understand his rights, nor the language in which the law [*loi*] is inscribed or the judgment pronounced, and so on. We could give multiple dramatic examples of situations of violence in which a person or group of persons assumed to fall under the law [*loi*] are judged in an idiom they do not understand, not very well or not at all. And however slight or subtle the difference of competence in the mastery of the idiom would be here, the violence of an injustice has begun when all the members [*partenaires*] of a community do not share, through and through, the same idiom. Since, in all rigor, this ideal situation is never possible, one can already draw some inferences about what the title of our conference calls "the possibility of justice." The violence of this injustice that consists of judging those who do not understand the idiom in which one claims, as one says in French, that "*justice est faite* [justice is done, made]" is not just any violence, any injustice. This injustice, which supposes all the others, supposes that the other, the victim of the injustice of language, if one may say so, is capable of a language in general, is man as a speaking animal, in the sense that we, men, give to this word "language." Moreover, there was a time, not long ago and not yet over, in which "we, men" meant "we adult white male Europeans, carnivorous and capable of sacrifice."

In the space in which I am situating these remarks or reconstituting this discourse one would not speak of injustice or violence toward an animal, even less toward a vegetable or a stone. An animal can be made to suffer, but one would never say, in a sense said to be proper, that it is a wronged subject, the victim of a crime, of a murder, of a rape or a theft, of a perjury—and this is true *a fortiori*, one thinks, for what one calls vegetable or mineral or intermediate species like the sponge. There have been, there are still, many "subjects" among humankind who are not recognized as subjects and who receive this animal treatment (this is the whole unfinished story and history I briefly alluded to a moment ago). What one confusedly calls "animal," the living thing as living and nothing more, is not a subject of the law or of right [*de la loi ou du droit*]. The opposition between just and unjust has no meaning as far as it is concerned. Whether it is a matter of trials of animals (there have been some) or lawsuits against those who inflict certain kinds of suffering on animals (legislation in certain Western countries provides for this and speaks not only of the "rights of man" but also of the rights of the animal in general), these are either archaisms or still marginal and rare phenomena not con-

stitutive of our culture. In *our* culture, carnivorous sacrifice is fundamental, dominant, regulated by the highest industrial technology, as is biological experimentation on animals—so vital to our modernity. As I have tried to show elsewhere,[17]
carnivorous sacrifice is essential to the structure of subjectivity, which is to say to
the founding of the intentional subject as well and to the founding, if not of the law
[*loi*], at least of right [*droit*], the difference between law and right [*la loi et le droit*],
justice and right, justice and law [*loi*], here remaining open over an abyss. I will
leave these problems aside for the moment, along with the affinity between carnivorous sacrifice, at the basis of our culture and our law, and all the cannibalisms,
symbolic or not, that structure intersubjectivity in nursing, love, mourning and, in
truth, in all symbolic or linguistic appropriations.

If we wish to speak of injustice, of violence or of a lack of respect toward
what we still so confusedly call the animal—the question is more current than ever
(and so I include in it, in the name of deconstruction, a set of questions on carno-
phallogocentrism)—one must [*il faut*] reconsider in its totality the metaphysico-
anthropocentric axiomatic that dominates, in the West, the thought of the just
and the unjust.

From this very first step, one can already glimpse a first consequence: by decon-
structing the partitions that institute the human subject (preferably and paradig-
matically the adult male, rather than the woman, child, or animal) at the measure
of the just and the unjust, one does not necessarily lead toward injustice, nor to the
effacement of an opposition between just and unjust but, in the name of a demand
more insatiable than justice, leads perhaps to a reinterpretation of the whole apparatus of limits within which a history and a culture have been able to confine their
criteriology. Under the hypothesis that I am superficially considering for the moment, what is currently called deconstruction would not at all correspond (though
certain people have an interest in spreading this confusion) to a quasi-nihilistic
abdication before the ethico-politico-juridical question of justice and before the
opposition between just and unjust, but rather to a double movement that I would
schematize as follows:

1. The sense of a responsibility without limits, and so necessarily excessive, incalculable, before memory; and so the task of recalling the history, the origin and the
   sense, thus the limits, of concepts of justice, law [*loi*] and right [*droit*], of values,
   norms, prescriptions that have been imposed and sedimented there, from then

---

17. On animality, cf. my *Of Spirit: Heidegger and the Question,* trans. F. Bennington and R. Bowlby
(Chicago: University of Chicago Press, 1989). As for sacrifice and carnivorous culture, see my "'Eating
Well,' or the Calculation of the Subject," trans. Peter Connor and Avital Ronell, in Jacques Derrida,
Points . . . : Interviews, 1974–1994.

on remaining more or less readable or presupposed. As to the legacy we have received under the name of justice, and in more than one language, the *task* of a historical and interpretative memory is at the heart of deconstruction. This is not only a philologico-etymological task or the historian's task but the responsibility in face of a heritage that is at the same time the heritage of an imperative or of a sheaf of injunctions. Deconstruction is already pledged, engaged [*gagée, engagée*] by this demand for infinite justice, which can take the aspect of this "mystique" I spoke of earlier. One must [*il faut*] be *juste* with justice, and the first justice to be done is to hear it, to try to understand where it comes from, what it wants from us, knowing that it does so through singular idioms (*Dikē, Jus, justitia, justice, Gerechtigkeit*, to limit ourselves to European idioms that it may also be necessary to delimit, in relation to others—we shall come back to this later). One must know that this justice always addresses itself to singularity, to the singularity of the other, despite or even because it pretends to universality. Consequently, never to yield on this point, constantly to maintain a questioning of the origin, grounds and limits of our conceptual, theoretical or normative apparatus surrounding justice—this is, from the point of view of a rigorous deconstruction, anything but a neutralization of the interest in justice, an insensitivity toward injustice. On the contrary, it hyperbolically raises the stakes in the demand for justice, the sensitivity to a kind of essential disproportion that must inscribe excess and inadequation in itself. It compels to denounce not only theoretical limits but also concrete injustices, with the most palpable effects, in the good conscience that dogmatically stops before any inherited determination of justice.

2. This responsibility before memory is a responsibility before the very concept of responsibility that regulates the justice and appropriateness [*justesse*] of our behavior, of our theoretical, practical, ethicopolitical decisions. This concept of responsibility is inseparable from a whole network of connected concepts (propriety and property, intentionality, will, freedom, conscience, consciousness, self-consciousness, subject, self, person, community, decision, and so forth). All deconstruction of this network of concepts in their given or dominant state may seem like a move toward irresponsibility at the very moment that, on the contrary, deconstruction calls for an increase in responsibility. But in the moment that the credit or credibility [*crédit*] of an axiom is suspended by deconstruction, in this structurally necessary moment, one can always believe that there is no more room for justice, neither for justice itself nor for the theoretical interest that is directed toward the problems of justice. It is a moment of suspense, this period of *epokhē*, without which there is, in fact, no possible deconstruction. It is not a simple moment: its possibility must remain structurally present to the exercise of all responsibility if such responsibility is never to abandon itself to

dogmatic slumber, and therefore to deny itself. From then on, this moment overflows itself. It becomes all the more anguishing. But who will claim to be just by economizing on anguish? This anguishing moment of suspense also opens the interval of spacing in which transformations, even juridicopolitical revolutions, take place. It cannot be motivated, it cannot find its movement and its impulse (an impulse that, however, cannot itself be suspended) except in the demand for an increase or a supplement of justice, and so in the experience of an inadequation or an incalculable disproportion. For in the end, where would deconstruction find its force, its movement or its motivation if not in this always unsatisfied appeal, beyond the given determinations of what one names, in determined contexts, justice, the possibility of justice?

And yet, one must [*encore faut-il*] interpret this disproportion. If I were to say that I know nothing more just than what I call today deconstruction (nothing more just—I am not saying nothing more legal or more legitimate), I know that I would not fail to surprise or shock not only the determined adversaries of said deconstruction or of what they imagine under this name, but also the very people who pass for or take themselves to be its partisans or its practitioners. And so, I will not say it, at least not directly and not without the precaution of several detours.

As is well known, in many countries, in the past and in the present, one of the founding violences of the law [*loi*] or of the imposition of state law has consisted in imposing a language on national or ethnic minorities regrouped by the state. This was the case in France on at least two occasions, first when the Villers-Cotteret decree consolidated the unity of the monarchic state by imposing French as the juridico-administrative language and by forbidding Latin, the language of law or of the Church. The decree allowed all the inhabitants of the kingdom to be represented in a common language, by a lawyer-interpreter, without the imposition of the particular language that French still was. It is true that Latin was already carrying a violence. The passage from Latin to French was only the passage from one violence to another. The second major moment of imposition was that of the French Revolution, when linguistic unification sometimes took the most repressive pedagogical turns, or in any case the most authoritarian ones. I am not going to engage in the history of these examples. One could also find others in the United States, yesterday and today; the linguistic problem is still acute there and will be for a long time, precisely in such a place where questions of politics, education, and law are inseparable.

Now let us go straight, without the least detour through historical memory, toward the formal, abstract enunciation of several aporias—those in which, between law and justice, deconstruction finds its privileged site, or rather, its privileged instability. Deconstruction is generally practiced in two ways or two styles, and it most often grafts one on to the other. One takes on the demonstrative and apparently ahistorical allure of logico-formal paradoxes. The other, more historical or more anamnesic, seems to proceed through readings of texts, meticulous interpretations and genealogies. Allow me to devote myself successively to both exercises.

First I will dryly and directly state, I will "address," the following aporias. In fact, there is only one aporetic potential that infinitely distributes itself. I shall only propose a few examples that will suppose, make explicit or perhaps produce a difficult and unstable distinction between justice and law, between justice (infinite, incalculable, rebellious to rule and foreign to symmetry, heterogeneous and heterotropic) on the one hand, and, on the other, the exercise of justice as law, legitimacy or legality, a stabilizable, statutory and calculable apparatus [*dispositif*], a system of regulated and coded prescriptions. I would be tempted, up to a certain point, to bring the concept of justice—which I am here trying to distinguish from law—closer to Levinas's. I would do so just because of this infinity and because of the heteronomic relation to the other [*autrui*], to the face of the other that commands me, whose infinity I cannot thematize and whose hostage I am. In *Totality and Infinity*, Levinas writes, "la relation avec autrui—c'est à dire la justice [the relation with the other—that is to, say, justice]"[18];—it is a justice he elsewhere defines as "*droiture de l'accueil fait au visage* [the straightforwardness of the welcome made to the face]."[19] Straightforwardness [*la droiture*] is not reducible to law, of course, nor to "address" nor to "direction" of which we have been speaking for a while, but the two values are not without relation, the common relation that they maintain with a certain *rectitude.*

Levinas speaks of an infinite right in what he calls "Jewish humanism," whose basis is not "the concept 'man'" but rather the other [*autrui*]: "the extent of the other's right" is "practically an infinite right."[20] Here *équité* is not equality, calculated proportion, equitable distribution or distributive justice, but rather, absolute dissymmetry. And the Levinasian notion of justice would rather come closer to the Hebrew equivalent of what we would perhaps translate as holiness [*sainteté*]. But since I would have other difficult questions about Levinas' difficult discourse, I cannot be content to borrow a conceptual trait without risking confusions or analogies. And so I will go no further in this direction.

Everything would still be simple if this distinction between justice and law were a true distinction, an opposition the functioning of which was logically regulated and

---

18. Emmanuel Levinas, *Totality and Infinity*, trans. A. Lingis (Pittsburgh: Duquesne University Press, 1969), 89.

19. Ibid., 82.

20. Emmanuel Levinas, *Nine Talmudic Readings*, trans. Annette Aronowicz (Bloomington: Indiana University Press, 1990), 98.

masterable. But it turns out that law claims to exercise itself in the name of justice and that justice demands for itself that it be established in the name of a law that must be put to work [*mis en oeuvre*] (constituted and applied) by force "enforced."[21] Deconstruction always finds itself and moves itself between these two poles.

Here, then, are some examples of aporias.

1. First Aporia: The E*pokhē* of the Rule.

Our most common axiom is that to be just or unjust, to exercise justice or to transgress it I must be free and responsible for my action, my behavior, my thought, my decision. One will not say of a being without freedom, or at least of one who is not free in a given act, that its decision is just or unjust. But this freedom or this decision of the just, if it is to be and to be said such, to be recognized as such, must follow a law [*loi*] or a prescription, a rule. In this sense, in its very autonomy, in its freedom to follow or to give itself the law [*loi*], it has to be capable of being of the calculable or programmable order, for example as an act of fairness [*équité*]. But if the act simply consists of applying a rule, of enacting a program or effecting a calculation, one will perhaps say that it is legal, that it conforms to law, and perhaps, by metaphor, that it is just, but one would be wrong to say that the *decision* was just. Simply because there was, in this case, no decision.

To be just, the decision of a judge, for example, must not only follow a rule of law or a general law [*loi*] but must also assume it, approve it, confirm its value, by a reinstituting act of interpretation, as if, at the limit, the law [*loi*] did not exist previously—as if the judge himself invented it in each case. Each exercise of justice as law can be just only if it is a "fresh judgment" (I borrow this English expression from Stanley Fish's article, "Force").[22] This new freshness, the initiality of this inaugural judgment can very well—better yet, must [*doit*] very well—conform to a preexisting law [*loi*], but the reinstituting, reinventive and freely deciding interpretation of the responsible judge requires that his "justice" not consist only in conformity, in the conservative and reproductive activity of judgment. In short, for a decision to be just and responsible, it must [*il faut*], in its proper moment, if there is one, be both regulated and without regulation, it must preserve the law [*loi*] and also destroy or suspend it enough to have [*pour devoir*] to reinvent it in each case, rejustify it, reinvent it at least in the reaffirmation and the new and free confirmation of its principle. Each case is other, each decision is different and requires an absolutely unique interpretation, which no existing, coded rule can or ought to guarantee absolutely. (At least, if the rule does guarantee it in a secure fashion, then

---

21. *Translator's note:* The word *enforced* is in English in the text.
22. *Translator's note:* Stanley Fish, "Force," in *Doing What Comes Naturally*, 503–24.

the judge is a calculating machine.) This is something that happens sometimes; it happens always in part and according to a parasitizing that cannot be reduced by the mechanics or the technology introduced by the necessary iterability of judgments. To this very extent, however, one will not say of the judge that he is purely just, free, and responsible. But one will also not say this if he does not refer to any law, to any rule, or if, because he does not take any rule for granted beyond his/its interpretation, he suspends his decision, stops at the undecidable or yet improvises outside of all rules, all principles. It follows from this paradox that at no time can one say *presently* that a decision is just, purely just (that is to say, free and responsible), or that someone *is* just, and even less, "*I am* just." Instead of *just* one can say *legal* or *legitimate*, in conformity with a law, with rules and conventions that authorize calculation, but with a law of which the founding origin [*l'origine fondatrice*] only defers the problem of justice. For in the founding [*au fondement*] of law or in its institution, the same problem of justice will have been posed and violently resolved, that is to say buried, dissimulated, repressed. Here the best paradigm is the founding [*fondation*] of the nation-states or the institutive act of a constitution that establishes what one calls in French *l'état de droit.*

2. Second Aporia: The Haunting of the Undecidable.

No justice is exercised, no justice is rendered, no justice becomes effective nor does it determine itself in the form of law, without a decision that cuts and divides [*une décision qui tranche*]. This decision of justice does not simply consist in its final form—for example, a penal sanction, equitable or not, in the order of proportional or distributive justice. It begins, it ought to begin, by right [*en droit*] or in principle, in the initiative that amounts to learning, reading, understanding, interpreting the rule, and even calculating. For if calculation is calculation, the *decision to calculate* is not of the order of the calculable, and it must not be so [*et ne doit pas l'être*].

One often associates the theme of undecidability with deconstruction. Yet, the undecidable is not merely the oscillation between two significations or two contradictory and very determinate rules, each equally imperative (for example, respect for equity and universal right, but also for the always heterogeneous and unique singularity of the unsubsumable example). The undecidable is not merely the oscillation or the tension between two decisions. Undecidable—this is the experience of that which, though foreign and heterogeneous to the order of the calculable and the rule, must [*doit*] nonetheless—it is of *duty* [*devoir*] that one must speak—deliver itself over to the impossible decision while taking account of law and rules. A decision that would not go through the test and ordeal of the undecidable would not be a free decision; it would only be the programmable application or the continuous unfolding of a calculable process. It might perhaps be legal; it would not be just. But in the moment of suspense of the undecidable, it is not just either, for only a decision is just. In order to maintain the proposition "only a decision is just," one need not refer decision to the structure of a subject or to the propositional form of a judgment. In a way, and at the risk of shocking, one could even say that a subject can never decide anything [*un sujet ne peut jamais rien décider*]: a subject is even that to *which* a decision cannot come or happen [*arriver*] otherwise than as a marginal accident that does not affect the essential identity and the substantial presence-to-self that make a subject what it is—if the choice of the word *subject* is not arbitrary, at least, and if one trusts in what is in fact always required, in our culture, of a subject.

Once the test and ordeal of the undecidable has passed (if that is possible, but this possibility is not pure, it is never like an other possibility: the memory of the undecidability must keep a living trace that forever marks a decision as such), the decision has again followed a rule, a given, invented or reinvented, and reaffirmed rule: it is no longer *presently* just, *fully* just. At no moment, it seems, can a decision be said to be presently and fully just: either it has not yet been made according to a rule, and nothing allows one to call it just, or it has already followed a rule—whether given, received, confirmed, preserved or reinvented—which, in its turn, nothing guarantees absolutely; and, moreover, if it were guaranteed, the decision would have turn back into calculation and one could not call it just. That is why the test and ordeal of the undecidable, of which I have just said it must be gone through by any decision worthy of this name, is never past or passed [*passée ou dépassée*], it is not a surmounted or sublated [*relevé*] (*aufgehoben*) moment in the decision. The undecidable remains caught, lodged, as a ghost at least, but an essential ghost, in every decision, in every event of decision. Its ghostliness [*sa fantomaticité*] deconstructs from within all assurance of presence, all certainty or all alleged criteriology assuring us of the justice of a decision, in truth of the very event of a decision. Who will ever be able to assure and ensure that a decision as such has taken place, that it has not, through such and such a detour, followed a cause, a calculation, a rule, without even that imperceptible suspense and suspension [*suspens*] that freely decides to apply—or not—a rule?

A subjectal axiomatic of responsibility, of conscience, of intentionality, of property and propriety, governs today's dominant juridical discourse; it also governs the category of decision right down to its appeals to medical expertise. Yet this axiomatic is fragile and theoretically crude, something I need not emphasize here. The effects of these limitations affect more than all decisionism (naive or sophisticated); they are concrete and massive enough to dispense here with examples. The obscure dogmatism that marks the discourses on the responsibility of an accused [*prévenu*], his mental state, the passionate character, premeditated or not, of a crime, the incredible depositions of witnesses and "experts" on this subject, would

suffice to testify, in truth to prove, that no critical or criteriological rigor, no knowledge, are accessible on this subject.

This second aporia—this second form of the same aporia—already confirms
this: if there is a deconstruction of all presumption to a determining certainty of a
present justice, it itself operates on the basis of an "idea of justice" that is infinite,
infinite because irreducible, irreducible because owed to the other—owed to the
other, before any contract, because it has *come*, it is a *coming* [*parce qu'elle est
venue*], the coming of the other as always other singularity. Invincible to all skepticism, as one can say by speaking in the manner of Pascal, this "idea of justice"
seems indestructible in its affirmative character, in its demand of gift without
exchange, without circulation, without recognition or gratitude, without economic
circularity, without calculation and without rules, without reason and without theoretical rationality, in the sense of regulating mastery. And so, one can recognize in
it, even accuse in it a madness, and perhaps another kind of mysticism [*une autre
sorte de mystique*]. And deconstruction is mad about and from such justice, mad
about and from this desire for justice. Such justice, which is not law, is the very
movement of deconstruction at work in law and in the history of law, in political
history and history itself, even before it presents itself as the discourse that the
academy or the culture of our time labels deconstructionism.

I would hesitate to assimilate too quickly this "idea of justice" to a regulative
idea in the Kantian sense, to whatever content of a messianic promise (I say *content*
and not form, for any messianic form, any messianicity, is never absent from a
promise, whatever promise it is) or to other horizons of the same *type*. And I am
only speaking of a *type*, of the type of horizon the kinds [*espèces*] of which would
be numerous and competing—that is to say similar enough in appearance and
always pretending to absolute privilege and to irreducible singularity. The singularity of the historical place—perhaps our own; in any case the one I am obscurely
referring to here—allows us a glimpse of the type itself, as the origin, condition,
possibility or promise of all its exemplifications (messianism or determinate messianic figures of the Jewish, Christian or Islamic type, idea in the Kantian sense,
eschato-teleology of the neo-Hegelian type, Marxist or post-Marxist, etc.). It also
allows us to perceive and conceive a law [*loi*] of irreducible competition [*concur-
rence*], but from an edge [*un bord*] where vertigo threatens to seize us the moment
we see nothing but examples and some of us no longer feel engaged in competition; this is another way of saying that from this point on we always run the risk
(speaking for myself, at least) of no longer being, as one says, "in the running [*dans
la course*]." But not to be "in the running" on the inside track does not mean that
one can stay at the starting line or simply be a spectator—far from it. It may be the

very thing that, as one also says, "keeps us moving [*fait courir*]" stronger and faster—for example, deconstruction.

3. Third Aporia: The Urgency That Obstructs the Horizon of Knowledge.

One of the reasons I am keeping such a distance from all these horizons—from the Kantian regulative idea or from the messianic advent, for example, at least in their conventional interpretation—is that they are, precisely, *horizons*. As its Greek name suggests, a horizon is both the opening and the limit that defines either an infinite progress or a waiting and awaiting.

Yet justice, however unpresentable it remains, does not wait. It is that which must not wait. To be direct, simple and brief, let us say this: a just decision is always required *immediately*, right away, as quickly as possible. It cannot provide itself with the infinite information and the unlimited knowledge of conditions, rules, or hypothetical imperatives that could justify it. And even if it did have all that at its disposal, even if it did give itself the time, all the time and all the necessary knowledge about the matter, well then, the moment of *decision as such*, what must be just, *must* [*il faut*] always remains a finite moment of urgency and precipitation; it must [*doit*] not be the consequence or the effect of this theoretical or historical knowledge, of this reflection or this deliberation, since the decision always marks the interruption of the juridico-, ethico-, or politico-cognitive deliberation that precedes it, that *must* [doit] precede it. The instant of decision is a madness, says Kierkegaard. This is particularly true of the instant of the *just* decision that must rend time and defy dialectics. It is a madness; a madness because such decision is both hyper-active and suffered [*sur-active et subie*], it preserves something passive, even unconscious, as if the deciding one was free only by letting himself be affected by his own decision and as if it came to him from the other. The consequences of such heteronomy seem redoubtable but it would be unjust to evade its necessity. Even if time and prudence, the patience of knowledge and the mastery of conditions were hypothetically unlimited, the decision would be structurally finite, however late it came—a decision of urgency and precipitation, acting in the night of nonknowledge and nonrule. Not of the absence of rules and knowledge but of a reinstitution of rules that by definition is not preceded by any knowledge or by any guarantee as such. If one were to trust in a massive and decisive distinction between performative and constative—a problem I cannot get involved in here—one would have to attribute this irreducibility of precipitate urgency, this inherent irreducibility of thoughtlessness and unconsciousness, however intelligent it may be, to the performative structure of "speech acts" and acts in general as acts of justice or of law, whether they be performatives that institute something or derived

performatives supposing anterior conventions. And it is true that any current performative supposes, in order to be effective, an anterior convention. A constative
can be *juste*, in the sense of *justesse*, never in the sense of justice. But as a performative cannot be just, in the sense of justice, except by grounding itself [*en se fondant*]
in on conventions and so on other performatives, buried or not, it always maintains within itself some irruptive violence. It no longer responds to the demands of
theoretical rationality. And it never did, it was never able to; of this one has an a
priori and structural certainty. Since every constative utterance itself relies, at least
implicitly, on a performative structure ("I tell you that I speak to you, I address
myself to you to tell you that this is true, that things are like this, I promise you or
renew my promise to you to make a sentence and to sign what I say when I say that
I tell you, or try to tell you, the truth," and so forth), the dimension of *justesse* or
truth of theoretico-constative utterances (in all domains, particularly in the
domain of the theory of law) always thus presupposes the dimension of justice of
the performative utterances, that is to say their essential precipitation, which never
proceeds without a certain dissymmetry and some quality of violence. That is how
I would be tempted to understand the proposition of Levinas, who, in a whole
other language and following an entirely different discursive procedure, declares
that "*la vérité suppose la justice* [truth presupposes justice]."[23] Dangerously parody-
ing the French idiom, one could end up saying: "*La justice, il n'y a que ça de vrai.*"[24]
This is, no need to insist, not without consequence for the status, if one can still say
that, of truth, of the truth of which Saint Augustine says that it must be "made."

Paradoxically, it is because of this overflowing of the performative, because of
this always excessive advance of interpretation, because of this structural urgency
and precipitation of justice that the latter has no horizon of expectation (regulative
or messianic). But for this very reason, it has perhaps an *avenir*, precisely [*justement*], a "to-come" [*à-venir*] that one will have to [*qu'il faudra*] rigorously distinguish from the future. The future loses the openness, the coming of the other (who
comes), without which there is no justice; and the future can always reproduce the
present, announce itself or present itself as a future present in the modified form of
the present. Justice remains *to come*, it remains *by coming* [*la justice reste à venir*], it
has to come [*elle a à venir*] it *is* to-come, the to-come [*elle est à-venir*], it deploys
the very dimension of events irreducibly to come. It will always have it, this à-venir,
and will always have had it. *Perhaps* this is why justice, insofar as it is not only a

---

23. Levinas, *Totality and Infinity*, 90.
24. *Translator's note:* Approximating the literal, this expression could be translated as "justice alone is
true" or "the only truth is justice." More idiomatically, it would be rendered "justice—that's what it's all
about."

juridical or political concept, opens up to the *avenir* the transformation, the recasting or refounding [*la refondation*] of law and politics.

"Perhaps"—one must [*il faut*] always say *perhaps* for justice. There is an avenir for justice and there is no justice except to the degree that some event is possible which, as event, exceeds calculation, rules, programs, anticipations and so forth. Justice, as the experience of absolute alterity, is unpresentable, but it is the chance of the event and the condition of history. No doubt an unrecognizable history, of course, for those who believe they know what they are talking about when they use this word, whether its a matter of social, ideological, political, juridical or some other history.

This excess of justice over law and calculation, this overflowing of the unpresentable over the determinable, cannot and should not [*ne peut pas et ne doit pas*] serve as an alibi for staying out of juridico-political battles, within an institution or a state, between institutions or states. Abandoned to itself, the incalculable and giving [*donatrice*] idea of justice is always very close to the bad, even to the worst for it can always be reappropriated by the most perverse calculation. It is always possible, and this is part of the madness of which we were speaking. An absolute assurance against this risk can only saturate or suture the opening of the call to justice, a call that is always wounded. But incalculable justice *commands* calculation. And first of all, closest to what one associates with justice, namely, law, the juridical field that one cannot isolate within sure frontiers, but also in all the fields from which one cannot separate it, which intervene in it and are no longer simply fields: the ethical, the political, the economical, the psycho-sociological, the philosophical, the literary, etc. Not only *must* one [*il faut*] calculate, negotiate the relation between the calculable and the incalculable, and negotiate without a rule that would not have to be reinvented there where we are "thrown," there where we find ourselves; but one *must* [*il faut*] do so and take it as far as possible, beyond the place we find ourselves and beyond the already identifiable zones of morality, politics, or law, beyond the distinctions between national and international, public and private, and so on. The order of this *il faut* does not *properly* belong either to justice or to law. It only belongs to either realm by exceeding each one in the direction of the other—which means that, in their very heterogeneity, these two orders are undissociable: *de facto* and *de jure* [*en fait et en droit*]. Politicization, for example, is interminable even if it cannot and should not ever be total. To keep this from being a truism, or a triviality, one must recognize in it the following consequence: each advance in politicization obliges one to reconsider, and so to reinterpret the very foundations of law such as they had previously been calculated or delimited. This was true for example in the French Declaration of the Rights of Man, in the abolition of slavery, in all the emancipatory battles that remain and will have to remain in progress, everywhere in the world, for men and for women. Nothing seems to me less outdated than the classical emancipatory ideal. One cannot attempt to disqualify it today, whether crudely or with sophistication, without at least some thoughtlessness and without forming the worst complicities. It is true that it is also necessary to re-elaborate, without renouncing, the concept of emancipation, enfranchisement, or liberation while taking into account the strange structures we have been describing. But beyond these identified territories of juridico-politicization on the grand geo-political scale, beyond all self-serving misappropriations and hijackings, beyond all determined and particular reappropriations of international law, other areas must constantly open up that can at first resemble secondary or marginal areas. This marginality also signifies that a violence, even a terrorism and other forms of hostage taking are at work. The examples closest to us would be found in the area of laws [*lois*] on the teaching and practice of languages, the legitimization of canons, the military use of scientific research, abortion, euthanasia, problems of organ transplant, extra-uterine conception, bio-engineering, medical experimentation, the "social treatment" of AIDS, the macro- or micro-politics of drugs, homelessness, and so on, without forgetting, of course, the treatment of what one calls animal life, the immense question of so-called animality. On this last problem, the Benjamin text that I am coming to now shows that its author was not deaf or insensitive to it, even if his propositions on this subject remain quite obscure or traditional.

II: FIRST NAME OF BENJAMIN [*PRÉNOM DE BENJAMIN*]

[Prolegomena.[25] *Rightly or wrongly, I thought that it would perhaps not be entirely inappropriate to interrogate a text by Walter Benjamin, singularly an essay written in 1921 and entitled* Zur Kritik der Gewalt [Critique of Violence] *at the opening of such a meeting on "Nazism and the Final Solution. Probing the Limits of Representation." I have therefore chosen to propose a somewhat risky reading of this text by Benjamin, this for several reasons that seem to converge here.*

1. I believe this uneasy, enigmatic, terribly equivocal text is haunted in advance (but can one say "in advance" here?) by the theme of radical destruction, extermination, total annihilation, and first of all the annihilation of the law, if not of justice; and among those rights, human rights, at least such as these can be interpreted within a

---

25. These prolegomena were intended to introduce a second part of the text, the part that was read on April 26, 1990, at the opening of the colloquium held at the University of California-Los Angeles, "Nazism and the 'Final Solution,' Probing the Limits of Representation."

tradition of natural law of the Greek type or the "Aufklärung" type. I purposely say that this text is haunted by the themes of exterminating violence because first of all, as I will try to show, it is haunted by haunting itself, by a quasi-logic of the ghost which, because it is the more forceful one, should be substituted for an ontological logic of presence, absence or representation. Yet I ask myself whether a community that assembles or gathers itself together in order to think what there is to be thought and gathered of this nameless thing that has been named the "final solution" does not first of all have to show itself hospitable to the law of the ghost [la loi du fantôme], *to the spectral experience and to the memory of the ghost, of that which is neither dead nor alive, more than dead and more than living, only surviving, hospitable to the law* [loi] *of the most imperious memory, even though it is the most effaced and the most effaceable memory, but for that very reason the most demanding.*

This text by Benjamin is not only signed by a thinker who is said and said himself to be, in a certain manner, Jewish (and it is about the enigma of this signature that I would like to talk above all); Zur Kritik der Gewalt *is also inscribed in a Judaic perspective that opposes just, divine (Jewish) violence, which would destroy the law, to mythical violence (of the Greek tradition), which would install and preserve the law.*

2. *The profound logic of this essay puts to work an interpretation of language—of the origin and the experience of language—according to which evil, that is to say lethal power, comes to language by way of, precisely,* representation *(theme of this colloquium), that is to say, by that dimension of language that is* re-presentative, mediating, thus technological, utilitarian, semiotic, informational—*all powers that uproot language and cause it to decline, to fall far from, or outside of, its originary destination. This destination was appellation, nomination, the gift or the call of presence in the name. We will ask ourselves how this thought of the name* [cette pensée du nom] *is articulated with haunting and the logic of the specter. This essay by Benjamin, treats, therefore, of evil—of that evil that is coming and that comes to language through representation. It is also an essay in which the concepts of responsibility and of culpability, of sacrifice, decision, solution, punishment or expiation play a discreet but certainly major role, one most often associated with the equivocal value of the undecidable, of what is demonic and "demonically ambiguous."*

3. Zur Kritik der Gewalt *is not only a critique of representation as perversion and fall of language, but of representation as a political system of formal and parliamentary democracy. From that point of view, this "revolutionary" essay (revolutionary in a style that is at once Marxist and messianic) belongs, in 1921, to the great antiparliamentary and anti-"Aufklärung" wave upon which Nazism will have, as it were, surfaced and even "surfed" in the 1920s and the beginning of the 1930s. Carl Schmitt, whom Benjamin admired and with whom he maintained a correspondence, congratulated him for this essay.*

   4. *This very polyhedric and polysemic question of representation is also posed from another point of view in this strange essay. Having begun by distinguishing between two sorts of violence, founding violence and preserving violence, Benjamin must concede at one moment that the one cannot be so radically heterogeneous to the other since the violence called founding violence is sometimes "represented," and necessarily repeated, in the strong sense of that word, by the preserving violence.*

   For all these reasons and according to all of these interlaced threads to which I am going to return, one can ask oneself a certain number of questions. They will be on the horizon of my reading even if I do not have the time or the means to make them explicit here. What would Benjamin have thought, or at least what thought of Benjamin is virtually formed or articulated in this essay (and can it be anticipated?) on the subject of the "final solution"? On its project, its setting to work, the experience of its victims, the judgments, trials, interpretations, the narrative, explicating, and literary representations which have attempted to measure up to it? How would Benjamin have spoken of it? How would he have wished one to speak, to represent, or to forbid oneself from representing the "final solution," to identify it, to assign places in it, origins to it, responsibilities for it (as a philosopher, judge or jurist, as moralist, man of faith, poet, filmmaker)? The so very singular multiplicity of the codes that converge in this text, and, to remain bound by this, the graft of the language of Marxist revolution on that of messianic revolution, both of them announcing not only a new historical epoch, but also the beginning of a true history void of myth—all this makes it difficult to propose any hypotheses about a Benjaminian discourse on the "final solution" and about a Benjaminian discourse on the possibility or impossibility of a discourse on the "final solution," of which it would be reckless to say, relying on the objective dates of the Wannsee Conference of 1942 and Benjamin's suicide on the Franco-Spanish border in 1940, Benjamin knew anything about. The chronology of such events cannot be taken for granted. And one will always find ways to support the hypothesis according to which Benjamin, already in 1921, was thinking about nothing other than the possibility of this final solution that all the better challenges the order of representation since it would perhaps have belonged in his eyes to radical evil, to the Fall as the fall of language in representation. There are many signs that indicate, were one to trust the constant logic of his discourse, that for Benjamin, after this unrepresentable thing that the "final solution" will have been, not only are discourse and literature and poetry not impossible but more originarily and more eschatologically than ever, they would see themselves open to the dictation of the return or the still promised advent of a language of names, a language or a poetics of appellation, in opposition to a language of signs, of informative or communicative representation.

   At the end, after the end of a reading during which the horizon of Nazism and of the final solution will only appear through signs and announcing flashes, and will only

be addressed in a virtual, oblique or elliptical fashion. I will propose a few hypoth[...]
on the way in which this text of 1921 can be read today, after the advent of Nazism and
the event of the "final solution."

Before proposing an interpretation of this singular text, and before articulating
some questions that concern it more strictly, I must also say a few words, in this already
too lengthy introduction, about the contexts in which I began to read the essay, prior
even to thinking about this colloquium.

That context was double and I will define it as schematically as possible, while limiting myself to the aspects that may interest us here this evening, because they will have
left some traces on my reading.

1. First of all, within a three-year seminar on "philosophical nationalities and
nationalisms," there was a year-long sequence subtitled Kant, the Jew, the German
during which, while studying the varied but insistent recurrence of the reference to
Kant, even to a certain Judaism in Kant, on the part of all those who, from Wagner and
Nietzsche to Adorno, sought to respond to the question "Was ist Deutsch?" I became
very interested in what I then called the Judeo-German "psyche," to wit, the logic of
certain phenomena of a troubling specularity ("psyche" also meaning a sort of mirror
in French), a specularity that was itself reflected in some of the great German Jewish
thinkers and writers of this century: Cohen, Buber, Rosenzweig, Scholem, Adorno,
Arendt—and, precisely, Benjamin. A serious reflection on Nazism, and on the "final
solution," cannot spare a courageous, interminable and polyhedral analysis of the
history and structure of this Judeo-German "psyche." Among other things that I
cannot speak of here, we studied certain analogies—sometimes of the most equivocal
and disquieting sort—between the discourses of some "great" German, non-Jewish
thinkers and some "great" German Jewish thinkers: a certain German patriotism,
often a German nationalism, and sometimes even a German militarism (during and
after the First World War) were not the only analogy, far from it, for example in Cohen
or Rosenzweig, and in the converted Jew, Husserl. It is in this context that certain
limited but determinate affinities between Benjamin's text and some texts by Carl
Schmitt, and even by Heidegger, seem to me to deserve a serious interrogation. Not
only because of the hostility to parliamentary democracy, even to democracy as
such, not only because of the hostility to the Aufklärung, because of a certain interpretation of the pólemos, of war, violence and language, but also because of a thematic
of "destruction" that was very widespread at the time. Although Heideggerian
Destruktion cannot be confused with the concept of "destruction" that was also at the
center of Benjaminian thought, one may well ask oneself what such an obsessive thematic might signify, what it prepares or anticipates between the two wars, all the more
so in that, in every case, this destruction also sought to be the condition of an authentic tradition and memory.

text: On the occasion of a recent colloquium held at the Cardozo Law
University in New York on "Deconstruction and the Possibility of
after a long consideration of the relations between deconstruction and
ne this text by Benjamin from another point of view. I followed there
cautiously as possible, a dismaying trajectory, one that is aporetic but
also p... of strange events in its very aporia, a kind of self-destruction, if not a
suicide of the text, that lets no other legacy appear than the violence of its signature—
as divine signature. The last words, the last sentence of this text devoted to the notion
of Gewalt, a notion that is so difficult to translate ("violence," but also "legitimate
force," authorized violence, legal power, as when one speaks of Staatsgewalt, state
power), resonate as the shofar on the evening or the eve of a prayer that is no longer or
not yet heard. Not only does it sign, this ultimate address, and so close to the first name
of Benjamin, Walter, but at the end of a text that strives to deconstruct and disqualify
all the oppositions it has put to work in a critical fashion (notably the opposition
between decidable and undecidable, between theoretical judgment and revolutionary
action, between founding violence and preserving violence within mythological law
which is itself opposed to the just, divine violence, etc.). At the end of a text of which
there remains no content (theoretical, philosophical, or semantic), perhaps even no
content that would be "translatable" outside of the singularity of its own event, outside
of its own ruin, one ultimate sentence, one eschatological sentence, names the signa-
ture and the seal, names the name, and what is called and calls itself "die waltende."
This "play" between walten *and* Walter *cannot provide any demonstration or any cer-*
tainty. Here is, besides, the paradox of its "demonstrative" force: this force has to do
with the dissociation between the cognitive and the performative. But this "play" is not
at all ludic. For we know, on the other hand, that Benjamin was very interested,
notably in his essay on "Goethe's Elective Affinities," *in the aleatory but significant*
coincidences of which proper names are properly the site.

But who signs violence [qui signe la violence]—*will one ever know it? Is it not*
God, the wholly other? As always, is it not the other who signs? Is it not "divine vio-
lence" that will always have come first but also given all the first names, by giving man
the sole power of naming? Here are the last words of this strange text: "Divine violence
(die göttliche Gewalt), which is the sign and seal (Insignium und Siegel), *but never*
the means of sacred execution, may be called sovereign (mag die waltende heissen)."

How to read this text according to a "deconstructive" gesture that would not be, no
more now than it has ever been, Heideggerian or Benjaminian—here is, in sum, the
difficult and obscure question that this reading would like to risk.]

If I have not exhausted your patience, let us now approach, in another style, another
rhythm, the promised reading of a brief and disconcerting Benjamin text. I am

speaking of "Zur Kritik der Gewalt" (1921), translated as "Critique of Violence."[26] One will not dare say that this text is *exemplary*. We are in a realm where, in the end, there are only singular examples. Nothing is absolutely exemplary. I will not attempt to justify absolutely the choice of this text. But it is not, for all that, the worst example of what could be exemplary in a relatively determined context such as ours.

Benjamin's analysis reflects the crisis in the European model of bourgeois, liberal, parliamentary democracy, and so the crisis in the concept of law that is inseparable from it. Germany in defeat is at this time a place in which this crisis is extremely sharp, a crisis whose originality also comes from certain modern features like the right to strike, the concept of the general strike (with or without reference to Sorel). It is also the aftermath of a war and a prewar era that saw the European development and failure of pacifist discourse, antimilitarism, the critique of violence, including juridico-police violence, which will soon be repeated in the years to follow. It is also the moment in which the questions of the death penalty and of the right to punish in general are painfully current. Change in the structures of public opinion, thanks to the appearance of new media powers such as radio, begins to put into question this liberal model of parliamentary discussion or deliberation in the production of laws [*lois*] and so forth. Such conditions motivated the thoughts of German jurists like Carl Schmitt, to mention only him—and because Benjamin had great respect for him, not hiding a debt toward him that Schmitt himself did not hesitate to recall on occasion. It is "Zur Kritik der Gewalt," moreover, that, upon its publication won Benjamin a letter of congratulations from the great conservative Catholic jurist, still a constitutionalist at the time (but one knows of his strange conversion to Hitlerism in 1933, and of his correspondence with Benjamin, with Leo Strauss and with Heidegger, among others). And so I was also interested by these few historical indices—this text, for example, at once "mystical" in the overdetermined sense that interests us here, and hypercritical, something which is far from being simply contradictory. In some of its features, it can be read as a grafting of neomessianical Jewish mysticism onto post-Sorelian neo-Marxism (or the reverse). As for analogies between "Zur Kritik der Gewalt" and certain turns of Heideggerian thought, they are impossible to miss, especially those surrounding the motifs of

26. First published in *Archiv für Sozialwissenschaft und Sozialpolitik*, 1921; reprinted in *Gesammelte Schriften* 2, no. 1, (Frankfurt a/Main: Suhrkamp, 1977), 179–203. French translation by Maurice de Gandillac, "Pour une critique de la violence," in Walter Benjamin, *Mythe et Violence* (Paris: Denoël, 1971); reprinted in *L'homme, le language et la culture* (Paris: Denoël Gonthier, Bibliothèque Médiations, 1974). We will refer to this last edition for the translation (at times with very slight modifications but only for reasons linked to our discussion). *Translator's note:* The English translation, "Critique of Violence," is by Edmund Jephcott in Walter Benjamin, *Reflections: Essays, Aphorisms, Autobiographical Writings*, ed. Peter Demetz (New York: Schocken, 1986). Page numbers for both will hereafter be cited parenthetically in the text, with *E* signifying the English translation.

Walten and *Gewalt.* "Zur Kritik der Gewalt" concludes with divine violence (*göttliche Gewalt*), and in the end Walter says of divine violence that it may be named *die waltende* ("*Die göttliche Gewalt . . . mag die waltende heissen* [Divine violence . . . may be called sovereign]"). These are the last words of the text—"*die waltende heissen*"—like the discreet seal and the first name of its signature.

It is this historical network of equivocal contracts that interests me in its necessity and in its very dangers. In the Western democracies of 1989, with work and a certain number of precautions, lessons can still be drawn from it.

Keeping in mind the thematic of our colloquium, this text seemed exemplary to me, up to a point, to the degree that it lends itself to an exercise in deconstructive reading, as I shall try to show.

This deconstruction does not *apply itself* to such a text, however. It never applies itself to anything from the outside. It is in some way the operation or rather the very experience that this text, it seems to me, first does itself, by itself, on itself.

What does this mean? Is it possible? What remains, then, of such an event? Of its auto-heterodeconstruction? Of its just and unjust incompletion? What is the ruin of such an event or the open wound of such a signature? That is one of my questions. It is a question about the possibility of deconstruction, on its impossible possibility.[27]

Benjamin's demonstration concerns the question of law (*Recht*). It even means to inaugurate, one shall be able to say it more rigorously in a moment, a "philosophy of law." And this philosophy seems to be organized around a series of distinctions that all seem interesting, provocative, necessary up to a certain point but, it seems to me, radically problematic:

1. There is, first, the distinction between two kinds of violence of law, in relation to law: the founding violence, the one that institutes and posits law (*die rechtsetzende Gewalt*)[28] and the violence that preserves, the one that maintains, confirms, insures the permanence and enforceability of law (*die rechtserhaltende Gewalt*).[29] For the sake of convenience, let us continue to translate *Gewalt* as "violence," but I have already mentioned the precautions this calls for. Gewalt

---

27. I schematize here a theme largely developed elsewhere. Cf. for example: "the most rigorous deconstruction has never claimed to be . . . possible. And I would say that deconstruction loses nothing from admitting that it is impossible. . . . For a deconstructive operation *possibility* would rather be the danger, the danger of becoming an available set of rule-governed procedures, methods, accessible approaches. The interest of deconstruction, of such force and desire as it may have, is a certain experience of the impossible: that is, . . . *of the other*—the experience of the other as the invention of the impossible, in other words, as the only possible invention." "Psyche: Invention of the Other," trans. Catherine Porter, in *Reading de Man Reading* (Minneapolis: University of Minnesota Press, 1989) 36.

28. *Translator's note:* Jephcott's translation refers here to "law-making" violence.

29. *Translator's note:* Jephcott: "law-preserving" violence.

can also mean the dominance or the sovereignty of legal power, the authorizing or authorized authority: the force of law [*loi*].

2. Next there is the distinction between the founding violence that makes law—it is named "mythic" (implicit meaning: Greek, it seems to me)—and the destructive violence that annihilates law (*Rechtsvernichtend*[30])—named "divine" (implicit meaning: Jewish, it seems to me).

3. Finally, there is the distinction between justice (*Gerechtigkeit*) as the principle of all divine positing of the end (*das Prinzip aller göttlicher Zwecksetzung*) and power (*Macht*) as principle of mythical positing of law (*aller mythischen Rechtsetzung*).[31]

In the title "Critique of Violence," *critique* does not simply mean negative evaluation, legitimate rejection or condemnation of violence, but judgment, evaluation, examination that provides itself with the means to judge violence. The concept of critique, insofar as it implies decision in the form of judgment and question with regard to the right to judge, thus has an essential relation, in itself, to the sphere of law. Fundamentally, this is something like the Kantian tradition of the concept of critique. The concept of violence (*Gewalt*) permits an evaluative critique only in the sphere of law and justice (*Recht, Gerechtigkeit*) or the sphere of moral relations (*sittliche Verhältnisse*).[32] There is no natural or physical violence. One can speak figuratively of violence with regard to an earthquake or even to a physical ailment. But one knows that these are not cases of a *Gewalt* able to give rise to a judgment, before some instrument of justice. The concept of violence belongs to the symbolic order of law, politics and morals—of all forms of *authority* and of *authorization*, of claim to authority, at least. And it is only to this extent that it can give rise to a critique. Up to this point this critique was always inscribed in the space of the distinction between means and end. But, objects Benjamin, to ask oneself if violence can be a means *with a view* toward ends (just or unjust) is to prohibit oneself from judging violence *itself*. The criteriology would then concern only the application of violence, not violence *itself*. One would not be able to tell if the latter, as means, is in *itself* just or not, moral or not. The critical question remains open—the question of an evaluation and a justification of violence in itself, whether it be a simple means and whatever its end may be. This critical dimension would have been foreclosed by the *jusnaturalist* tradition. For defenders of natural law, recourse to violence poses no problems, since natural ends are just. Recourse to violence is as justified, as normal as man's "right" to move his body to reach a given goal. Violence (*Gewalt*) is from

30. *Translator's note:* Jephcott: "law-destroying" violence.
31. *Translator's note:* Jephcott: "Justice is the principle of all divine end making, power the principle of all mythical lawmaking" (E295).
32. *Translator's note:* Jephcott: "moral issues" (E277).

this point of view a "natural product [*Naturprodukt*]" (180/E278). Benjamin gives several examples of this naturalization of violence by *jusnaturalism*:

1. The state founded on natural law, which Spinoza talks about in the *Theologico-Political Treatise* in which the citizen, before a contract is formed by reason, exercises *de jure* a violence he disposes of *de facto*.
2. The ideological foundation of the Terror under the French Revolution, and
3. The exploitations of a certain Darwinism, and so on.

Yet if, at the opposite end from jusnaturalism, the tradition of positive law is more attentive to the historical evolution of law, it also falls short of the critical questioning called for by Benjamin. Doubtless it can only consider all means to be good once they conform to a natural and ahistorical end. It prescribes that one judge means, that is to say judge their conformity to a law that is in the process of being instituted, to a new (consequently not natural) law that it evaluates in terms of means. It does not exclude, therefore, a critique of means. But the two traditions share the same dogmatic presupposition, namely, that just ends can be attained by just means: "Natural law attempts, by the justness of the ends (*durch die Gerechtigkeit der Zwecke*), to 'justify' ('*rechtfertigen*') the means, positive law to 'guarantee' ('*garantieren*') the justness of the ends through the justification (*Gerechtigkeit*) of the means" (180/E278). The two traditions would turn in the same circle of dogmatic presuppositions. And there is no solution for the antinomy when a contradiction emerges between just ends and justified means. Positive law would remain blind to the unconditionality of ends, natural law to the conditionality of means.

Nevertheless, although he seems to dismiss both cases symmetrically, from the tradition of positive law Benjamin retains the sense of the historicity of law. Inversely, it is true that what he says further on about divine justice is not always incompatible with the theological basis of all jusnaturalisms. In any case, the Benjaminian critique of violence claims to exceed the two traditions and no longer to arise simply from the sphere of law and the internal interpretation of the juridical institution. It belongs to what he calls in a rather singular sense a "philosophy of history" and is expressly limited, as it is by Schmitt always, to the given of European law.

At its most fundamental level, European law tends to prohibit individual violence and to condemn it not because it poses a threat to this or that law [*loi*] but because it threatens the juridical order itself (*die Rechtsordnung*).[33] Whence the law's interest, for it does have an interest in laying itself down and preserving itself, or in representing the interest that, *justement*, it represents. To speak of law's interest may seem "surprising" (Benjamin's word), but at the same time it is normal, it is in the nature of its own interest, to pretend to exclude any individual violence threatening

---

. *Translator's note:* Jephcott: "the legal system" (E280).

its order and thus to monopolize violence, in the sense of *Gew*
say authority. Law has an "interest in a monopoly of violence (*In*
der Monopolisierung der Gewalt)" (183/E281). This monopoly
protect any given just and legal ends (*Rechtszwecke*) but law itself.

This seems like a tautological triviality. Yet is not tautology t
structure of a certain violence of the law that lays itself down, by a
violent, this time in the sense of outlaw [*hors-la-loi*], anything that do　　 .recog-
nize it? Performative tautology or a priori synthesis, which structures any founding
[*fondation*] of the law [*loi*] upon which one performatively produces the conventions (or the "credit" of which we spoke earlier) that guarantee the validity of the
performative, thanks to which one gives oneself the means to decide between legal
and illegal violence. The expressions tautology, *a priori synthesis*, and especially the
word *performative* are not Benjaminian, but I dare believe that they do not betray
his purposes.

The admiring fascination exerted on the people by "the figure of the 'great'
criminal (*die Gestalt des 'grossen' Verbrechers*)" (183/E281), can be explained as follows: it is not someone who has committed this or that crime for which one feels a
secret admiration; it is someone who, in defying the law [*loi*], lays bare the violence
of the juridical order itself. One could explain in the same way the fascination
exerted in France by a lawyer like Jacques Vergès who defends the most unsustain-
able causes by practicing what he calls the "strategy of rupture"—that is, the radical contestation of the given order of the law [*loi*], of judicial authority and
ultimately of the legitimate authority of the state that summons his clients to
appear before the law [*loi*]. Judicial authority before which, in short, the accused
appears without appearing [*comparaît alors sans comparaître*], appears only to testify (without testifying) of his opposition to the law [*loi*] that summons him to
appear. By the voice of his lawyer, the accused claims the right to contest the order
of law—sometimes the identification of the victims. But what order of law? The
order of law in general, or this order of law instituted and set to work ("enforced")
by the power of this state? Or order as inextricably mixed with the state in general?

The discriminating example here would be that of the right to strike. In class
struggle, notes Benjamin, the right to strike is guaranteed to workers who are therefore, besides the state, the only legal subject (*Rechtssubjekt*) to find itself guaranteed
a right to violence (*Recht auf Gewalt*) and so to *share* the monopoly of the state in
this respect. Some could have thought that since the practice of the strike, this
cessation of activity, this "nonaction" (*Nicht-Handeln*), is not an action (184/E281).
That is how the concession of this right by the power of the state (*Staatsgewalt*) is
justified when that power cannot do otherwise. Violence would come from the
employer and the strike would consist only in an abstention, a nonviolent withdrawal by which the worker, suspending his relations with the management and

.cnines, would simply become alien to them. The man who will become ..echt's friend defines this withdrawal (*Abkehr*) as an "*Entfremdung* [estrangement]." He puts the word in quotation marks (184/E281).

Yet Benjamin clearly does not believe this argument on the nonviolence of the strike. The striking workers set the conditions for the resumption of work; they will not end their strike unless a list, an order of things, has changed. And so there is violence against violence. In carrying the right to strike to its limit, the concept or watchword of *general* strike thus manifests its essence. The state can hardly stand this passage to the limit. It judges it abusive and claims that there was a misunderstanding of the original intention, and that the right to strike was not "so" intended (*das Streitrecht 'so' nicht gemeint gewesen sei*) (184/E282). It can then condemn the general strike as illegal and, if the strike persists, we have a revolutionary situation. Such a situation is in fact *the only one* that allows us to conceive the homogeneity of law and violence, violence as the exercise of law and law as the exercise of violence. Violence is not exterior to the order of law. It threatens law from within law. Violence does not consist essentially in exerting its power or a brutal force to obtain this or that result but in threatening or destroying an order of given law and precisely, in this case, the order of state law that was to accord this right to violence, for example the right to strike.

How to interpret this contradiction? Is it only *de facto* and exterior to law? Or is it rather immanent in the law of law, in the right to law [*au droit du droit*]?

What the state fears, the state being law in its greatest force, is not so much crime or robbery, even on the grand scale of the Mafia or heavy drug traffic, as long as they transgress the law [*loi*] with an eye toward particular benefits, however important they may be. (It is true that today these state-like and international institutions have a more radical status than that of crime and represent a threat with which so many states negotiate by allying themselves to it—and by submitting to it, for example, by making their own profit in money-laundering—while dissembling as fighting it by any means.) The state is afraid of *founding* violence—that is, violence able to justify, to legitimate (*begründen*), or transform the relations of law (*Rechtsverhältnisse*),[34] and so to present itself as having a right to right and to law [*comme ayant un droit au droit*]. This violence thus belongs in advance to the order of a law that remains to be transformed or founded, even if it may wound our sense of justice (*Gerechtigkeitsgefühl*) (185/E283). Only this violence calls for and makes possible a "critique of violence" that determines it to be something other than the natural exercise of force. For a critique of violence—that is to say, an interpretive and meaningful evaluation of it—to be possible, one must first recognize meaning

---

34. *Translator's note:* Jephcott: "legal conditions" (E283).

in a violence that is not an accident arriving from outside the law. That which threatens law already belongs to it, to the right to law [*au droit au droit*], to the origin of law. The general strike thus provides a valuable guiding thread, since it exercises the conceded right to contest the order of existing law and to create a revolutionary situation in which the task will be to found a new law, if not always, as we shall see in a moment, a new state. All revolutionary situations, all revolutionary discourses, on the left or on the right (and from 1921, in Germany, there were many of these that resembled each other in a troubling way, Benjamin often finding himself between the two) justify the recourse to violence by alleging the founding, in progress or to come, of a new law, of a new state.[35] As this law to come will in return legitimate, retrospectively, the violence that may offend the sense of justice, its future anterior already justifies it. The foundation of all states occurs in a situation that one can thus call revolutionary. It inaugurates a new law; it always does so in violence. *Always*, which is to say even when there have not been those spectacular genocides, expulsions or deportations that so often accompany the foundation of states, great or small, old or new, right nearby or very far away.

In these situations said to found law or state, the grammatical category of the future anterior all too well resembles a modification of the present to describe the violence in progress. It consists, precisely, in, feigning the presence or simple modalization of presence. Those who say "our time," while thinking "our present" in light of a future anterior present do not know very well, by definition, what they are saying. It is precisely in this nonknowledge that the eventness of the event consists, what one naively calls its presence.[36]

These moments, supposing we can isolate them, are terrifying moments because of the sufferings, the crimes, the tortures that rarely fail to accompany them, no doubt, but just as much because they are in themselves, and in their very violence, uninterpretable or undecipherable. This is what I am calling the "mystical." As Benjamin presents it, this violence is certainly legible, even intelligible since it is not alien to law, no more than *pólemos* or *éris* are alien to all the forms and signification of *dikē*. But it is, in law, what suspends law. It interrupts the established law to found another. This moment of suspense, this *epokhē*, this founding or revolutionary moment of law is, in law, an instance of nonlaw [*dans le droit une instance de non-droit*]. But it is also the whole history of law. *This moment always takes place and*

---

35. One finds the principle of an analogous argument in Carl Schmitt. Cf. *Politics of Friendship*, trans. George Collins (London: Verso, 1997), 119ff.

36. On this logic and "chrono-logic," I allow myself to refer to "Declarations of Independence," trans. Tom Keenan and Tom Pepper, in *New Political Science*, 15 (summer 1986): 7–15. Heidegger often recalls that "our own historical time" determines itself only from a future anterior. We never know at the moment, presently, what is our own historical time.

never takes place in a presence. It is the moment in which the foundation of law remains suspended in the void or over the abyss, suspended by a pure performative act that would not have to answer to or before anyone. The supposed subject of this pure performative would no longer be before the law [*devant la loi*], or rather he would be before a law [*loi*] still undetermined, before the law as before a law still nonexisting, a law still ahead, still having to and yet to come [*une loi encore devant et devant venir*]. And the being "before the law" that Kafka talks about resembles this situation,[37] both ordinary and terrible, of the man who cannot manage to see or above all to touch, to catch up with the law [*loi*]: it is transcendent in the very measure that it is he who must found it, as yet-to-come [*comme à venir*], in violence. One "touches" here without touching on this extraordinary paradox: the inaccessible transcendence of the law [*loi*], before which and prior to which "man" stands fast, only appears infinitely transcendent and thus theological to the extent that, nearest to him, it depends only on him, on the performative act by which he institutes it: the law [*loi*] is transcendent, violent and nonviolent, because it depends only on who is before it (and so prior to it), on who produces it, founds it, authorizes it in an absolute performative whose presence always escapes him. The law [*loi*] is transcendent and theological, and so always to come, always promised, because it is immanent, finite, and thus already past. Every "subject" is caught up in this aporetic structure in advance.

Only the "to-come" [*avenir*] will produce the intelligibility or the interpretability of this law [*loi*]. Beyond the letter of Benjamin's text, which I stopped following in the style of commentary a moment ago but which I am interpreting from the point of its avenir, one will say that the order of intelligibility depends in its turn on the established order which it serves to interpret. This readability will then be as little neutral as it is nonviolent. A "successful" revolution, the "successful" foundation of a state (in somewhat the same sense that one speaks of a "felicitous performative speech act") will produce after the fact [*après coup*] what it was destined *in advance* to produce, namely, proper interpretative models to read in return, to give sense, necessity and above all legitimacy to the violence that has produced, among others, the interpretative model in question, that is, the discourse of its self-legitimation. Examples of this circle, this other hermeneutic circle, are not lacking, near us or far from us, right here or elsewhere, whether it is a question of what happens from one neighborhood to another, one street to another in a great metropolis, or from one country or one camp to another in a world war (in the course of which states and nations are founded, destroyed, or redesigned). This must be taken into account in order to delimit an international law constructed on the Western concept of state

---

37. Cf. "Before the Law," trans. Avital Ronell, in *Acts of Literature*, ed. Derek Attridge (New York; Routledge, 1992).

sovereignty and nonintervention, but also in order to think its infinite perfectibility. There are cases in which it is not known for generations if the performative of the violent founding of a state is successful ("felicitous") or not. Here we could cite more than one example. This unreadability of violence has to do with the very readability of a violence that belongs to what others would call the symbolic order of law, and not to pure physics. We might be tempted to turn around like a glove this "logic" ("logic" in quotation marks, for this "unreadable" is also very much "illogical" in the order of *logos*, and this is also why I hesitate to call it "symbolic" and precipitately send it into the order of Lacanian discourse), the "logic" of this readable unreadability. In sum, it signifies, a juridicosymbolic violence, a performative violence at the very heart of interpretative reading. And the example or index could be carried by metonymy back toward the conceptual generality of the essence.

One would then say that there is a possibility of "general strike," a right analogous to that of general strike in any interpretative reading, the right to contest established law [*le droit de contester le droit établi*] in its strongest authority, that of the state. One has the right to suspend the legitimating authority and all its norms of reading, and to do this in the most incisive [*les plus lisantes*], most effective, most pertinent readings, which of course will sometimes argue [*s'expliquent*] with the unreadable in order to found another order of reading, another state, sometimes without doing it or in order not to do it. For we shall see that Benjamin distinguishes between two sorts of general strikes, some destined to replace the order of one state with another (general *political* strike), the other to abolish the state (general *proletarian* strike).

In sum, the two temptations of deconstruction.

There is something of the general strike, and thus of the revolutionary situation, in every reading that founds something new and that remains unreadable in regard to established canons and norms of reading—that is to say the present state of reading or of what figures the State (with a capital *S*), in the state of possible reading. Faced with such a general strike, and depending on the case, one can speak of anarchism, skepticism, nihilism, depoliticization, or, on the contrary, of subversive overpoliticization. Today, the general strike does not need to demobilize or mobilize a spectacular number of people. It is enough to cut the electricity to a few privileged places, such as the postal service, radio and television, and other networks of centralized information; to introduce a few efficient viruses into a well-chosen computer network; or, by analogy, to introduce the equivalent of AIDS into the organs of transmission, into the hermeneutic *Gespräch*.[38]

Can what we are doing here resemble a general strike or a revolution, with regard to models and structures, but also modes of readability of political action? Is

---

38. Cf. my "The Rhetoric of Drugs" in *Points*.

that what deconstruction is? Is it a general strike, or a strategy of rupture? Yes and no. Yes, to the extent that it assumes the right to contest, and not only theoretically, constitutional protocols, the very charter that governs reading in our culture and especially in the academy. No, at least to the extent that it is in the academy that it has been developed (and let us not forget, if we do not wish to sink into ridicule or indecency, that we are comfortably installed here on Fifth Avenue—only a few blocks away from the inferno of injustice). And besides, just as a strategy of rupture is never pure, since the lawyer or the accused have to "negotiate" it in some way before a tribunal or in the course of a hunger strike in the prison, so too there is never a pure opposition between the general *political* strike looking to refound another state and the general *proletarian* strike looking to destroy the state.

And so these Benjaminian oppositions appear more than ever to have to be deconstructed [*paraissent donc plus que jamais à déconstruire*]; they deconstruct themselves, even as paradigms for deconstruction. What I am saying here is anything but conservative and antirevolutionary. For beyond Benjamin's explicit purpose, I shall propose the interpretation according to which the very violence of the foundation or *positing of law* (*Rechtsetzende Gewalt*) must envelop the violence of the *preservation of law* (*Rechtserhaltende Gewalt*) and cannot break with it. It belongs to the structure of fundamental violence in that it calls for the repetition of itself and founds what ought to be preserved, preservable, promised to heritage and to tradition, to partaking [*partage*]. A foundation is a promise. Every positing (*Setzung*) permits and promises, posits ahead [*permet et pro-met*]; it posits by setting and by promising [*en mettant et en promettant*]. And even if a promise is not kept in fact, iterability inscribes the promise as guard in the most irruptive instant of foundation. Thus it inscribes the possibility of repetition at the heart of the originary. Better, or worse, it is inscribed in this law [*loi*] of iterability; it stands under its law or before its law [*sous sa loi ou devant sa loi*]. Consequently [*du coup*], there is no more pure foundation or pure position of law, and so a pure founding violence, than there is a purely preserving violence. Positing is already iterability, a call for self-preserving repetition. Preservation in its turn refounds, so that it can preserve what it claims to found. Thus there can be no rigorous opposition between positing and preserving, only what I will call (and Benjamin does not name it) a *differential contamination* between the two, with all the paradoxes that this may lead to. No rigorous distinction between a general strike and a partial strike (again, in an industrial society, we would also lack the technical criteria for such a distinction), nor, in Georges Sorel's sense, between a general *political* strike and a general *proletarian* strike. Deconstruction is also the thought *of* this differential contamination—and the thought *taken by* the necessity of this contamination.

It is in thinking about this differential contamination, as the contamination at the very heart of law that I single out this sentence of Benjamin's, to which I hope to come back later: there is, he says "something rotten in law (*etwas Morsches im Recht*)" (188/E286). There is something decayed or rotten in law, which condemns it or ruins it in advance. Law is condemned, ruined, in ruins, ruinous, if one can risk a sentence of death on the subject of law, especially when it is a question of the death penalty. And it is in a passage on the death penalty that Benjamin speaks of what is "rotten" in law.

If there is something of strike and the right to strike in every interpretation, there is also war and *pólemos*. War is another example of this contradiction internal to law. There is a law of war, a right to war [*droit de la guerre*].[39] (Schmitt will complain that it is no longer recognized as the very possibility of politics.) This law involves the same contradictions as the right to strike. Apparently subjects of law declare war in order to sanction violence, the ends of which appear natural (the other wants to lay hold of territory, goods, women; he wants my death, I kill him). But this warlike violence that resembles "predatory violence (*raubende Gewalt*)" outside the law [*loi*] is always deployed *within* the sphere of law (185/E282). It is an anomaly *within* the legal system with which it seems to break. Here the rupture of the relation is the relation. The transgression is before the law [*loi*]. In so-called primitive societies, where these meanings would be more clearly brought out, according to Benjamin, the peace settlement shows very well that war was not a natural phenomenon. No peace is settled without the symbolic phenomenon of a ceremonial, which recalls the fact that there was already ceremony in war. War, then, did not simply amount to the clash of two interests or of two purely physical forces. Here an important parenthesis emphasizes that, to be sure, in the pair *war/peace*, the peace ceremonial recalls the fact that the war was also an unnatural phenomenon; but Benjamin apparently wants to withdraw a certain meaning of the word *peace* from this correlation, in particular in the Kantian concept of "perpetual peace." Here it is a matter of a whole other "unmetaphorical and political (*unmetaphorische und politische*)" signification (185/E283), the importance of which we may weigh in a moment. At stake is international law, where the risks of diversion or perversion for the benefit of individual interests, whether those of a state or not, require an infinite vigilance, all the more so as these risks are inscribed in its very constitution.

After the ceremony of war, the ceremony of peace signifies that the victory establishes a new law. And war, which passes for originary and archetypal (*ursprüngliche*

---

39. *Translator's note:* Jephcott: "military law" (E283).

und urbildliche) violence in pursuit of natural ends,[40] is in fact a violence that serves to found law (*rechtsetzende*). From the moment that this positive, positing (*setzende*) and founding character of another law is recognized, modern law refuses the individual subject all right to violence [*tout droit à la violence*]. The people's shudder of admiration before the "great criminal" is addressed to the individual who takes upon himself, as in primitive times, the stigma of the lawmaker or the prophet.

Yet the distinction between the two types of violence (founding and preserving) will be very difficult to trace, to found or to preserve. We are going to witness an ambiguous and laborious movement on Benjamin's part to save at any cost a distinction or a correlation without which his whole project could collapse. For if violence is at the origin of law, understanding demands that the critique of this double violence be brought to its logical conclusion. To discuss the law-preserving violence, Benjamin sticks to relatively modern problems, as modern as the problem of the general strike was a moment ago. Now it is a matter of compulsory military service, the modern police or the abolition of the death penalty. If, during and after World War I, an impassioned critique of violence was developed, it took aim this time at the law-preserving form of violence. Militarism, a modern concept that supposes the exploitation of compulsory military service, is the forced use of force, the "compulsory" use (*Zwang*) of force or violence (*Gewalt*) in the service of the state and its legal ends. Here military violence is legal and preserves the law. It is therefore more difficult to criticize than the pacifists and activists believe in their "declamations," for which Benjamin does not hide his low esteem. The ineffectiveness and inconsistency of antimilitary pacifists has to do with their failure to recognize the legal and unassailable character of this law-preserving violence.

Here we are dealing with a *double bind* or a contradiction that can be schematized as follows: On the one hand, it appears *easier* to criticize the violence that founds since it cannot be justified by any preexisting legality and so appears savage. But on the other hand, and this reversal makes the whole worth of this reflection, it is *more difficult*, more illegitimate to criticize this same founding violence since one cannot summon it to appear before the institution of any preexisting law: it does not recognize existing law in the moment that it founds another. Between the two limits of this contradiction, there is the question of this ungraspable *revolutionary instant*, of this *exceptional decision* which belongs to no historical, temporal continuum but in which the foundation of a new law nevertheless *plays* [*joue*], if one can say so, on something from an anterior law that it extends, radicalizes, deforms, metaphorizes or metonymizes—this figure here taking the names of war or general strike. But this figure is also a contamination. It effaces or blurs the distinction,

---

40. *Translator's note:* Jephcott: "primordial and paradigmatic" (186/E283).

pure and simple, between foundation and preservation. It inscribes iterability in originarity, and this is what I would call deconstruction at work, in full negotiation: in the "things" themselves and in Benjamin's text.

As long as they do not give themselves the theoretical or philosophical means to conceive this coimplication of violence and law, the usual critiques remain naive and ineffectual. Benjamin does not hide his disdain for the declamations of pacifist activism and for the proclamations of "quite childish anarchism" that would like to exempt the individual from all constraints. The reference to the categorical imperative ("Act in such a way that at all times you use humanity both in your person and in the person of all others as an end, and never merely as a means," 187/E285), however uncontestable it may be, allows for no critique of violence. Law in its very violence claims to recognize and defend said humanity as end, in the person of each individual. And so a purely moral critique of violence would be as unjustified as impotent. For the same reason, one cannot provide a critique of violence in the name of liberty, of what Benjamin here calls "formless 'freedom'" (gestaltlose 'Freiheit') that is, in sum, a purely formal freedom, an empty form, following a Marxist-Hegelian vein that is far from absent throughout this meditation (187/ E285). These attacks against violence lack pertinence and effectiveness because they remain alien to the juridical essence of violence, to the "order of law." An effective critique must take issue with the body of law itself, in its head and in its members, with the laws [lois] and the particular usages that law adopts under the protection of its power (Macht). This order is such that there exists only one fate, a unique fate or history (nur ein einziges Schicksal, 187/E285). This is one of the major concepts of the text, but also one of the most obscure, whether it is a question of fate itself or of its absolute uniqueness. That which exists, which has consistency (das Bestehende) and that which at the same time threatens what exists (das Drohende) belong inviolably (unverbrüchlich) to the same order, and this order is inviolable because it is unique. It can only be violated within itself. The notion of threat appears here indispensable. But it also remains difficult to delimit for the threat does not come from outside. The law [le droit] is both threatening and threatened by itself. This threat is neither intimidation nor dissuasion, as pacifist, anarchists or activists believe. The law shows itself to be threatening in the way fate is threatening. To reach the "deepest meaning" of the indeterminacy (Unbestimmtheit) of the legal threat (der Rechtsdrohung),[41] it will later be necessary to meditate upon the essence of fate that is at the origin of this threat.

In the course of a meditation on fate, which includes along the way an analysis of the police, the death penalty, and the parliamentary institution, Benjamin will

---

41. *Translator's note:* Jephcott: "the uncertainty of the legal threat" (E285).

thus come to distinguish between divine justice and human justice, between the divine justice that destroys law and the mythic violence that founds it.

Law-preserving violence, this threat that is not intimidation, is a threat *of law*. Double genitive: it both comes from law and threatens law. A valuable index arises here from the domain of penalty law, the right to punish [*le droit de punir*] and the death penalty. Benjamin seems to think that the arguments against penalty law, and notably against the death penalty, are superficial, and not so by accident. For they do not admit an axiom essential to the definition of law. Which? Well, when one tackles the death penalty, one does not dispute one penalty among others but law itself in its origin, in its very order. If the origin of law is a violent positing, it manifests itself in the purest fashion when violence is absolute, that is to say when it touches on the right to life and to death. Here Benjamin does not need to invoke the great philosophical arguments that before him have justified, in the same way, the death penalty (Kant and Hegel, for example, versus the first abolitionists like Cesare Beccaria).

The legal system [*l'ordre du droit*] fully manifests itself in the possibility of the death penalty. By abolishing it, one would not be touching upon one *dispositif* among others. Rather, one would be disavowing the very principle of law. Thus is confirmed that something is "rotten" at the heart of law. The death penalty must [*doit*] testify that law is a violence contrary to nature. But what today testifies to this in a manner that is even more "spectral" (*gespenstische*) (189/E286) by mixing the two forms of violence (preserving and founding) is the modern institution of the police. This is a mixture of two heterogeneous violences, "in a kind of spectral mixture (*in einer gleichsam gespenstischen Vermischung*)," as if one violence haunted the other (though Benjamin does not put it this way in commenting on the double meaning of the word *gespenstich*). Spectrality has to do with the fact that a body is never present for itself, for what it is. It appears by disappearing or by making disappear what it represents: one for the other. One never knows who one is dealing with, and that is the definition of the police, singularly of state police the limits of which are, at bottom, unlocatable [*inassignables*]. This absence of a border between the two types of violence, this contamination between foundation and preservation is ignoble; it is, he says, the ignominy (*das Schmachvolle*) of the police. Prior to being ignoble in its procedures, in the unnameable inquisition that police violence allows itself without respect for anything, the modern police force is structurally repugnant, filthy [*immonde*] in essence because of its constitutive hypocrisy. Its lack of limit does not only come from surveillance and repression technology— such as was already being developed in 1921, in a troubling manner, to the point of doubling and haunting all public and private life (what we could say today about the development of this technology!). It comes from the fact that the police are the state, that they are the specter of the state and that, in all rigor, one cannot take issue with the police without taking issue with the order of the *res publica*. For today the police are no longer content to enforce the law and thus to preserve it; the police invent the law, publish ordinances, and intervene whenever the legal situation is unclear to guarantee security—which is to say, these days, nearly all the time. The police are the force of law [*loi*], they have force of law, the power of the law. The police are ignoble because in their authority, "the separation of law-founding violence and law-preserving violence is suspended [*in ihr die Trennung von rechtsetzender und rechtserhaltender Gewalt aufgehoben ist*]" 189/E286). In the *Aufhebung* that the police signifies in itself, the police invent law; they make themselves "rechtsetzend," legislative. The police arrogate the right, arrogate the law [*elle s'arroge le droit*], each time the law is indeterminate enough to open a possibility for them. Even if they do not make the law [*loi*], the police behave like a lawmaker in modern times, if not the lawmaker of modern times. Where there are police, which is to say everywhere and even here, one can no longer discern between two types of violence—preserving and founding—and that is the ignoble, ignominious, revolting ambiguity. The possibility, which is also to say the ineluctable necessity of the modern police force, ruins, in sum—one could say deconstructs—the distinction between these two kinds of violence that nevertheless structures the discourse that Benjamin calls a new critique of violence.

Such discourse Benjamin would like either to found or to preserve, but in all purity he can do neither. At most, he can sign it as a spectral event. Text and signature are specters, and Benjamin knows it, so well that the event of the text "Zur Kritik der Gewalt" consists of this strange *ex-position*: before your eyes a demonstration ruins the distinctions it proposes. It exhibits and archives the very movement of its implosion, leaving in place what one calls a text, the ghost of a text that, itself in ruins, at once foundation and preservation, accomplishes neither, occurs to and reaches neither one nor the other [*n'arrive ni à l'une ni à l'autre*] and remains there, up to a certain point, for a certain amount of time, readable and unreadable, like the exemplary ruin that singularly warns us of the fate of all texts and all signatures in their relation to law—that is, necessarily (alas), in their relation to a certain police force. Such would be, let it be said in passing, the status without statute, the statute without status of a text said of deconstruction and of what remains of it. The text does not escape the law [*loi*] that it enunciates. It ruins itself and contaminates itself; it becomes the specter of itself. But of this ruin of signature, there will be more to say.

What threatens the rigor of the distinction between the two types of violence— and which Benjamin does not say, excluding it or misrecognizing it—is, at bottom, the paradox of iterability. Iterability makes it so that the origin must [*doit*] repeat itself originarily, must alter itself to count *as origin*, that is to say, to preserve itself. Right away there is the police and the police legislates, not content to enforce a law [*loi*] that would have had no force before the police. This iterability inscribes preservation in the essential structure of foundation. This law [*loi*] or this general necessity is certainly not reducible to a modern phenomenon; it has an a priori worth, even if one understands that Benjamin gives examples that are irreducibly modern in their specificity, and explicitly targets the police of the "modern state." Rigorously speaking, iterability precludes the possibility of pure and great founders, initiators, lawmakers ("great" poets, thinkers or men of state, in the sense Heidegger will mean in 1935, following an analogous schema concerning the fatal sacrifice of these founders).

Ruin is not a negative thing. First, it is obviously not a thing. One could write, maybe with or following Benjamin, maybe against Benjamin, a short treatise on the love of ruins. What else is there to love, anyway? One cannot love a monument, a work of architecture, an institution as such except in an experience itself precarious in its fragility: it has not always been there, it will not always be there, it is finite. And for this very reason one loves it as mortal, through its birth and its death, through one's own birth and death [*à travers sa naissance et sa mort*], through the ghost or the silhouette of its ruin, one's own ruin [*sa ruine*]—which it already is, therefore, or already prefigures. How can one love otherwise than in this finitude? Where else would the right to love, even the love of law, come from [*d'où viendrait autrement le droit d'aimer, voire l'amour du droit*]?

Let us return to the thing itself—that is to say, to the ghost; for this text tells a ghost story, a history of ghosts. We can no more avoid ghost and ruin than we can elude the question of the rhetorical status of this textual event. To what figures does it turn for its *exposition*, for its internal explosion or its implosion? All the exemplary figures of the violence of law are singular metonymies, namely, figures without limit, unfettered possibilities of transposition and figures without face or figure [*figures sans figure*]. Let us take the example of the police, this index of a ghostly violence because it mixes foundation with preservation and becomes all the more violent for this. Well, the police that thus capitalize on violence are not simply the police. They do not simply consist of policemen in uniform, occasionally helmeted, armed and organized in a civil structure on a military model to whom the right to strike is refused, and so forth. By definition, the police are present or represented everywhere there is force of law [*loi*]. They are present, sometimes invisible but always effective, wherever there is preservation of the social order. The police are not only the police (today more or less than ever), they are there [*elle est là*], the figure without face or figure of a *Dasein* coextensive with the *Dasein* of the *polis*.

Benjamin recognizes this in his way, but in a double gesture that I do not think is deliberate and in any case is not thematized. He never gives up trying to contain in a pair of concepts and to bring back down to distinctions the very thing that incessantly exceeds them and overflows them. In this way he admits that the ill or evil [*le mal*] with the police is that it is a figure without face or figure, a violence that is formless (*gestaltlos*). As such, the police is nowhere graspable (*nirgends fassbare*). In so-called civilized states the specter of its ghostly apparition is all pervasive (*allverbreitete gespenstische Erscheinung im Leben der zivilisierten Staaten* 189/E287). And still, as this formless ungraspable figure of the police, even as it metonymizes itself—*spectralizes itself*—as the police everywhere become, in society, the very element of haunting, the milieu of spectrality, Benjamin would still want for it to remain a determinable and proper figure to the civilized states. He claims to know what he is speaking of when he speaks of the police in the proper sense, and would want to determine the phenomenon. It is difficult to know whether he is speaking of the police of the modern state or of the state in general when he mentions the civilized state. I would be inclined toward the first hypothesis for two reasons:

1. Benjamin selects modern examples of violence: for example, that of the general strike or the "problem" of the death penalty. Earlier on, he speaks not only of civilized states, but of another "institution of the modern state," the police. It is the *modern* police force, in *modern* politico-technical situations, that has been led to make the law it is only supposed to enforce.

2. While recognizing that the ghostly body of the police, however invasive it may be, always remains equal to itself, Benjamin admits that its spirit (*Geist*), the spirit of the police, police spirit, does less damage in absolute monarchy than in modern democracies where its violence degenerates. Would this be only, as we may be tempted to think today, because modern technologies of communication, of surveillance and interception of communication, ensure the police absolute ubiquity, saturating public and private space, pushing to its limit the coextensivity of the political and the police domain [*la coextensivité du politique et du policier*]? Would it be because democracies cannot protect the citizen against police violence unless they enter this logic of *policio-political coextensivity* [*co-extensivité politico-policière*], that is to say by confirming the police essence [*l'essence policière*] of the public thing (police of police, institutions of the type "informatique et liberté," monopolization by the state of technologies of protection of private life secrecy, as the federal government and its police forces are currently suggesting to American citizens while also offering to

produce the necessary electronic chips; they would then decide the moment when the security of the state would require the interception of private exchanges, or authorize, for example, the installation of invisible microphones, the use of directional microphones, the intrusion into computerized networks or, more simply, the practice, so common in France, of good old phone taps)? Is this the contradiction of which Benjamin thought? The internal degeneration of the democratic principle inevitably corrupted by the principle of police power, intended, in principle, to protect the former but uncontrollable in its essence, in the process of its becoming technologically autonomous?

Let us stay with this point for a moment. I am not sure that Benjamin intended the *rapprochement* I am attempting here between the words *gespenstische*, spectral, and *Geist*, spirit, in the sense of the ghostly double. But this analogy hardly seems contestable even if Benjamin did not recognize it. The police become hallucinatory and spectral because they haunt everything; they are everywhere, even there where they are not, in their *Fort-Dasein*, upon which one can always call. Their presence is not present, any more than any presence is present, as Heidegger reminds us, and the presence of their ghostly double knows no boundaries. They conform to the logic of "Zur Kritik der Gewalt" to note that anything that touches on the violence of law—here the police force itself—is not natural but spiritual. There is a spirit, both in the sense of specter and in the sense of the life that rises, through death, precisely, through the possibility of the death penalty, above natural or "biological" life. The police testify to this. Here I shall invoke a "thesis" defended by the *Ursprung des deutschen Trauerspiel* regarding the manifestation of spirit that shows itself to the outside under the form of *power*. The faculty of this power (*Vermögen*) determines itself in actuality as the *faculty* to exercise *dictatorship. Spirit is dictatorship*. Reciprocally, dictatorship, which is the essence of power as violence (*Gewalt*), is of spiritual essence. The fundamental spiritualism of such an affirmation resonates with what grants the authority (legitimized or legitimizing) or the violence of power to an instituting decision that, by definition, does not have to justify its sovereignty before any preexisting law [*loi*] and only calls upon a "mysticism," only utters itself as a series of orders, edicts and prescriptive dictations or dictatory performatives. "Spirit (*Geist*)—such was the thesis of the age—shows itself in power (*weist sich aus in Macht*); spirit is the capacity to exercise dictatorship, (*Geist ist das Vermögen, Diktatur auszuüben*). This capacity requires both a strict inner discipline and the most unscrupulous external action (*skrupelloseste Aktion*)."[42]

---

42. Walter Benjamin, *Ursprung des deutschen Trauerspiels, GS* 1.1, 276; trans. by John Osborne as *The Origin of German Tragic Drama* (London: Verso, 1977), 98. I thank Tim Bahti for having directed me to

Instead of being itself and being contained within democracy, this spirit of the police, this police spirit, this police violence *as spirit*, degenerates there. It testifies in modern democracy to the greatest thinkable degeneration of violence (*die denkbar grösste Entartung der Gewalt bezeugt*, 190/E287). The degeneration of democratic *power* (and the word *power* would often be the most appropriate to translate *Gewalt*, the internal force or violence of its authority) would have no other name than the police. Why? In absolute monarchy, legislative and executive powers are united. In it violence is therefore normal, conforming to its essence, its idea, its spirit. In democracy, on the contrary, violence is no longer accorded nor granted to the spirit of the police. Because of the presumed separation of powers, it is exercised illegitimately, especially when instead of enforcing the law, it makes the law. Benjamin here indicates at least the principle of an analysis of police reality in industrial democracies and their military-industrial complexes with high computer technology. In absolute monarchy, police violence, terrible as it may be, shows itself as what it is and as what it ought to be in its spirit, whereas the police violence of democracies denies its own principle, making laws surreptitiously, clandestinely.

The consequences or implications are twofold:

1. Democracy would be a degeneration of law, of the violence, the authority and the power of law.
2. There is not yet any democracy worthy of this name. Democracy remains to come: to engender or to regenerate.

Benjamin's discourse, which then develops into a critique of the parliamentarism of liberal democracy, is therefore *revolutionary*, even tending toward Marxism [*marxisant*], but in the two senses of the word "revolutionary," which also includes the sense "reactionary"—that is, the sense of a return to the past of a purer origin. This equivocation is typical enough to have fed many revolutionary discourses on the right and the left, particularly between the two wars. A critique of "degeneration" (*Entartung*) as critique of a parliamentarism powerless to control the police violence that substitutes itself for it, is indeed a critique of violence on the basis of a "philosophy of history": a putting into archeo-teleological, indeed archeo-eschatological perspective that deciphers the history of law as a decline or decay (*Verfall*) since the origin. The analogy with Schmittian or Heideggerian schemas does not need to be emphasized. This triangle would have to be illustrated by a correspondence, I mean

this passage. The same chapter discusses earlier the apparition of specters [*Geisterscheinungen*] 273/ "ghost-scenes" E94). And further it is again a question of the evil genius (*böse Geist*) of despots, and of the becoming-ghost [*devenir-revenant*] of the dead.

the epistolary correspondence that linked these three thinkers (Schmitt/Benjamin, Heidegger/Schmitt). It is still a matter of spirit and of revolution.

The question, at bottom, would be, What about liberal and parliamentary democracy today? As means, all violence founds or preserves the law. Otherwise it would renounce all value. There is no problematic of law without this violence of means, without this principle of power. Consequence: every juridical or legal contract (*Rechtsvertrag*) (190/E288) is founded on violence. There is no contract that does not have violence as both an origin (*Ursprung*) and an outcome (*Ausgang*). Here a furtive and elliptical allusion by Benjamin is decisive, as is often the case. As founding or positing law, instituting violence (*rechtsetzende*) does not need to be immediately or directly present in the contract (*nicht unmittelbar in ihm gegenwärtig zu sein*) (190/E288). But without being immediately present, it is replaced (*vertreten*), represented by the supplement of a substitute. The forgetting of originary violence produces itself, lodges and extends itself in this *différance*, in the movement that replaces presence (the immediate presence of violence identifiable as such in its *traits* and its spirit), in this *differantial* representativity. The loss of conscience or of consciousness does not happen by accident, nor does the amnesia that follows. It is the very passage from presence to representation. Such a passage forms the trajectory of decline, of institutional degeneration, their *Verfall*. Benjamin had just spoken of a degeneration (*Entartung*) of originary violence, for example, that of police violence in absolute monarchy, which is corrupted in modern democracies. Here is Benjamin deploring the *Verfall* of revolution in parliamentary spectacle: "When the consciousness of the latent presence of violence in a legal institution disappears, the institution falls into decay (*schwindet das Bewusstsein von der latenten Anwesenheit der Gewalt in einem Rechtsinstitut, so verfällt es*)," (190/E288). The first example chosen is that of the parliaments of the time. If they offer a deplorable spectacle, it is because these representative institutions forget the revolutionary violence from which they are born. In Germany in particular, they have forgotten the aborted revolution of 1919. They now lack the sense of the founding violence of law that is represented in them (*Ihnen fehlt der Sinn für die rechtsetzende Gewalt, die in ihnen repräsentiert ist*). The parliaments live in forgetfulness of the violence from which they are born. This amnesiac denegation does not betray a psychological weakness; it is inscribed in their statute, and in their very structure. From then on, instead of reaching decisions commensurable or proportional to this violence and worthy of it, they practice the hypocritical politics of *compromise*. The concept of compromise, the *denegation* of open violence, the recourse to dissimulated violence belong to the spirit of violence, to the "mentality of violence (*Mentalität der Gewalt*)" that promotes acceptance of the adversary's coercion both in order to avoid the worst and while saying, with the sigh of the parliamentarian, that this is certainly not ideal, that, no doubt, things would have been better otherwise but that, precisely, one could not do otherwise.

Parliamentarism is therefore in the violence of authority and in the renunciation of the ideal. It fails to resolve political conflicts by nonviolent speech, discussion, and deliberation—in short, by setting liberal democracy to work. In the face of the "decay of parliaments (*der Verfall der Parlamente*)," Benjamin finds the critique of the Bolshevist and the trade unionist both pertinent (*treffende*) overall and radically destructive (*vernichtende*).

We now have to introduce a distinction that once again brings Benjamin to a certain Carl Schmitt and minimally gives a more precise sense of what the historical configuration could have been in which all these different modes of thinking were inscribed (the exorbitant price Germany had to pay for defeat, the Weimar Republic, the crisis and impotence of the new parliamentarism, the failure of pacifism, the aftermath of the October Revolution, competition between the media and parliamentarism, new particulars of international law, and so forth). Although the undeniable link to such conjuncture may be thin, the consequences of these discourses and of the symptoms they indicate (which they are as well) does not exhaust itself in them—far from it. Careful transpositions can make their reading ever more necessary and fruitful today. If the content of their privileged examples has somehow aged, their argumentative schemas seem today more than ever to deserve interest and discussion.

We just saw, in sum, that in its origin and its end, in its foundation and its preservation, law is inseparable from violence, immediate or mediate, present or represented. Does this exclude all non-violence in the elimination of conflicts, as one might easily be tempted to conclude? Not at all. But the thought of non-violence must exceed the order of public law. An agreement, a union without violence (*gewaltlose Einigung*) is possible everywhere the culture of the heart (*die Kultur des Herzens*) gives men pure means with accord (*Übereinkunft*) in view (191/E289). Does this mean that one must stop at this opposition between private and public to protect a domain of non-violence? Things are far from that simple. Other conceptual partitions will delimit, in the sphere of politics itself, the relation of violence to non-violence. This would be, for example, in the tradition of Sorel or Marx, the distinction between the general *political* strike—violent since it wants to replace the state with another state (for example the one that had just flashed forth in Germany)—and the general *proletarian* strike, the revolution that instead of strengthening the state aims at its suppression—as it aims at the elimination of "sociologists, says Sorel, elegant amateurs, of social reforms or intellectuals who have made it their profession to think for the proletariat" (194/E292).

Another distinction seems even more radical and closer to a critique of violence as means. It opposes the order of means, precisely, to the order of *manifestation*. Once again it is very much a matter of the violence of language, but also of the advent of non-violence through a certain language. Does the essence of language consist in signs, considered as *means* of communication as re-presentation, or in a manifestation that no longer (or not yet) has anything to do [*qui ne relève plus ou pas encore*] with communication through signs, that is to say, from the means/end structure?

Benjamin intends to prove that a non-violent elimination of conflicts is possible in the private world when it is ruled by the culture of the heart, cordial courtesy, sympathy, love of peace, trust, friendship. We enter here into a realm where, since the means/ends relation is suspended, one is dealing with pure means that, as it were, exclude violence. Conflicts between men now go through objects or things (*Sachen*) and it is only in this most "realist" or most "object-ive [*chosique*]" relation that the domain of pure means—that is to say, the domain of "technology" par excellence—opens. Technology is the "most proper domain" of pure means. As technology, a technology of civil agreement, conversation (*Unterredung*) would be the "most profound example" of this "most proper domain."

Yet how does one recognize that violence is excluded from the private or proper sphere (*eigentliche Sphäre*)? Benjamin's response may be surprising. The possibility of this non-violence is attested to by the fact that the lie is not punished, nor is deception or fraud (*Betrug*). Roman law and Old German law did not punish them. This confirms at least that something of private life or of personal intention escapes the space of power, of law, of authoritarian violence. The lie is here the example of what escapes the policio-juridico-political right of inspection [*droit de regard*]. From then on, to consider a lie an offense is a sign of decadence: a decline is in process (*Verfallsprozess*) when state power seeks to control the veracity of discourses to the point of ignoring the boundaries between the proper sphere of the private and the field of the public thing [*la chose publique*]. Modern law loses confidence in itself, it condemns deception not for moral reasons but because it fears the violence that it might unleash on the victims' part. These victims may in turn threaten the order of law. It is the same mechanism as the one at work in the concession of the right to strike. It is a matter of limiting the worst violence with another violence. What Benjamin seems to be dreaming of is an order of non-violence that subtracts from the order of law, and so from the right to punish the lie—not only private relations but even certain public relations as in the general proletarian strike of which Sorel speaks, a strike that would not attempt to refound a state and a new law; or again, certain diplomatic relations in which, in a manner analogous to private relations, some ambassadors settle conflicts peacefully and without treaties. Arbitration is nonviolent in this case because it is situated beyond all order of law and therefore beyond violence (195/E293). We shall see in a moment how this nonviolence is not without affinity to pure violence.

Here Benjamin proposes an analogy over which one should linger for a moment, particularly because in it intervenes this enigmatic concept of fate. What would happen if a violence linked to fate (*schicksalsmässige Gewalt*), one using just (*berechtigte*) means, found itself in an irresolvable conflict with just (*gerechten*) ends? And in such a way that one would have to envision another kind of violence, which, regarding these ends, would be neither a justified nor an unjustified means? As neither a justified nor an unjustified means, undecidably, it would no longer even be a means but would enter into a whole other relation with the pair means/ end. One would then be dealing with a whole other violence, a violence that would no longer allow itself to be determined in the space opened up by the opposition means/end. The question is all the more grave in that it exceeds or displaces the initial problematic that Benjamin had constructed up to that point on the subject of violence and of law. This problematic was entirely governed by the concept of means. Here one notices that there are cases in which, posed in terms of means/ end, the problem of law remains undecidable. This ultimate *undecidability*, which is that of all problems of *law* (*Unentscheidbarkeit aller Rechtsprobleme*), is the insight of a singular and discouraging experience. Where is one to go after recognizing this ineluctable undecidability?

Such a question opens, first, upon another dimension of language, upon a beyond of mediation and so beyond language as sign. Sign is here understood, as always in Benjamin, in the sense of mediation, as a means toward an end. It seems at first that there is no way out, and so there is no hope. But at the end of the impasse, this despair and hopelessness (*Aussichtslosigkeit*) calls for decisions of thought that concern nothing less than the origin of language in its relation to truth, destinal violence (*schicksalhafte Gewalt*) that puts itself above reason, and then, above this violence itself, God: another, a wholly other "mystical foundation of authority."

It is not, to be sure, Montaigne's or Pascal's, but we should not trust too much in this distance. That is what the *Aussichtslosigkeit* of law opens upon, as it were; that is where the impasse of law leads.

There would be an analogy between "the undecidability [*Unentscheidbarkeit*] of all the problems of law" and what happens in nascent language (*in werdenden Sprachen*) in which it is impossible to make a clear, convincing, determinant decision (*Entscheidung*) between true and false [*le juste et le faux*], right and wrong (*richtig/falsch*). This is only an analogy proposed in passing. But it could be developed on the basis of other Benjamin texts on language, notably "The Task of the

Translator" (1923) and especially the famous essay of 1916 (five years earlier, therefore, "On Language As Such and On the Language of Man"). Both put into question the notion that the essence of language is originally communicative, that is to say semiological, informative, representative, conventional, hence *mediatory*. Language is not a means with an end (a thing or signified content, even an addressee) to which it would have to make itself correctly adequate. This critique of the sign was political then as well: the conception of language as means and as sign would be "bourgeois." The 1916 text defined original sin as that fall into a language of mediate communication where words, having become means, incite chatter (*Geschwätz*); the question of good and evil after the creation arises from this chatter. The tree of knowledge was not there to provide knowledge of good and evil but as the symptomatic sign (*Wahrzeichen*) of judgment (*Gericht*) borne by he who questions. "This immense irony," Benjamin concludes, "is the sign by which the mythical origin of law is recognized (*das Kennzeichen des mythischen Ursprungs des Rechtes*)."[43]

Beyond this simple analogy, Benjamin here wants to conceive of a finality, a justice of ends that is no longer tied to the possibility of law, in any case to what is always conceived of as universalizable. The universalization of law is its very possibility; it is analytically inscribed in the concept of justice (*Gerechtigkeit*). But in this case what is not understood is that this universality is in contradiction with God himself, that is, with the one who decides the legitimacy of means and the justice of ends *over and above reason and even above destinal violence*. This sudden reference to God above reason and universality, beyond a sort of *Aufklärung* of law, is nothing other, it seems to me, than a reference to the irreducible singularity of each situation. And the audacious thought, as necessary as it is perilous, of what one would here call a sort of justice without law, a justice beyond law [*une sorte de justice sans droit, une justice au-delà du droit*] (this is not one of Benjamin's expressions) is just as valid for the uniqueness of the individual as for the people and for the language, in short, for history.

To explain this "nonmediate function of violence (*eine nicht mittelbare Funktion der Gewalt*)," (196/E294) Benjamin again takes the example of everyday language as if it were only an analogy. In fact, it seems to me, we have here the true mechanism, and the very place of decision. Is it by chance and unrelated to such a figure of God that he speaks then of the experience of *anger*, this example of a manifestation that passes as immediate, and alien to any correlation between means and end? Is it by chance that he takes the example of anger to show that, before any mediation, language is manifestation, epiphany, pure presentation? The explosion of violence, in anger, would not be a means toward an end; it would have no other aim than to

---

43. Benjamin, "On Language as Such," *GS* 2.1, 154; tr. E. Jephcott in *Reflections*, 328.

show and to show itself. Let us leave the responsibility for this concept to Benjamin: the manifestation of self, the in some way disinterested, immediate and uncalculated manifestation of anger. What matters to him is a violent manifestation of violence that thus shows itself and that would not be a means toward an end. Such would be mythic violence as manifestation of the gods.

Here begins the last sequence, the most enigmatic, the most fascinating and the most profound in this text. One must underscore two of its traits: on the one hand a terrible ethico-political ambiguity, which at bottom reflects the terror that constitutes, in fact, the theme of the text; and on the other hand the exemplary instability of its status and its signature—what, finally, you will permit me to call this heart or courage [ce cœur ou ce courage] of a thinking that knows there is no justesse, no justice, no responsibility except in exposing oneself to all risks, beyond certainty and good conscience.

In the Greek world, the manifestation of divine violence in its mythic form founds a law rather than applies, by force of force [à force de force], rather than "enforces,"[44] an existing law by distributing awards and punishments. It is not a distributive or retributive justice, and Benjamin evokes the legendary examples of Niobe, Apollo and Artemis, and Prometheus. As it is a matter of founding a new law, the violence that befalls Niobe comes from fate. This fate can only be uncertain and ambiguous (zweideutig), since it is not preceded or regulated by any anterior, superior or transcendent law. This founding violence is not "properly destructive (eigentlich zerstörend)," since, for example, it respects the mother's life at the moment it brings a bloody death to Niobe's children (197/E294–95). But this allusion to blood spilled is here discriminating. It seems to be the only basis for identifying the mythical and violent foundation of law in the Greek world, for distinguishing it from the divine violence in Judaism. The examples of this ambiguity (Zweideutigkeit) multiply, the word returns at least four times. There is thus a "demonic" ambiguity of this mythical positing of law, which is in its fundamental principle a power (Macht), a force, a positing of authority, and so, as Sorel himself suggests, with Benjamin's apparent approval here, a privilege of kings, of the great or powerful: at the origin of all law is a privilege, a prerogative (in den Anfängen alles Recht 'Vor' recht der Könige oder der Grossen, kurz der Mächtigen gewesen sei, 198/E296). At this originary and mythical moment, there is still no distributive justice, no punishment or penalty, only "expiation" (Sühne) rather than "retribution."

To this violence of the Greek mythos Benjamin opposes, feature for feature, the violence of God. From all points of view, he says, it is its opposite. Instead of founding law, it destroys it; instead of setting limits and boundaries, it annihilates them;

---

44. *Translator's note:* The word *enforce* is in English in the text.

instead of leading to fault and expiation, it causes to expiate; instead of threatening, it strikes; above all—and this is the essential issue—instead of killing with blood, it kills and annihilates *without bloodshed*. Blood would make all the difference. The interpretation of this thought of blood is as troubling, despite certain dissonances, in Benjamin as it is in Rosenzweig. Blood is the symbol of life, Benjamin says, of mere life, life pure and simple, life as such (*das Symbol des blossen Lebens*) (199/ E297). In making blood flow, the mythological violence of law is exercised for its own sake (*um ihrer selbst willen*) against mere life (*das blosse Leben*), which it causes to bleed, while remaining precisely within the order of life of the living as such [*l'ordre de la vie du vivant en tant que tel*]. In contrast, purely divine (Judaic) violence is exercised on all life but to the profit or for the sake of the living (*über alles Leben um des Lebendigen willen*). In other words, the mythological violence of law is satisfied in itself by sacrificing the living, whereas divine violence sacrifices life to save the living, for the sake of the living. In both cases there is sacrifice, but in the case where blood is exacted, the living is not respected. Whence Benjamin's singular conclusion, and again I leave to him the responsibility for this interpretation, particularly for this interpretation of Judaism: "The first [the mythological violence of law —J. D.] demands [*fordert*] sacrifice, the second [i.e., divine violence —J. D.] accepts it, assumes it [*nimmst sie an*]." In any case, this divine violence, which would be attested to not only by religion but also in present life or in manifestations of the sacred, annihilates, perhaps, goods, life, law, the foundation of law, and so on, but it never attacks—for the purpose of destroying it—the soul of the living (*die Seele des Lebendigen*). Consequently, one has no right [*on n'a pas le droit*] to conclude from this that divine violence leaves the field open for all human crimes. "Thou shalt not kill" remains an absolute imperative once the principle of destructive divine violence commands the respect of the living being, beyond law, beyond judgment, for this imperative is followed by no judgment. It provides no criterion for judgment; one could not find in it the authority to automatically condemn any putting to death. The individual or the community must keep the "responsibility" (the condition of which being the absence of general criteria and automatic rules), must assume their decision in exceptional situations, in extraordinary or unheard-of cases (*in ungeheuren Fällen*). That, for Benjamin, is the essence of Judaism, which would explicitly refuse to condemn murder in cases of legitimate self-defense, and which, according to him, sacralizes life to the point that certain thinkers extend this sacralization beyond man to include animal and vegetable.

But one should sharpen to the utmost what Benjamin means by the sacrality of man, of life or rather of the human *Dasein*. He stands up vigorously against all sacralization of life *for itself*, natural life, the simple fact of living. Commenting at length on the words of Kurt Hiller, according to which "higher even than the happiness and the justice of existence (*Dasein*) stands existence itself" (201/E298), Benjamin judges the proposition that a simple Dasein would be higher than a just Dasein (*als gerechtes Dasein*) to be false and ignoble, if by *Dasein* one understands the simple fact of living. And while noting that these terms *Dasein* and *life* remain very ambiguous, he judges the same proposition, however ambiguous it may remain, in the opposite way, as full of a powerful truth (*gewaltige Wahrheit*) if it means that man's nonbeing would be still more terrible than man's not-yet-being just, purely and simply, in unconditional fashion. In other words, what makes the worth of man, of his Dasein and of his life, is that he contains the potential, the possibility of justice, the avenir of justice, the avenir of his being-just, of his having-to-be just. What is sacred in his life is not his life but the justice of his life. Even if beasts and plants were sacred, they would not be so for their mere life, says Benjamin. This critique of vitalism or biologism, if it also resembles one by a certain Heidegger and if it recalls some Hegel propositions, here proceeds like the awakening of a Judaic tradition. And it does so in the name of life, of the most living of life [*du plus vivant de la vie*], of the value of the life that is worth more than life (pure and simple, if such exist and that one could call natural and biological), but that is worth more than life because it is life itself, insofar as life prefers itself. It is life beyond life, life against life, but always in life and for life.[45] Because of this ambiguity in the concepts of life and Dasein, Benjamin is both drawn to, and reticent before, the dogma that affirms the sacred character of life, as natural life, pure and simple. The origin of this dogma deserves inquiry, notes Benjamin, who is ready to see in it the relatively modern and nostalgic response of the West to the loss of the sacred.

Which is the ultimate and most provocative paradox of this critique of violence? The one that offers the most to think about? It is that this critique presents itself as the only "philosophy" of history (the word "philosophy" remaining in unforgettable quotation marks) that makes possible an attitude that is not merely "critical" but, in the more critical and diacritical sense of the word "critique," *krinein*, an attitude that will permit to choose (*krinein*), and so to decide and to cut in history and on the subject of history. It is the only one, Benjamin says, that permits, in respect to present time, the taking of a position, of a discriminating, deciding, and decisive position (*scheidende und entscheidende Einstellung*, 202/E299–300). All undecidability is situated, blocked in, accumulated on the side of law, of mythological

---

45. As paradoxical as it is in itself, as quick as it is to having to turn into its opposite, this logic is typical and recurring. Among all the affinities (surprising or not) that it can favor, let us mention once again an analogous gesture in Schmitt, a gesture that is in itself paradoxical and necessary for a thinker of politics as war: the *physical* putting to death is here a prescription that is explicitly and rigorously taken into account by Schmitt. But this putting to death would be only an opposition of life to life. There is no death [*il n'y a pas la mort*]. There is only life, its position—and its opposition to itself which is only a mode of the position to self. Cf. *Politics of Friendship*, 135, n. 18.

violence, that is to say the violence that founds and preserves law. But on the other hand all decidability stands on the side of the divine violence that destroys the law, we could even venture to say, that deconstructs the law. To say that all decidability is found on the side of the divine violence that destroys or deconstructs the law is to say at least two things:

1. *History* is on the side of this divine violence, and precisely in opposition to myth. It is indeed for this reason that it is a matter of a "philosophy" of history and that Benjamin appeals in fact to a "new historical era [*ein neues geschicht-liches Zeitalter*]" (202/E300) that should follow the end of the mythic reign, the interruption of the magic circle of the mythic forms of law, the abolition of the *Staatsgewalt*, of the violence, power, or authority of the state. This new historical era would be a new political era on the condition that one not link the political to the state, as Schmitt for example tends to do, to the contrary and teleologi-cally, even if he defensively argues that he does not confuse the two.

2. If all decidability is concentrated on the side of divine violence in the Judaic tra-dition, this would come to confirm and give meaning to the spectacle offered by the history of law, which deconstructs itself and is paralyzed, in undecidability. What Benjamin calls, in fact, the "dialectic of up and down (*ein dialektisches Auf und Ab*)" in the founding or preserving violence of law constitutes an oscillation in which the preserving violence must constantly give itself up to the repression of hostile counterviolences (*Unterdrückung der feindlichen Gegengewalten*). But this repression—and law, the juridical institution, is essentially repressive from this point of view—never ceases to weaken the founding violence that it repre-sents, so it destroys itself in the course of this cycle. For here Benjamin to some extent recognizes this law [*loi*] of iterability that insures that the founding vio-lence is constantly represented in a preserving violence that always repeats the tradition of its origin and that ultimately keeps nothing but a foundation des-tined from the start to be repeated, preserved, reinstituted. Benjamin says that founding violence is "represented (*repräsentiert*)" in preserving violence.

To think at this point that one has cast light and correctly interpreted the mean-ing, the *vouloir-dire* of Benjamin's text, by opposing in a decidable way the decid-ability of divine, revolutionary, historical, anti-state, anti-juridical violence on one side and on the other the undecidability of the mythic violence of state law, would still be to decide too quickly and not to understand the power of this text. For in its last lines a new act of the drama is played, or a *coup de théâtre* that I could not swear was not premeditated from the moment the curtain went up. What does Benjamin in fact say? First he speaks *in the conditional* about "revolutionary violence (*revolu-tionäre Gewalt*)": *if,* beyond law, violence sees its status insured as pure and immediate violence, then this will prove that revolutionary violence is possible. Then one would know, but this is a conditional clause, what this revolutionary violence is whose name is the purest manifestation of violence among men (202/E300).

Yet why is this statement in the conditional? Is it only provisional and contingent? Not at all. For the decision (*Entscheidung*) on this subject, the determinant decision, the one that allows knowing or recognizing such a pure and revolutionary violence *as such*, is a *decision not accessible to man*. Here we must deal with a whole other undecidability. It is better to cite Benjamin's sentence *in extenso*: "Less possible and also less urgent for man, however, is to decide when pure violence was effected in a determined case (*Nicht gleich möglich, noch auch gleich dringend ist aber für Menschen die Entscheidung, wann reine Gewalt in einem bestimmten Falle wirklich war*)" (202–3/E300).

This has to do with the essence of divine violence, of its power and of its justice. Divine violence is the most just, the most historic, the most revolutionary, the most decidable or the most deciding. Yet, as such, it does not lend itself to any human determination, to any knowledge or decidable "certainty" on our part. It is never known in itself, "as such," but only in its "effects" and its effects are "incomparable." They do not lend themselves to any conceptual generalization. There is no certainty (*Gewissheit*) or determinant knowledge except in the realm of mythic violence—that is to say, of law, that is, of the historical undecidable. "For only mythical violence, not divine, will be recognizable as such with certainty, unless it be in incomparable effects. . . . " (E300).

To be schematic, there are two violences, two competing *Gewalten*: on one side, decision (just, historical, political, and so on), justice beyond law and the state, but *without decidable knowledge*; on the other, decidable knowledge and certainty in a realm that *structurally remains that of the undecidable*, of the mythic law and of the state. On one side is the decision without decidable certainty, on the other the certainty of the undecidable but without decision. In any case, in one form or another, the undecidable is on each side, and is the violent condition of knowledge or action, but knowledge and action are always dissociated.

Questions: What one calls in the singular, if there is one and only one, deconstruction, is it the former or the latter? Something else entirely or something else in the end? If one trusts the Benjaminian schema, is the deconstructive discourse on the undecidable rather Jewish (or Judeo-Christian-Islamic), or rather Greek? Rather religious, mythical, or philosophical? If I do not answer questions that take this form, it is not only because I am not sure that such a thing as deconstruction, in the singular, exists or is possible. It is also because I believe that deconstructive discourses, as they present themselves in their irreducible plurality, participate in an impure, contaminating, negotiated, bastard and violent fashion in all these filiations—let us call them Judeo-Greek to save time—of decision and the undecid-able. And then, that the Jew and the Greek may not be quite what Benjamin wants us to believe. And finally for what remains to come of or from deconstruction [*pour ce que de la deconstruction reste à venir*], I believe that something else runs through its veins, perhaps without filiation, an entirely different blood or rather something else entirely than blood, be it the most fraternal blood.[46]

And so in saying *adieu* or *au-revoir* to Benjamin, I nevertheless leave him the last word. I let him sign, at least if he can. It is always necessary that the other sign and it is always the other that signs last. In other words, first.

In his last lines, Benjamin, just before signing, even uses the word *bastard*. That in short is the definition of the myth, and thus of the founding violence of law. Mythic law—we could say juridical fiction—is a violence that will have "bas-tardized (*bastardierte*)" the "eternal forms of pure divine violence." Myth has bas-tardized divine violence with law (*mit dem Recht*). Misalliance, impure genealogy: not a mixture of bloods but bastardy, which at its root will have created a law that makes blood flow and exacts blood as payment.

And then, as soon as he has taken responsibility for this interpretation of the Greek and the Jew, Benjamin signs. He speaks in an evaluative, prescriptive, non-constative manner, as we do each time we sign. Two energetic sentences proclaim what the watchwords *must* [*doivent*] be, what one *must do* [*ce qu'il faut faire*], what one *must* [*faut*] *reject*, the evil or perversity of what is to be rejected (*Verwerflich*). "But one must reject [*Verwerflich aber*] all mythical violence, the violence that founds law, which one may call governing [*schaltende*] violence. One must also reject [*Verwerflich auch*] the violence that preserves law, the governed violence [*die verwaltete Gewalt*] in the service of the governing."

Then there are the last words, the last sentence. Like the evening *shofar*, but on the eve of a prayer one no longer hears. No longer heard or not yet heard—what is the difference?

Not only does it sign, this ultimate address, and very close to the first name of Benjamin, Walter. It also names the signature, the sign and the seal, it names the name and what calls itself *die waltende*.[47]

---

46. In putting this text of Benjamin to the test of a certain deconstructive necessity, at least such as it is here determined for me now, I am anticipating a more ample and coherent work: on the relations between this deconstruction, what Benjamin calls "destruction [Zerstörung]" and the Heideggerian "Destruktion."

47. Chance of language and of the proper name, chance [*aléa*] at the juncture of the most common and the most singular, law [*loi*] of the unique fate, this "play" between *Walten* and *Walter*, this very game, here, between *this* particular Walter and what he says of *Walten*, one must [*il faut*] know that it cannot provide any knowledge, any demonstration or any certainty.

That is the paradox of its "demonstrative" force. This force has to do with the dissociation between the cognitive and the performative of which we spoke a moment ago (and elsewhere too, precisely in

But who signs? It is God, the Wholly Other, as always. Divine violence will always have preceded but will also have *given* all the first names. God is the name of this pure violence—and just in essence: there is no other, there is none prior to it and before that it has to justify itself. Authority, justice, power, and violence all are one in him.

The other signs always, here is what signs perhaps this essay: essay of signature, which carries itself in its truth, to wit, that always the other signs, the wholly other, and *tout autre est tout autre*. This is what one calls God—no, what calls itself God when necessarily he/it signs in my place even when I believe I name him. God is the name of the absolute metonymy, what it names by displacing the names, the substitution and what substitutes itself in the name of this substitution. Even before the name, as soon as the first name [*dès le prénom*]: "*Die göttliche Gewalt, welche Insignium und Siegel, niemals Mittel heiliger Vollstreckung ist, mag die waltende heissen*, divine violence, which is the sign and seal but never the means of sacred execution, can be called sovereign violence [*die waltende heissen*]."

It can be called—sovereign. In secret. Sovereign in that it calls itself and it is called there where sovereignly it calls itself. It names itself. Sovereign is the violent power of this originary appellation. Absolute privilege, infinite prerogative. The prerogative gives the condition of all appellation. It says nothing else, it calls itself, therefore, in silence. Nothing resonates, then, but the name, the pure nomination of the name before the name. The pre-nomination of God—here is justice in its infinite power. It begins and ends at the signature.

At the most singular, the most improbable of signatures, at the sovereign. At the most secret, too: sovereign *wants to say/means* [*veut dire*], for whoever knows how to read, secret. *Veut dire*, that is to say (*heisst*) calls, invites, names, addresses, addresses itself.

For whoever can read, at once [*aussitôt*] crossing the name of the other.

For whoever receives the power [*force*] to unseal, but as such also keeping it intact, the undecipherability of a seal, the sovereign and not an other.

POST-SCRIPTUM

This strange text is dated. Every signature is dated, even and perhaps all the more so if it slips in among several names of God and only signs by pretending to let God himself

---

regard to the signature). But, touching on the absolute secret, this "play" is in no way ludic and gratuitous. For we also know that Benjamin was very interested, notably in his "Goethe's Elective Affinities," in the contingent [*aléatoire*] and significant coincidences of which proper names are properly the site. I would be tempted to give this hypothesis a new chance after the recent reading (August 1991) of the very fine essay by Jochen Hörisch, "L'ange satanique et le bonheur—Les noms de Walter Benjamin" in *Weimar: Le tournant critique*, ed. G. Raulet (Paris: Anthropos, 1988).

sign. If this text is dated and signed (Walter, 1921), we have only a limited right to convoke it to bear witness either to Nazism in general (which had not yet developed as such), or to the new forms assumed there by the racism and the anti-Semitism that are inseparable from it, or even less to the "final solution": not only because the project and the deployment of the "final solution" came later and even after the death of Benjamin, but because within the history itself of Nazism the "final solution" is perhaps something that some can consider an ineluctable outcome and inscribed in the very premises of Nazism, if such a thing has a proper identity that can sustain this sort of utterance, while others—whether or not they are Nazis or Germans—can think that the project of a "final solution" is an event, even a new mutation within the history of Nazism and that as such it deserves an absolutely specific analysis. For all of these reasons, we would not have the right or we would have only a limited right to ask ourselves what Walter Benjamin would have thought—in the logic of this text (if it has one and only one)—of both Nazism and the "final solution."

And yet. Yet, in a certain way I will do just that, and I will do it by going beyond my interest for this text itself, for its event and its structure, for that which it gives us to read of a configuration of Jewish and German thinking right before the rise of Nazism, as one says, of all the partakings and all the partitions that organize such a configuration, of the vertiginous proximities, the radical reversals of pro into con on the basis of sometimes common premises. Presuming, that is, that all these problems are really separable, which I doubt. In truth, I will not ask myself what Benjamin himself thought of Nazism and anti-Semitism, all the more so since we have other means of doing so, other texts by him. Nor will I ask what Walter Benjamin himself would have thought of the "final solution" and what judgments, what interpretations he would have proposed. I will seek something else, in a modest and preliminary way. However enigmatic and overdetermined the logical matrix of this text might be, however mobile and convertible, however reversible it is, it has its own coherence. This coherence is itself coherent with that which governs a number of other texts by Benjamin, both earlier and later. It is by taking account of certain insistent elements in this coherent continuity that I will try out several hypotheses in order to reconstitute not some possible utterances by Benjamin but the larger traits of the problematic and interpretive space in which he could perhaps have inscribed his discourse on the "final solution."

On the one hand, he would probably have taken the "final solution" to be the extreme consequence of a logic of Nazism that, to take up again the concepts from our text, would have corresponded to a multiple radicalization:

1. *The radicalization of evil linked to the fall into the language of communication, representation, information (and from this point of view, Nazism has indeed been the most pervasive figure of media violence and of political exploitation of the mod-*

ern techniques of communicative language, of industrial language and of the language of industry, of scientific objectification to which is linked the logic of the conventional sign and of formalizing matriculation);

2. *The totalitarian radicalization of a logic of the state (and our text is indeed a condemnation of the state, even of the revolution that replaces a state by another state, which is also valid for other totalitarianisms—and already we see prefigured the question of the* Historikerstreit*);*

3. *The radical but also fatal corruption of parliamentary and representative democracy by a modern police force that is inseparable from it, that becomes the true legislative power and whose ghost commands the totality of the political space. From this point of view, the "final solution" is both a historico-political decision by the state and a police decision, a decision of the police, of the civil and the military police, without anyone ever being able to discern the one from the other and to assign the true responsibilities to any decision whatsoever.*

4. *A radicalization and total extension of the mythical, of mythical violence, both in its sacrificial founding moment and its most preserving moment. And this mythological dimension, that is at once Greek and aestheticizing (like fascism, Nazism is mythological, Grecoid, and if it corresponds to an aestheticization of the political, it is in an aesthetics of representation), also responds to a certain violence of state law, of its police and its technology, of law totally dissociated from justice, as the conceptual generality propitious to the mass structure in opposition to the consideration of singularity and uniqueness. How can one otherwise explain the institutional, even bureaucratic form, the simulacra of legalization, of juridicism, the respect for expertise and for hierarchies, in short, the whole judicial and state organization that marked the techno-industrial and scientific deployment of the "final solution"? Here a certain mythology of law was unleashed against a justice, which Benjamin believed ought to be kept radically distinct from law, from natural as well as historical law, from the violence of its foundation as well as from that of its preservation. And Nazism was a conservative revolution that was preserving this law.*

Yet, on the other hand and for these very reasons, because Nazism leads logically to the "final solution" as to its own limit and because the mythological violence of law is its veritable system, one can only think, that is, also recall the uniqueness of the "final solution" from a place other than this space of the mythological violence of law. To take the measure of this event and of what links it to fate, one would have to leave the order of law, of myth, of representation (of juridico-political representation with its tribunals of historian-judges, but also of aesthetic representation). Because what Nazism, as the final achievement of the logic of mythological violence, would have attempted to do is to exclude the other witness, to destroy the witness of the other order, of a divine violence whose justice is irreducible to law, of a violence heterogeneous to the order both of law and right (be it that of human rights) or of the order of representation and of myth. In other words, one cannot think the uniqueness of an event like the "final solution" as extreme point of mythic and representational violence, within its own system. One must try to think it beginning with its other, that is to say, starting from what it tried to exclude and to destroy, to exterminate radically, from that which haunted it at once from without and within. One must try to think it starting from the possibility of singularity, the singularity of the signature and of the name, because what the order of representation tried to exterminate was not only human lives by the millions—natural lives—but also a demand for justice, and also names: and first of all the possibility of giving, inscribing, calling, and recalling the name. Not only because there was a destruction or project of destruction of the name and of the very memory of the name, of the name as memory, but also because the system of mythical violence (objectivist, representational, communicational, etc.) went all the way to its own limit, in a demonic fashion, on the two sides of the limit: at the same time, it kept the archive of its destruction, produced simulacra of justificatory arguments, with a terrifying legal, bureaucratic, statist objectivity and (at the same time, therefore) it produced a system in which its logic, the logic of objectivity, made possible the invalidation and therefore the effacement of testimony and of responsibilities, the neutralization of the singularity of the final solution; in short, it produced the possibility of the historiographic perversion that has been able to give rise both to the logic of revisionism (to be brief, let us say of the Faurisson type) as well as a positivist, comparatist, or relativist objectivism (like the one now linked to the Historikerstreit) according to which the existence of an analogous totalitarian model and of earlier exterminations (the Gulag) explains the "final solution," even "normalizes" it as an act of war, a classic state response in time of war against the Jews of the world, who, speaking through the mouth of Weizman in September 1939, would have, in sum, like a quasi-state, declared war on the Third Reich.

From this point of view, Benjamin would perhaps have judged vain and without pertinence, in any case without a pertinence commensurable to the event, any juridical trial of Nazism and of its responsibilities, any judgmental apparatus, any historiography still homogenous with the space in which Nazism developed up to and including the final solution, any interpretation drawing on philosophical, moral, sociological, psychological, or psychoanalytical concepts, and especially juridical concepts (in particular those of the philosophy of law, whether it be that of natural law, in the Aristotelian style or the style of the Aufklärung). Benjamin would perhaps have judged vain and without pertinence, in any case without pertinence commensurable to the event, any historical or aesthetic objectification of the "final solution" that, like all objectifications, would still belong to the order of the representable and even of the determinable, of the determinant and decidable judgment. Recall what we were saying a moment ago: in the order of the bad violence of law, that is, the mythological violence, evil had to do with a certain undecidability from the fact that one could not distinguish between founding violence and preserving violence, because corruption was dialectical and dialectically unavoidable there, even as theoretical judgment and representation were determinable or determinant there. On the contrary, as soon as one leaves this order, history begins—and the violence of divine justice—but here we humans cannot measure judgments, which is to say also decidable interpretations. This also means that the interpretation of the "final solution," as of everything that constitutes the set and the delimitation of the two orders (the mythological and the divine) is not in the measure of man. No anthropology, no humanism, no discourse of man on man, even on human rights, can be proportionate to either the rupture between the mythical and the divine, or to a limit experience such as the "final solution." Such a project attempts quite simply to annihilate the other of mythic violence, the other of representation: fate, divine justice and that which can bear witness to it, in other words man insofar as he is the only being who, not having received his name from God, has received from God the power and the mission to name, to give a name to his fellow [semblable] and to give a name to things. To name is not to represent, it is not to communicate by signs, that is, by means of means in view of an end, and so forth. In other words, the line of this interpretation would belong to that terrible and crushing condemnation of the Aufklärung that Benjamin had already formulated in a text of 1918 published by Scholem in 1963 honoring Adorno on his sixtieth birthday.[48]

This does not mean that one must simply renounce the Enlightenment and the language of communication or of representation in favor of the language of expression. In his Moscow Diary in 1926–27, Benjamin specifies that the polarity between the two languages and all that they command cannot be maintained and deployed in a pure state, but that "compromise" is necessary or inevitable between them. Yet this remains a compromise between two incommensurable and radically heterogeneous dimensions. It is perhaps one of the lessons that we could draw here: the fatality of the compromise between heterogeneous orders, which is a compromise, moreover, in the name of the justice that would command one to obey at the same time the law of representations (Aufklärung, reason, objectification, comparison, explication, the taking into account of multiplicity and therefore the serialization of the unique) and the law [loi] that transcends representation and withholds the unique, all uniqueness, from its reinscription in an order of generality or of comparison.

---

48. *Translator's note:* Walter Benjamin, "On the Program of the Coming Philosophy" *GS* 2.2, 157–71, trans. Mark Ritter in *Walter Benjamin: Selected Writings,* vol. 1, ed. Marcus Bullock and Michael W. Jennings (Cambridge, Mass.: Harvard University Press, 1996), 100–10.

in conclusion, the most redoubtable, indeed perhaps almost unbearable
beyond the affinities it maintains with the worst (the critique of
theory of the Fall and of originary authenticity, the polarity between
language and fallen language, the critique of representation and of parliamen-
tary democracy, etc.), is a temptation that it would leave open, and leave open notably to
the survivors or the victims of the "final solution," to its past, present or potential victims.
Which temptation? The temptation to think the holocaust as an uninterpretable mani-
festation of divine violence insofar as this divine violence would be at the same time
annihilating, expiatory and bloodless, says Benjamin, a divine violence that would
destroy current law, here I re-cite Benjamin, "through a bloodless process that strikes and
causes to expiate." ("The legend of Niobe may be confronted, as an example of this vio-
lence, with God's judgment on the company of Korah (Numbers 16:1–35). It strikes
privileged Levites, strikes them without warning, without threat and does not stop short
of annihilation. But in annihilating it also expiates, and a deep connection between the
lack of bloodshed and the expiatory character of this violence is unmistakable," E297).

When one thinks of the gas chambers and the cremation ovens, this allusion to an
extermination that would be expiatory because bloodless must cause one to shudder.
One is terrified at the idea of an interpretation that would make of the holocaust an
expiation and an indecipherable signature of the just and violent anger of God.

It is at that point that this text, in all its polysemic mobility and all its resources for
reversal, seems to me finally to resemble too closely, to the point of specular fascination
and vertigo, the very thing against which one must act and think, do and speak. This
text, like many others by Benjamin, is still too Heideggerian, too messianico-Marxist
or archeo-eschatological for me. I do not know whether from this nameless thing that
one calls the "final solution" one can draw something that still deserves the name of a
lesson [enseignement]. But if there were a lesson to be drawn, a unique lesson among
the always singular lessons of murder, from even a single murder, from all the collective
exterminations of history (because each individual murder and each collective murder
is singular, thus infinite and incommensurable), the lesson that we could draw
today—and if we can do so then we must [et si nous le pouvons nous le devons]—is
that we must think, know, represent for ourselves, formalize, judge the possible com-
plicity among all these discourses and the worst (here the "final solution"). In my view,
this defines a task and a responsibility the theme of which I have not been able to read
in either Benjaminian "destruction" or Heideggerian "Destruktion." It is the thought
of difference between these destructions on the one hand and a deconstructive affirma-
tion on the other that has guided me tonight in this reading. It is this thought that the
memory of the "final solution" seems to me to dictate.

Translated by Mary Quaintance

6

A Note on "Taking a Stand for Algeria"

What is the relation between the theological and the autobiographical? Is there a necessity, an imperative, even, that, coming from religion, would demand the telling of one's life? There is a personal dimension to many of the writings that illuminate the question of religion in Derrida's work. In "Taking a Stand for Algeria," Derrida acknowledges the temptation of testimony, "the temptation to turn a demonstration into a sensitive or pathetic testimony," and to oneself reduce what needs to be thought and said to such testimony. Derrida acknowledges the temptation of testimony and reinscribes it as dictation. It is "impossible to dissociate here the heart, the thinking, and the political position-taking," Derrida writes. This impossibility is dictated by the other, it is an invention of the other—"here," Algeria ("which in the end I know to have never really ceased inhabiting or bearing in my innermost"), and a love for Algeria, that "dictates all that I will say in a few words."

The temptation of the autobiographical cannot be disentangled from other—political—dimensions that also dictate, often in the most violent and coercive ways, the particulars of a religious tradition as it took place and takes place in Algeria. Algeria thus becomes a name for religion, for Derrida's "own" religion, the fragility of which may be revealed by paraphrasing the still "autobiographical" if impossible confession of *Monolingualism of the Other*: "I have only one religion; it is not mine." But the testimony and the autobiographical is also the writing of the name—here, *Algeria*—which in turn testifies and dictates all that the "I" says and asks, including the question of "in the name of whom and in the name of what we speak here." If Algeria, a love for Algeria, dictates all that is said in this text by acknowledging the "temptation" of testimony, this text also becomes the occasion to reaffirm a link that was never quite severed, a link between religion and autobiography.

And yet, it is important to note that Derrida also writes here that he will "refrain" from temptation. One could therefore suggest that a different imperative is at work, another necessity of dissociation if not severing. Such an imperative is in fact articulated in this text as taking a stand "for the effective dissociation of the political and the theological." Such dissociation, Derrida makes clear, is still to come, and it would have to be very distinct from the history that has opposed, until now, reason and revelation, Church and State, religion and politics.

G. A.

TAKING A STAND
FOR ALGERIA

This text was read by Jacques Derrida during a public meeting organized by the ICSAI (International Committee in Support of Algerian Intellectuals) and the League of Human Rights, on 7 February 1994, after the publication of an appeal for civil peace in Algeria. Following are excerpts of the appeal referred to in the text:

> *Concerning the crisis which Algeria experiences today, only the Algerians can find political solutions. Yet these cannot be born in the isolation of the country.*
>
> *Everybody recognizes the complexity of the situation: diverging analyses and perspectives can legitimately be expressed about its origins and developments. Nevertheless, an agreement can be reached on a few points of principle.*
>
> *First of all, to reaffirm that any solution must be a civil one. The recourse to armed violence to defend or conquer power, terrorism; repression, torture and executions, murders and kidnappings, destruction, threats against the life or security of persons, these can only ruin the possibility which are still within Algeria's reach in order to build its own democracy and the conditions of its economic development.*
>
> *It is the condemnation by all of the practices of terrorism and repression which will thus begin to open a space for the confrontation of each and everyone's analyses, in the respect of differences.*
>
> *Proposals will be made to increase the number of acts of solidarity in France and elsewhere. Some initiatives are required without delay to make public opinion sensitive to the Algerian tragedy, to underscore the responsibility of governments and international financial institutions, to further the support of all for the Algerian democratic demands.*

I am asked to be brief; I will be. When I ask, as I will do, in the name of whom and in the name of what we speak here, I would simply like to let some questions be heard, without contesting or provoking anybody.

In the name of whom and of what are we gathered here? And whom do we address?

These questions are not abstract, I insist on this—and I insist that they engage first of all only me.

For several reasons. Due to decency or modesty *first*, of course, and because of a worry about what an Appeal like ours may contain in both strengths and weaknesses. However generous or just it may be, an Appeal—particularly when it resonates from here, from the walls of this Parisian auditorium, that is, for some of us, not for all precisely, but for many of us, when it is thus cast from far—I always fear that such an Appeal, however legitimate and well meaning it may be, may still contain, in its very eloquence, too much authority, and I fear that as such it also defines a place of arbitration (and there is indeed one in our Appeal; I will say something about it later). In its apparent neutrality in arbitration, such an Appeal runs the risk of containing a lesson, an implicit lesson, whether it be a lesson learnt, or worse, a lesson given. So it is better to say it, it is better not to hide it from ourselves. Above all, decency is required when one risks matching a few words to such a real tragedy about which the Appeal from the ICSAI and the League of Human Rights rightly underlines *two characteristics*.

1. *The entanglement* (the very long history of the premises, of the "origins" and of the "developments" which have led to what looks like a terrifying deadlock and to the entwined sharing of responsibilities in this matter, in Algeria as well as outside); which implies that the time of the transformation and the coming of this democracy, the response to the "Algerian democratic demand" mentioned several times in the Appeal, this time *for* democracy will be long, discontinuous, difficult to gather into the act of a single decision, into a dramatic reversal which would respond to the Appeal. It would be irresponsible to believe or to make believe the opposite. This long time *for* democracy, we will not even be able to gather it in Algeria. Things will have to take place *elsewhere, too*. None of the autonomy of Algerians is taken away in such a serious reminder. Even if we could doubt this and even if we kept dreaming of one such reversal in the course of events, the very time of this meeting would be enough to remind us of it. Indeed, we come after the so-called reconciliation talks, that is, after a failure or a simulacrum, a disaster at any rate so sadly foreseeable, if not calculated, which sketches, as if negatively, the dream of the impossible which we can neither abandon nor believe in.

2. Our Appeal also underscores the fact that in front of such an entangled situation, the diversity of perspectives and analyses is "legitimate." And how true that is! But at that point, the Appeal carefully stops and goes back to what it defines as a possible "agreement" on a "few points of principle." Yet, nobody, even

among the first to sign the Appeal (I am one of them), is fooled by the fact that the "diversity of analyses and perspectives," if it is taken to be legitimate, can lead some to diverge on the "few points of principle" at stake (for instance, about what is to be understood by the three major words or motifs of the Appeal: that of *violence* [all forms of violence are condemned: but what is violence, that armed violence which is the most general concept in the Appeal? Does it cover *any* police operation even if it claims to protect the security of citizens, and to insure—or claims to insure—the legal and normal processes of a democratic society, etc?], then that of *civil* peace [What of the civil in general? What is the civil? What does civil mean today? etc.], and above all that of the idea of *democracy* [Which democracy is referred to?].

In the end, these words only engage myself, for if I have supported and even participated in the preparation of the Appeal for civil peace in Algeria; if I approve of all its formulations (which seen to me both prudent and demanding), I cannot be sure ahead of time that, as far as implications and consquences are concerned, my interpretation is in all respects the same as that of the others who have signed it.

Thus, I will try to tell you briefly how I understand some crucial passages of the Appeal. I will do so in a dry and analytical manner, to save time but also in order to refrain from a temptation I have which some might deem sentimental: the temptation to turn a demonstration into a sensitive or pathetic testimony, and to explain how all I will say is inspired above all and after all by a painful love for Algeria, an Algeria where I was born, which I left, literally, for the first time only at nineteen, before the war of independence, an Algeria to which I have often come back and which in the end I know to have never really ceased inhabiting or bearing in my innermost, a love for Algeria which, if not the love of citizen, and thus the patriotic tie to a nation-state, is none the less what makes it impossible to dissociate here the heart, the thinking, and the political position-taking—and thus dictates all that I will say in a few words. It is precisely from this point that I ask in the name of what and of whom, if one is not an Algerian citizen, one joins and supports this Appeal.

Keeping this question in mind, I would thus like to demonstrate telegraphically, in four points, why our Appeal cannot limit itself to a praiseworthy *neutrality* in front of what, indeed, must be above all the responsibility of the Algerians themselves. Hence, "not to limit oneself to political neutrality," which does not mean that one has to chose a side—we refuse this, I believe—between *two* sides of a front supposed to define, for a large part of the public opinion, the fundamental

fact of the current conflict. On the contrary, it seems to me that political responsibility today consists in not accepting this fact as natural and unchangeable. It
consists in demonstrating, by saying it and by turning it into acts, that it is not
so and that the democratic way has its place and its strengths and its life and its
people elsewhere.

But saying this is not to be politically neutral. On the contrary it means to take a
stand *four times*: to take a stand

1. for a new international solidarity;
2. for an electoral agreement;
3. for a dissociation of the theological and the political; and
4. for what I would more or less properly call a new Third Estate.

The Appeal says that the solutions belong to the Algerians alone, a correct claim
in principle, but it adds several times that these solutions cannot be born in the
"isolation of the country." This reminds us of what must be made explicit in order
to draw its consequence: political solutions do not depend in the last instance on
the citizens of this or that nation-state. Today, with respect to what was and
remains up to a point a just imperative, that is, non-intervention and the respect of
self-determination (the future of Algerian men and women of course belongs in
the end to the Algerian people[1]), a certain manner of saying it or of understanding
it runs the risk of being, from now on, at best the rhetorical concession of a bad
conscience, at worst, an alibi. Which does not mean that a right of intervention or
of intrusion, granted to other states or to the citizens of other states *as such*, should
be reinstated. That would indeed be inadmissible. But one should reaffirm the
international aspect of the stakes and of certain solidarities that tie us all the more
in that they do not only tie us as the citizens of determinate nation-states. Which
does complicate things, but also sets the true place of our responsibility: neither
simply that of Algerian citizens, nor that of French citizens; and this is why my
question, and my question as one who has signed the Appeal, comes from neither
an Algerian nor a French as such, which does not free me *on the other hand* of my
responsibilities, civil or more than civil, as a French citizen born in Algeria, and
obliges me to do what must be done according to this logic in my country, toward

---

1. *Translator's note*: The French text says "*l'avenir*," Derrida having made elsewhere an operative
distinction between the *futur* which more or less duplicates the present and an *avenir* which leaves open
a space for alterity. However, the word is quite difficult to render into English (literally: "to-come"), so
we have opted throughout for a simpler translation which fits—we hope—with the political urgency of
the style.

the public opinion and the French government (as we try to do here; all that remains to be done in this regard has been and will still have to be said). For example (for lack of time, it will be my only example) the logic of the Appeal leads us to take sides—it is indeed necessary—about Algeria's foreign debt and what is linked to it. This matter is also, as is well known (unemployment, despair, dramatically increasing poverty), an essential component of the civil war and all of today's sufferings. But we cannot seriously take a position on the economic recovery of Algeria without analyzing the national and international responsibilities in this situation, and, above all, without pointing to means of politico-economic interventions which go beyond Algeria, going even beyond France. It is a matter of European and world-wide stakes, and those who call, as we do, for such international endeavours and call to what the Appeal carefully names "international financial institutions," those who call for these responsibilities and these solidarities, those do not speak anymore *solely* as Algerians or French, nor even as Europeans, even if they *also* and *thereby* speak as all of these.

WE TAKE A STAND FOR AN ELECTORAL AGREEMENT

One cannot invoke, however abstractly, democracy, or what the Appeal calls the "Algerian democratic demand" without taking a stand in the Algerian political sphere. A consistent democracy demands at least, in its minimal definition: 1. a schedule, that is, an electoral engagement; 2. a discussion, that is, a public discourse armed only with reasoned arguments, for example in a free press; 3. a respect of the electoral decision, and thus of the possibility of transition within a democratic process which remains uninterrupted.

This means that we, who have signed the Appeal, have already taken a stand twice on this matter, and it was necessary. *On the one hand*, against a state apparatus which would not urgently create the necessary conditions, in particular those of *appeasement* and of discussion, in order to re-initiate *as quickly as possible* (and this *rhythm* poses today the most effective problem, the one to discuss democratically) an interrupted electoral process. *Voting* is not indeed the whole of democracy, but without it and without this form and this accounting of voices, there is no democracy. *On the other hand*, by the very reference to a democratic demand, we also take a stand against whoever would not respect the electoral decision, but would tend, directly or indirectly, before, during or after such elections, to question the very principle presiding over such plebiscite, that is, democratic life, a legal state, the respect for free speech, the rights of the minority, of political transition, of the plurality of languages, mores and beliefs, etc. We are resolutely opposed—it is a stand we take clearly, with all of its consequences—to whoever would pretend to profit from democratic processes without respecting democracy.

To say that we are logically against both of these perversions insofar as we refer to democracy in Algeria, is not to speak as either a citizen of this or that nation-state, or as an Algerian, or as a French, or as a French from Algeria, whatever the added depth and intensity of our responsibility in this respect may be. And we are here in the international logic that has presided over the formation of the ICSAI, a committee first and foremost international. By the same token, beyond the painful Algerian example in its very singularity, we generally call–as the International Parliament of Writers does in its fashion, sharing our demands and associated with us today–for an international solidarity seeking its supports neither in the current state of international law and the institutions that represent it today, nor in the concepts of nation, state, citizenship, and sovereignty which dominate this international discourse, *de jure* and *de facto*.

WE TAKE A STAND FOR THE EFFECTIVE DISSOCIATION OF THE POLITICAL AND THE THEOLOGICAL

Our idea of democracy implies a separation between the state and religious powers, that is, a radical religious neutrality[2] and a faultless tolerance which would not only set the sense of belonging to religions, cults, and thus also cultures and languages, away from the reach of any terror—whether stemming from the state or not—but also protects the practices of faith and, in this instance, the freedom of discussion and interpretation within each religion. For example, and here first of all, in Islam whose different readings, both exegetical and political, must develop freely, and not only in Algeria. This is in fact the best response to the racist anti-Islamic movements born of that violence deemed Islamic or that would still dare to affiliate themselves with Islam.

WE TAKE A STAND FOR WHAT I WOULD TENTATIVELY CALL, TO BE QUICK, THE NEW THIRD ESTATE IN ALGERIA

This same democratic demand, as in fact the Appeal for civil peace, can only come, from our side as well as from those with whom we claim solidarity, from those active

---

2. *Translator's note:* This translates "*laïcité*," a word which summons a long-standing French tradition of *engaged* religious non-alignment best illustrated in the 1905 law separating church and state.

forces in the Algerian people who do not feel represented in the parties or structures engaged on either side of a non-democratic front. Hope can come only from these live places, these places of life, I mean, from an Algerian society which feels no more represented in a certain political state (which is also a state of fact) than in organizations that struggle against it through killing or the threat of murder, through execution in general. I say *execution in general*, for if we must not delude ourselves about the notion of violence, and about the fact that violence begins very early and spreads very far, sometimes in the least physical, the least visible, and the most legal forms of language, then our Appeal, at least as I interpret it, still positions itself *unconditionally* in terms of a limit to violence, i.e., the death penalty, torture, and murder. The logic of this Appeal thus requires the unflinching condemnation of the death penalty no less than of torture, of murder or the threat of murder. What I call with a more or less appropriate name the new Third Estate, is what everywhere carries our hope because it is what says no to death, to torture, to execution, and to murder. Our hope today is not only the one we share with all the friends of Algeria throughout the world. It is first and foremost carried, often in a heroic, admirable, exemplary fashion, by the Algerian man and woman who, in his or her country, has no right to speak, is killed or risks his or her life because he or SHE speaks freely, he or SHE thinks freely, he or SHE publishes freely, he or SHE associates freely. I say the Algerian man or woman, insisting, for I believe more than ever in the enlightened role, in the enlightening role which women can have, I believe in the clarity of their strength (which I hope tomorrow will be like a wave, crashing peacefully and irresistibly), I believe in the space which the women of Algeria can and must occupy in the future we call for. I believe in, I have hope for their movement: irresistibly crashing. In the houses and in the streets, in workplaces and in the institutions. (This civil war is for the most part a war of men. In many ways, not limited to Algeria, this *civil* war is also a *virile* war. It is thus also, laterally, in an unspoken repression, a mute war against women. It excludes women from the political field. I believe that today, not solely in Algeria, but there more sharply, more urgently than ever, reason and life, political reason, the life of reason and the reason to live are best carried by women; they are within the reach of Algerian women: in the houses and in the streets, in the workplaces and in all institutions.)

The anger, the suffering, the trauma, but also the resolution of these Algerian men and women, we have a thousand signs of them. It is necessary to see these signs, they are directed at us too, and to salute this courage—with respect. Our Appeal should be made first *in their name*, and I believe that even before being addressed to them, it comes from these men, it comes from these women, whom we also have to hear.

This is at least what I feel resonating, from the bottom of what remains Algerian in me, in my ears, my head, and my heart.

Translated by Boris Belay

7

A Note on "A Silkworm of One's Own"

"Wouldn't the apocalyptic be a transcendental condition of all discourse, of all experience even, of every mark or every trace? And the genre of writings called apocalyptic in the strict sense, then, would be only an example, an *exemplary* revelation of this transcendental structure. In that case, if the apocalypse reveals, it is first of all the revelation of the apocalypse. . . ." From the questions raised here in "Of an Apocalyptic Tone," Derrida's momentous reflections and reinscriptions of the notion of revelation have been constant (see also "How to Avoid Speaking," *Politics of Friendship*, and "Faith and Knowledge"). "A Silkworm of One's Own" constitutes a high point in these reflections, which encompass apocalypse, revelation, *Offenbarung* and *Offenbarkeit*. "A Silkworm of One's Own" is also one of Derrida's most extended discussions of an artifact of Jewish ritual—here the prayer shawl (Heb. *tallith*) as it is deployed in daily practices and legal discussions. As such, it continues to interrogate the relation and the limit between life and work with the peculiar inflections added to these terms by "religion." As this text demonstrates, revelation is another site of a thinking at the limit and of the limit, a thinking of separation.

If a dissociation of the theological from the political is, in fact, what is still called for, what remains to come (something which means refiguring the history of the West as still remote from such "to-come," such *avenir*), it is because the very notion of dissociation and separation remains wanting. How does one cross ("for it will be a crossing") the veil of separation that separates from nothing? "For that, with that in view, you have to wait for the Messiah as for the imminence of a verdict which unveils nothing consistent, which tears no veil." This is the impossible, of course: "you want to have finished with the veil, and no doubt you will finish, but without having finished with it. To have finished with oneself, that's the veil. . . . Just where you have finished with it, it will survive you, always." There is a history of separation, as there is a history of confession, and a history of knowledge (*savoir*, a word that receives a manifold of reinscriptions in the extended and continuing dialogue that takes place here and elsewhere between Hélène Cixous and Derrida).

But insofar as there is also that which "has nothing to do with revelation or unveiling," a different order of truth in all its figures, separation, "the veil" may be revealed as history "itself." At the same time, what then appears without being revealed, without revelation, is another history.

Is the tallith, the Jewish prayer shawl, Derrida's "own" prayer shawl, different from the veil? Can it be considered to have another history, one that could be considered as separate from the veil? But what would separate the tallith and the veil? It is this separation otherwise, the way in which the tallith is "unlike a veil" ("at least this is what I would like to teach or say in myself"), that Derrida offers in this text. "The difference of the event," not a veil, is what separates "the logic or topic of the veil from those of the shawl, that shawl called tallith." This event is what Derrida calls here "verdict," no longer "the revelation of a truth, a verdict without truth," but also the saying of a worm (*ver*)—"But I am a worm, and not human" (Psalms 22:6)—a worm of one's own.

G. A.

A SILKWORM OF ONE'S OWN

(Points of View Stitched on the Other Veil)[1]

Sero te amavi.

ON THE WAY TO BUENOS AIRES,
24–28 NOVEMBER 1995

1. —Before the verdict, my verdict, before, befalling me, it drags me down with it in its fall, before it's too late, stop writing. Full stop, period. Before it's too late, go off to the ends of the earth like a mortally wounded animal. Fasting, retreat, departure, as far as possible, lock oneself away with oneself in oneself, try finally to understand oneself, alone and oneself. Stop writing here, but instead from afar defy a weaving, yes, from afar, or rather see to its diminution. Childhood memory: raising their eyes from their woollen threads, but without stopping or even slowing the movement of their agile fingers, the women of my family used to say, sometimes, I think, that they had to *diminish*. Not undo, I guess, but *diminish*, i.e., though I had no idea what the word meant then but I was all the more intrigued by it, even in love with it, that they needed to *diminish* the stitches or reduce the knit of what they

---

1. [*Translator's note:*] The title and subtitle of the piece already introduce a number of more or less untranslatable motifs which will run throughout the text. The title, *Un ver à soie* literally means "A silkworm," but the play on *soi*, "oneself," is important (as in *Une chambre à soi*, A Room of One's Own). The subtitle, *Points de vue piqués sur l'autre voile*, is more difficult. *Points de vue* more or less corresponds to the English "Points of View," but "points" is also the term for a stitch, and, aurally, runs into *point de vue* where the "point" can be mildly old-fashioned intensifier of *pas*, not—given the developments to come in the text, *point de vue* could reasonably be taken as "no view at all"; *piquer* here most obviously means to stitch, but carries an overtone of its colloquial meaning to steal, to pinch; and *voile* could here be either masculine (veil), or feminine (sail). In this context, the frequent use of *voilà*, "there," "see" (from *vois là*, "see there," but homophonous with *voile à . . .* , "[a] veil on") has seemed worth signalling by keeping the word in French. To the translator's relief and despair, some of these possibilities and difficulties are later explicitly discussed in the text, along with their untranslatability.

were working on. And for this *diminution*, needles and hands had to work with two loops at once, or at least play with more than one.

—Which has nothing to do, if I understand aright, with the mastery of a Royal Weaver or with Penelope's ruse, with the *metis* of weaving-unweaving. Not even a question of pretending, as she did one day, to be weaving a shroud by saving the lost threads [*les fils perdus*: the lost sons], thus preparing a winding sheet for Laertes, King of Ithaca and father of Odysseus, for the very one that Athena rejuvenated by a miracle. Don't lose the thread, that's the injunction that Penelope was pretending to follow, but also pretence or fiction, ruse ("I should be grateful to you young lords who are courting me, now that King Odysseus is dead, if you could restrain your ardour for my hand till I have done this work, so that the threads I have spun may not be utterly wasted. It is a winding-sheet for Lord Laertes. When he succumbs to the dread hand of Death that stretches all men out at last, I must not risk the scandal there would be among my countrywomen here if one who had amassed such wealth were put to rest without a shroud")[2]).

Whereas in *diminution*, if I understand aright, the work is not undone ...

—No, nothing is undone, on the contrary, but I would also like, in my own way, to name the shroud, and the voyage, but a voyage without return, without a circle or journey round the world in any case, or, if you prefer, a return to life that's not a resurrection, neither the first nor the second, with and without the grand masters of discourse about the Resurrection, Saint Paul or Saint Augustine ...

—My God, so that's all your new work is, is it, neither an Odyssey nor a Testament ...

—No, just the opposite, it *is*: I'd like to call them to the witness-stand, knowing that what they say will always be bigger than the tapestry I'll be trying to sew them into, while pretending to cross through them—for it will be a crossing. And as we're starting to talk in the plane, let's call that crossing a flight and that tapestry a flying carpet. We're just leaving the West to lose our Orient-ation.

—Talking music, you can, *decrescendo, diminuendo*, attenuate little by little the intensity of the sound, but also "diminish" the intervals. Whilst in the language of rhetoric, a little like litotes, like extenuation or reticence, a "diminution" consists in saying less, sure, but with a view to *letting* more be understood.

—But "letting" thus—and who lets what, who lets who, be understood?—one can always speak of diminution *by diminution*. And, by this henceforth uncatchable stitching, still let rhetoric appropriate the truth of the verdict. A trope would still in

---

2. [*Translator's note:*] *Odyssey*, II, 96–104, tr. E. V. Rieu (Harmondsworth, Middlesex, England: Penguin, 1946), pp. 39–40. Penelope's speech here is in fact being reported to the Assembly at Ithaca by Antinous, the leader of the Suitors.

this case be coming to dictate to it the true-say of its *veridictum*, of this verdict which seems to have been at the beginning, like your first word. By virtue of this strange verdict, without truth, without veracity, without veridicity, one would never again reach the thing itself, one would above all never touch it. Wouldn't even touch the veil behind which a thing is supposed to be standing, not even the veil before which we sigh together, before which we are together sighing. For the same cause, a common cause. Ah, how tired we are, how I would like finally to touch "veil," the word and the thing thus named, the thing itself and the vocable! I would like not only to see them, see in them, towards them or through them, the word and the thing, but maintain a discourse about them which would, finally, touch, in short a "relevant" discourse which would say them properly, even if it no longer gives anything to be seen.

—We'll have to give up touching as much as seeing, and even saying. Interminable diminution. For you must know right now: to touch "that" which one calls "veil" is to touch everything. You'll leave nothing intact, safe and sound, neither in your culture, nor in your memory, nor in your language, as soon as you take on the word "veil." As soon as you let yourself be caught up in it, in the word, first of all the French word, to say nothing yet about the thing, nothing will remain, nothing will remain any more.

—We'll soon see how to undo or rather diminish. Diminish the infinite, diminish *ad infinitum*, why not? That's the task or the temptation, the dream, since ever. You're dreaming of taking on a braid or a weave, a warp or a woof, but without being sure of the textile to come, if there is one, if any remains and without knowing if what remains to come will still deserve the name of text, especially of the text in the figure of a textile. But you insist on writing to it, doing without undoing, from afar, yes, from afar, like before life, like after life, on writing to it from a lower corner of the map, right at the bottom of the world, in sight of *Tierra del Fuego*, in the Magellan strait, in memory of the caravels. In memory of him for whom everything turned out so badly, once he'd gone through the strait. Poor Magellan, you can say that again. Because I can still see those caravels. On writing to him from afar *as if*, caught in the sails and pushed towards the unknown, at the point of this extremity, *as if* someone were waiting for the new Messiah, i.e., a "happy event": nicknamed the verdict. Unbeknownst to everything and everyone, without knowing or being sure of anything. The infinite finite time of a trial which consists less in waiting for this or that verdict than in the straits of an implacable suspicion: and what if you were imposing the duration of this trial on yourself so as not to want what you know you want or to want what you believe you no longer want, i.e. the due date of such and such a verdict, that one and no other? Not with a view to not wanting what you want but because you no longer want your wanting, whence the interminable imminence of the verdict?

—Yes, but the due date of a verdict which will therefore no longer be the revelation of a truth, a verdict without truth, as we were saying, without veracity or veridicity, yes but a date which is no longer caught up in the fold or unfolding of a veil. Quite differently, still earlier, or later, I see him waiting for an event of quasi-resurrection which, for once, therefore in view of a first and last time, would have nothing to do with an unveiling, nothing to do with what they call a truth, with the dictation of a truth, if you're fixed on that, or with an unburying. What would *as if* mean from the moment—a revolutionary or messianic moment—when I was determining the *as if* on the basis of exemplary phrases such as 'it's as if I were alive' or 'it's as if I were dead'? What would "as if" mean then, I ask. To whom would I ever dare address such phrases? Now, in order to start a diminution *ad infinitum*, you'd have to write him from the very distant place of this *as if*. For that, with that in view, you have to wait for the Messiah as for the imminence of a verdict which unveils nothing consistent, which tears no veil.

—You poor thing, you poor thing: finishing with the veil will always have been the very movement of the veil: un-veiling, unveiling oneself, reaffirming the veil in unveiling. It finishes with itself in unveiling, does the veil, and always with a view to finishing off in self-unveiling. Finishing with the veil is finishing with self. Is that what you're hoping for from the verdict?

—Perhaps, no doubt. I fear so, I hope so.

—There's no chance of that ever happening, of belonging to oneself enough (in some *s'avoir*,[3] if you want to play) and of succeeding in turning such a gesture towards oneself. You'll end up in imminence—and the un-veiling will still remain a movement of the veil. Does not this movement always consist, in its very consistency, in its texture, in finishing itself off, lifting itself, disappearing, drawing itself aside to let something be seen or to let it be, to *let*?

—Yes and no. A signature, if it happens, will have pushed that destiny off course. Of course, we have always to remember the other veil, but by forgetting it, where you're expecting something else again, preparing yourself for a form of event without precedent, without eve, and keep vigil for the coming of the "without eve." vigil over it, see to it that it surprises you. Of course you will not forget that the Temple veil was torn on the death of the Messiah, the other one, the ancestor from Bethlehem, the one of the first or second resurrection, the true-false Messiah who heals the blind and presents himself saying "I am the truth and the life," the very one in whose name the christophelical caravels discovered America and everything that followed, the good and the worst. At the moment of his death, the Temple veil is supposed to have torn . . .

---

3. [*Translator's note:*] *Savoir*, to know, *S'avoir*, to have or possess oneself.

—Shall we say that in tearing thus the veil revealed at last what it ought to hide, shelter, protect? Must we understand that it tore, simply, as if the tearing finally signed the end of the veil or of veiling, a sort of truth laid bare? Or rather that it was torn in two, as Matthew and Mark say, down the middle says Luke, which maybe gives two equal veils at the moment when, as the sun goes black, everything becomes invisible?[4] Now this veil, remember, was one of the two veils of Exodus,[5] no doubt the first, made of blue and purple and scarlet, a veil made of "fine-twined" or "twisted" linen. Inside it was prescribed to install the ark of the testimony. This veil will be for you, says Yahve to Moses, the *separation* between the holy and the most holy, between the tabernacle and the tabernacle of tabernacles.[6] The

---

4. "Kai idou to katapetasma tou naou eskhisthe [ap'] anothen eos kato eis duo . . . Et ecce velum templi scissum est in duas partes a summo usque desorsum." (Matthew, 27:51); "tout heliou eklipontos . . . eskhisthe de to katapetasma tou naou meson . . . Et obscuratus est sol; et velum templi scissum est medium . . . " (Luke, 23:45); "Kai to katapetasma tou naou eskhisthe eis duo ap'anothen eos kato . . . Et velum templi scissum est in duo, a summo usque deorsum" (Mark, 25:38).

5. Exodus, 26:31.

6. We would need to cite more than one translation. Some oppose the veil to the curtain (A. Chouraqui, *Noms*, Desclée de Brouwer; Louis Segond, Nouvelle édition de Genève, 1979, Société biblique de Genève), the other distinguishes curtain (instead of veil) from drape (E. Dhormes, in the Bibliothèque de la Pléiade). [The Authorised translation has "vail" and "hanging"; the New Revised version has "curtain" and "screen." —tr.] In the case of the first veil or first curtain, we're dealing with the work of an artist or an inventor; the second (curtain or drape) is merely the work of an embroiderer: "work of embroidery," "embroiderer's work." The difference appears to be clearly made [though perhaps less so in the English translations: the Authorised version is less clear: "And thou shalt make a vail of blue, and purple, and scarlet, and fine twined linen of cunning work: with cherubims shall it be made" (XXVI, 31); "And thou shalt make an hanging of the door of the tent, of blue, and purple, and scarlet, with fine twined linen, wrought with needlework" (XXVI, 36). The New Revised Edition has "You shall make a curtain of blue, purple, and crimson yarns, and of fine, twisted linen; it shall be made with cherubim skillfully worked into it" (XXVI, 31); "You shall make a screen for the entrance of the tent, of blue, purple, and crimson yarns, and of fine twisted linen, embroidered with needle-work." (XXVI, 36). On the one hand, art and inaugural invention, on the other, a secondary know-how or technique. Two examples (italics mine [I have translated these French translations as literally as is feasible —tr.]):

> Make a veil: / azure, purple, scarlet cochenille, / byssus twist, / it will be an inventor's work: griffons./ You will give it on four acacia columns, / covered with gold, their hooks of gold, / on four silver plinths. Give the veil, under the hooks, have come there, inside the veil, / the ark of testimony. And the veil will distinguish for you / between the sanctuary and the sanctuary of sanctuaries, / Give the veil on the ark of testimony, / in the sanctuary of sanctuaries. / Place the table outside the veil, / and the candelabrum opposite the table, / on the wall of the dwelling, towards the South. Give the table on the wall to the North. / Make a curtain for the opening of the tent: / azure, purple, scarlet cochenille, / byssus twist, / embroiderer's work . . . (Chouraqui: in a later edition, in 1985, the translation is substantially modified: "veil" is replaced now by "screen," now by "absolutory," "inventor" by "weaver.")

> You will also make the Curtain of violet purple and red purple, of scarlet vermilion and fine linen twist. It will be made [ornamented] with Cherubim, artist's work. / You will place it on four acacia columns covered with gold, with golden hooks on four silver bases. You will place the Curtain under the hooks and there, within the Curtain, you will place the Ark of the Testimony. The Curtain will be for you the separation between the Holy and the Holy of Holies. / You will place the Propitiatory on the Ark of the testimony in the Holy of Holies. / You will put the Table outside the Curtain and the Candelabrum opposite the Table on the side of the Dwelling to the South; you will place the Table on the north side. / Then you will make a Drape at the entry of the Tent, of violet purple and red purple, in crimson vermilion and fine linen twist, embroiderer's work. (Dhormes)

veil tearing down the middle, is that the end of such a separation, of that isolation, that unbelievable solitude of belief?

—I know of no other separation in the world, or which would be commensurable with that one, analogous, comparable to that one which allows us to think nonetheless every other separation, and first of all the separation which separates from the wholly other. Thanks to a veil given by God, and giving here is ordering [*donner c'est ici ordonner*]. Whether or not this unbelievable separation (belief itself, faith) came to an end with the death of Christ, will it ever be comprehended, will it ever be comprehensible in the veiled folds of a Greek *aletheia*? No being, no present, no presentation can here be indicated in the indicative. It was, is, shall be, shall have been, should have been for all time the sentence, the saying of God, his verdict: by God *order (is) given to give* the veil, the veil (is) the gift (that it is) ordered to give. Nothing else that is. God would thus be the name of what gives the order to give the veil, the veil between the holy and the holy of holies. Now "God," the name of God, distinguishes between the artist or inventor of the veil, on the one hand, and the embroiderer on the other. Both are men, if I have understood aright, human beings, and men rather than women. But they do not work in the same fashion. Their fashion is different. Like their manner, their hands, their handwork and the place of their work: inside, within the secret for the artist or the inventor, and almost outside, at the entrance or the opening of the tent for the embroiderer, who remains on the threshold. And that in view of which they work in this way: veil, curtain, drape, is nothing less than the dwelling of God, his dwelling, his *ethos*, his being-there, his sojourn, his halt to come: "For me they shall make a sanctuary. I shall dwell in their bosom."[7] He who lives there, in this *ethos*, and this Who is also a What, like a Third Party, is the Law, the text of the law.

—Here, in this very place where we are . . .

— . . . where we're taking ourselves . . .

— . . . where we are going, do I understand aright, it would be something else, even if the concern remained still to distinguish between the holy and the holy of holies. Will you ever give up on this concern? This concern that Hegel in the tradition of a Pompey he understood so well, will never really have accepted, concerned as he was to distinguish between the secret of the Jews and the mystery of the Gods of Eleusis.[8] Thinking this concern meant also traversing it, transfixing it with truth,

---

7. Tr. A. Chouraqui. "And they will make me a sanctuary and I shall dwell in the midst of them" (Dhormes). "They will make me a sanctuary, and I shall live in their midst."

8. [Editor's note by René Major for the French publication of this text in *Le contretemps*, 2 (1997)] The consequence of this is analysed in *Glas* (Galilée, 1974 [tr. John P. Leavey, Jr. and Richard Rand, University of Nebraska Press, 1986]), for example around the following passage:

going towards something else and ending up forgetting it. An absolute knowledge [*savoir*] will never accept this unique separation, that in the veiled place of the Wholly Other, nothing should present itself, that there be Nothing there that is, nothing that is present, nothing that is in the present.

—Truth, if we need it and if you still care, still seems to wait. In sericulture before the verdict, *another figure* . . .

—Sericulture, you mean the culture of silk?

—Patience, yes, the culture of the silkworm, and the quite incomparable patience it demands from a *magnanier*, the sericultivator. Where we're going, before the verdict falls, then, at the end of this time that is like no other, nor even like the end of time, another figure perhaps upsets the whole of history from top to bottom, and upsets even the meaning of the word "history" neither a history of a veil, a veil to be lifted or torn, nor the Thing, nor the Phallus nor Death, of course, which would suddenly show itself at the last *coup de théâtre*, at the instant of a revelation or an unveiling, nor a theorem wrapped up in shroud or in modesty, neither *aletheia*, nor *homoiosis*, nor *adequatio*, nor *Enthüllung*, nor *Unverborgenheit*, nor *Erschlossenheit*, nor *Entdecktheit* nor *Übereinstimmung*, nor modesty, halt or reticence of *Verhaltenheit*, but another unfigurable figure, beyond any holy shroud, the secret of a face which is no longer even a face if face tells of vision and a story of the eye. Wait without horizon, then, and someone else one knows too well, me for example, why not, but come back from so far, from so low, quick or dead, wait for the other who comes, who comes to strike dumb the order of knowledge: neither known nor unknown, too well-known but a stranger from head to foot, yet to be born. It will be

---

But this place and this figure have a singular structure: the structure encloses its void within itself, shelters only its own interiorised desert. It opens onto nothing, encloses nothing, contains as its treasure only nothingness: a hole an empty spacing, a death. A death or a dead man, because according to Hegel space is death and because this space is also one of absolute vacuity. Nothing behind the curtains. Hence the ingenuous surprise of the non-Jew when he opens, when he is allowed to open or when he violates the tabernacle, when he enters the dwelling or the temple and after so many ritual detours to reach the secret centre, he discovers nothing—only nothingness.

No centre, no heart, an empty space, nothing.

You undo the bands, move the cloths, pull back the veils, part the curtains: nothing but a black hole or a deep gaze, colourless, formless and lifeless. This is the experience of the powerful Pompey at the end of his avid exploration: 'If no form (*Gestalt*) was offered to sensibility (*Empfindung*), meditation and adoration of an invisible object had at least to be given a direction (*Richtung*) and a delimitation (*Umgrenzung*) enclosing that object—Moses gave them this in the form of the Holy of Holies of the Tabernacle, and subsequently the temple. Pompey was surprised when he got into the most inner place of the Temple, the centre (*Mittelpunkt*) of adoration and there, at the root of the national spirit, in the hope of recognising the living soul of this exceptional people at its centre and perceiving a being [an essence, *Wesen*] offered to his meditation, something full of meaning (*Sinvolles*) offered to his respect, and when entering the secret [the familiar and secret intimacy, *Geheimnis*] before the ultimate spectacle he felt himself mystified (*getäuscht*) and found what he was looking for in an empty space (*in einem leeren Raume*) (p. 60 [pp. 49–50; tr. mod.]).

the end of history in this sense. Verdict: end of the end of history, everything is going to start again, and with no shroud we would know what to do with. More or less than—diminished. Enough heritage, dream your caravel, unless a heritage is still looming and expected at this instant, at this point of verdict.

—You don't believe in it yourself. I'm warning you, you won't escape, even if the verdict is favourable, i.e., negative. At least as for what you will be too quick to nickname "aporia," that is, that, well, in any case the veil lifts. *It's either or*. Either the veil remains a veil, therefore destined to lift, thus following its own movement (and tearing basically changes nothing here), or else you want to undo yourself from it without undoing it, as you've been claiming for a moment, in which case it still lifts or removes itself, you allow it to sublate itself [*se relever*], intact or torn, which comes to the same thing. Two liftings, then, the one no longer belonging to the other but because it belongs to the other, by belonging to the other. *L'une se garde de l'autre*.[9] The one toward the other. With a view to the other. Will you be able to interrupt it? You want to have finished with the veil, and no doubt you will finish, but without having finished with it. To have finished with oneself, that's the veil. That's it, just that, itself in oneself. Just where you have finished with it, it will survive you, always. That's why, far from being one veil among others, example or sample, a shroud sums up the essence of the veil. So you haven't stopped trembling since your departure for the other side of the world. You're not trembling because of leaving, but at what is waiting for you on your return . . .

—No, because the point is that it is no longer me in question, but what we're here calling the verdict. A still unknown verdict for an indeterminable fault, all the perjuries in the world, blasphemies, profanations, sacrileges, there have been so many. In any case, as for me, I'm lost. But I'd still like it to happen to me and cause my downfall *thus* and not otherwise. Because I feel that the time of this verdict, if it could finally open up a new era, is so paradoxical, twisted, tortuous, against the rhythm, that it could mime the quasi-resurrection of the new year only by sealing forever the "so late, too late," in what will not even be a late conversion. A "so late, too late, *sero*" (life will have been so short), a delay I am complaining about, feeling sorry for myself while complaining about it [*me plaignant moi-même en me plaignant de lui*], accusing, *Klagen, Anklagen*. But to whom do I make this complaint?

---

9. [*Translator's note:*] *Deux relèves, donc, l'une ne relevant plus de l'autre mais* parce *qu'elle relève de l'autre, pour* relever de l'autre. L'une se garde de l'autre. The first sentence plays across the noun *relève*, proposed by Derrida to translate Hegel's *Aufhebung*, and the verb *relever de*, to belong to, to be a matter for, to come under. The formula *L'une se garde de l'autre*, used by Derrida in, for example, *Mal d'archive* (Paris: Galilée, 1995), 124–25, condenses *se garder de quelque chose*, to beware of something, to steer clear of something, to protect oneself against something, here the other, and *se garder quelque chose* (with the *de l'* now becoming a partitive article), to keep something for oneself, here to keep some other for oneself. "The one keeps the other (off)," perhaps. Here the feminine *l'une* refers to the *relève* mentioned earlier.

Would it suffice to be able to reply to this question for the complaint immediately to have no further *raison d'être*? Is it to God? Was it even to Christ that my poor old incorrigible Augustine finally addressed his "too late," "so late" when he was speaking to beauty, *sero te amavi, pulchritudo tam antiqua et tam nova . . . ?* "So late have I loved thee, beauty so ancient and so new," or rather, because it is *already* late, "Late *will I* have loved thee . . . " A future perfect is wrapped up in the past, once "late" means (as it always does, it's a tautology) "so late" and "too late." There is no lateness in nature—neither in the thing itself, nor in the same in general. "Late" is already said in the comparative, or even the absolute superlative, "late" always means "later than . . . " or "too late, absolutely." Before and earlier than objective time, before all metrical knowledge about it, before and rather than *noting* the chronology of whatever it may be, "late" evaluates, desires, regrets, accuses, complains—and sighs for the verdict, so late, very late, late, quite simply (*ateknôs*), always comes the time for loving. You were with me and I was not with you:

Sero te amavi, pulchritudo tam antiqua et tam nova,
sero te amavi! et ecce intus eras et ego foris et ibi te
quaerebam et in ista formosa, quae fecisti, deformis
inruebam, mecum eras, et tecum non eram.[10]

You were with me and I was not with you.

Will we still recount an eye-operation as a story of veils? I know Hélène Cixous, I have known her, note the improbable tense of that verb,[11] for more than thirty-three years, but since ever without knowing [*savoir*]. I have known her forever without ever knowing what she *confides* here in *Savoir*, i.e.,—and this would be, feeble hypothesis, today's revelation,[12] the revolution of an avowal at last disarmed—that she could not see: all this time she will have been short-sighted, in truth almost blind. Blind to the naked eye up to the day she had an operation—yesterday. The day before, she was still blind to the naked eye, I mean blind when she was not wearing her lenses, her own proper lenses, appropriate lenses or "contact lenses," an expression I like to hear in English, in memory of a certain *Conversation in the Mountains*.[13] What Hélène Cixous has just confided here, she also *confesses* it,

---

10. *Confessions*, X, xxvii, 38.
11. [*Translator's note:*] More improbable in French: *Je connais H.C.*, "I know H. C.", but the present tense is maintained in *Je connais H. C. depuis 33 ans*, "I have known H. C. for 33 years."
12. [*Translator's note:*] *La révélation du jour*, also "The revelation of the (day)light."
13. For at least three reasons. (1) Because of the name *Lenz*, of course. Celan has it appear right at the start of *Gespräch im Gebirg*, "For the Jew, you know this well, what does he own that is really his, that is not lent, borrowed, never returned, went off then and came along, came from yonder on the road, the beautiful, incomparable road, went off, like Lenz, through the mountains, they'd let him live down

no doubt, and therefore *avows* it. But, first virtue in the abyss of such a *Savoir*, the fault she avows was already an avowal, a "position of avowal" in which she (she who almost never says "I" for herself) had lived until then, and lived without seeing, and especially without knowing that one day, thanks to an unforeseeable piece of eye-surgery, she would see, she would see without yet knowing what she would see and what seeing would mean. Others would judge that through this avowal, this avowal of avowal at the moment of seeing, she lifts the veil on a myopia which was both a fault and a veil: "Myopia was her fault, her lead;[14] her imperceptible native veil."

—How can a veil hold one on a lead? What does *laisse* mean when we're talking about a veil?

—*Voilà* the whole question, every word counts. It holds, touches, pulls, like a lead, it affects and sometimes tears the skin, it wounds, it penetrates under the epidermic surface, which a veil never does when it suffices to veil one's gaze. *Savoir* could be read as a poem of touch,[15] it sings sight like a touch "without intermediary, without non-contact lenses":

> The continuity of her flesh and the world's flesh, touch then, was love, and that was the miracle, giving. Ah! She hadn't realised the day before that eyes are miraculous hands, had never enjoyed the delicate tact of the cornea, the eyelashes, the most powerful hands, these hands that touch imponderably near and far-off heres. She had not realised that eyes are lips on the lips of God.

Reminding us that blindness placed her in a "position of avowal," and that "she was the first to accuse herself," there she goes [*la voilà*] avowing the avowal. She

---

below, where by force he belongs, in the depths, he, the Jew, went off and went off (French translation by J. E. Jackson and A. du Bouchet, in *Strette* [Paris: Mercure de France, 1971], p. 171). (2) Then because of the name *Klein*, another proper name immediately renamed by Celan and which was also that of Hélène Cixous's mother or grandfather. As if the name of Paul Celan had met the name of Hélène Cixous, following the poetic necessity of a time I do believe to be incontestable: "To meet him [i.e., Lenz] came his cousin [...] to meet the other, Gross came with Klein, and Klein, the Jew, made his stick silent before the stick of the Jew Gross. (3) Finally and above all, this story of cousins german (*Geschwisterkinder*) is told also as a story of eyes, of weaving and of veils: "But they, cousins german, may the complaint reach back to God [*Gott sei's geklagt*], have no eyes [*keine Augen*]. Not, in truth, that they do not possess eyes, but in front there hangs a veil, not in front, no, behind, a moving veil [*ein beweglicher Schleier*]; scarcely has an image burst in than it remains suspended in the web [*im Geweb*], and a thread [*ein Faden*] is already in place, which weaves itself there [*der sich da spinnt*], around spins itself around the image, a veil thread [*ein Schleierfaden*]; itself weaves itself around, round the image, makes a child with it, half image and half veil [*halb Bild und halb Schleier*]" (ibid., p. 172).

14. [*Translator's note:*] *Sa laisse*, her leash, but picking up the earlier play on the verb *laisser*, to let, to allow, and introducing the following development.

15. "Technics," the surgery of our time, my chances and my friends. None of this could have happened, happened to them or happened to me, only ten years ago. If Hélène Cixous got her sight back, I was able to dedicate to Jean-Luc Nancy, who inherited another heart, a *text*, *Touch*, still unpublished in French (tr. Peggy Kamuf in *Paragraph*, 16, no. 2 [1993], 122–57). [See now *Le Toucher, Jean-Luc Nancy* (Paris: Galilée, 2000).]

repents of the past avowal as though it were a first fault. In the experience of blind-ness, avowal was part of the game. It formed part, a first part, a first act, of her blindness. The avowal itself was the fault, *voilà* the sentence, *voilà* the judgment, another verdict, and one miraculously contemporaneous with the one awaiting me, the sentence [*l'arrêt*] of a text which thereby turns out to be the most innocent, but also the most cleverly calculated: infinite knowing which carries itself off in an operation, knowing which knows how to lose itself although it remains infinitely calculated from its title on, *Savoir*, and calculated not to play on its force or to show it, but with a view to outplaying it in what it offers.

—I am indeed playing in my turn with the letters or even the syllables of this title, *Savoir*. In a word as in so many words, and some of them appear to be visible, others audible, in a skein of shards of words of all sorts, a noun, *le savoir*, a verb in the infinitive, *savoir*, a (demonstrative) pronoun, *ça*, a (possessive) adjective, *sa*, punctuation marks, invisible homonyms and apostrophes, *S'avoir*, all that becomes here, only here, in the sentences of this text here, the unique body of an unheard-of word, more or less than a word the grammar of a syntagm in expansion. A sentence in suspense which flaps its wings at birth, like the silk-worm butterfly, above the cocoon, i.e. the poem. From that height, the mobile of a bewinged signature thus illuminates the body of the text . . .

—a bit like the lamp of a hovering helicopter, immobile and throbbing, the fly-ing spotlamp looking down, one-eyed lamp watching over the verdict to come . . .

— . . . right on the body of the text without which it would be nothing, not even born. The body of the text, the irreplaceable poem entitled *Savoir* . . .

—Why "irreplaceable"? Must one give in to praise in this way, as a law of the genre?

—No, nothing is more foreign to my concern than praise, just when I am talk-ing from so far away, and evaluation. No, this irreplaceability depends on its poetic act, of course, but specifically where it allows itself also to be ruled, held back, never letting itself let go, by the lead of a referent, an event, the *operation*, which precisely no longer depended on her (she was operated, not operating, in it), a sort of acci-dent, and such a dangerous one, which took place for her alone and once only. The instant of this irreplaceable operation, hers, this time, the poetic one, will in return have cut into language with a laser. That instant will have moved, burned, wetted, then cut up the old-new French language, the well-beloved language whose inheri-tors we are, but also the thieves, the usurpers, the spies, the secret agents, the colonised-colonisers, the artisans, the obscure weavers, deep in their shop, for it owes everything to us, does frenchlanguage, she to whom we owe even more at the moment we get into it, i.e.,[*à savoir*] . . .

—Her avowal of avowal gives us food for reading. Food for thought, suddenly, or for dreaming something that's obvious: this pre-operatory vigilance is what will have borne an immense poetic corpus, which I thought I knew and which I persist in thinking has not yet been read: not [*point*] recognized in this century, ill-known especially in this country for reasons which, if brought out, would reveal everything that, in this century and especially in this country, *is forbidden*. Before this avowal of avowal, my blind friend had hidden from me that very thing, that she could not see [*point*], not without glass or lens, the one I hold (and it doesn't date from today) for the most far-seeing among the poets, the one in whom I read foreseeing thought, prophesy in language, in more than one language within the frenchlanguage. Where we know, that's our secret, what it can mean to lose one's Latin.[16] She had not told me the secret of her every day, and nor had I seen it, or seen it coming. And yet what she declares today has nothing to do with revelation or unveiling. This event belongs to a quite different space, it comes following a different order, that order under which falls too what I am calling the *verdict*. It is neither a torn cloth, nor a lifted curtain nor a split veil . . .

—But would you dare claim that it is not still hung between the holy and the holy of holies?

—Who knows? Perhaps we have to dare, indeed. As for the verdict thus suspended, what we ought to risk will always depend on a "perhaps." The fulgurating newness of this day depends, or tends. Towards who or what I know not yet. But it tends and depends on what no doubt I knew without knowing. I was expecting it without knowing: so without expecting, some will say. Yes, a bit like in the strait-time that separates me from this verdict, the expected, feared, hoped-for verdict at the end of the trip to Latin America, on my return from Buenos Aires, Santiago de Chile and São Paulo. Where one knows nothing of the future of what is coming, before the throw of the dice or rather the shot fired at the temple in Russian roulette. So, what? Who does this re-commencement without precedent look like if still it expects a return? But "resurrection" is not the right word. Neither the first nor the second resurrection Saints Paul and Augustine talk to me about.

—**Too obvious, that's my age, true enough:** know enough, more than enough, it's obvious, about the truth you're so attached to, the truth as a history of veils. What fatigue. Exhaustion. Proofs tire truth, as Braque said, more or less. That's why I've gone so far to wait for the verdict, to the tropics. From Saint James [Santiago] to Saint Paul [São Paulo]. Maybe with a view not to return. But "fatigue" still doesn't mean anything in this case. Like the "as if" just now. You still don't know the "fatigue" I'm talking about. The exhaustion of this fatigue will gain its meaning, tomorrow, perhaps, from the truth that engenders it and when one has understood

---

16. [*Translator's note:*] *Perdre son latin*, not to be able to make head nor tail of something.

what it means, for someone like me, at the moment when he is dreaming of writing it in Spanish, one of his forgotten ancestral languages, from the bottom of the map of the world, **what to be fatigued, yes, fatigued of the truth,** *voilà,* fatigued like truth, exhausted from knowing it, for too long, that history of the veil, and all the folds [*plis*], explications, complications, explicitations of its revelations or unveilings. If you only knew how fatigued I feel at these revelations and unveilings, how many I have to put up with, how badly I put up with them when they have to do not only with opening onto this or that but onto the veil itself, a veil beneath the veil, like the thing itself to be unburied. It's too old for me, you see, too old like me, that truth. For my old age is measured by the age of that veil, however young I remain, and green and naive. I am weary, weary, weary of the truth and of the truth as untruth of a being-there, a *Dasein* which is "each time in the truth and the untruth (*in der Wahrheit und Unwahrheit*),"[17] "co-originarily in truth and untruth,"[18] in uncovering and re-covering, unveiling and veiling (*Enthüllung/ Verhüllung*), dissimulation or withdrawal (*Verborgenheit*) and non-withdrawal (*Unverborgenheit*) of the opening (*Erschlossenheit*), weary of this opposition which is not an opposition, of revelation as veiling, *vice versa* (*Wahrheit/ Unwahrheit, Entdecktheit/ Verborgenheit*) as, *a fortiori* of all its supposed derivatives, such as truth as accord, concord or adequate correspondence (*Übereinstimmung*), *and so on, und so weiter. Et passim.*

You must understand me, you see, and know what it is to be weary, in this case, to be weary of a figure and its truth, of a strophe, a trope and the folds of the said truth when it plays itself out with so many veils. Infinite weariness, what do you expect, I want to end it all. Protest, attestation, testament, last will, manifesto against the shroud: I no longer want to write on the veil, do you hear, right on the veil or on the subject of the veil, around it or in its folds, under its authority or under its law, in a word neither on it nor under it. With other *Schleiermachers* of all sorts I have used and abused truth—as untruth of course, come come, *et passim,* and of revelation and unveiling as veiling, of course, in so many languages. Go and see if I'm lying.[19]

---

17. For example *Sein und Zeit,* p. 222 and passim [tr. Macquarrie and Robinson (Oxford: Blackwell, 1980), p. 265].

18. Ibid., p. 229 and passim [p. 272].

19. Complaint and accusation. *Klagen Anklagen.* I complain about myself to myself and I want, finally, to escape, that's my only excuse. Avowal, immodesty and impudence. The fatigue of exhaustion is here the thing itself. It is identical with the very thing complained about. How can one complain about the thing itself? How can one lodge [*déposer*] such a complaint and hold the fatigue of exhaustion to be such a deposit? You have to *know* the thing itself, that thing thus called (the thing *itself, meisme,* with the phantasm of possibility, the phantasm of power and possession lodged at the root, *metipse* of ipseity itself). But you have to *know,* too, and first, that the thing itself is always announced as what can stand behind the transparent, translucent or opaque veil: the thing itself *behind* the veil or the thing itself the phantasm of which is itself an effect of the veil, as much as to say enveiled *thing* as *veiled*

Fed up with veils and sails.[20] Where do I still get, and from what distance, the force and the desire to come from far behind to have finished with it and precipitate the verdict? Precipitate it without end? And precipitate imminence until the end of time? Sails [*la voilure*] will have clothed my entire history, veils and sails of every sex and gender,[21] more ample than any veiling [*voilage*] of my texts which have, however, done nothing other than try to enfold them in turn and pocket them, to put the whole history of our culture, like a pocket-handkerchief, in a pocket. But with a view to putting yet another handkerchief on top: bigger and smaller than anything, shedding tears beyond being, save—

—Save what? Save whom? You're not even leaving anyone the right to claim that "veil" still has something to hide for you, and that it will suffice for you to have done with the veil to have access to that other Thing itself, that Cause safe and intact. You'd be merely repeating the scene you're trying to look as though you're saying farewell to, making us into your witness, from so high and so far . . .

—Save that something else already really had to be at work, something else that this old so old history of veils, that tiresome, tireless, tired out history which I'm leaving behind me and which is running after me, a history which I knew, which I will have known too well how to do. Do too well, there's the fault, begin to do too well . . . [22]

—Exhaustion [*Epuisement*] that's all you can say. *Epuisement* does not only recall the water and the well [*le puits*] of truth, it brings us back to the pit, the chimney or the mine-shaft, the hole (*puteus*), i.e., if we are to believe them, to what a veil is always destined to dissimulate, in the place of the Thing itself. So it's not your *épuisement* that'll save you from the veil . . .

---

cause—of nudity, of modesty, of shame, of reticence (*Verhaltenheit*), of the law, of everything that hides and shows the sex, of the origin of culture and so-called humanity in general, in short of what links evil, radical evil, to *knowledge*, and knowledge to avowal, knowing-how-to-avow [*le savoir-avouer*] to knowledge avowed [*le savoir avoué*].

As the fatigue of exhaustion is here lodged, or lodges here its complaint against all this discourse, in truth against the matrix of this discourse, it owes it to itself to give up all modesty, to give up the most elementary politeness.

That's what allows me, in my great fatigue (great, believe me, you see), to refer to this or that of my still penelopean works those who want to see if I'm lying when I say I have already written too much on the veil, about it, thematically, inexhaustibly, and woven *right on* the veil, for example in all the texts on Heidegger, which is far from being insignificant here, in *Dissemination* (first in "Plato's Pharmacy," which begins with the *istos* or the tissue of the textile, and especially in "The Double Session," short treatise of the veil, the hymen, the wing and the eyelid, etc., and short treatise written in "ver," that is played according to the syllable, the vocable or the letters "ver," the "ver" versified or vitrified, exhibited in a glass case in all its states), in *Spurs*, stuck in the "veils of all sorts," in *Glas, La Carte postale D'un ton apocalyptique* . . . , *Mémoires d'aveugle, etc.* On what footing to make a fresh start, that's the question of this trip.

20. In English in the text.

21. See note 1 above.

22. "Commencer . . . à bien faire"; also alluding to the idiom "Ça commence à bien faire!" It's getting a bit much.

—But I'm not exhausted at all, me, myself, I'm as young as can be, as though on the eve of a resurrection that has not yet spoken its name. You still don't known me by my name. I am only tired of the veil, it is the veil which is exhausted for me, *in my place*. It has stolen my name from me. I am pretending to confess; failing to have been able to do too well what is beginning to get a bit much with veils of all sorts, as if apparently the fate of humanity, of so-called humanity supposedly born with shame, reticence, *Verhaltenheit*, nudity, evil-knowledge, the knowledge of evil, the tree of knowledge, sin, fall or *Verfallen*, therefore the veil, as though the fate of humanity was again going to depend on whoever holds power over women about the veil. And I am not just talking about an abusive interpretation of the Koran. Saint Paul had something to do with it, we'll have to talk some more about him, and what I admire most in Nietzsche is his lucidity about Paul. Save, then, I no longer know what, not yet who, but that we needed, on return from the ends of the earth and life something else, which would have an impact [*faire date*], expected at its date and singular like an absolutely unforeseeable verdict, absolutely, that is with no relation to foresight, nor therefore to sight. Life or death question, but one which is decided otherwise than by tearing, bursting, lifting, folding, unfolding anything like "veil." This coming would have to come from elsewhere, at its date, like an operation of the other, entrusted to the other, in the other's hand, contrary to prostheses, glasses, lenses and other lasers . . .

—But what place are they still taking, these old prostheses? In short, we'd have had our fill, we'd have had *enough* (*satis*, saturation, satire, etc.), if I understand aright, enough of inheriting or, what comes to the same thing, of bequeathing. As for inheriting, a single question today, I see no other: that of knowing whether— and by what right, at the origin and the end of right—knowing whether you will continue, survive, persecute, hunt, hound, knowing whether, and at the end of the day by what right, you will overload the others, become "yours," with your own death, the mourning for your body in ash or buried, with your own winding-sheet until the presumed end of time, with the imprint of your face on the linen of a shroud, until the end of time. As someone will already have always done.

—Break with this One without leaving a trace, not even a trace of departure, not even the seal of a break, *voilà* the only possible decision, *voilà* the absolute suicide and the first meaning there can be in letting the other live, in letting the other be, without even counting on the slightest profit from this lifting of veil or shroud. Not even want a departure without shroud and in fire, not far from Tierra del Fuego. Not even leave them my ashes. Blessing of the one who leaves without leaving an address. No longer be oneself or have oneself [*s'être ou s'avoir*], voilà the truth without truth which is looking for me at the end of the world. Do one's mourning for truth, don't make truth one's mourning, and the mourning of ipseity itself, but (or therefore) without wearing or making anyone else wear mourning, and without truth ever suffering itself, I mean truth in itself, if there ever was any.

Textile, tactile, tallith; tear my tallith away from any story of the eye, from the theft of absolute *usure*. For after all: before the experience of what remains to be seen, my reference cloth was neither a veil nor a canvas [*une toile*], but a shawl. A prayer shawl I like to touch more than to see, to caress every day, to kiss without even opening my eyes or even when it remains wrapped in a paper bag into which I stick my hand at night, eyes closed. And it is not an article of clothing, the tallith, although one wears it, sometimes right against one's skin. *Voilà* another skin, but one incomparable to any other skin, to any possible article of clothing. It veils or hides nothing, it shows or announces no Thing, it promises the intuition of nothing. Before seeing or knowing [*le voir ou le savoir*], before fore-seeing or fore-knowing, it is worn in memory of the Law. You still have to see it in another way for that, have it to yourself, have oneself [*s'avoir*] that skin, and see it indeed: "It will be *your* fringe, and when you *see* it, you will remember all Iahve's commandments, you will carry them out . . ."[23] When one cannot read the original language, one rapidly loses one-self in translations (veils, fringes or clothing, then panels, wings, corners). "It will be *your* fringe, and when you *see* it . . . ," He says, or, other translation, "When you have this fringe, you will *look* at it . . . ," or again, "It is *for you* in fringe. You *will see it,* / and you will memorise all the orders of I h v H / adonai, and you will do them . . ."[24]

So there would be, on sight, *your* sight ("see," "look"), an appropriation ("to you," "you will have," "for you"), a taking possession. But this is the property (the for-self) which at bottom does not belong and is there only to recall the Commandments. This coming to self of the shawl, every man having his own tal-lith, that's a necessary condition for the sight of the shawl (you will "see" this fringe, you will "look" at it), but only with a view to recalling oneself to the law (it will be *your* fringe, *yours*, and when you *see* it, you will remember—the law: you will be recalled to the law by the for-self of the shawl). As if everyone discovered his own shawl to his own sight, and right on his own body, but only with a view to hearing and recalling the law, of *recalling* oneself to it or of *recalling* it to oneself. And so to do more or something different, through memory, than "seeing." Each time is signed the absolute secret of a shawl—which can of course, at time for prayer, say the precepts, be lent, but not exchanged, and especially not become the property of

---

23. Numbers, 15:39. [Derrida here quotes the Dhormes translation, which I have rendered rather lit-erally. The Authorised version has: "And it shall be unto you for a fringe, that ye may look upon it, and remember all the commandments of the LORD, and do them . . . "; the New Revised version, "You have the fringe so that, when you see it, you will remember all the commandments of the LORD and do them . . . ".]

24. [Translations of the] translations by Segond and Chouraqui, respectively.

someone else.[25] The secret of the shawl envelops one single body. One might think
that it is woven *for* this one body proper, or even *by* it, from which it seems to
emanate, like an intimate secretion, but this is less through having engendered it
thus right close up to oneself than through having already opened it or given it
birth to the divine word which will have preceded it. For a secretion, as is well-
known, is also what separates, discerns, dissociates, dissolves the bond, holds to the
secret. One says "*my* shawl" only by obeying Iahve's order. And by beginning to
wonder: who am I, I who have already said "here I am"? What is the self?

My shawl. Mine was white first, completely white, only white, virgin and without
those black or blue stripes[26] that are printed, it seems to me, on almost all the talliths
in the world. It was in any case the only white tallith in my family. It was given to me
by my mother's father, Moses. Like a sign of having been chosen, But why? I say it
was white because with time it is going a little yellow. I do not know why, but after
I left the house in El Biar where I had left it, my father borrowed it from me for a
few years. It is true that he still had reason to wear it, and he took it across the
Mediterranean at the time of the exodus. After his death, I took it back as though I
were inheriting it a second time. I hardly ever wear it (is *wear* the right word? Do you
wear this thing? Does it need it? Does it not carry off [*emporte*] before being worn
[*portée*])? So I no longer wear it. I simply place my fingers or lips on it, almost every
evening, except when I'm travelling to the ends of the earth, because like an animal
it waits for me, well hidden in its hiding place, at home, it never travels. I touch it

25. "It is permitted to take occasionally the tallith of another to pray, even without his knowing it and
to say the blessing for him, for in general it is admitted that people like the commandments to be
accomplished with what remains to them, so long as it costs them nothing. But it must not be taken out
of the house in which it is kept . . . "; Rabbi Chlomoh Ganzfried, *Abrégé du Choul'han Aroukh*, tr. G.A.
Guttel and L. Cohn (Paris: Libraire Colbo, 1966), Vol. 1, p. 40.

26. Numbers, 15:37–9: "And the LORD spake unto Moses, saying / Speak unto the children of Israel,
and bid them that they make them fringes in the borders of their garments throught their generations,
and that they put upon the fringe of the borders a riband of blue: / And it shall be unto you a fringe . . . "
(Authorised version); The LORD said to Moses: / Speak to the Israelites, and tell them to make fringes
on the corners of their garments throughout their generations and to put a blue cord on the fringe at
each corner. / You have the fringe . . . " (New Revised version). In the talmudic treatise *'Houlin* (88b and
89a), one can read: 'What is more, Raba says: to recompense the saying of our father Abraham: 'That I
will not take from a thread even to a shoelatchet . . . ' (Genesis, 14, 23), Abraham obtained two commandments: that of the 'riband of blue . . . ' (the *tzitzit*), and that of the 'band of *tephillin*' (phylacters).
For it is said (Deuteronomy, 28:10): 'And all the peoples shall see that the name of the Eternal is associated with yours', and on this matter there is teaching: Rabbi Eliézer has said: 'They are [the phylacters] of
the head.' But what about the 'riband of blue'? It is taught: rabbi Meir has said: in what does blue differ
from all colours? For blue is like the sea, and the sea like the firmament of the sky, and the firmament of
the sky like sapphire, and sapphire like the throne of God, for it is said (Exodus, 24,10): 'And they saw
the God of Israel: and *there was* under his feet as it were a paved work of a sapphire stone . . . ', and there
is later (Ezechiel, 1, 26): 'there was the likeness of a throne, as the appearance of a sapphire stone . . . '

In his *Nouvelles Lectures Talmudiques*, which appeared a few days before his death, Levinas interrogates this passage, among others, to elaborate the question "Who is oneself?", what is the "self," the "oneself," the *quant-à-soi* (reserve)? (Paris: Minuit, 1995), p 77ff.

without knowing what I am doing or asking in so doing, especially not knowing into whose hands I am entrusting myself, to whom I'm rendering thanks. But to know at least two things—which I invoke here for those who are foreign (get this paradox: even more ignorant, more foreign than I) to the culture of the tallith, this culture of shawl and not of veil: *blessing* and *death.*

Blessing: first, for example, the Day of Atonement (and the etymology of the word *kippur* is interwoven, it seems to me, with the whole lexicon of the tallith), a father can thus bless his two sons—not his daughter: daughters, women and sisters are not in the same place in the synagogue; and moreover they have no tallith; and I'm thinking of this passage of Deuteronomy (22:5) in which it is said, just before the prescription of the "fringes upon the four quarters of thy vesture [of the veil with which you veil yourself]," that the woman will not wear the dress of a man, nor the man that of a woman, for whoever does so is an abomination for "Iahvé, your God." I can still see this father, but I could not see him, by definition, by situation, he blessed his two sons one day bigger than he, lifting with both arms his tallith stretched above the two heads. Bigger than he, and one bigger than the other, the sons are stifling a little under the solemn protection, under the roof of that temple so close, during the interminable prayer, in what was called the "great temple," an old mosque right in the middle of an Arab district, anciently Judeo-Arab, a mosque in the Spanish style since become a mosque again.

Death: then, for example, the same father buried, like all men, in his own tallith. What will become of the one my grandfather had given me if he did not know what he was doing when he chose a white one, and if he chose me for the choice of this white tallith? The decision is not yet taken, and will not be mine: ashes after fire? Earth? Virgin soil with a burial in the white tallith? I ought to have pretended to dictate this decision, but I have suspended it designedly. I have decided that the decision would not be mine, I have decided to dictate nothing as to my death. Giving myself up thus to the truth of the decision: a verdict is always of the other. Life will have been so short and someone is saying to me, close to me, inside me, something like: "It is forbidden to be old" (Rabbi Nahman of Breslau).

If there had been one, what colour would have been the tallith of someone who said: I am the truth and the life, I have come, they saw me not, I am the coming, etc., so long after another had said, first: here I am?

SANTIAGO DE CHILE–VALPARAISO, 29 NOVEMBER–4 DECEMBER 1995

Some people are so meticulous as to keep them in a book and make bookmarks of them: since they have served once to accomplish a commandment, may another commandment be accomplished with them!

2. Fault or election, a veil is worn as a sign of mourning. Now you've just reread *Savoir*, and *voilà*, for example! What has just happened, change of voice, unforeseeable coming of the other, is this event: eye-surgery, an operation of the hand, a hand armed with a laser, so a sort of ray of light, of *Light Amplification by Stimulated Emission of Radiation*. Let's never forget: in the amplifying cave or in the resonating cavity which engenders this radiance, there'll already have been need of two reflecting surfaces, two mirrors parallel to each other and perpendicular to the rays. Two mirrors echo each other in parallel, an echo of light, *in parallel*: one next to the other. Before there be light, before the luminous beam is projected and powerful enough, with a view to cutting, for example, they will have needed, like in nature, this double mirror with two voices . . .

—Basic question, of the base of the eye too: what is a laser? Will someone one day have to confess that he was circumcised with a laser?

—Such a manual operation can perform what we call a miracle of knowledge, of course—and the author of *Savoir* often talks of a *miracle*,[27] because what is extraordinary here touches on seeing—a marvel of the eye produced by techno-science, but, by allowing seeing in her, Hélène Cixous, at the basis of the joy of her seeing, at the heart of her vision come about but not come back (for it was not there before), there is mourning. At the base of the eye restored, mourning. We have to *learn from her*: a knowing and a piece of news: learn from her that the vision of seeing, her seeing, her vision, was from the start in mourning of the unseen. This operation had to be paid for by a loss. This operation thus engenders the opus, i.e., the poem which was born of it and here beats its wings. This celebration poem allows a song of mourning to throb in it—and the party a lament. As if, instead of having long ago to lose her sight, which basically never happened to her, she had just today, at the moment of the laser, and for the first time, suddenly lost the unseen. Like me, but quite differently, she does her mourning for the veil (as for me, I'd like to have done with mourning, she has perhaps already succeeded in that). She says:

> That's when she shuddered as an unexpected mourning stabbed through her: but I'm
> *losing* my myopia!
>
> [. . .] Now it was time to bid cruel and tender farewell to the veil she had cursed so
> much.
>
> "Now at last I can love my myopia, that gift in reverse, I can love it because it is
> going to come to an end."

---

27. "It was *seeing-with-the-naked-eye*, the miracle. [. . .] and that was the miracle, the donation. [. . .] And to say that this miracle struck only hers [. . .] Quick, a miracle! she would cry Whoa! gently miracle, she cried."

She had fallen into a state of farewell.

The mourning for the eye which becomes another eye: "I'll never be shortsighted again!"

And as always with great blind figures, the sense of having been chosen infuses what she says. It makes the source of each word tremble, it gives strength to reinvent the language in its unprecedented *veridictum*. A bene-malediction elects to genius this great lineage of prophetic poets I recently ran out of breath trying to track, through eye, mourning and ancestor [*l'oeil, le deuil et l'aieul*] in *Memoirs of the Blind*: Homer, Milton, Nietzsche, Joyce, Borges. I would have inscribed her there without hesitation, as the only woman, in this genealogy of night, if I had not been ignorant all this time, these thirty-three years, of the fact that she was all but blind and had hidden it from me. For the operation has less restored her sight than it has deprived her, whence the mourning, of this "malediction," of this "myopia which chose her and set her apart . . . ," of the "veil she had cursed so much."

A strait, what a word. Mine and hers. I was talking about my Tierra del Fuego and Strait of Magellan, without knowing if I would come back alive from them. Now here she is having crossed them, and, getting her sight back, she finally hears herself *hearing* and touches *touch*.

Hearing first:

The joy of the unbridled eye: you can hear better like this. To hear you have to see clearly.

Now she could hear clearly even without glasses.

But while her unbound soul soared, a fall formed: getting away from her "my-myopia," she was discovering the bizarre benefits her internal foreigner used to heap on her "before," that she never been able to enjoy with joy, but only in anguish: the non-arrival of the visible at dawn, the passage through not-seeing, always there has been a threshold, swim across *the strait between the blind continent and the seeing continent, between two worlds, a step taken, come from outside*, another step [*un pas encore*], an imperfection, she opened her eyes and saw the not yet [*le pas encore*], there was this door to open to get into the visible world. ([Author's] emphasis)

She also touches touch. First, the "veil from birth" she has just lost, she wears [*porte*] its mourning, and it is a door [*une porte*], the mourning of the veil is even bigger than she is, like the mourning of its truth, its veridicity, under the adornment of glasses or lenses.

The lenses seemed like a fraud to her. People said to her: you have beautiful eyes, and she would reply: I am short sighted. People did not believe her: they didn't listen. They didn't know. She spoke "the truth." She be-lied her face, her eyes. As if her real . . . As if her false . . . As if she were lying. Wandering, flickering of the lie. Where is the truth. Myopia was her truth.

Then the lie—where is the truth. And in depriving her of "her truth," of "the truth," what knowledge, what technoscience with the laser has just given her (the "miracle," as she is quite right to call it often, since it has to do with the admirable and admiring faculty of admiring), was less sight, less hearing too, than touch. Let's re-read: she has just seen with her "own eyes," without her "non-contact lenses," her own glasses which still remained foreign to her:

> . . . she had seen the world with her own eyes, without intermediary, without her non-contact lenses. The continuity of her flesh and the flesh of the world, touch then, was love, and there was the miracle, the giving [. . .]. She had just touched the world with her eye . . .

Thanks to mourning, the fire of the New World at last and touch ground.

Transfer and translations of the Sandman, that is: an accident can always happen. The hand of Oedipus, eye-surgeon, son and inheritor of another eye-surgeon, the author of *Savoir* knows that it can, this hand, be tempted to poke its eye out, her own as much as the other's. He can forget, the son, it happened to him, it's just happened to him, he can be absent-minded enough to forget in his eye a contact lens when he shouldn't have, or a grain of sand. The immobile archaism of the fantasy can outplay with its infinite anachronism all the lasers in the world. It can not allow itself to be translated in an age of technoscience before which we must never disarm: the unconscious, for its part, never disarms. It is more powerful than technical all-powerfulness. It resists translation.

Fair wind to translation. To that of the old world in any case. Veils of all sorts belong for ever more to the inheritors of a single tongue, if only they know how to make it multiply in itself. The tongue *is there* or, if you prefer, the velums [*voiles*] of the palate. And with the economy of the so-called French language, what holds truth to veils. Literally, to the letter, to each letter and each word.

In its received truth, translation bets on a received truth, a truth that is stabilised, firm and reliable (*bebaios*), the truth of a meaning which, unscathed and immune, would be transmitted from one so-called language to another in general, with no veil interposed, without anything sticking or being erased that is essential, and resisting the passage. Now the braid which here links us to the word *truth,* in the language we inherit, she and I, and whose economy we are here and now putting to work *à contretemps,* this unique braid ties the same word, the true of truth or the veridicity of *veridictum,* not only to the semantic motifs of veil (revelation, unveiling, unburying, nudity, shame, reticence, halt, what is untouchable in the safe and sound, of the immune or the intact, and so the holy and the sacred, *heilig, holy,* the law, the religiosity of the religious, etc.), but also, *in-dis-sociably,* to all the formal and phonematic motifs, to all the related vowels and consonants, almost infinite in number: *voiles* in the masculine [veils] or the feminine [sails], *savoir* [knowing] and *vouloir* [willing], *la vérité* [truth] and *le vrai* [the true] of the *verdict, la voix* [the voice], *les voies* [the ways] and *le voir* [seeing], *le pouvoir* [power] and *le devoir* [duty], *la venue* [the coming] or the "*viens*" ["*come*"] of the "*me voici*" [here I am] or the "*me voilà*" [there I am], and I leave you to carry on without end. It's the same braid, but infinite. All these vocables echo each other in *Savoir,* these words and many others set each other off endlessly along a chain of echoes, in a beam of light whose power is increased by the mirrors it hits on its way, where "she had lived," "in the cave of the species." The braid of phonemes is not always invisible, but primarily it gives itself to be heard, it is knotted out of sight, becoming thus a thing of myopia and blindness. More obvious to the blind, it remains forever, like the warp of this text, you must know it, untranslatable. No-one will ever export it entire outside the so-called French language, in any case in its economy (so many meanings, so many in so few words) but also outside its corpus, expanding and which cannot get over it. No-one, that's the challenge, will extranslate it from the language we inherit—that we inherit even if or precisely because it is not and never will be ours. We must give up appropriating it other than to put it outside its self which cannot get over it and no longer recognises its filiation, neither its children nor its idiom.

Don't lose the thread, not one thread, she—another—said, remember Penelope. One thread runs through this braid, one thread she never loses, the thinnest, the V which, sharp-pointed downwards, runs its genius through *Savoir.* It is not a *velar* phoneme, fine temptation, but a *labial* phoneme. The labial consonant is sung in this poem. Hélène Cixous sings the knowledge of lips. In Hebrew language is called lip. And this curing of the blind is a miracle of the lips. The touch of *Savoir* is a self-touching of the lips:

> Ah! She hadn't realised the day before that eyes are miraculous hands, had never enjoyed the delicate tact of the cornea, the eyelashes, the most powerful hands, these hands that touch imponderably near and far-off heres. She had not realised that eyes are lips on the lips of God.

One can scarcely count the V's of *Savoir*,[28] but the lips do what they say in it. They weave by secretion an irreplacable tunic of consonants, an almost invulnerable tunic lacking nothing, save precisely one word, as though deliberately.

Save which word? And is it really lacking? Who can be sure of it? All these labial consonants, all these lip movements—it is not enough merely to count them, not enough merely to accumulate their statistics, you have to give yourself over to the very necessity of the written at the very place where it falls silent again (read it twice, with your eyes, then aloud, and several times, as here, like this, in different tones). So you must also let yourself be drawn along by the meaning, according to the destinal chance of this unique language. You must *Savoir*. It is done, given, signed. With a movement of the lips, indeed. But also, so that the lips become at last visible and tangible, so that they may touch each other, so that they be no longer loud-hailers or spokespersons [*porte-voix ou porte-parole*], she signs with a movement of lips which separate on touching, in the hiatus or the gape of a strange silence.

Omitted, for one word is omitted, I do indeed say omitted, doubtless omitted deliberately, *la voile* [sail] is not named. Does that mean there is no sail? And that *Savoir* is ignoring it? No, *Savoir* knows how to ignore it with its learned ignorance.

There is a spectacular homonymy, one which works in French, only in French and even more orthographical than that between *soi* [self] and *soie* [silk]: between *voile* and *voile*, *le* voile and *la* voile. This homonymy which is effaced in pluralising itself, *les voiles*, or in making itself indefinite, *quelque voile* (some veil, some sail), this homonymy one can play like gender difference, or sex in grammar, that's the only possibility, as you have been able to admire, that *Savoir* does not put to work.

---

28. Pointing out only one occurrence of words in *v* that sometimes return, from beginning to end of *Savoir*, here's a simple cumulative list: *savoir, voile, voyait, pouvait, devant, aveu, vois, visage, venir, devrais, aveugle, devait, venait, suivant, arriver, privée, vit, invisible, vivante, voilà, ville, intervalle, avaient, voilette, pauvres, savait, mévoyait, vit, voir, vivre, réservait, vérités, découvertes, vain, vous, vîtes, saviez, gravement, rendez-vous, nouvelle, vaincre, l'invincible, vivant, vécu, caverne, venu, versé, veines, voici, avoir, pouvoir, devenir, avait, événement, vies, vu, vinrent, réserve, lèvent, lever, viens, visibles, vision, verre, vue, veille, lèvres, venait, voyante, violente, retrouver, équivalent, invu, invention, vie, avant, avez, vérité, visibilité, advenir, irréversible, vite, révoltait, vaines, veine, malvenue, dévoilée, envers, achever, délivré, vissements, vains, découvrait, avant, voyant, voyait, virginité, vivait, voyance, sauvée, savent, verrait, janvier, rives, bouleversait, reviendrait, révélée, levait, veut vouloir . . .* I may have missed some. But what is she fabricating in this fabric? What is she fabricating with these Vs? Imagine someone wanting to translate them, translate their warp and their woof! Good luck and courage to this new royal weaver! For translation always fails when it gives up giving itself over to a certain alliance of lips and meaning, of palate and truth, of tongue to what it *does*, the unique poem.

Imagine too a parchment on which all the other words, the words without "V" have been burned, you reinvent them, you make other sentences, you want to *know* [*savoir*]. What has happened? What is happening? Nothing is impossible, and translation is not ruled out, but you need another economy for it, another poem. One could in this way deem a passage from *Messie* (Editions des femmes, pp. 142ff.) to be a poetic translation of *Savoir*. Unless it's the other way round. It's another version, another poem, infinitely different and yet twin, almost contemporary, through the operation, the "miracle," and the mourning it names.

Unless that's all it's thinking about. *La voile*, that's the only possibility that a *Savoir* does not exhibit. It does not unfold it *explicitly*, and that's the whole question, the whole art of weaving and braiding that the tradition thinks it ought to reserve for women. It made a certain Freud dream, where he was not far from admitting the fantasy, and even the *idée fixe*, precisely on the subject of a modesty which was feminine, more feminine, feminine rather than not, come along to "hide" (*verdecken*) a certain "lack of penis" (*Penismangel*). If I am in that case prey to a fantasy or an *idée fixe* about this, confesses the man, for it is also a confession, "I am naturally without defence" (*natürlich wehrlos*), disarmed, unarmed.

[Great and inexhaustible penelopean scene which is played in the tissue of this text, for it is also a *text*, on *Femininity* . . . (Is it unfair to see in it the matrix of all the Lacanian theorems on a libido supposedly only masculine, on a phallus which, unlike the penis, belongs to no sex, and on castration, and truth, and the veil and the cause?) Freud's reference to braiding (*Flechten*) or weaving (*Weben*) closely follows the statement according to which "there is only one libido," but in the service of both sexual functions, so that we can assign it no sex, unless, adds Freud, relying too much on the conventional equivalence of activity and virility, one says that it is masculine. But in that case never forget, he goes on more precisely still, that this libido comprises "tendencies with passive aims." In any case, if one can at a pinch invoke a masculine libido, Freud insists, there is no sense and no justification in talking about a "feminine libido." After which, with a certain prudence, alleging imputations, commonly accepted truths, but also the necessity of distinguishing between the sexual function and discipline or social education, Freud mentions successively the frequency of feminine frigidity, the development of feminine narcissism [Psyché, you'll say, or the woman with the built-in mirror: the laser, see above!] and especially modesty [*pudeur*] (*Scham*) which passes for a feminine property *par excellence*. In these two last cases, the cause does not appear to be in doubt for Freud: "penis envy," penis envy I say, late compensation for an "originary" sexual inferiority, manoeuvre with a view to hide (*verdecken*) a "defect of the genital organs." Freud's metalanguage then resorts to the opposable figures of hiding or veiling (*verdeken, verhüllen*) on the one hand, and of uncovering (*Entdeckung, Erfindung*) on the other, still with a view to analysing the motivations which might push the woman to invent, discover, unveil—and hide. No doubt one thinks that women have contributed little to the history of civilisation by their "discoveries and inventions" (*Entdeckungen und Erfindungen*). But they have discovered (*erfunden*), uncovered one technique, that of braiding and weaving. The unconscious motive of this "discovery"? Hiding, veiling a "defect of the genital organs." So they *discovered with a view to veiling*. They have unveiled the means of veiling. In truth, looking more closely, over Freud's shoulder, they have discovered *nothing at all*, all they did was imitate, since Nature, dame "Nature," making pubic hair grow at puberty, had already "given," he says, a model, a paradigm (*Vorbild*) for what was basically only an "imitation" (*Nachahmung*). This pubic hair already hides, it dissimulates, it veils (*verhüllt*) the genital organs. For this feminine "technique," only one further "step" was necessary: make the threads or fibres (*Fasern*) hold together, intertwine them from where they were stuck on the body right on the skin, merely bushy, mixed up, felted (*verfilzt*).

But what authorises Freud to speak here, against the very logic of his argument, of a "technique"? Is it still an art or an artifice, is it a discovery, this so-called 'technique' which invents only the means of imitating nature, and in truth of unfolding, making explicit, unveiling a natural movement of nature? And unveiling a movement which itself consists in veiling? Of decrypting a nature which, as is well-known, likes to encrypt (itself), *physis kruptesthai phileï*? This "technique" is less a break with *physis* than an imitative extension of it, thus confirming, perhaps, a certain animality of woman even in her artifices. (And what if a *tekhnè* never broke radically with a *physis*, if it only ever deferred it in differing from it, why reserve this animal naturality to woman?) A woman would weave like a body secretes for itself its own textile, like a worm, but this time like a worm without worm, a worm primarily concerned to hide in itself its non-being. What the woman would like to veil, according to Freud who, of course, does not mention the animal here, is that she does not have the worm she perhaps is. (I do not know what can be done with this piece of data, but in German one says *Fasernackt* for "naked as a worm" or "starkers.") Freud's conclusion, which I have already quoted, would deserve interminable analysis. It calls on the reader to witness: "If you reject this idea as imaginary [as a fantastical fantasy, *als phantastisch*], and if you impute to me as an *idée fixe* (*als eine fixe Idee*) the influence of the lack of a penis on the formation of femininity, then I am naturally disarmed (*natürlich wehrlos*)." Freud names arms (*Wehr*). He is not, supposedly is not, without the truth of the true (*Wahrlos*, if you like) but without arms (*wehrlos*) and naturally "naturally" (*natürlich*) disarmed, vulnerable, naked.

What should we retain from this rhetoric? What should we conclude from this last hypothesis in the form of a fictive avowal? At least this: the fantasy can be in this case an arm (*Wehr*), and the arm a fantasy. And without getting to the bottom of things here (where the question of the bottom and the bottomless bottom remains entire), let us propose a protocol or a premise for any discussion that may happen: perhaps we should no longer exclude the possibility that, instead of simply being opposites or being mutually exclusive, both the truth (to be unveiled) and the fantasy and the arm be *on the same side*. Instead of having to choose between two sides, one having a bone to pick [*maille à partir*, a stitch to separate] with the other, we would have to find out how to get by on the side of this same, on the side of the same rib [*du côté de la même côte*] (man woman) when it can always become coat of mail [*cotte de maille*] or an uneasy settlement [*cote mal taillée*]. We have to disentangle, disencumber, extricate before opposing absence to presence: of the Penis, of the Phallus, of the Thing or the Cause behind the Veil.

In counterpoint to "Femininity," that New "Introductory" Lecture on psycho-analysis, I will here counsel reading or re-reading *La*.[29] Here Hélène Cixous deals in her poetic and thinking way, getting her hands and languages involved, with all these huge questions. I can only quote a few lines of what is more, in truth, than a counterpoint; but this to incite you to read it all, for quoting is not reading, and it would not suffice to recall the innumerable veils of *La*, "the children with veiled faces,"[30] the equivocal multiplicity or the enveloped duplicity of sexes ("And under the sheet who knows what sexes are rocked, are troubled?"[31]), it would also be nec-essary to deploy too the innumerable folds of a reply to *this* Freud, the one of the equivalence mother = matter = *materia* = Madeira = *Holz* = *hylé*, etc., who is none other than the Freud of *Penismangel* and the pseudo-discovery of weaving:

> [...] Madeira!
> She exhibits her primary content, her crowns of veils, of branches, her vegetable furs, and makes possible and inevitable the work of the languages which cover her in words of love. Which elaborate the matters she is made of in all technical, filial, artis-tic, linguistic manners, as its pressing charm suggests, precisely.
> Mysteriously, imposes it.
> As though the future were inscribed There. In front of her, almost visible. And yet already inscribed in all the languages.

And then everything that is written under the title "Being her butterfly" ("Towards the bed of straw, of fur, of fresh straw buzzing towards the bisexual bed ... "[32]), and then the discovery of sight foreseen in the work twenty years before the "operation," when "sight" means as much the sight of the other as my own, that I see you and that you see, and that you can see me also see you see me, in the double mirror before all lasers:

> I am coming! I'm getting there! I am in sight of you, and of seeing you, I see!
> So I had never seen anything, the suns were rising for nothing! Your sight! Your sight! Oh naked! [Ta vue! Ta vue! Oh nue!][33]

---

29. Hélène Cixous, *La* (Paris; Gallimard, 1976, reprint éd. des femmes, 1979).
30. Ibid., p. 132.
31. Ibid., p. 131.
32. Ibid., pp. 147–48; 193–94.
33. Ibid., p. 201.

And finally for what is without end, this speech in *L'amie de l'abîme*:

Often her abyss becomes for her an arm in the struggle against the pursuer [...]

In truth, the abyss is as natural for her as her family relation with the infinite. She is herself a mixture of edge, abyss and leap into the infinite. But natural feminine leap.

How does a girl jump? Without calculating, without measuring the abyss, without preparation. Let's start with the leaps of the Maid. [...]

The rider sees he is lost.

(You have to wonder over whom the young rider is going to jump. Every woman will have guessed that the lion is none other than the figure of the Scolding Master. See his Introductory Lectures on Psychoanalysis).[34]

The great art of *Savoir*, one might say then, is this: not to name *la voile*, reticence and modesty, stop there, know how not to go too far, how to hold in reserve what would be too visible, and keep it *silent*, another way of veiling, of veiling one's voice. How can one speak of a veiled voice,[35] still veiled even in song, and even when shouting? *Savoir*: prefer diminution, in the *keeping silent* of reticence, i.e., that figure of rhetoric which consists in saying more through silence than eloquence itself. The sails of Tristan and Isolde, Hélène Cixous has renamed them elsewhere,[36] veils in the feminine. There is indeed the covering of "eyelids," there is indeed a *voilette*, in *Savoir*, a feminine "voilette de brume," but not sails caught

---

34. Ibid., pp. 227–28.

35. [*Translator's note:*] A *voix voilée* is a husky voice.

36. From everywhere there comes upon her, in her language, pulled in by the very breath of the poem, a flotilla of black and white sails, black or white, black/white, a flotilla but always the same sail. For example, to cite only the most recent:

Others, apart from me, really have died from a sail that was not white. The shirt you'd promised me you'd wear on Sunday should have been white, my love, and it was black. That was an error.

What? For a shirt? No, I swear not. No-one can die from a shirt, nor even from a sail nor even from a letter. Dying from a sail is such a betrayal! (*Beethoven à jamais ou l'existence de Dieu* [Paris: Editions des femmes, 1993], pp. 24–25)

Or again, in the same book, the song of *Betrayal* (rendered innocent, if that were possible or necessary, by the sublimity of the silence or of the veiled avowal, by a keeping-silent that's able to speak or make understood without betraying):

A brush of a finger—the sun goes down—Cut—Cut of faith—A finger. A word. A fake. An optical error. Instead of seeing one thinks one sees. And *voilà* the white black sail.

As for me, when I am betrayed, I do not know if I am betrayed by treachery or treason, or by myself. [...] I would never have believed that one day I would see as black the white sail between us ... ' (Ibid., pp. 210–14).

A plane was passing, I flung myself into its belly, blood was running from my wings [...] This is not a complaint. It is a confession: I indeed almost betrayed my love [...] No-one will ever know. [...] The other:

'As soon as I saw you see me, I fled.' (Ibid., pp. 229–33)

in the wind, the sails of sailing, the sails of gliding, the sails of the caravels. It is true that there are wings: " ... the others had all their wings." And we know with this knowledge that if we have to count on absence, there can be no question of counting here presences and absences. There is no table to table them, no slide-rule for this knowledge.

All my nicknames, I have so many: what I am nicknaming here the tallith, my tallith, my own tallith, my very own, is not a veil, nor a sail—nor a canvas [*toile*], it's a prayer-shawl.

It is unique. I think I never talk to it, but it is unique, I know that and it knows that I know and it knows that I know without my having to tell it, that it is unique. It doesn't speak either but it could, we both know that.

Liaison or alliance with the unpronounceable. My tallith does not cover my whole body and leaves me vulnerable. I belong to it and I live in it before claiming it as my property. Perhaps it gives me in secret, I don't know, a roof or protection but, far from assuring me of anything at all, it recalls me to the mortal wound. Recalling me thus, everything in it recalls me to the "One," the "only once," "for one only." Unlike a veil, at least this is what I would like to teach or say in myself, this tallith depends on the One of the unique, the singular event whose repetition repeats only, and that's history, the "once only" of the Law given, the 613 or so commandments that make up the Law (they say that the numerical value of the word designating the fringes of the tallith, the Tsitsiths, is 600, plus 8 threads and 5 knots, making 613).

> *Before* hiding from sight like an opaque veil,
> *before* letting light through like a translucent veil
> *before* showing the thing like a transparent veil
> *before* hinting to sight like a veil which lets one
> make out, through the diaphanous light, the thing
> and the forms it is embracing,
> *before all else,* my tallith touches itself.

We indeed say "before," "before all else," in front of everything, for that does not mean that the tallith and its fringes have simply nothing to do with seeing. Simply one sees them and one sees *through* them differently than (*through*) a veil or behind a veil to be lifted.[37] Before and in front of the veil. This tactile thing is not properly

---

37. Perhaps this is the place to situate an allusion of Emmanuel Levinas to this "trellis" of fringes through which a gaze would give itself over to God. After mentioning an irrectitude this time going "higher than rectitude" and leading, in separation, towards the He at the base of the You, Levinas notes, "Franz Rosenzweig interprets the *reply* given by Man to the Love with which God loves him, as the movement to one's neighbour [...]. This picks up the structure which rules a homelitic theme of Jewish thought: 'the fringes at the corners of clothes' the sight of which ought to recall to the faithful 'all

speaking or *stricto sensu* a textile, not yet or already no longer. Nor is it worn like a tunic but, as tactile, tactile before being visible, like a blind person's thing. Right on the body or far from the body. When it is worn right on the body, the tallith *touches itself* like the sacred texts of the tephillin (phylacteries). Sometimes on top of, sometimes underneath, the other clothes. Underneath, that's the one I never had, the little one, they call it, the one you should wear all day. One can sleep in the little tallith, so I've never done that. If one has slept in the little tallith, one does not have to bless it on getting up. But the blessing for the big tallith must in that case include the little one. In a book my father left me, I learn that if one must of course take off one's tallith to go "to the lavatory," one does not have to bless it when one puts it back on, since "going to the lavatory is not an interruption." I also learn that a tallith must be cut to the prescribed size and above all woven of white sheep's wool.

White sheep's wool: this last recommendation appears to be a major one. To understand it, one must untangle the threads of more texts or make sense of more prescriptions than I can decipher here. For this point appears to be a point of dispute, if not of controversy. I am not sure that my tallith is made of pure and "natural" silk (what's natural silk?), but I do believe that it is made of neither linen nor wool. In truth, I'm starting to fear not. When one is obliged to make do with a linen tallith on which it is impossible to attach woollen fringes, some people claim that in that case you must sew leather corners on—skin, basically—and then sew woollen fringes onto this animal skin. The impossibility, or what is really the forbidding of woollen fringes directly on the linen tallith, in this case, could come from certain prescriptions in Deuteronomy (22:2) concerning the sheep, the lamb, the tunic of brother and neighbour. I believe I have already said that women do not have a tallith, but I do not know who makes the tallith. In the same passage of Deuteronomy—*Words*, in Chouraqui's translation—the following verse solemnly forbids both men and women, as an "abomination for Jahvé, your God," from exchanging their clothes. Their "tunic" says Chouraqui: "Man's clothes will not be on a woman, man will not put on a woman's tunic: yes, whoever does that is in abomination for I h v H/adonaï, your Elohim."

At the moment of transcribing this transcription, as faithfully as I can, I look at these sacred letters, these blessed letters [*ses lettres sacrées, ces sacrées lettres*], I stare at the acronym of these consonants: I H V H. Both immobile and mobile, without

---

the commandments of the Eternal' (Numbers, 15:38–40), are called "tsitsith." This word is linked, in the ancient rabbinic commentary called *Siphri*, to the verb "tsouts," one form of which, in the *Song of Songs*, II, 9, means "observe" or "look"; 'My true love . . . looks through the trellis.' The faithful looking at the 'fringes' which remind him of his obligations thus renders his gaze to the True Love observing him. And this would be the vis-à-vis or face to face with God!" *De Dieu qui vient à l'idée* (Paris: Vrin, 1982), p. 114.

possible permutation, the holy acronym never trembles, it ought never to tremble. And yet it trembles, today, its order makes something tremble.

As for swapping one's tunic with a woman, who can be sure of never having been "in abomination"? Not me, I fear.

A number with the power of the infinite, the number of recommendations concerning the corners and holes of the tallith, the tears, the edges, the hems, the knotting and unknotting of the fringes: we'd need pages, volumes, impossible and interminable analysis because every analysis, every untying of the threads must first appear before their law. Before the orders they give, for it is a gift they order [*c'est un don qu'ils ordonnent*]. The big tallith, mine, the one I've already spoken about, one wraps oneself in it during prayer. I think I haven't worn mine for almost half a century. And I do not know what it is made of. But it is there. Tangible and close, even though in order to get on with each other we never speak to each other. When as a young man I did sometimes wear it, I was always careful to unfold its greatest surface, amply. I never imitated those who sometimes roll it round their neck like a white woollen scarf.

Before wrapping oneself up in the tallith, at the moment of saying the blessing, which one must do standing up and taking care that the fringes do not drag on the ground (in which case they must be picked up and can, it is said, be placed in the belt), one must examine not only the fringes but also the threads in the holes and the twists. It is above all necessary to analyse, undo knots, separate threads, prevent them from sticking to each other. On one condition: that it not delay the prayer. Because one must never pray too late *or à contretemps*, that is, if I understand aright, alone, praying alone, absolutely alone—as apparently I've always done, but that's doubtless merely a superficial appearance. Here's what is prescribed in the *Kitsour Choul'hane Aroukh,* this black, all black book my father left me: "If one arrives late at the synagogue such that separating the fringes and examining them would prevent one from praying with the community, one does not need to examine them and separate them." Categorical imperative, then: don't be late. At all events not for prayer. You don't keep a prayer waiting, what's more it never lets itself be waited for, it comes before everything, before the order, before the question, before the reply, before dialogue, before knowledge, before the "this is" or the "what is . . . ?," it is neither true nor false, as a Greek philosopher even said. Even a Greek knew that! This is how I try to calculate the formidable time, the time of the verdict awaiting me, to be on time when the time comes [*pour étre à l'heure à l'heure*], but the "too late," "so late," the evening of the verdict remains so internal to it that I despair of ever effacing it, *sero te amavi.*

I do not know what my tallith is made of, I was saying, especially not of what substance, natural or artificial. It can be touched, but touch does not allow me to conclude. According to the Torah and the "works of the deciders," it would seem that wool is required.

"Wool": that's what the cloth should be made of, an animal tissue, then, and only yesterday, at the origin, a living tissue.

"Linen": this is permitted, at a pinch, but only when wool is lacking and it is impossible to do otherwise. In that case, as we have seen, the fringes must be woollen and sewn onto leather, an animal skin, then, only yesterday, at the origin, that living skin the four corners are made of.

As for "silk" (be it "natural" or "artificial"), the duties are even more tangled. For we must distinguish the warp from the woof. For if the woof of the tallith is, as should be, made of wool, whereas the warp is of cotton, silk or "something similar," or vice versa, if the warp is made of wool whereas the woof is made of a textile (in the strict sense), silk or cotton, then, in these two cases, he who fears God will not bless such a Tallith. For they say that woollen fringes only free you from this prescription for one sort of cloth. What appears to matter, after wool, after animality, is therefore the *homogeneity* of the textile (in the broad sense). When a silken tallith has woollen fringes, one will not bless it. In such a case, you have first to wrap it in another tallith, a woollen tallith, bless it, then wrap oneself in one's own silken tallith. But, homogeneity again, if the fringes are also of silk, like the tallith itself, the blessing is permitted. My *Kitsour Choul'hane Aroukh* specifies in brackets: "Silken Tsitsith (fringes) are not common in our provinces, for the Tsitsith must be spun with a view to what they are to be used for." The worst case, it's clear, is mixing wool and silk in the Tsitsith.

As for the sewing of the corners and the threads themselves, that would be another book. To the contrary of what is imposed on the rest of the tallith, and especially its fringes, here rules the law of *heterogeneity* or dissimilarity: silken thread (or similar) for a linen tallith; for a silken tallith, however, avoid silken thread, and for a woollen tallith avoid woollen thread. Same thing for the hem around the hole. But that's true only if it's sewn with white thread, for "with coloured thread," affirms the same text, "there is nothing to fear."

Have I insisted sufficiently on what matters to me here, i.e., the living creature? What in the first place is commanded by the categorical imperative of wool and leather? Fur and skin: the tallith must be something living taken from something living worn by something living. But, more precisely and later, taken from something dead which was one day living, and burying the dead that was one day living. Living, that is something that will have had some relation to itself [*à soi*]. The living is the possibility of auto-affection, of time and delay: what, in self-affection, will have been able to touch itself.

—That's twice you've spoken of categorical imperative: just now you had not to be late (*sero*), now it's the law of skin, the law of the living . . .

—That may be the same thing, and I'm just saying why I hold these two imperatives to be untenable (but you know how important I think the untenable is: it's the
very possibility of the promise, which must be able to be untenable and threatening,
contrary to what they say). Here are the hypotheses or daydreams I'm offering. The
imperative of fur, wool and skin seems indeed to mean that, unlike veil, sail or canvas, a tallith is primarily animal. Like the tephilline: a skin on skin. As the skin comes
not from just any animal but from sheep, ewe or ram, it in some sense commemo-
rates an experience one would call sacrificial if the word "sacrifice" were not a bad
translation for *Korban* (approach, coming together) and a translation which moreover takes us back toward the cultures of the veil. So a living creature wears something living, a living creature wraps up, until death,[38] in what was something living
offered to something living, a mortal wraps up in what will have been living and put
to death by its own, as a sacrifice—or rather as what gets translated as sacrifice. If
there is a "truth" of this shawl, it depends less on the lifting or the unfolding of a veil,
on some unveiling or revelation, than on the unique event, the gift of the law and the
"coming together" it calls back to itself. Even if one translates this gift of the Law as

---

38. I recalled this fact earlier: a tallith could become a shroud. But as I cannot help comparing (comparing, neither more nor less) the time of what I'm calling here the Verdict with the time of the "fearful
days" between the New Year and the day of Expiation, as they are interpreted by Rosenzweig, I will be
content to *quote* a passage from *The Star of Redemption*, merely to quote it whereas it ought to demand
book after book of exegesis, and especially when it uses an *analogy* to *translate* the prayer-shawl into its
Greek equivalents, chlamyse and chiton: "Throughout these days, a wholly visible sign expresses the
underlying motif, namely, that for the individual, eternity is here shifted into time. For on these days the
worshipper wears his shroud. It is true that even on ordinary days, the moment when the prayer-
shawl—chlamys and toga of antiquity—is donned, that moment directs the mind to the shroud, and to
eternal life when God will sheath the soul in his mantle. Thus the weekday and the weekly Sabbath, as
well as creation itself, illumine death as the crown and goal of creation. But the entire shroud, compris-
ing not only the shawl but also the under-robe—chiton and tunic of antiquity—is not the costume of
every day. Death is the ultimate, the boundary of creation. Creation cannot encompass death as such.
Only revelation has the knowledge—and it is the primary knowledge of revelation—that love is as
strong as death. And so a man wears, already once in his life, on his wedding day under the bridal
canopy, the complete shroud which he has received from the hands of the bride." (*The Star of
Redemption*, tr. William W. Hallo (London: Routledge, 1970), pp. 325–26.
I often wonder what is going through the mind of the enigmatic "Jewish fiancée" by Rembrandt (and
Hélène Cixous's [*La fiancée juive—de la tentation* (Paris: Editions des femmes, 1995)], with her two
rings and her hand on the other's hand over her heart. Is she soon going to take the veil? A mourning
veil, the veil of a bride or of a nun, or, for now, of a secular sister? What would she have thought if she'd
read what comes next in Rosenzweig's text, at least up to the point where he talks about the "shroud,"
worn as "a challenge to death"; what would she have thought of this, for example, which comes shortly
after the allusion to the fiancée: "Only the man needs to be aware that the Torah is the basis of life. When
a daughter is born, the father simply prays that he may lead her to the bridal canopy and to good works.
For a woman has this basis of Jewish life for her own without having to learn it deliberately over and
over, as the man who is less securely rooted in the depths of nature is compelled to do [well, that seems
to recall—or rather to anticipate, for the lecture is later than Rosenzweig's text, though it is true that
these statements are ageless—Freud's 'Femininity': woman closer to Nature, more rooted in it, for better
and for worse]. According to ancient law, it is the woman who propagates Jewish blood. The child of a
Jewish mother is Jewish by birth, just as the child of parents who are both Jewish." (Ibid., p. 326)

Revelation, the figure of the veil, the intuition and the movement of vision count for less than the taking-place of the event, the singular effectivity of the 'once only' as history of the unique: the time, the trace of the date and the date itself as trace.

I continue to murmur, under the protection of hypothesis: when prayer tends to replace, in "coming together," the bloody sacrifice and the putting to death of the living creature, then the prayer shawl, the tallith and the tsitsith commemorate both the privileged animal of the sacrifice—the wool of sheep or ram, the leather, etc.,—*and*, leaping with one wing-beat to the eschatalogical term of the story, the sacrifice of sacrifice, the end of sacrifice in coming together, its unterminated and perhaps interminable sublimation, the coming together of the infinite coming together in the orison of prayer. (Following a suggestion of Maimonides, God himself preferred mankind not to end in one go the murderous sacrifice[39] and it's true it's taking a long time—how long, my God ...). We'd still need to find out, if we held to this hypothesis, where to inscribe a circumcision in this history of the tallith. Is it still a "sacrifice," a "coming together," and the attenuation, the delay, the infinite moratorium on crueller mutilations? I'm thinking of all those cloths that are wrapped round the penis of the baby circumcised on the eighth day, of that sort of shroud too, all bloody, in which the removed piece of flesh might be buried. Detached skin, but assumed (taken from oneself, alliance of floating skin, a scarf or a muffler), the tallith hangs on the body like a memory of circumcision. A circumcision reserved for the man, this one too. Basically it is the same thing, the same, and being-oneself. Ordered to the given order of the other, himself. *Ipse,* the power itself, and the law, the law of the father, of the son, of the brother or the husband, the laws of hospitality (*hospes, hosti-pet-s, posis, despotes, utpote, ipse,* etc., the "mysterious -*pse* of *ipse*," says Benveniste, naively astonished[40]).

But never. Up to the end, never, whatever may happen: in no case, whatever the verdict at the end of so formidable a journey,[41] never can one get rid of a tallith. One must never, ever, at any moment, throw it away or reject it. On must especially not ill-treat the fringes, even if they have become useless: "Some people are so meticulous as to keep them in a book and make bookmarks of them: since they

---

39. See Catherine Chalier, *Judaisme et altérité* (Paris: Verdier, 1982), p. 242: "Prayer, indeed as 'promise of our lips' destined to 'replace the bulls,' must be as agreeable to God as the smell of the sacrifices ... ," specifies Catherine Chalier whose words in quotation marks refer to Hosea 14:2. In Chouraqui's translation, the verse says: "Take with you the words and return to I h v H/adonai./Say to him: 'Tolerate all the wrong and take what is good! / Let us pay the bullocks of our lips!" [The Authorised version has: "Take with you words, and turn to the LORD: say unto him, Take away all iniquity, and receive us graciously: so will we render the calves of our lips," and the New Revised: "Take words with you and return to the LORD; say to him, 'Take away all guilt; accept that which is good, and we will offer the [bulls] of our lips.'"]

40. *Le vocabulaire des institutions indo-européennes* (Paris: Minuit, 1969), vol. 1, chapter 7, "Hospitality."

41. [*Translator's note:*] In English in the text.

have served once to accomplish a commandment, may another commandment be accomplished with them."[42]

Which is what I am doing here, basically, and signing and booking and dating,[43] as always, *à contretemps*.

SÃO PAULO, 4 DECEMBER–8 DECEMBER 1995

> Von Querah
> komm ein, als die Nacht
> das Notsegel
> bauscht sich. . . . [44]

> Das seidenverhangene Nirgend
> widmet dem Strahl seine Dauer,
> ich kann dich hier
> sehn.[45]

3. Have I managed to demonstrate it? What separates the logic or topic of the veil from those of the shawl, that shawl called tallith, this tallith unique up to and including the number of its corners, wings, fringes, so many commandments, is the difference of the event, the irreducible reference to the One, to the One + n which multiplies only the first time, and gives me my tallith, my own, to me alone, both as order and as gift, whereas I can and must never reappropriate it for myself, assigning myself thus my ipseity in what we really must call a history, a single history. The uniqueness of this reference, the untranslatable carry of this ference prevents a tallith, which one cannot and must not get rid of, from being or becoming, like every veil, merely a figure, a symbol, a trope.

Does this mean that the literality *of* "tallith," my tallith, is irreducible?

How to avoid hearing even here, in the name of this city, the *Epistle to the Romans*? Its author thought he knew the literality of the letter. He prided himself on being able to distinguish, for the first time, he no doubt thought, wrongly, the circumcision of the heart, according to the breath and the spirit, from the circumcision of body or flesh, circumcision "according to the letter."[46]

---

42. *Kitsour Choul'hane Aroukh,* vol. 1, p. 45.

43. [*Translator's note:*] *et signe et livre et date;* taken verbally rather than nominally, this gives "sign(s) and deliver(s) and date(s)."

44. "Indirectly / Come, by night, to / the sail of distress / is filling" (Paul Celan).

45. "The silk-hung nowhere / Dedicates its duration to the ray, / here I can / see you" (Paul Celan)

46. Romans 2:25–9; see too Galatians, 6:11–17 ("You see with what large letters I write with my hand! Those who wish to look good towards the flesh / oblige you to get yourselves circumcised/with the sole aim of not being persecuted for the messiah's cross / No, those of circumcision do not themselves keep

In the *Epistle to the Corinthians*, the same Paul (my young dead brother, dead before my birth, was also called Paul, Paul Moses), the same one who attacked the literal circumcision of men, that same one wanted to veil woman and un-veil man. During prayer or the prophetic act.

He writes in his letter: "the head of every man, is messiah; / the head of woman, is man; the head of the messiah, is Elohim. / Any man who prays or transmits his inspiration head covered [*pas aner proseukhomenos e propheteuon kata kephales ekhon . . . omnis vir orans, aut prophetans velato capite*] dishonours his head. / Every woman who prays or transmits her inspiration head uncovered / dishonours her head, yes, as though she were shaven. / If then the woman is not veiled, let her also shave herself! / But if it is shameful for a woman to be shorn or shaved, / let her veil herself! / For the man is not obliged to veil his head: / he is the image and the glory of Elohim; / Woman is the glory of man. / For man was not drawn from woman, / but woman comes from man. / Man was not created for woman, / but woman for man. / So the woman must have on her head a power [an insignium of power, a sign of authority, *potestatem, exousiam*], / because of the messengers."[47]

---

the tora; / but they want to have you circumcised so as to be proud of your flesh/ But for myself I am proud of nothing / except the cross of our Adôn Ieshoua the messiah / on which the universe was cruci-fied for me and the universe. Yes circumcision is nothing, nor the foreskin, but a new creation" (tr. Chouraqui). [Authorised version: "Ye see how large a letter I have written unto you with mine own hand./As many as desire to make a fair shew in the flesh, they constrain you to be circumcised; only lest they should suffer persecution for the cross of Christ. / For neither they themselves who are circumcised keep the law; but desire to have you circumcised, that they may glory in your flesh. / But God forbid that I should glory, save in the cross of our Lord Jesus Christ, by whom the world is crucified unto me, and I unto the world. / For in Christ Jesus no other circumcision availeth any thing, nor uncircumcision, but a new creature"; New Revised: "See what large letters I make when I am writing in my own hand! / It is those who want to make a good showing in the flesh that try to compel you to be circumcised— only that they may not be persecuted for the cross of Christ. / Even the circumcised do not themselves obey the law, but they want you to be circumcised so that they may boast about your flesh. / May I never boast of anything except the cross of our Lord Jesus Christ, by which the world has been crucified to me, and I to the world. / for neither circumcision nor uncircumcision is anything; but a new creation is everything!"]

47. [*Translator's note:*] I Corinthians 11:3–10. Authorised version: "But I would have you know, that the head of every man is Christ; and the head of the woman is the man; and the head of Christ is God. / Every man praying or prophesying, having his head covered, dishonoureth his head. / But every woman that prayeth or prophesyeth with her head uncovered dishonoureth her head; for that is even all one as if she were shaven. / For if the woman be not covered, let her also be shorn: but if it be a shame for a woman to be shorn or shaven, let her be covered. / For a man indeed ought not to cover his head, foras-much as he is the image and glory of God: but the woman of the man. / Neither was the man created for the woman; but the woman; but the woman for the man. / For this cause ought the woman to have power on her head because of the angels"; New Revised version: "But I want you to understand that Christ is the head of every man, and the husband is the head of his wife, and God is the head of Christ. Any man who prays or prophesies with something on his head disgraces his head, but any woman who prays or prophesies with her head unveiled disgraces her head—it is one and the same thing as having her head shaved. For if a woman will not veil herself, then she should cut off her hair; but if it is dis-graceful for a woman to have her hair cut off or to be shaved, she should wear a veil. For a man ought not to have his head veiled, since he is the image and reflection of God; but woman is the reflection of

And this very mild, this terrible Paul dares, for he dares with all the daring whose monstrous progeniture are our history and culture (see the erections of São Paulo the proud), this Paul who preferred a good Greek to a bad Jew, this Paul who claimed to know literally what is the breath of spirit and teach it to the Jew so that he would become a good Jew, better than the good Greek, this Paul dares to leave us to judge, he dares to say, to say to us (Jews or Greeks?) that he leaves us to judge. He goes so far as to invoke again, like so many others closer to us, both Rosenzweig and Freud, for example, Nature, Nature herself (*e physis aute, ipsa natura*), he turns us toward it at the moment he lets us judge: "Judge for yourselves [*En umin autois krinate, vos ipsi judicate*]: / is it appropriate for a woman to pray to Elohim unveiled? / Does not nature herself teach us/that it is a dishonour for the man to have long hair? / But the woman who wears long hair, that's a glory for her, / "for her hair was given her as adornment."[48]

—Your epistle against Saint Paul is double-edged, like what you say about circumcision. In everything you're suggesting, with little airs of elliptical reticence, it's as though you were against circumcision but also against those who are against circumcision, you ought to make your mind up. You're against everything ... Like what you say against the veil, in your Penelopean discourse, make your mind up ... Make your mind up and develop a coherent comparatist hypothesis, with as its key a politics of the tallith, of the veil, the tchador or the kipa in a secular and democratic school system ... [49]

—Not in a hurry. Yes, I'm against, yes, yes I am. Against those who prescribe the veil and other such things, against those who forbid it too, and who think they can forbid it, imagining that this is good, that it is possible and that it is meaningful. Not in a hurry: the scholarly, the secular and the democratic belong through and through to cultures of the tallith and the veil, etc., people don't even realise any longer. ... Contamination is everywhere. And we hadn't finished, I haven't finished with Saint Paul. The one who wanted to veil the heads of the women and unveil those of the men, that very one denounced Moses and the children of Israël. He accused them of having given in to the veil, of not having known how to lift the

---

man. Neither was man created for the sake of woman, but woman for the same of man. For this reason a woman ought to have a symbol of authority on her head, because of the angels."

48. Ibid., 13–15. [Authorized version: "Judge in yourselves: is it comely that a woman pray unto God uncovered? / Does not even nature itself teach you, that, if a man have long hair, it is a shame unto him? / But if a woman have long hair, it is a glory to her: for her hair is given her for a covering."; New Revised version: "Judge for yourselves: is it proper for a woman to pray to God with her head unveiled? Does not nature itself teach you that if a man wears long hair, it is degrading to him, but if a woman has long hair, it is her glory? For her hair is given to her for a covering."]

49. [*Translator's note:*] This is an allusion to the ongoing *affaire des foulards* in the French school system, which has on several occasions controversially attempted to prevent Muslim girls from wearing the veil in school, in the name of the secular nature of the system as a whole.

veil, the veil over the face of God, the veil over the covenant, the veil on the heart. The Messiah, the Man-God and the two Resurrections, *voilà* the great Unveiler. Perhaps it's because of this that, at his death, the veil of the temple tore. After having recalled that the "service of death, engraved in letters on stones," was "in such glory that the Benéi Israël were unable to fix their eyes on the face of Moshè because of the glory of his face, ephemeral however,"[50] Saint Paul wonders how the service of the breath or the spirit (therefore of life and not of death) would not be still more glorious, more luminous. And this light is *unveiling*:

> Having such a hope, we employ a full frankness; / but not like Moshè putting a veil over his face / so that the Benéi Israël could not stare at the end of the ephemeral ... / But their thoughts hardened. For up to the present day / the same veil remains, on reading the antique pact./ It is not unveiled (*idipsum velamen in lectione veteris testamenti manet non revelatum, to auto kalumma epi te anagnosei tes palaias daithekes menei*), for it is in the Messiah that he disappears. / But still today, when Moshè is read, a veil lies on their heart. / It is when he turns towards the Adôn that the veil is removed. [...] But if our announcement is veiled, it is for the lost ones that it is veiled, / those whose thoughts the Elohim of that era blinded ...[51]

Un-veiled *Savoir* of language beyond language, of the frenchlanguage when it overtakes the french-language. For notwithstanding what we said above about the untranslatable, it would be naive to suppose that *Savoir* can be read only "in

---

50. II Corinthians 3:7. [Authorised version: "But if the ministration of death, written and engraven in stones, was glorious, so that the children of Israel could not steadfastly behold the face of Moses for the glory of his countenance; which glory was to be done away."; New Revised version: "Now if the ministry of death, chiseled in letters on stone tablets, came in glory so that the people of Israel could not gaze at Moses' face because of the glory of his face, a glory now set aside ... "]

51. Ibid., 3:12–18; 4:3–4. [Authorised version: Seeing then that we have such hope, we use great plainness of speech: / And not as Moses, which put a vail over his face, that the children of Israel could not steadfastly look to the end of that which is abolished: / But their minds were blinded: for until this day remaineth the same vail untaken away in the reading of the old testament; which vail is done away in Christ. / But even unto this day, when Moses is read, the vail is upon their heart. / Nevertheless when it shall turn to the Lord, the vail shall be taken away. [...] But if our gospel be hid, it is hid to them that are lost: / in whom the god of this world hath blinded the minds of them which believe not ... "; New Revised version: "Since, then, we have such a hope, we act with great boldness, not like Moses, who put a veil over his face to keep the people Israel from gazing at the end of the glory that was being set aside. But their minds were hardened. Indeed, to this very day, when they hear the reading of the old covenant, that same veil is still there, since only in Christ is it set aside. Indeed, to this day whenever Moses is read, a veil lies over their minds; but when one turns to the Lord, the veil is removed. [...] And even if our gospel is veiled, it is veiled to those who are perishing. In their case the god of this world has blinded the minds of the unbelievers ... "]

French," in the French language such *in fact* as it is given. You have to know what she does to the French language. *Savoir* will be read only in a French to come, whether it recognise itself therein or not, and this can only happen *in delayed form*. Whence this inimitable gesture consisting in inheriting without inheriting, reinventing mother and father. *Savoir* gives the language the advance of an unpickable and unprecedented tunic, almost invulnerable (it has not to be so absolutely), unique, hard-wearing through the supple and tight weaving of all the given threads. No doubt the form and the meaning hold together in the same sewing, indissociably, in the weaving of one and the same text, a poem without example. But this one holds, it holds to itself by holding to what has happened, holds on to it and holds itself on to it by virtue of an operation of writing which indebts itself to a "real" operation, "in the world," right on one body: ference or reference of a one-off. Through the carry [*portée*], the graciously carried grace of this ference, *Savoir* indebts itself, recognising its debt, to an event which remains unique, forever unique, forever heterogeneous to every language, i.e., the operation which gave her her sight back, one day, not long ago, to herself, the signatory of *Savoir*, in one go, through the armed hand of the other, armed with a laser forever depriving her of the unseen.

—When you refer thus to the irreducible reality of an event (outside discourse but not outside text), I am really worried. It looks so unlike you, you look so unlike yourself, it looks so unlike the image of you that circulates in these regions. It's as though you were talking about the scenario for a soap in which (as happens) you have to change a character because the actor died or broke his contract.

—You mustn't believe in images, especially not when they circulate "in these regions." Above all you have to wonder what other image, what other and what other of the image is being forbidden in that case. One is only astonished if one has not yet thought through the strange event nicknamed *signature*. It is auto-hetero-referential. Why must one say, in all rigour, as I have just done, "the signatory" of *Savoir*? In order to analyse a sort of hem: on the edge where it stands, the signature does not belong simply within the cloth on the edge of which it is sewn. It will remain forever heterogeneous to it even if, however, it is not external to it, any more than the date. We have already verified this fact, and we could repeat this verification almost infinitely with so many texts by the same author, other sentences, other poems. They could have the same meaning ("at last I see, miracle," etc.), be so alike as to be mistakable for each other as to their form, but what *Savoir* says, referring directly to it, by its date, its signature, I can, as can others, know it *elsewhere*, thanks to other witnesses, other words given. Although they overflow *Savoir*, these attestations nonetheless form a text, traces, an infinite corpus. They attest that the eye-operation, sight returned, the "miracle," the "giving," took place only once in "reality." That "reality" exceeds *Savoir* but that excess remains caught, even as an overlap, a hem or the tear they suture, in the poetic stitching of an experience which could announce it in the same words of the same language. Whence the effects of anticipated iterability we have pointed out.

Each time it's like that, the operation of this operation, the operation of poetic writing. Indebting itself to the other operation, the so-called "real" operation, it also indebts itself to the other's operation, that event which happens where I am no longer operating, where I am operated. Which does not mean that the hand of the other knows what it's doing, and that knowledge belongs to the other. An accident is always possible, as we have said, it has even taken place and catastrophe was avoided at the last minute, through strikes and traffic-jams. Each time this unheard-of operation operates in this way, thus and otherwise, in each text signed by Hélène Cixous, in her opus which is also the body proper of her corpus, but a body proper exposed, vulnerable, expropriable in advance: readable unreadable. Vulnerable: an almost invulnerable tunic, we were saying, and it must not be absolutely invulnerable, such is the condition of the signature. I sign, an "I" signs, she signs always in the very place of the wound, in the place of the wound which is only possible, of course, but so virtual that it remains, the possible wound is assigned, it bears the bereaved memory of an unrefusable lesion: you'd think it was older than self, you can have forgotten it but it carries on dictating the place of all the blows to which we are sensitive, all the blows of fate we await and fear as though we necessarily desired even the worst of them. That explains in part, surprise or not, that the reading of what happens thus, through *this* corpus *here*, to the french-language, to its in-self-out-of-self ipseity, to the putting-outside-self of its being-in-self, that that very thing remain to come in the French of the France of this century. I know of no more perverse and unjust misprision. But I do not foresee the future thus promised, I foretell it. Foretelling it, I do not describe a next day which will be, as if in advance one were lifting a veil to allow the predictable future to be seen, a being to come one would see coming. No, the gage of my foretelling *destines*. It calls to make come, it destines itself here differently: beyond any truth as onto-logical revelation. It destines itself to those men or women who will know how to read, of course. But knowing how to read here, *voilà* the circle, is learned only on the basis of the gage given, and given in the first instance to what it's a question of *reading finally*, equal to [*à la hauteur de*] what *you have to read*: this corpus which is given to you, not this corpus finally un-veiled, but this corpus which has undone itself from the veil, this corpus which has known, from the operation of the other, how to undo itself from veiling and from unveiling. That is [*à savoir*], to reply about the veil: to Saint Paul as much as to Saint Freud, as to the same. (But Paul remains, and Freud.) For this to happen, equal to this corpus, the corpus thus dis-enveiled, you have to write and sign in turn, countersign in writing something else, in another language, without betraying the injection or the call of the first seal. One will never be able to *prove* that it happened, but only *swear* that it did. Perjury *must* remain possible. That's a duty that must be respected.

Of man and woman: the tallith is proper to man, like circumcision. As for knowing whether some discourse on fetishism . . .

—Haven't you exhausted them, as you claim?

—It's true, but I would still like to know if a "theory-of-fetishism" could ever measure up to the infinite tenderness that can be inspired, on contact, on caressing, by a tallith, mine, and every "my own tallith" (as if some "my own tallith" preceded ipseity and the ability to say "I"). I would like to sing the very solitary softness of my tallith, softness softer than softness, entirely singular, both sensory and non-sensory, calm, acquiescent, a stranger to anything maudlin, to effusion or to pathos, in a word to all "Passion." And yet, compassion without limit, compassion without idolatry, proximity and infinite distance. I love the peaceful passion, the distracted love my tallith inspires in me, I get the impression it allows me that distraction because it is sure, so sure of me, so little worried by my infidelities. It does not believe in my inconstancies, they do not affect it. I love it and bless it with a strange indifference, my tallith, in a familiarity without name or age. As if faith and knowledge, another faith and another knowledge, a knowledge without truth and without revelation, were woven together in the memory of an event to come, the absolute delay of the verdict, of a verdict to be rendered and which is, was, or will make itself arrive without the glory of a luminous vision. My white tallith belongs to the night, the absolute night. You will never know anything about it, and no doubt neither will I.

And yet, of course, it will not suffice to profess that a theoretical knowledge about the truth of fetishism here reveals itself or turns out to be impotent—and that a "my own tallith" will always remain incommensurable with it. One will always be able to take the tallith for a fetish, on condition of an upheaval in the axioms of the theorem of restricted fetishism and a formalisation—I attempted it in *Glas* and elsewhere—of generalised fetishism. At the moment of the verdict, this theory would no longer be merely a theory, it would take into account, at the end of the day, with the whole history engaged in it (from Exodus to Saint Paul to Freud to everything that is implied and placed *en abyme* in *A Silkworm of One's Own*), this thought of the event without truth unveiled or revealed, without phallogocentrism of the greco-judeo-paulino-islamo-freudo-heideggeriano-lacanian veil, without phallophoria, i.e., without procession or theory of the phallus, without veiling-unveiling of the phallus, or even of the mere place, strictly hemmed in, of the phallus, living or dead. This culpable edging of the phallus, the edges of this cut which support the veil and hold it out like a tent or an awning, a roof, a canvas, this theoretical toilet of the phallus is none other than the concept, yes, the concept in itself, the possibility of the concept, of the concept in itself. The phallus is the concept, you can't oppose it, any more than you can oppose a "sexual theory." Unless you do something different, you can only oppose to it another concept or another theory, a knowledge like another. Very little. It is not enough to have concepts at one's disposal, you have to know how to set them, like one sets sails, often to save oneself of course, but on condition of knowing how to catch the wind in one's sails: a question of force, concepts and veils are there only in view of this question of force. All I'm doing here, they'd say, is cite Benjamin: "For the dialectician, the point is to have the wind of universal history in his sails (*den Wind der Weltgeschichte in den Segeln zu haben*). Thinking for him means to set sail (*Denken heisst bei ihm, Segel setzen*). What is important is the *way* they are set. Words are his sails (*Worte sind seine Segel*: unless one translates also, "his sails are (merely) words"). The way they are set transforms them into concepts. [...] Being a dialectician means having the wind of history in one's sails. Sails are concepts (*Die Segel sind die Begriffe*). But it is not enough to have sails at one's disposal (*über die Segel zu verfügen*). What really matters is the art of knowing how to set them (*die Kunst, sie setzen zu können*)."[52]

What knowledge does not know, is what happens. *Voilà* what happens. For what happens (the operation I don't operate, the one that operates me), you must *Savoir*, another *Savoir*, here it is, the other's.

Abyss and gap in memory, ripening [*véraison*]: all that goes before has not been dreamed, it is the narrative of a true dream I've only just woken from. A "bad" dream, enough to make you thrash about like a wounded devil in an invisible straitjacket, when you can't stop crumpling the sheets around you to make a hole in the violence and find the way out. Far from Europe, from one ocean to another, over the Cordillera dos Andes, weeks of hallucinatory travel during which I was dreaming of the interruption of the dream, the sentence of life or death, the final whistle blown by a verdict which never stopped suspending its moratorium and stretching out its imminence. It has not yet taken place but I am almost awake. I am writing with a view to waking up and the better to prepare myself for the reality of the verdict, or better, for the verdict when it will have become reality itself, that is severity without appeal. But also without truth, or veracity, or veridicity, without the slightest promised reappropriation. Of course, I still dream of resurrection. But the resurrection I dream of, for my part, at the ends of the verdict, the resurrection I'm stretched out towards, would no longer have to be a miracle, but the reality of

---

52. Walter Benjamin, *Das Passagen-Werk*; Fr. tr. J. Lacoste, *Paris, Capitale du XIXe siècle, Le livre des passages* (Paris: Éditions du Cerf, 1989), p. 491.

the real, quite simply, if it's possible, ordinary reality finally rendered, beyond fantasy or hallucination. The weaving machine comes to a stop, unexpectedly, the bobbin comes to rest between dream and reality, but in a now unrecognisable silence, without the slightest image still. The interruption of the dream will always remain improbable, like the end of the journey I'm still flying towards. But the duration counts, and the endurance of the voyage, the return flight. Already I'm getting ready. I am ready, I say to myself, I'm quite close to enjoying in peace, I'm already enjoying the turbulence and the burst cloud, the accepted self-evidence, the new finitude affirmed. What luck, this verdict, what feared chance: yes, now, there will be for me worse than death, I would never have believed it, and the enjoyment here nicknamed "resurrection," i.e., the price to pay for the extraordinarily ordinary life toward which I should like to turn, without conversion, for some time still—such an enjoyment will be worth more than life itself.

Everything had begun the night before. I had just read *Savoir*. And before closing my eyes to give in to sleep, I let myself be invaded, as they say, gently, in gentleness, by a childhood memory, a true childhood memory, the opposite of a dream, and here I embroider no longer:

Before I was thirteen, before ever having worn a tallith and even having dreamed of possessing my own, I cultivated (what's the link?) silk worms, the caterpillars or larvae of the bombyx. *I now discover that that's called sericulture (from Seres, the Seres, it appears, a people of Eastern India with whom there was a silk trade). In the four corners of a shoebox, then, I'd been shown how, I kept and fed silkworms. Every day, but I would have liked to make myself the infatigable officiant of this service. Several times a day, the same liturgy, you had to offer them mulberry leaves, these little indifferent idols. For weeks, I would leave the room where the box was kept only to look for mulberry trees. These trips were journeys and adventure: we didn't know where to look for them any more, or whether we were going to find any more. My silkworms stayed there, then, with me, in my place as in their place, in the rack of the* magnagnerie, *so many words I knew nothing of in those days. In truth, they needed lots of mulberry, too much, always too much, these voracious little creatures. They were especially voracious between moultings (at the moment called the* frèse). *You could hardly see the mouths of these white or slightly greyish caterpillars, but you could sense they were impatient to nourish their secretion. Through their four moultings, the caterpillars, every one for itself, were themselves, in themselves, for themselves, only the time of a passage. They were animated only in view of the transformation of the mulberry into silk. We would sometimes say the worm, sometimes the caterpillar. I would observe the progress of the weaving, of course, but basically without seeing anything. Like the movement of this production, like this becoming-silk of a silk I would never have believed natural, as this extraordinary process remained basically invisible, I was above all struck by the impos-*

sible embodied in these little creatures in their shoe-box. It was not impossible, of course, to distinguish between a head and a tail, and so, virtually, to see the difference between a part and a whole, and to find some sense in the thing, a direction, an orientation. But it was impossible to discern a sex. There was indeed something like a brown mouth but you could not recognise in it the orifice you had to imagine to be at the origin of their silk, this milk become thread, this filament prolonging their body and remaining attached to it for a certain length of time: the extruded saliva of a very fine sperm, shiny, gleaming, the miracle of a feminine ejaculation which would take the light and which I drank in with my eyes. But basically without seeing anything. The serigenous glands of the caterpillar can, I've just learned, be labial or salivary, but also rectal. And then it was impossible to distinguish between several states, between several movements, between several self-affections of the same minusucule living spontaneity. The self-displacement of this little fantasy of a penis, was it erection or detumescence? I would observe the invisible progress of the weaving, a little as though I was about to stumble on the secret of a marvel, the secret of this secret over there, at the infinite distance of the animal, of this little innocent member, so foreign yet so close in its incalculable distance. I cannot say that I appropriated the operation, nor will I say anything other or the contrary. What I appropriated for myself without turning it back on myself, what I appropriated for myself over there, afar off, was the operation, the operation through which the worm itself secreted its secretion. It secreted it, the secretion. It secreted. Intransitively. It dribbled. It secreted absolutely, it secreted a thing which would never be an object to it, an object for it, an object it would stand over against. It did not separate itself from its work. The silkworm produced outside itself, before itself, what would never leave it, a thing which was no other than itself, a thing that was not a thing, a thing which belonged to it, to whom it was properly due. It projected outside what proceeded from it and remained at bottom at the bottom of it: outside itself in itself and near itself, with a view to enveloping it soon entirely. Its work and its being toward death. The living, tiny but still divisible formula of absolute knowledge. Absolute nature and culture. Sericulture was not man's thing, not a thing belonging to the man raising his silkworms. It was the culture of the silkworm qua silkworm. Secretion of what was neither a veil, nor a web (nothing to do with the spider), nor a sheet nor a tent, nor a white scarf, this little silent finite life was doing nothing other, over there, so close, right next to me but at an infinite distance, nothing other than this: preparing itself to hide itself, liking to hide itself, with a view to coming out and losing itself, spitting out the very thing the body took possession of again to inhabit it, wrapping itself in white night. With a view to returning to itself, to have for oneself what one is, to have oneself [s'avoir] and to be oneself [s'être] while ripening but dying thus at birth, fainting to the bottom of oneself, which comes down to burying oneself gloriously in the shadow at the bottom of the other: "Aschenglorie: (. . .) grub ich mich in dich und in dich." *Love itself. Love made itself make love right next to the watching dreaming child. For the child could not believe what he was seeing, he could not see what he thought he was seeing, he was already telling himself a story, this story, like a philosophy of nature for a shoebox (romanticism in Algeria, in the middle of summer—for I was forgetting to say that, by its essence, all this could only have been possible, in my memory in any case, in summer, in the heat of the holidays in El-Biar), namely that the silkworm buried itself, came back to itself in its odyssey, in a sort of absolute knowledge, as if it had to wrap itself in its own shroud, the white shroud of its own skin, in order to remain with itself, the being it had been with a view to re-engendering itself in the spinning of its filiation, sons or daughters—beyond any sexual difference or rather any duality of the sexes, and even beyond any coupling. In the beginning, there was the worm which was and was not a sex, the child could see it clearly, a sex perhaps but which one? His bestiary was starting up. This philosophy of nature was for him, for the child I was but that I remain still, naivety itself, doubtless, but also the time of infinite apprenticeship, the culture of the rag trade, culture made up according to fiction, the autobiography of the lure,* Dichtung und Wahrheit, *a novel of education, a novel of sericulture that he was beginning to write with a view to addressing it to himself, to stand up in it himself in a Sabbath of colours and words: the word mulberry was never far from ripening and dying* [mûrir . . . mourir] *in him, the green of the mulberry whose green colour he warded off like everyone in the family, a whole history and war of religions, he cultivated it like a language, a phoneme, a word, a verb (green* [vert] *itself, and greenery* [verdure], *and going green* [verdir], *and worm* [ver] *and verse* [vers] *and glass* [verre] *and rod* [verge] *and truth* [vérité], *veracious or veridical* [vérace ou véridique], *perverse and virtue* [pervers et vertu], *all the crawling bits of words with* ver- *in even greater number, that he will celebrate later and recalls here, one more time, without veil or shame.*[53]

("Virus" belongs in his imagination to the same family, it's a little perverse and pernicious worm [un petit ver pervers et pernicieux], *neither living nor dead, which carries delayed death in its self-multiplication. It is also, moreover a slime from slugs, in Latin, and for Virgil or Pliny the seed of animals, for Cicero a venom or a poison.)*

Just now I've found the most beautiful of them, which was looking for me from the start: **véraison.** *Véraison (from vérir, varire, to vary, change colour) is the moment of ripening, the moment of maturation. Fruits, especially fruits of the vine, begin then to*

---

53. [*René Major's note:*] "La double séance," in *La dissémination* (Paris: Seuil, 1972), especially around [Mallarmé's] *Crise de vers*, the "crisis [. . .] of the versus (V)," ["brise d'hiver," "bise d'hiver," "averse," "vers," "verre," "envers," "pervers," "travers," etc., p. 310 ff. and passim. It is recalled that this "versification" "deconstructs" the opposition of metaphor and metonymy (p. 314, note 65).

take on the colour they will have when they reach maturity. The berry starts to grow again, the grape becomes translucent in white vines, red in black vines.

Now long after the formation of the cocoon, an incalculable time for the child, a time without common measure, when the damp patch would finally appear, when an unknown blood, a red almost black, came from within to soften and penetrate the skin, then open the way for the moth's wings, at this moment of awakening as much as of birth, at the moment at which the unforeseeable reappropriation took place, the return to itself of the silkworm which lets fall its old body like a bark with holes in it, what happened then, what in truth, I must tell you, happened once, once only, the véraison in the blinking of an eye, the grain of a telephone ring, that one and only time, like the surprise I had to expect, for it never makes a mistake, never misleads me, that véraison that took place only once but will demand all the time given to become what it was, I will never tell you that tale.

I have promised.

A lapse of time: it was only an interval, almost nothing, the infinite diminution of a musical interval, and what a note, what news, what music. The verdict. As if suddenly evil never, nothing evil ever, happened again. As though evil would only happen again with death—or only later, too late, so much later.

Translated by Geoffrey Bennington

8

A Note on "Hostipitality"

The thread of hospitality—here explicitly linked to forgiveness and friendship, to humor and to transcendence—can be followed in Derrida's work since at least *Writing and Difference*, most notably, though not exclusively, in his readings of Levinas. It has emerged in a more explicit fashion in *Politics of Friendship*, *Adieu to Emmanuel Levinas*, and recently in *Of Hospitality* (which includes two earlier sessions of Derrida's seminar on hospitality). But who or what is the subject of hospitality? To one reading of this question, the French language provides a disarmingly and quantitatively simple answer: the *hôte*. In French, the *hôte* is both the one who gives, *donne*, and the one who receives, *reçoit*, hospitality. As Derrida argues, however, this distinction finds its condition in the aporetic laws of hospitality that, prior to either, give to both *hôtes* the possibility and impossibility of the gift of hospitality. Who, then, is the *hôte* whose "violence" Derrida recalls at the beginning of *Adieu*, and who "dare[s] to say welcome" and thus "to insinuate that one is at home here . . . thus appropriating for oneself a place to *welcome* the other, or, worse, *welcoming* the other in order to appropriate for oneself a place"? To translate this *hôte* as either "host" or "guest" would be to erase the demand made by hospitality as well as the violence that is constitutive of it, "the notion of the *hostis* as host or as enemy." Hence, Derrida's neologism: *hostipitalité* raises in a radically new way the question of the subject of hospitality.

The following text is the first publication of Derrida's "notes" for sessions of his regular and widely followed seminars in Paris and in the United States.

Derrida teaches. This means, first of all, that his writing is fundamentally pedagogical, taking his readers on a course that, at various speeds and stages, constitutes itself as a pedagogical situation (recall the opening paragraphs of "Cogito and the History of Madness"). It also means that there are explicit links that tie his writing to his teaching. No doubt, a powerful example of this is found in *Politics of Friendship*, a book which, "in its present form," documents "what was only the first session of a seminar conducted with this title" (vii).

Aside from their status as a glimpse into Derrida's classroom, and as evidence of a teaching practice that is uncompromising in its meticulous preparation and its detailed elaborations, these four sessions constitute an exceptional, liminal text—not a polished essay—that provides a view of the reach of Derrida's "background" work prior to publication (hence the choice made here to preserve the unedited form of the material). In this particular case, Derrida's remarks on Louis Massignon, on Arabic hospitality and on aspects of Islam reveal themselves as essential parts of the reflections and readings that have appeared in print elsewhere as asides or marginal notes (for example in *Monolingualism of the Other* and *Adieu to Emmanuel Levinas*). Derrida's seminar is also a course in the comparative study of religion.

G. A.

HOSTIPITALITY

SESSION OF JANUARY 8, 1997

Where are we going? What awaits us at the beginning, at the turn [*au tournant*], of this year?

You are thinking perhaps that these are questions to laugh about.

But perhaps we are going to laugh, today.

We have not yet encountered this strange possibility, regarding hospitality, the possibility of laughter. We have encountered tears (those, for example, of the women who, during Tupinamba ceremonies of hospitality and "when they receive friends who go to visit them," begin to cry as a sign of welcome [*en signe de bienvenue*], "with both hands over their eyes, in this manner weeping their welcome to the visitor").[1] We have often spoken of mourning, of hospitality as mourning, of burial, of Oedipus and Don Juan, and recently even about the work of mourning as a process of hospitality, and so on.

But we have not evoked laughter. Yet it is difficult to dissociate a culture of hospitality from a culture of laughter or a culture of smile. It is not a matter of reducing laughter to smile or the opposite, but it is hard to imagine a scene of hospitality during which one welcomes [*accueille*] without smiling at the other, without giving a sign of joy or pleasure, without smiling at the other as at the welcoming of a promise [*comme à la bienvenue d'une promesse*].

If I say to the other, upon announcement of his coming [*sa venue*], "Come in [*Entrez donc*]," without smiling, without sharing with him some sign of joy, it is not hospitality. If, while saying to the other, "Come in [*Entre donc*]," I show him that I am sad or furious, that I would prefer, in short, that he not come in, then it is

---

1. Jean de Léry, *History of a Voyage to The Land of Brazil, Otherwise Called America*, trans. and intro. by Janet Whatley (Berkeley and Los Angeles: University of California Press, 1990), 164.

assuredly not hospitality. The welcome must be laughing or smiling [*l'accueil doit être riant ou souriant*], happy or joyous. This is part of its essence in a way, even if the smile is interior and discreet, and even if it is mixed with tears which cry of joy, unless—as one can always suppose with our Tupinamba weepers, and as the hypothesis was offered—their welcoming ritual be associated with a cult of the dead, the stranger being hailed like a *revenant*.[2] "In the first place, as soon as the visitor has arrived in the house of the *moussacat* whom he has chosen for his host (the *moussacat* being the head of the household, who offers food to people passing through the village ...), he is seated on a cotton bed suspended in the air, and remains there for a short while without saying a word. Then the women come and surround the bed, crouching with their buttocks against the ground and with both hands over their eyes; in this manner weeping their welcome to the visitor, they will say a thousand things in his praise."[3]

Laughter and tears, then—through the tears, the welcoming smile, the *hôte* as *ghost* (spirit or *revenant*, holy spirit, holy ghost or *revenant*),[4] here is what awaits us perhaps, what awaits us at the turn of the year, under the heading and in the name of waiting [*au titre de l'attente*];[5] for the question of hospitality is also the question of waiting, of the time of waiting and of waiting beyond time.

Where are we going? What awaits us at the turn of this year, we were asking, and are we going to laugh? Are we going to cry? And if laughter were a new question for this seminar, what should one await from it, expect of it [*que faut-il en attendre*]?

We know nothing about this, of course, but we know enough to tell ourselves that hospitality, what belabors and concerns hospitality at its core [*ce qui travaille l'hospitalité en son sein*], what works it like a labor, like a pregnancy, like a promise as much as like a threat, what settles in it, within it [*en son dedans*], like a Trojan horse, the enemy (*hostis*) as much as the *avenir*, intestine hostility, is indeed a contradictory conception, a thwarted [*contrariée*] conception, or a *contraception* of awaiting, a contradiction of welcoming itself. And something that binds perhaps, as in Isaac's pregnancy [*la grossesse d'Isaac*], the laughter at pregnancy, at the

---

2. *Translator's Note:* The English edition of Léry offers the following note, which covers the issues here alluded to by Derrida:

> [Alfred] Métraux [in *La religion des Tupinamba* (Paris: Ernest Leroux, 1928)] gives an overview of the ceremony of the tearful greeting, which was widespread among South American tribes east of the Andes, and among some North American tribes (see also Georg Friederici, *Der Tränengruss der Indianer*) ... Métraux thinks that this ritual is associated with the cult of the dead, who names and exploits figure so often in the laments. [Charles] Wagley, in *Welcome of Tears*, notes the survival of this custom in 1953 in a Tupi-related tribe, the Tapirapé (de Léry, *History,* 252 n. 6).

3. De Léry, *History,* 164.
4. *Translator's Note:* The word *ghost* is in English in the text.
5. *Translator's Note:* "au titre de" could also mean "on behalf of" as in "je parle au titre de la Francophonie,": "I speak on behalf of Francophony."

announce of childbirth. Abraham, of whom we will speak a lot today, laughs, like Sarah, at the announce of Isaac's birth (*Yiṣḥaq* means "he laughs").

Hospitality must wait *and* not wait. It is what must await *and still* [*et cependant*] not await, extend and stretch itself [*se tendre*] and still stand and hold itself [*se tenir*] in the awaiting and the non-awaiting. Intentionality *and* non-intentionality, attention *and* inattention. Tending and stretching itself between the tending [*le tendre*] *and* the not-tending or the not-tending-itself [*ne pas se tendre*], not to extend this or that, or oneself to the other. It must await and expect itself to receive the stranger.[6] Indeed, if we gather [*nous recueillons*] all these words, all these values, all these significations (to tend and extend, to extend oneself, attention, intention, holding [*tenue*], withholding [*retenue*]),[7] the entire semantic family of *tenere* or of the *tendere* (Gr. *teinô*), we see this same contradictory tension at once working, worrying, disrupting the concept and experience of hospitality, while also making them possible. (I remember all of a sudden [*tout d'un coup*] that in English one says "to extend an invitation": to tend or extend [*tendre ou étendre*] an invitation—and we will see or recall in a moment that if hospitality seems linked to invitation, an invitation offered, extended, presented, sent; if it seems linked to the act of invitation, to the inviting of invitation, one must also make a note [*prendre acte*] of this: that radical hospitality consists, *would have* to consist, in *receiving without invitation,* beyond or before the invitation.)

If then we gather this entire semantic family of the holding [*tenir*], of the tending, the extending [*du tendre*], and the awaiting [*de l'attendre*], one must well expect [*s'attendre à*] an unlivable contradiction. I say "unlivable" because once more it is in death and on the edge of death [*au bord de la mort*], it is to death that hospitality destines itself—death thus also bearing the figure of visitation without invitation, or of haunting well- or ill-come, coming for good or ill [*la hantise bien ou mal venue*].

Let us unfold this contradiction that makes me contradict myself not only every time that I speak of hospitality, that I make it into a theme, be it a phenomenological, theoretical, speculative, or philosophical theme, but also every time that I offer hospitality.

Indeed, *on the one hand*, hospitality must wait, extend itself toward the other, extend to the other the gifts, the site, the shelter and the cover; it must be ready to welcome [*accueillir*], to host and shelter, to give shelter and cover; it must prepare

---

6. *Translator's Note:* See Derrida's discussion of his own translation of "s'attendre" and "s'at-tendre" in *Aporias*, trans. Thomas Dutoit (Stanford: Stanford University Press, 1993), p. 64ff.

7. *Translator's Note:* The word *tenue* has many meanings in French. It has to do with duration and continuity, holding a session (in court, for example), with behaving oneself and good manners, house keeping and dress or uniform, and the handling of the road (for a car). *Retenue* has to do with holding and withholding and confiscating merchandise, holding a student at the end of the day in punishment, or, more seriously, a prisoner; *avoir de la retenue* is to behave with moderation and reserve, even wisdom.

itself and adorn itself [*se préparer et se parer*] for the coming of the hôte; it must even develop itself into a culture of hospitality, multiply the signs of anticipation, construct and institute what one calls structures of welcoming [*les structures de l'accueil*], a welcoming apparatus [*les structures d'acceuil*]. Not only is there a culture of hospitality, but there is no culture that is not also a culture of hospitality. All cultures compete in this regard and present themselves as more hospitable than the others. Hospitality—this is culture itself.

Since I *also* happened to have said that burial and the cult of the dead is culture, that there is no culture without a culture of death,[8] one will perhaps be surprised—but not for too long—when realizing that these two enunciations say the same thing, that they converge at the point where hospitality and the culture of the dead, of the abode as last resting place [*de la demeure comme dernière demeure*], beginning with mourning and memory itself, are the same thing (we will return to this in a moment). Hospitality therefore presupposes waiting, the horizon of awaiting and the preparation of welcoming [*accueil*]: *from life to death.*

But, *on the other hand,* the opposite is also nevertheless true, simultaneously and irrepressibly true: to be hospitable is to let oneself be overtaken [*surprendre*], *to be ready to not be ready,* if such is possible, to let oneself be overtaken, to not even *let* oneself be overtaken, to be surprised, in a fashion almost violent, violated and raped [*violée*], stolen [*volée*] (the whole question of violence and violation/rape and of expropriation and de-propriation is waiting for us), precisely where one is not ready to receive—and not only *not yet ready* but *not ready, unprepared* in a mode that is not even that of the "not yet."

One must not only not be ready nor prepared to welcome [*accueillir*], nor well disposed to welcome—for if the welcome is the simple manifestation of a natural or acquired disposition, of a generous character or of a hospitable *habitus*, there is no merit in it, no welcome of the other as other. But—supplementary aporia—it is also true that if I welcome the other out of mere duty, unwillingly, against my natural inclination, and therefore without smiling, I am not welcoming him either: One must [*il faut*] therefore welcome without "one must" [*sans "il faut"*]: neither naturally nor unnaturally. In any case, the awaited hôte (thus invited, anticipated, there where everything is ready to receive him) is not a hôte, not an other as hôte. If, in hospitality, one must say *yes,* welcome the coming [*accueillir la venue*], say the "welcome"; one must say *yes,* there where one does not wait, *yes,* there where one does not expect, nor await oneself to, the other [*là où l'on ne s'attend pas soi-même à l'autre*], to let oneself be swept by the coming of the wholly other, the absolutely unforeseeable [*inanticipable*] stranger,[9] the uninvited visitor, the

---

8. *Translator's Note:* See Derrida, *Aporias,* esp. 43–44/F83–84.

unexpected visitation beyond welcoming apparatuses. If I welcome only what I welcome, what I am ready to welcome, and that I recognize in advance because I expect the coming of the hôte as invited, there is no hospitality.

It is as if there were a competition or a contradiction between two neighboring but incompatible values: *visitation and invitation*, and, more gravely, it is as if there were a hidden contradiction between hospitality and invitation. Or, more precisely, between hospitality as it exposes itself to the visit, to the visitation, and the hospitality that adorns and prepares itself [*se pare et se prépare*] in invitation. These two hôtes that the visitor and the invited are, these two faces of hospitality, visitation and invitation, are not moments of hospitality, dialectical phases of the same process, the same phenomenon. Visitor and invited, visitation and invitation, are simultaneously in competition and incompatible; they figure the non-dialectizable [*non-dialectisable*] tension, even the always imminent implosion, in fact, the continuously occurring implosion in its imminence, unceasing, at once active and deferred, of the concept of hospitality, even of the *concept* in *hospitality*. To wait without waiting, awaiting absolute surprise, the unexpected visitor, awaited without a horizon of expectation: this is indeed about the Messiah as hôte, about the messianic as hospitality, the messianic that introduces deconstructive disruption or madness in the concept of hospitality, the madness *of* hospitality, even the madness *of the concept of* hospitality.

I do say "even of the concept in hospitality" because the contradiction (atopical: madness, extravagance, in Greek: *atopos*) of which we are speaking produces or registers this autodeconstruction in every concept, in the concept of concept: not only because hospitality undoes, should undo, the grip, the seizure (the *Begriff*, the *Begreifen*, the capture of the *concipere, cum-capio*, of the *comprehendere*, the force or the violence of the taking [*prendre*] as comprehending [*comprendre*]), hospitality is, *must* be, *owes to itself* to be, inconceivable and incomprehensible, but also because in it—we have undergone this test and ordeal so often—each concept opens itself to its opposite, reproducing or producing in advance, in the rapport of one concept to the other, the contradictory and deconstructive law of hospitality. Each concept becomes hospitable to its other, to an other than itself that is no longer *its* other. With this apparent nuance we have a formula of the entire contra-

---

9. *Translator's Note:* "L'étranger" can often, and more appropriately, be translated as "the foreigner" and even (although not in this particular instance) as "the foreign." It can also be read as "abroad" as in "voyager à l'étranger," to travel abroad. The expression "à l'étranger" could thus be read "to the stranger," "to the foreign," or simply "abroad." Because of those and other echoes (of Levinas as well), I have chosen to consistently translate "l'étranger" as "stranger" but minimally the more contained or current meaning of "foreigner" should always be kept in mind.

diction, which is more than a dialectical contradiction, and which constitutes perhaps the very stakes of all consistent deconstructions: the difference between something like "its" other (the very Hegelian formula of "its other"), the difference, therefore, between hospitality extended to one's other (to everybody their own, their chosen and selected hôtes, their integratable immigrants, their assimilable visitors with whom cohabitation would be livable) and hospitality extended to an other who no longer is, who never was the "its other" of dialectics.

Hospitality—if there is any—must, would have to, open itself to an other that is not mine, my hôte, my other, not even my neighbor or my brother (Levinas always says that the other, the other man, man as the other is *my* neighbor, my universal brother, in humanity. At bottom, this is one of our larger questions: is hospitality reserved, confined, to man, to the universal brother? For even if Levinas disjoints the idea of fraternity from the idea of the "fellow [*semblable*],"[10] and the idea of neighbor [*prochain*] or of proximity from the idea of non-distance, of non-distancing, of fusion and identity, he nonetheless maintains that the hospitality of the hôte as well as that of the hostage must belong to the site of the fraternity of the neighbor). Hospitality, therefore—if there is any—must, would have to, open itself to an other that is not mine, my hôte, my other, not even my neighbor or my brother, perhaps an "animal"—I do say animal, for we would have to return to what one calls the animal, first of all with regards to Noah who, on God's order and until the day of peace's return, extended hospitality to animals sheltered and saved on the ark, and also with regards to Jonah's whale, and to *Julien l'hospitalier* in Gustave Flaubert's narrative (*The Legend of St Julian Hospitator* [*La légende de Saint Julien l'Hospitalier*]). Saint Julian was a great hunter before the Lord. A large stag was struck by his last arrow, a large black stag in the forehead of whom the arrow remains stuck though it "did not seem to feel it," a large stag, whose "blazing eyes, solemn as a patriarch or a judge." This stag announces three times to him that he, Julian, will kill his father and mother: "Accursed, accursed, accursed! One day, cruel heart, you will kill your father and mother."[11] And Julian (this is the whole story that you know or should read) does in fact kill them and later finds himself devoted to a duty of hospitality, to the point of receiving the visit, the visitation of a leper

---

10. *Translator's Note:* On the French "semblable," see what Emmanuel Levinas writes: "Le tiers est autre que le prochain, mais aussi un autre prochain, mais aussi un prochain de l'Autre et non pas seulement son semblable [The third party is other than the neighbor, but also another neighbor, and also a neighbor of the other, and not simply his fellow]" (Emmanuel Levinas, *Autrement qu'être ou au-delà de l'essence* [The Hague: Martinus Nijhoff, 1974], 200; *Otherwise than Being or Beyond Essence*, trans. Alphonso Lingis [Pittsburgh: Duquesne University Press, 1998], 157).

11. Gustave Flaubert, "The Legend of St Julian Hospitator" in *Three Tales*, trans. Robert Baldick (New York: Penguin Books, 1961), 67.

Christ who tells him "I am hungry," "I am thirsty," "I am cold," "take me in your bed and in your arms, embrace me."

If every concept shelters or lets itself be haunted by another concept, by an other than itself that is no longer even its other, then no concept remains in place any longer. This is about the concept of concept, and this is why I suggested earlier that hospitality, the experience, the apprehension, the exercise of impossible hospitality, of hospitality as the possibility of impossibility (to receive another guest whom I am incapable of welcoming, to become capable of that which I am incapable of)—this is the exemplary experience of deconstruction itself, when it is or does what it has to do or to be, that is, the experience of the impossible. Hospitality—this is a name or an example of deconstruction. Of the deconstruction of the concept, of the concept of concept, as well as of its construction, its home, its "at-home" [son chez-soi]. Hospitality is the deconstruction of the at-home; deconstruction is hospitality to the other, to the other than oneself, the other than "its other," to an other who is beyond any "its other." We have undergone such a test or ordeal a thousand times when, for example (to remain close to Levinas for a little longer), we saw that the border between the ethical and the political is no longer insured, that the third [le tiers], who is the birth of justice and finally of the state, already announces himself in the duel of the face-to-face and the face, and therefore disjoints it, dis-orients it, "destin-errs" it; that the beyond the state (the condition of ethics) had to produce itself in the state—and that all the topological invaginations, which made the outside produce an enclave in the inside of the inside, were affecting the order of discourse, were producing deconstructive ruptures in the discourse and the construction of concepts.[12]

There is no apparent inconsistency, no absolute discontinuity between Totality and Infinity—which insisted upon the welcome [l'accueil] (the governing word) and upon the subjectivity of the subject as hôte—and then, ten years later, the definition of the subject as hostage, vulnerable subject subjected to substitution, to trauma, persecution, and obsession. Yet, there is a change of accent and a change of scenery [paysage]. After peace, after the peaceable and peaceful experience of welcoming, there follows (but this following [succession] is not a new stage, only the becoming-explicit of the same logic) a more violent experience, the drama of a relation to the other that ruptures, bursts in or breaks in, or still, you may recall some of those citations, an experience of the Good that elects me before I welcome it, in other words, of a Goodness, a good violence of the Other that precedes welcoming.

In fact, beginning with the texts that follow Totality and Infinity, for example in "The Trace," we had already lent our attention to the Levinasian definition of the

12. Translator's Note: See Derrida, Adieu: To Emmanuel Levinas.

face as *visit* and *visitation*: the face "visits me as already ab-solute" or "the face is of itself visitation and transcendence."[13] The concepts (disrupting of concepts) constituted by the motifs of hostage and substitution belong to [*relèvent de*] the same thought of visitation, that is to say, to the coming of an other as a hôte who is not invited [*comme hôte qui n'est pas invité*], a visitor who is not an expected guest, an invited guest [*un invité invité*], a guest the welcoming of whom I am ready for. This is indeed a thought of hospitality, and of hospitality to the infinite, to God, perhaps even more consistent, but it is a thought of hospitality where the one welcoming [*l'accueillant*] is second, where the welcoming [*l'accueil*] is second, no longer subject to the visit, to the visitation, and where one becomes, prior to being the *hôte*, the hostage of the other. There is no disagreement here with the logic of *Totality and Infinity*, but the displacement of accent intervenes in the self-contradiction, the self-deconstruction of the concept of hospitality. And with this concept of subjectivity or of ipseity as hostage, we have the inseparable concept of *substitution*, of the unique as *hostage* responsible for all, and therefore substitutable, precisely there where [*là même où*] he is absolutely irreplaceable.

Why does it appear to me necessary, today, to return to these motifs of hostage and of substitution?

To say it first in one word, before I explain myself better, I return to these two motifs of hostage and of substitution, from the point of view, obviously, of hospitality, in order to initiate, at the turn of this year, a turn in our trajectory, at any case in the references that guide us. We have spoken a lot about the Bible, what one calls the Old and the New Testaments, what Levinas himself, precisely in "The Trace" (in the passage I quoted earlier), had called "our Judeo-Christian spirituality." But we have not yet come to the culture of this other Abrahamic monotheism that is Islam, about which even the most ignorant know that it too has always presented itself—perhaps even more than Judaism and Christianity—as a religion, an ethics, and a culture, of hospitality.

The mediation that seems to me here, and which is (perhaps, perhaps) the most appropriate in our context, is found, I will explain, in the figure of a spirituality that is, this time, Christiano-Islamic: the oeuvre, the thought, the extraordinary life of Louis Massignon.

Massignon was, if one can trust these words, an Islamologist and an Orientalist. He also oriented his entire life, his entire spiritual adventure, his entire testimony

---

13. In *Humanisme de l'autre l'homme*, 1963–64, but gathered in this collection in 1972; see Emmanuel Levinas, "Meaning and Sense," trans. Alphonso Lingis, *Collected Philosophical Papers* (Pittsburgh: Duquesne University Press, 1998), 106; "La signification et le sens," *Humanisme de l'autre homme* (Paris : Fata Morgana-Le livre de poche, 1972), 69.

toward an experience of hospitality, of Abrahamic hospitality. As strange or pre-dictable as it may seem, he also made use of the words *substitution* and *hostage* in order to define, and to call for, a new approach to Islam, a new understanding [*intel-ligence*] of Islam on the part of non-Muslim Christians. But this understanding would be more than a theoretical or objective one; it would be or aspire to be a new form of partaking [*partage*] or participation between the three Abrahamic religions reinterpreted from [*à partir de*] a Christianity (Massignon was a Christian and he had undergone a sort of Christian conversion [*une sorte de conversion de chrétien*] to Christianity—a conversion that is somehow comparable to that of Paul Claudel—and which followed what he himself called a "visitation of the stranger"; we will come to this in a moment), from a re-thinking of Christianity nourished by Islam.

This is all difficult and complicated, as you imagine, but we must approach it [*il nous faut nous en approcher*], because it is all made in the name of a thought that is at its core an original and strong thought of hospitality, and because the words *hostage* and *substitution* do not appear here by chance.

I have no hypothesis for now regarding the possible rapports or meetings between Massignon and Levinas. To my knowledge, but I have not reread everything from this perspective, and I want to remain prudent, Levinas does not refer to Massignon, even though the latter's oeuvre, his teaching and his person were quite present and radiating in pre- and postwar Paris, in the very same circles in which Levinas was a participant.[14] In any case, what I will say about it, most notably around hospitality, the hostage and substitution, has nothing to do with an investigation regarding pri-ority or influence. It is rather a matter of a configuration that is structural, historical and even historial, a configuration that I judge significant, illuminating, and pro-vocative for us. It makes one think [*elle donne à penser*]. It invites one to think.

What matters to me here today, more precisely, is to find a way to link what we have said so far with the question we have not yet come to, that of hospitality according to Islam, a question that is intrinsically interesting and urgent today, when the gravest ethicopolitical stakes concern *both* the tradition of internal or external—if one may say so—hospitality, in the Arabo-Islamic countries, cultures, and nations *and* the hospitality extended or—most often—refused to Islam in non-Islamic lands, beginning here "at home" [*"chez nous"*]. The analogies (limited but determined) toward which we will direct our interest cannot diminish in any way the singularity and originality of the two thoughts, Levinas's and Massignon's.

---

14. The *Collège de philosophie* was directed just after World War Two by Jean Wahl, great friend and protecting elder of Levinas. Massignon gave some lectures there; and Levinas' great friend, Blanchot, among others, participated with Bataille in the famous discussions about sin with Massignon, in 1944, at the home of Marcel Moré: with Bataille but also with Father Daniélou—Levinas knew Daniélou well; he often conversed with him—with Hyppolite, Sartre, Adamov, Klossowski, Camus, et al.

Whether Levinas knew Massignon or not, whether he cites him or not (as for me, I have never encountered a reference to Massignon in Levinas, nor reciprocally—the usefulness of indexes and computers, scanners, all the more so for amnesiacs like me). It is true that Levinas speaks little about Islam (like Rosenzweig, whose condescending, even pejorative pages on Islam we have studied before);[15] but if this is true that he speaks little about it, a lot less than about Christianity, Levinas declares nothing but the greatest respect for Islam. Two examples, from *Difficult Freedom*; The first, the most marked, is found in "Monotheism and Language" (1959):

> Islam is above all one of the principal factors involved in this constitution of humanity. Its struggle has been arduous and magnificent. It long ago surpassed the tribes that gave birth to it. It swarmed across three continents. It united innumerable peoples and races. It understood better than anyone that a universal truth is worth more than local particularisms. It is not by chance that a talmudic apologue cites Ishmael, the symbol of Islam, among the rare sons of Sacred History, whose name was formulated and announced before their birth. It is as if their task in the world had for all eternity been foreseen in the economy of Creation. (. . .) It is this that I should like to say, by way of explaining Judaism's attitude to Islam, to a meeting of Jewish students—that is to say, clerics and a people of clerics. The memory of a common contribution to European civilization in the course of the Middle Ages, when Greek texts entered Europe via the Jewish translators who had translated Arab translations, can be exalting only if we still manage today to believe in the power of words devoid of rhetoric or diplomacy. Without reneging on any of his undertakings, the Jew is open to the word and believes in the efficacy of truth.[16]

The other text, also in *Difficult Freedom*, seems interesting mostly because of the accent it places on heteronomy.

> Like Jews, Christians and Muslims know that if the beings of this world are the results of something, man ceases to be just a result and receives "a dignity of cause," to use Thomas Aquinas's phrase, to the extent that he endures the actions of the cause, which is external *par excellence,* divine action. We all in fact maintain that human autonomy rests on a supreme heteronomy and that the force which produces such marvelous

---

15. *Translator's Note:* Derrida is here referring to Franz Rosenzweig, *The Star of Redemption,* trans. William W. Hallo (New York: Holt, Rinehart and Winston, 1971). For a short discussion of Rosenzweig's treatment of Islam and some bibliographic references, see Barbara Galli's "'The New Thinking': An Introduction," in *Franz Rosenzweig's "The New Thinking,"* ed. Alan Udoff and Barbara E. Galli, eds. (Syracuse: Syracuse University Press, 1999), esp. 186, n. 22.

16. Emmanuel Levinas, *Difficult Freedom: Essays on Judaism,* trans. Seán Hand (Baltimore: Johns Hopkins University Press, 1990), 179; *Difficile liberté* (Paris: Albin Michel, 1976), 205–206.

effects, the force which institutes force, the civilizing force, is called God. (…) At the moment of this experience, whose religious range has for ever left its mark on the world, Catholics, whether secular, priests or monks, saved Jewish children and adults both in France and outside France, and on this very soil Jews menaced by racial laws heard the voice of a Muslim prince place them under his royal sovereignty.[17]

For those who may not know who Louis Massignon is, I will recall that he died at the age of seventy-nine, in 1962, that is to say at the end of the Algerian War during and against which he was very actively engaged (for this he was detained in the Hôpital Beaujon in 1959, having demonstrated with Sartre and François Mauriac and having almost lost an eye following an attack by demonstrators in 1958. He was also very active on behalf of Morocco and on behalf of the Palestinian refugees). Massignon was born in 1883 and after traveling to Algeria and Morocco, after failing at the *agrégation* in history, he began, in 1906, a great career as an Orientalist. He was a member of the Institut Français d'Archéologie Orientale in Cairo; he published numerous texts, among them, in 1908, "Saints Buried in Baghdad" and "Migrations of the Dead in Baghdad." He developed a relationship with Charles de Foucauld and with Claudel and experienced a kind of ecstatic conversion (one of his biographers reservedly writes: "1909: night of admiration with Foucauld"). He met André Gide, Henri Bergson, Charles Pierre Péguy, and gave mass for Charles de Foucauld in 1913. That same year he met the woman who will become his wife in 1914, though his life would be marked, in a way that is both intense and tragic, by homosexuality. During the war his first child was born and he begun to publish on Hallaj, the mystic to whom he would dedicate an immense thesis (five volumes published as *La passion de Hallaj, martyr mystique de l'islam*),[18] and the attention of a lifetime. The thesis was published in 1922 but the manuscript had been burned at Louvain in 1914. From then on, I cannot follow the considerable body of texts, travels, lectures, and events that mark this uncommon life.[19] At this time, he also began a military and diplomatic career in the Middle East during which he met T. E. Lawrence (the two are dissimilar but comparable figures). He taught at the Collège de France after doing some substitute teaching there. He published numerous texts on Arabic as a liturgical language or as a philo-

---

17. Levinas, *Difficult Freedom*, 11–12/*Difficile liberté*, 24–25. *Translator's Note:* Levinas's lecture was delivered in Morocco. Levinas is referring to Mohammed V, king of Morocco, known to have refused to turn over his Jewish subjects to the French authorities during the war.

18. Louis Massignon, *The passion of al-Hallaj: mystic and martyr of Islam*, trans. Herbert Mason (Princeton: Princeton University Press, 1982).

19. I refer you for example, among other sources, to Pierre Rocalve, *Louis Massignon et l'islam* (Damascus: Institut Français de Damas, 1993) where you will find a bio-bibliography and a concordance both precise and precious, and to Charles Destremau and Jean Moncelon, *Massignon* (Paris: Plon, 1994).

sophical language, on "basic root-terms of the Muslim philosophical vocabulary."
In 1923, he published a text that should be important to us, "The Three Prayers of
Abraham Father of all Believers."[20] In this text, one reads the formulation of a central theme that inspires Massignon's entire exegesis and spiritual struggle, namely
that the three monotheistic religions, as Abrahamic religions, are issued from a
patriarch that came to this earth as a "stranger, a hôte, *gêr*," and a kind of saint of
hospitality. We will return to this major reference of Genesis 12:1, which plays a
determining role in both Rosenzweig and Levinas (another time, we shall also
return to the notion of *stranger* in Levinas), where Yahweh orders Abraham to
depart, to leave his land and the house of his father, transforming him into a hôte
(but, obviously, while promising him a land).

In order to outline the absolute, and absolutely originary role that the establishment of hospitality plays in Massignon's thought, in his spiritual, politicospiritual
adventure, I am going to quote a few texts, beginning with one he wrote in June
1949 after a long visit in the camps of Arab refugees in Palestine: "God did find a
hôte in Abraham and these Arabs are the last witnesses of this cult of hospitality
that our racisms deny. . . . But how many Christian exegetes are left who believe in
Abraham's existence?"[21]

The same year, in Paris, during the study week of Catholic intellectuals, he
asserted the following, which shows his devotion to Abraham, the absolute hôte
and the father of the three religions, the traces of whom he constantly followed
during his travels and missions:

> During my missions, I tried to cover the itinerary of Abraham, from the *Lekh lekha*
> (Genesis 12:1 [when God tells him, therefore, "Go," "leave this land," get out of Ur] to
> "Hineni" ["Here I am"—not Genesis 21:2 as Massignon or Rocalve mistakenly
> asserts, since 21:2 is when Sarah, visited by Yahweh, gives birth to Isaac and says (we
> will return to this long scene of Isaac's laugh, of Isaac as a laugh that lasts for a long
> time, and is punctuated by Sarah who, alluding to a prior scene to which I would like
> to return as well), in Chouraqui's translation: "Elohim made me a laugh, any hearer
> will laugh about me;" in Dhormes' translation: "Elohim gave me reason to laugh;
> whoever learns of this will laugh about me."[22] "Hineni" is from Genesis 22, the

---

20. "Les trois prières d'Abraham père de tous les croyants," in Louis Massignon, *Parole donnée* (Paris:
Seuil, 1983) 257–72; trans. Allan Cutler in *Testimonies and Reflections: Essays of Louis Massignon*, ed.
Herbert Mason (Notre Dame: University of Notre Dame Press, 1989), 3–20.

21. Quoted in Louis Massignon, *L'hospitalité sacrée* (Paris: Nouvelle Cité, 1987), 30, n. 26.

22. *Translator's Note:* I translate here from the French translations used by Derrida, namely André
Chouraqui (Paris: Desclée de Brouwer, n. d.) and Edouard Dhormes (Paris: Gallimard, "Bibliothèque
de la Pléiade," 1972). The NSRV translates Genesis 21:6 as follows: "God has brought laughter for me;
everyone who hears will laugh with me. "

moment when Yahweh puts Abraham to the test by asking him to cut Isaac's throat — J. D.]. I started in Ur in Chaldea, and went very close to Haran and to Beersheba where Abraham abandoned his elder son Ishmael [the story of Hagar and the geneal- ogy of Muslim Ishmaelites —J. D]. I went to Mamre where he asks for the forgiving of Sodom [this is one of the prayers that counted most for Massignon, and for Levinas as well. Levinas alludes to this prayer in the *New Talmudic Readings*: "Prayer of Abraham on behalf of the perverse Sodom threatened with just sanctions by the Lord, prayer by means of a sublime and famous bargaining, lasting ten verses (Genesis 18:22–32), with God himself, a very firm pleading in favor of Sodom before the Creator of the world, disputing about the notion of divine justice. It is precisely here that Abraham declares himself "dust and ashes": "I who am but dust and ashes" (verse 27)"[23] —J. D.], and finally to Jerusalem. There I understood that he was the Father of all faiths, that he was the pilgrim, the *gêr* [the stranger, the hôte], the one who left his own, who made a pact of friendship with the foreign countries where he came as a pilgrim, that the Holy Land was not the monopoly of one race, but the Land prom- ised to all pilgrims like him.

A few years later, in 1952, Massignon, whom Claudel used to call "the knight of God," published in the *Revue internationale de la Croix Rouge* an article entitled "Respect of the Human Person in Islam and the Priority of Asylum Right over the Duty of Just War." There he wrote, "Whereas degenerate Christianity sees in Abraham no more than a incoherent folk image, the Muslim world in its entirety believes in its father Abraham, invokes him in a social and solemn fashion, for the salvation of each and all, the God of Abraham, at the annual Feast of sacrifices, 'Id al Qurban, at the end of the five daily prayers, at engagement celebrations and at funerals."[24]

In the same text, it is indeed the hospitality of the hôte Abraham that is placed at the center of Islam and that makes of Islam the most faithful heir, the exemplary heir of the Abrahamic tradition. "The European no longer understands that, thanks to the heroic manner in which he has practiced the notion of hospitality, Abraham deserved as his inheritance not only the Holy Land but also the entering in it of all the foreign hôtes who are "blessed" by his hospitality. . . . Abraham's hos- pitality is the sign announcing the final completion of the gathering of all nations, all blessed in Abraham, in this Holy Land that must be monopolized by none. . . . The Qur'ān mentions three times (XI, 72; XV, 51; LI, 24) the passage from Genesis

---

23. Emmanuel Levinas, *New Talmudic Readings*, trans. Richard A. Cohen (Pittsburgh: Duquesne University Press, 1999), 114; *Nouvelles lectures talmudiques* (Paris : Minuit, 1996) 83.

24. Quoted in Rocalve, *Louis Massignon*, 30.

(18:1–33).[25] It is from this fundamental text that Islam has deduced the principle of *Iqrā* (*dakhalk, jiwar*), right of hospitality, *ikram al dayf,* respect of the human person, of the *hôte,* sent by God."[26]

But what is this "fundamental text" from which Islam deduced the right of hospitality? It is a text from *Genesis* often quoted by Massignon, a scene during which Abraham extends hospitality to three visitors, three hôtes sent by God. Before reading and commenting upon this text about an originary and triple hospitality, I would like to read some passages from Massignon's letters where it is discussed in a certain manner, in his manner—this will give you an image of his quite singular fervor. These letters are reproduced in *L'hospitalité sacrée:*

> The three Angelus at the core of my life are the three prayers of Abraham, which will burst on Judgment Day like fountains of consolation for broken hearts from the very pure heart of Mary our Mother. To these Angelus, instead of vocal prayers, a small shudder of the heart, which palpitates for the glory of the saints toward the All-Saint; let us not refuse it to the Holy Spirit; let us always say to Him the "fiat" in our worst distress. [August 20, 1948]

> Our Badaliya is a reminder for everyone, and, first of all, for us, of the first, of the sweetest Christian duty: welcoming the other, the stranger, the neighbor who is closer than all our close ones [*accueillir l'autre, l'étranger, le prochain qui est plus proche que tous nos proches*], without reserve nor calculation, whatever it cost and at any price. [September 8, 1948]

> Exactly forty years ago, I was still in Brittany. I had planted a large cross in the wasteland; it is still there. On October 7 and 9, I spent the day invoking the protection of Saint Abraham (who saved me from the Dead Sea) for my entire life, committing

---

25. *Translator's Note:* The Qur'ānic references to the Genesis passage are the following:

XI, 71–72: "And his wife, standing by, laughed when We gave her good tidings (of the birth) of Isaac, and, after Isaac, of Jacob. She said: Oh, woe is me! Shall I bear a child when I am an old woman, and this my husband is an old man? Lo! This is a strange thing!"

XV, 51–52: "And tell them of Abraham's guests, (How) when they came in unto him, and said: Peace. He said: Lo! we are afraid of you.'"

LI, 24–27: "Hath the story of Abraham's honoured guests reached thee (O Muhammad)? When they came in unto him and said: Peace! He answered, Peace! (and thought): Folk unknown (to me). Then he went apart unto his housefolk so that they brought a fatted calf; And he set it before them, saying: Will ye not eat?

The Meaning of the Glorious Koran, trans. Marmaduke Pickthall (New York: Everyman's Library, 1992).

26. *Translator's Note:* Quoted in Rocalve, 33.

myself to pray this great prayer, still relevant. This year, Ibrahim who took his name for himself, who suffered with it, who offered with it his first born, renews his consecration to the father of all believers, to whom Mary shouted her joy on the day of the "Magnificat." "*Tou'azzimou nafsia erreb*, my soul glorifies the Lord." I pray of him that he offers us to God with the three Angelus, to repeat with him these three prayers which are one, the prayer of Sodom, the exile of Ishmael and the sacrifice of Isaac, in one and unique offering to the three divine Hôtes that Abraham received at Mamre where we prayed as if upon his grave on March 7, 1934. [October 8, 1948][27]

Let us now return to the text of Genesis 17 and 18. At age eighty-six, Abraham has had a son, Ishmael, from his servant Hagar since Sarai could not bear children. After he turns ninety-nine, Abraham receives the visitation of Yahweh, and this apparition ("He appeared" says one translation [by Edouard Dhormes]; "he makes himself seen" says another [by André Chouraqui]), this unexpected apparition by an uninvited visitor who makes himself seen, who shows himself, who comes ("shows up"),[28] this nonawaited irruption is, in itself, already a visitation.

And during this visitation, Yahweh announces other arrivals [*d'autres venues*], other hôtes, in sum, other visits or visitations. This visitation of Yahweh is so radically surprising and over-taking [*sur-prenante*] that he who receives does not even receive it himself, in his name [*celui qui la reçoit ne la reçoit même pas lui-même, en son nom*]. His identity is as if fractured. He receives without being ready to welcome since he is no longer the same between the moment at which God initiates the visit and the moment at which, visiting him, he speaks to him. This is indeed hospitality *par excellence* in which the visitor radically overwhelms the self of the "visited" and the *chez-soi* of the hôte (host).[29] For as you know these visitations and announcements will begin with changes of names, heteronomous changes, unilaterally decided by God who tells Abram that he will no longer be called Abram but Abraham (with wordplay, it seems, on Ab-hamon, "father of the multitudes"), much as later, before Isaac's birth, he will change the name of Sarai into Sarah ("my princess" into "princess").

This is the moment at which the visitation of the absolute hôte to the stranger that Abraham is not only changes—in a way, or, in any case, affects—the identity and the appellation of the hôte, but does so heteronomously at the moment the father of creation institutes Abraham as father of a multitude of nations. This institution of paternity constitutes the pact or covenant, sealed by the circumcision of the male child at eight days: "Any uncircumcised male who is not circumcised

---

27. Massignon, *L'hospitalité sacrée*, 253–56.
28. *Translator's Note:* The expression *shows up* is in English in the text.
29. *Translator's Note:* The word *host* is in English in the text.

in the flesh of his foreskin shall be cut off from his people; he has broken my covenant" (Genesis 17:14).

Then Yahweh announces the coming of Isaac, but this visitation, which announces a birth, announces, in fact, another announcement and another visit or visitation, that of hôtes, of three visitors (*tres vidit et Unum adoravit*, as Massignon will translate in a text I will address later) who will come to announce to Abraham both that Sarai will have to change her name and that she will give birth to Isaac, he who laughs—and this already made Abraham laugh who, in a scene that is truly a scene of hospitality (titled by Chouraqui, in fact, "Abraham's hospitality"—the very scene discussed by Massignon in a letter from October 8, 1948), will soon receive these three visitors and extend to them hospitality, drink and food.

With these texts, with Genesis 17:15–27 and Genesis 18, we have what are for Massignon the founding texts, and they all speak at once the universal paternity of Abraham at the origin of the three religions, the pact, and the pact as experience of sacred hospitality. Since there are so many of them, I cannot quote or analyze all the passages of Massignon's texts where the word "hôte" is made into the fundamental word of the fundamental experience. You will find many such passages, all perfectly explicit, in *L'hospitalité sacrée*, which intersect with some of those I have read earlier. Here are two examples:

> The hôte is the messenger of God (*Dheïf Allah*). Abraham's hospitality is a sign announcing the final completion of the gathering of all nations, blessed in Abraham, in this Holy Land which must be monopolized by none. (. . .) This notion of sacred hospitality seems to me essential for a search after truth between men, in our itineraries and our work, here below, and toward the threshold of the hereafter. (. . .) With hospitality, we find the Sacred at the center of our destinies' mystery, like secret and divine alms. (. . .) This mystery touches the very bottom of the mystery of the Trinity, where God is at once Guest [*Hôte*], Host [*Hospitalier*], and Home [*Foyer*].[30]

> Of the three solemn prayers of Abraham, before the prayer for Ishmael, the Arab and the Muslims, before the prayer for Isaac and the Twelve Tribes descended from his son Jacob, the first prayer which we must take up once again is the prayer for Sodom, without either unhealthy curiosity or hypocritical disdain, in the evening Angelus, "che volge il disio" (Dante, *Purgatorio* 8:1). This is not the place to examine the conditions under which the texts of these three prayers have been handed down to us through all the mishaps to which the copyists and translators have been exposed. (. . .) The first prayer of Abraham is the prayer which he uttered on behalf of Sodom. . . . He had abandoned the townsman's life of Chaldea to take up the life of a

---

30. Massignon, *L'hospitalité sacrée*, 121.

wandering shepherd. He planted the first stake which rooted him in the Promised Land very near his own future tomb. The perfect hospitality which he offered to his three mysterious visitors ("tres vidit et Unum adoravit"), who came to overwhelm him with the promise of Isaac, led them to test him: Is Abraham, now that he is assured an heir, going to continue to look after the people of Sodom, allies of his nephew Lot, whom he has already saved only by force of arms, or will he disavow his pact of fidelity with them when he learns that they have gone astray by iniquity? Then the angels told him that the people of Sodom had committed terrible sins and that the Lord was going to destroy them. But Abraham himself had come into this land as a stranger, a *ger*: a guest [*hôte*]. The guest [*hôte*] is sacred and still remains so. (. . .) Sodom is the city of self-love which objects to the visitation of angels, of guests [*Hôtes*], of strangers, or wishes to abuse them.[31]

I would like to do at least *two things* for now, regarding the logic of this reference to sacred hospitality.

1. *On the one hand*, to recall that this was not, on Massignon's part, a neutral and expert discourse of exegetical knowledge, but rather the testimonial confession, the testimony, one would almost say the martyr of a burning experience, a passion of fire, a conversion that he himself describes, in the language of hospitality, as a memory of events and visitations that fractured his identity and that almost, as you will hear it, changed his name (much as occurred to Abraham and Sarah). Naturally, this fervent Christian who saw in Islam the best heir of the Father and of Abraham's hospitality, finds this language of hospitality again when he approaches both the mystery of Mary and Jesus (in the two post-Judaic religions) and the manifestation of Christ in Islam.

Here, for example, is a text from *La parole donnée*, entitled "Visitation of the Stranger [*Visitation de l'étranger*]." In it, Massignon answers a query regarding the meaning of the word "God," our representation of God and the correspondences, in him, of the word "God." "Before the Lord who has struck the blow, the soul . . . starts only to commemorate in secret this Annunciation, viaticum of hope, that she has conceived in order to give birth to the immortal. This frail Guest [*Hôte*] that she carries in her womb determines thereafter all of her conduct. It is not a made-up idea that she develops as she pleases according to her nature, but a mysterious Stranger whom she adores and who guides her: she devotes herself to Him. . . . The soul sanctifies herself to protect her Sacred Guest. . . . She does not speak about her Guest "didactically" . . . but rather testimonially, waiting for the moment when He

---

31. Massignon, "The Three Prayers of Abraham," 7–10/F260–63.

suggests to her that she invoke Him, making her progress in experiential knowledge through compassion."[32]

Sacred hospitality, at once received and given, is founded not only on the Father or the patriarch Abraham but also on the Christian figure of the Trinity about which, as we saw, Massignon notes on February 2, 1962 (a few months before his death, when he summoned the Assembly of the Badaliya—the community of substitution of which I will speak in a moment), "God is at once Guest, Host, and Home."

This visitation of the stranger, this language of sacred hospitality is inseparable from an experience (no doubt one that is brief in its actuality, if I may say so, but interminable in its temptation) of homosexuality. I refer you here to Destremeau-Moncelon, from whom I read the few lines that recall, discreetly but, in a way, clearly, some recognized facts. They also quote Massignon when he explains the double reference that marks his language when he speaks of "sacred hospitality":

> The faults of which Massignon accused himself are now known: his liaison in Egypt with Yā-Sīn bin Ismail, his Alexandrian nights with Luis de Cuadra in 1907, and because it immediately precedes his conversion, his attraction to Djabbouri, during the raid to the desert of El-Okhaydir. He will not keep the mystery from his friends. Paul Claudel, for example, wrote to the Abbé Fontaine on 9 February 1914, concerning André Gide: "He confessed to me the reasons for his resistance. They are the same ways [les mêmes mœurs] that [Massignon] practiced in the past." Massignon will even contribute some clarifications at the end of his life: "The problem for me was that I was using the language of my sins, the language of the hopeless life I had led, in the homes of strangers [chez des étrangers], in search of something I did not know, that I had found in the shared agony of observing sacred hospitality.[33]

2. Finally, on the other hand, I would like to make manifest, in this testimonial logic of sacred hospitality, these two motifs of substitution and of hostage which cross so strangely, and in spite of so many differences, the same words in Levinas.

First, the word substitution, which Massignon could have encountered first in someone who had a certain influence upon him and who was one of three great figures he admired as a young man, namely, with Charles de Foucauld and Léon Marie Bloy, J. K. Huysmans (whom Massignon visits in 1900 just after his baccalauréat, when Huysmans, already suffering from throat cancer, has converted to Catholicism under the influence of one Père Boullan, who professed "mystical substitution" and

32. Massignon, "Visitation de l'étranger: Réponse à une enquête sur Dieu," Parole donnée, 281–82; trans. Herbert Mason and Danielle Chouet-Bertola in Testimonies and Reflections, 39–40.

33. Destremau and Moncelon, Massignon, 65–66.

the redemptive role of suffering).[34] Here is how Huysmans elaborates the doctrine of
"mystical substitution" (you will find here again something of Levinas's logic of the
hostage "responsible for all"): "Humanity is governed by two laws that it ignores in its
carelessness: the law of solidarity in evil, the law of reversibility in the good; solidarity
in Adam, reversibility in Our Lord. Otherwise put, up to a point, each is responsible
for the faults of the others, and must also, up to a point, expiate them. . . . God first
submitted to these laws when he applied them to himself in the person of the Son. . . .
He wanted for Jesus to give the first example of mystical substitution, the substitution
[*suppléance*] of him who owes nothing for him who owes everything. . . .[35]

This concept of substitution will be found everywhere in Massignon's spiritual
itinerary. It is the first movement of absolute hospitality. Aside from the texts and
speeches where this logic and this lexicon of substitution are operative, in 1943,
Massignon founded, with Mary Kahil in Cairo, under the Arabic name for substitution, *Badaliya*, a kind of spiritual community (a Christian one, gathering
Christians in the East, but turned toward Islam, such that some have seen here
wrongly—well, actually . . . —an attempt at proselytizing that should be fought
against). The wish to found this Badaliya dated from ten years earlier (1934, already
with Mary Kahil). The first statutes of the Badaliya that came into existence in
Damietta, Egypt, were published in April 1943; they announce that which is to be
"realized and completed" in its "providential truth," namely the "vocation of
Christians in the East of Arab race or language, reduced by the Muslim conquest to
being only a small flock": "union of prayers, between weak and poor souls, who
seek to love God and to give him glory, more and more, in Islam."

The word *hostage* appears immediately, with a particular connotation, in order
to designate who they are—who we are—who offer ourselves and commit ourselves, we who offer our life as a pledge. "We offer ourselves as pledge"—this is what
the word *hostage* means—but as pledge, voluntary prisoners, guarded hôtes, in a
kind of captivity or spiritual residency, in a foreign milieu that we respect, namely,
Islam; a milieu that we want to bring back to the truth to which it is itself the heir
and the trustee. Hostages, we offer ourselves as hostages—this means: we substitute
ourselves for the others in order to give ourselves as pledge in this foreign milieu,
with a mission, a duty which is not that of converting the Muslims (actually, it is,
but without external pressure),[36] but rather of awakening, in the Muslim people

---

34. See Destremau and Moncelon, *Massignon*, 22ff.

35. Quoted in Destremau and Moncelon, 23.

36. Letter of May 20, 1938: "(Badalyia) The "conversion" of these souls, yes, it is the goal, but it is for
them to find it themselves, without their suffering our insistence as an external pressure. It must be the
secret birth of a love, shared Love. . . . " (Massignon, *L'hospitalité sacrée*, 208).

who are cut off and excluded, the truth of Christ, of the sacred face of Christ, of which this Muslim people keeps an imprint, even if it keeps an imperfect tradition.

The strong words of the text I will read are the following: hostage, substitution or *suppléance*, intercession or incorporation, tradition, transmission, heritage and precious deposit.

"Al-Badaliya" (Statutes)

To realize and complete, in all its providential truth, the vocation of Christians in the East, of Arab race or Arabic language, whom the Muslim conquest has reduced to no more than a very *small flock*.

This union of prayers between weak and poor souls who seek to love God and to glorify him, more and more, in Islam, was born in Damietta, Egypt.

Assembled, gathered, and governed by the same impetus, toward the same goal which binds us, and through which we offer and commit our lives, from now on, *as hostages*.

—This goal, Christ's manifestation in Islam ("Blessed be Jesus Christ, true God and true Man, in Islam"), demands a deep penetration, made of fraternal understanding and of careful attentiveness, in the lives of families, of Muslim generations, past and present, whom God has placed on each of our paths. He has thus brought us to the subterranean waters of the grace granted by the Holy Spirit. We are trying to find the living sources of these waters for this people who were excluded, cut off long ago from the promise of the Messiah as children of Hagar, for, in their Muslim, imperfect, tradition, they preciously keep something like an imprint of the sacred face of Christ whom we adore, of "Issa Ibn Maryam" whom we want them to rediscover in themselves, in their heart.

—In this mission of intercession for them, where we ask God, without respite nor interruption, for the reconciliation of this dear souls, for whom we wish to substitute ourselves "*fil badaliya*," by paying their ransom in their place and at our expense, it is in replacement [*suppléance*] of their future "incorporation" in the Church that we wish to assume their condition, by following the example of the Word made flesh, by living among them each day, by partaking of their lives—us, baptized—like salt partakes of the taste of food.

—It is with this vocation for their salvation that we must and wish to sanctify ourselves, aspiring to become additional Christ [*d'autres Christ*] (like living Gospels), so that they recognize *Him* through us, and that we safeguard, with this silent and obscure apostleship, the sincerity of our own donation.

—Facing them, we must perfect and complete the Passion of Christ, since our ancestors, the Christians of the East have transmitted it to us as their unfinished legacy: they did not dare to take up Mohammed's challenge, when, one day in Medina, he called upon them to prove the Incarnation by exposing themselves to the Judgment of God: that is to say through the ordeal of fire.

This test and ordeal, demanded by the founder of Islam, has been postponed until us. It was desired by Saint Francis who gave himself [*qui s'y offrit*] to it in Damietta, and by many others who, in silence, have given themselves for the sake of Muslim souls. It was given to us as a precious deposit, transmitted from age to age, and it is incumbent upon us to perfect and realize it.

—A role is reserved for us in this mysterious duel, where for centuries Christendom has been facing the refusal of the Muslim world. Through many an ordeal and many an apostasy, this struggle has provided Christendom with many a joy and much glory for Eternity, with the institution of liturgical festivals, the founding of religious orders and the death of many a martyr.

—Waiting for this hour, we pray for them and with Him during the three Angelus of the day, affirming, through Mary's "Fiat," the mystery of divine Incarnation that the Muslims wish to deny; at the same hours the call to prayer of the Muezzin gathers the hearts in the same adoration of the One God of Abraham; during our Friday communions, day of Christ's Passion, which is also their day of gathering, chosen unconsciously to testify of their own faith.

—Living in Muslim land, under the pressure of an atmosphere which would obscure and suffocate our Christian faith were we not hoping for this *shahāda* (testimony [*témoignage*]) of martyrdom, in a hope that remembers the oath sworn long ago by the Mercedarians to replace, if necessary, in the Muslim jails, the prisoners that they wanted to redeem. We must follow the behavior of Saint Francis and of Saint Louis, facing these millions of souls who wait for us and look at us, as we are called to testify through our life, and, if God permits, through our death, like Foucauld, to whom it was granted and who also asked for it for his friends: to return to Christ who asks us to continue his Passion, this *shahāda* which we desire to offer him, as unworthy as we are.

Goals:

1) The Badaliya addresses itself to the Christians of the East.

2) It proceeds from the consciousness of a particular responsibility of these Christians toward their Muslim brothers in the midst of whom they live. These Christians have a providential mission toward them and they want to be faithful to it.

3) Moreover, because they have suffered and are still suffering at their hands, they want to practice toward them the highest Christian charity according to the command of our Lord "Love your enemies and pray for those who persecute you"

(Matthew 5:44) and according to his example: "While we were enemies, we were reconciled to God through the death of his Son" (Romans 5:10).

4) Thus, counting on the divine grace, these Christians want to consecrate them-selves to the salvation of their brothers, and in this hope of salvation, to give to Jesus Christ, in the name of their brothers, the faith, the Adoration and the love that, because of their imperfect knowledge of the Gospels, they are prevented from giving it themselves. Salvation does not necessarily mean external conversion. It is already a lot to obtain that a greater number belong to the soul of the Church, that they live and die in a state of grace.

5) Through these characteristics, the Badaliya distinguishes itself from the various associations and leagues of prayers already existing in Europe and with which the members of the Badaliya gratefully unite.[37]

The idea of a sacred deposit and of a guardian of the deposit recurs regularly, for example in a letter to Mary Kahil, probably from 1934, where Massignon defends himself against the accusation of religious syncretism and where the logic of the deposit is interlaced with that of the mystical substitution and of the hostage as *dis-appropriation* (this is Massignon's word).[38]

The word *hostage*, always emphasized, is applied by Massignon to himself. He wants to be and says himself to be a voluntary hostage, for example in another let-ter of 1947 to Mary Kahil where Massignon writes, "Hold on to your internal voca-tion to intercede for these Muslim souls. With me, you have been devoted to them by your compassion for the renegade Luis de Cuadra, to whom I had become hostage [*dont j'étais constitué l'otage*]."[39]

It is not only the word *hostage* that recalls (*mutatis mutandis* and with each dif-ference being vigilantly respected) Levinas's discourse, starting with *Otherwise than Being*. It is also the word *persecution*. I am hostage and I am persecuted, says Massignon, for example in a letter where he speaks of a "Islamico-Christian prayer" and even of a "Islamico-Christian prayer front." Here, then, I will read this letter before letting you think about this strange configuration of Judeo-Islamico-Christian hospitality, about peace too, but also about the war of hostages that is waged in it with pitiless compassion. "I am persecuted in all kinds of ways at the moment, but I am at peace. I was born into this world in order to share in Love and also in the Cross. Love is an inexorable fire and it burns like Sodom, for Sodom, for this world which tears itself in the midst of the love of God. (...) I am giving one

---

37. Quoted in *L'hospitalité sacrée*, 373–76.
38. *Translator's Note:* The letter is entitled "Depositum Custodi" in Massignon, *L'hospitalité sacrée*, 171–73.
39. Letter of June 29, 1947, in Massignon, *L'hospitalité sacrée*, 241.

of your friends some documents about the supreme effort that I attempted with my admirable Muslim friend, *Sheikh* el Okbi, in order that the Islamico-Christian prayer front maintain and affirm itself in the East, under the sign of 'Issa Ibn Maryam' (Jesus son of Mary)."[40]

SESSION OF FEBRUARY 12, 1997

The question of forgiveness—the immense, classical but also impossible question of forgiveness, pregnant with an abyssal history—appeared to provoke us, to push us to gather and to formalize the difficulties, the paradoxes and aporias holding us on the "lookout." I would like to return to this question for a few moments, not in order to pretend to be done or even to begin with it, but rather in order to reinscribe the hand that has been dealt [*la donne*] in our trajectory, between Levinas and Massignon, and on the way toward an approach of the Muslim culture of hospitality.

First of all, regarding what links the test and the ordeal [*l'épreuve*] of hospitality to that of forgiveness, one should not only say that forgiveness granted to the other is the supreme gift and therefore hospitality par excellence. Forgiving would be opening for and smiling to the other, whatever his fault or his indignity, whatever the offense or even the threat. Whoever asks for hospitality, asks, in a way, for forgiveness and whoever offers hospitality, grants forgiveness—and forgiveness must be infinite or it is nothing: it is excuse or exchange.

But if there is a scene of forgiveness at the heart of hospitality, between hôte and hôte, host and guest,[41] if there is failing, fault, offense, even sin, to be forgiven on the very threshold, if I may say so, of hospitality, it is not only because I must [*je dois*] forgive the other in order to welcome him, because the welcoming one [*l'accueillant*] must forgive the welcomed one [*l'accueilli*]. It is also because, inversely and first of all, the welcoming one must ask for forgiveness from the welcomed one even prior to the former's own having to forgive. For one is always failing, lacking hospitality [*car on est toujours en faute d'hospitalité*]: one never gives enough. Not only because welcoming is welcoming the infinite, and therefore welcoming, as Levinas says, beyond my capacity of welcoming [*ma capacité d'accueil*] (something that results in my always being behind, in arrears, always inadequate to my hôte and to the hospitality I owe him), but also because hospitality, as we saw, does not only consist in welcoming a guest, in welcoming according to the invitation, but rather, following the visitation, according to the surprise of the visitor, unforeseen,

---

40. Letter of April 30, 1958, in Massignon, *L'hospitalité sacrée*, 305.
41. *Translator's Note:* The words *host* and *guest* are in English in the text.

unforeseeable [*imprévu, imprévisible*], unpredictable, unexpected and unpredict-able,[42] unawaited [*inattendu*]. Hospitality consists in welcoming the other that does not warn me of his coming. In regard of this messianic surprise, in regard of what must thus tear any horizon of expectation, I am always, if I can say so, always and structurally, lacking, at fault [*en défaut, en faute*], and therefore condemned to be forgiven [*voué à me faire pardonner*], or rather to have to ask for forgiveness for my lack of preparation, for an irreducible and constitutive unpreparedness.

In both cases—that I cannot ever give enough to the welcomed or awaited guest nor expect enough [*m'attendre assez*] or give enough to the unexpected visitor or arriving one—in these two hypotheses, which are, by the way, structurally hetero-geneous to the rapport to the other, I am positioned so as to abandon the other, so as not to give him enough, and thus to leave him abandoned. Therefore, I have to ask for forgiveness for abandonment [*j'ai donc à demander pardon de l'abandon*], forgiveness for not giving, forgiveness for not having known how to give [*pardon de n'avoir pas su faire don*].

I will start again from this Jewish joke reported by Theodor Reik (who wrote exten-sively on the *Grand Pardon* and on the *Kol Nidre*).[43] "Two Jews, longtime enemies, meet at the synagogue, on the Day of Atonement [*le jour du Grand Pardon*]. One says to the other [as a gesture, therefore, of forgiveness —J. D.]: 'I wish for you what you wish for me.' The other immediately retorts: 'Already you're starting again?'"

An unfathomable story, a story that seems to stop on the verge of itself, a story whose development consist in interrupting itself, in paralyzing itself in order to refuse itself all *avenir*; absolute story of the unsolvable, vertiginous depth of the bottomlessness [*sans-fond*], irresistible whirlpool that carries forgiveness, the gift, and the re-giving, the re-dealing of forgiveness, to the abyss of impossibility.

How to acquit oneself of forgiveness? And does not forgiveness have to exclude all acquitting, all acquitting of oneself, all acquitting of the other?

Forgiving is surely not to call it quits, clear and discharged [*pardonner, ce n'est sûrement pas tenir pour quitte*]. Not oneself, nor the other. This would be repeating evil, countersigning it, consecrating it, letting it be what it is, unalterable and iden-tical to itself. No adequation is here acceptable or tolerable. What, then?

As I have said, I think that we will agree in finding this Jewish joke not only funny, but also memorable and unforgettable, precisely where it treats of this treatment of memory and the unforgettable that one calls forgiveness. Forgiveness

---

42. *Translator's Note:* The words *unexpected* and *unpredictable* are in English in the text.

43. *Translator's Note:* Yom Kippur, the Jewish Day of Atonement, is called in French "le Grand Pardon," the Great Forgiveness. On the eve of Yom Kippur, the famous *Kol Nidre* (Aramaic, "all the vows") is recited.

is above all not forgetting, on the contrary. There is no forgiveness without memory, certainly, but no forgiveness is reducible to an act of memory. To forgive is not to forget, above all not to forget. A story "for laughs," no doubt, but what, in it, makes us laugh, laugh or cry, and laugh through the tears or anguish?

This, no doubt, has to do first of all with economy [*épargne*], an economy that was powerfully analyzed by Freud, and by Sarah Kofman interrogating Freud.[44] By the way, in her chapter on the "three knaves [*les trois larrons*]," a note also speaks of forgiveness. It speaks of the economy of "pleasure allowed by the super-ego, the *forgiveness* of sorts that is granted by it and that brings humor closer to the manic phase, since thanks to its '*gifts* [*dons*],' the diminished 'ego' finds itself if not euphoric at least inflated anew."[45]

Without pursuing this direction, I will remain, for the moment, with the wild analysis of this Jewish story: two enemies make the gesture of forgiving each other, they fake it, "for laughs," but they reopen, or internally persist with, the conflict. They avow to each other [*ils s'avouent*] this inexpiable war; they symmetrically accuse each other of it. The avowal goes through a symptom rather than through a declaration, but this changes nothing of the truth: they have not disarmed; they continue to wish each other ill.

One of the allegorical powers of this story is perhaps the following: the test and ordeal that these two Jews undergo, and that which makes us laugh, is indeed the radical impossibility of forgiveness. And yet, as I have suggested earlier, in this impossible, and commonly endured as impossible, forgiveness, in this common non-forgiveness, this mutual non-forgiveness, these two Jews, face to face (with or without a third), experience, perhaps, a kind of compassion. Perhaps. And perhaps a kind of forgiveness filters unconsciously through this compassion, supposing that an unconscious forgiveness were not nonsense.

A Jew, a Jew of any time but, above all, in this century, is also someone who undergoes the test and the ordeal of the impossibility of forgiveness, of its radical impossibility. Besides, who would give this right to forgive? Who would give—and to whom—the right to forgive for the dead, and to forgive the infinite violence done to them, depriving them of burial and of name, everywhere in the world and not only in Auschwitz? And thus everywhere the unforgivable would have occurred? Besides, regarding everything for which Auschwitz remains both the proper name and the metonymy, we would have to speak of this painful but essential experience which consists in reproaching oneself as well, in front of the dead, as it were, with having survived, with being a survivor. There would be, there sometimes is, a feeling

44. Sarah Kofman, *Pourquoi rit-on ? Freud et le mot d'esprit* (Paris: Galilée, 1986), esp. 100–13.
45. Kofman, *Pourquoi*, 104; emphases added.

of guilt, muted or acute, for living, for surviving, and therefore an injunction to ask for forgiveness, to ask the dead or one knows not who, for the simple fact of being there [*être là*], alive, that is to say, for surviving, for being here, still here, always here, here where the other is no longer—and therefore to ask for forgiveness for one's being-there [*être-là*], a being there originarily guilty. Being-there: this would be asking for forgiveness; this would be to be inscribed in a scene of forgiveness, and of impossible forgiveness. If there is, in a Nietzschean or Heideggerian, even Levinasian, sense (three very different, even irreducible, senses), a kind of a priori debt or indebtedness, prior even to any contract, as Levinas would say, prior to any borrowing, then, any *existant*, any subject, any *Dasein*, is in the process of asking for forgiveness for what he is [*pour ce qu'il est*], of asking for forgiveness insofar as he is [*en tant qu'il est*]. He confesses, even when he does not confess or denies confessing. Forgiveness asked [*le pardon demandé*] does not occur at a given moment for such particular fault or unacquittable debt, but for the unacquittable that is the fact of being there. Even if forgiveness is not asked for by way of an explicit formulation, by way of an "I beg your pardon," even if it is not asked of a determined addressee, the prayer, a kind of silent "Our Father," would be operative in the murmur or the whispering of any existence, day and night, unto sleep and unto dream.

And this constancy of begged forgiveness also testifies to the impossibility of forgiveness, received or granted. If—whether or not I want to—I am always asking for forgiveness, it is because forgiveness remains denied [*refusé*], and therefore apparently impossible.

Regarding the guilt of the survivor, which is not only that of the concentration camp survivor, but, first of all, of any survivor, of anyone who is mourning, of all work of mourning—and the work of mourning is always an "I survive," and is therefore of the living in general—regarding the originary guilt of the living as survivor who must therefore be forgiven simply for the fact of living and of surviving the death of the other, I will quote a long parenthesis of Levinas in his "Cours sur la mort et le temps" (in the book *Dieu, la mort et le temps*). You will see again that the logic of substitution and of hostage is here operative. This is a parenthesis where Levinas again speaks in his own name, as it were, while in the process of pedagogically exposing Heidegger:

(Sympathy and compassion, to suffer for the other or "to die a thousand deaths" for the other [*l'autre*], have as their condition of possibility a more radical substitution for an other [*autrui*]. This would be a responsibility for another in bearing his misfortune or his end *as if one were guilty of causing it* [*comme si on en était coupable*; underscored in italics: one thus asks for forgiveness, "as if"? —J. D.]. This is the ultimate proximity. *To survive as a guilty one.* In this sense, the sacrifice for another [*autrui*] would create an other relation with the death of the other: a responsibility that would perhaps answer the question of why one can die. In the guiltiness of the survivor, the death of the other [*l'autre*] concerns me [*est mon affaire*]. *My* death is my *part* in the death of the other, and in my death I die the death that is my fault. The death of the other is not only a moment of the mineness of my ontological function.)⁴⁶

This survivor's guilt for the death of the other, this forgiveness asked a priori by the living as survivor—this is what, making us *a priori* guilty of the death of the other, transforms this death into something other than a natural death: forgiveness begged confesses [*avoue*] guilt and transforms the death of the other into the equivalent of a murder. When someone dies (when I mourn him, that is to say, when it is someone whom I am supposed to love, whom I am supposed to hold dear, someone close or one of my own, in all the senses of these words), then my sadness and my guilt signify that I am responsible for this death, that I feel responsible, as one says, for this death which is therefore a murder. They signify that I have killed, symbolically or not, the other, or, in any case, that I have "let him die." As soon as I feel responsible for a death, it means that I interpret it as a murder. There always is at least nonassistance to an endangered person in the phantasm that links us to the death of our own [*qui nous rapporte à la mort des nôtres*]. I say "our own" not because I know or can determine first what this means (loved ones, family, compatriots, etc.). No, it is the opposite, rather. My own, our own, are those who never die of natural death since I accuse myself of having killed them or having let them die. My own are the victims of murder, those who do not die of natural death, since, actively or passively, I feel I have lent my hand to their death. This is also what one calls love. Thus I would define my own, those whom I hold dear: they are those who always die by my fault, those of whom I ask forgiveness for their death which is my fault. Such, at least, is the ineluctable empire of the phantasm at the origin of meaning.

One also finds in Blanchot and in Levinas this thought of death that is always a murder. In Blanchot I do not remember where—even though I have quoted this sentence I no longer know where.⁴⁷ In Levinas, still in the "Cours sur la mort et le temps," "In the death of another, in his face that is exposition to death, it is not the passage from one quiddity to another that is announced; in death is *the very event*

46. Emmanuel Levinas, *God, Death, and Time*, trans. Bettina Bergo; slightly altered (Stanford: Stanford University Press, 2000) 39; *Dieu, la mort et le temps* (Paris: Grasset, 1993), 50. Levinas is here commenting on *Being and Time*, §47.

47. *Translator's Note:* Derrida may be referring here to Blanchot as he is quoted in "Living On: Border Lines": "There is death and murder (words which I defy anyone to distinguish . . .)" (J. Derrida, "Living On: Border Lines," trans. James Hulbert, in *Deconstruction and Criticism*, ed. Harold Bloom et al. (New York: Continuum, 1979)/*Parages* (Paris: Galilée 1986), 163, quoting Maurice Blanchot, *The Writing of the Disaster*, trans. Ann Smock [Lincoln: University of Nebraska Press, 1995], 71).

of passing (our language says, moreover, "he has passed" ["*il passe*"]) with its own acuteness that is its scandal (each death is the first death). One must think of all the murder there is in death: every death is a murder, is premature, and there is the responsibility of the survivor."[48] But the impossibility of forgiveness, let us not hide this from ourselves, must be thought yet otherwise, and unto the most radical root [*la racine la plus radicale*] of its paradox, in the very formation of a concept of forgiveness. What a strange concept! Since it does not resist the impossibility of what wants to be conceived in it, since it explodes or implodes in it, it is an entire chain of concepts which explodes with it, and even the concept of concept that thus finds itself undergoing the test and ordeal of its essential precariousness, of its finitude and its deconstructability.

The impossibility of forgiveness offers itself to thought, in truth, as its sole possibility. Why is forgiveness impossible? Not merely difficult for a thousand psychological reasons, but absolutely impossible? Simply because what there is to forgive must be, and must remain, unforgivable. If forgiveness is possible, if there is forgiveness, it must forgive the unforgivable—such is the logical aporia. But, in spite of appearances, this is not only a cold and formal contradiction or logical dead end. It is a tragedy of compassion and of inter-subjectivity as destiny of the hostage, hôte, and madness of substitution of which we speak with Levinas and Massignon. If one had to forgive only what is forgivable, even excusable, *venial,* as one says, or insignificant, then one would not forgive. One would excuse, forgive, erase, one would not be granting forgiveness. If, in the process of any given transformation, the fault, the evil, the crime are attenuated or extenuated to the point of veniality, if the effects of the wound were less hurting, were even accompanied by some surplus of jouissance, then that which itself becomes forgivable frees itself of all guilt [*se met hors de cause*] and needs no forgiveness. The forgiveness of the forgivable does not forgive anything: it is not forgiveness. In order to forgive, one must [*il faut*] therefore forgive the unforgivable, but the unforgivable that remains [*demeuré*] unforgivable, the worst of the worst: the unforgivable that resists any process of transformation of me or of the other, that resists any alteration, any historical reconciliation that would change the conditions or the circumstances of the judgment. Whether remorse or repentance, the ulterior purification of the guilty has nothing to do with this. Besides, there is no question of forgiving a guilty one, a subject subject to transformation beyond the fault. Rather, it is a matter of forgiving the fault itself— which must remain unforgivable in order to call for forgiveness on its behalf. But to forgive the unforgivable—is this not, all logic considered, impossible? If it remains thus impossible, forgiveness must therefore *do the impossible*; it must undergo the

---

48. Levinas, *God, Death, and Time,* 72/*Dieu, la mort et le temps,* 85.

test and ordeal of its own impossibility in forgiving the unforgivable. It must therefore undergo the test and ordeal, merge [*se confondre*] with the very test and ordeal of this aporia or paradox: the possibility, if it is possible and if there is such, the possibility *of* the impossible. And the impossible of the possible.

Here perhaps is a condition that forgiveness shares with the gift [*une condition que le pardon partage avec le don*]—and therefore with hospitality, which gives without return or else is nothing. Beyond the formal analogy, this perhaps also means that one affixes its condition of impossibility to the other: the gift to forgiveness or forgiveness to the gift, hospitality to forgiveness and forgiveness to hospitality—hospitality as the opposite of abandonment. Not to mention that one must also be forgiven for the gift (which cannot avoid the risk of causing pain, of doing wrong [*risquer de faire mal, de faire le mal*], for example in giving death) and that a gift remains perhaps more unforgivable than nothing in the world [*plus impardonable que rien au monde*].

The question that imposed itself on me one day (what is "to give in the name of the other?" "Who knows what we do when we give in the name of the other?") to suggest that here was perhaps the only chance of the gift—doesn't it let itself be translated by forgiveness? If I forgive in my name, my forgiveness expresses what I am capable of, me, and this decision (which is therefore no longer a decision) does no more than deploy my power and abilities, the potential energy of my aptitudes, predicates, and character traits. Nothing is more unforgivable, more haughty [*hautain*] sometimes, more self-assured than the "I forgive you." (We shall encounter again this theme of height [*hauteur*].) I can no more decide, what is called deciding, in my name, than I can forgive in my name but only in the name of the other, there where alone I am capable neither of deciding nor of forgiving. What must be [*il faut*], therefore, is that I forgive what is not mine to forgive, not the power of giving or forgiving: what must be is that I forgive beyond me [*il faut que je pardonne au-delà de moi*] (this is close to what Levinas says, that I must welcome the infinite, and this is the first hospitality, beyond the capacity of the I—which is obviously the impossible itself: how could I do what I cannot do? How to do the impossible? Only the other in me can do it, and decide—this would be to let him do it [*le laisser faire*], without the other doing it simply in my place: here is the unthinkable of substitution. Perhaps, one must [*peut-être faut-il*] think substitution from these limit-experiences, possible-impossible, the impossible of the possible, that are the decision, the gift, forgiveness—and what I want to signal here is that the allusions, at least, to forgiveness in Levinas and Massignon are remarkable). And that this, this gift, this forgiveness, this decision, would be done in the name of the other does not exonerate in any way my freedom or my responsibility, on the contrary.

The impossibility of the possible, the possible of the impossible: here is a definition that resembles what one often gives for death, Heidegger in particular. And
there is nothing fortuitous in this. We have to think this affinity, therefore, between
the impossibility named death and the impossibility named forgiveness, between
the gift of death and the gift of forgiveness as possibility of the impossible, possibility of the impossible hospitality. It is a little as if "hospitality," the name *hospitality*,
came to name [*surnommer*], but also to give a kind of proper name to this opening
of the possible onto the impossible, and reciprocally: when hospitality takes place,
the impossible becomes possible but *as* impossible. The impossible, for me, for an
"I," for what is "my own" or is properly my own in general.

For where is forgiveness more impossible, and therefore possible *as* impossible,
than beyond the border between one living and one dead? How could the living forgive the dead [*comment un vivant pourrait-il pardonner à un mort*]? What sense and
what gift would there be in a forgiveness that can no longer hope to reach its destination, except inside oneself [*sinon au-dedans de soi*], toward the other [*vers l'autre*]
that is welcomed or rescued as a narcissistic ghost inside oneself? And reciprocally,
how can the living hope to be forgiven by the dead or by a specter inside itself? One
can follow the consequence and consistency of this logic to the infinite.

Well then, I wage that this limit which cannot be crossed [*infranchissable*]—and
nonetheless is crossed insofar as it cannot be crossed [*et franchie pourtant comme
infranchissable*], in the enfranchisement of the uncrossed that cannot be crossed
[*dans l'affranchissement de l'infranchissement de l'infranchi*]—is the very line that
our two Jews have crossed, with or without confession, without repentance, regarding their mutual accusation. To avow, to share, to confide in each other this test and
ordeal which cannot be crossed [*cette épreuve infranchissable*] of the unforgivable,
to describe oneself as unforgivable for not forgiving—this is perhaps not forgiveness, since forgiveness seems impossible, even there where it takes place, but it is to
bear with [*compatir avec*] the other in the test and ordeal of the impossible.

This would be here—here we are—the ultimate compassion. And this compassion is perhaps also the very test of substitution: to be one at the place of the other,
the hostage and the hôte of the other; therefore the subject of the other, subject to
the other, there where not only cannot places be exchanged—insofar as they
remain unexchangeable and where everything withdraws from a logic of exchange—
but where this unicity, this irreplaceability of the nonexchange poses itself, affirms
itself, tests and suffers itself, in substitution. I am *like* [*comme*] the other, there
where I cannot be, and could never be *like* him, in his resemblance, his identification or in his place. There where there is room [*place*] for the replacement of what
remains irreplaceable. There is where we say I, him, her and me, here is what says

"I," the same and the other, and this cease only at death. What also allows to think that this play of substitution, which resembles an exchange of place between two inexchangeable absolutes, is perhaps also the first intrusion of the third in the face-to-face, this intrusion of which we have underscored that it was at once ineluctable and a priori, archi- or preoriginary, an intrusion not occurring to the dual but *connaissant* with it, knowing it and being-born-together with it, insinuating itself in it from the first instant—and immediately poses, without waiting, the question of justice linked to the third. But in one stroke, as we saw, betraying, by demand of justice, the fidelity to the other's singularity, the absolute and infinite, finite-infinite singularity of the other. This is what I have called the congenital perjury of justice, justice [*le juste*] as perjury. But this is also where I have to ask for forgiveness for being just, to ask forgiveness of the other, of every other; where, for justice, I have to take account of the other of the other, of another other, of a third. Forgiveness for infidelity at the heart of fidelity, for perjury at the heart of sworn faith [*foi jurée*]— it would suffice to say "at the heart," period. Perjury is a heart, it is at the heart of the heart, and it is from this tragedy, which "discords" the heart in its very accord [*qui désaccorde le coeur dans l'accord même*], that the prayer of mercy [*miséricorde*] rises, even for the nonbeliever, and even if he knows nothing of it. As soon as there is substitution, and as soon as there is a third [*un troisième*], I am called by justice, by responsibility, but I also betray justice and responsibility. I have to ask, therefore, for forgiveness even before committing a determinable fault. One can call this original sin prior to any original sin, prior to the event, real or mythical, real or phantasmatic, of any original sin. Since it is from this substitution that subjectivity (in the sense Levinas gives to it) is determined, subjectivity as hôte or subjectivity as hostage, one must indeed think this subjectivity-substitution as a being-under, being-below [*un être-sous, être-dessous*]: not being-under and being-below in the sense of the classical subject, of the *subjectum* or *substantia* or *hypokeimenon*, as what is extended, lying, standing under its predicates, its qualities, attributes or accidents. Rather, as what is put under, submitted [*soumis*], subjected [*assujetti*], under the subjection of the law that is above it, at this height of which Levinas speaks, the height of the Most-High as the height of the other or of God. And this is indeed submission, subjection, sub-jection of one who is who he is only insofar as he asks for the forgiveness of the other: "on one's knees," as one says, while entrusting himself [*se livrant*] to the sovereignty of the other who is higher. This verticality of the body and of the asymmetric gaze that gazes at the other without exchanging looks [*sans croiser le regard*], of the face-to-face that does not exchange looks with, nor sees, the face of God—this is the orientation of subjectivity in substitution, which can ask for forgiveness but can never grant itself [*s'accorder*] the assurance of granting [*accorder*] forgiveness. One must [*il faut*] ask for forgiveness but even if one must [*il faut*] forgive, one must do so without knowing, without having or pretending to have the assurance. "I beg your pardon" is a decent statement—"I forgive you" is an indecent statement because of the haughty and complacent height it denotes or connotes. Who am I, who do I pretend to be to thus grant myself the right to forgive?

If forgiveness can be asked for by me but granted only by the other, then God, the God of mercy, is the name of he who alone can forgive, in the name of whom alone forgiveness can be granted, and who can always abandon me, but also—and this is the equivocal beauty of this word *abandonment*—the only one to whom I can abandon myself, to the forgiveness of whom I can abandon myself.

Thus, I have to ask the hôte for forgiveness because, unable to ever receive and give him enough, I always abandon him too much, but inversely, in asking the other for forgiveness and in receiving from him the forgiveness of him, I abandon myself to him.

This is also what one calls love, and, first of all, mystical love, which gives itself without giving anything else but itself; which abandons itself while asking for forgiveness at the height of the other, for forgiveness kneeling, for forgiveness on one's knees, the kneeling of prayer—essential prostration to begged forgiveness—and forgiveness granted from God.

If you read again some of Massignon's letters, you will find—this time in what he calls "the Islamico-Christian front of prayer"—the structure, the inter-subjective, inter-substitutive but dissymmetric scene, and the lexicon of this love-gift, forgiveness, abandonment [*amour-don, pardon, abandon*] in kneeling prostration. I will give a few examples taken from *L'hospitalité sacrée*.

> The offering of a soul by another that offers it still. That night, while praying in front of a burning Paschal cierge to gain the ability to love that other soul more than oneself, so that it grows in beauty and in wisdom before God, surpassing in grace the fragile vow, the fraternal clumsiness prostrated in the night. . . . [January 28, 1946]

> This grief came to you suddenly, taking [your mother] away from you, she who was the luminous center of your family life. One must kneel in silence before the mysterious divine will who had given her to you—as a deposit—for so many years. . . . [May 31, 1946]

> To bring oneself to the divine presence and to invoke it from the bottom of one's heart. To compose a space for the "fiat," kneeling in front of Mary. To consider her trusting humility, her maternal intercession in our poor lives as sinners. To beg her to say for us, for all of us, sinners "*fil badaliya*," this humble, divine word of all vocation: "Fiat." [October 6, 1946]

This is the moment when God's gift [*le don de Dieu*], the Holy Spirit brings us to conceive of abandon with Mary's approval. I have found that I am nothing. I cannot go to Him with my intelligence, I know nothing: nor with my feeling, I feel nothing. I touch him directly with abandon, in an instant, and it is enough. Why ask him for a sign? Why ask to be a martyr? To be burned? Why ask for ecstasy? Abandon is more than ecstasy. It is what already makes us—the becoming that we are—immortal ... (in Arabic: *islam*). [January 4, 1947]

The sword's blow of conversion entirely enlightened me, for a brief moment, with the gaze of my Judge. Silently, coming from his mouth, his liberating word was at least bringing me into the communion of the Church where he had left me alone, searching among his faithful creatures for who would extend to me the adorable and living sign of his mercy—his pierced hand; for who would grant me the consoling word of forgiveness: "I love you." [January 31, 1947]

"To find oneself again [*se retrouver*]": We have learned, haven't we, everything that this poignant word contains of intoxicating immortality to share together. For to love is to find and to find oneself again, it is to enter into solitude, there where faith, hope, and charity become—in our hearts abandoned by all perishable and infinitely poor things—the burning love of the three divine Persons. The three guests of Abraham went to burn Sodom. ... [May 28, 1947][49]

Besides, if one were to look, in ethics according to Levinas, for the trace of this "forgiveness to be asked for [*ce pardon à demander*]" from the threshold of existence, which is from the first, for every mortal, a surviving [*une survie*], one would find it very early in his texts, as early as *De l'existence à l'existant*, for example (written in captivity between 1940 and 1945). I have not been able to extract all the passages that explicitly name forgiveness but here are a few examples. In *De l'existence à l'existant*, the lexicon of "forgiveness" as originary structure, in a way, surges in an unusual but necessary manner, there were it is a question of freedom and of time. Before speaking, as he already does, of the face-to-face, Levinas redefines freedom in its rapport to time, to the present and to the instant, the limit of freedom: "The freedom of the present finds a limit in the responsibility for which it is the condition."[50]

As soon as the present of freedom at once conditions responsibility and finds itself limited, even negated by it, I am responsible before the other, at the heart of my freedom and even before, if one may say so, being free, in order to be free. Here is

---

49. Quoted in *L'hospitalité sacrée*, 232–40.

50. Emmanuel Levinas, *Existence and Existents*, trans. Alphonso Lingis (Dordrecht: Kluwer Academic Publishers, 1988), 79; [*De l'existence à l'existant* (Paris: Vrin, 1990), 135.

what Levinas precisely calls, already, a paradox: "This is the most profound paradox in the concept of freedom: its synthetic bond with its own negation. A free being alone is responsible, that is, already not free."[51] No doubt one must be free [*sans doute faut-il être libre*] in order to ask for forgiveness and free to grant it. But the paradox of a freedom limited by an originary responsibility before the other is that the relation of the I to the other before whom one is responsible is a rapport of infinite and originary duty and indebtedness, therefore incommensurable, irredeemable [*inacquittable*] and therefore delivered over to the "asking for forgiveness," "asking to be forgiven," saved or redeemed by forgiveness as soon as I say "I" and "I am free" or "responsible." From the most solitary threshold of solitude, I am constituted by this request for forgiveness, this "asking for forgiveness" or by this "being forgiven" for existing, this having to be forgiven—as survivor. Such that the rapport to forgiveness is no longer a secondary, contingent, moment in a kind of chapter of ethics, it is rather constitutive of my being-myself [*mon être-moi-même*] in my rapport with the other. I have to ask for forgiveness for being myself, before asking for forgiveness for what I am, for what I do or what I have. This "forgiveness to be asked for" belongs to a kind of "*cogito*," "*ego cogito*" before the "*ego cogito*": as soon as I say *I*, even in solitude, as soon as I say *ego cogito*, I am in the process of asking for forgiveness or of being forgiven, at least if the experience lasts for more than an instant and temporalizes itself. Such at least is the way I read the following passage, "Solitude is accursed not of itself, but by reason of its ontological significance as something definitive. Reaching the other is not something justified of itself; it is not a matter of shaking me out of my boredom. It is, on the ontological level, the event of the most radical breakup of the very categories of the ego, for it is for me to be somewhere else than my self [already substitution —J. D.]; it is *to be pardoned*, to not be a definite existence. The relationship with the other is not to be conceived as a bond with another ego, nor as a comprehension of the other which makes his alterity disappear, nor as a communion with him around some third term."[52]

The word *ontological*, it seems to me, here means that everything that is being, like "being forgiven" or "to be forgiven" is a category that is not only psychological or moral, but rather ontological. Yet, this is an event (this is the word: "ontologically the even of the most radical rupture of the very categories of the ego . . . ") that, insofar as it is ontological, breaks with traditional ontology and finally, Levinas will says this later, with ontology itself in the name of ethics, metaphysics, or first philosophy.

This thought of forgiveness, from this time on, is therefore a thought of time as the structure of the ego. The "I" temporalizes itself in the leap, the salvation and the

---

51. Levinas, *Existence*, 79/ *De l'existence*, 135.
52. Levinas, *Existence*, 85/*De l'existence*, 144; emphasis added.

surviving, the resurrection from one instant to the other. This temporal structure as leap, promised salvation, redemption and resurrection, implies the "forgiveness," or the having to be forgiven, or the having to ask for forgiveness. I will read a passage where this phenomenology of temporalization and of responsible freedom inscribes forgiveness in a thought of salvation, of redemption, of the Messiah and above all of resurrection: resurrection is the miracle of each instant.

> The economic world then includes not only our so-called material life, but also all the forms of our existence in which the exigency of salvation [*l'exigence du salut*] has been traded in, in which Esau has already sold his birthright. The world is the secular world, where the "I" accept wages. Religious life itself, when it is understood in terms of the category of wages, is economic. Tools serve this yearning for objects as wages. They have nothing to do with ontology; they are subordinate to desire. They not only suppress disagreeable effort, but also the waiting time. In modern civilization they do not only extend the hand, so that it could get at what it does not get at of itself; they enable it to get at it more quickly, that is, they suppress in an action the time the action has to take on. Tools suppress the intermediary times; they contract duration. Modern tools are machines, that is, systems, arrangements, fittings, coordinations: light fixtures, telephone lines, railroad and highway networks. The multiplicity of organs is the essential characteristic of machines. Machines sum up instants. They produce speed; they echo the impatience of desire.
>
> But this compensating time is not enough for hope. For it is not enough that tears be wiped away or death avenged; no tear is to be lost, no death be without a resurrection. Hope then is not satisfied with a time composed of separate instants given to an ego that traverses them so as to gather in the following instant, as impersonal as the first one, the wages of its pain. The true object of hope is the Messiah, or salvation [*L'object veritable de l'espoir, c'est le Messie, ou le salut*].
>
> The caress of a consoler which softly comes in our pain does not promise the end of suffering, does not announce any compensation, and in its very contact, is not concerned with what is to come with *afterwards* in economic time; it concerns the very instant of physical pain, which is then no longer condemned to itself, is transported "elsewhere" by the movement of the caress, and is freed from the vice-grip of "oneself," finds "fresh air," a dimension and a future [*avenir*]. Or rather, it announces more than a simple future [*avenir*], a future [*avenir*] where the present will have the benefit of a recall. This effect of compassion, which we in fact all know, is usually posited as an initial datum of psychology, and other things are then explained from it. But in fact it is infinitely mysterious.
>
> Pain cannot be redeemed. Just as the happiness of humanity does not justify the mystery of the individual, retribution in the future [*avenir*] does not wipe away the

pains of the present. There is no justice that could make reparations for it. One should have to return to that instant, or be able to resurrect it. To hope then is to hope for the reparation of the irreparable; it is to hope for the present. It is generally thought that this reparation is impossible in time, and that eternity alone, where instants distinct in time are indiscernible, is the locus of salvation [le lieu du salut]. This recourse to eternity, which does not seem to us indispensable, does at any rate bear witness to the impossible exigency for salvation which must concern the very instant of pain, and not only compensate for it. Does not the essence of time consist in responding to that exigency for salvation? Does not the analysis of economic time, exterior to the subject, cover over the essential structure of time by which the present is not only indemnified, but resurrected? Is not the future [avenir] above all a resurrection of the present [une resurrection du présent]?

Time and the "I"
We believe that time is just that. What is called the "next instant" is an annulment of the unimpeachable commitment to existence made in the instant; it is the resurrection of the "I." We believe that the "I" does not enter identical and unforgiven [identique et impardonné]—a mere avatar—into the following instant, where it would undergo a new experience whose newness will not free it from its bond with itself—but that its death in the empty interval will have been the condition for a new birth. The "elsewhere which opens up to it will not only be a "change from its homeland" [un "dépaysement"] but an "elsewhere than in itself ["ailleurs qu'en soi"], which does not mean that it sank into the impersonal or the eternal. Time is not a succession of instants filing by before an I, but the response to the hope for the present, which in the present is the very expression of the "I," and is itself equivalent to the present. All the acuteness of hope in the midst of despair comes from the exigency that the very instant of despair be redeemed. To understand the mystery of the work of time, we should start with the hope for the present, taken as a primary fact. Hope hopes for the present itself. Its martyrdom does not slip into the past, leaving us with a right to wages. At the very moment where all is lost, everything is possible.

There then is no question of denying the time of our concrete existence, constituted by a series of instants to which the "I" remains exterior. For such is the time of economic life, where the instants are equivalent, and the "I" circulates across them to link them up. There time is the renewal of the subject, but this renewal does not banish tedium; it does not free the ego from its shadow. We ask then whether the event of time cannot be lived more deeply as the resurrection of the irreplaceable instant [l'irremplaçable instant]. In place of the "I" that circulates in time, we posit the "I" as the very ferment of time in the present, the dynamism of time. This dynamism is not that of dialectical progression, nor that of ecstasy, nor that of duration, where the present encroaches upon the future [*avenir*] and consequently does not have between its being and its resurrection the indispensable interval of nothingness. The dynamism of the "I" resides in the very presence of the present, in the exigency which this presence implies. This exigency does not concern perseverance in being, nor, properly speaking, the impossible destruction of this presence, but the unraveling of the knot which is tied in it, the definitive, which its evanescence does not undo. It is an exigency for a recommencement of being, and a hope in each recommencement of its non-definitiveness. The "I" is not a being that, as a residue of a past instant, attempts a new instant. It is this exigency for the non-definitive. *The "personality" of a being is its very need for time* as a miraculous fecundity in the instant itself, by which it recommences as other.

But it cannot endow itself with this alterity. The impossibility of constituting time dialectically is the impossibility of saving oneself by oneself and of saving oneself alone [*l'impossibilité de se sauver par soi-même et de se sauver tout seul*]. The "I" is not independent of its present, cannot traverse time alone, and does not find its recompense in simply denying the present. In situating what is tragic in the human in the definitiveness of the present, and in positing the function of the I as something inseparable from this tragic structure, we recognize that we are not going to find in the subject the means for its salvation. It can only come from elsewhere, while everything in the subject is here.[53]

Forgiveness is therefore inscribed in the becoming-responsibility of freedom—that is to say, in the very movement of temporalization as well. Here is what all classical philosophy of time, until Bergson and Heidegger, will have missed. They have missed forgiveness, all these philosophers of time; in sum, they have not thought forgiveness. And thereby [*et du coup*], they have missed time, they have lacked the time to think time, which thinks only from [*depuis*] forgiveness. It is their fault, the ontological fault of ontology. Levinas does not say that it is an unforgivable fault, but one can say it while smiling in his place [*mais on peut le dire en souriant à sa place*]:

Traditional philosophy, and Bergson and Heidegger too, remained with the conception of a time either taken to be purely exterior to the subject, a time-object, or taken to be entirely contained in the subject. But the subject in question was always a solitary subject. The ego all alone, the monad, already had a time. The renewal which time brings with it seemed to classical philosophy to be an event which it could account for by the monad, an event of negation. It is from the indetermination of nothingness, which the instant which negates itself at the approach of the new instant ends up in, that the subject was taken to draw its freedom. Classical philosophy left

53. Levinas, *Existence*, 90–93/ *De l'existence*, 155–59.

aside the freedom which consists in not negating oneself, but in having one's being *pardoned* by the very alterity of the other. It underestimated the alterity of the other in dialogue where the other frees us, because it believed there existed a silent dialogue of the soul with itself. In the end the problem of time is subordinate to the task of bringing out the specific terms with which dialogue has to be conceived.[54]

One will find these motifs, somehow transformed, but faithfully so, a long time later, at least in *Totalité et infini*, precisely in the passages devoted to "The Ethical Relation and Time."[55] Here, in a gripping manner, it is at the heart of the analysis of betrayal, of an essential betrayal, linked to essence and to the possibility of the will, that the figure of forgiveness appears as an essential figure of history, of what does and undoes history.

This is the paradox and the essence of time itself proceeding unto death, where the will is affected as a thing by the things—by the point of steel or by the chemistry of the tissues (due to a murderer or to the impotency of the doctors)—but gives itself a reprieve and postpones the contact by the against-death of postponement. The will essentially violable harbors treason in its own essence. It is not only offendable in its dignity—which would confirm its inviolable character—but is susceptible of being coerced and enslaved as a will, becoming a servile soul. (. . .) And yet in its separation from the work and in the possible betrayal that threatens it in the course of its very exercise, the will becomes aware of this betrayal and thereby keeps itself at a distance from it. Thus, faithful to itself, it remains in a certain sense inviolable, escapes its own history, and renews itself. There is no inward history. The inwardness of the will posits itself subject to a jurisdiction which scrutinizes its intentions, before which the meaning of its being coincides totally with its inward will. The volitions of the will do no weigh on it, and from the jurisdiction to which it opens comes pardon, the power to efface, to absolve, to undo history. The will thus moves between its betrayal and its fidelity which, simultaneous, describes the very originality of its power. But the fidelity does not forget the betrayal . . . and the pardon which ensures [the will] this fidelity comes to it from the outside. Hence the rights of the inward will, its certitude of being a misunderstood will, still reveal a relation with exteriority. The will awaits its investiture and pardon. It awaits them from an exterior will, but one from which it would experience no longer shock but judgment, an exteriority withdrawn from the antagonism of wills, withdrawn from history. This possibility of justification and

---

54. Levinas, *Existence*, 95/*De l'existence*, 160–61; *Translator's Note:* Levinas's emphasis is not reproduced in Lingis' English translation.

55. Levinas, *Totality and Infinity*, trans. Alphonso Lingis (Pittsburgh: Duquesne University Press, 1969), 220ff; *Totalité et infini* (The Hague: Martinus Nijhoff, 1961), 195ff.

pardon, as religious consciousness in which interiority tends to coincide with being, opens before the Other, to whom I can speak. I speak a word that, in the measure that it welcomes the Other as Other, offers or sacrifices to him a product of labor, and consequently does not play above economy. Thus we see expression, the other extremity of the voluntary power that is separated from its work and betrayed by it, nonetheless referring to the inexpressive work by which the will, free with regard to history, partakes of history.[56]

This inscription, so necessary, of forgiveness in betrayal and of betrayal in forgiveness, is what enables saying to the other or of hearing oneself tell the other and hearing the other tell oneself [*s'entendre dire par l'autre*, hearing oneself told by the other] and hearing, understanding what is thus said: you see, you start again, you don't want to forgive me, even on the day of Atonement, but me too, me neither, a "me" neither, we are in accord, we will forgive each other nothing, it is impossible, let us not forgive each other, agreed [*d'accord*]? And then comes the complicitous burst of laughter, the mad laughter, laughter becoming mad, demented laughter [*le rire dément*].

Le rire dément, demented laughter, laughter denies. Yes, laughter denies. It is mad, this demented laughter, and it denies lying [*et il dément mentir*]. This laughter is, like every laughter, a kind of denegation of lying which lies still while denying lying or while avowing lying—or, if you prefer, which says the truth of lying, which says the truth in lying, thus recognizing that a logic of the symptom will always be stronger than an ethic of truthfulness [*véracité*]. Whatever I would want to say, sincerely or not, this will mean [*cela voudra dire*] or rather this will signify without *vouloir-dire* more and something else than what I want to say, through my body, my history, the economy of my existence, of my life or of my relation to death. And here is another lie to be forgiven.

These two Jews are also just and righteous, in their own manner, righteous ones who are just enough [*des justes assez justes*] to avow, to avow to the other and avow to the other in themselves that they are incapable of forgiving, that they are not just enough, not even sincere enough, since they continue to lie at the moment of avowal. The extreme vigilance is always at fault—this is why forgiveness is always to be asked for and why it always leaves something to be desired, why, besides, it belongs from the beginning to the scene of desire, to the disproportion of desire and of love: I love you, forgive me, *pardon*, I love you. Forgive me for loving you, forgive me for loving you too much, that is say, not enough, for loving you as the

---

56. Levinas, *Totality*, 229–32/*Totalité*, 205–208.

other, for loving the other in you, of missing you, failing to reach you [*de te man-quer*, also: for your missing me] always, etc.

And yet, the avowal, even the reciprocal and almost simultaneous avowal of the common and mutual fault (as in the Jewish story), deserves compassion, we said, and a kind of forgiveness granted by one knows not who, a forgiveness which takes place even there where nobody can forgive anyone [*là où personne ne peut pardon-ner à personne*], the granting of a granted forgiveness [*l'accord d'un pardon accordé*] by an X, a great Third, God, if you will, that renders substitution possible. For it is not by chance, nor contingent, nor avoidable, that it would be always and finally of God that we ask for forgiveness, even when we are linked by a scene of forgiveness, to one or the other [*à tel ou tel*] on earth, as we recalled last time when evoking "Our Father who art in Heaven":

> Our father who art in heaven, hallowed be your name. Your kingdom come. Your will be done, on earth as it is in heaven. Give us this day our daily bread. And forgive us our debts *as* we have also have forgiven our debtors. And do not bring us to the time of trial, but rescue us from the evil one.[57]

This paradoxical agreement in the compassion that I imagine or dream between the two Jews in the synagogue—is it not peace? Yes, it is peace, it is life: at bottom, this is the great forgiveness [*le grand pardon*], if there is one, but on a day of great forgiveness, one must always say "the great forgiveness, if there is one"—to the grace of God. And what is more comical than the great forgiveness as test and ordeal of the unforgivable? What is more alive, what better reconciliation? What an art of living! How to do otherwise, besides, what better to do, as soon as one lives or survives? Without having chosen? This is the definition of today [*c'est la définition d'aujourd'hui*], of a today, a *sursis de vie*, this reconciliation in the impossible.

But I want to suppose that these two Jews, in their infinite compassion for each other, at the very moment when they decide that they do not know how to stop [*au moment même où ils arrêtent qu'ils ne savent pas s'arrêter*], at the very moment when they recognize that they cannot disarm nor stop [*désarmer*], as life itself never disarms nor stops [*ne se désarme jamais*], these two Jews will have forgiven each other, but without saying so to each other. They have at least spoken to each other, even if they have not spoken forgiveness. They have told each other—in silence, a silence of innuendo [*sous-entendu*] where misunderstanding [*le malen-tendu*] can always find space to reside—that forgiveness granted does not signify

---

57. *Translator's Note:* Matthew 6:9–13; Derrida emphasizes "as [*comme*]."

"reconciliation" (Hegel) nor "work itself," "the deep work of time" discontinuous, delivered and delivering of continuity by the interruption of the other, in view of the "messianic triumph" "forewarned against the revenge of evil" (Levinas).

For here is the last aporia of forgiveness, the most artful perhaps, the most gifted to provoke laughter to the point of madness.

On the one hand, when someone forgives someone else (for example, the worst possible wound, or, still more simply, what may repeat it even perversely, the recall of a wound), well then, one must above all not tell the latter. The other must not hear [*il ne faut pas que l'autre entende*], one must not say, that one forgives, not only in order not to recall the (double) fault but also not to recall or to manifest that something was given (forgiven, given as forgiveness), something was given back again, that deserves some gratitude or risks obligating the one who is forgiven. At bottom, nothing is more vulgar and impolite, even wounding, than to obligate someone by telling them "I forgive you," which implies an "I give you" and already opens a scene of acknowledgment [*reconnaissance*], a transaction of gratitude, a commerce of thanking that destroys the gift. Similarly, one must never say: "I grant you hospitality" or "I invite you." When one says "I invite you," it means: I pay and we are inscribed in the circular commerce of the most inhospitable exchange possible, the least giving. When one invites, not only mustn't one send invitation cards and say "I invite you," it is me who invites. Not only must one not say this, but one must also not think it nor believe it, nor make it appear—to oneself or to the other. One must therefore say nothing [*il faut donc se taire*], one must say nothing of forgiveness [*il faut taire le pardon*] where it takes place, if it takes place. This silence, this inaudibility that calls itself, that is allowed by, death. As if one could forgive only the dead (acting, at least, as if the other were dead ("for laughs"), as if he were in a situation of no longer being here ever to hear, at the moment of receiving forgiveness), and as if one could forgive only the dead while playing dead oneself [*tout en faisant soi-même le mort*] (as if one were not forgiving, as if one were not letting the other know or, at the limit, as if one did not even know oneself). From this point of view, two living beings cannot forgive each other nor declare to each other that they forgive each other insofar as they are living. One would have to be dead to believe that forgiveness is possible. The two Jews had the depth, the rigor, and the honesty of noticing that, better, of declaring it.

But, *on the other hand*, and inversely, what would a silent forgiveness be, an unperceived forgiveness, an unknown forgiveness, granted unbeknownst to the one receiving it? What would be a forgiveness of which the forgiven one would know nothing? It would no longer be forgiveness. Such silence, in forgiveness, would be as disastrous [*néfaste*] as what silence would have wanted to avoid. A forgiveness that would address itself only to the other dead (once dead, and even if his specter survives "in me"), wouldn't that be a gesticulation of comedy, a miserable simulacrum, at most a phantasm destined to consol oneself for not having known how to forgive on time? A reconciliation with oneself with which the other has nothing to do? If there were to be forgiveness, I would therefore have to forgive when it is still time, *before* the death of the other. And of course *before* my death: what would forgiveness be that would come from the dead? It is true that this forgiveness from dead to dead, from one bank of death to the other, is, in fact, the most common recourse—our life is made of it—a spectral and phantasmatic recourse, a forgiveness of *procedure*, a historical forgiveness there where forgiveness must remain irreducible to history, a forgiveness that loses itself in oblivion and denatures itself in excuse and veniality, as soon as from living to living, true forgiveness, forgiveness of the unforgivable, remains forbidden. A priori, and thus *forever* forbidden.

What, then? Do precisely what is *always* forbidden, forbidden *forever*? Forgive, there where it is forbidden, there where it is possible *because* impossible? And worse yet, do what is forbidden on a day of great forgiveness [*un jour de Grand Pardon*]? There is no worse sin, more dangerous profanation, so close to the moment when God inscribes you—or does not—in the book of the living.

Let us summarize the properly scandalous aporia, the one upon which we cannot but stop while falling upon it: impossible, possible only *insofar as* impossible, impossible concept of the impossible which would start to resemble a *flatus vocis* if it were not what one desires the most in the world, as impossible as the forgiveness of the unforgivable—forgiveness remains, impossible, in any case [*de toutes les façons*]: between two living, between the dead and the living, between the living and the dead, between two dead. It is only possible, in its very impossibility, at the invisible border between life and death (for one has seen, one can forgive only there where the forgiven and the forgiving are not there to know it) but this border of scandal does not let itself be crossed: neither by the living nor by the dead [*ni par du vivant ni par du mort*].

It is not even crossed, though there lies perhaps the undiscoverable site which all these questions watch [*veillent*], by the specter [*par du spectre*]. At what moment does Abraham waken the memory of his being foreign abroad, to the stranger [*son être-étranger à l'étranger*]? For Abraham calls himself again, he recalls that he is destined by God to be a hôte (*ger*), an immigrant, a foreign body abroad, a strange body to the stranger [*un corps étranger à l'étranger*] ("Go from your country and your kindred and your father's house.... your offspring shall be hôtes in a land that is not theirs...." [Genesis 12:1, 15:13]).

Presenting himself thus as a stranger without a home, watching [*veillant*] the body of his dead Sarah (the woman who laughs at the announcement of a birth while pretending that she didn't laugh), Abraham asks for a site for her. A last *demeure*. He wants to be able to give her a burial worthy of her, but also a site that would separate him from her, like death from life, a site "facing me," says one translation, "out of my sight," says another (Genesis 22:4). And for this, one knows the scene; he wants to pay, the husband of Sarah, the woman who laughs, he insists firmly, he does not want that this be given to him, under any condition, not at any price [*à aucun prix*]. Besides, Abraham too had laughed, at the announcement of the same news, the late birth of Isaac (*Yiṣḥaq*: he laughed. Isaac, the coming of Isaac, causes both of them to shake with laughter, one after the other; Isaac is the name of he who *comes* to make them laugh, laugh at his coming, at his very coming, as if laughter had to greet a birth, the coming of a happy event, a coming [of, from, to (*du*)] laughter: come-laugh-with-me). The moment came to laugh—this was also the moment Elohim named Sarah. He gave her a name [*il la surnomma*], deciding rather that Abraham, who just received an other name (changed from Abram to Abraham), would no longer call her Sarai, my princess, but Sarah, princess.

To this question in the form of an aporia, I know no appeasing answer. Not even mad laughter. Nothing is given in advance for forgiveness, no rule, no criteria, no norm. It is the chaos at the origin of the world. The abyss of this non-response, such would be the condition of responsibility—decision and forgiveness, the decision to forgive this concept, if there ever is one. And always in the name of the other.

(Last vertigo, last breath: forgiving in the name of the other: is this only forgiving in one's/his place [*à sa place*], for the other, in substitution? Or is it forgiving the other one's/his name, that is to say what survives of him, forgiving [in] the name of the other [*pardonner au nom de l'autre*] as [to] his first fault?)

The answer must be each time invented, singular, signed—and each time once only [*et chaque fois une seule fois*] like the gift of a work, a donation of art and of life, unique and replayed until the end of the world [*et jusqu'à la fin du monde rejouée*].

Given and dealt again [*redonnée*]. To the impossible, I want to say unto the impossible.

If one wanted systematically to pursue a search about forgiveness in Levinas, and from the point of view of hospitality, it is to the theme of cities of refuge [Deuteronomy 19] that one would have to return.[58] These cities are not sites where one forgives the involuntary murderer who is welcomed. Rather, one grants him respite, an excuse, a relative and temporary absolution. I do not want to go over this again here, we have read the texts closely enough. I would have been tempted, however, to insist on the fact that, in Levinas' eyes—and this is why, though he lauds

---

58. *Translator's Note:* See Emmanuel Levinas, "Cities of Refuge," in *Beyond the Verse: Talmudic Readings and Lectures,* trans. Gary Mole (Bloomington: Indiana University Press, 1994), 34–52; "Les villes-refuges" in *L'au-delà du verset: Lectures et cours talmudiques* (Paris : Minuit, 1982).

those cities, he still finds the law equivocal—there is no innocent murder, and one is guilty even of murders committed by accident (you remember), which would mean that any murder, any transgression of the "thou shall not kill" is unforgivable (war? State of David? Messianic peace? And animal sacrifice . . . ?)

I just recalled the word *ger* (stranger, *hôte*) which names in Abraham or Ibrahim he who is destined by God to be a hôte (ger), an immigrant, a foreign body abroad. But it seems that in Arabic, and in the Islamic world (I say "it seems," and I speak only very indirectly because my competence in Arabic is no less than my competence in Hebrew, and I move forward here, prudently, only under the control of those who know and will correct me or will help me on occasion), it seems, I say, that one could make the link between *ger* and the names *giwār* and *dakhīl*. *Giwār*, noun of action, means both protection and neighborliness, protection of him who is *gār*, protected, customer, subtantive that is often linked to the Hebrew usage of *ger* (protected by the tribe and the community). An expert on Semitic languages, Theodor Nöldeke, asserts that the two words are used in the "same juridical sense (*im wesentlich demselben rechtlichen Sinne*: in a legal, juridical sense that is essentially the same)."[59] The two words also share a connotation of holiness when they are both invoked, it seems, to refer to the protection of a holy site or to what is protected by a holy site or by a deity. I have learned also that the Phoenician cognate of these two words, appearing in many proper names, designates whoever is protected by the holiness of a site, by sacred hospitality, in sum. Charles Virolleaud, eminent expert and pioneer in the study of *Ras sarma*, writes the following: "*Gr* already appears in the fourteenth century B.C.E. in a poem where one reads *gr bt il*, which I have translated in 1936 in my *La légende de Danel*, 'the *hôte* of the house of God.' . . . Cyrus H. Gordon rendered this as 'a person taking asylum in a temple.'" What is clear, in any case, is that the hôte or stranger is holy, divine, protected by divine blessing.

A last remark to conclude for today. It does seem that the meaning of "protected" privileged by Nöldeke, without putting into question the origin and the socioreligious value of the term, underscores its conservation as a phenomenon of the nomadic tradition, of the nomadic customary law. This would also be the case for *dakhīl* (interior, intimate, hôte to whom protection is due, stranger, passing traveler. The right of the *dakhīl* would be a right of asylum witnessed everywhere in the Semitic world). However, although some Arab lexicographers see here a derivation of the meaning "to pause at the place of a hôte" from the prior sense of "deviate," it may still be about, and here I quote from the *Encyclopedia of Islam*, "the almost universal semantic link between 'stranger, enemy' (cf. Latin *hostis*) and '*hôte*,

---

59. Theodor Nöldeke, *Neue Beiträge zur Semitischen Sprachwissenschaft* (Strassburg: K. J. Trubner, 1910), 38.

customer," since the root *gwr* has in both languages also the sense of hostility, injustice. Gesenius suggests the link to Akkadian *geru*, but it is rather *gār*, enemy, that would be appropriate."

We are back, then, as nomadic as sedentary, to the sites of our *hostipitality*. We will depart again in order to err again, going from substitution to substitution: "substitution frees the subject from boredom [*la substitution affranchit le sujet de l'ennui*]" says Levinas.[60] Let us hope.

SESSION OF MARCH 5, 1997

In the indirect and diverted trace of a motif from the Arabo-Islamic culture of hospitality, we were in the process of attending to the double motif of pervertibility and deviation, of swerving off the road, the migratory errancy of the foreign errant [*l'errant étranger*] who makes a halt and who has the right to hospitality for three days. Between the two motifs, let us first note this, between the pervertibility of an hospitality that can both poison the hôte and therefore also poison itself, corrupt itself, pervert itself, between deviation, digression (from oneself) and corruptibility, there is an obvious and unavoidable passage. It is inscribed in the very meaning [*valeur*] of stranger, foreign, or foreigner [*étranger*], that is to say what is foreign to the proper, foreign to and not proper to, not close to or proximate to [*non proche à*]. The stranger is a digression that risks corrupting the proximity to self of the proper.

Mais que veut dire l'étranger? But what does the stranger mean? What does the foreigner want to say? What does he mean, and does he want to speak, the stranger? What impression does the usage of this worn word [*l'usage de ce mot usé*] leave behind? Do the logic and rhetoric which make use of this worn word have a sense, one sense and a pure one [*un sens un et pur*], which does not pervert itself nor contaminate itself immediately?[61]

We are still facing the question of the stranger, that which comes to us from the stranger, there where he interrogates us first, even puts us into question, and the question of what the stranger wants to say/mean [*et celle de ce que* veut dire "*l'étranger*"].

Que veut dire l'étranger?

60. Emmanuel Levinas, *Otherwise than Being or Beyond Essence*, trans. Alphonso Lingis (Pittsburgh: Duquesne University Press, 1998), 124; *Autrement qu'être ou au-delà de l'essence* (The Hague: Martinus Nijhoff, 1974), 160.

61. *Translator's Note:* At this point in the lecture, Derrida recommends Sophie Wahnich, *L'impossible citoyen, L'étranger dans le discours de la Révolution française* (Paris: Albin Michel, 1997). On the difficulties of reading "la question de l'étranger" see Anne Dufourmantelle and Jacques Derrida, *On Hospitality*, trans. Rachel Bowlby (Stanford: Stanford University Press, 2000).

Here the temptation emerges of going back on the tracks of seminars from ten years ago (Georg Trakl, and *Unterwegs zur Sprache (La parole dans le poème, Die Sprache im Gedicht: Est ist die Seele ein Fremdes auf Erden*, the soul is, in truth, a foreigner on the earth ... the step of the stranger resonates through the silver night, *und es läutet der Schritt / Des Fremdlings durch die silberne Nacht*).

One would have to go over—this time by letting ourselves be guided by our meditation on hospitality—all that we tried to think in an earlier lecture about the difference between the stranger and the others, the blow [*Schlag, la frappe*] of *Geschlecht* as human species and as sex, sexual difference, the rapport between brother and sister.[62] We wouldn't have time, and I don't have the courage. Were we to do it, however, and I do invite you to try for yourselves, one would perhaps have to read with one hand Heidegger and Trakl (and I believe there is already more than one hand) and with the other a text by Levinas entitled "The Foreignness to Being," which says something of the reference to Trakl[63]:

> Let us finally venture to raise some questions with regard to Heidegger. Is man's foreignness in the world [*l'étrangeté de l'homme au monde*] the effect of a process that began with the Presocratics, who spoke of the openness of being without preventing the forgetting of this openness in Plato, Aristotle, and Descartes? The soul exiled here below, which Plato transmits to metaphysical thought, already attests to the forgetting of being. But does the notion of the subject reflect only what Heidegger calls the history of being, whose metaphysical forgetting marks the epoch of the history of philosophy? Does the crisis of inwardness mark the end of this foreignness, ex-ception or exile, of the subject and of man? Is it for stateless man the return to a fatherland on the earth [*est-ce pour l'homme apatride le retour à une patrie sur terre*]?
>
> Are not we Westerners, from California to the Urals, nourished by the Bible as much as by the Presocratics, foreigners in the world [*étrangers au monde*], but in a way that owes nothing to the certainty of the *cogito*, which, since Descartes, is said to express the being of entities? The end of metaphysics does not succeed in dissipating this foreignness to the world. Are we standing before non-sense infiltrating into a world in which hitherto man was not only the shepherd of being, but elected for himself? Or shall the strange defeat or defection of identity confirm the human election— my own, to serve, but that of the other for himself? The verses of the Bible do not here

---

62. See Jacques Derrida, *Of Spirit*, trans. G. Bennington and R. Bowlby (Chicago: University of Chicago Press, 1989). *Translator's Note:* On Heidegger, Trakl, *Schlag* and *Geschlecht*, see Jacques Derrida, "*Geschlecht* II: Heidegger's Hand," trans. John P. Leavey Jr. in *Deconstruction and Philosophy: The Texts of Jacques Derrida*, ed. John Sallis (Chicago: University of Chicago Press, 1987), esp. 185ff.

63. Emmanuel Levinas, "No Identity," trans. Alphonso Lingis, in *Collected Philosophical Papers* (Pittsburgh: Duquesne University Press, 1998), esp. 148.

have as their function to serve as proofs; but they do bear witness to a tradition and an experience. Do they not have a right to be cited at least equal to that of Hölderlin and Trakl? The question has a more general significance: have the Sacred Scriptures read and commented on in the West influenced the Greek scripture of the philosophers, or have they been united to them only teratologically? Is to philosophize to decipher a writing hidden in a palimpsest?

In Psalm 119 we read: "I am a stranger on the earth [*étranger sur la terre*], do not hide from me your commandments." Would historical criticism show this text to be a late one, and would it already date from the Hellenistic period, in which the Platonic myth of the soul exiled in the body would have been able to seduce the spirituality of the West? But the psalm echos texts recognized as prior to the century of Socrates and Plato; in particular Leviticus 15:23: "No land will be alienated irrevocably, for the earth is mine, for you are but strangers, domiciled in my land." It is not here a question of the foreignness of the eternal soul exiled among passing shadows, nor of a displaced state which the building of a house and the possession of land will enable one to overcome, by bringing forth, through building, the hospitality of sites which the earth envelops. For like in Psalm 119, which calls for commandments, this difference between the ego and the world is prolonged by obligations toward the others. They echo the Bible's permanent *saying* [*dire*]: the condition (or the uncondition) of being strangers [*d'étrangers*] and slaves in the land of Egypt brings man close to his neighbor [*rapproche l'homme du prochain*]. In their uncondition of being strangers men seek one another. No one is at home. The memory of this servitude assembles humanity. The difference that opens between the ego and itself, the non-coincidence of the identical, is a fundamental non-indifference with regard to men. . . .

A stranger to itself, obsessed by others, dis-quiet, the ego is a hostage [*le Moi est otage*], a hostage in its very recurrence as an ego ceaselessly missing itself. For it is thus always closer to the other, more obliged, aggravating its own insolvency. This debt is absorbed only by being increased; such is the pride of non-essence! It is a passivity no "healthy" will can will; it is thus expelled, apart, not collecting the merit of its virtues and talents, incapable of recollecting itself so as to accumulate itself and inflate itself with being. It is the non-essence of man, possibly less than nothing. "It may be," Blanchot also wrote, "that, as one is pleased to declare, 'man is passing.' Man is passing, man has even always already passed, in the measure that he has always been appropriated to his own disappearance. . . . This then is not a reason to repudiate humanism, as long as it is recognized in the least deceptive mode, never in the zones of inwardness, power and law, order, culture, and heroic magnificence." (. . .) Man has to be conceived on the basis of the self putting itself, despite itself, in place of everyone, substituted for everyone by its very non-interchangeability [*substitué à tous de par sa non-interchangeabilité même*]. He has to be conceived on the basis of the condition or uncondition of being hostage, hostage for all the others [la condition ou l'incondition d'otage—d'otage de tous les autres] who, precisely qua others, do not belong to the same genus as I, since I am responsible even for their responsibility. It is by virtue of this supplementary responsibility that subjectivity is not the ego, but me [*la subjectivité n'est pas le Moi, mais moi*].[64]

Concerning the Arabo-Islamic tradition of hospitality,[65] aside from the three or four paths I just outlined (pre-Islamic nomadism, conditionality, deviation or halt and pervertibility), I would like to bring some additional, though clearly insufficient, details about some essential motifs that would obviously call for wider research. I always bring such details with shyness and prudence dictated by my incompetence, and while inviting those who can to make more precise, to discuss and enrich, these poor preliminary threads.

As to pre-Islamic hospitality, I would like to evoke, as I should have done earlier, the figure of the poet Ḥātim al-Ṭā'ī, who lived in the second half of the sixth century, and who seems to me interesting, among other things because of the scene of posthumous hospitality with which he is associated. At bottom, since the beginning, we have been trying to think not only the link between hospitality and death, mourning, spectrality, hospitality to the dead and hospitality of the dead.

HĀTIM AL-ṬĀ'Ī b. 'Abd Allāh b. Sa'd, Abū Saffāna or Abū 'Adī, poet who lived in the second half of the 6th century A.D., traditionally the most finished example of the pre-Islamic knight, always victorious in his undertakings, magnanimous toward the conquered and proverbial for his generosity and hospitality. . . . In the *adab* books there are a number of traditions giving instances of his generosity, and it is even said that after his death he used to entertain travelers who asked for hospitality; he would rise from his tomb, slaughter a camel, and his son 'Adī would be ordered in a dream to replace the dead animal. This tomb was probably on a hill where he had lived. Four stone figures stood on either side of his tomb, young girls with their hair loose, representing mourners.[66]

---

64. Ibid. , 148–50.

65. *Translator's Note:* At this point, Derrida's notes provide the following:

Summary of previous session:
Islam (commented quotes) around a few themes.
Origin in nomadic law and its transformation in Qur'anic law. Qur'an citations
   1. *Conditionality (three days)*
   2. *the idea of deviation (path and road: chance, etc.)*
   3. *pervertibility (and therefore perfectability), from which "sickness" ("lovesickness" in Song of Songs, quoted by Levinas. Analysis of lexicon of "pathology" (of the pathological in general, in opposition to the autonomous [l'autonomique] in Autrement qu'être, where Levinas cites the Song).*
Sketch of a question: cloning and substitution.

66. *Encyclopedia of Islam*, vol. 3 (Leiden: E. J. Brill, 1971), 274.

One would first have to engage the enormous semantic, historical, sociopolitical and, first of all, religious web that is organized and developed here around a few radiating notions.

1. Beginning with the notion of *da'wa*, from the root *da'a* (to call, invite: *heissen*, and thus, first, invitation). In the Qur'ān XXX, 24: a call to the dead in order to take them out of their tomb at the time of the last judgment:

> He bringeth forth the living from the dead, and He bringeth forth the dead from the living, and He reviveth the earth after her death. And even so will ye be brought forth. And of His signs is this: He showeth you the lightning for a fear and for a hope, and sendeth down water from the sky, and thereby quickeneth the earth after her death. Lo! Herein indeed are portents for folk who understand. And of His signs is this: The heavens and the earth stand fast by His command, and afterward, when He calleth you, lo! From the earth ye will emerge [*thumma idhā da'akum da'watan min al-ard*].[67] DA'WA, pl. *da'awāt*, from the root *da'ā*, to call, invite, has the primary meaning call or invitation. In the Kur'ān, XXX, 24, it is applied to the call to the dead to rise from the tomb on the day of Judgement. It also has the sense of invitation to a meal and, as a result, of a meal with guests. . . . The *da'wat al-mazlūm*, prayer of the oppressed, always reaches God. The *da'wa* of the Muslim on behalf of his brother is always granted. The word is applied to a vow of any kind. It can also have the sense of imprecation or curse. . . . In the religious sense, the *da'wa* is the invitation addressed to men by God and the prophets, to believe in the true religion: Islam . . . Muḥammad's mission was to repeat the call and invitation: it is the *da'wat al-Islām* or *da'wat al-Rasūl*. As we know, the Infidels' familiarity with, or ignorance of, this appeal determined the way in which the Muslims should fight against them. Those to whom the *da'wa* had not yet penetrated had to be invited to embrace Islam before fighting could take place. . . . The word *da'wa* is also applied to propaganda, whether open or not, of false prophets. . . . In the politicoreligious sense, *da'wa* is the invitation to adopt the cause of some individual or family claiming the right to the imāmate over the Muslims.[68]

2. Then the notion of *dhimma*, which names this kind of permanent contract, constant and indefinitely renewed commitment which obligates the Muslim community to grant hospitality to the members of the other revealed religions,

---

67. *The Meaning of The Glorious Koran*, XXX, 19–25.
68. *Encyclopedia of Islam*, vol. 2, 168.

conditional and strongly conditioned hospitality: hospitality is owed and granted only on the condition that non-Muslims respect the superiority of Islam.

DHIMMA. The term used to designate the sort of indefinitely renewed contract through which the Muslim community accords hospitality and protection to members of other revealed religions, on condition of their acknowledging the domination of Islam.... The bases of the treatment of non-Muslims in Islam depend partly on the attitude of the Prophet, partly on conditions obtaining at their conquest. Muḥammad is known to have first tried to integrate the principal Jewish groups at Medina into a rather loose organization, then opposed them violently, and finally, after the expansion of his authority across Arabia, concluded agreements of submission and protection with the Jews of other localities such as Khaybar, and with the Christians of *e.g.* Nadjrān; this last action alone could and did serve as precedent in the subsequent course of the Conquest. The essential Kur'ānic text is IX, 24: "Fight those who do not believe ... until they pay the *djizya* ... " which would imply that after they had come to pay there was no longer reason for fighting them.[69]

We will return to this on the way, no doubt. Earlier, however, I was thinking about the lovesickness of which we spoke last time in the fervent echo or the melancholy wake of the *Song of Songs,* the *Poem of Poems,* as if the poetical of the poetical [*le poétique du poétique*] of all declaration of love had to do with this sickness of the other, if not of the foreigner in me, of another in me, outside of me, of the other who angers me and puts me out of myself [*qui me met hors de moi*], the other who puts me out of myself in me, of the other always both more ancient and more to come than me, whom I thus mourn [*dont je porte ainsi le deuil*] as a mourning of me [*comme le deuil de moi*], as if I carried with me the mourning of me carried by the other, there where would thus begin an ageless hospitality, or a hospitality of all ages, a hospitality which could only survive itself before its time, and of which the poem would say, in sum, from one to the other in me: I love you, I am sick of love from you, sick of love for you, for while wholly wanting, with all my desire, to die before you so that I don't see you die, for you know that one of us will see the other die, well then, while wholly wanting, with all my hopeless desire, to die first, I would also want to survive you, to have at least the time to be there to console you at the time of my death, to assist you and so that you would not be alone [*seul(e)*] at the time of my death: I would want to survive you just enough to help you, the time that it will take, to bear my death. "I love you" would thus signify

---

69. Ibid., 227–28.

this impossible grammar, a grammar that one can find at once tragic and comic, as time itself: I would want to survive you at my death, to survive me in you, to guard in me your mourning of me, etc. And this "I love you, and therefore I guard you/keep you in surviving you" is unforgivable, therefore I ask you for forgiveness there where it is possible to ask for and to grant forgiveness, there where only, you recall, it is unforgivable.[70]

This is what I was saying to myself, when I arrived, about the possible/impossible hospitality (writing from now on: im-possible: in/possibilizing). Another thought of the possible and of the virtual ... avowing the im-possible (for example the unforgivable—does it make the impossible possible? I cannot forgive you, I cannot give you, I cannot receive you, etc.).

Another example of the im-possible: to be present or absent for the hôte, close or far (*fort/da*). Absent as present, present as absent (example of the plane: how much time is needed to speak of the hôte as hôte? No rule: invention, but invention of the possible: impossible.

Being-present as absent to the hôte? Must one be there (living, or surviving, or not)? *Unheimliche*: absence as presence. Must one be present or not, and how, to the hôte? The hôte always passing through (road and itinerary, iterability: come: come back [*viens: re-viens*]). But must one hold back [*re-tenir*] the passing hôte? When does holding back and retaining [*retenir*] him become detaining [*détenir*] the other as hostage? (to hold, to hold the other, to entertain and support [*entre-tenir*] the hôte (entertain and sustain[71]: art of conversation, without labor nor program, no constraint nor commerce: leisure, gratuitousness, grace, art salon, music salon, etc.)

Moments of hospitality follow each other but do not resemble each other.

The question: does hospitality presuppose improvisation? Yes and no.

The unforeseen [*l'imprévu*], providential hospitality, the messianic "unawares [*à l'improviste*]."

Greetings (who greets first?). "A-dieu": what does the *à* signify? Analyze at length: Latin (*ad, toi*, intentionality, direction, sense, movement, to come, opening, etc. Ah, but also belonging [*appartenance*] and dative: I am God's, for and to God [*à Dieu*], yours, for and to you, the infinite, for and to the infinite. Therefore, substitution and

---

70. *Translator's Note:* At this point, Derrida has the following note:

Comment on the first strophe of the Song of Songs in both [French] translations while insisting upon the differences in time and in mode (future indicative or subjunctive and future perfect) and the name/the thing, the symbolical/the physical ... and above all "rightly do they love you [c'est avec raison qu'on t'aime (Dhormes)/Les rectitudes t'aiment (Chouraqui)]" (*Song of Songs* 1:5). Straightforwardness [*droiture*] and face-to-face, love and betrayal (reason of the infinite, reason and sickness, ...).

71. The words *entertain* and *sustain* are in English in the text.

cloning, series and irreplaceability: is a clone identical or different only *solo numero* (homozygotic twin). Without entering the scientific debate (contestation as to the novelty, the consequences, etc.). Ask whether this changes anything for ethics of substitution (Levinas-Massignon), birth and death, letting be born, letting die.

Two questions: 1. Where and when does the living begin? Let live, let be born, let die, leaving in peace: a seminar on hospitality is a mediation and an exercise of language or of writing about all the possible statements that one can let "hold" (to hold dear, to maintain, retain, entertain and support, detain [*tenir à, maintenir, retenir, entretenir, détenir*] but also "letting [*laisser*]" (*lassen, let*, which do not play in the same way with their Latin root *laxare*, to let go, to loosen, to relax [*lâcher, relâcher, détendre*], Italian *lasciare*, with its enormous semantic tree: not to prevent, letting be or *laisser faire*, to let pass, to wait, to allow, to abandon (and therefore also: to lose or bequeath, to transmit or to give) to abandon oneself, but also to maintain ("let them together [*laissez les ensemble*]"). 2. Second question: Where does the human begin (the "thou shalt not kill": the human or the living? abortion: subject *hôte*-hostage? Father and infinite fecundity. Clone without father?

SESSION OF MAY 7, 1997

What is a substitution? Can one speak of substitution as such [*La substitution*]? Does it have an essence, an essence that would be one? A unique model, unsubstitutable to itself? Can one ask the question What is it? on the subject of substitution? Can one ask this question there where the very proximate words substance or subjectivity (to wit, what is *under* [*ce qui se tient* sous], what comes under [*ce qui vient sous*], the *hypokeimenon* that situates itself "below," places itself or poses itself underneath, takes places and occurs [*prend place et à lieu*] under qualities, attributes or predicates) not only calls (for) the ontological question, the question What is? What is the being of? but already gives an answer to this question: substance is the very being of that which is because it sustains every thing that occurs. Why does the substitute, why does the substitution of the substitute appear thus to resist the prerogative of philosophical or ontological interrogation?

I do not know why—(I entrust you with this symptom in confidence, I give it to you, and you will do with it as you please)—I do not know why the first example that came to my mind to illustrate the concept of substitution, the first among all the examples of substitution for which one could infinitely substitute any other (and an example is always a kind of substitutable substitute: when I say "for example," I immediately say that I could substitute an other example; if I say "you, for example," I imply that it could be someone else; which is why it is such a terrible phrase that says to someone "you, for example," since it inscribes chance and substitution, possible replaceability in the address to the other. It is often the violent address of who has the authority and power to take hostage: "you, for example," says the teacher in his class at the time of asking a question and verifying knowledge, while authoritatively designating someone summoned to respond, someone who can no longer avoid and must say "present," "here I am." "You, for example, tell me what does 'substitution' mean?" or the attitude of the occupier designating hostages: "you, for example, get out of the lineup," etc.). Well, I admit then that the first example that came to my mind, if one can say so, to my consciousness, when I thought of giving you an example of substitution, is the example of child substitution: when one steals a child from his parents and substitutes another instead. For some, this is the utmost violence possible, an exceptional and exceptionally cruel violence. For others, this welcoming [*accueillir*] the substitute child, the child who replaces another or who is taken from his parents in order to be welcomed [*accueilli*], to be taken in [*recueilli*] by others, is the gift of hospitality *par excellence*. One is more hospitable toward the adopted child than toward the so-called natural or legitimate child. And one can also attempt to demonstrate, as we have in the past, that there is no such thing as a natural and immediate filiation: every child is a substituted substitute [*tout enfant est substitut substitué*].

Let us leave this for now, but this example will catch up with us quickly. I wanted therefore to entrust you with this example, the first that came to my mind whereas there are so many other possible examples of substitution, by definition (the sign, the representing, prosthesis, money, everything that comes in the place of, etc.). But immediately after having lent my attention to the fact that the first example of substitution that came to my mind was the child, I wanted to search the dictionary, as I do often, as a matter of duty and to verify, to search for example. First in *Littré*, I looked for the examples given, the exemplary phrases too, cited in order to illustrate what one calls substitution. What, then, do I find as a first definition or as first example? Child substitution. As if child substitution were not an example among other, a substitution for which one could substitute as many others as one would want, but were rather substitution par excellence, the exemplary substitution, paradigmatic or arche-substitution, irreplaceable substitution, there where the logic of substitution seems, on the contrary, to place under question the irreplaceability of *arkhè* and of the originary.

If the first substitution remained child substitution, then any substitution would amount perhaps to re-produce, to figure, to recall some child substitution, what would lead one to think or dream that the child itself was the *first* substitute. One is all the more encouraged in the direction of this dream when, as if by chance, the same *Littré*, after this first example of substitution, child substitution, the first citation is from Rousseau, the very same Rousseau who said—you will recall this phrase from *Emile* that we have commented on at length: "there is no substitute for a mother's love,"—which implies that it is irreplaceable, nonsubstitutable.[72] Then the same Rousseau, thinker of the substitutive supplement, said in the *New Héloïse*, "It would seem life is a possession one receives only on condition of passing it on, a sort of substitution which must pass from generation to generation [*une sorte de substitution qui doit passer de race en race*]."[73]

This sentence inscribes in any case the process of substitution in a *genealogy*, in a genealogical sequence of the genealogic, even of the genetic. Substitution would be, first of all, a living replacement of life by life, of the living by the living, of a living by another: a living one for another [*un vivant pour un autre*] (which is not far from the sacrifice of life and thus from "dying for the other"—we will return to this). To replace something with something, a number or a figure [*un nombre ou un chiffre*] with another in a homogenous series, would not be a substitution, in any case not a grave substitution. A substitution worthy of the name would be not of something but of someone with someone, even with something [*la substitution non de quelque chose mais de quelqu'un par quelqu'un, voire par quelque chose*]. Unless the most terrifying stakes lied, with this equivocation, the ineluctable substitution of someone with something [*la substitution ineluctable de quelqu'un par quelque chose*] (fetishism would be only a figure of this), with substitution itself, as if substituting someone with someone always amounted to contaminating the logic of the *who* with the logic of the *what*, or ethics with arithmetic (one would have to write *arithméthique*, with an *h*). One *for* the other: the three senses of the "for" (all of which inter-cross, over-determine or ally themselves, more or less underground in Levinas in order to speak substitution: the prosthetic sense (one thing put—or putting itself—in the place of the other, for the other), the dative sense (one giving itself, devoting itself, sacrificing itself for the benefit of the other, for the other), the phenomenological or ontophenomenological sense (the "for the other [*pour autrui*]," the appearing or being "for the other"). These three "for" intercross as in the expression "witness for the other [*témoin pour l'autre*]"; "no one is a witness for the witness" (Celan).

72. *Translator's Note:* Jean-Jacques Rousseau, *Emile ou de l'Education* in *Œuvres complètes* 4 (Paris : Gallimard, 1969), 257, *Emile*, trans. Barbara Foxley (London: Everyman's Library, 1950), 13. See also *De la grammatologie*, (Paris: Minuit, 1967)/*Of Grammatology*, trans. G. C. Spivak (Baltimore: Johns Hopkins University Press, 1976) 209/E145.

73. Jean-Jacques Rousseau, *Julie or the New Heloise*, trans. Philip Stewart and Jean Vaché, *The Collected Writings of Rousseau*, vol. 6 (Hanover, N. H. : Dartmouth College/University Press of New England, 1997), 539.

There is nothing fortuitous in that, immediately after the arche-example of the child—of substitution of child if not of substitution as child—the same dictionaries would mention substitution as a legal matter, but not just any legal matter. After all, in the (French) legal code, the *substitut* is he who is granted the right to replace the other in the latter's functions, and more precisely, in French law, the justice [*magistrat*] in charge of replacing the attorney general. There is a long tradition, a French and literary tradition, which complains and accuses, complains of *substituts*, of deputies [*représentants*] of the law as *substituts*. Molière compares them to clawed beasts [*animaux à griffes*], these clerks [*greffiers*]—another figure of life, of animal life. "How many beautiful animals the claws of which you must pass: sergeants, attorneys, advocates, registrars, deputies [*substituts*], assessors, judges and their clerks!"[74] (There would be much to say about zoological figuration, the animal representation of men of law in general, the representation of the space of law as animal space, from Molière to Kafka). As for Rousseau, who has composed a great list of charges against the substitute in politics, against the elected who alienates the popular voice and the general will, he also writes in *The Social Contract* that: "everyone knows what happens when the King appoints agents [*quand le roi se donne des substituts*]."[75]

There is nothing fortuitous, then, in the mention of substitution as a matter of law, not just any legal matter but of it as it concerns inheritance, family succession, the parental chain or filiation, substitution as filiation—jurisprudence concerning here those who are called upon to substitute for the first heirs. Substitution also signifies, in the case of the child, succession. It then designates the disposition according to which one calls upon the heirs to succeed—themselves, in a way—in such manner that the first child, the first heir will be unable to alienate the property promised or subject to substitution. This word has an entire legal history, from Roman law, where substitution often designates the replacement of the heir (*substituere heredem*, to designate an heir replacing the first designated heir, even the eldest), a history into which we will not delve but that I had to recall because, even though the word substitution belongs to as many codes as one wills, and for reasons which we will discuss, to codes of law, law of things and law of persons [*droit des choses et droit des personnes*] (to substitute is to replace something or someone, even someone with something: one would perhaps say "killing" in so doing, killing to substitute a thing for someone, a dead thing for a living one), nevertheless, therefore, its privileged link to law and right, to rights of inheritance and of family succession, did deserve to be noted, for reasons that will not cease to

---

74. Molière, *Les fourberies de Scapin* II, 8; trans. G. Graveley in *Six Prose Comedies of Molière* (London: Oxford University Press, 1956), 349.

75. Jean-Jacques Rousseau, *Social Contract*, trans. Judith R. Bush, Roger D. Masters, and Christopher Kelly, in *The Collected Writings of Rousseau*, vol. 4, 177.

reappear and to be important to us. Besides, most literary examples given by *Littré* for the verb "to substitute" are also borrowed from estate law [*droit de succession*]. Of course, this presupposes that the chain of successive inheritors would be sufficiently alike to substitute for each other, with the required family resemblance, but would not substitute each other serially, as in a series of clones. You see the question returning. Bossuet was not naming clones but apostles when he said, "They [the apostles] will leave heirs behind; they will not cease to substitute successors for each other and this race will never end." The word "generation [*race*]," as in Rousseau's phrase quoted earlier, does indicate nevertheless the call to a genealogy or to a quasi-genetics that reproduces itself infinitely as the same, that inherits itself thanks to substitution, to a kind of autosubstitution. What can this mean: an autosubstitution? Can one, must one, substitute oneself to oneself? What then does oneself mean in this case? Obviously, the "generation" in question, as a site of substitution, defines a space of inheritance as space of the same. To the same extent, the simple reproduction of the identical by autosubstitution (the phantasm of cloning) forbids the inheritance, which it otherwise seems to make possible; it interrupts parental filiation, which seems to announce itself with substitution. One finds in the vocation to inheritance which announces itself under the word *substitution* and under the operation of substituting, this crossing of natural and reproductive automaticity, and of perversion or institutional artificiality, of natural or institutional reproduction—unless substitution were the very thing that ruins or threatens this opposition between nature and institution. At the heart of the logic of substitution or of the supplement, there is, therefore, apparently, this crossing of natural reproduction and technological reproductibility, of natural series and institutional deviation, of bio-engineering and freedom, of so-called natural filiation and adoption as legal fiction.[76] One finds all this in this sentence by Vertot (in his *Révolutions Romaines* XIV, 282) quoted again in *Littré*: "One found [in Caesar's will] that he had adopted Octavius, the son of his sister's daughter, as his son and primary heir, and that he substituted to him, in the case of death with progeny, Decimus Brutus, one of the main conspirators." And there is Montaigne: "In case one of them [i.e., instituted heirs] were to die [*vienne à défaillir*, that is to say, to miss or lack, to default for one reason or another, one of which being death, disappearance by death; and the substitute always replaces a fault, supplements a disappearance —J. D.], I substitute he who survives him for his share." I quote this sentence because of the allusion to surviving, because the substitute, as inheritor (and that too is the dream of a certain cloning) ensures the surviving, even the indefinite surviving of what it replaces et repeats at once, what it serves as.

---

76. *Translator's Note:* Derrida adds the English "legal fiction" to the French "fiction légale. "

The word *substitution* has occupied us much in the previous sessions. I say "the word" rather than the concept, because under this word one can substitute more than one concept of substitute and of substitution. The word and the presumption of a concept or a logic of substitution, a certain substitution, in any case, enabled us to link to each other these thoughts of hospitality that are at once ethics of substitution and ethics of holy or sacred hospitality—of Jewish filiation or of Christian and Islamic filiation, such as they are represented, under the common sign of Abraham, the father of nations, by the discourses of Levinas and of Massignon. Yes, under the sign of Abraham, of father Abraham, the absolute Patriarch, since the reference to Abraham the foreigner but also to Abraham the hôte, who receives the hôtes or messengers of God in Mamre, this reference to inheritence, to memory and to the founding example of the patriarchal hôte Abraham, was central and unerasable in both discourses, on both "prayer fronts," to recall Massignon's phrase, the Christiano-Islamic prayer front and the Jewish prayer front. But from the perspective of hospitality, these thoughts of substitution were turning toward Abraham the hôte or the stranger, to whom Yahweh said; "Go from your country and your kindred and your father's house" (Genesis 12:1) and be a stranger. Or yet Abraham, to whom Yahweh said later, "Know this for certain, that your offspring [*ceux de ta race*] shall be aliens [*des hôtes*, or strangers: it is always the word *ger* that designates the stranger received in a land, the immigrant, the alien [*métèque*][77] — J. D.] in a land that is not theirs" (Genesis 15:13), words that Abraham will recall at the time of Sarah's death, in Hebron, when addressing the Hittites to ask for a burial ground: "I am a stranger and an alien [*je suis hôte*] residing among you [Chouraqui says: "I am an alien [*je suis un métèque*], a resident with you" —J. D.]; give me property among you for a burying place, so that I may bury my dead out of my sight [Chouraqui: "and I will bury my dead in front of me"—here too, if we had time for a digression, we would insist on the taking root in a foreign land not by way of birth but by way of death and burial, displacement upon which we reflected last year around *Oedipus at Colonus*—and here too, it is a question, if not of a secret burial, at least of a burial with which one parts in order for it to be distant from the bereaved ("in front of me," says Chouraqui) or invisible to him ("out of my sight" says Dhormes) —J. D.]" And every time, one has the impression that the work of mourning and of fidelity will only be possible if the other is separated from the bereaved, out of me [*hors de moi*], before me or, if not out of me, out of my sight; as if the work of mourning, often presented as an interiorization, an idealizing incor-

---

77. *Translator's Note:* The word *métèque* in its common French usage is a pejorative for foreigner. Etymologically, it is related to the Greek *metoikos*, one who changes home.

poration, that is to say also a substitution of the image of the other with the other in me, had a chance to operate, had a chance to shelter the memory or the I of the other in me only to the extent that the dead other remains in his place out of me—in me, out of me. If mourning is hospitality, a burial in oneself and out of oneself, it is necessary [il faut] for both burials, and therefore for both hospitalities, to remain quite distinct, separated, split, that the decomposition of the body (external hospitality of physical burial) occur elsewhere in order to let the idealizing memory appropriate the hôte dead in oneself, in an operation that is entirely one of substitution. In both founding references to Abraham that I have just cited, however, it is a question of hospitality to the stranger Abraham, in a foreign land [à l'étranger] (the two messengers of God in Mamre). It is not a question of sacrifice, nor of sacrificial substitution like the moment of Isaac's sacrifice, to which I will return once more.

However, in the scene of Genesis 23, Sarah's burial, as a scene of hospitality—since Abraham opens by saying, "I am myself an alien among you" when he asks for a burial ground—this scene which follows the so-called interrupted sacrifice of Isaac, that is the substitution of the ram for the son ["Abraham went and took the ram and offered it up as a burnt offering instead of his son (22:13)—"in place of (à la place)," says Dhormes, "at the site (au lieu de)," says Chouraqui, his "unique son," "your only one" as God said: it is a matter of substituting an animal for the unique beloved, the preferred unique one —J. D), the scene of Sarah's burial, Sarah whom Yahweh had, you recall, "visited" (Dhormes), "sanctioned" (Chouraqui), in order to give her Isaac in her old age—the scene of Sarah's burial can also be read as a scene of sacrifice and of substitution. Indeed, Abraham absolutely insists on paying for the field and the cave, the site of burial that the Hittites absolutely insist on giving him. In this extraordinary scene (that I will read in part) in which one insists on paying, the others on giving without being paid, one has the feeling that Abraham insists on sacrificing what he calls "the full price" or "four hundred shekels of silver," in order at once to mourn Sarah and to owe nothing. Both parties want to cancel the debt with a gift, but a sacrificial gift, a gift that presupposes some sacrifice. And it is Hebron, the site of Sarah's burial but also of Abraham's, upon which the scene of sacrificial appropriation has not ceased perpetuating itself until now, just yesterday, through so many substitueries.[78]

Let us start again. What is a substitution? What does one say when saying "substitution"? What does one do when substituting? If, to this question, I substitute, as I

78. *Translator's Note:* This untranslatable neologism combines "substitution" with "tueries," killings.

must, its development, to wit, "who substitutes what?" it risks still not being enough: one must [*il faut*] add, "Who substitutes what to what? To what, and to whom?

In all the substitutions I have just performed (regarding the subject and the object of the verb, "Who substitutes? And what? And to what or to whom?), you will have noted the suspended indecision between the "what" and the "who." It matters to us first and foremost. Besides, if one opens the *Littré* at the definition for *substitution*, one will read just this alternative between the "who" and the "what"; more precisely, between the person and the thing. You will also notice that the living said to be animal is here absent, who is neither a person nor a thing, but who nonetheless occupies, as you know and as we will explore, the most significant place regarding sacrificial or fetishistic substitution. I read *Littré*, therefore: "Substitution: action that consists in putting a thing, a person *in the place of* [*à la place de*] another. A child substitution."

In the place of—locution which names the occupied space, the destined location [*emplacement*], natural or not, even the lodging, the habitat, the *lieu* (one also says, for substitution, "*ceci au lieu de cela*"), "at the place of" ["*à la place de*," "*au lieu de*," "*en lieu et place de*"], this can also be said "for [*pour*]": this *for* that, the one *for* the other, and so on. And this *for* is in itself sufficiently equivocal, indicating both substitution and gift, the dative ("one for the other" is both substitution and dative destination); this *for* is equivocal enough to offer us some resistance, entering and not entering in an economy of gift and sacrifice, entering it in order to [*pour*] exceed it.

Let us reconsider this flat definition: "action that consists in putting a thing, a person in the place of another." Through the indefinite multiplicity of the examples of substitution, which one can justly substitute for all the others (signs instead of things, words instead of sense, a word for another, prostheses serving as what they replace, representatives [*représentants*] and lieutenants of everything,[79] re-presentations in general), we see some invariables settling. First, the number or the multiplicity, at least two, at least a series of two, one plus one, even one plus one plus one infinitely. This "one +"—its substitute may be what one calls a "what" and not a "who," even a "what" instead of a "who," where one usually hears, in the word *what*, an inert object-thing, without consciousness and without speech, without humanity, and in the word *who*, a human *existant* (person, subject, I, ego, conscience, unconscious, although the "id [*ça*]" of the unconscious could be situated under the category of the "what"). Here too, one would encounter difficulties—

---

79. *Translator's Note:* Aside from etymological connections (*lieu-tenant*, place-holder), a lieutenant is, according to the *OED*, "one who takes the place of another; usually, an officer civil or military who acts for a superior; a representative, substitute, vicegerent. "

and this is, no doubt, the heart of the problem—in situating the living in general, for example, in the figure of what one commonly calls the animal, in this alternative of the "what" and the "who." We will return to this. For the moment, I want to underscore a warning. Since we are going very quickly, coming back to the problem of Abrahamic hospitality, the hôte and the hostage, the thought of hospitable substitution, for example, in Levinas and Massignon, the difference between the "what" and the "who" does not amount simply to the difference between the thing (what) and the person (who), the object (what) and the subject (who), the not-conscious and the not-free (what) and the conscious or the free (who), not even, above all, between the common and the proper, even between on the one hand the common, the general, the generic or the homogenous (what) and, on the other hand, the singular, the heterogeneous or the exceptional. It is of this last distinction that we must be suspicious, for one could indeed think that when Levinas and Massignon speak of substitution—what they have in mind—the terms of substitution are not common, substitutable things which enter into a homogeneous series (as if I replaced a stone or a brick by another resembling it, or even a numerical identity, three with four, a white ball by a black ball, a ballot paper by a ballot paper). When they speak of substitution, it is a matter of an absolutely singular and irreplaceable existence that, in a free act, substitutes itself for another, makes itself responsible for another, expiates for another, sacrifices itself for another outside of any homogeneous series. Substitution is not the indifferent replacement of an equal thing by an equal or identical thing (as one can, for example, imagine—ideological phantasm—that a clone can replace the individual from which it comes or another identical clone, the difference between the two being null, save the number; the difference between them being only in the number, *solo numero*, as one says). No, the Abrahamic substitution implicates [*engage*] exceptional, elected existences that make themselves or expose themselves of themselves [*s'exposent d'elles-mêmes*], in their absolute singularity and as absolutely responsible, the gift or the sacrifice of themselves. That they would be implicated [*engagées*], that they would give themselves as pledge [*comme gage*] does not mean that substitution would be a free and voluntary act. It is also a grace and a certain passivity, a reception or a visitation, but in any case, it is not the passivity of an effect to which an inert thing would be submitted. It is a matter of another passivity, anything but a mechanical reproduction or this biotechnological reproductibility of phantasmatic cloning.

To underscore this point better, in order to settle it before moving on to complicate things further, I would like to quote and comment successively on some passages by Massignon and Levinas regarding substitution (in passing we will encounter some motifs that will matter to us and that we could problematize, such as compassion, sacrifice, fraternity, and above all, expiation. These significations of sacrifice and expiation, which cross all the Abrahamic thoughts of substitution, would suffice to make them into something else than arithmetologies of cloning series.

> "The why? We are told that the Badaliya is an illusion, since one cannot put oneself in the place of another, and that it is a lover's dream. One must answer that it is, that it is not a lover's dream, but a suffering that one receives without having chosen it and of which one conceives the grace, the hidden visitation from the bottom of the anguish of compassion which grabs us, and that it is the entrance to the Kingdom of God and that this suffering grabs us. Indeed, it appears powerless, but because it demands everything Someone who is on the Cross shares it with us, and He will transfigure it on the Last Day. This is suffering together human pain often not apparent for beings such that they have no pitiable companions such as us."[80]

Since we are talking about Massignon, and about the Abrahamo-Arabo-Islamic prayer front, I would like, during a brief digression, to answer a concern that you might share with me, I imagine, regarding the ellipsis, if not the exclusion, in any case the active silence within which this Badaliya suppresses [*tait*], walls in, chokes all fraternity with those who have, after all, some right to figure in an Abrahamic prayer front—to wit, the Jews. Why are they so visibly absent from the compassion and the substitution of Massignon? Without advancing too much, but also without withdrawing, I could say that the general sociological configuration of this trajectory (Bourgeois French Catholicism, the filiation of "Huysmans, Claudel, Father de Foucauld," etc.), to which one could add other characteristics, leaves us with the feeling of some probability of anti-Semitism, one that would be vaguely sociological and atmospheric. I would have stayed with this hypothesis and with this probability, I would have kept this statistical feeling for myself had I not found under Massignon's own pen, on the significant date of March–April 1938, just before the war, therefore (and one must be very attentive here), the two following confidences, which are also two confessions, both close to expiation and both turning toward Abraham, toward a still incomplete prayer to Abraham:

> One must know how to harden the will (regarding France and the Christians of the East), back to the wall, face-to-face with danger. I am thinking less of external perils than of the internal danger—where, to thank us for having given them asylum, so may Jewish refugees are working toward our destruction. Singular destiny of this

---

80. Massignon, *L'hospitalité sacrée*, 293.

unsatisfied people, non-social and yet predestined (when will I conclude my third prayer of Abraham!). [March 15, 1938]

The intrigues of Jewish refugees in France have pushed me into a crisis of anti-Semitism in which I fought with the Maritains and with Georges Cattawi. [April 15, 1938)[81]

We were saying that the substitution of which Massignon and Levinas speak, in the name of hospitality, is not the simple, objective and technological replacement of a homogenous element by another homogenous element in a series, through the effect of a simple, functional calculation, as one replaces a chessboard piece by another which comes in its place, something which a calculating machine could do, like the computer against which Kasparov was recently playing. There is no general equivalence for the substitution of which Massignon and Levinas speak, no general equivalence, no common currency, which would ensure this exchange as replacing two comparable values. And yet, and yet (Christ for Massignon, money for Levinas, the third, justice, whoever, subject in the current sense, election, etc.)

One would also have to make an additional step while in a way displacing the axiomatic certainty with which we have opposed the ethical substitution to arithmetic substitution. The criteria of exceptionality, of irreplaceable singularity, of unicity, does not seem to me sufficient.

At bottom, in every substitution, whatever its terms, the units or identities, the conceptual equivalence of the contents, the homogeneity of seriality, in every substitution, one finds singularity and exceptionality of the units of the substitutions. Even if I replace a grain of sand by a grain of sand, an hour by another, a hand by another (to recall the Kantian example of dissymmetry), each unit, each identity, each singularity is irreplaceable in its factual existence; it is even elected in a certain manner, even if this election becomes precarious or unconscious. It is therefore not the criteria of irreplaceability, of singularity and unicity (*solo numero*) which distinguishes the "ethical" substitution—let us call it that, to go quickly—from simple, arithmetic substitution. One must take into account, if one can say so, with these values of compassion, expiation and sacrifice, another deal or hand [*une autre donne*]. And with it, we will find ourselves again at the heart of the question of hospitality, of hostipitality [*hostipitalité*].

For it does not suffice that the subject of substitution (the term, the X subject to substitution) be unique, irreplaceable, elected to come or to offer itself in the place of the other, irreplaceable for being replaced. It is also necessary [*il faut aussi*]

81. Massignon, *L'hospitalité sacrée*, 206–207.

that this irreplaceable be aware of *itself* [*se sente*], that it be aware and be aware of itself [*qu'il sente et se sente*], and therefore that it be a self with a rapport to itself, which is not the case of every unique and irreplaceable being in its existence. This self, this ipseity, is the condition of ethical substitution as compassion, sacrifice, expiation, and so on.

The question is, therefore, once again: What is a self? An ipseity? What is it if auto-affection, auto-motion, the fact of being able to move oneself, to be moved [*s'émouvoir*] and to affect oneself, is its condition, in truth, the definition? It is the proper of what one calls the living in general, and not only of man but also of the animal, of the compassion for the animal. It is the measure of this question that we will address next time, first in a discussion, the problems of the double, cloning, genealogy and kinship, filiation and sacrifice (animal and/or human) and "thou shall not kill."

I ask you therefore to prepare this discussion.

Translated by Gil Anidjar

BIBLIOGRAPHY

SELECTED TEXTS BY JACQUES DERRIDA

Adieu à Emmanuel Levinas. Paris: Galilée, 1997. Trans. Pascale-Anne Brault and Michael Naas as *Adieu to Emmanuel Levinas*. Stanford: Stanford University Press, 1999.

Apories: Mourir—s'attendre aux « limites de la vérité ». Paris: Galilée, 1996. Trans. Thomas Dutoit as *Aporias*. Stanford: Stanford University Press, 1993.

"Artefactualités." *Echographies de la télévision*, avec Bernard Stiegler. Paris: Galilée—Institut National de l'Audiovisuel, 1996. 9–35.

"Avances." In Serge Margel, ed., *Le tombeau du dieu artisan*. Paris: Editions de Minuit, 1995. 7–43.

"Circonfession." *Jacques Derrida*, avec Geoffrey Bennington. Paris: Seuil, 1991. Trans. Geoffrey Bennington as "Circumfession." In *Jacques Derrida*, by Geoffrey Bennington and Jacques Derrida. Chicago: University of Chicago Press, 1993.

"Comment ne pas Parler: Dénégations." In *Psyché: Inventions de l'autre*. Paris: Galilée, 1987. Trans. Ken Frieden as "How to Avoid Speaking: Denials." *Derrida and Negative Theology*. Ed. Harold Coward and Toby Foshay. Albany: State University of New York Press, 1992. 73–142.

Cosmopolites de tous les pays, encore un effort! Paris: Galilée, 1997.

De l'esprit: Heidegger et la question. Paris: Galilée, 1987. Trans. Geoffrey Bennington and Rachel Bowlby as *Of Spirit: Heidegger and the Question*. Chicago: The University of Chicago Press, 1989.

De l'hospitalité: Anne Dufourmantelle invite Jacques Derrida à répondre. Paris: Calmann-Lévy, 1997. Trans. Rachel Bowlby as *Of Hospitality: Anne Dufourmantelle Invites Jacques Derrida to Respond*. Stanford: Stanford University Press, 2000.

"Des tours de Babel." *Psyché: Inventions de l'autre*. Trans. Joseph F. Graham, in this volume.

"Différance." *Marges de la philosophie*. Paris: Minuit, 1972. Trans. Alan Bass as *Margins of Philosophy*. Chicago: University of Chicago Press, 1982.

Donner la mort. Paris: Galilée, 1999. Partial trans. David Wills as *The Gift of Death.* Chicago: University of Chicago Press, 1995.

D'un ton apocalyptique adopté naguère en philosophie. Paris: Galilée, 1983. Trans. John P. Leavy, Jr. as "Of an Apocalyptic Tone Newly Adopted in Philosophy." *Derrida and Negative Theology.* Ed. Harold Coward and Toby Foshay. Albany: State University of New York Press, 1992. 25–71.

"Edmond Jabès et la question du livre." *L'écriture et la différence.* Paris: Seuil, 1967. Trans. Alan Bass as "Edmond Jabès and the Question of the Book" *Writing and Difference.* Chicago: University of Chicago Press, 1978.

"Ellipse." *L'écriture et la différence.* Trans. Alan Bass as "Ellipsis." *Writing and Difference.* Chicago: University of Chicago Press, 1978.

"En ce moment même dans cet ouvrage me voici. In *Psyché: Inventions de l'autre.* Trans. Ruben Berezdivin as "At this very moment in this work here I am." *Re-Reading Levinas.* Ed. Robert Bernasconi and Simon Crichtley. Bloomington: Indiana University Press, 1991. 11–48.

Feu la cendre. Paris: des femmes, 1987. Trans. Ned Lukacher as *Cinders.* Lincoln: University of Nebraska Press, 1991.

"Foi et savoir: Les deux sources de la « religion » aux limites de la simple raison." *La religion.* Sous la direction de Jacques Derrida et Gianni Vattimo. Paris: Seuil, 1996. Trans. Samuel Weber as "Faith and Knowledge," in this volume.

Force de loi. Paris: Galilée, 1994. Trans. Mary Quaintance as "Force of Law" in this volume.

"Interpretations at War: Kant, le Juif, l'Allemand." *Phénoménologie et Politique: Mélanges offerts à Jacques Taminiaux.* Bruxelles: Ousia, 1989. Trans. Moshe Ron as "Interpretations at War: Kant, the German, the Jew," in this volume.

Khōra. Paris: Galilée, 1993. Trans. Ian Mc Leod. *On the Name.* Ed. Thomas Dutoit. Stanford: Stanford University Press, 1995.

Le monolinguisme de l'autre ou la prothèse d'origine. Paris : Galilée, 1996. Trans. Patrick Mensah as *Monolingualism of the Other, or the Prosthesis of Origin.* Stanford: Stanford University Press, 1998.

Le toucher, Jean-Luc Nancy. Paris: Galilée, 2000.

Mal d'archive : Une impression freudienne. Paris: Galilée, 1995. Trans. Eric Prenowitz as *Archive fever: A Freudian impression.* Chicago: University of Chicago Press, 1996.

Mémoires d'aveugle: L'autoportrait et autres ruines. Paris: Réunion des musées nationaux, 1990. Trans. Pascale Anne-Brault and Michael Naas as *Memoirs of the Blind: The Self-Portrait and Other Ruins.* Chicago: University of Chicago Press, 1993.

"My Chances/*Mes Chances:* A Rendezvous with Some Epicurean Stereophonies."
    Trans. Irene Harvey and Avital Ronell. *Taking Chances: Derrida, Psychoanalysis,*
    and Literature. Ed. Joseph H. Smith and William Kerrigan. Baltimore: The Johns
    Hopkins University Press, 1984. 1–32.

"No Apocalypse, Not Now (full speed ahead, seven missiles, seven missives)."
    Diacritics 14, no. 2 (1984): 20–31.

"Nombre de oui." *Psyché.* Trans. Brian Holmes. "A Number of Yes." *Qui Parle* 2.2
    (1988): 118–133.

"Parti pris pour l'Algérie." *Les temps modernes* as 580 (1995), 233–41. Trans. Boris
    Belay as "Taking a Stand for Algeria," in this volume.

Passions. Paris: Galilée, 1993. Trans. David Wood as "Passions." *On the Name* (Stan-
    ford: Stanford University Press, 1995).

Points de suspension: Entretiens. Ed. Elisabeth Weber. Paris: Galilée, 1992. Trans.
    Peggy Kamuf et al. as *Points . . . Interviews, 1974–1994.* Stanford: Stanford Uni-
    versity Press, 1995.

Politiques de l'amitié. Paris : Galilée, 1994. Trans. George Collins as *Politics of*
    Friendship. London: Verso, 1997.

"Qu'est-ce qu'une traduction 'relevante'?" *Quinzième Assises de la Traduction Litté-*
    raire (Arles 1998). Arles, 1999. Trans. Lawrence Venuti as "What Is a 'Relevant'
    Translation?" *Critical Inquiry* 27, no. 2 (2001) 174–200.

Sauf le nom. Paris: Galilée, 1993. Trans. John P. Leavey, Jr. *On the Name.* Stanford:
    Stanford University Press, 1995.

Schibboleth: pour Paul Célan. Paris : Galilée, 1986. Trans. Joshua Wilner as "Shib-
    boleth: For Paul Celan." *Midrash and Literature.* Ed. Geoffrey H. Hartman and
    Sanford Budick. New Haven: Yale University Press, 1986. 3–72.

Spectres de Marx: L'état de la dette, le travail du deuil, et la nouvelle Internationale.
    Paris : Galilée, 1993. Trans. Peggy Kamuf as *Specters of Marx: The State of the Debt,*
    the Work of Mourning, and the New International. New York: Routledge, 1994.

"Théologie de la traduction." In *Du droit à la philosophie.* Paris : Galilée, 1990.
    Trans. Joseph Adamson et al. as "Languages and Institutions of Philosophy (IV.
    Theology of Translation)." *Recherches Sémiotiques / Semiotic Inquiry* 4, no. 2
    (1984): 139–52.

"Typewriter Ribbon: Limited Ink (2) ('Within Such Limits')." *Material Events: Paul*
    de Man and the Afterlife of Theory. Ed. Tom Cohen et al. Minneapolis: University
    of Minnesota Press, 2001.

Ulysse Gramophone: Deux mots pour Joyce. Paris: Galilée, 1987. Trans. Tina Kendall
    and Shari Benstock as "Ulysses Gramophone: Hear Say Yes in Joyce." *Acts of*
    Literature. Ed. Derek Attridge. New York: Routledge, 1987. 253–309.

"Un ver à soie: Points de vue piqués sur l'autre voile." *Voiles*, avec Hélène Cixous. Paris: Galilée, 1998. Trans. Geoffrey Bennington as "A Silkworm of One's Own," in this volume.

"Violence et métaphysique: Essai sur la pensée d'Emmanuel Levinas." *L'écriture et la différence*. Trans. Alan Bass as "Violence and Metaphysics: An Essay on the Thought of Emmanuel Levinas." *Writing and Difference*. Chicago: University of Chicago Press, 1978.

DERRIDA AND RELIGION: SELECTED BIBLIOGRAPHY

Arkoun, Mohammed. "Logocentrisme et vérité religieuse dans la pensée islamique." *Studia Islamica* 35 (1972): 5–51.

Beardsworth, Richard. *Derrida and the Political*. London: Routledge, 1996.

Bennington, Geoffrey. *Interrupting Derrida*. London: Routledge. 2000.

———. *Legislations: The Politics of Deconstruction*. London: Verso, 1994.

Benslama, Fethi, ed. *Idiomes, Nationalités, Déconstructions: Rencontre de Rabat avec Jacques Derrida (Cahiers Intersignes 13)*. Casablanca: Toubkal/L'aube, 1998.

Boyarin, Daniel. *Intertextuality and the Reading of Midrash*. Bloomington: Indiana University Press, 1990.

Bracken, Christopher. *The Potlatch Papers: A Colonial Case History*. Chicago: University of Chicago Press, 1997.

Brault, Pascale-Anne and Naas, Michael. "To Believe: An Intransitive Verb? Translating Skepticism in Jacques Derrida's *Memoirs of the Blind*." *Paragraph* 20, no. 2 (1997): 101–19.

Caputo, John D., and Charles E. Winquist. "Derrida and the Study of Religion." *Religious Studies Review* 16, no. 1 (1990): 19–25.

Caputo, John D. *Against Ethics*. Bloomington: Indiana University Press, 1993.

———. *The Prayers and Tears of Jacques Derrida: Religion Without Religion*. Bloomington: Indiana University Press, 1997.

Carlson, Thomas A. *Indiscretion: Finitude and the Naming of God*. Chicago: University of Chicago Press, 1999.

Clément, Bruno. *L'invention du commentaire: Augustin, Jacques Derrida*. Paris: PUF, 2000.

Critchley, Simon. *The Ethics of Deconstruction: Derrida and Levinas*. Oxford: Blackwell, 1992.

Dufrenne, Mikel. "Pour une philosophie non-théologique." *Le poétique*. 2nd ed. Paris: Presses Universitaires de France, 1973.

Fenves, Peter, ed. *Raising the Tone of Philosophy: Late Essays by Immanuel Kant, Transformative Critique by Jacques Derrida*. Baltimore: Johns Hopkins University Press, 1993.

Foshay, Toby, and Harold Coward, eds. *Derrida and Negative Theology*. Albany: State University of New York Press, 1992.

Gasché, Rodolphe, "God for Example." *Inventions of Difference: On Jacques Derrida*. Cambridge, Mass.: Harvard University Press, 1994.

Geller, Jay. "Identifying 'Someone Who is Himself One of Them': Recent Studies of Freud's Jewish Identity." *Religious Studies Review* 23, no. 4 (1997): 323–31.

Handelman, Susan A. *The Slayers of Moses: The Emergence of Rabbinic Interpretation in Modern Literary Theory*. Albany: State University of New York Press, 1982.

Hart, Kevin. *The Trespass of the Sign: Deconstruction, Theology and Philosophy*. New York: Fordham University Press, 2000 [1989].

Hartman, Geoffrey. *Saving the Text: Literature/Derrida/Philosophy*. Baltimore: Johns Hopkins University Press, 1981.

Hobson, Marian. *Jacques Derrida: Opening Lines*. London: Routledge, 1998.

Iser, Wolfgang, and Sanford Budick, eds. *Languages of the Unsayable: The Play of Negativity in Literature and Literary Theory*. New York: Columbia University Press, 1989.

Kepnes, Steven, ed. *Interpreting Judaism in a Postmodern Age*. New York: New York University Press, 1996.

Khatibi, Abdelkebir. "Frontières." *Cahiers Intersignes* 1 (1990): 13–22. *Maghreb Pluriel*. Paris: Denoël, 1983.

Kronick, Joseph G. *Derrida and the Future of Literature*. Albany: State University of New York Press, 1999.

Marion, Jean-Luc. "Esquisse d'un concept phénoménologique du don." *Archivio di filosofia* 62, nos. 1–3 (1994): 75–94.

Meschonnic, Henri. *Le signe et le poème*. Paris: Gallimard, 1975.

Miller, J. Hillis. "Theology and Logology in Victorian Literature." *Journal of the American Academy of Religion* 47, no. 2 (1979): 345–61.

Nancy, Jean-Luc. *Des lieux divins*. Mauvezin: Trans-Europ-Repress, 1997.

New, Elisa. "Pharaoh's Birthstool: Deconstruction and Midrash." *SubStance* 57 (1988): 26–36.

Ofrat, Gideon. *Derrida the Jew: On Judaism and Wound and on the Thought of Jacques Derrida* (in Hebrew). Jerusalem: Ha-akademia, 1998.

Robbins, Jill. *Altered Reading: Levinas and Literature*. Chicago: University of Chicago Press, 1999.

———. "Circumcising Confession: Derrida, Autobiography, Judaism." *diacritics* 25, no. 4 (1995): 20–38.

———. *Prodigal Son/Elder Brother: Interpretation and Alterity in Augustine, Petrarch, Kafka, Levinas*. Chicago and London: University of Chicago Press, 1991.

Rojtman, Betty. *Black Fire on White Fire: An Essay on Jewish Hermeneutics from Midrash to Kabbalah*. Trans. Steven Rendall. Berkeley and Los Angeles: University of California Press, 1998.

Ronell, Avital. *Dictations: On Haunted Writing*. Lincoln: University of Nebraska Press, 1993.

————. *Finitude's Score: Essays for the End of the Millennium*. Lincoln: University of Nebraska Press, 1994.

————. *Stupidity*. Champaign: University of Illinois Press, 2001.

Scanlon, Michael J., and John D. Caputo, eds. *God, the Gift, and Postmodernism*. Bloomington: Indiana University Press, 1999.

Scharlemann, Robert P., ed. *Negation and Theology*. Charlottesville: University Press of Virginia, 1992.

Smith, James K. A. "Determined Violence: Derrida's Structural Religion." *The Journal of Religion* 78, no. 2 (1998): 197–212.

Spivak, Gayatri Chakravorty. *A Critique of Postcolonial Reason: Toward a History of the Vanishing Present*. Cambridge, Mass.: Harvard University Press, 1999.

Taylor, Mark. *Altarity*. Chicago: University of Chicago Press, 1987.

————. *Erring: A Postmodern A/Theology*. Chicago and London: University of Chicago Press, 1984.

————. *Nots*. Chicago: University of Chicago Press, 1993.

Vries, Hent de. *Philosophy and the Turn to Religion*. Baltimore: Johns Hopkins University Press, 1999.

————. "Theotopographies: Nancy, Hölderlin, Heidegger." *Modern Language Notes* 109 (1994): 445–77.

Weber, Elisabeth, "Elijah's Futures" in *Futures: Of Jacques Derrida*, ed. Richard Rand. Stanford: Stanford University Press, 2001.

————, ed. *Questions au Judaïsme*. Paris: Desclée de Brouwer, 1996.

Weber, Samuel, and Hent de Vries, eds. *Violence, Identity, and Self-Determination*. Stanford: Stanford University Press, 1997.

Wolosky, Shira. "Derrida, Jabès, Levinas: Sign-Theory as Ethical Discourse." *Prooftexts* 2 (1982): 283–302.

————. *Language Mysticism: The Negative Way of Language in Eliot, Beckett, and Celan*. Stanford: Stanford University Press, 1995.

Zarader, Marlène. *La dette impensée: Heidegger et l'héritage hébraïque*. Paris: Seuil, 1990.

PERMISSIONS

INDEX

Abraham, 8, 10, 15, 360, 369–75, 399–400, 414–15

Abram, 372, 400

Address to the German Nation (Fichte), 173–76

Adieu to Emmanuel Levinas (Derrida), 356–57

Adorno, Theodor, 147, 154, 261, 297

Agamben, Giorgio, 19

"Al-Badaliya" (Statutes), 377–79

"An Unpublished Letter from Gershom Scholem to Franz Rosenzweig, on the Subject of Our Language, a Confession [Une lettre inédite de Gershom Scholem à Franz Rosenzweig, à propos de notre langue, une confession]," 191

Anthropology from a Pragmatic Point of View (Kant), 166, 220–21

Apollo, 287

Aquinas, Thomas, 5–6

Arendt, 261

Aristotle, 237

Arnaud, 239

Artemis, 287

Augustine, 2, 30–31, 255, 312

Austin, J. L., 29

Baudelaire, 111

Beccaria, Cesare, 276

"Before the Law" (Derrida), 235

Beiträge zur Philosophie (Heidegger), 55

Benjamin, Walter: on name of God, 211; and Nazism, 294–98; and Schmitt, 281–83; on semiotics, 223–24; on translation, 102, 111–33; on violence, 228–29, 234, 258–98

Bennington, Geoffrey, 32–33

Benveniste, Emile, 46, 68–69, 71, 73–74, 99

Bergson, Henri, 24, 41, 77, 170, 368, 394

Bible, the, 9–11, 90, 102–33, 144, 164–65, 365

Bismarck, 180–81

Blanchot, Maurice, 118

Bloy, Léon Marie, 375

Borges, 330

Boullan, Père, 375–76

Brecht, 268

Brentano, 130

Buber, 142, 146, 160, 170–71, 261
Budick, Sanford, 138

"Ce qui reste à force de musique"
    (Derrida), 228
Chouraqui, André, 106–108, 339,
    372–73, 414–15
Christ, 363–64
Cicero, 71, 73, 106, 354
"Circumfession" (Derrida), 36, 38,
    102
Cixous, Hélène, 17, 309–10, 319–22,
    329–38, 349
Claudel, Paul, 366, 368, 370, 418
Cohen, Hermann, 24, 135–36, 139–88,
    261
Cohen, Martha, 146
Colombet, Claude, 127–28
"Comment ne pas parler" ["How to
    Avoid Speaking"] (Derrida),
    26–27, 29–31
Concept of Law (Hart), 242
"Confession on the Subject of Our
    Language [Bekenntnis über unsere
    Sprache]" (Scholem), 226–27
Confessions (Augustine), 30–31
Conversation in the Mountains
    (Cixous), 319–22
Cornell, Drucilla, 230, 236
"Cours sur la mort et le temps"
    (Levinas), 383–85
Critique of Practical Reason (Kant),
    165–66, 187–88
Critique of the Faculty of Judgement,
    The (Kant), 165–66
"Critique of Violence [Zur Kritik der
    Gewalt]" (Benjamin), 228–29, 234,
    258–98

Daniel, 204–205
David, 164, 205
De Gaulle, Charles, 216
De l'existence à l'existant (Levinas),
    390–91
Declaration of the Rights of Man,
    257–58
"Declarations of Independence"
    (Derrida), 235
"Deconstruction and the Possibility of
    Justice" (colloquium, Cardozo Law
    School), 230, 244, 262
Derrida, Jacques: on Algeria, 299–300;
    on force of law, 228–29; on
    German–Jews, 135–36; on God,
    102–103; on hospitality, 356–57;
    identities of, 32–38; and Jewish rit-
    ual, 309; on language, 189–90; on
    religion, 1–31, 39–41; translation
    of, 134
"Des Tours de Babel" (Derrida),
    102–103
Desbois, 128–30
Destremeau and Moncelon, 375
Deuteronomy, Book of, 328, 339,
    400–401
Deutschtum und Judentum (Cohen),
    135–36, 139–40, 146–71
Dhormes, Edouard, 372, 414–15
Dieu, la mort et le temps (Levinas),
    383–84
Difficult Freedom (Levinas), 367–68
Discourse to the German Nation
    (Cohen), 181
Don Juan, 358
Donner la Mort (Derrida), 102
Du droit à la philosophie (Derrida),
    33–35

Ecce Homo (Nietzsche), 25

Elohim, 400

Emile (Rousseau), 411

"Encre blanche et Afrique originelle:
    Derrida et la postcolonialité"
    (Zabus), 32

Encyclopedia of Islam, 401–402

Epistle to the Corinthians, 345–50

Epistle to the Romans, 344

Ernout-Meillet, 71

Exodus, Book of, 315, 350

"Eyes of Language, The" (Derrida),
    189–90

Faith and Knowledge (Hegel), 53–54

"Faith and Knowledge: The Two
    Sources of 'Religion' at the Limits
    of Reason Alone" (Derrida),
    20–27, 102

"Femininity" (Cixous), 336

Ferraris, Maurizio, 75

Fichte, Johan Gottlob, 173–76, 184

Finnegans Wake (Joyce), 108

Fish, Stanley, 236, 242, 251

Flaubert, Gustave, 363–64

"Force" (Fish), 242, 251

"Force and Signification" (Derrida),
    228–29

"Force of Law" (Derrida), 228–29

"Foreignness to Being, The" (Levinas),
    403–405

Foucauld, Charles de, 368, 418

Frederick II, 181

Freud, Sigmund: and the Abrahamic,
    11–20; and economy, 382; and the
    "Egyptian," 32; and evil, 90; and
    Nature, 346; on "penis envy,"
    334–36; and the veil, 349–50

Friedlander, Saul, 230

From Berlin to Jerusalem (Scholem),
    192–93

From the Sacred to the Holy (Levinas),
    99

Gandillac, Maurice de, 111–33

Genesis, Book of, 105–33, 369–74,
    399–400, 414–15

Genet, Jean, 24–26, 101

Genet à Chatila (Genet), 25–26,
    101

Gide, André, 368

Glas (Derrida), 24, 235, 350

God: and Abraham, 370–75, 414–15;
    as being, 162–63; covenant with,
    223–24; death of, 53, 78–79; as
    jealous, 203; name of, 102–109,
    118–19, 132–33, 189, 211; and
    Noah, 363; oneness of, 164;
    power of, to name, 297; thought
    of, 116–17; as witness, 65

"Goethe's *Elective Affinities*"
    (Benjamin), 262

Gospels, the, 10

Grotius, 168

Hagar, 372

Hart, H. L. A., 242

Ḥātim al-Ṭāʾī, 405–406

Hebrew Bible, the, 2

Hegel, G. W. F.: and classification,
    178–79; and death penalty, 276;
    Derrida and, 24, 41; and the
    holy, 316–17; and Kant, 165; on
    reconciliation, 398; on religion,
    6, 53–54, 61; on right, 235; on
    vengeance, 207–208

Heidegger, Martin: 122; and avoidance, 26–27, 29; and Benjamin, 261, 278, 298; and Christianity, 51, 53–55, 57, 61, 91–99; on death, 387; Derrida and, 41; on duties, 177; on foreignness, 403–404; and forgiveness, 394; and Greeks, 152–53; and Hitler, 180–81; and Idea, 154–57; on "last god," 91; Levinas on, 383; and neo–Kantianism, 140–41; on nothing-ness, 178–79; on presence, 280; on sacred language, 217–18, 220; and Schmitt, 263, 281–82; and silence, 163; and thought, 172; and vocabulary of being, 44; and *Walten/Gewalt*, 234

Heraclitus, 234

Herrstein-Smith, Barbara, 236

Hiller, Kurt, 288–89

Hitler, 180–81, 263

Hofmann, J.-B., 71

Hölderlin, 122, 132

Homer, 330

"Hostipitality" (Derrida), 356–57

Husserl, Edmund, 61, 130, 140–41, 147, 155–56, 261

Huysmans, J. K., 375–76, 418

Ibn Ezra, 164

I H V H, 339–40

Institution and Interpretation (Weber), 242

International Committee in Support of Algerian Intellectuals (ICSAI), 301, 302

"Interpretations at War" (Derrida), 135–36

Introduction to the Theory of Right (Kant), 233

Isaac, 9, 359–60, 372–73, 400, 415

Iser, Wolfgang, 138

Ishmael, 9, 372

Jakobson, 110–11

James, 322

Jesus, 2

"Jewish–German Psyche, The: The Examples of Hermann Cohen and Franz Rosenzweig" (Derrida), 135–36

Joyce, James, 108, 330

Jüdische Schriften, 146

Kabbalah, the, 2, 214

Kafka, Franz, 17, 172–73, 235, 270, 412

Kahil, Mary, 376, 379

Kant, Immanuel: anti–Semitism of, 220–21; Derrida and, 24, 41; on dignity of life, 87; on duty, 245; as German Jew, 135–88; on law, 233, 276; and pacifism, 183, 186–88; Protestant descendance of, 165–66; and regulative idea, 254–55; on religion, 48–50, 52–53, 59–61, 77, 88

Kepler, 154–55, 173

Khatibi, Abdelkebir, 37

Kitsour Choul'hane Aroukh, the, 340, 341

Kobbert, 71

Kofman, Sarah, 382

La (Cixous), 336

La Folie du jour (Blanchot), 118

La Fontaine, 241

La passion de Hallaj, martyr mystique de l'islam (Massignon), 368

La parole donnée (Massignon), 374–75

Lactantius, 71, 73–74

Laertes, 312

"Language and Secularization in Gershom Scholem [Langage et sécularisation chez Gershom Scholem]" (Mosès), 191, 224–26

Lassalle, Ferdinand, 181

Lawrence, T. E., 368

"Laws of Reflection, The: Nelson Mandela, in Admiration" (Derrida), 235

Le Pen, 166

League of Human Rights, 301, 302

Legend of St Julian Hospitator, The (Flaubert), 363–64

Leibniz, 156–57, 162, 173

Levi, Primo, 18–19

Levinas, Emmanuel: on foreignness, 403–405; on forgiveness, 385–96, 400; and hospitality, 39, 364–68, 375–85; on Islam, 367–68; and Judaism, 91; on justice, 250, 255; and the sacred, 54, 99, 200; on substitution, 409–420; and violence, 235

L'hospitalité sacrée (Massignon), 371–74, 389–90

Libellus de Optimo Genera Oratorum (Cicero), 106–107

Littré, 410–11, 413, 416

Love in Two Languages (Amour bilingue) (Khatibi), 37

Luke, 315

Luther, 152–53, 160, 163, 184

Magellan, 313–14

Maimonides, 151, 162–64, 184, 343

Mallarmé, 112–13

Mark, 315

Marochitanus, Samuel, 16

Marx, Karl: critique of religion, 52–53; Jewish origin of, 181; on strikes, 283

Massignon, Louis, 39, 357, 365–80, 385–90, 409, 414–20

Matthew, 315

Mauriac, François, 368

Memoirs of the Blind (Derrida), 102

Mendelssohn, 163, 180, 221

Messiah, the, 313–14, 347, 362

Messianic Idea in Judaism, The (Scholem), 204

"Migrations of the Dead in Baghdad" (Massignon), 368

Milton, 330

Molière, 412

Monolingualism of theOther (Derrida), 36–38, 189, 299–300

Montaigne, 239–42, 285, 413

Moscow Diary (Benjamin), 297

Moses, 15, 164, 165, 170, 315, 346–47

Mosès, Stéphane, 191, 193, 208, 213, 224–26

Mother Nature, 172

Nahman of Breslau, Rabbi, 328

Nancy, Jean–Luc, 2

Napoleon, 181

"Nazism and the 'Final Solution': Probing the Limits of Representation" (colloquium, UCLA), 230, 258
New Héloïse (Rousseau), 411
New Testament, the, 2
Nicholas of Cusa, 156, 162, 173
Nietzsche, Friedrich: blindness of, 330; and Germans, 154, 261; on the Indo–European, 71–75; and Kant, 50, 165; and Paul, 325
Niobe, 287
Noah, 363
Nöldeke, Theodor, 401

Odysseus, 312
Oedipus, 209, 330, 358
"Of an Apocalyptic Tone" (Derrida), 102, 309
Of Hospitality (Derrida), 356–57
Of Spirit (Derrida), 26–27, 228
Ofrat, Gideon, 35
"On Language as Such and On the Language of Man" (Benjamin), 286
On Translation (Jakobson), 110–11
Othello, 11, 13, 15
Otherwise than Being (Levinas), 379–80
Otto, W., 71
"Our Father who art in Heaven," 397

Pascal, Blaise, 238–42, 285
Paul, 2–3, 85, 312, 322, 325, 345–50
Pauly–Wissowa, 71
Péguy, Charles Pierre, 368
Penal Code, the, 128
Penelope, 312, 330

Pentateuch, the, 164
Phenomenology of Spirit, The (Hegel), 53–54
Philo Judaeus, 148, 162, 173, 184
Philosophical Dictionary [Dictionnaire philosophique] (Voltaire), 59–60, 105
Plato, 57, 148, 162–63, 184
Pliny, 354
Politics of Friendship (Derrida), 39, 228, 356–57
Pompey, 316
Post Card (Derrida), 36
Prometheus, 287
Propriété littéraire et artistique (Colombet), 127–28
Psychopathology of Everyday Life, The (Freud), 11–12

Quaintance, Mary, 229
Qur'ān [Koran], the, 11, 325, 370, 406–407

Rawls, John, 242
Rectorate Speech (Heidegger), 177
Reik, Theodor, 381
Religion (Derrida), 21–22
Religion der Vernunft aus den Quellen des Judentums (Cohen), 140
Religion within the Limits of Reason Alone (Kant), 48–50, 52–53, 77, 165–66
Remnants of Auschwitz (Agamben), 19
Renan, 184–86
"Replying to the Question: Who is German?" (Adorno), 147
"Respect for the Human Person in

Islam and the Priority of Asylum
    Right over the Duty of Just War"
    (Massignon), 370
Revue internationale de la Croix Rouge,
    370
Rilke, 122
Rosenzweig, Franz: 261; and Benjamin,
    288; and Genesis, 369–70; and
    Jewish-German psyche, 135–36,
    139–46, 149, 170–74, 178–80; on
    Luther, 160; and Nature, 346;
    and Scholem, 189–227; and State,
    187
Rousseau, 130, 411–413
Rushdie, Salman, 82

"Saints Buried in Baghdad"
    (Massignon), 368
Sarah, 360, 372–73, 399–400
Sarai, 372, 400
Sartre, Jean–Paul, 368
Scheler, 147
Schmitt, Carl, 6, 63–64, 228, 259–61,
    263, 281–83
Scholem, Gershom, 135, 142, 146,
    189–227, 261, 297
Segond, Louis, 106
Sein und Zeit (Heidegger), 51, 54–55,
    96, 218
Shakespeare, 11, 13, 15
Shem, 106–108
Shylock, 11, 13, 15
"Signature, Event, Context" (Derrida),
    228
"Silkworm of One's Own, A" (Derrida),
    309–10, 350
Social Contract, The (Rousseau),
    412

Song of Songs, 407–408
Sophocles, 132
Sorel, Georges, 272, 283
Spinoza, 163–65, 199, 203, 206, 266
Star of Redemption (Rosenzweig),
    143–46
Strauss, Leo, 263

Tableaux parisiens (Baudelaire),
    111
"Taking a Stand for Algeria" (Derrida),
    299–300
Talmud, the, 2
"Task of the Translator, The"
    (Benjamin), 102, 111–33,
    285–86
Tertullian, 71, 73–74
Theologico-Political Treatise (Spinoza),
    164, 203, 266
"Three Prayers of Abraham Father of
    All Believers, The" (Massignon),
    369
Timaeus (Plato), 57
"To Speculate—On Freud" (Derrida),
    235
Totality and Infinity[Totalité et infini]
    (Levinas), 250, 364–65, 395–96
"Trace, The" (Levinas), 364–65
Trakl, Georg, 219, 403
Tristan and Isolde, 337
*Two Sources of Morality and Religion,
    The* (Bergson), 77

Vattimo, Gianni, 44
Vergès, Jacques, 267
Vertot, 413
Virgil, 354
Virolleaud, Charles, 401

"Visitation of the Stranger [Visitation de l'étranger]" (Massignon), 374–75

Voltaire, 59–60, 105

Vor dem Gesetz [Before the Law] (Kafka), 172–73, 235, 270

Wagner, 154, 261

Was ist Metaphysik (Heidegger), 217, 218, 220

Weber, Sam, 236, 242

Weizman, 296

What Is a Nation (Renan), 184–86

"Wolf and the Sheep, The" (La Fontaine), 241

Writing and Difference (Derrida), 356–57

Yahve, 315

Yahweh, 133, 162, 369, 372, 414

YHWH, 107–109

Zabus, Chantal, 32